Shattered Hope

Captain Jacobo Arbenz, October 1944. Arbenz was, the CIA later wrote, "brilliant . . . cultured."

Shattered Hope

THE GUATEMALAN REVOLUTION AND THE UNITED STATES, 1944–1954

Piero Gleijeses

PRINCETON UNIVERSITY PRESS

PRINCETON, NEW JERSEY

Copyright © 1991 by Princeton University Press
Published by Princeton University Press, 41 William Street,
Princeton, New Jersey 08540
In the United Kingdom: Princeton University Press, Oxford

Library of Congress Cataloging-in-Publication Data

Gleijeses, Piero.
Shattered hope : the Guatemalan revolution and the United States, 1944–1954 / Piero Gleijeses.
Includes bibliographical references (p.   ) and index.
1. United States—Foreign relations—Guatemala. 2. Guatemala—Foreign relations—United
States. 3. United States—Foreign relations—1945–1953. 4. Guatemala—Politics and
government—1945–1985. I. Title.
E183.8.G9S48   1991   327.7307281'09044—dc20   90—8901

ISBN 0-691-07817-3

The author gratefully acknowledges permission from the following publications in which
portions of chapters 1, 3, 5, and 8 previously appeared:
    Mesoamérica, ''La aldea de Ubico: Guatemala, 1931–1944,'' June 1989 (chapter 1);
    Journal of Latin American Studies, ''The Death of Arana,'' October 1990 (chapter 3);
    Journal of Latin American Studies, ''Juan José Arévalo and the Caribbean Legion,'' February
1989 (chapter 5);
    Journal of Latin American Studies, ''The Agrarian Reform of Jacobo Arbenz,'' October 1989
(chapter 8).
    The photographs appearing in this book were graciously provided from private collections.

This book has been composed in Linotron Times Roman

Princeton University Press books are printed on
acid-free paper and meet the guidelines for
permanence and durability of the Committee on
Production Guidelines for Book Longevity of
the Council on Library Resources

Printed in the United States of America by Princeton University Press,
Princeton, New Jersey

10   9   8   7   6   5   4   3   2   1

To Setsuko Ono and Letterina Gleijeses

Contents

Illustrations

Frontispiece. Captain Jacobo Arbenz, October 1944

Following page 148

Jacobo Arbenz and his wife María, shortly after their marriage in 1939

Jacobo and María, September 1945

Jorge Toriello flanked by Francisco Arana and Jacobo Arbenz

Guatemalan soldiers being greeted by Jorge Toriello, October 22, 1944

Juan José Arévalo returned to become the first president of the Guatemalan revolution

Francisco Arana, chief of the armed forces under Arévalo

Arévalo "had the physique of a very big man"

Arana courted U.S. officials

Arana and Arévalo

Carlos Paz Tejada and Arévalo

President Arbenz on his inauguration day

María de Arbenz on inauguration day

Arbenz in exile, painted by his wife in 1965

Arbenz in Havana, 1962

Figures

Acknowledgments

IT IS a pleasant task to thank those who have supported me during the writing of this volume. My wife, Setsuko Ono, stood by me at the inception; suffered through the first, most painful drafts; offered sensitive, intelligent, and frank criticism; and saved the manuscript at a decisive stage when I had worked myself into a dead end.

I received financial assistance from the Central American and Caribbean Center of Johns Hopkins University and from the Plumsock Foundation, whose director, Christopher Lutz, also shared his deep knowledge of Guatemalan history.

Doña María de Arbenz, Major Carlos Paz Tejada, and Robert Woodward, three of the protagonists of this story, graciously read the entire manuscript. Three U.S. officers who served in Guatemala in the early 1950s—Colonel Aloysius McCormick, Colonel Thomas Hanford, and Major Manuel Chavez— read those sections that dealt with the Guatemalan army. To them, and to all those Guatemalans, Americans, and others who agreed to be interviewed, my sincere thanks.

I talked late into many nights with my two closest Guatemalan friends. Their deep knowledge and love of their country inspired me. It is indicative of the culture of fear in Guatemala today that they have asked me not to mention them by name.

I was fortunate to benefit from the assistance and advice of friends and colleagues at the Johns Hopkins University, four above all—Bonnie Tenneriello, Thomas Thornton, Marta Velazquez, Bernard Wolfson. My task was made easier by two outstanding librarians, Linda Carlson and Barbara Prophet. After several barren years, I was finally able to count on the assistance of an excellent secretary, Paula Smith; when she left, I was taken under the wing of Florence Rotz, by general acclaim the best secretary to have graced these halls in a great many years.

My intellectual debt to Nancy Mitchell is truly deep. Her analytical skills, her great literary talent, her probing, irreverent questions, and her own deep knowledge of U.S. policy in the region gave new life to the manuscript. First as my research assistant, then as a colleague, we began an intellectual collaboration that I hope will last through many books—hers and mine.

Washington, D.C.
September 1990

Acknowledgments

A Note on Documentation

DOCUMENTS from the National Archives (NA) are always from Record Group (RG) 59.

Intelligence documents from the State Department (OSS, OIR) located in the NA do not have file numbers. They are in RG59, Research and Analysis File. They are identified only with NA.

The file number of the embassy's *Joint Weeka* (*JW*) is always 714.00(W). Prior to January 1954, the *JW* was divided into two sections, political (I) and economic (II). When citing *JW*, I and II refer to these sections, not to volume numbers.

The origin of all documents is either Washington, D.C., or Guatemala City, unless otherwise indicated.

Prior to June 1944, the NA gave each document in its Decimal Files a unique identifying number following its decimal number; after June 1944, only the date of the document is repeated after the decimal number. Whereas I cite the former, I do not cite the latter except in those rare instances when it differs from the actual date of the document.

Documents received through the Freedom of Information Act frequently have no file numbers and have not yet been filed. These documents are cited with no archival information.

Document numbers are given whenever they exist. Informal correspondence carries no document numbers, nor do memos of conversations; whenever the former has a title, it is included; for the latter, either the participants in the conversation or the title of the conversation, whichever is shorter, is included.

Whenever a document appears in its entirety in *Foreign Relations of the United States* (*FRUS*), I use the *FRUS* citation. When, however, the *FRUS* version is incomplete, I cite the original.

For articles from the press that are not cited in full in the notes, see the Bibliography. The place of publication is the United States or Guatemala, unless otherwise indicated.

Abbreviations

AGA	Asociación General de Agricultores
AGCA	Archivo General de Centroamérica
AHA	Archivo Histórico Arquidiocesano
AmEm	American embassy
AmEmG	American embassy, Guatemala
ARA	American Republics Area
AWD	Allen Welsh Dulles
CAD	departmental agrarian committee
CAL	local agrarian committee
CF	Confidential File
CGTG	Confederación General de Trabajadores de Guatemala
CM:G	Correspondencia Dirigida al Señor Ministro: Gobernación
CNCG	Confederación Nacional Campesina de Guatemala
CO:G	Copiador de Oficios: Gobernación
CPR	Correspondencia del Presidente de la República
CR	*Congressional Record*
CSC:DAT	Correspondencia Sindical Campesina: Departamento Administrativo del Trabajo
CSM	*Christian Science Monitor*
CT:DAT	Contratos de Trabajo: Departamento Administrativo del Trabajo
CTG	Confederación de Trabajadores de Guatemala
DCA	*Diario de Centro América*
DCM	Deputy Chief of Mission
DDE:DS	Dwight David Eisenhower Diary Series
DF	Decimal File
DP:SACS	Dulles Papers Special Assistant Chronological Series
DP:SS	Dulles Papers Subject Series
DP:TCS	Dulles Papers Telephone Conversation Series
DOS	Department of State
EL	Eisenhower Library
EL I	*El Imparcial*
FPL	Frente Popular Libertador
FRUS	*Foreign Relations of the United States*
GF	General File
GT	Guatemala Transcripts
HCFA	U.S. House Committee on Foreign Affairs

ID	Intelligence Document Files
IGT	Inspección General de Trabajo
IMJP:G	Informes Mensuales de Jefes Políticos: Gobernación
IRCA	International Railways of Central America
JFD:CS	John Foster Dulles Chronological Series
JP	Jefaturas Políticas
JW	*Joint Weeka*
MemoConv	Memorandum of conversation
MemoTel	Memorandum of telephone conversation
ML	Mudd Library, Princeton University
MP:G	Ministerio Público: Gobernación
NA	National Archives
NA-S	National Archives at Suitland
NYT	*New York Times*
OAS	Organization of American States
ODECA	Organización de Estados Centroamericanos
OF	Official File
OIR	Office of Intelligence and Research
OJR	Organismo Judicial de la República
PAR	Partido de Acción Revolucionaria
PGT	Partido Guatemalteco del Trabajo
PIN	Partido de Integridad Nacíonal
PRG	Partido de la Revolución Guatemalteca
RF	Regional Files
RG	Record Group
RN	Renovación Nacional
SCFR	U.S. Senate Committee on Foreign Relations
TL	Truman Library
UFCO	United Fruit Company
USIA	United States Information Agency
WF	Whitman File
WP	*Washington Post*
WSJ	*Wall Street Journal*

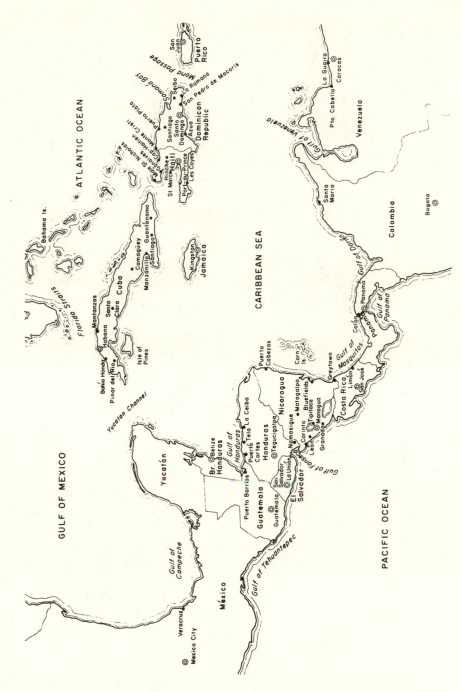

Map of Central America and the Caribbean. (From Dana Munro, *The United States and the Caribbean Republics, 1921–1933*

Shattered Hope

Witnesses

"It wasn't a great conspiracy, and it wasn't a child's game. We were just a group of young men searching for our destiny." So said Alfredo Guerra Borges one evening in January eighteen years ago. He had been a leader of the Communist Party of Guatemala (PGT) in the early 1950s. Ours was not a formal interview. I was curious about the Guatemalan revolution; he was eager to relive a past of which he was still proud.

He spoke of Jacobo Arbenz—the Red Jacobo. He spoke of himself and of his friends, of what they accomplished, and of what they failed to achieve. He spoke of Moscow and of Alejandro, the Cuban communist who sat in on the councils of the PGT. He spoke of Washington and of Ambassador John Peurifoy, whom he had ridiculed in the columns of the PGT's *Tribuna Popular*. And he spoke, as in wonder, of the fall of Arbenz.

The CIA engineered the coup against Arbenz that ended the Guatemalan revolution—a revolution that had seen the PGT bask in the president's favor while communists were pariahs elsewhere in Latin America; a revolution that had seen the first true agrarian reform of Central America: half a million people (one-sixth of Guatemala's population) received the land they desperately needed.

Jacobo Arbenz and Juan José Arévalo presided over Guatemala during those ten "years of spring in the land of eternal tyranny."[1] Arévalo—eloquent and charismatic—was a prominent intellectual; Arbenz—introverted and, even by CIA accounts, brilliant[2]—was an unusual young colonel who cared passionately about social reform. The virus of communism had infected both of them, especially Arbenz, or so said American observers. A few months before the coup, the *New York Times* delivered its indictment: Arbenz was "a prisoner of the embrace he so long ago gave the Communists."[3]

Thirty-six years have passed. It is no longer fashionable to disparage Arévalo: he was, we are told, a Rooseveltian, a democrat whom Washington had misunderstood. But Arbenz is still controversial. Many believe that he too was misjudged and that the CIA plotted his overthrow because he had expropriated the land of the United Fruit Company. Others disagree. The former general

[1] Cardoza y Aragón, *La Revolución Guatemalteca*, p. 9.
[2] CIA, "Guatemala," SR-46, July 27, 1950, p. 39, Truman Papers, President's Secretary's File, Intelligence File, Box 261, TL.
[3] "Guatemala Reds Increase Powers," *NYT*, Nov. 6, 1953, p. 3.

secretary of the PGT, Arbenz's closest friend, observes dryly, "They would have overthrown us even if we had grown no bananas."[4]

Since I first spoke with Alfredo Guerra Borges in January 1973, several excellent studies have appeared that examine U.S. policy toward the Guatemalan revolution, but the contours of the revolution itself—the Guatemalan side of the story—remain hazy.[5] This is the story that I have sought to uncover.

My search led me to the Guatemalan and American press of the period; to the *Guatemalan Transcripts* (ninety-four boxes of documents seized by the CIA after the fall of Arbenz); to presidential libraries, the National Archives of the United States and of Guatemala, and to other public and private libraries.

But the mysteries of the revolution remained unsolved. Who killed Francisco Arana, the man who had hoped to be Arévalo's successor? Why did Arbenz import weapons from Czechoslovakia? How close was he to the Communist party? Why did the army turn against him? Why did he resign? The written record does not answer these questions. Much that transpired was not recorded at the time, and the protagonists have remained silent through the years. Even the loquacious Arévalo, who has written voluminous memoirs, has not written about his own presidency.

And so I pursued the survivors—in Guatemala, in Mexico, in the United States, in Cuba, in the Dominican Republic, in Nicaragua, in Costa Rica. I began in 1978, and my last interview was in 1990. Some people spoke for one hour, others for many hours, in interviews that spanned twelve years. This allowed me to check and cross-check their stories and to probe more deeply as I learned more.

Let me give, as an example, the case of Arbenz's widow, María. I first tried to interview her in August 1978, when I arrived at her house in San Salvador with a warm letter of introduction from a mutual friend, only to be told, "La señora is away. We don't know when she will be back." I persisted during the following years, as she moved to San José, Costa Rica. At last, in February 1982, I was invited to her sister-in-law's house for lunch. "Come," I was told. "Doña María will be here." I arrived—with two Guatemalan friends who knew her and who had helped arrange the encounter—like a prospective

---

[4] Interview with Fortuny.

[5] In the early 1980s several books were published that made good use of newly declassified documents to shed light on U.S. policy toward Guatemala: Immerman, *CIA in Guatemala*; Schlesinger and Kinzer, *Bitter Fruit*; Cook, *Declassified Eisenhower*, pp. 217–92. While these books overshadow everything that had been written previously on the subject, three earlier works deserve to be remembered: Jonas and Tobis, *Guatemala*, and Blasier, *Hovering Giant*, for their intelligent analyses; and Wise and Ross, *Invisible Government*, pp. 177–96, for its investigative skill. More recent works that rely on this new scholarship include Rabe, *Eisenhower and Latin America*, pp. 42–63, and Wood, *Dismantling*, pp. 152–90.

bridegroom, surrounded by matchmakers. Doña María did not appear. "She couldn't make it," her sister-in-law explained. "But, please, stay for lunch. Let's talk." I stayed. We talked through the afternoon and into the evening. As I was leaving, my hostess made a phone call. She then handed me a slip of paper. "Call this number tomorrow morning at nine."

At nine, I made my call, nervous, half-expecting to be told, "La señora is away." But Doña María came to the phone, and that same afternoon I went to her house. It was February 9, 1982. To my knowledge, I am the only person to whom she has granted an interview since the fall of Arbenz.

For three days she did not allow me to take notes, whereas she taped our conversations for her records. There was not a word about the Communist party; we were fencing. Gradually, she began to tell me her story. I interviewed her for three weeks in 1982, for ten days in 1984, and more briefly on later occasions when I was in San José. Most interviews lasted for three or four hours. But one, the one during which we discussed the fall of Arbenz, began, as always, at three-thirty in the afternoon and ended well past midnight.

By the time I met Doña María, I had been working on the book for several years. I could engage her in discussion rather than merely take notes. As the days and weeks passed, María's story unfolded. It corroborated what José Manuel Fortuny, the general secretary of the PGT, had already told me.

Of course, memory is treacherous and men lie. Are María de Arbenz and Fortuny entirely reliable? No, of course not. Do they have their own agendas? Yes, of course. But there are safeguards: (1) They were interviewed repeatedly, and always separately. Doña María did not see the notes of my interviews with Fortuny, and Fortuny did not see the notes of my interviews with Doña María. And yet their testimonies are strikingly similar. (2) Cui bono? María de Arbenz and Fortuny have no common agenda: María de Arbenz is no longer a communist and lives a quiet bourgeois life in Costa Rica; Fortuny is still a communist and lives in Mexico. They are not friends; they have not seen each other since the death of Jacobo Arbenz in 1971. While it might be in Fortuny's interest to stress Arbenz's communist past (although it could be used to justify the U.S. intervention),[6] it is certainly not in Doña María's interest. Yet their accounts concur both in broad outline and in most details. (3) There are very few points for which I rely exclusively on the testimonies of María de Arbenz and Fortuny. Even when addressing Arbenz's motivations for the agrarian reform program, an issue that is not discussed in the written record, the testimonies of Fortuny and María de Arbenz were weighed against those of Guerra Borges (who left the party in the mid-1960s and is no friend

[6] Indeed, the man who gave me the letter of introduction for Doña María in 1978 told me that he did not think it was wise to write about Arbenz's political sympathies. "It would play right into the CIA's hands."

of Fortuny), Alejandro (who has seen neither María nor Fortuny since the mid-1960s), Augusto Charnaud MacDonald (a noncommunist), and Guillermo Noriega Morales (the only surviving noncommunist who had helped to prepare the first draft of the agrarian reform program).

María de Arbenz is a key witness, but so are Guatemala's army officers, for the army held the balance of power in Arbenz's time. Most of the military officers of the period are still in Guatemala, and they are garrulous. Most had never been interviewed before. They arrived with a prepared script, but, to a man, they departed from it. Colonel Enrique Parinello, the army chief of staff under Arbenz, initially insisted that he had been loyal to the president, but as the interview progressed, he admitted that he had known that the army was going to betray Arbenz and that he had said nothing because the situation had seemed so hopeless—the United States had decided that Arbenz had to go. Colonel Rubén González Siguí began by regaling me with the standard army version of the fall of Arbenz. As he droned on, I put down my pen. I had delayed my flight from Guatemala in order to see him. It was September 1982, during Guatemala's dirty war, and I was uneasy, coming as I was from Mexico, where I had interviewed Guatemalan exiles. "Look," I told him. "What you're telling me makes no sense." I itemized the inconsistencies of this well rehearsed account. "I can leave now, if you want. Or we can talk. I won't quote you without your permission." We talked. With bitter pride, González Siguí recollected how Arbenz had stood up to the United States, and how the army had not.

There is a man in Guatemala City who has in his desk drawer a gun and a handkerchief stained with blood. When I first went to interview him, before bidding me welcome he opened the drawer and flourished the gun. I flinched. It was August 1978. Violence was increasing in the capital, and my host was a man of the far right, a fervent supporter of the Movimiento de Liberación Nacional, which had a long history of political assassinations. He wanted to impress upon me that in Guatemala one must live by the gun, that in Guatemala one must kill or be killed. The handkerchief, he explained, was stained with the blood of Carlos Castillo Armas, the man who had overthrown Arbenz and who was himself mysteriously assassinated three years later. And so I met Guayo Taracena de la Cerda, an enthusiastic supporter of Castillo Armas and a dedicated foe of Arbenz. Taracena is an idealist who has killed but not stolen, a man who fought for a cause, not for personal gain. I spent many hours with him through the summer of 1978 and again in 1982.

It is not only the Guatemalans who have a story to tell. So too do the Americans, from embassy officials who witnessed the unfolding of the revolution to CIA agents who plotted its demise. They were interviewed for this book, several on repeated occasions. They were, for the most part, professional and dispassionate. Richard Bissell, who participated in the CIA plot against Arbenz, spent six hours analyzing the weaknesses of the operation—weaknesses, he concluded, that were many and glaring. Ambassador Peurifoy's deputy, Bill Krieg, remarked that the communist leaders "were very honest, very committed. This was the tragedy: the only people who were committed to hard work were those who were, by definition, our worst enemies."[7]

Unlike the Guatemalan participants, most of the Americans had been interviewed by other researchers, but an understanding of the Guatemalan revolution casts new light on their accounts. My analysis of the Guatemalan side of the story has convinced me that the accuracy and subtlety of U.S. intelligence on Guatemala improved from Truman to Eisenhower and that in the course of the revolution, the influence of the communists in shaping Guatemalan policy increased, while the influence of the United Fruit Company in shaping American policy decreased. There is no convenient villain of the piece, but rather a complex interplay of imperial hubris, security concerns, and economic interests. It is against this constellation of forces that the story of the Guatemalan revolution was played out to its tragic end. The record—Guatemalan and American, oral and written—shows that Fortuny was right: "They would have overthrown us even if we had grown no bananas."

[7] Interview with Krieg.

CHAPTER 1

The Era of Ubico

ON JANUARY 22, 1932, a peasant revolt erupted in El Salvador. The uprising was quickly suppressed, as the government slaughtered from ten to thirty thousand peasants. The young Communist Party of El Salvador, which had participated in the revolt, was branded by the Salvadoran authorities as its sole organizer and the source of its every atrocity.[1]

Neighboring Guatemala shuddered. Fear spread through its upper class: a similar upheaval could take place at home. But President Jorge Ubico had already acted: on January 29, the Guatemalan government announced that a Bolshevik revolt had been narrowly averted "in one of the most efficient and beneficial operations executed in the Americas since the arrival of the conquistadores." The communists, it explained, had gained control of the trade unions and had been agitating in the countryside; their leader, the carpenter Antonio Obando Sánchez, had been appointed "High Commissar and Great Teacher of the Steppes in the Soviet of Guatemala" by the Kremlin.[2]

And so hundreds were arrested, as the upper class quaked. "There was a house," the police disclosed,

> in which the cook, the chauffeur, a maid and a gardener had joined the communists; they were ready to betray their masters—raping, murdering and robbing on the day of the uprising. In another household, a black servant was found carrying the tools needed to break into the bedroom of two of our most beautiful high society girls. In another house, the police confiscated ropes which were going to be used to hang a rich man and his family who lived in the heart of our capital city.[3]

The demonic nature of the communist leaders was exposed. Obando Sánchez, it was stated, "preaches slaughter first, and then the complete redistribution of private property, including—like pieces of furniture or slaves (and only to satisfy the biological needs of the species)—all the women of the defeated

[1] On the revolt, see Anderson, *Matanza*; Dalton, *Miguel Mármol*, pp. 229–367; "Los sucesos," *Abra*; Arias Gómez, *Farabundo Martí*; McClintock, *American Connection*, 1:99–121.

[2] *La Gaceta: Revista de policía y variedades*, Feb. 7, 1932, pp. 251–323, p. 306 (quoted). See also "Vasto plan del terrorismo comunista para Guatemala," *El I*, Jan. 29, 1932, p. 1; "Todos los cabecillas capturados," *El I*, Jan. 30, 1932, p. 1; "Sigue la limpia de agitadores del terrorismo," *El I*, Feb. 2, 1932, p. 1.

[3] *La Gaceta* (see n. 2 above), p. 306. This issue includes a long list of the detained "communist plotters."

bourgeoisie from age eight to thirty, sentencing those who are older to death by fire." Juan Pablo Wainwright, a young upper-class Honduran who had joined the party a few months earlier, was just as bloodthirsty: "His only interest is burning, destroying, breaking, raping, cutting in two, in four, beating and redistributing private property."[4]

There had been no plot: the Guatemalan Communist Party was far weaker than its Salvadoran counterpart. In 1932, the communists were thinking not of revolution but of survival.[5] Yet the Guatemalan upper class believed the government's propaganda. Then, as now, its acumen was warped by its fear of losing any of its privileges, by its proclivity to brand all suggestions of reform as communist subversion, and by its tendency to believe anything that might confirm its deformed view of reality.[6]

The upper class, the press, and the Church warmly praised the government's "activism and vigor" against international communism. They warned, however, that there must be no slackening of the vigilance and the repression needed to prevent further outbursts.[7]

They had no reason to fret. Ubico, himself a prominent landowner, crushed both the fledgling labor movement and the tiny Communist party. Most leading party members fell into the hands of the police and were tortured. Not one begged for mercy; not one repented. Among them was Wainwright, who is remembered for an act of courage unique in the thirteen years of Ubico's rule. "Cruelly tortured," relates an inveterate anticommunist writer,

Wainwright sent a note to General Ubico offering him sensational revelations. Ubico arrived at the penitentiary and entered the gloom of cell number 13.

"What do you have to tell me?" asked the dictator.

"I sent for you," replied Wainright, "to tell you that you are a miserable murderer and an animal." He spat in Ubico's face. The dictator whipped him merci-

---

[4] Ibid., pp. 309, 279.

[5] Interview with a party leader, Vásquez, who notes that the party, which had been founded in 1922, never had more than one hundred members. The best source on the Communist Party of Guatemala in the twenties is Taracena Arriola: "Les origines," pp. 282–390, 425–29 and "El primer partido." Obando Sánchez, a leader of the party, includes valuable information in his *Memorias*, pp. 43–109. Useful studies by Guatemalan communists of the post–World War II period are: Alvarado Arellano, *Apuntes*, pp. 5–11 and *Esbozo histórico*, pp. 3–6; Gutiérrez, *Breve historia*, pp. 21–27 and *Apuntes*, pp. 14–20. The only worthwhile source in English is Alexander, *Communism*, pp. 350–53.

[6] See Gleijeses, *Politics and Culture*, pp. 24–26.

[7] Quoted from "El comunismo," *El Apostol*, Jan. 31, 1932, p. 17. See also "Manifestación social contra el comunismo," *El I*, Feb. 1, 1932, p. 1; "Es una suerte para Guatemala represión oportuna al comunismo," *El I*, Feb. 5, 1932, p. 1; "Orden de la gran parada anticomunista el domingo," *El I*, Feb. 11, 1932, p. 1.

lessly. He was almost dead when a bullet ended his suffering. Wainwright lived and died with honor.[8]

Several communists were executed a few days later. The party had been destroyed. It was the second year of the era of Ubico.

Lacking gold, sugar, and spices, Guatemala had been an impoverished and neglected colony throughout the three centuries of Spanish rule. Even after independence it remained an impoverished backwater. Coffee was to change this.

In the last decades of the nineteenth century, the rising demand for coffee wrenched Guatemala into the world economy. Great coffee estates were created, and, to bring the coffee to the sea, railroads were built. Agrarian "reforms" that dispossessed the Indians of their land and labor codes that legalized forced labor ensured that the Indian would supply the workforce.[9]

While the Indian tilled the land, the foreigner built the railroad. By 1912, the American-owned International Railways of Central America controlled Guatemala's railroads. Over the next two decades, the United Fruit Company acquired immense tracts of state land, offering in return paltry sums of money and perfunctory thanks. The State looked on, untroubled by the mergers and the acquisitions that tightened foreign control of the economy.

In 1920, Guatemala entered a period of limited political democracy. The Congress and the press were relatively free. Repression remained, but less than in the past, at least in the cities. The urban population demanded economic concessions and dared to stage strikes. Often the police intervened and arrested people, but wages did increase and several labor unions were legalized.[10] In 1922, thirteen Ladino artisans and a Salvadoran law student created the Communist Party of Guatemala. It was illegal, persecuted, and penniless. ("We were ignorant; we didn't know anything about Marxist theory; we didn't even own any Marxist books," recalls one of the party's founders.)[11] But due to the skill of its leaders, the party acquired influence in the labor movement out of proportion to its meager numbers. It had, however, no contacts in the

[8] Schlesinger, *Revolución comunista*, pp. 44–46, quoted from p. 46. On Wainwright, see also García, *Páginas de lucha*, pp. 73–75; Gaitán, "Los mártires"; Oqueli, "Un señor"; Rosenthal, *Guatemala*, pp. 192–93.

[9] The best works on the coffee era are by McCreery and Castellanos Cambranes. By McCreery, see esp. *Development and the State*, "Debt Servitude," and "An 'Odious Feudalism.' " By Castellanos Cambranes, see *Desarrollo* and *Café y campesinos*. A classic study is Rubio Sánchez, "Breve historia."

[10] On the democratic interlude of the 1920s, see Figueroa Ibarra, "Contenido de clase" and "La insurrección"; Arévalo Martínez, *Ecce Pericles!*, esp. vol. 2; Taracena Arriola, "Les origines," pp. 104–424; Quintana, *La generación de 1920*; Pitti, "Ubico."

[11] Interview with Vásquez.

rural areas. There, no unions were allowed, and democracy meant herding the Indians to the polls on election day.

With the crash of 1929, the coffee market collapsed, the Guatemalan economy went bankrupt, and unemployment spread through the land. "There is a great deal of unrest among the working classes," reported the U.S. embassy in April 1930.[12] Fearing "the gathering of red storm clouds,"[13] the Guatemalan elite knew that the times demanded a strong leader. That man was Jorge Ubico. As a governor, he had gained "a reputation for efficiency and cruelty." The U.S. embassy gave him its hearty endorsement.[14] In February 1931, he triumphed in a presidential election in which he was the sole candidate.

During his thirteen-year dictatorship, Ubico built a number of roads using largely unpaid Indian labor provided in lieu of a road tax; this age-old practice he enforced with particular vigor. He also erected several public buildings. Again, much of the labor was unpaid, supplied by convicts whose ranks were swelled by periodic police raids on Saturday evenings in poor sections of the capital and other towns to arrest drunken laborers and others who might have become drunk had they had the time. This, too, was an old practice, which had fallen into disuse during the more permissive twenties.[15]

By 1934, Ubico had balanced the national budget by slashing government expenditures. He had also reduced graft, which had been rampant in the twenties. For many members of the Guatemalan middle class, this austerity meant dismissal from the bureaucracy. For others, Ubico's rule meant a sharp reduction in salaries and pensions. Blue collar workers fared worse. When the workers of Novella & Company, the largest cement factory of Central America, went on strike in March 1931 to protest a wage cut, the newly inaugurated Ubico ordered the arrest of the ringleaders.[16] Then came the great wave of repression that accompanied the discovery of the 1932 "communist plot"; the

[12] Hawks to SecState, no. 19, Apr. 2, 1930, p. 4, NA 814.00/1011.

[13] David Vela, "Canción de alba porvenirista," *El I*, Nov. 27, 1930, p.3.

[14] Grieb, "American Involvement," p. 12. The best source on Ubico prior to his presidency is Pitti, "Ubico."

[15] See esp. Grieb, *Guatemalan Caudillo*, pp. 126–40, 163–76. This is superior to the only comparable study of the Ubico era: Arévalo Martínez, *Ubico*. It is less penetrating, however, than Pitti's magisterial "Ubico," which ends, unfortunately, with Ubico's accession to the presidency. The writings of former *Ubiquistas* convey the flavor of the times: Col. Ardón, *El señor general*, is a vivid apology by an unreconstructed *Ubiquista*; Col. Flores Avendaño, *Memorias*, 1:143–270, describes the Ubico era through one man's eyes; Samayoa Chinchilla, *El dictador*, is well written and at times incisive.

[16] See "Una protesta," *Nuestro Diario*, Mar. 20, 1931, p. 3; López Larrave, *Breve historia*, p. 23; Obando Sánchez, *Memorias*, pp. 77–78; Dosal, "Political Economy," pp. 341–43.

urban labor movement was destroyed. Thereafter, notes a labor lawyer, "began the long night of Guatemalan labor." The words "trade union, strike, labor rights, petitions" were proscribed, "and those who dared use them were automatically branded as 'communists.' "[17]

Ubico watched carefully that no naive soul spoiled the Guatemalan workers. He intervened in 1942, when the U.S. army (which was building military bases in the country) sought to pay its laborers more than the prevailing wage of twenty-five cents per day.[18] Wages failed to increase even when the Second World War brought sharp inflation to Guatemala.[19] His rule did, however, bring the workers one improvement: disgusted by the subversive connotation of the word, Ubico decreed that there would no longer be "obreros" in Guatemala; they all became "empleados."[20]

However important politically, cities and towns were only specks in the immense *finca* that was Guatemala. In 1940, about 90 percent of the approximately 2.25 million Guatemalans lived in communities of fewer than ten thousand inhabitants. Two-thirds of these Guatemalans were Indians, the descendants of the vanquished Maya.[21] Above the Indians were the Ladinos, an ambiguous category that encompassed all those who were not officially classed as Indians, blacks, or Chinese; it ranged from upper-class whites who boasted of their European lineage to landless Indians who had renounced the culture of their people.

Rare was the Ladino, whatever his status, who felt no contempt for the Indian. Contempt and fear. One day the Indians might rise in blind, destructive fury. No one could divine what lurked behind their subservient smiles, their tame demeanor, their silence. The aboriginal race was "cowardly, sad, fanatical, and cruel. . . . [It was] closer to beast than to man," lamented a young Guatemalan intellectual in 1927. "For the Indians there is only one law—the lash."[22]

---

[17] López Larrave, *Breve historia*, p. 24.

[18] FBI, "Guatemala Today," July 1944, p. 31, NA 814.00/8-944.

[19] For the inflation of the war years, see the Weekly Stability Reports of the U.S. military attaché in Guatemala, 1942–44, RG319 RF, Boxes 749 and 1564, NA-S. See also Bulmer-Thomas, *Political Economy*, pp. 95–100, and CT:DAT, 1944, AGCA.

[20] See Monteforte Toledo, *Guatemala*, p. 290, n. 1, and González Orellana, *Historia de la educación*, p. 374.

[21] Before they were published, these census figures were laundered by Ubico; he swelled the population by 1 million and cut the proportion of Indians from more than two-thirds of the total to one-half. See Naval Attaché June, "Intelligence Report" no. 464-42-R, Dec. 14, 1942, RG165 RF, Box 1574, NA-S; Early, *Demographic Structure*, pp. 20–21; "2.781.665 habitantes en Guatemala," *El I*, June 17, 1950, p. 1; Monteforte Toledo, *Guatemala*, pp. 61–70.

[22] Quotations from García Granados, *Evolución sociológica*, pp. 25–26, and a Guatemalan official quoted in Jones, *Guatemala*, p. 106.

On this beast rested the prosperity of Guatemala. "The Indian," the U.S. embassy noted, "illiterate, unshod, diseased, is the Guatemalan laborer."[23] Until 1934, he was bound to his master by debt peonage. After 1934, he was bound to the State by Ubico's vagrancy laws: all those Indians who owned no land or less than a prescribed amount were ordered to hire themselves out to landowners for at least one hundred days a year.[24] Theoretically, the Indians could choose their employers and negotiate their contracts according to the laws of supply and demand. But in a world ruled by the masters' violence, these laws hardly applied. When there was any trouble, the landowners banded together. Thus, in the department of Quezaltenango, they "joined forces to create a trust . . . which would maintain a wage level of 15 centavos per day. . . . Penalties were agreed upon for anyone who broke this rule."[25]

Only exceptionally were such steps necessary. The Indian laborers could not read the contracts to which they apposed their thumbs; they could not verify whether the written words matched the *patrón*'s oral promises. Moreover, all Indian men between eighteen and sixty years of age had to prove that they had hired themselves out for the prescribed number of days. To this end, they were required to carry cards on which their employers noted the days they had worked, and "it was the common occurrence that the *patrón* would keep a laborer on simply by refusing to sign the books."[26] If a dispute arose, the authorities sided with the landowners. But disputes were usually settled within the closed world of the fincas: whips and stocks were a standard part of the landowner's equipment.

Ubico, sympathetic to the landowners' concerns, legalized murder: Decree 1816 of April 1932 exempted landowners from the consequences of any action taken to protect their goods and lands.[27] From this to the cold-blooded murder of a stubborn Indian was a moot step. Yet, one wonders why this decree was necessary. Civilized Guatemalans had always understood the occasional need to kill an Indian.

By replacing debt peonage with the vagrancy laws, Ubico sought to improve Guatemala's image abroad. He also satisfied the requests of many land-

---

[23] Capt. Rose, "Military Attaché Report" no. 922, Oct. 25, 1943, p. 2, RG319 DF, Box 226, NA-S.

[24] See Skinner-Klée, *Legislación indigenista*, pp. 108–14 and 118–19 for Decree 1995 (May 7, 1934), Decree 1996 (May 10, 1934) and "Reglamento relativo a los jornaleros para trabajos agrícolas" (Sept. 24, 1935). In theory, the vagrancy laws applied to all Guatemalan citizens; in practice, they applied almost exclusively to Indians. Only those Indians who could convince the unsympathetic authorities that they did not earn their living through agriculture escaped the law. See also Jones, *Guatemala*, pp. 160–67, and Whetten, *Guatemala*, pp. 120–22.

[25] Jones, *Guatemala*, pp. 165–66.

[26] Adams, *Crucifixion*, p. 178.

[27] *DCA*, May 7, 1932, p. 14.

owners who had argued since the 1920s that debt peonage was ineffective and uneconomic.[28] The vagrancy laws increased the influence of the central government, which was given the responsibility of allocating Indians among competing landowners. This was part of Ubico's effort "to shift the locus of power that had generally rested locally and regionally in the hands of the local upper class," and as such it paralleled the 1935 Municipal Law, which replaced the country's elected mayors with *intendentes* appointed by the central government.[29] Just as the *intendente* system was not introduced to improve the lot of the lower classes, so the vagrancy laws were not concerned with the welfare of the Indians.

This is not to say that Ubico was unpopular with the Indians. The daily oppression they endured—an oppression that seemed as eternal as the land and the sky—came from their immediate masters: the landowners, the local authorities, and their Ladino neighbors. The president of the republic was a remote figure, nearly as remote as the concept of a country called Guatemala. Ubico, who traveled extensively through the country, may even have appeared as a benevolent figure who came from afar and spoke words that, though stern, lingered as an echo of hope after the great man had departed.[30] These are impressions; no one, save a few foreign anthropologists who eschewed political analysis, attempted to penetrate the world of the Indian.[31] For the Ladinos, the Indians were inferior beings, a featureless mass that understood only force.

The instruments of control were at hand. This was a militarized society. Every governor of Guatemala's twenty-two departments was a general. The

[28] See Pitti, "Ubico," pp. 230–32, 286, 369, 376, 404–5, 408, 487–88; McCreery, "Debt Servitude," esp. pp. 756–59; Castellanos Cambranes, "Los empresarios agrarios," pp. 276–79; Dawson, "Labor Legislation," esp. pp. 135–37.

[29] For an excellent analysis, see Adams, *Crucifixion*, pp. 174–79, quoted from p. 175.

[30] On these travels, see the apologetic but interesting Hernández de León, *Viajes*. For less partisan sketches published in later years by participants and other witnesses, see Samayoa Chinchilla, *El dictador*, pp. 93–94, 147–59; Torres Moss, "Justicia salomónica"; González, "Recuerdos."

[31] Outstanding among these anthropological studies is Tax, *Penny Capitalism*. More recent studies also offer insight. For example, in a superb book based on field research done in the 1960s, Carmack writes of the area of Momostenango: "The Indians seem to have believed that their problems were due to local ladino officials, but not to Ubico himself." (*Historia social*, p. 300.) For U.S. embassy accounts of unreported Indian riots and the attending executions and imprisonments, see Davis to Burnett, Aug. 13, 1936, RG165 RF, Box 1562, NA-S; R.McN, "Labor-General," July 8, 1942, RG165 RF, Box 1563, NA-S; F.G.M., "Roads and Highways," Sept. 7, 1942, RG165 RF, Box 1568, NA-S. For a poignant account written by Indians of the massacre at Tacaná in 1937 (that was officially described as the army's appropriate response to a riot), see Diego López P. et al. to Procurador General de la República, Tacaná, Dec. 2, 1945, MP:G, Leg. 32562, AGCA.

National Radio and the Department of Roads were staffed by military officers; officers led convicts and Indians to perform forced labor in the cities and the countryside. Secondary education was placed under military control: school principals were senior army officers; lieutenants and captains were in charge of discipline; students were required to undergo reserve training.[32] "With the militarization of these minor civil officials," the U.S. naval attaché explained, "President Ubico further extends his military control over the everyday life and every thought and action of the people of Guatemala."[33]

Not only did these measures enforce military discipline in the bureaucracy, they also employed some of the eighty generals who infested the Guatemalan army in the early 1940s. (Those who had no specific duties congregated every morning in the dictator's anteroom to await his pleasure.) Hated by their own officers, Ubico's generals were notorious for their ignorance, incompetence, and cruelty. Their sole qualification was their mindless obedience to Ubico's orders.

The Guatemalan army, noted a 1944 U.S. intelligence report, was a dismal affair, 798 officers and 5,528 enlisted men who were "poorly trained and poorly equipped." ("It is doubtful," the report pointed out, "whether many of the soldiers have ever fired their rifles.")[34] The officers were Ladinos; nearly all the soldiers were Indian conscripts drafted by force. Military service, Ubico explained, was enlightening for the Indians: "They arrive rude and brutish, but when they leave they are no longer like donkeys, they have good manners and are better equipped to face life."[35] Life in the barracks was similar, however, to life on the *patrones*' estates: despised and paid miserably, they slept on the floor, ate terrible food, donned ragged and dirty uniforms, and were whipped mercilessly at the least infraction. In the words of a Gua-

[32] González Orellana, *Historia de la educación*, pp. 360–62, 439–40; Valdes López, "Aspectos socioculturales," pp. 32–35; Carrillo Ramírez, *Evolución histórica*, 1: 242–57.

[33] Lamson-Scribner, "Attaché's Report" no. 670, July 14, 1938, RG165 RF, Box 1571, NA-S.

[34] FBI, "Guatemala Today" (see n. 18 above), pp. 77–81, quoted from p. 77. Counting the number of officers and men in the Guatemalan army was not an exact science: just as he did with the census (see above, n. 21), so Ubico inflated the size of the army, padding it with imaginary reserves. (See Military Intelligence Division, "Military Forces of the Central American Republics," no. 265-231, Oct. 15, 1940, RG165 RF, Box 1574, NA-S; Woodward to SecState, no. 538, Aug. 28, 1945, RG84 CF, Box 13, NA-S; HQs Panama Canal Department, "Weekly Intelligence Summary" no. 263, July 15, 1947, p. 5, RG319 ID 384002, NA-S.) There is no adequate study of the army in the Ubico era. Interviews with the following officers who were on active duty at the time were particularly useful: Lorenzana, Silva Girón, Paz Tejada, Cruz Salazar.

[35] Ubico, quoted in Hernández de León, *Viajes*, 2:17.

temalan officer who served under Ubico and who is not given to sentimentality, "Their treatment was atrocious"; they were, observes another officer, "inept, ill-prepared, illiterate and whipped into stupidity."[36]

Ubico's notorious parsimony was also evident in the treatment of his officers, at least until they reached the rank of colonel. Their salaries were mediocre, and they endured an oppressive discipline. Their role was to inspire fear on behalf of the dictator, but they, too, lived in a world of fear, where "the slightest hint of dissatisfaction could prove fatal."[37] To avoid contamination, officers were not sent to study abroad. They were jailers, forbidden to wander outside the prison walls. The "merciless system" worked. The officers were automata, ready to obey all orders, refraining from all initiative: "We were always scared; the military code was draconian, prescribing the death penalty for virtually every offense. Spies were everywhere."[38]

For added security, Ubico relied on an elite unit that served as his presidential guard. The Guardia de Honor received the bulk of the weapons given to Guatemala by the United States during the Second World War, including the only twelve tanks in the country. Its soldiers "slept on cots, not on the floor . . . and were somewhat better dressed and better fed."[39] The officers received higher pay; in return, they were expected to be particularly loyal to Ubico.

Special loyalty was also expected from the officers *de linea*. These were generally lower-middle-class Ladinos who rose through the ranks. For them, the life of an officer represented both an attractive station and one of the very few avenues of upward mobility in Guatemala. By contrast, the officers *de escuela*—those who had graduated from the military academy—were generally of middle-class extraction. Had it not been for the economic crisis of the 1930s, many would have attended the university; a military career offered them neither social nor economic advancement, particularly toward the end of the era, when the plethora of generals and colonels stifled the possibility of promotion.

However pitiful as a professional military force, the Guatemalan army was more than adequate to control the unarmed populace; indeed, it was impressive compared to the other ragtag armies of Central America. Moreover, it was supplemented by the police which, drawn almost exclusively from poor

[36] Quotations from interview with Lorenzana and from Silva Girón, *12 Horas*, p. 28.

[37] Lt. Col. Cruz Salazar, "El ejército," p. 77.

[38] Quotations from Lt. Col. Hardy, "Military Attaché Report" no. A/G 2028, Apr. 12, 1944, RG319 DF, Box 749, NA-S, and from interview with Col. Lorenzana. For a dramatic example, see the story of Roberto Barrios Peña recounted in Hunter, "Intelligence Report" no. 13-43-R, Jan. 15, 1943, RG165 RF, Box 1565, NA-S.

[39] Silva Girón, *12 Horas*, p. 32. Zamora Alvarez, *Las memorias de Andrés*, pp. 47-71, describes the life of a soldier in the Guardia de Honor in the last months of the dictatorship. For the early years of the Guardia de Honor, see Gen. Zamora Castellanos, *Nuestros cuarteles*, pp. 254–74.

Ladinos, had "the reputation of being one of the most efficient and secretive in Latin America."[40] Together, the army and the police formed a formidable barrier to domestic unrest, and they faced no difficult challenges. After the destruction of the 1932 "communist plot," Ubico crushed a true conspiracy in 1934. There were no other plots of any significance, and there were no disturbances, until 1944.[41]

Nor was there much crime, at least not in the usual sense: common criminals were swiftly and ruthlessly punished. Accounts abound of how safe Guatemala became under Ubico's rule. It was not safe, however, for the victims of the dictator's whims, for "subversive" Indians, or for poor Ladinos. "We had to endure not only the all-encompassing will of the dictator," recalls a former official, "but also the numerous 'Little Ubicos' who imitated him while doing his bidding: the chief of police, the governors of the departments, the local police chiefs and hundreds more. . . . In the early days of the dictatorship I became aware of murders perpetrated by the rural police. They had to set an example, their chiefs said, in order to escape the Man's wrath."[42]

Communists and criminals (insofar as he distinguished between them) were two of Ubico's phobias. The third was intellectuals, for whom he "felt an Olympian contempt."[43] His disdain was tinged with mistrust; people who read might fall prey to subversive ideas, that is, to communism. Thus he made sure that no subversive books entered Guatemala, and that no subversive ideas perturbed the Guatemalan youth. "We were political illiterates," recalls a student leader.[44]

Arrogant and suspicious, Ubico was loath to delegate authority. As a loyal minister stated, "His overestimation of himself led him to take care of everything without seeking advice." He had developed, noted the FBI, a clever system of "checking up on his ministers": he appointed their enemies as their deputies. "In this way they keep a check on each other and report to the President."[45] A U.S. official had seen this side of Ubico as early as 1923:

[40] FBI, "Guatemala Today" (see n. 18 above), pp. 66–77, quoted from p. 66. Ubico's jails were also famous for their efficiency; China requested permission to study them. (Tchou Che-Tsien, Consul General of China, to Ministro Gobernación, Jan. 7, 1944, CM:G, Leg. 32357, AGCA.)

[41] On the 1934 plot, see de los Rios, *Ombres*, 1:379–97 and 2:171–207; Sandoval Vásquez, *Leifugados*, pp. 74–78 and 217–57; Arévalo Martínez, *Ubico*, pp. 34–38; Aguilar P., *Vida*, pp. 25–52.

[42] Flores Avendaño, *Memorias*, 2:240–41.

[43] González Campo, "El general," p. 346.

[44] Interview with Galich, one of the leaders of the 1944 movement against Ubico in the university.

[45] Quotations from González Campo, "El general," pp. 347–48 and FBI, Hoover to Berle, Jan. 13, 1942, p. 2, NA 814.00/1371.

During the hour and a half that I spent with the General, I was impressed with . . . the almost Anglo-Saxon frankness of the man. He is what is known here as the white type, untainted by mixed blood. . . . The accession of General Ubico as President would be, however, the accession of a dictator. He has the suggestion complex, imagining that he is Napoleon, whom he does strongly resemble. This physiological [sic] state of mind is immediately apparent when one enters his drawing room. In conspicuous places are busts of Napoleon. . . . Above these statues is a large photograph of General Ubico.[46]

Ubico may have had delusions of grandeur, but his world was narrow; "he lacked the statesman's vision."[47] His was the Guatemala of the past, and he was suspicious of all change. "He opposed industrial development because factories spawned a proletariat from which the communists would emerge"; when Bata, a leading shoe manufacturer, sought to establish itself in Guatemala in the early 1940s, "Ubico categorically rejected the proposal."[48]

Ubico's bravery was legendary, as was his bravado: "I have no friends, but only domesticated enemies. . . . Be careful! I am a tiger, you are monkeys."[49] Considering Guatemala to be his personal domain, Ubico "ruled the country as if it were his hamlet. He controlled everything. It is true that there was less theft under Ubico. The only man with the freedom to steal was Ubico himself."[50] A 1944 U.S. intelligence report noted that after taking office, Ubico "became the greatest private landowner in Guatemala, despite his much-publicized campaign for honesty in government." He bought "many properties at a price fixed by himself." He also made sure that his salary and perquisites were generously increased while he slashed the bureaucrats' salaries, and he graciously accepted, in 1940, a gift of $200,000 from a servile Congress. This spontaneous token of gratitude aroused resentment, but the begrudgers were swiftly silenced: "The Legation has heard," the U.S. minister reported, "that some ninety persons in Guatemala have been put in jail for speaking out of turn regarding this gift."[51]

[46] G-2 Intelligence Report, "Interview with General Jorge Ubico," no. 839, Dec. 17, 1923, p. 3, RG165 RF, Box 1565, NA-S.

[47] González Campo, "El general," p. 346.

[48] Quotations from Alfonso Solorzano in Quan Rossell, *Guatemala*, 1:218, and González Campo, "El general," p. 354. The former was a foe of Ubico, the latter an apologist, but on this point they are in full agreement.

[49] Samayoa Chinchilla, *El dictador*, pp. 62, 107.

[50] José Luis Balcarcel in Quan Rossell, *Guatemala*, 2:497–98.

[51] Quotations from: Office of Strategic Services, Research and Analysis Branch, "The First Two Months of the New Guatemalan Government (November–December 1944)," no. 2791, Dec. 23, 1944, p. 6, NA; Cabot to SecState, no. 1599, Dec. 4, 1940, p. 3, NA 814.00/1340; DesPortes to SecState, no. 1250, May 8, 1940, p. 1, NA 814.001/101. For Ubico's salary and perquisites in July 1938 (totaling $11,790), see Samayoa Chinchilla, *El dictador*, p. 109.

Those who offended the dictator were harshly punished. The secret police "has earned for itself the odious title of the Guatemalan Gestapo," a U.S. official noted.[52] "The spy network was organized wisely and carefully. There were informers in all social classes. . . . The servant was a spy, and so was his master; the lady was a spy, and so was the whore; the priest was a spy, and so was the teacher."[53] As a result, recalls the son of a senior official, "In my friends' homes—and even in my home—in the streets, everyone spoke in hushed tones. . . . Suspicion was rife."[54] The immense majority of the elite submitted to the dictator's will, participated in his personality cult, and turned against those whom he branded as his enemies—even when they were friends or relatives. In return, they were allowed to live the lives of petty feudal lords.

Cold and contemptuous toward the Guatemalan upper class, Ubico was gentle with the United States. To be sure, the men he admired were not Roosevelt and Cordell Hull, but Franco and Mussolini. Admiration, however, did not stand in the way of common sense; the Caribbean belonged to the United States. Moreover, Ubico saw the Americans as a valuable shield against Mexico, a neighbor that in the nineteenth century had annexed vast regions claimed by Guatemala and had become—or so Ubico and his class believed—a breeding ground for communist infection.[55] The United States, by contrast, was relatively healthy, even though Ubico at times doubted Roosevelt's steadfastness. He was worried, he told a U.S. diplomat in 1941, "about communistic activities and so many strikes in the United States." The American Communist Party may have been small, but "the smallest rat left unmolested in a mansion would in time do considerable boring." Whether in Guatemala or the United States, he stressed, the communists should be given a "dose of lead," not freedom of speech.[56]

Only about communism did Ubico dare to offer advice to the United States. Otherwise, his attitude was that of the obsequious pupil. He "diligently courted American officials, diplomats, and businessmen, exhibited preference for Yankee investors, and showed considerable imagination in discovering ways to demonstrate his support."[57] For example, he appointed a U.S. officer as director of the Escuela Politécnica, an unprecedented gesture. Except for a few months in 1943, U.S. officers occupied that prestigious post throughout

[52] FBI, "Guatemala: Police and Penal System," no. 2710, Dec. 4, 1943, p. 4, RG165 RF, Box 1562, NA-S.

[53] Samayoa Chinchilla, *El dictador*, p. 68.

[54] Julio Gómez Padilla in Quan Rossell, *Guatemala*, 1:333.

[55] For Ubico and Mexico see Pitti, "Ubico," pp. 9–11, 63–64, 462–63; Grieb, *Guatemalan Caudillo*, pp. 206–18, 235–47; Zorrilla, *Relaciones*, pp. 691–734.

[56] MemoConv, Aug. 12, 1941, quoted from pp. 3–4, enclosed in DesPortes to SecState, no. 2057, Aug. 14, 1941, NA 814.00/1358.

[57] Grieb, *Guatemalan Caudillo*, p. 72.

Ubico's thirteen years; other U.S. officers were among the academy's professors.[58]

After hostilities broke out in Europe, Ubico asserted that Guatemala "was with the United States in any needed capacity 'all of the way.' "[59] He declared war on Japan on December 8, one day after Pearl Harbor; on Italy and Germany on December 11, the day they declared war on the United States. "General Ubico," the U.S. military attaché reported, "has always been quick to follow the lead of the United States in the war measures dictated by that country. He has given many unheard of concessions to the U.S. Army." American troops were stationed in Guatemala, and Ubico "cooperated in the maintenance of harmonious relations with United States military personnel."[60]

At Washington's behest, Ubico moved against the German community in Guatemala—five to six thousand individuals, mainly Guatemalans of German origin. This small but economically influential group had supported the dictator loyally, and there is no indication that he considered them a threat to his rule. The Americans wanted action, and he complied. Following Guatemala's declaration of war on Germany, Ubico allowed the FBI to deport several hundred German citizens and Guatemalans of German origin to the United States. Others faced discriminatory measures that culminated, in June 1944, in the expropriation of all the coffee estates belonging to the German community.[61]

[58] There is no good study of the Escuela Politécnica; still, the following are useful: Samayoa Coronado, *Escuela Politécnica*; Zamora Castellanos, *Nuestros cuarteles*, pp. 45–133; Escuela Politécnica, *La Escuela Politécnica* and *Centenario*. Carrillo Ramírez, *Evolución histórica*, 2:153–226, describes the curriculum at the academy. Francisco Morazán, who entered the Academy in 1933, has written a graphic account of his experiences, "Apuntes," pp. 104–570. For the U.S. view of the school in the Ubico era, see Harris, "The Military School," no. 1473, Dec. 1, 1931, and Lt. Col. Marsh, "National Military Academy," no. 414, May 18, 1942, both RG165 RF, Box 1572, NA-S.

[59] MemoConv, p. 1, included in DesPortes to SecState, no. 2057, Aug. 14, 1941, NA 814.00/1358.

[60] Quotations from Rose, "Military Attaché Report" no. 1105, Mar. 7, 1944, RG319 RF, Box 748, NA-S, and from FBI, "Guatemala Today" (see n. 18 above), p. 191.

[61] For the most comprehensive treatment, see FBI, "Guatemala Today" (see n. 18 above), pp. 82–193. See also June, "Intelligence Report" no. 582-41, Sept. 20, 1941, RG165 RF, Box 1566, NA-S; FBI, Hoover to Berle, Jan. 13, 1942, pp. 4–6, NA 814.00/1371; United States Tariff Commission, *Economic Controls*, pp. 18–19. Decree 3115 of June 22, 1944, stipulated that the former owners would be compensated after the war, according to the value they had declared for tax purposes. (See *DCA*, June 23, 1944, p. 805, and "Razones de la expropiación," *El I*, June 23, 1944, p. 1.) There is no definitive study of the German presence in Guatemala. The best sources

In the late 1930s, occasional articles in the U.S. press had castigated Ubico as sympathetic to the Axis powers. His behavior during the war allayed such fears. As a result, between 1940 and mid-1944, the American press displayed warm appreciation for Jorge Ubico, an exotic strongman who built roads, maintained stability and exhibited a touching admiration for the United States and Franklin Delano Roosevelt. Ubico, John Gunther told his many readers, "is the biggest man in Central America. Given local conditions, he has done a lot. . . . Relations between the United States and Guatemala are in every way excellent, better than they have ever been before."[62]

Ubico's treatment of American companies was exemplary. Not only did he respect their immense privileges, but he was forthcoming in the one case in which, for a less supple man, confrontation would have been inevitable. The matter involved a 1930 contract with the United Fruit Company (UFCO): in return for a grant of two hundred thousand hectares at Tiquisate on the Pacific coast, the company pledged to build a Pacific port within seven years.[63] For the landed elite, this had one significant benefit: cheaper transportation costs. The coffee grown on the Western Piedmont would no longer have to be carried by rail all the way to Puerto Barrios on the Atlantic, an economic absurdity from which the International Railways of Central America (IRCA) extracted a hefty profit.

Had UFCO honored the agreement, IRCA's losses would have been substantial. But the two American companies reached a friendly understanding, which was formalized in a September 1936 contract. UFCO, which already owned 17 percent of IRCA's stock, bought additional shares, bringing its total participation to 42.68 percent. It also pledged not to build a port on the Pacific. Thus the bananas from Tiquisate would have to be transported, like the coffee, all the way to Puerto Barrios—but IRCA would charge UFCO less than half its usual freight rate. It was a deal that promised to benefit both companies.[64]

Without Ubico's gentle forbearance, the agreement would not have been possible. In March 1936, Guatemala had freed UFCO of its obligation to build the port "because of the prevailing economic crisis" (which was less severe than in 1930, when the original contract had been signed). UFCO paid $50,000 and retained the land it had received for agreeing to build the port. The negotiations, UFCO's local manager told the American chargé, "had

---

are Castellanos Cambranes, *El imperialismo alemán*; Náñez Falcón, "Dieseldorff"; Wagner, "Actividades empresariales."

[62] Gunther, *Inside Latin America*, pp. 122, 126. See also Lawrence and Sylvia Martin, "Ubico—Boss of Guatemala," *CSM*, Oct. 18, 1941, p. 5; John Gunther, "Four Strong Men and a President," *Harper's*, Sept. 1942, pp. 418–27; Frank Taylor, "Guatemala's Hardheaded Ubico," *Reader's Digest*, Feb. 1944, pp. 25–27.

[63] See de León Aragón, *Los contratos*, pp. 261–73.

[64] For the 1936 agreement, see LaBarge, "A Study of United Fruit," pp. 19–20.

been carried on most amicably . . . [and the company] had not been subjected to any particular pressure."[65]

Once again, as so often in its empire-building in the Caribbean basin, UFCO reaped the benefits of dictatorial rule. Whereas the 1930 contract had been preceded by long and acrimonious debates in the Guatemalan Congress and the press, the 1936 agreement was approved swiftly and without debate.

There is no indication that U.S. officials intervened to help the company. Nor was such help requested by UFCO. Having just "reelected" himself in violation of the constitution, Ubico was particularly eager for American goodwill; he was also aware that in the early 1920s the State Department had applied massive pressure when the Guatemalan government had failed to satisfy the demands of American companies.[66] Moreover, UFCO and IRCA were powerful enough in their own right to elicit sympathetic treatment.

During his presidency, Ubico proved himself worthy of the Americans' favor, and the United States was not ungrateful. U.S. officials had welcomed Ubico's accession to the presidency in 1931, praising him in extravagant terms as the man who could best maintain pro-American stability in Guatemala during the world recession.[67] Their approval was steadfast until the last months of the dictator's rule.

Even useful dictators can become expendable. Throughout Latin America, the Depression had spawned strongmen; by the mid-1940s the economic crisis had waned, and the Allied victory over Hitler was spreading antidictatorial feelings among even the upper class. In the Caribbean arc, through the mid-1940s, dictators faltered and fell: Anastasio Somoza's control of Nicaragua was seriously threatened; Rafael Trujillo experienced difficulties in the Dominican Republic; in Cuba, Fulgencio Batista accepted defeat at the polls; while Isaias Medina Angarita was toppled in Venezuela.

At the University of San Carlos, Guatemala's only center of higher education, some students began to shake off the torpor that had becalmed the country. The creation of the Law Students' Association in October 1942 and of a Federation of University Students thirteen months later were tentative steps along a narrow path. The students appeared to eschew political issues and to seek only minimal academic freedom, but below the surface, tensions were rising.[68] U.S. officials reported that Ubico's decision to continue for a third

[65] O'Donaghue to SecState, no. 941, Apr. 8, 1936, p. 2, NA 814.6156/13. For the text of the contract and a critical analysis, see de León Aragón, *Los contratos*, pp. 95–105, 171–90, 274–84.

[66] For the State Department's efforts on behalf of Empresa Electrica and IRCA, see Pitti, "Ubico," pp. 68–72, 83, 88–104; see also below, p. 86.

[67] See Grieb, "American Involvement."

[68] The best source on the period of awakening within the university and on the weeks of unrest that preceded Ubico's resignation is Galich, *Del pánico al ataque*. Also useful

term (from March 1943 to March 1949) created "considerable public tension" and "latent opposition."[69] Ubico's police chief pointed to the Atlantic Charter as "the cause of political unrest. . . . He advised that the people [had] read Allied propaganda posters about the Four Freedoms and their ensuing thoughts on the matter led them to feel discontented under the present Guatemalan government."[70] In fact, the middle class hated Ubico, and even the upper class was turning against him. It no longer needed the arrogant strongman.

Ubico's departure was preceded by that of his Salvadoran colleague, General Maximiliano Hernández Martínez. After crushing a military revolt in April 1944, Martínez faced a mounting wave of urban strikes. Students and blue collar workers led the unrest, the army wavered, and the U.S. embassy, seeking an orderly transition, urged the beleaguered dictator to leave. On May 11, Martínez sought refuge in Guatemala.[71]

The fall of a neighboring dictator unnerved Ubico and inspired his restive subjects. Guatemala's university students were the first to react. Until late June their demands were confined to academic issues, but their assertiveness itself was a political challenge. The authorities responded with surprising irresolution, combining hesitant concessions with light punishments. A few students were detained briefly, and others lost their jobs as schoolteachers. The overall impression was one of weakness. The students were emboldened, and the grip of fear over the population began to loosen.

In mid-June the ferment spread to the capital's teachers. The preparations for Teachers' Day (June 30) provided the spark: "As in every year, the teachers' martyrdom had begun. Without regard for age or sex, they had to assem-

---

are Morales, *Derrocamiento*; Mejía, *El movimiento obrero*, pp. 41–76; Ruiz Franco, *Hambre*, pp. 17–51; Gómez Padilla in Quan Rossell, *Guatemala*, 1:333–46; Zea González, *El espejismo*, pp. 128–71; Arévalo Martínez, *Ubico*, pp. 64–137, 166–69. Of particular interest is a series of articles by university students in *Studium*, April 1945, no. 1. Samayoa Chinchilla, *El dictador*, pp. 178–81, describes Ubico's last days in power from the vantage point of an official in the presidential palace. Two accounts by loyal *Ubiquistas* are González Campo, "La caída," and Salazar, *Memoria*, pp. 316–23. The definitive study of the fall of Ubico has yet to be written.

[69] FBI, "Guatemala Today" (see n. 18 above), p. 48. See also June to Navy Department, no. 259-42, June 1, 1942 enclosed in DesPortes to SecState, no. 2949, June 10, 1942, NA 814.00/1390; June to Navy Department, 16-43-R, Jan. 19, 1943, NA 814.00/1429; Drew to SecState, no. 3593, Feb. 9, 1943, NA 814.00/1405; Drew to SecState, no. 3707, Mar. 19, 1943, NA 814.00/1419; FBI, Hoover to Berle, Oct. 25, 1943, NA 814.00/1449; FBI, Hoover to Berle, Mar. 6, 1944, NA 814.00/1401.

[70] FBI, Hoover to Berle, June 2, 1944, p. 8, NA 814.00/6-2444. See also June, "Intelligence Report" no. 16-43-R, Jan. 19, 1943, pp. 1–2, RG165 RF, Box 1565, NA-S.

[71] On the fall of Martínez, see Morán, *Las jornadas cívicas*, and Parkman, *Nonviolent Insurrection*.

ble every afternoon at the *Instituto Nacional Central de Varones*. There they practiced marching for two hours without a break. Led by army officers, they would have to parade on Teachers' Day in perfect order, carrying heavy flags under the blazing sun.''[72] In growing numbers, the teachers boycotted the exercises. Soon other professionals, especially young lawyers, began to express their support for the students and to present demands of their own. But no one dared, as yet, to call for the dictator's resignation.

Ubico responded on June 22 by suspending constitutional guarantees. While no such guarantees had existed during his rule, their formal suspension indicated that a showdown was imminent. In the words of a student leader, "Everyone held their breath" that day and the next. "Beneath the anxiety, a new spirit was rising, nurtured by the bravery of the students and the whole-hearted support of the teachers.''[73] On Saturday, June 24, two brave souls brought a petition signed by 311 prominent Guatemalans to the presidential palace. In a respectful but firm tone, the document called for the reestablishment of constitutional guarantees. It was an act of audacity that Ubico viewed as painful betrayal. That same day, for the first time in the Ubico era, crowds gathered in the capital to demonstrate against the government. Also for the first time, voices were heard—a few at first, then a swelling chorus—demanding the dictator's resignation. The poor joined the students, teachers, and other professionals in the streets. "The first organized demonstration" of the day, reported U.S. Ambassador Boaz Long, took place around noon "when students marched quietly through the streets, cheering the United States and President Roosevelt as they passed the American Consulate General and the office occupied by the Military and Naval Attachés."[74] Throughout the day there was little violence. During the night, the police sent thugs to loot and riot in some areas of the capital. Several people were killed. The authorities blamed the demonstrators.[75]

By the next morning, Sunday, June 25, "tension throughout the city had mounted with almost incredible rapidity," Long observed. Large crowds gathered. The police and the army intervened, wounding many. "To any person who has been familiar with the thirteen years of iron-bound discipline maintained by the Ubico administration," noted Long, "it was difficult to believe that an incident at first confined to a small group comprised of University students should so swiftly have spread as to involve the entire city in a serious

[72] Galich, *Del pánico al ataque*, pp. 256–57.

[73] Ibid., p. 332. For an eye-witness account of the students' reaction to the suspension of constitutional guarantees, see Catalán M., "Huelga."

[74] Long to SecState, no. 1256, June 27, 1944, p. 1, NA 814.00/6-2344.

[75] See "Actos de pillaje cometidos el sábado," *El Liberal Progresista*, June 26, 1944, p. 1, and "Fue una farsa vulgar de la policía el asalto al barrio de La Palmita y Colonia de Ubico," *El I*, July 3, 1944, p. 1.

situation marked by public disorder and general civic disobedience.''[76] In the afternoon, a thirty-one-year-old schoolteacher, María Chinchilla, was killed by a soldier. On Monday, June 26, ''all stores and business houses, gasoline stations and newspaper offices closed.''[77] Guatemala City was challenging Ubico.

The confrontation would be brief and bloodless. For the next few days the police and the army were the unchallenged masters of the streets of the capital, but most offices and shops remained closed. Then, on June 30, the news spread: Ubico, it was said, had resigned.

And resign he did, on July 1. He abandoned a struggle he had not yet lost and might eventually have won. The capital was defiant, but the rest of the country was quiet, and the army had shown no sign of rebellion.[78] Nor had the Americans asked Ubico to step down. They did not, however, intervene to prop him up. Throughout June they were noncommittal. The State Department had told the embassy to limit its good offices, which had been requested by Ubico, ''exclusively to the transmission of messages between the contending factions.''[79] U.S. officials were beginning to see the dictator as an anachronism, they considered his handling of the crisis ineffectual, and they were confident that should Ubico be replaced, his successors would be friendly to Washington.

American aloofness struck Ubico as a sharp rebuff, but it brought little comfort to his foes. A leader of the opposition contrasted the attitude of Ambassador Long to that of the Mexican ambassador after meeting them both in late June: ''Long was tight-lipped; he neither said nor did anything that could give

[76] Long to SecState, no. 1256, June 27, 1944, p. 2, NA 814.00/6-2344.

[77] Long to SecState, no. 412, June 26, 1944, NA 814.00/1474. As the newspapers were either shut down or under government control, embassy memos and dispatches (NA 814.00 and RG84 GR, Box 106, NA-S) are the best source for the developments of the last week of June.

[78] For an overview, see the June reports of the Jefes Políticos (IMJP:G, Leg. 32376, AGCA). For the army, interviews with the officers listed in n. 34 above were instructive. For a corroborating sketch of the situation in the Guardia de Honor, see Zamora Alvarez, *Las memorias de Andrés*, pp. 73–76. Accounts by opposition leaders do not refer to any contact with active duty officers or to any wavering within the armed forces. The same telling silence is found in two army publications that deal at length with the events of 1944: *Revista de la Revolución*, Jan. 1945, and *Revista Militar*, Jan./Feb. 1945. In his Weekly Stability Reports for May and June 1944, the U.S. military attaché continued to assert that the army was loyal to Ubico (RG319 RF, Box 1564, NA-S). The only glimmer of a plot against Ubico was in the Escuela Politécnica among a mere handful of officers led by Jacobo Arbenz. They failed to gain adherents. (See below p. 139.)

[79] Quoted from Hull to AmEmG, no. 367, June 25, 1944, NA 814.00/1470. See also Long to SecState, no. 400, June 25, 1944, NA 814.00/1461; and Long to SecState, no. 402, June 25, 1944, NA 814.00/1470.

us the least comfort. But the Mexican Ambassador emphatically expressed his sympathy—and that of his government—for the Guatemalan people and the triumph of democracy in our country.''[80] Mexican sympathy was welcome, but it was the attitude of the United States that could be decisive. Washington had not turned against the dictator. The army was still loyal. Ubico had a good chance to ride out the storm.

Why then did he step down? Was he convinced that his position had become hopeless? Was he moved by bitter disappointment, having swallowed his sycophants' assurances that the people loved him? Ubico, reported Long on the morning of June 30, was ''deeply disillusioned and hurt with the realization that the majority of the country was against him.'' He was particularly embittered, Long added, by the petitions for his resignation submitted over the preceding days by a long list of prominent Guatemalans, including many whom he had considered absolutely loyal.[81]

Perhaps Ubico's decision was also influenced by his poor health, or even by the hope that soon he would be begged to return by a repentant people. No definitive answer has been offered by friend, foe, or even by Ubico himself; he left the presidential palace on the morning of July 1 with neither words nor overt emotion. He did not seek the safety of an embassy but went to his private residence in the capital—hardly the behavior of a cowed tyrant.

What is certain, however, is that he selected his successor in a most bizarre fashion. After signing his resignation decree on the morning of July 1, he ordered an aide, General Roderico Anzueto, ''to choose three generals to take over the presidency.'' Anzueto decided to select men he thought he would be able to control. Stepping out of the president's office, he performed his task: to their great surprise, three undistinguished generals—Federico Ponce Vaides, Eduardo Villagran Ariza, and Buenaventura Pineda—learned that henceforth they would constitute a three-man military *junta* and take the place of Ubico. When another general started to ask Ubico to stay, the dictator ''cut him short: 'Shut up!' he exclaimed. And he left.'' The first act of the new rulers, recalls the war minister, ''was to get drunk.''[82]

---

[80] Ernesto Viteri Bertrand, quoted by Morales, *Derrocamiento*, p. 108; see also pp. 95–97, 107–9, and Galich, *Del pánico al ataque*, p. 243. The role of the Mexican ambassador and his government's sympathy for the opposition to Ubico were widely noted. See Long to SecState, no. 1251, June 24, 1944; Long to SecState, no. 1261, June 27, 1944; FBI, Hoover to Berle, Aug. 23, 1944, p. 15; AmEm Mexico, Messersmith to SecState, no. 941, July 1, 1944; AmEm Mexico, Messersmith to SecState, no. 18733, July 12, 1944; Long to SecState, no. 1380, Aug. 1, 1944. All NA 814.00. See also: ''Triunfo del civismo,'' *El I*, July 3, 1944, p. 1; Muñoz Meany, *El hombre*, pp. 141–44; Roberto Quintana, ''Gesto heróico,'' *Studium*, Apr. 1945, no. 1, pp. 75–81; *Revista de la Revolución*, Jan. 1945, p. 28.

[81] Long to SecState, no. 1269, June 30, 1944, p. 2, NA 814.00.

[82] Quotations from: Rivas, ''Versión inédita''; Villegas Rodas, ''Como se produjo,''

On July 4, the most ambitious member of the *junta*, General Ponce, easily convinced a timorous Congress to elect him provisional president. "A Thompson sub-machine gun is a very good persuader," the U.S. military attaché observed dryly. Ponce was effusive. "I never dreamt, I never imagined, that one day I would be entrusted with the weighty responsibility which you now offer to me," he told the congressmen in his inaugural speech a few hours later.[83] In the weeks that followed, Ponce permitted the formation of political parties and trade unions and promised to hold free elections. Once again, students and teachers led the struggle. "The students," wrote Ambassador Long in August, "have injected themselves into all sorts of situations—labor, political, personal, congressional—ever since they succeeded in starting a movement which culminated in the resignation of President Ubico."[84] The country's two strongest opposition parties were the Frente Popular Libertador, whose leaders were university students, and Renovación Nacional, led by schoolteachers. Their candidate, university professor Juan José Arévalo, emerged as the leading contender for the presidency.

It became evident, however, that should elections indeed take place, they would be free only for those who were willing to choose General Ponce as Guatemala's next president.

Emboldened by their victory over the formidable Ubico, the inhabitants of the capital responded with mounting unrest. Ferment spread to many provincial towns, but the countryside remained quiet. Hoping to quell the opposition, Ponce exploited the Ladinos' fear of an Indian revolt. Beginning in late August, truckloads of Indians were carted to the capital to march in support of him; they were then shipped back to their villages, pawns in a struggle among

---

p. 3; Corado, "Yo no firmé." (These three senior government officials were eyewitnesses.) On Anzueto, interview with Rolz Bennett was useful. The U.S. embassy was told that the *junta* had been selected by the army's general staff, but this was certainly not the case. (See Salazar to Long, July 1, 1944, enclosed in Long to SecState, no. 1275, July 3, 1944; Long to SecState, no. 461, July 2, 1944; FBI, Hoover to Berle, July 15, 1944. All NA 814.00.) The manner in which Ubico chose his successors, coupled with the fact that there is no evidence that he tried to influence them after his resignation, disproves the theory that he stepped down in order to maintain power behind the throne.

[83] Quotations from Rose, "Weekly Conditions Report" no. 3020, July 6, 1944, p. 3, RG84 GR, Box 106, NA-S, and from "Discurso del General Ponce ante la Cámara," *El I*, July 5, 1944, p. 1. The best sources for the Ponce presidency are Arévalo Martínez, *Ubico*, pp. 166–343; Arévalo, *El candidato*, pp. 113–314; Ruiz Franco, *Hambre*, pp. 51–168; Flores Avendaño, *Memorias*, 2:271–317; Zea González, *El espejismo*, pp. 172–99. As with the fall of Ubico, much remains to be written; however in this case the Guatemalan press, which had become quite outspoken, is far more useful. For both periods, U.S. documents are a very important source.

[84] Long to SecState, no. 1428, Aug. 15, 1944, p. 2, NA 814.00.

Ladinos. The tactic culminated on Independence Day, September 15, with a parade of two thousand "imported" Indians marching through Guatemala City swinging clubs and machetes and shouting slogans in honor of "My President Ponce."[85] The government press praised "the magnificent parade . . . [and] the sincerity of the peasantry," and castigated those "power-hungry politicians who have contempt for the Indian."[86] The opposition offered a different assessment: "Sadness. . . . This is the only possible response to the pathetic parade of September 15. . . . What a sad spectacle! Illiterates, ignorants, marching through the streets of the capital without knowing why, shouting slurred slogans that they do not understand, repeating them by rote under the shadow of the whip." In tones of horror, of indignation, another paper described the marchers as "an unthinking mob . . . a host of illiterate Indians . . . armed with machetes, sticks, and clubs . . . with pictures of the provisional president hanging from their rags."[87]

Tensions grew. On October 1, the editor of the country's major opposition daily, El Imparcial, was assassinated by order of the government. Opposition leaders began to seek refuge in foreign embassies and in neighboring countries; others were deported. "Arévalo is in the Mexican Embassy," reported a U.S. official on October 18, "and his seeking refuge there is thought by many to mark the end of his serious candidacy."[88] It seemed increasingly likely that Ponce would triumph.

A conspiracy was hatching, however, among young army officers. It was spearheaded by Jacobo Arbenz Guzmán, a captain who had resigned from the army in early July, and by Major Carlos Aldana Sandoval, who belonged to the powerful Guardia de Honor. A few civilian leaders, particularly students, joined the officers. On the night of October 19, the plotters, minus Aldana Sandoval, struck. Frightened by his own audacity, Aldana Sandoval had fled to the safety of the Salvadoran border a few hours before the appointed time. His defection might have spelled disaster had it not been for an officer who had joined the plot in its later stages: Major Francisco Arana, the commander of the twelve tanks of the Guardia de Honor. Led by Arana, the Guardia de Honor rose in revolt. Throughout the night weapons were distributed to civil-

[85] The term "imported" is from Long to SecState, no. 1555, Sept. 22, 1944, p. 3, NA 814.00.

[86] "El día de la patria, los hijos del pueblo y el Ejército Nacional," El Independiente, Sept. 21, 1944, p. 2. See also "El indígena y su participación en la política" (edit.), La Nación, Sept. 18, 1944, p. 1.

[87] Quotations from "Magno desfile del día 15," Circuito Estudiantil, Sept. 22, 1944, p. 1, and from "Desvirtuación del 15 de Septiembre," El Libertador, Sept. 19, 1944, p. 1. See also Frente Unido de Partidos y Agrupaciones Cívicas to Diplomatic Corps, Sept. 21, 1944, enclosed in Long to SecState, no. 1554, Sept. 22, 1944, and Long to SecState, no. 1560, Sept. 25, 1944. All NA 814.00.

[88] Affeld to SecState, no. 687, Oct. 18, 1944, p. 1, NA 814.00.

ian volunteers; overall, between two and three thousand were armed. At first, the outcome was uncertain, as the other army units in the capital remained loyal to Ponce. But their resistance weakened as the hours went by. In the early afternoon of October 20, Ponce surrendered and was allowed to leave the country with his closest associates.[89]

On October 24, a car stopped for Ubico at the British embassy, where he had sought refuge when Ponce fell. It was bound for the airport. Upon leaving the country that he had ruled for thirteen years, Ubico lamented: "What they are doing to me is scandalous: to get rid of me as if I were a dog! They had better watch out: they have seized power; now they better muster the ability and the nerve to retain it. Beware of zealots and communists!"[90] Ubico flew to New Orleans, where he began pestering the U.S. government about his property, which had been confiscated in Guatemala.[91]

He died in New Orleans on June 14, 1946. In 1963, his remains were returned to Guatemala, where they were placed in a mausoleum and accorded full military honors.[92] The men who had ruled Guatemala since the overthrow of Arbenz admired Ubico's firm hand. They welcomed the old dictator home.

[89] On the plot and the fighting, see *Revista de la Revolución*, Jan. 1945; *Revista Militar*, Jan./Feb. 1945, pp. 3–7; *Studium*, Apr. 1945, pp. 36–39; U.S. embassy dispatches and internal memos Oct. 20–24, 1944 (esp. Affeld to SecState, no. 1658, Oct. 23, 1944, NA 814.00; Rose, "Revolution of October 20, 1944," enclosed in Affeld to SecState, no. 1662, Oct. 24, NA 814.00; all of Box 107, RG84 GR, NA-S). See also Arévalo, *El candidato*, pp. 297–327; Zea González, *El espejismo*, pp. 200–227; Arévalo Martínez, *Ubico*, pp. 299–343; Silva Girón, *12 horas*; Zamora Alvarez, *Las memorias de Andrés*, pp. 73–121. The best press coverage of the fighting was provided by *El I* in its issues of Oct. 21–24, 1944. Retrospective press accounts of the plot and the fighting include "Génesis de la revolución," *Nuestro Diario*, Oct. 27, 1944, p. 8; *El I*, Oct. 20, 1945, special supplement, section 3; Lt. Enrique de León Aragón, "Situaciones sobre el origen de la Revolución del Veinte de Octubre," *El Libertador*, Oct. 23, 1945, pp. 8, 10; Oscar de León Aragón, "Participación de los estudiantes universitarios en los sucesos del 20," ibid., pp. 9, 12–15; "Tengo pruebas de que Córdova fue todo un patriota, declara Silverio Ortiz," *El I*, June 8, 1946, p. 1; Toriello, "Revelaciones"; "Que pasó el 20 de Octubre?" *El Gráfico*; Pinto Recinos, "Lo que yo sé." Interviews with the following officers who participated in the revolt were particularly useful: Aldana Sandoval, Barrios Peña, Paz Tejada, Lorenzana, Mendoza. Also useful was an interview with Rolz Bennett, a civilian plotter against Ponce.

[90] "Sale el exdictador," *El I*, Oct. 25, 1944, p. 1 (quoted from p. 2).

[91] See Marta de Ubico to Eleanor Roosevelt, Dec. 15, 1944, enclosed in McLaughlin to Rockefeller, Jan. 20, 1945, NA 814.001/12-1544; MemoConv ("Conditions in Guatemala: President Ubico"), Jan. 5, 1945, p. 3, NA 814.00; MemoConv (Mrs. Ubico, Daniels, Newbegin), May 19, 1948, RG84 GR, Box 193, NA-S.

[92] "Ceremonial del ejército para inhumar los restos de Ubico," *El I*, Aug. 13, 1963, p. 1; "Inhumados los restos de Ubico hoy," *El I*, Aug. 14, 1963, p. 1. See also Zea Carrascosa, *Semblanzas*, pp. 223–25.

CHAPTER 2

The Presidency of Juan José Arévalo

THE FALL of Ponce marked the beginning of the Guatemalan revolution. It was a peculiar revolution, which saw urban workers, the middle class, the landed elite, and the officer corps celebrating together. "The quest for democracy had united them,"[1] but the definition of democracy would divide them.

The victorious rebels replaced Ponce with a three-man *junta*: Major Arana and Captain Arbenz, the two military heroes of the revolt, flanked the civilian Jorge Toriello, an upper-class youth who had played a prominent role in the struggle against Ponce. Toriello, the U.S. embassy later noted, "had an arbitrary, ruthless, impetuous character," but he also represented "an energetic conservative element in the Guatemalan government."[2]

Those were weeks of heady enthusiasm in the capital and the towns of the republic. A new Guatemala, it was said, was being born, a democratic Guatemala in which people would no longer live in fear. The *junta* promised free elections for a Constituent Assembly, a Congress, and a president. Political parties grew more vigorous, and trade unions stepped up their activities in the cities and on the plantations of the United Fruit Company.

Adorned by a new revolutionary veneer—had they not welcomed the fall of Ubico and Ponce?—Guatemala's latifundistas did not feel threatened. By eliminating the constraints imposed by the whims of a strongman, "democracy" might enhance their power and privilege. Furthermore, between 1940 and 1944 the international price of coffee had nearly doubled, promising Guatemala an economic boom, as in the 1920s.[3] Prosperity would enable the landed elite to buy off the middle class and the urban workers.

[1] Guerra Borges, *Pensamiento económico social*, p. 9.

[2] Quotations from Wells to DOS, no. 318, Mar. 10, 1950, p. 2, NA 714.00, and Woodward to SecState, no. 317, July 13, 1945, p. 2, NA 814.00. After the *junta*'s term had ended, Toriello's political role became marginal. Ambitious, shrill, violent, he was unable to retain a following even among conservative groups. For perceptive U.S. reports on Toriello and his political demise, see Cochran, "Guatemala-Political," June 29, 1945, p. 2, NA 814.00/6-1945; Woodward to SecState, no. 493, Aug. 17, 1945, pp. 2–4, NA 814.00; Donovan to SecState, no. 1025, Jan. 21, 1946, RG84 CF, Box 14, NA-S; Donovan to SecState, no. 1482, June 25, 1946, RG84 CF, Box 14, NA-S; DOS, Office of Research and Analysis, "Current US Policy toward Guatemala," no. 3569, Feb. 20, 1946, pp. 3–5, NA.

[3] See United Nations, FAO, *The World Coffee Economy*, pp. 55–56, 73, and Hennessey, "National Economy," p. 48.

To keep a democracy healthy, the upper class believed, the government had to promote the enlightened development of rural Guatemala. It must provide the *patrones* with easy credit and good prices for their products; it must let them look after the welfare of their workers without interference; it must clamp down on "all subversive propaganda."[4]

The countryside had remained quiet while urban Guatemala had turned against Ponce. But on October 22, 1944, two days after Ponce's demise, violence erupted at Patzicía, a small, predominantly Indian community about fifty miles west of the capital. "Armed with axes, machetes, clubs, stones and knives," approximately 1,000 Indians rose in a spontaneous outburst, killing more than twenty Ladinos. They chanted slogans in honor of "our General Ponce," but above all they cried: "We want land!"[5] The *junta* reacted swiftly. Soldiers were dispatched at once, and the rebellious Indians were punished in the traditional manner: with a bloodbath. "The troops summarily shot the rebels. They killed women, children and men indiscriminately," relates one of the few accounts of the episode; the exact death toll will never be known, but at least nine hundred Indians were killed. "This . . . would act as a warning throughout the Republic for any other disorders of this nature," the chief of staff of the Guatemalan army explained. In urban Guatemala no voices questioned the ferocity of the repression. This silence was considered auspicious by the landed elite, as was the fact that the revolt had encountered "the most drastic response of which the white and Ladino population is capable," in the words of the U.S. ambassador. After the slaughter of Patzicía, peace and tranquillity returned to the countryside.[6]

Middle-class youth had led the struggle against Ubico and Ponce, but the army emerged unscathed from the turmoil. Ponce had been overthrown neither

---

[4] For representative statements see Guatemala, *El triángulo de Escuintla*, esp. pp. 1, 123 (quoted), 135–37; Marroquín Rojas, *Crónicas*, pp. 98, 106; "Finqueros de Escuintla denuncian propaganda roja," *El I*, June 2, 1945, p. 1.

[5] "Al grito: Queremos las tierras que nos ofrecieron," *El I*, Oct. 24, 1944, p. 1. The passivity of the countryside during the struggle against Ponce is described in the monthly reports of the Jefes Políticos. (See IMJP:G, July–Oct. 1944, Leg. 32379, AGCA.)

[6] Quotations from: Hernández Sifontes, *Realidad jurídica*, p. 264; Rose, "Immediate Conditions in the Interior," no. 1348-44, Oct. 27, 1944, RG84 CF, Box 15, NA-S; Long to SecState, no. 1774, Nov. 24, 1944, NA 814.00. See also Long to SecState, no. 1682, Oct. 31, 1944, RG 84, Box 107, and Everardo Jiménez de León to Secretario de Estado de Gobernación y Justicia, Chimaltenango, Nov. 18, 1944, IMJP:G, Leg. 32379, AGCA. The Patzicía revolt is taboo in Guatemalan writing. Two brief accounts are Zamora Alvarez, *Las Memorias de Andrés*, pp. 147–53, and Santa Cruz Morales, "Hace 42 años." The figure of nine huundred killed is from Hernández Sifontes, *Realidad jurídica*, p. 264, and confirmed by interview with María de Rivera, a Guatemalan anthropologist who has interviewed survivors of the massacre.

by a general strike nor by an armed populace. The Guardia de Honor had spearheaded the insurrection, and army officers had led the rebel forces throughout the fighting. The purge within the military that followed Ponce's surrender was conducted without civilian interference, and it was limited to the crowd of generals, all of whom were dismissed, and several colonels.

The rebel officers had given arms to civilian volunteers during the fighting. But upon Ponce's defeat the *junta* moved to restore the military's monopoly of weapons. Its first bulletin demanded that all arms be returned within twenty-four hours: "all those who fail to comply . . . will be punished with the full weight of the law." Furthermore, those who returned the weapons would receive a small monetary compensation. Most of the weapons were returned.[7]

Thus the military remained the arbiter of the country's political life. For the landed elite, this was welcome. The Guatemalan army had never betrayed the country's latifundistas in favor of the lower classes. Should young hotheads try to turn democracy into license, the officers would restore order.

Nor was the upper class alarmed by the prospect that Juan José Arévalo, the charismatic presidential candidate, might win the December 1944 elections. Arévalo had the physique, voice and eloquence of a *caudillo*, but in Guatemala only the man on horseback could be a *caudillo*. Arévalo was a forty-year-old university professor who had written several books, not one of them about politics. Literature and the philosophy of education seemed to be his passions.

Arévalo, who was of middle class extraction, had become a primary schoolteacher in 1922. Five years later, at age twenty-three, he went to Argentina, having won a scholarship to university. He left behind the memory of a brilliant and dynamic teacher and a gifted writer.[8]

Arévalo spent six years in Argentina, where he earned a doctorate in the philosophy of education; he was one of a handful of Guatemalans who had completed postgraduate studies in any field. From Argentina he sent 150 copies of his first book, *Viajar es vivir*, to Guatemala. "The Guatemalan press reviewed the book enthusiastically," he later wrote, but "after a few months

[7] Quoted from "Dan término perentorio de 24 horas," *El I*, Oct. 22, 1944, p. 1. See also "Severa medida," *El I*, Oct. 26, 1944, p. 1. Interviews with Galich, Paz Tejada, Charnaud, Fortuny, and other participants confirmed that almost all of the weapons were returned.

[8] There is no definitive biography of Arévalo. With more or less grace, his biographers lapse into uncritical praise. The list includes Dion, *Las ideas sociales*; Delli Sante-Arrocha, *Arévalo*; Mejía, *Juan José Arévalo*; Ordóñez Argüello, *Arévalo visto por América*; Alvarez Elizondo, *El Presidente Arévalo*; Barrios Archila, *Biografía mínima*. Arévalo has written his memoirs: *Memorias de aldea* and *La inquietud normalista* describe his life before he left for Argentina in 1927; *La Argentina* covers the 1927–1944 period; *El candidato* spans the months from June 1944 to March 1945; *Escritos complementarios* deals with 1951 to 1963.

no one read it. There was no one left who could appreciate its melding of philosophy and literature."[9]

In 1934 Arévalo returned to his homeland, confident of both his excellence and his brilliant future. He dutifully went to pay his respects to Ubico, sure that the dictator would appoint him undersecretary of education, a post which was vacant. He presented Ubico with a copy of his doctoral dissertation; his alma mater, he explained, intended to publish the manuscript. "Therefore I urged Ubico to have the government rush the book to print so that Guatemala would have the honor of the first edition."[10]

Arévalo received a rude shock: Ubico was not interested in his dissertation. Worse, two days later he appointed Arévalo to a mid-level post in the Ministry of Education.

"Stunned . . . I offered my thanks," relates Arévalo in his memoirs. "I would have only a typewriter and two chairs—no subordinates, not even a secretary. . . . I felt humiliated. Ubico had dealt me a blow that was as unexpected as it was undeserved. . . . I was a Doctor of Philosophy of Education, I had studied abroad for six years, and I had been deemed unworthy to be the undersecretary of education."[11]

Two years later, in 1936, Arévalo returned to Argentina—to escape dictatorship, his admirers have claimed;[12] to seek a better job, retort his critics, noting that while in Argentina he never once spoke out against the dictator.[13] Probably both the desire for a better job and aversion to Ubico's rule motivated Arévalo. Back in Guatemala after the fall of Ubico, he was categorical: "I left because I refused to submit to dictatorship."[14]

On July 2, 1944, in Guatemala City, eight friends—five of whom were teachers—assembled at the house of Mario Efraín Nájera Farfán. Ubico had stepped down the previous day; it was time, they argued, to create a political party, a

[9] Arévalo, *La Argentina*, pp. 258–59.

[10] Ibid., p. 281.

[11] Ibid., p. 282.

[12] See for instance "Rasgos biográficos del Dr. Juan José Arévalo," *El Libertador*, Dec. 9, 1944, p. 3; Mejía, *Juan José Arévalo*, p. 40; Alvarez Elizondo, *El Presidente Arévalo*, pp. 42–43.

[13] The one possible exception is a 1937 letter that Arévalo sent to a professor in Costa Rica. (See Arévalo, *Escritos políticos*, pp. 55–56, and Arévalo, *La Argentina*, pp. 405–6.)

[14] "Declaraciones del Dr. Juan José Arévalo," *Circuito Estudiantil*, Sept. 12, 1944, p. 2. But in fact Arévalo did submit: after the aborted 1934 plot against Ubico, he signed, as did many other government employees, a public statement that combined abject professions of loyalty to the dictator with furious invective against the defeated plotters. (See Arévalo, *La Argentina*, pp. 298–99. For the text of the statement, see "Una página del Partido Liberal," *La Hora*, Jan. 15, 1945, p. 1.)

party that should immediately select a presidential candidate in a bid to capture the people's attention.[15]

"We all agreed that our candidate had to be a new man," recalls Nájera Farfán. Such a man was his friend Arévalo, who was a distinguished professor at the University of Tucuman, Juan José Orozco asserted. Most of those present knew Arévalo personally, and some had been his colleagues when he had been a schoolteacher. A few were familiar with his books—"well-written, elegant and instructive."[16]

By the time the meeting adjourned, the eight had formed Renovación Nacional, the teachers' party, and they had a candidate, Juan José Arévalo. On July 3, they sent Arévalo a telegram announcing their momentous decision and urging him to return at once. Arévalo accepted.[17]

In a matter of days, in a phenomenon unprecedented in Guatemala, the suggestion of one man became the cry of many. Arévalo's candidacy was endorsed by the Frente Popular Libertador (FPL, the students' party) in early August. By September 3, when he returned to Guatemala, Arévalo's name had become a household word in the capital, spread through the front pages of the opposition press and invoked at political rallies. He, who had fought neither in word nor in deed against Ubico, was suddenly the leader of a movement in search of a soul; he was the symbol of the new Guatemala.

In 1944, recalls a witness, "there were many who remembered Arévalo as an honorable man who had not been tainted by Ubiquismo."[18] Those who had forgotten Arévalo and those who had never heard of him suddenly felt that they had long known and admired the man. Arévalo, the FPL's newspaper, *El Libertador*, announced on August 4, was "a man without blemish, with the experience, the talent, the strength of character, and the idealism that our people need. . . . While we Guatemalans were unaware of the virtues of Doctor Juan José Arévalo, several sophisticated nations, including Argentina, have benefitted from the intellectual achievements of our compatriot and have honored him."[19]

Little if anything was known of his political views; indeed, notes a judicious observer, Arévalo "had been away long enough to have become personally

[15] The best accounts of the meeting are by Nájera Farfán: *Los estafadores*, pp. 69–71, and "El Arevalismo y el momento actual," *El Libertador*, Jan. 25, 1945, p. 3. See also Alvarez Elizondo, *El Presidente Arévalo*, p. 93, n. 6; "Proyecciones de la Revolución del 44," *El Gráfico*.

[16] Quotations from Nájera Farfán, "El Arevalismo" (see n. 15 above), and Nájera Farfán, *Los estafadores*, p. 71.

[17] Nájera Farfán, "El Arevalismo," (see n. 15 above); Arévalo, *La Argentina*, pp. 514–18; Arévalo, *El candidato*, pp. 6–18.

[18] Interview with Lorenzana.

[19] "Por qué apoyamos la candidatura de Juan José Arévalo," *El Libertador*, Aug. 4, 1944, p. 1.

anonymous, an immeasurable help in his candidacy,'' since he could be all things to all people.[20] The fact that he was a professor fired the enthusiasm of students and teachers, the two groups that had led the struggle against Ubico and were now in the forefront of the opposition to Ponce. ''In Argentina Arévalo is thought of as the new Sarmiento of the Americas,'' proclaimed an enthusiastic teacher. ''Being a philosopher, Doctor Arévalo understands the deepest yearnings of the human soul,'' explained *El Libertador* with similar hyperbole a month before the philosopher had returned to Guatemala.[21]

Arévalo's relative youth was also to his advantage. ''At that time the word youth was a political catchword which held out the promise of something new and bypassed the discussion of social and economic problems.''[22] The fact that Arévalo was white and that his place of self-imposed exile had been Argentina, a white country ruled by conservatives (and not Mexico, mestizo and revolutionary), was reassuring to the Guatemalan landed elite. His books, which very few Guatemalans had read, had esoteric titles that bespoke of spiritual concerns, not socioeconomic issues, and this too comforted the upper class.[23]

The crowds that welcomed Arévalo when he arrived in Guatemala were not disappointed. ''Arévalo won the elections the moment he stepped off the plane,'' recalls an eyewitness.[24] Even his critics acknowledge his charisma. One noted ''his powerful physique, his eloquence, his exuberance, and his acute intelligence.'' Another remarked, ''If nothing else, Arévalo looked every inch the president. Six feet tall, and weighing nearly 200 pounds, Arévalo furnished the young revolutionaries with a leader they could look up to, both literally and figuratively.''[25]

The candidate ''stumped the country,'' a U.S. embassy official recalled, ''spellbinding the common people with his impressive physical appearance and excellent oratory.''[26] His oratory, however, was as elusive as it was stir-

[20] Silvert, *Study in Government*, p. 8.

[21] Quotations from ''Juan José Arévalo, candidato del F.P.L.,'' *El Libertador*, Aug. 4, 1944, p. 3, and ''Juan José Arévalo y su candidatura,'' *El Libertador*, Aug. 7, 1944, p. 1.

[22] Alfonso Solorzano in Quan Rossell, *Guatemala*, 1:235.

[23] *Viajar es vivir, La pedagogía de la personalidad, La filosofía de los valores en la pedagogía, La adolescencia como evasión y retorno.*

[24] Interview with María de Rivera, Washington, D.C., Dec. 23, 1984. For press accounts, see ''Desborde cívico,'' *El I*, p. 1; ''Apoteósica recepción,'' *El Libertador*, p. 3; ''Apoteósico recibimiento,'' *El Americano*, p. 1. All Sept. 4, 1944.

[25] Quotations from Samayoa Chinchilla, *El Quetzal no es rojo*, p. 91, and Schneider, *Communism*, p. 16.

[26] Siracusa, ''Summary of Statements Made by Mr. Siracusa in Presentation of Guatemalan Situation,'' enclosed in Siracusa to Patterson, Aug. 22, 1949, p. 3, RG84 GR, Box 216, NA-S. Siracusa's remarks provide a revealing and comprehensive window

ring. He mentioned the economy, but stressed "the primacy of spiritual matters."[27] He suggested the need for social reforms but emphasized his opposition to "the naive redistribution of property. . . . The old class hatreds have been overcome," he asserted, and "spouting about materialism has been unmasked as the new propaganda tool of totalitarianism."[28] Sibylline statements reinforced the spiritual side of his message. "In Guatemala there are no longer conservatives, even though there is an aristocracy. Aristocracy is not a political category. It is an aesthetic category," he proclaimed on one occasion, stating on another, "The primary problems of Guatemala are spiritual problems. This is my theory, which is a little revolutionary and clashes with the materialist theories."[29]

As the December presidential elections drew near, several candidates withdrew in favor of Arévalo. The strongest of the remaining contenders was Adrian Recinos. A scholarly man who had long been Ubico's ambassador to the United States, Recinos was intelligent but uncharismatic. He enjoyed the support of a group of upper class friends, but not of the upper class as a whole. And he was tainted by his long collaboration with Ubico. He was, in short, no match for Arévalo, who won the presidency with 85 percent of the votes cast by literate men (the only enfranchised people). Arévalo's triumph represented the victory of the "revolution"—that is, no one's victory in particular. Time alone would reveal who Arévalo truly was and what the Guatemalan revolution would mean.[30]

On March 15, 1945, Arévalo assumed the presidency of Guatemala. The country presented a desolate spectacle. Despite Ubico's roads, internal transportation was woefully inadequate. Illiteracy was over 70 percent. Although the republic's agricultural potential was impressive—"In soils and climate," noted the World Bank, "few countries are better equipped for agricultural development"—agriculture was stifled by the pattern of landownership: 2 percent of landowners owned 72 percent of agricultural land; less than 1 percent of the land was cultivated, while half of those who owned land were crowded

---

on the embassy's attitude toward the Arévalo government. They were well received by the department.

[27] "Declaraciones del Dr. Juan José Arévalo," *Circuito Estudiantil*, Sept. 12, 1944, p. 4.

[28] "Pensamiento de J. José Arévalo," *La República*, Nov. 13, 1944, pp. 3–4.

[29] Quotations from "Socialismo espiritual preconiza el candidato Arévalo para Guatemala," *El I*, Oct. 30, 1944, p. 1 (quoted from p. 2) and "Declaraciones del Dr. Juan José Arévalo," *Circuito Estudiantil*, Sept. 12, 1944, p. 4.

[30] For two inside accounts of the electoral campaign, see Arévalo, *El candidato*, pp. 36–484, and Flores Avendaño, *Memorias*, 2:275–327. (Flores Avendaño was one of the defeated candidates.)

nomic."[40] This may have been true of the government's efforts in the country-side, but the reforms in favor of the urban middle and lower classes showed a clear grasp of the importance of economics.

The striking contradiction between Arévalo's urban and rural policies did not arise from the confused nature of Spiritual Socialism; its causes were concrete. In comparison to his predecessors, the president was exceptionally sympathetic to the rural masses. Yet, except geographically, the largely Indian world of the peasantry was far removed from that of Arévalo and the other middle class leaders who formed the new political elite. This distance muted the echo of the peasants' suffering. Among the government forces, only the trade unions showed an active desire for real change in the countryside, but their influence was limited, and their immediate interest was in the cities. The only powerful pressure group with direct interests in the countryside was the upper class, and it opposed all change.

Rather than a political theorist, Arévalo was a populist leader, personally honest, and without a comprehensive socioeconomic program for his country. He was a master, however, of politics—that is, he possessed an uncanny ability to manipulate men, including his own key supporters, the leaders of the revolutionary parties.[41]

These parties, which enjoyed a massive majority in Congress throughout Arévalo's term, were the Frente Popular Libertador (FPL), Renovación Nacional (RN), and the Partido Acción Revolucionaria (PAR). Created in November 1945 by the merger of the FPL and RN, the PAR survived the split of the FPL and RN eighteen months later. In terms of age and social extraction, the leadership of the three parties was similar: middle-class urban youth, particularly those university students and teachers who had distinguished themselves in 1944. The splintering of the PAR was due to personal ambitions, political differences, and the "influence of President Arévalo." Arévalo, noted a prominent administration figure, preferred to manipulate competing parties rather than to confront only one.[42]

[40] Quotations from interview with Woodward, and from Silvert, *Study in Government*, p. 11. Dion, *Las ideas sociales*, and Delli Sante-Arrocha, *Arévalo*, make sustained but vain attempts to penetrate the mysteries of Spiritual Socialism.

[41] The term *revolutionary parties* refers to all noncommunist parties that supported the Arévalo and Arbenz administrations.

[42] Monteforte Toledo, *Guatemala*, p. 311. See also Donovan to SecState, no. 2490, June 3, 1947, NA 814.00; Donovan to SecState, no. 2499, June 6, 1947, NA 814.00. There is no comprehensive study of the revolutionary parties. Important primary sources can be found in the *GT*, esp. boxes 9, 12, 66, 67, 68, 69. Despite a marked bias, reports from the U.S. embassy are valuable, as are some U.S. government studies, notably a 117-page analysis by the State Department's Office of Intelligence and Research ("Guatemala: Communist Influence," no. 5123, Oct. 23, 1950, NA). For the Arbenz years, see, in particular, the embassy's weekly *Joint Weeka* (*JW*). Among

Until 1949, when it was crippled by internal strife, the FPL was the largest of the revolutionary parties. Increasingly resistant to social reform, it competed with the more centrist RN for Arévalo's affection. To the left of both stood the PAR, which was more sympathetic to organized labor, locked in a bitter feud with the FPL, and ever more distant from Arévalo.

Within each party, rival factions clashed over the scope and speed of social reforms and over the division of the spoils of political power. Corruption was rampant, and graft became "the order of the day at high levels. While most, if not all, officials of the present government came into power as poor men," a U.S. official wrote in 1949, "few of them remain so today."[43] The story of Mario Méndez Montenegro is a case in point. As a student leader in 1944, he had displayed bravery and charisma. He became, under Arévalo, one of the leaders of the FPL, but when he served as mayor of Guatemala City (1946–1948), he demanded bribes from those who sought to do business with the city government.[44]

Among and above the squabbling factions, Arévalo adroitly mediated, using his well-honed political skills, his great personal charm, and "his largesse" with political leaders.[45] True, as time went on, he lost some of his prestige. But from the pack of revolutionary politicians, no civilian emerged who could challenge the president. Like Arévalo, most of these politicians lacked a comprehensive program for the country. They had grown up in Ubico's Guatemala—that is, in an intellectual desert. After 1944 much of their energy went to personal aggrandizement. There were exceptions, but they were few.

Arévalo and the revolutionary parties were urged forward by a combative labor movement regrouped in two rival confederations, the Federación Sindical de Guatemala (FSG) and the Confederación de Trabajadores de Guatemala (CTG). By early 1950 the FSG and the CTG claimed approximately ninety thousand members. While many of their unions existed on paper only, the number of effectively organized workers still ran into several tens of thousands; most were blue and white collar urban workers.[46]

---

published works, the most useful are Bishop, "Guatemalan Labor," pp. 109–58 (focusing on the relationship of the revolutionary parties to the labor movement); Schneider, *Communism*, esp. pp. 218–49; LeBaron, "Impaired Democracy," pp. 141–61. Particularly helpful were interviews with Galich, Charnaud, Fortuny, Bauer Paiz, Capuano, Monteforte Toledo.

[43] Siracusa (see n. 26 above), p. 4.

[44] On Méndez Montenegro, see Siracusa to SecState, no. 249, May 20, 1948, p. 2 ("Case 1") and p. 3 ("Case 4"), NA 814.00. For a devastating indictment of the corruption that permeated the 1950 Central American and Caribbean Games, see "Danza olímpica de los millones que se tornó despilfarro," *El I*, Apr. 2–12, 1951.

[45] Monteforte Toledo, *Guatemala*, p. 312.

[46] There was another labor confederation, the Federación Regional Central de Trabajadores, but in size and influence it was insignificant. In May 1950 still another labor

Important differences separated the leaders of the FSG and the CTG. As U.S. scholars have observed, the leaders of the CTG were more honest and more committed to the workers' interests, but also more open to communist influences. The following comparison is representative: Arturo Morales Cubas, the FSG's secretary general from its inception until January 1948, "was considered moderate in his views. . . . He might in time have furnished wider leadership to the labor movement had not his reputation and position been undercut by opportunism and corruption. He was unfortunately . . . a union leader who used his position to pilfer union funds." By contrast, Víctor Manuel Gutiérrez, who became secretary general of the CTG in October 1946, was "known as the Franciscan . . . because of his strict personal habits and devotion to work; he had a sense of the times and an urgent message for the laboring class." Gutiérrez and the leaders of the CTG "were the only ones who had a sure path to follow, a firm sense of direction." The FSG leaders, on the other hand, "never appeared to exercise a firm and well formulated approach either to their internal affairs or to the national problems. They were always the reluctant followers unable to seize the initiative."[47]

Their differences notwithstanding, the FSG and the CTG repeatedly joined together to press their demands on an often reluctant government. Using their leverage as the only group that could provide active support as well as votes to the various revolutionary parties, they achieved significant victories.

The most important was the Labor Code promulgated on May 1, 1947. In a more advanced country, the code would have been a moderate document; in Guatemala, it was radical. It affirmed the right to unionize (but set crippling limitations on agricultural unions). It afforded protection from unfair dismissals and guaranteed the right to strike within a conciliation mechanism. ("While helpful to labor," this mechanism "also served to set a limit on labor's right to strike," noted a U.S. government report.[48]) The code also stipulated a forty-eight-hour week, regulated the employment of women and adolescents, and established basic standards of health and safety in the workplace.[49]

---

confederation was created, the Confederación Nacional Campesina de Guatemala (CNCG), which is discussed below, pp. 172–73.

The best sources on organized labor in the Arévalo years are Bishop, "Guatemalan Labor," pp. 9–129, and Bush, "Organized Labor." Ramos Guzmán de Schmoock, "El movimiento sindical," pp. 21–119, taps some sources not used by Bishop and Bush. Ruiz Franco, *Hambre*, which covers the early stages of the labor movement, is a classic. Pearson, "*Confederación*," pp. 1–40, focuses on the countryside.

[47] Bishop, "Guatemalan Labor," pp. 23, 25, 91, 130. Bishop's views are supported by those of the other authorities listed in n. 46 above.

[48] DOS, Office of Intelligence and Research, "Guatemala: Communist Influence," Oct. 23, 1950, p. 56, NA.

[49] The full text of the law, approved by Congress on Feb. 1, 1947, as Decree 330, is printed in *DCA*, Feb. 25, 1947, pp. 1113–30, and Feb. 26, 1947, pp. 1143–60.

The Labor Code was followed, in January 1948, by the inauguration of the Guatemalan Institute of Social Security (IGSS). Financed by the state, the employers, and the workers, the IGSS was designed and directed by two young bureaucrats from Costa Rica.[50] It soon earned the praise of even harsh critics of the Arévalo administration. The U.S. embassy reported that it was "undoubtedly the best administered and most effective of the social reforms of the Arévalo administration," and the conservative *El Imparcial* noted its "very constructive role."[51] Competently staffed by a well-paid bureaucracy, and shielded from outside interference, the IGSS was a signal exception to the morass of corruption, nepotism, and incompetence that engulfed the Arévalo administration.

By March 1951, when Arévalo's term ended, several tens of thousands of blue and white collar urban workers were insured by the IGSS, but rural workers remained unprotected. As time went by, the IGSS's financial straits worsened. The employers, particularly those in rural areas, did not pay their quotas; nor did many workers. In the summer of 1950, the IGSS asked the government for a special grant of $1 million; the alternative, it stressed, was "closing down or cutting sharply into its services."[52] The government did not help; worse, it too was behind in the payment of its quotas.

Likewise, many of the provisions of the Labor Code were implemented minimally or not at all. This was even true in the case of the urban workers, who were the main beneficiaries of the new legislation. Nonetheless, despite the inflation that plagued the Arévalo years, real wages for urban workers increased, at times significantly. The extent of the improvement often depended on the political muscle of individual unions; hence teachers and railwaymen were among those who fared best.[53]

Moreover, through occasional strikes, and more often through the conciliation mechanism established by the code, unionized workers were generally

[50] An excellent study of the IGSS is Suslow, "Social Security."

[51] Quotations from Fisher, "Memo: Oscar Barahona Streber," Aug. 17, 1950, RG84 CF, Box 15, NA-S, and from "Labor de seis años" (edit.), *El I*, Mar. 15, 1951, p. 2.

[52] Suslow, "Social Security," p. 118.

[53] On inflation and wages under Arévalo see Hendon, "Some Recent Economic Reforms," pp. 132–58; Bush, "Organized Labor," part 3, pp. 74, 77; Bishop, "Guatemalan Labor," pp. 54–56. Also valuable are economic and labor reports of the U.S. embassy. See, for instance: Donovan to SecState, A-539, Dec. 6, 1946, p. 3, NA 814.50; Wells to SecState, A-240, Oct. 14, 1948, pp. 6–7, NA 814.50; Larsen to SecState, no. 101, Jan. 26, 1950, p. 11, NA 814.10; "Quarterly Labor Review. Third Quarter—1950," no. 470, Nov. 3, 1950, p. 22, NA 814.06; "Annual Economic Report—1950," no. 980, Apr. 10, 1951, pp. 11–12, NA 814.00; "Annual Labor Report—1950," no. 989, Apr. 10, 1951, p. 26, NA 814.06.

able to secure protection from arbitrary dismissals—and this, in Guatemala, was a dramatic improvement.

The Arévalo years also brought political freedoms to the urban population: freedom to vote, freedom to express one's opinions, freedom to read a broader range of books and newspapers. Many members of the upper class soon branded these freedoms as intolerable excesses and began to reminisce about the times of Ubico, when "social peace" had reigned supreme. But to the lower and middle classes, Ubico had brought only hardship, and the political freedoms instituted by the 1944 revolution were very welcome.

There was also change in the countryside. Forced labor and the vagrancy laws were not enforced after the fall of Ponce. The 1945 constitution replaced Ubico's *intendentes* with elected mayors. In 1947 the Labor Code established the right of agricultural workers to unionize as long as the union had at least fifty members, two-thirds of whom were literate (a virtual impossibility that was removed the following year). Finally, Arévalo sought to bring education to the countryside and asserted that the Indians were Guatemalans and citizens, as the law stated.

But the cancer that rotted the countryside and the entire republic was the distribution of land. Prodded by organized labor, Congress established a committee to study the problem of agrarian reform. The members read books, made speeches, wrote reports. "We proceeded very slowly," the chairman of the committee recalls.[54] Nothing happened. "Except for the passage of compulsory land rental legislation in 1950, no positive action was taken by the Arévalo Administration" in the field of agrarian reform, concluded the Office of Intelligence and Research of the U.S. State Department in 1953. The land rental legislation, a mild measure designed to assist sharecroppers, was "honored far more in breach than in observance."[55]

When Arévalo assumed office, the Guatemalan state administered about 130 large estates—the Fincas Nacionales: the coffee estates of the German community that had been expropriated by Ubico in June 1944 and the estates of Ubico and some of his generals, which were confiscated a few days after the overthrow of Ponce. Together, these estates produced about 25 percent of the country's coffee crop. Had they been well administered, the Fincas Nacionales would have been a model of economic development and source of revenue; they could have improved the lot of tens of thousands of agricultural

---

[54] Interview with Monteforte Toledo.

[55] Quotations from DOS, Office of Intelligence and Research, no. 6001, Mar. 5, 1953, p. 1, NA, and from interview with Steins. On the lack of implementation of the land rental law enacted on Dec. 21, 1949, as Decree 712, see Comité Interamericano de Desarrollo Agrícola, *Tenencia de la tierra*, p. 37; García Añoveros, *La reforma agraria*, pp. 162–63. For the text of the law, see Méndez Montenegro, *444 años*, pp. 707–10.

laborers and demonstrated that not only the landed elite could manage Guatemala's most important export crop.

This opportunity was squandered. The administrators of the Fincas Nacionales were—almost to a man—as ignorant of agriculture as they were eager to enrich themselves. Following a tour of the Finca Santa Fe, a foreign scholar noted: ''The administrator appeared to know nothing and care less. The house and garden of the Germans was in an abandoned state. . . . The majority of the machines were broken.'' After visiting several other Fincas Nacionales, the same scholar concluded: ''The Directors of the various farms all hedged when questioned about production. Most of them seemed to lack knowledge of the functioning of their farms. . . . Only one of the Directors that I met . . . appeared capable.'' This grim assessment was shared by most outside observers, including the World Bank.[56]

Corruption and incompetence also characterized the bureaucracy that oversaw the Fincas from Guatemala City. Its director was inept and surrounded by corrupt aides. His one qualification was his birthright: he was the president's brother.[57]

It is hardly surprising that the output of the Fincas Nacionales decreased steadily. By 1950 their share of Guatemala's coffee production had fallen to 20 percent. Thus the state lost precious revenue and confirmed the landed barons in their conviction that they alone could manage Guatemala's agriculture.

In lieu of agrarian reform, Arévalo attempted colonization, spending several million dollars to establish an agricultural colony on untilled state land at Poptún, in faraway El Petén. The project began, with much fanfare, on November 14, 1945. ''Road-building is a major expense,'' an observer noted three years later. ''Most of the labor and equipment is devoted to this activity. The major problem is getting equipment. All equipment has to be flown to the colony. . . . Actual colonization has not yet begun.''[58] Expenses soared because of the prohibitive transportation costs, inefficiency, and corruption.

---

[56] Quoted from Suslow, ''Aspects of Social Reforms,'' pp. 67–68. See also IBRD, *Economic Development*, pp. 36–37; Biechler, ''Coffee Industry,'' pp. 49–50; Hendon, ''Some Recent Economic Reforms,'' pp. 177–81; Whetten, *Guatemala*, p. 128. A folder in the *GT*, Box 20, provides a glimpse of life on the Fincas Nacionales.

[57] In addition to many of the sources listed in n. 56 above, a 1953 series of front-page articles in *La Hora* is particularly instructive: ''Vacías las cajas de Fincas Nacionales,'' Jan. 3; ''Getellá ordena acción judicial pronta,'' Jan. 7; ''Investigan maquinaria y ganado en Fincas,'' Jan. 9; ''Aclara y la vez confirma una noticia de 'La Hora,' '' Jan. 10; ''Liquidador Getellá cuenta que es lo que sabe de los asuntos que él asumió,'' Jan. 12; ''El ex-gerente Arévalo llamado a dar aclaraciones importantes,'' Jan. 13; ''Grave denuncia recibe Getellá,'' Jan. 14; ''Mariano Arévalo da declaraciones,'' Jan. 15.

[58] Suslow, ''Aspects of Social Reforms,'' p. 75.

Arévalo was undaunted. Poptún was "the country's greatest political and economic undertaking," yet another proof of "the creative power of Arevalismo."[59] More soberly, the World Bank concluded, "The $3,000 spent on each of the present Poptún houses would probably have been enough to set a farmer up in business."[60] Guatemala was fortunate that this was Arévalo's only foray into colonization. As the president's term ended, Poptún accommodated only a few hundred colonists. "All kinds of supplies had to be brought by plane and there were no great hopes of future market outlets. Consequently, the colony was successful only so long as it received a heavy subsidy and it has been gradually dying as public funds assigned to it have been diminished," reported a Guatemalan economist a few years later.[61]

Of course, Arévalo was not an agronomist; he was an educator. And it was education, he asserted, that would transform the Indian into a citizen. The needs were immense, and his hopes were generous. But Arévalo's ambitious plans clashed with his country's strained budget and lack of human resources. Overwhelmingly Ladinos, rural teachers could overcome neither the cultural barriers to the Indian world nor their own prejudice. Most of these teachers, moreover, were among Guatemala's least qualified; they were the *empiricos*, who lacked even a secondary school degree and worked in the countryside because they could not find employment elsewhere.[62]

"All educational reform will ultimately fail," Arévalo had written in 1939, ". . . unless laws and governments help to eliminate . . . all types of economic exploitation."[63] As president, he chose to overlook these wise words. And in the absence of significant social reforms, minimal literacy in Spanish (which would soon be forgotten for lack of use) would not help the Indians to improve their lot. Their world would remain that of the agricultural laborer and minifundista eking out a substandard living. Books and newspapers would still belong to an alien world.

Most Indian parents believed that schools would offer their children little beyond the teacher's scorn. And an Indian child, as Ruben Reina noted in a classic study, "is needed for general assistance in the household and cannot

[59] Guatemala, *Primera colonia agrícola de Poptún*, pp. 3, 95.

[60] IBRD, *Economic Development*, p. 85.

[61] Fuentes-Mohr, "Land Settlement," p. 31.

[62] On rural education under Arévalo, see esp. González Orellana, *Historia de la educación*, pp. 394–423. Suslow, "Aspects of Social Reforms," pp. 18–27, 33–43, is informative and incisive; Noval, *Tres problemas*, makes valuable comments of a general nature that apply to the Arévalo period; Jimenez, *La educación rural*, pp. 66–307, is analytically poor but rich in detail; Casey, "Indigenismo," pp. 299–356, is a sympathetic study.

[63] "Marco social de la educación en nuestra América," *Revista de pedagogía*, Nov. 1939, reprinted in Arévalo, *Escritos pedagógicos y filosóficos*, pp. 33–45, quoted from p. 40.

easily be spared without causing sacrifice to his family." It was from the family, moreover, that children acquired the skills necessary for adult life.[64] In 1950 90 percent of the Indian children did not attend school.[65] All too often, there were no schools; when they existed, attendance was very low.

While Arévalo's interest in rural education was genuine, his commitment to rural labor unions was less certain. Labor organizers in the countryside faced formidable obstacles. Legal restrictions were compounded by the remoteness of the rural world in a country sorely deficient in transportation. The labor confederations did not have the resources for a sustained campaign in the countryside; indeed, noted a November 1948 report, the CTG "had no vehicles of any kind, not even a horse, and . . . the CTG delegates operating in the rural areas could only depend upon their legs"; the FSG "faced the same financial difficulties as the CTG."[66] And the Arévalo Administration refused to lend vehicles to the labor organizations.[67]

Most landowners resisted unionization "by every means at their disposal, including floggings" and "even killings." They enjoyed the support of the Church and the local authorities, who were unimpressed by the feeble admonitions emanating from the central government. There is no record of landowners or local officials who were successfully prosecuted or otherwise punished for acts of violence against their workers.[68]

As a result, organized labor made only scant inroads in the countryside. The major exceptions were the labor unions that developed on the plantations of United Fruit. (UFCO's workers had been militant in the 1920s and had begun organizing in the summer of 1944, shortly after the fall of Ubico.)[69] Elsewhere, noted a careful scholar, "only on the coffee fincas owned by the national government did unionism make some headway, and even here the policies of the government were often contradictory and restrictive of unionism."[70]

By the late 1940s, the vagrancy laws were no longer enforced, but population growth and soil erosion had made them unnecessary. Lacking sufficient land to support themselves and their families, many Indians—and some Ladinos—had no choice but to sell their labor in a market characterized by excess supply; the absence of labor unions sealed the landowners' advantage. Nomi-

[64] Reina, "Chinautla," p. 91.

[65] See González Orellana, *Historia de la educación*, pp. 401–2.

[66] Bishop, "Guatemalan Labor," pp. 82, 95.

[67] Pearson, *"Confederación,"* p. 31.

[68] Quotations from Bishop, "Guatemalan Labor," p. 76, and Bush "Organized Labor," part 3, p. 38. See also the IMJP:G, the JP, and the CPR; all AGCA.

[69] On UFCO's unions see Bush, "Organized Labor," part 2, pp. 13–39.

[70] Bishop, "Guatemalan Labor," p. 74. For scattered reports on peasant unions, see CSC:DAT, AGCA.

nal wages for agricultural workers did increase in the Arévalo years, but inflation took its toll on the rural population. "The Indian who does not own enough land to be self-sufficient in staple products must pay the higher price for the corn," noted a perceptive study. The dearth of adequate statistics prevents a definitive judgement, but the existing data support the conclusion of a scholar who was quite sympathetic to Arévalo. Corn, he wrote, "sold on the market for between 1¢ and 2¢ per pound prior to the war. It now [mid-1949] costs between 5¢ and 6¢ per pound . . . while cash wages have generally risen in most areas, many [agricultural] workers have experienced an overall decline in real wages." The payment in kind that many of these workers received generally failed to increase through the 1940s.[71]

Arévalo's failure to bring real change to the countryside was not due solely to the opposition of the powerful in Guatemalan society. "Arévalo came from a family of middle-class landowners," recalls the president of the Guatemalan Congress. "He had no interest in agrarian reform."[72] Arévalo had indicated as much in an unusually candid speech in April 1945. "In Guatemala there is no agrarian problem," he averred. "The problem is that the peasants have lost their desire to till the soil because of the attitudes and politics of the past. My government will motivate them, but without resorting to any measures that hurt other classes."[73]

The urban-based labor movement—above all the CTG—was virtually alone in pressing for agrarian reform and rural unionization. These measures, the

[71] Quotations from Suslow, "Aspects of Social Reforms," p. 95, and Bush, "Organized Labor," part 2, p. 42. Reports by local authorities indicate that the vagrancy laws were enforced in the countryside at least through mid-1947. See, for instance, Gobernador Departamental de Izabal to Alcalde Municipal Morales, Feb. 11, 1946, JP (Puerto Barrios), AGCA; Gobernador Departamental de Izabal to Alcalde Municipal Morales, Mar. 23, 1946, p. 2, ibid.; Gobernador Departamental de Izabal to Alcalde Municipal Morales, Apr. 30, 1946, ibid.; Gobernador Departamental de Huehuetenango, no. 2372, Sept. 12, 1946, p. 1, IMJP:G, Leg. 32721, AGCA; Gobernador Departamental de Mazatenango, no. 2383/1, Oct. 14, 1946, p. 1, ibid.; Gobernador Departamental de Mazatenango, Dec. 15, 1946, p. 1, ibid.; José Angel Ico Delgado et al. to Ministro de Agricultura, May 8, 1947, IGT, Leg. 48750, AGCA; Manuel Mayo Cuc et al. to Inspector General del Trabajo, May 28, 1947, ibid. On agricultural wages and inflation under Arévalo see AmEmG to DOS, no. 162, Aug. 11, 1950, Table 1, p. 6, NA 814.231; AmEmG to DOS, no. 718, Jan. 22, 1951, pp. 23-25, NA 814.2333; Bush, "Organized Labor," part 2, pp. 40–55; Suslow, "Social Security," pp. 100–3, 110–14. (Suslow uses documents from the IGSS.) For the effects of population growth and erosion in a particular area, see Colby and van den Berghe, *Ixil Country*, pp. 74, 108–10. For an interesting editorial on the problem of erosion, see "Erosión: Enemigo público número uno de la vitalidad de la tierra," *DCA*, Aug. 11, 1948, p. 3.

[72] Interview with Monteforte Toledo.

[73] "Ideal de una Centroamerica como una sola nación culta, democrática, grande," *El I*, Apr. 4, 1945, p. 1.

CTG leaders argued, were also in the interest of the urban workers, for the labor movement would remain small, and hence weak, without the participation of the rural masses. Moreover, they stressed, agrarian reform would increase agricultural productivity and result in more abundant and cheaper foodstuffs for the cities. A less poor peasantry, they also noted, would be able to buy some of the products of the Guatemalan industries; production would increase and so would employment and wages in the cities. Finally, agrarian reform and rural unions would sap the power of the landed elite, organized labor's most bitter foe.[74]

Only a few PAR leaders truly supported these demands. In the final analysis, the Arévalo administration sought to cure some of the symptoms of the sickness that consumed Guatemala's rural world, not the sickness itself. For little could be done to improve the Indians' lot without first dealing with the country's land tenure system. Eloquent laws stating that the Indian was a citizen could not temper the contempt that most Ladinos felt for the Indians, that is, the age-old racism that justified extreme exploitation. Only a lessening of this exploitation could eventually transform the Indian into a full-fledged citizen.

If Arévalo's measures were sadly inadequate in terms of the peasants' needs, they seemed revolutionary to the Guatemalan latifundistas. To them any concession was excessive and dangerous. "The conservative elements," the U.S. military attaché reported, "attribute labor unrest to communism, look with horror on social reforms and reflect that it was easier to do business, easier to make money, and easier and safer to live during the dictator era."[75]

And so the upper class's honeymoon with Arévalo gave way, in 1946, to rising hostility. *El Imparcial*, the republic's major newspaper, reflected the mounting disappointment of its owners and their conservative friends. As Congress debated about the labor code, *El Imparcial* fustigated against the "impatience of the workers, both in city and country."[76] On February 1, 1947, the code was approved by the Congress, and the labor confederations

---

[74] For a representative statement of the CTG's position, see "La CTG frente a la política nacional e internacional," *El Libertador*, Oct. 31, Nov. 5, and Nov. 12, 1946. For a revealing document, see Gutiérrez to Arévalo, July 17, 1947, CPR, 1947, AGCA. For a comprehensive discussion, see Ramos Guzmán de Schmoock, "El movimiento sindical," pp. 37, 41–42, 49, 51–52, 63–70, 99–100, 107–9, 111–13, 116–17.

[75] Col. Devine, "Alleged Communist Penetrations," no. 104–46, Mar. 29, 1946, p. 2, RG84 CF, Box 14, NA-S.

[76] "A donde va Guatemala?" (edit.), *El I*, Oct. 24, 1946, p. 1. For an instructive comparison, see the still friendly editorial of *El I* on the first anniversary of the fall of Ponce ("Un año de revolución," Oct. 20, 1945, p. 1).

intensified their demands for social and economic change in the countryside. "How far have the seeds of subversion been cast?" asked *El Imparcial*.

> The impact has been worst in the countryside. Day after day we read of discord, strikes and riots occurring in many areas where the Indians are a majority. . . . Not that the Indian is to blame: intellectually and socially he is a child. He believes what he is told by those who seek to excite his base desires and passions. . . . No one can foresee the consequences of a struggle that would engulf the entire republic. Until now we Guatemalans have looked to our army as the source of stability in the hour of danger. Who can be sure that the will of the army has not been sapped by the subversives? Will Indian soldiers participate in a war of extermination against their own race?[77]

Seeking the support of the Church, the upper class rose in defense of the values of "Christian" Guatemala, which were endangered by the government's "threats and attacks" against "the Catholic sensibilities of our people."[78] Led by Archbishop Mariano Rossell y Arellano, this was a deeply conservative church, whose model of political democracy and social justice was Franco's Spain. Deprived of its property in the 1870s, the Church had achieved a comfortable modus vivendi with Ubico, who had eased some of the restrictions to which it had been subjected. The 1945 constitution had further improved the Church's position, but it had not gone far enough in the eyes of Rossell y Arellano and his clergy. Therefore, the Church began its feud with the revolution.[79]

For too long the Guatemalan elite had lived under the shadow of dictators. Under Arévalo, right-wing parties remained ephemeral, unable to unite and reminiscent of social clubs. The scions of the upper class were not willing to invest energy or money in electoral politics, a distasteful and bothersome distraction from social and economic pursuits. They countered the *Arevalista* threat with invectives in the media and overtures to the Church. Above all, they resorted to their traditional ploy: they sought a military *caudillo* who would seize power and protect them. To this end they plotted, while raising their monotonous and shrill refrain. The government, they claimed, had fallen into the hands of communists.

[77] "Agitación campesina" (edit.), *El I*, Feb. 27, 1947, p. 1.

[78] "Cuatro puntos de la oposición," *El I*, Oct. 7, 1946, p. 1 (quoted from p. 7).

[79] For the Church under Ubico and Arévalo, see Holleran, *Church and State*, pp. 210–54; Frankel, "Political Development," pp. 169–265; Bendaña Perdomo, "Historia general," pp. 41–50; Miller, "Catholic Leaders"; Estrada Monroy, *Datos para la historia*, 3:495–640.

CHAPTER 3

The Death of Francisco Arana

"FROM THIS day forward the Guatemalan army will be an institution of impeccable professionalism," Arévalo promised in his inaugural address. "Led by men who have proven their patriotism and their love of the Guatemalan people, it will be the guardian of our domestic peace, and it will join in the great cultural awakening of our country."[1] Heady words, but as Arévalo knew, more tangible inducements were necessary to assure the army's loyalty. And so the officer corps became the pampered child of the revolution through large salary increases, generous scholarships to study abroad, well-paid positions in the government bureaucracy, and other alluring benefits. Aware of the limits of his power, the civilian president carefully refrained from interfering in military matters. It was, for the officer corps, a welcome change.

Major Francisco Arana and Captain Jacobo Arbenz were the two most influential officers when Arévalo's presidency began. Within the officer corps they were perhaps equal in prestige, but not in power. Arana was not only Arbenz's senior in age and rank, but luck had allowed him to play the decisive role in the overthrow of Ponce.

"Arana's emergence as one of the three leaders of the revolution . . . was," as the U.S. embassy reported, "something of an accident." He joined the plot only in its late stages, at the insistence of Major Aldana Sandoval. He was, however, the commander of the tank unit at the Guardia de Honor—that is, of the country's only tanks. The sudden defection of Aldana Sandoval on the eve of the revolt propelled Arana into the role of a leader, "a leader found at the last minute."[2] In the hours that followed, he fought with bravery and imagination.

Since 1937, Jacobo Arbenz had been a professor at the Escuela Politécnica, a post that gave him prestige but no troops. In the summer of 1944, he and Aldana Sandoval began to organize the uprising. He plotted as a civilian, having resigned from the army in early July to protest Ponce's takeover. Dressed as a civilian, leading a group of students, he had appeared on the night of October 19 at the Guardia de Honor, where Arana was already in charge. His brilliant career at the military academy and his role against Ponce earned Ar-

---

[1] Arévalo, *Discursos en la presidencia*, pp. 7–21. Quoted from pp. 13–14.

[2] Quotations from Affeld, "Confidential Biographic Data: Francisco Javier Arana," Apr. 4, 1945, p. 1, RG84 GR, Box 217, NA-S, and from interview with Mendoza.

benz the respect of many officers, particularly those *de escuela*, who, like him, had graduated from the academy.

During the uprising Arbenz and Arana fought with equal distinction. But Arana led the Guardia de Honor. As a result he became the senior member of the three-man *junta*.[3]

Arévalo first met Arbenz and Arana in the presidential palace a few days after the fall of Ponce. "The first to appear was a blond and blue-eyed young man, wearing a blue suit and a narrow red tie," Arévalo later wrote.

> He greeted me respectfully. . . . I had come, I told him, to meet and congratulate the two officers, Arbenz and Arana. The young man smiled and said: "I am Arbenz, Doctor Arévalo. . . ." Then Arana appeared. He was a man of average height and wide girth; a leather belt below his navel cinched his paunch. . . . His round face was expressionless, his eyes were evasive, and his smile fleeting. His handshake was limp. . . . When we were introduced he looked at me carefully and formally expressed his pleasure to meet me. He accepted my congratulations. But his reaction was not like that of Arbenz.[4]

The son of lower-middle-class parents, the thirty-nine-year-old Arana was "of mixed Spanish and Indian blood," an embassy official observed, "with the latter strain somewhat in predominance."[5] He had ascended from the ranks. He was "not a 'crusader' in any sense of the word."[6] The U.S. military attaché succinctly captured his personality:

EDUCATION: Little culture or polish . . .

MENTAL CHARACTERISTICS: Above average in general intelligence. Has initiative and a good intuitive grasp of the whole picture.

EMOTIONAL NATURE: Courageous and steady. Stolid Indian type.

PERSONALITY TRAITS: High ambition and tenacity of purpose. High sense of responsibility . . .

INTERPERSONAL RELATIONS: A good mixer, liked by superiors, equals and juniors. Has high qualities of leadership . . .

LOYALTY: Loyal under normal conditions.

POLITICAL VIEWS: Strongly nationalistic. Slightly pro-American.[7]

[3] "Had Major Aldana not been removed effectively from the fighting, no doubt he would have emerged in the place subsequently occupied by Major Arana." (Affeld [see n. 2 above], p. 2.)

[4] Arévalo, *El candidato*, pp. 327–29.

[5] Affeld (see n. 2 above), p. 1.

[6] Woodward to SecState, no. 2426, Apr. 24, 1945, p. 2, RG84 GR, Box 134, NA-S.

[7] Lt. Col. Morgan, "Lt. Col. Francisco Javier Arana," no. 313-46, Sept. 13, 1946, p. 1, RG84 GR, Box 217, NA-S.

Arana's Guatemalan contemporaries concurred.[8] "He was intelligent, canny like a peasant, and he could be charming," a political foe remembers. A poor speaker in public, he was "persuasive in small groups."[9] He might have lacked formal education, but he was intellectually curious and well-read by the pitiful standards of the Guatemalan officers, particularly those *de linea*. Generous with his friends, convivial—he excelled at telling jokes—he projected the image of a "good fellow" who had some charisma.[10]

This good fellow was now the most powerful man in the Guatemalan army. "Time alone will tell," an embassy official mused in March 1945, "whether Arana possesses the capacity to fill his role as intended, rather than using it . . . to handpick the next candidate for the Presidency." There was an undercurrent of uncertainty in embassy dispatches about Arana. "Arana has sufficient of the phlegmatic Indian strain to give him the laconic dignity, fearlessness and astuteness which seem frequently to be qualities that gravitate into positions of dictatorial control in the Latin American melting pot."[11]

Had Arana had his way, Arévalo would not have become president. After the fall of Ponce, Arana urged Arbenz and Toriello first to postpone the elections, then to disavow the results. "Don't forget," he wrote Toriello in a personal letter dated April 26, 1947, "what a hard time you had—the discussions, the arguments—convincing me to accept this situation [the election of Arévalo], which I never wanted because I knew that it meant handing the revolution over to civilians who would reap the benefits of what we, the military, had accomplished."[12]

---

[8] The portrait of Arana is based on (1) interviews with Guatemalans of different political sympathies, notably Cols. Lorenzana and Mendoza, Lt. Col. Cruz Salazar, Maj. Paz Tejada, Lt. Montenegro, and Charnaud, Galich, and Barrios Peña; (2) U.S. documents, esp. embassy reports; (3) works by Guatemalans, particularly a series by a well-informed if partisan friend of Arana, Avila Ayala, "La muerte del coronel Arana." A brazen apology of Arana that includes some useful information is Alvarado Rubio, *El asesinato*. For biographical data, see Zea Carrascosa, *Semblanzas*, pp. 279–80.

[9] Quoted from interview with Galich.

[10] Interview with Paz Tejada.

[11] Quotations from Affeld (see n. 2 above), p. 2, and Woodward to SecState, no. 215, June 19, 1945, p. 4, RG84 GR, Box 134, NA-S. For early expressions of this uncertainty, see also Col. Devine, "Intelligence Report" no. R75-46, Mar. 5, 1946, RG319 DF, Box 1621, NA-S; Lt. Col. Morgan, "Intelligence Report" no. R135-46, Apr. 29, 1946, RG319 ID 26044, NA-S; Col. Devine, "Intelligence Report" no. R254-46, July 11, 1946, RG319 DF, Box 1893, NA-S; Donovan to SecState, no. 1553, July 16, 1946, RG84 CF, Box 14, NA-S; enclosure no. 1 in Donovon to Sec-State, no. 2075, Jan. 2, 1947, NA 814.00; HQs Panama Canal Department, "Weekly Intelligence Summary" no. 255, May 21, 1947, RG319 ID 371556, NA-S.

[12] Arana to Jorge Toriello, Apr. 26, 1947, *El I*, Apr. 29, 1947, p. 9. See also "Carta abierta del Sr. Jorge Toriello al Jefe de las Fuerzas Armadas," Apr. 25, 1947, *El I*,

After Toriello indiscreetly published this letter, Arana issued a terse statement to the effect that, since the armed forces were apolitical, he would remain silent.[13] The damage had been done: Arana's letter to Toriello, noted the U.S. embassy, "quite frankly indicates . . . his belief that the government should not have been turned over to the civilian elements."[14]

Toriello and Arbenz demanded that the duly elected Arévalo be allowed to assume the presidency, and Arana finally agreed, but he exacted a price: the new constitution must guarantee his dominant position in the military. "After two private meetings" with Arana, President-elect Arévalo had little choice but to agree.[15] The 1945 constitution, prepared by an assembly dominated by Arévalo's supporters, established a new military position, patently absurd in an army of a few thousand men. Henceforth, there would be a chief of the armed forces, largely free of civilian control and more powerful than the minister of defense: "Military appointments," the constitution stipulated, "shall be made by the chief of the armed forces, through the minister of defense." His term would be six years. Unlike any other appointed official, he could be removed only by Congress, and then only if he had broken the law.[16] Upon Arévalo's inauguration, Arbenz became the minister of defense; Arana, the chief of the armed forces.

Arana's ambitions continued to grow. Soon an opportunity presented itself. On December 16, 1945, while cavorting in the countryside with a young American journalist, Arévalo drove his car into a deep ravine. It seemed at first that the president would be incapacitated for a long time.[17] Fearing that

---

Apr. 29, 1947, p. 1; Toriello, "Comentarios a la carta que recibí," Apr. 26, 1947, *El I*, Apr. 29, 1947, p. 9. On Arana's reluctance to hand the presidency to Arévalo, see also Affeld, "Memorandum for the Record," Jan. 26, 1945, RG84 GR, Box 134, NA-S.

[13] "Comunicado del Jefe de las Fuerzas Armadas coronel Francisco J. Arana," *El I*, Apr. 30, 1947, p. 1.

[14] Donovan to SecState, no. 2440, May 12, 1947, p. 2, NA 814.00.

[15] Cruz Salazar, "El ejército," p. 84.

[16] See arts. 149–61 of the 1945 constitution; quoted from art. 157. According to Cruz Salazar, the creation of this post was the result of Arana's pressure on Arévalo. Cruz Salazar served as intermediary in two secret meetings between Arana and Arévalo. (Interview with Cruz Salazar.) Arévalo refused to comment, beyond saying that Cruz Salazar's account was "largely correct" and that the decision to create the post of Chief of the Armed Forces was taken without him; "in fact, I wasn't even consulted." (Interview with Arévalo; see also Arévalo, *El candidato*, pp. 384–86, 610–14.) Cols. Lorenzana and Aldana Sandoval confirmed Cruz Salazar's account. (Interviews with Lorenzana and Aldana Sandoval.)

[17] For press accounts of the accident, see esp. *La Hora*, Dec. 17, 18, 1945, p. 1, and *El I*, Dec. 18, 19, 1945, p. 1. The press demurely overlooked the presence of the young lady. This was during the political honeymoon, and Arévalo was a married man. U.S. embassy reports were less discreet: "The young woman is understood to have

Arana might exploit the situation to seize power, a group of leaders of the PAR approached him. A secret deal was struck: the *Pacto del Barranco* (Pact of the ravine). In exchange for Arana's promise to refrain from a military coup, these leaders pledged in writing that their party would support his candidacy in the November 1950 presidential elections. Arévalo, who in fact recovered swiftly, reluctantly endorsed the arrangement.[18]

The U.S. State Department did not learn of the *Pacto del Barranco* until January 15, 1947:

> Lt. Col. Morgan, former Assistant Military Attaché in Guatemala, called on Mr. Newbegin [at the Central American desk of the State Department] . . . and told him that there was one bit of highly secret political information on Guatemala which had never been reported but was of great importance in analyzing current political trends in that country. This was the existence of an agreement between Col. Arana . . . and PAR, the dominant political party. Under this agreement Arana would be the candidate of PAR in the presidential election of 1951 [sic].
>
> This agreement, according to Colonel Morgan, explains Arana's unwillingness to join any movement to overthrow Arévalo. Arana does not want to incur unpopularity with his strongest supporters, the political party and liberal elements in the country, nor does he wish to endanger the institution of a six-year presidential term.
>
> This agreement, Colonel Morgan stated, is written and is known only to a very few people in Guatemala and is not known to anyone at the American Embassy.[19]

Left alone, Arana might indeed have remained content in his role as the heir apparent. But Guatemala's landed elite sought a champion to defend their privileges, and they turned to Arana "to use him as an instrument of disruption." With an ardor that blossomed as their hostility toward Arévalo deepened, the proud scions of the coffee elite began their humiliating courtship. They flocked around Arana, whom, in happier circumstances, they would have shunned as a parvenu. They invited him to their parties and their country

---

been Miss Lynn Cady Schnider, an American citizen who is rumored to have been very closely acquainted with President Arévalo. It is understood that Miss Schnider was not seriously injured and that she departed from Guatemala for Mexico or the United States on December 21, 1945." (Woodward to SecState, no. 965, Dec. 29, 1945; see also Woodward to SecState, no. 927, Dec. 18, 1945 and Woodward to SecState, no. 945, Dec. 22, 1945. All NA 814.001.)

[18] The existence of the pact is mentioned only by a few writers, notably Nájera Farfán, *Los estafadores*, pp. 105–6, Galich, *¿Por qué lucha Guatemala?*, p. 201, and Villagrán Kramer, "Los pactos," no. 1, July 12, 1987, p. 11. My sources include interviews with Galich, Charnaud, Fortuny, Monteforte Toledo, Barrios Peña, and Paz Tejada who, upon succeeding Arana as chief of the armed forces in August 1949, found the pact itself in a drawer of Arana's desk. (Among the signatures was that of Galich.)

[19] Williams, "Guatemalan Politics—Agreement between Arana and PAR," Jan. 16, 1947, NA 814.00.

estates. They showered him with praise, urging him to save Guatemala and overthrow the communist, Arévalo.[20]

Arana's drama had begun. He had no desire to sully his hands with a military coup. He wanted to retain his cachet as the democratic hero of the uprising against Ponce. He was not a violent man, as long as he could get what he wanted by other means, and the *Pacto del Barranco*, Arévalo's repeated assurances, and his own military power seemed to guarantee that he would be president in 1951—a president elected by an admiring populace, not a usurper ruling through force.

Yet Arana was not immune to the charm and the flattery of the elite. Lacking strong views on political and social affairs, he would not have complained about the government's reforms had it not been for the shrill protests of his new friends. He wanted their approval, but had no desire to antagonize the administration parties and the labor unions, the foot soldiers who would deliver the vote in the 1950 presidential elections. Caught between these contradictory desires, his behavior was inconsistent. He grumbled to his friends about the government's radicalism and labor's excesses ("What they are doing is unconscionable; I disapprove"), and occasionally he was outspoken to members of the government and to U.S. officials ("The present situation . . . [is] intolerable").[21] But these complaints rarely—very rarely—translated into action. Arana was openly defiant on only a few occasions. In September 1947, for instance, he hid a right-wing plotter in his house and demanded that several labor leaders be deported. As a rule, he did not actively oppose the government's policies, and, whatever he may have said behind Arévalo's back, "he visited the president in his house, in a respectful manner."[22]

Arana's grumblings, his occasional defiance, and his ties to some of the government's most bitter foes bred suspicion among administration politicians and labor leaders. In 1948, a few began to criticize him openly. "We believe it to be a mistake," admonished the prominent PAR leader Augusto Charnaud MacDonald, "to govern by force. Colonel Arana tried to deport two members of the FPL and the PAR whom he considered hostile to him. . . . A violent

[20] Quoted from Rivera to Ambassador and Donovan, May 9, 1946, RG84 CF, Box 14, NA-S. This is confirmed by the sources listed in n. 8 above, including Arana's adviser Barrios Peña, a prominent member of the upper class. See also FBI, Hoover to Neal, July 19, 1946, NA 814.00; FBI, Hoover to Neal, July 30, 1946, NA 814.00; Lt. Col. Morgan, "Lt. Col. Francisco Javier Arana," no. 313-46, Sept. 13, 1946, RG84 GR, Box 217, NA-S.

[21] Quotations from interviews with Barrios Peña and from Donovan to SecState, no. 1529, July 8, 1946, p. 2, NA 814.00.

[22] Quoted from interview with Galich. On the September 1947 incident, see HQs Panama Canal Department, "Weekly Intelligence Summary" no. 273, Sept. 25, 1947, pp. 7–8, RG319 ID 0400768, NA-S.

act such as forcing two citizens to leave their country . . . stabs democracy in the back.''[23]

For his part, Arana began to doubt the revolutionary parties' commitment to his presidential aspirations. In the November 1948 congressional elections, he ran his own slate of supporters. It was an inept effort, directed by men, like Ricardo Barrios Peña, who were more adept at plotting than at running a campaign. The outcome has been described by Clemente Marroquín Rojas, the most brilliant of Guatemala's right-wing journalists: "In 1948 half of the Congress was up for reelection. . . . Colonel Arana lent his support to several candidates, but he chose undistinguished individuals who were virtually unknown; worse, he gave his money away indiscriminately, both to his friends and to his enemies—more than $30,000 from the Defense Ministry went to his enemies. Not one of Arana's candidates . . . was elected to Congress.''[24]

This futile attempt further strained Arana's relations with the revolutionary parties. A few days before the elections, the Guatemalan Congress overwhelmingly approved an unprecedented resolution that was clearly intended as a rebuke to Arana: "The Legislature," it stated, "has learned that some members of the army have been interfering in the Congressional campaign." Arana responded promptly with a curt statement that "can only be interpreted," explained the U.S. embassy, "as a sharp rebuff.''[25] A few days later, the embassy added:

Concurrent with increasing political activity in connection with the forthcoming Congressional elections are persistent reports of a possible early revolutionary attempt to be headed by Colonel . . . Arana. . . . While much of this talk is believed to be within the realm of speculation, it seems clear that recent political developments have distinctly cooled the relations between President Arévalo and Colonel Arana on one hand, and Congress and Colonel Arana on the other. The President is said to be annoyed by the "Arana-for-President" movement which has been launched by several independent groups in Guatemala City recently, probably with the encouragement of Arana. One informant of reliability reports that Arana approached a leading citizen . . . urging the latter to organize a political party to espouse Arana's candidacy in 1950. . . . Many observers believe that he much prefers to gain his ends through democratic elections, but that he is determined by any means to succeed Arévalo.

[23] Charnaud MacDonald, "Arana y la unidad de las fuerzas revolucionarias," *El Libertador*, Aug. 21, 1948, p. 21.

[24] "Ya no pierdan su tiempo, señores finqueros," *La Hora Dominical*, June 1, 1952, p. 1. An interview with Barrios Peña was particularly useful.

[25] Quotations from "40 diputados firman punto resolutivo," *El I*, Nov. 4, 1948, p. 1, and Wells to SecState, no. 561, Nov. 10, 1948, NA 814.00/11-1248, p. 1. For Arana's response, see "Proceder del Congreso causa extrañeza a Arana," *El I*, Nov. 8, 1948, p. 1.

Some months ago, there was considerable talk of an understanding between Colonel Arana and the *Frente Popular Libertador*. However recent developments cast doubts upon this possibility. . . . Arana's relations with the more leftist *Partido Acción Revolucionaria* and *Renovación Nacional* also obviously have cooled during recent weeks. . . .

The action of Congress in protesting the alleged intervention of the Armed Forces in politics . . . unquestionably has worsened Arana's relations with the Arevalista political parties. It is common knowledge that Congress gave serious consideration to adopting a curt resolution reaffirming its previous charge, in response to Arana's official communication of denial. . . . However, wiser counsel prevailed (one dissenter Deputy is reported to have observed that Congress could censure Arana if it wished, but to do so would invite dissolution the following day) and for the moment, at least, the incident is officially closed.

With the foregoing as background, it is difficult not to attach greater significance to current rumors that Colonel Arana has reached the end of his patience with the present "revolutionary" government, and is seeking the right opportunity and a reasonable excuse for a military coup d'etat. Although the Embassy believes that Arana sincerely desires to preserve constitutional government, and hopes to become President by means of the ballot, it must be admitted that all indications point to his having personal ambitions, as well as personal antipathy toward the extremism which all too frequently is identified with the Arévalo regime. For this reason, one may not rule out the possibility that the force of political developments may turn his ambitions in revolutionary channels.[26]

After his electoral fiasco, Arana still sought, through a combination of veiled threats and suasion, to secure the support of the leaders of the revolutionary parties, and they too wanted to avoid an open break. In early 1949, for instance, Arana twice approached José Manuel Fortuny, the leader of the radical wing of the PAR. In Fortuny's words, Arana asked, " 'Why don't you and your friends like me? I'm not a man of the right.' Arana was very direct: 'I am going to be a candidate,' " and he asked for the PAR's support. " 'The truth,' he complained, 'is that you people are ingrates.' " Fortuny responded: " 'We are not against you. We appreciate the role that you played in the revolt against Ponce. It's just that you have no sympathy for labor.' " He avoided stating categorically that the PAR would not support Arana. The party, he claimed, had not yet made a decision.[27]

The faltering minuet that had begun with the *Pacto del Barranco* was draw-

---

[26] Wells to SecState, no. 564, Nov. 12, 1948, NA 814.00. See also "Crisis between Col. Arana and President Arévalo May Result in a Coup d'état by the former," enclosed in Wells to de Zengotita, Nov. 5, 1948 (1); Wells to de Zengotita, Nov. 5, 1948 (2); Wells to de Zengotita, Nov. 15, 1948; Wells to de Zengotita, Nov. 19, 1948; Patterson to SecState, no. 462, Nov. 26, 1948. All RG84 GR, Box 192, NA-S.

[27] Interview with Fortuny.

ing to a close. The hostility of the PAR and RN toward Arana was obvious. Within the FPL, the most conservative of the revolutionary parties, only the faction led by Mario Méndez Montenegro still supported Arana. Some of them were motivated by loyalty; others, by opportunism. Their reasoning was, chided a critic, "The man with the weapons will win; it's best to back the winner; we're for Arana."[28] But in April 1949, the FPL held its first national convention and the *Aranistas* were soundly defeated.[29] They bolted from the party and created the FPL Ortodoxo. In the following weeks, recalls an observer sympathetic to Arana, "in almost all the departments of the republic the dissidents began to organize Arana's supporters. This premature campaign caused a lot of tension."[30] He was not a candidate, Arana explained to inquiring journalists, but he would run should the people of Guatemala so demand.[31] Meanwhile, writes another friendly witness, "many complained that his behavior was dishonorable because he was, in fact, running a presidential campaign while he was still chief of the armed forces, and he was funding it with government money. . . . Throughout the country one saw army jeeps carrying *Aranista* propaganda . . . and Arana himself would appear in uniform . . . in order to open branches of the FPL Ortodoxo."[32]

Yet Arana's chances appeared increasingly slim. The FPL Ortodoxo lacked popular appeal; the revolutionary parties were hostile, as was the labor movement. When some members of the powerful railway union (SAMF) declared their support of Arana's candidacy in January 1949, they were promptly rebuked by the SAMF leadership and by the country's two labor confederations.[33] Meanwhile, interest was growing in the government camp about the possible candidacy of Lieutenant Colonel Arbenz, the enigmatic minister of defense, who seemed to be sympathetic to labor and respectful of the constitution.

The first overtures toward Arbenz had taken place in September 1947, after the discovery of both a right-wing conspiracy to overthrow the government and an attempt by a few individuals to create a communist party. Directing his anger only at the "subversives" of the left, Arana had demanded that the

[28] "FPL define su postura," *Nuestro Diario*, June 11, 1949, p. 9.

[29] For the convention, see the issues of *Nuestro Diario* and *El I* of Mar. 31, Apr. 1, 2, 4, 1949. See also Wells to SecState, no. 179, Apr. 5, 1949, NA 814.00, and "Realizada la convención del Frente Popular Libertador," *El Libertador*, Apr. 16, 1949, p. 1.

[30] Nájera Farfán, *Los estafadores*, pp. 107–8.

[31] See, for instance, "Arana no gusta de camarillas," *El I*, Apr. 1, 1949, p. 1. and "Opinión que tiene Arana," *Nuestro Diario*, June 11, 1949, p. 1.

[32] Avila Ayala, "La muerte del coronel Arana," Aug. 2, 1954, p. 4.

[33] "Una rama del SAMF proclama la candidatura del coronel Arana," *Nuestro Diario*, Jan. 12, 1949, p. 9; "SAMF ajeno a los grupos políticos," *Nuestro Diario*, Jan. 13, 1949, p. 7.

government deport several labor leaders whom he considered particularly dangerous. Arbenz, who was usually reserved when nonmilitary matters were discussed in the cabinet, clashed violently with Arana. His intervention limited the purge. A few days later, several PAR leaders (notably Charnaud, Morgan, and Fortuny) sought a meeting with Arbenz to become better acquainted with the colonel who had sprung to the defense of the labor movement.[34]

By mid-1949, many PAR, RN, and labor leaders had privately decided to back Arbenz. In a country in which the military was the most powerful institution, only a military man would have any chance to beat Arana, and in their opinion Arbenz was "the most progressive officer."[35]

It never came to a vote. On July 18, 1949, Arana was killed at the Puente de la Gloria, not far from the capital. His murderers were never apprehended.

Ignoring the published accounts of Arbenz and other government officials, some authors imply that the assassins were from the upper class: "Many of Arana's 'friends' felt that they would profit from his death in that he had obstructed several *coups* against Arévalo, thus casting a shadow on his 'loyalty.' His murder would at one stroke remove him and cast blame and subsequent public revulsion on Arbenz."[36] This reasoning defies logic. Arana was the elite's only hope to seize power. Arévalo had faced a plethora of plots, perhaps as many as thirty. As the former president himself remarked, "Some were family affairs, concocted behind closed doors; the police would arrive and cart them away. Others were military affairs. Tangay, for example, entered from Mexico and seized several villages in the department of San Marcos; the local police hauled him in before the army arrived."[37] Not one of these plots threatened Arévalo because not one had the support of either of the army's major factions, led by Arana and Arbenz. Arbenz would not plot against Arévalo. Therefore, the elite's only hope was Arana—a live Arana; not a martyr, but a *caudillo* who could lead a revolt. And while it is true that Arana had withstood many pleas to overthrow Arévalo, his scruples had weakened as his electoral chances had waned.

[34] Interviews with Charnaud, Morgan, and Fortuny. For the government's reaction and the debate in the congress, see esp. *DCA* and *El I*, issues of Sept. 16 to Oct. 2, 1947. For Arbenz's demeanor in the cabinet, see MemoConv (Hill, Silva Peña), Dec. 28, 1953, enclosed in Krieg to Fisher, Dec. 29, 1953, NA 714.00; also helpful were interviews with two cabinet members, Charnaud and Osegueda. For Arbenz's role in limiting the purge, see also Dalton, *Miguel Mármol*, pp. 518–20.

[35] Interviews with Charnaud (quoted), Morgan, Fortuny, Guerra Borges. See also Pellecer, "Crónica," pp. 91–92, and Bishop, "Guatemalan Labor," pp. 126–27.

[36] Melville, *Guatemala—Another Vietnam?* p. 59. See also Jonas, "Guatemala," p. 156, n. 8, and Immerman, *CIA in Guatemala*, pp. 59–60. For published accounts by Arbenz and others, see below nn. 78–81.

[37] Arévalo, "La revolución le enseñó al pueblo."

One evening in September or October 1948, Captain Carlos Paz Tejada, a respected young officer, was invited to dine with Arana. They spent the evening at a country estate, the Quinta Samayoa. Also present were leading *Aranista* officers and Ricardo Barrios Peña, the scion of one of Guatemala's most illustrious families and a close adviser to Arana. After listening to bitter denunciations of the government by Arana and his friends, Paz Tejada made an impassioned plea to the colonel not to become another Ubico. "You took the wind from our sails," Barrios Peña told Paz Tejada a few years later. "We were about to launch the coup."[38] Indeed, Barrios Peña stresses, "We already had Paco [Arana] convinced."[39]

In the late spring of 1949, senior *Aranista* officers, on Arana's instructions, assembled one night at the Guardia de Honor: Arana would come, he had promised, to lead them against the government. They waited until dawn, but Arana did not appear. He had spent the night, they later learned, drinking with Arévalo in the presidential palace.[40]

Arana knew that if he were to launch a coup, he would succeed. True, Arbenz had many supporters within the officer corps; there were also minor cliques that retained their independence, and many officers who remained indifferent. But Arana had used his authority as chief of the armed forces to place his supporters in key positions. They controlled the Guardia de Honor and the Base Militar, the two important military units in the capital. *Aranistas* were the commanders of each of the country's seven Zonas Militares. The sole *Arbencista* officer in command of troops was Colonel Francisco Cosenza, the head of the minuscule air force. The police force, under Arévalo's brother-in-law Colonel Víctor Aldana Sandoval, was not *Aranista*, but, poorly armed and poorly trained, its power was negligible. And Arévalo's Presidential Guard consisted of only a few men under a loyal officer.

What held Arana back was not fear of defeat, but his "inner conflict."[41] As long as he hoped that he could reach the presidency by more respectable means, Arana could not bring himself to launch a coup. This explains why at the Quinta Samayoa he was moved by the plea of Paz Tejada, an officer with much prestige but little power.

By July 1949, however, Arana could dally no longer. Facing the opposition of the revolutionary parties and labor unions, and unable to create a strong

[38] Interview with Paz Tejada.

[39] Interview with Barrios Peña, who confirmed Paz Tejada's account and added a wealth of detail.

[40] Interviews with Lt. Montenegro, who was at the Guardia de Honor, and with Col. Mendoza, whose brother, Col. Miguel Mendoza, was one of the senior officers who spent the night at the Guardia de Honor waiting for Arana.

[41] Interview with Col. Mendoza.

Aranista party, he would need the army to deliver the peasant vote. Yet his control of the military was threatened.

The constitution stipulated that a military officer could be elected president only if he quit active duty at least six months before election day; Arana would have to step down as armed forces chief by May 1950. His successor would be selected by the Guatemalan Congress from a list of three names submitted by the Consejo Superior de la Defensa (CSD), an advisory body composed of twenty-three officers. (Ten were members ex-officio, the others were elected every three years by all active duty officers.)[42] The 1946 elections for the CSD had attracted little attention, but by the spring of 1949 the CSD had acquired unforeseen importance. For it was obvious that the Guatemalan Congress, if offered the opportunity, would appoint a *non-Aranista* as chief of the armed forces. From Arana's perspective, therefore, it was imperative that the CSD submit the names of three *Aranista* officers. Arana lacked a clear majority within the CSD, but some of its members were up for reelection in early July 1949.

Through May and June 1949, "a quiet tug of war was waged" within the CSD. Ostensibly at issue were the rules for the forthcoming elections. The *Aranistas* wanted to ensure that the commanders of the Zonas Militares and the unit commanders had as much influence as possible over the ballot. Their opponents wanted to ensure that the vote be secret and free. The outcome of an unfettered ballot among the more than seven hundred active duty officers was unpredictable. As a witness recalls, "the situation within the officer corps was confused." The discussions in the CSD grew increasingly acrimonious. Arana and Arbenz, both members ex-officio, rarely attended; they were kept informed by their supporters.[43]

As election day approached, Arana convoked an extraordinary session of the CSD. This time both he and Arbenz participated. "It was an extremely tense session," recalls the president of the CSD, Paz Tejada.[44] Arbenz remained cold, impassive, arguing points of law. No agreement was reached beyond the decision to postpone the elections until late July.[45]

[42] See arts. 131/6, 152, 156, and 161 of the 1945 Constitution, and Congressional Decree no. 116, May 22, 1945. (*Recopilación de leyes*, vol. 64, p. 486.)

[43] Quotations from Clemente Marroquín Rojas, "Los lobos se han ido," *La Hora*, July 14, 1954, p. 4, and Avila Ayala, "La muerte del coronel Arana," Aug. 5, 1954, p. 4. My sources for this struggle include interviews with two members of the CSD: Maj. Paz Tejada (president) and Lt. Col. Paiz Novales; with Arana's adviser, Barrios Peña; and with María de Arbenz, Galich and Charnaud. Avila Ayala, "La muerte del coronel Arana," Aug. 5, 1954, p. 4 and Aug. 6, 1954, p. 4, is particularly useful. See also Galich, *Por qué lucha Guatemala?*, p. 203.

[44] Interview with Paz Tejada.

[45] See "Prórroga en las elecciones del Consejo Superior de la Defensa," *DCA*, July 13, 1949, p. 1, and "Elecciones del Consejo de Defensa prorrogan," *Nuestro Diario*,

On Friday, July 15, came the anticlimactic denouement: in a session of the CSD, the *Aranistas* suddenly accepted their opponents' demands. The elections would not be supervised by the local commanders; instead, teams of officers would be sent from the capital to oversee the vote in the different Zonas Militares; they would bring back the ballot boxes; each commission would include both *Aranistas* and *non-Aranistas*. The elections would begin in three days.

That same Friday Arana suddenly replaced Colonel Cosenza, the *Arbencista* commander of the air force, with one of his men, Colonel Arturo Altolaguirre Ubico. His order was promptly executed even though it had not been issued through the Defense Ministry, as required by the constitution.[46]

The following morning, Paz Tejada expressed his surprise at the unexpected turn of events within the CSD to Arbenz: "They gave in without a struggle." Arbenz replied: "They don't care any more. They've made up their minds to go for a coup."[47]

Arbenz was right. "Arana had tired of waiting, of arguing, pleading and threatening," his adviser Barrios Peña explains. He had been, or so he believed, exceedingly patient, listening to his own scruples rather than to his friends' advice. He had accepted rebuffs from upstart politicians who had conveniently forgotten that it was he who had overthrown Ponce in 1944, thereby enabling them to embark on their profitable careers. Their impudence was now imitated within the CSD by a clique of officers without troops. To be sure, Arévalo continued to reassure him of his presidential prospects, but the facts belied the president's promises. It was time to act. On the afternoon of Saturday, July 16, Arana went to the presidential palace and confronted Arévalo in his office.[48]

Had he launched a straightforward coup, Arana would have succeeded. But overconfidence and the lingering remnants of his "inner conflict" led him along a more tortuous path. He still longed to be a properly elected president.

July 13, 1949, p. 7. The rumor later spread that the elections for the CSD had taken place in the week before July 18 and had been won by the *Aranistas*. (See Wells to SecState, no. 311, July 18, 1949, NA 814.00 and Alvarado Rubio, *El asesinato*, pp. 29–30.)

[46] Monteforte Toledo, *Una democracia*, p. 23; Wells to SecState, no. 311, July 18, 1949, NA 814.00; Altolaguirre, "Entrevistamos." Arana also demanded that the police hand over some of their weapons to him. (See Víctor Sandoval, Director General de la Guardia Civil, to César Solís, Ministro de Gobernación, July 15, 1949, CO:G, June–July 1949, p. 919, AGCA, and Solís to Jefe de las Fuerzas Armadas, July 16, 1949, ibid., pp. 919–20.) Arana's motivation must have been to flaunt his power; the weapons of the poorly armed police would not have altered the balance of power in the country.

[47] Interview with Paz Tejada.

[48] An interview with Barrios Peña was particularly useful for this paragraph and the next.

Instead of toppling Arévalo, he delivered an ultimatum: Arévalo must dismiss his cabinet and replace his ministers with those of Arana's choice. Arbenz and his followers would be retired from the army. If Arévalo complied, he would be allowed to complete his presidential term. If he refused, he would be deposed.[49]

Arévalo listened with apparent resignation and asked only for a few days' time so that he could implement the changes in an orderly manner. Arana consented. The ultimatum would expire at 10 p.m. on Monday, July 18 (the day the elections for the CSD were to begin). Arana left triumphant. "Arévalo," remarks Barrios Peña, "willfully deceived Arana."[50]

In vain had Arana's advisers pleaded with him, before he went to the presidential palace, to forego complicated games and simply seize power. In vain did they argue, after he returned from the palace, that he could not rely on Arévalo's promises. In vain did they stress "that in a coup d'état there's no time for talk—you act or you fail."[51]

Arrogance and wishful thinking blinded Arana. He believed that Arévalo, lacking the means to resist, would capitulate. He believed that Arbenz, who could count only on officers without troops, would acquiesce in his own dismissal, just as he had acquiesced to the removal of Colonel Cosenza. The departure of Arbenz and senior *Arbencistas*, Arana concluded, would cinch his control of the military; congress would be cowed, and Arévalo would be in his pocket. Who, then, would dare resist his presidential ambitions? He would be a constitutional president, not a *golpista*. This Arana predicted on Sunday afternoon, July 17, to his skeptical friend Barrios Peña in the latter's estate in the department of Escuintla, a few hours from the capital. "It was the last time I saw Paco; he was sure that he had won."[52]

Arévalo had no intention of giving up so easily. While the details vary according to the informants, the main lines of what took place within the government are clear. After Arana left, Arévalo summoned Arbenz and other key aides and informed them of the ultimatum. They readily agreed that Arana must be sent into exile. The next day, while Arana dallied at Barrios Peña's estate, the Permanent Committee of the Guatemalan Congress met in secret session and voted unanimously that Arana be dismissed. At the request of his friend Arévalo, Cuban President Carlos Prío Socarrás agreed to give Arana asylum in his country. Colonel Cosenza would fly the disgraced plotter to Havana.[53]

---

[49] No one witnessed this conversation between Arana and Arévalo. My major sources are interviews with Barrios Peña, Galich, Charnaud, María de Arbenz, Lorenzana, and Mendoza. See also Arbenz, "Habla Arbenz," p. 120.

[50] Quoted from interview with Barrios Peña.

[51] Interviews with Col. Mendoza (quoted) and Barrios Peña.

[52] Interview with Barrios Peña.

[53] The main sources for this paragraph and the two that follow are interviews with Galich, Charnaud, María de Arbenz, Paz Tejada, Monteforte Toledo, Lorenzana, and

A formidable problem remained: how would these bold decisions be enforced? The government's hope was to seize Arana without warning, and even then, the likely response of the *Aranista* commanders would be a military uprising. No clear plan of action emerged, only the decision that somehow, somewhere, Arbenz would capture Arana the next day, Monday, July 18.

It was Arana himself, on Monday morning, who gave the government the help it needed. Appearing unexpectedly at the presidential palace, he told Arévalo that he was on his way to El Morlón, the presidential chalet on the shores of nearby Lake Amatitlán, to seize a cache of weapons that was hidden there.

The previous spring, with Arana's grudging consent, Arévalo had provided weapons and other assistance to Dominican exiles seeking to free their country from the Trujillo dictatorship.[54] Some of these weapons had been seized by the Mexican authorities while the exiles were in Cozumel, Yucatán. In early July, the weapons were returned to the Guatemalan government, and they were placed at the small air base of San José. "On Arbenz's orders, and with the complicity of Colonel Cosenza, the weapons were spirited away to El Morlón," the chief of army intelligence told Arana on July 14.[55] But Arana's attention was focused on his ultimatum to Arévalo, not on a paltry cache of arms.[56] He took no steps to seize the weapons for three days. Then, on the morning of the eighteenth, he went to see Arévalo.

Arévalo says now that "on the 18th Arana and I did not quarrel, much less exchange insults."[57] But at the time he told his aides that Arana had spoken to him "in an abusive and very threatening manner," that the armed forces chief had upbraided him as though he had been a disrespectful student, alternating threats with sarcastic remarks about his propensity to hide weapons. Whatever the true tone of the conversation (and Arévalo's private account at the time is more credible than the public disclaimer of a much changed Arévalo three decades later), Arana announced that he was on his way to El Morlón to recover the weapons.[58]

Mendoza. See also Arbenz, "Habla Arbenz," p. 120; Marroquín Rojas, *La "Carta política,"* p. 33; Pellecer, "Dos yanquis," Sept. 2, 1982, p. 2; Pérez, "Los oscuros acontecimientos." The account by Pellecer given in this chapter is indirectly confirmed by Arévalo in his "De Juan José Arévalo."

[54] See below, p. 114.

[55] Interview with Col. Lorenzana, chief of army intelligence.

[56] Interview with Barrios Peña. The sources listed in n. 49 above believe that Arana did not mention the arms in El Morlón when he saw Arévalo on July 16.

[57] Arévalo, "De Juan José Arévalo." Arévalo was responding to Pellecer's statement, "The conversation between the two was heated. The colonel . . . raised his voice and insulted and threatened the president." (Pellecer, "Dos yanquis," Sept. 2, 1982, p. 2.)

[58] Quoted from interview with Galich. The other sources are those listed in nn. 49 and 53 above (excepting Barrios Peña and Pérez).

The real reasons for Arana's visit to Arévalo can only be surmised. Arana knew that the arms stored at El Morlón—two hundred rifles without ammunition—in no way altered the balance of power; nor did he anticipate any resistance to his July 16 ultimatum. Furthermore, he had no need to go in person to El Morlón or, for that matter, to inform Arévalo of his whereabouts. Arana, an "impulsive" man whose patience was exhausted, went to the palace to flaunt his power and hurry the humbled president into the swift execution of his ultimatum.[59]

Once again, Arévalo deceived Arana. He raised no objection to Arana's decision to go to El Morlón and even suggested that the commander of his Presidential Guard, Colonel Felipe Antonio Girón, go with him.[60] Arana left the presidential palace savoring another Pyrrhic victory. He drove to El Morlón accompanied only by his driver Francisco Palacios, his aide Major Absalón Peralta, and the hapless Girón. "Arana," recalls a colonel who knew him well, "was very sure of himself. He knew that the officers in command of the troops were loyal to him. He never imagined that Arbenz and Arévalo would stand up to him, and his confidence was reinforced by the fact that he was accompanied on his trip to El Morlón by Arévalo's chief of staff."[61]

Upon Arana's departure, Arévalo contacted Arbenz. Now was the time. On Arbenz's orders, several armed men sped from the capital in two cars to intercept Arana as he returned from El Morlón. They were led by the deputy chief of police, Lt. Colonel Enrique Blanco, and by the chairman of the congressional Armed Forces committee, Alfonso Martínez, who was a retired army officer and a close friend of Arbenz.[62] Near a small bridge, the Puente de la Gloria, they waited. Their wait was not long.

Arana's business at El Morlón was swiftly concluded. According to his driver, they had found the chalet locked. "After blowing the horn several times, a man appeared from the garden, and they went to one of the boathouses where a red truck loaded with rifles was found." Soon thereafter Colonel Juan José de León "appeared with an army truck and two or three soldiers . . . and Colonel Arana said to him 'You already know what I ordered you.' " Leaving de León at the boathouse to load the weapons, Arana and his party began the return trip to Guatemala City. As they reached the Puente de la Gloria, "there was, on the other side, a grey Dodge, because of which, seeing that it was impossible to cross the bridge, Col. Arana stopped his car."[63]

[59] This is also the interpretation of Barrios Peña (quoted), and Cols. Lorenzana and Mendoza.

[60] My sources disagree as to who initiated this suggestion.

[61] Interview with Col. Mendoza. See also Alvarado Rubio, *El asesinato*, p. 49.

[62] Interview with Lt. García, who was Arbenz's aide and with him at the time; interviews with María de Arbenz, Guerra Borges, Charnaud, Galich, Paz Tejada. See also Pellecer, "Crónica," pp. 99–101, and Arbenz, "Habla Arbenz," p. 121.

[63] "Statement of Lt. Colonel Alberto Bone Summarizing Statement Made by Mr.

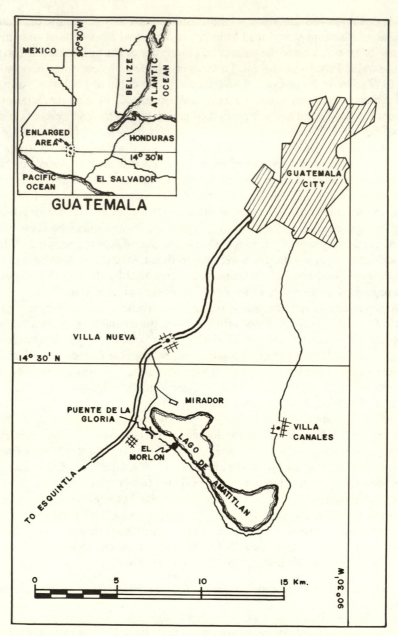

Map of Puente de la Gloria, where Arana was killed.

A brief shootout ensued and three men lay dead: Arana, his aide Peralta, and Lt. Colonel Blanco; others were wounded, including Arbenz's friend Alfonso Martínez. Did the ambushers open fire, without warning, as Arana's driver has claimed? Or did Peralta fire first, after Blanco had told Arana that he was under arrest and an argument had broken out? There is no definitive proof, but even some of Arana's friends believe that "the order was to capture Arana, not to kill him," that "his death was accidental."[64] Absalón Peralta and Blanco "first traded insults, then shots."[65]

News of Arana's death spread through the capital in a matter of hours. The Guardia de Honor rose in revolt.[66] For more than twenty-four hours the battle raged in the city. The rest of the country waited in tense expectation. More than once on the eighteenth, Arana's supporters seemed close to victory, but several factors were against them. Their intended victims had struck first, killing their *caudillo* and forcing them into a hasty reaction. While Arbenz led the loyalist forces with sang-froid and skill, no one rose to lead the rebels. Lt. Colonel Carlos Castillo Armas, possibly the most able of Arana's officers, was in Mazatenango, overseeing the elections for the CSD; he lacked the nerve to return to the capital.[67] The commander of the Guardia de Honor, Colonel Juan

---

Palacios J., Chauffeur of Colonel Arana, Concerning Events Associated With Arana's Death," pp. 1–2, enclosed in "Intelligence Report" no. IR-77-49, July 28, 1949. See also "Francisco Palacios hace sensacionales declaraciones," *Diario Latino*, San Salvador, Aug. 27, 1949, p. 1.

[64] Interview with Col. Lorenzana.

[65] Interview with Col. Mendoza. Also useful were interviews with Barrios Peña, Paz Tejada, Galich, García, María de Arbenz, Guerra Borges, Pellecer, Charnaud, and Aldana Sandoval (who pointed out that cold-blooded murderers would not have spared the life of Arana's driver). See also Pellecer, "Crónica," pp. 101–2, which gives a slightly different version of the scene.

[66] There is no definitive account of the fight. Following Arana's death, the government suspended publication of all newspapers, except the official *DCA*, which provided only sparse coverage. Upon resuming publication on August 1, the other newspapers wrote little on the subject. Coverage by the foreign press and by the U.S. embassy was superficial.

The government's version of the fighting was first outlined in "Mensaje del gobierno de la república a la ciudadanía," *DCA*, July 22, 1949, p. 1, and then in *Una democracia*, a 47-page pamphlet written by the president of the Guatemalan Congress, Monteforte Toledo. Useful information is included in Bush, "Organized Labor," part 4, pp. 11–14, in Sierra Roldán, *Diálogos*, pp. 44–46 and in Pellecer, "Dos yanquis," Sept. 3, 1982, p. 2. For an excellent series of articles by an *Aranista* officer, see Col. Pinto Recinos, "La rebelión." Particularly helpful were interviews with the following officers: García, Aldana Sandoval, Lorenzana, Mendoza, Montenegro, Paz Tejada; and with civilians Barrios Peña, Galich, and Charnaud.

[67] Castillo Armas was one of the few officers *de escuela* who was *Aranista*. An outstanding cadet (1933–1936), he attended classes at Fort Leavenworth, Kansas, from

Francisco Oliva, had been summoned by Arbenz to the Defense Ministry less than an hour after Arana's death; unaware of what had happened, he went and was arrested. Another *Aranista*, Colonel Gabino Santizo, the commander of the Base Militar, sided with the government. A few days later, with his customary eloquence, Arévalo told the people of Guatemala about the dialogue that, he said, had taken place between Arbenz and Santizo at the outset of the revolt: "Colonel Arbenz got in touch with . . . Colonel Gabino Santizo, a loyal soldier who immediately swore, 'My duty is to defend the government and the Constitution, and I guarantee you that all my commanders and officers will do their duty.' " The truth was more tawdry: Santizo had been bought for $75,000. That afternoon, while the *Aranista* officers at the base watched in sullen passivity, a group of loyalist officers arrived from the Defense Ministry "to place themselves under Santizo's orders," as the official story gently stated—or, more truthfully, to take control of his troops.[68]

Still, it was hours before the Base Militar stood solidly on the government's side, and in the meantime Arbenz had only the police, the tiny Presidential Guard, and loyal officers without troops. There were only a few weapons to arm the growing number of civilian volunteers.

The rebel officers squandered their advantage in ill-planned and poorly led attacks. Such were the incompetence and the disarray that effective command of the Guardia de Honor was assumed by a civilian, Mario Méndez Montenegro, the leader of the *Aranista* FPL Ortodoxo. Méndez Montenegro was brave, but untrained in military matters. Meanwhile, "some of the rebel colonels . . . were busy drinking."[69]

By dawn on July 19, the government was winning. The presidential palace and the police headquarters, the main targets of the rebels' attacks the previous

---

Oct. 1945 to Apr. 1946, and served as director of the Escuela Politécnica from Mar. 1947 to Mar. 1949. In Apr. 1949 he was appointed commander of the Fourth Military Zone (Mazatenango). His reaction to the news of Arana's death was provided by Paz Tejada, who was with him at the time. (Interview with Paz Tejada; see also Cáceres, *Aproximación*, pp. 46–47.)

[68] Quotations from "Mensaje del Gobierno" (see n. 66 above), p. 1 and from Monteforte Toledo, *Una democracia*, p. 19. A Guatemalan officer has written tactfully that on July 18, 1949, "the freedom of action of the Commander of the Base Militar was neutralized," without explaining how this was accomplished (Cruz Salazar, "El ejército," p. 86). Particularly informative were interviews with María de Arbenz, Paz Tejada, Guerra Borges, and Aldana Sandoval, the leader of the officers who took control of the Base Militar. See also Marroquín Rojas, "Los lobos se han ido," *La Hora*, July 17, 1954, p. 4. Santizo had a long pedigree as an *Aranista* plotter; he was one of the officers who were at the Quinta Samayoa in late 1948 (interview with Paz Tejada), and who later spent the night at the Guardia de Honor waiting for Arana (interview with Mendoza).

[69] Quoted from Pinto Recinos, "La rebelión," June 21, 1985, p. 2.

day, were in government hands. Government officers were now firmly in control of the Base Militar. The air force was also loyal: on Arbenz's orders, Colonel Cosenza arrested the officer whom Arana had appointed as his successor and resumed command. Civilian volunteers, mainly labor union members, had swelled the government ranks; they were armed with weapons from the Base Militar and the arms depot at Fort Matamoros, a small army barracks that Arbenz had seized during the night. Loyal officers and the cadets from the military academy hurriedly trained the volunteers.

By late morning soldiers from the Base Militar and armed civilians began to attack the Guardia de Honor. The air force's venerable planes strafed the rebel barracks and dropped a few bombs that rarely exploded. Even though the planes caused little physical damage, they deepened the rebels' demoralization. Through the Nuncio, at 1 p.m., the rebels sought negotiations. Desultory conversations ensued between representatives of both sides at the Salvadoran embassy; the government demanded unconditional surrender; the fighting resumed. At 5 p.m. the white flag was raised at the Guardia de Honor. The rebellion of the *Aranistas* had collapsed with approximately 150 dead and over two hundred wounded. In the words of a foe of Arbenz, the rebels' ineptitude "and the skill of the minister of defense determined the outcome of the battle."[70]

It remained for Arévalo to explain to the people of Guatemala the circumstances of Arana's death. On July 21, he declared five days of "national mourning."[71] Then, in a lengthy communiqué, he spun his tale.

Arana, Arévalo stated, was not blameless. Waylaid by the lure of the presidency and by self-seeking sycophants, "each day that passed he linked himself more and more closely with the political circles hostile to the president." But he resolutely resisted their entreaties that he overthrow the government. This refusal had cost him his life.

Arévalo did not name Arana's assassins, but he impugned the conservative opposition: the murderers were "reactionaries" who had finally realized that the colonel would never lead a coup d'état. Arana's death, the communiqué concluded, was a grave loss "for the nation, for the army, for the government and above all for his friend, President Arévalo."[72]

Before its publication, notes a PAR leader, "the official communiqué . . . was discussed in the cabinet; it was opposed by Arbenz, Foreign Minister Enrique Muñoz Meany and Carlos Aldana Sandoval, Minister of Public Works." These three asserted that Arévalo should tell the true story of Arana's death. ("There was no reason to lie," Aldana Sandoval exclaimed with a rare

[70] Cruz Salazar, "El ejército," p. 86.

[71] "Duelo nacional por la muerte del coronel Arana," *DCA*, July 21, 1949, p. 1.

[72] "Mensaje del Gobierno" (see n. 66 above), p. 3. "The official communiqué on Arana's death was written entirely by Arévalo" (Arévalo, "De Juan José Arévalo").

flash of emotion, more than forty years later.) Arévalo insisted on his version that, he explained, would avoid further inflaming passions; the other ministers agreed with the president.[73]

The next day, the official *Diario de Centro América* praised Arévalo's communiqué and drew a moral lesson: "Its eloquence has calmed us and given us the gift of truth, which comforts us. . . . Honesty seems defenseless, but it possesses a hidden weapon: truth, which always triumphs."[74]

Few Guatemalans agreed; few were so naive as to believe that Arana had been killed by his conservative friends. This contradicted both common sense and widely known facts. It was no secret, for instance, that Alfonso Martínez had been wounded at the Puente de la Gloria and that Martínez was close to Arbenz, not to the conservative opposition. Thus, the rumors and speculation surrounding the death of Arana took root.

At a massive rally in support of the administration, a prominent PAR leader, Carlos Manuel Pellecer, flatly contradicted the official story and alluded to Arana's disloyalty and to the true circumstances of his death. The government "rejects and officially condemns" Pellecer's declarations, a senior official announced the following day, on Arévalo's instructions. Pellecer was fired from his post in the Ministry of Education. "You were right to tell the truth," Arbenz later told him.[75]

In July 1950, on the first anniversary of the shootout at the Puente de la Gloria, opposition groups organized demonstrations accusing the government of the murder of Arana. Arévalo stuck to the official version. Arbenz remained silent, seeking to avoid an open break with the president. In the years that followed, first as president and then in lonely exile, Arbenz persisted in his silence even though he, far more than Arévalo, was branded as Arana's murderer. Shy, introverted, with a strict personal code of honor, he kept his promise not to speak out unless Arévalo agreed; the longer his silence, moreover, the more awkward a sudden reversal.[76] On one occasion, recalls his wife, he tried to convince Arévalo "to give a full and public account of the circumstances of Arana's death." It was in Montevideo, in the late 1950s, in one of the two ex-presidents' rare encounters during the years of exile. "But Arévalo said that it was better not to discuss it and changed the subject."[77]

[73] Pellecer, "Dos yanquis," Sept. 4, 1982, p. 2, and interview with Aldana Sandoval. As already noted, Arévalo indirectly endorsed Pellecer's account in "De Juan José Arévalo."

[74] "El gobierno dice al pueblo la verdad" (edit.), *DCA*, July 23, 1949, p. 3.

[75] Quotations from "El gobierno desaprueba el discurso del profesor Carlos Manuel Pellecer," *DCA*, July 25, 1949, p. 1 (quoted from p. 7), and Pellecer, "Dos yanquis," Sept. 4, 1982, p. 2.

[76] Interviews with María de Arbenz, Fortuny, and Guerra Borges.

[77] Interview with María de Arbenz.

Only in 1968, three years before his own death, did Arbenz finally state what had happened to Francisco Arana in those distant days of July 1949.[78]

Others did not wait so long. In July 1950, the communist weekly *Octubre* wrote that "prior to July 18 . . . Arana was ready to seize power," but it provided no details.[79] That same year, the communist leader Víctor Manuel Gutiérrez told a labor congress that Arana had died in an armed confrontation with "Police Coronel Enrique Blanco, who had a warrant for his arrest because he was plotting to overthrow Arévalo. . . . Therefore, comrade delegates, Arana was not assassinated: he died resisting arrest."[80] Information on the true circumstances of Arana's death was also provided in a 1956 book by Manuel Galich who, as secretary general of the FPL, had played a key role in July 1949.[81]

But Arévalo has remained evasive. At times he claims, as in a 1979 interview, that Arana's death is still an enigma, and probably "will remain a mystery forever."[82] On other occasions, as in a 1982 public letter, he has stated that he will reveal the truth in his memoirs, which will be published after his death.[83]

Why did Arévalo choose to cover up the facts? Perhaps in 1949 he honestly believed that his tale was the best way to restore domestic peace. Or perhaps he was keeping his options open: perhaps he believed that the *Aranistas* would one day regain power and that it was therefore not in his interest to malign their fallen hero. Or perhaps, as Arbenz speculated years later, "Arévalo played a very dirty trick on me."[84] For the residue of the official communiqué tarred Arbenz: in the absence of a plausible alternative and in the presence of the president's avowal of Arana's loyalty, speculation centered on the theory that Arana had been killed by *Arbencistas* in a showdown between military factions. As a key adviser to Arana muses, "Arévalo was very wily. He shifted all suspicion onto Arbenz."[85]

[78] Arbenz, "Habla Arbenz," pp. 119–22.

[79] "El 19 de Julio de 1949: Un gran golpe al imperialismo," *Octubre*, July 19, 1950, p. 1 (quoted from p. 3).

[80] Gutiérrez, "Informe rendido por el secretario general ante la novena asamblea confederal de la CTG," nd, p. 2, *GT*, Box 15.

[81] Galich, *¿Por qué lucha Guatemala?*, pp. 201–4.

[82] Interview with Arévalo.

[83] "De Juan José Arévalo." See also Alvarado Rubio, *El asesinato*, pp. 33–36, 41–48, 65–127.

[84] Interview with Fortuny quoting Arbenz.

[85] Interview with Barrios Peña. Since the late 1960s, Arévalo has spent most of his time in Guatemala, where the friends of Arana are again powerful. He has received honors and lives well. His lack of candor in July 1949 has served him well. See below, p. 394.

CHAPTER 4

The Election of Jacobo Arbenz

IT WAS THE HOUR of Jacobo Arbenz, the surviving military hero of 1944, the man who had led the government's defense against the *Aranistas*. After the rebels' defeat senior officers loyal to Arana were deported; others were retired, like Castillo Armas, or were shifted to positions of little importance.[1] Men loyal to Jacobo Arbenz now held the key military posts. On July 25, 1949, at Arbenz's request, Congress chose thirty-one-year old Paz Tejada as chief of the armed forces. Major Paz Tejada, noted the U.S. embassy, "was likeable . . . well-educated . . . well prepared for his job," and enjoyed "an unusual reputation for incorruptibility." He was also known for his independence of mind. Paz Tejada had joined the *Arbencista* group in order to counter the dictatorial propensities of Francisco Arana, but he remained very much his own man, and although he respected Arbenz, they were not close friends. He might become a powerful military leader, the embassy speculated, particularly if Arbenz's hold over the army were to weaken.[2] This appeared, for the moment, an unlikely prospect.

While the balance of power in the military had changed dramatically, the army's position in the country was unaffected. The military was, if anything, more powerful than before, because it was more united. And it retained its monopoly of the country's weapons.

During the revolt, as many as two thousand civilians, mainly students and union members, had been armed in the capital. At times, particularly on July 19, the volunteers had been asked their names and their addresses; on other occasions, the distribution had been indiscriminate.[3] But after the rebels' defeat, the government, prodded by the army, cajoled and threatened the civilians to return their weapons. As in October 1944, the labor leaders assisted the government; they feared a confrontation with the military that they were

[1] For a good summary, see Pinto Recinos, "La rebelión," July 3, 1985, p. 2.

[2] Patterson to SecState, no. 349, July 28, 1949, NA 814.00; quoted from Steins to SecState, no. 416, Aug. 3, 1949, p. 2, NA 814.20; Patterson to SecState, no. 421, Aug. 4, 1949, NA 814.20. Also useful were interviews with Paz Tejada, María de Arbenz, Guillén, Mendoza, Galich, García, Charnaud. For Paz Tejada's brilliant performance as a cadet and a young officer, see Samayoa Coronado, *La Escuela Politécnica*, 2:124, 370.

[3] In addition to the sources listed in p. 67, n. 66, see Patterson to SecState, no. 327, July 21, 1949, NA 814.00, and Tomás Yancos, "Una jornada gloriosa," *DCA*, July 28, 1949, p. 6.

bound to lose. While troops searched entire blocks of the city, the labor unions organized searches of their own and threatened to denounce all those found to be hiding weapons. In a matter of days, most of the arms had been returned. "We are surrendering the weapons that were given to us to defend our government," wrote the country's two foremost labor leaders to Arbenz. "We trust that they will be returned to us," should seditious officers again threaten "our freedom."[4]

Arbenz's behavior during the July uprising—firm in his support of the government, decisive in his military leadership—had reinforced his prestige, and the fact that there was no civilian who could unify the quarrelsome components of the government coalition and restrain the competing ambitions of a host of politicians further enhanced his status. Leaders such as Charnaud and Fortuny from the PAR and Gutiérrez from organized labor had first approached Arbenz out of expediency but had become his friends. They believed that they knew the true Jacobo, and that this man, so silent in public, would be not only an able leader but also a progressive one. By late 1949, the powerful PAR, the RN, and the country's two largest labor confederations were ready to declare their support of Jacobo Arbenz.[5]

Still another group was ready to raise Arbenz's standard: a handful of rich landowners and industrialists, most of whom, like Arbenz, hailed from Quezaltenango, Guatemala's second largest city. Having known the defense minister for many years, they too believed that they knew the private Jacobo. Arbenz, they argued, was courting the PAR and the labor movement because he needed their votes. As president, he would tolerate only modest social change. These men, unlike the immense majority of their peers, believed that limited concessions to the lower classes not only were politically necessary, but also would be economically beneficial. What Arbenz needed, they concluded, was the advice of well-bred and pragmatic friends. They were ready to educate the prince. In late 1949 these men—including Nicolás Brol, Joaquín Rivera Kunze, and Héctor Mazariegos—created the Partido de Integridad Nacional (PIN) to back Arbenz. Reflecting the geographical base of its leaders, the PIN was a regional party, with headquarters in Quetzaltenango.[6]

Who would launch Arbenz's candidacy? The PAR, RN, and PIN bickered for the honor, until Arbenz, heeding the advice of a few friends—the leaders of Guatemala's clandestine Communist party—chose the PIN because it

[4] Gutiérrez and Pinto Usaga to Arbenz, Aug. 16, 1949, *GT*, Box 1. See also "La CTG denunciará a las personas que no han devuelto armas," *DCA*, July 26, 1949, p. 1; Paz Tejada to Gutiérrez and Pinto Usaga, Aug. 18, 1949, *GT*, Box 2. Interviews with Paz Tejada, Galich, Charnaud, and Guerra Borges were helpful.

[5] Particularly useful were interviews with Fortuny, Charnaud, Guerra Borges, Morgan, Galich, and María de Arbenz.

[6] On the PIN (which is virtually ignored in the literature), see *GT*, Boxes 9 and 69.

would lend an image of moderation to his candidacy.[7] On February 5, 1950, the PIN proudly nominated Jacobo Arbenz. This was followed, in short order, by the endorsements of the PAR, RN, and organized labor.[8]

Only the most conservative revolutionary party, the decaying FPL, held back. After protracted infighting, it nominated Health Minister Víctor Manuel Giordani. But some party members had already defected in order to support another moderate civilian, Jorge García Granados, and still others endorsed Arbenz. Meanwhile the FPL's frustrated secretary general, the able and ambitious Manuel Galich, expelled Giordani and was proclaimed presidential candidate by his own supporters. (As the polls opened on November 10, Galich abandoned his hopeless quest and rallied to Arbenz.)[9]

On February 20, Arbenz resigned as defense minister and announced his decision to run for the presidency. Arévalo responded with an effusive letter addressed to "My Great and Dear Friend."[10] While it was obvious that Arbenz was the administration's candidate, it was equally obvious that he was not Arévalo's choice. The relationship between the exuberant, self-centered president and his laconic minister, while always correct, lacked warmth. "Arévalo didn't trust Arbenz," the president of Congress remembers, "because he considered him too leftist." Nor did Arévalo, by 1950, have much in common with the PAR, whose leaders he also judged too radical and too independent. His sympathies went instead to the moribund FPL. Left to his own devices, he would have endorsed his close friend Giordani.[11] But the army and the civilian groups that formed the backbone of the administration supported Arbenz. Giordani stood no chance. Under Arbenz, Arévalo would

[7] Interviews with two of these friends, Fortuny and Guerra Borges. Confirmed by interview with María de Arbenz.

[8] "Arbenz nominado candidato del PIN," *El I*, Feb. 6, 1950, p. 1; "Postulación comunicarán a Arbenz" and "Nominación simultánea en el RN," *El I*, Feb. 20, 1950, p. 1; "Arbenz recibe la postulación suya de manos de laborantes," *El I*, Feb. 27, 1950, p. 1.

[9] For the García Granados split, see esp. *El I*: "Candidatura no apoyarán los partidos Arevalistas," Nov. 14, 1949, p.1; "Aceptará su candidatura a presidente" and "Hacia el candidato único va la trinca," Nov. 15, 1949, p. 1. For Giordani's nomination, the best coverage is again by *El I*: "Giordani gana la partida a Galich," Apr. 21, 1950, p. 1, and "Candidato de un partido y no partido de un candidato," May 2, 1950, p. 1. For Galich's antics, see "Galichistas violaron el estatuto del partido al expulsarlo, declara Giordani," *El I*, Sept. 30, 1950, p. 1; "Galich nominado candidato," *DCA*, Oct. 2, 1950, p. 1; "Las UPAS del FPL llegaron cuando ya el Arbencismo amarraba la victoria," *La Hora*, Nov. 13, 1950, p. 1; "Indignación y desbandada populista," *La Hora*, Nov. 14, 1950, p. 1.

[10] "Entrevista hoy con el presidente," *El I*, Feb. 21, 1950, p. 1, and "Aceptada la renuncia al candidato por el presidente," *El I*, Feb. 27, 1950, p. 1 (quoted from p. 9).

[11] Interviews with Monteforte Toledo (quoted), María de Arbenz, Galich, Charnaud, Fortuny, Guerra Borges, Arévalo, and Osegueda.

play no major political role; he could expect, however, honors and material rewards, provided he behaved graciously while Arbenz was still a candidate. He behaved graciously, and he was rewarded.[12]

While a few members of the upper class supported Arbenz, many more believed that he too was a communist like Arévalo. Others were unsure, and some were even hopeful. Though of merely middle-class extraction, Arbenz was white and had married an upper-class Salvadoran. Above all, he was a military officer. As president, he might behave as army officers had always behaved in Guatemala—and control the rabble. But rather than bank on an uncertain prospect, most members of the elite sought a candidate they could trust unconditionally.

They found him in fifty-five-year old Miguel Ydígoras Fuentes. Of Ubico's many generals, Ydígoras alone had discovered the virtues of democracy—at dawn on October 20, 1944, a few hours after the first rebel troops had left the Guardia de Honor to overthrow Ponce. "The [State] Department will recall," a U.S. official later wrote, that "Ydígoras Fuentes put in an appearance at our Embassy divested of all insignia . . . to offer his services as 'mediator,' to be useful, as he put it, in any negotiations that might be undertaken." He made the same offer to the rebels. Indeed, he was very active throughout the day, but he did not fight. (It would have been the first battle of his long military career.)[13] In short, noted the same U.S. official, Ydígoras' role had been "ambiguous and odd."[14] Yet his last moment betrayal of Ponce and his eagerness to serve the new rulers proved fruitful. The *junta* eventually appointed him Guatemala's minister to London, and he continued in the same post under Arévalo. In addition to his diplomatic duties, he cultivated Trujillo. He told the Dominican that Arévalo was a communist, that his immediate ouster was imperative, and that he, Ydígoras, was the man for the job. He would need, he added, $50,000.[15]

In the spring of 1950, the frustrated rebel returned from London to make his bid for the presidency, supported "by conservatives and ex-partisans of the dictator Ubico," as a State Department official put it.[16] He was not, by

[12] For Arévalo after 1950, see below, pp. 392–94.

[13] AmEm Tegucigalpa, Erwin to DOS, no: 181, Nov. 5, 1953, pp. 2–3, NA 714.00. See also Affeld to SecState, no. 1672, Oct. 25, 1944, NA 814.00; Mannion, "Memorandum for the Charge d'Affaires," enclosed in Affeld to SecState, no. 1672, Oct. 25, 1944, NA 814.00; *Revista de la revolución*, Jan. 1945, pp. 20, 21 and 27. For Ydígoras's military career, see the hagiography by de Zirión, *Datos biográficos*.

[14] Erwin to DOS (see n. 13 above), p. 3. See also CIA, SR-46, "Guatemala," July 27, 1950, p. 10, Truman Papers, President's Secretary's File, Intelligence File, Box 261, TL.

[15] Andrés Pastoriza, memo, enclosed in Pastoriza to Rafael Trujillo, London, Aug. 21, 1947, Vega File.

[16] Burr to Holland, June 1, 1954. For relevant newspaper articles, see "Carta abierta

Ubiquista standards, a bloody man; he was merely corrupt. Bewailing the stupidity of his conservative friends, Marroquín Rojas later wrote, "When they should have chosen a well-known, experienced and resolute candidate, they chose the shadow of dictatorship. When many people told me that they were supporting Ydígoras because he would resort to arms if he lost the elections, I assured them that Ydígoras . . . was not the man to lead a heroic rebellion."[17] Marroquín Rojas was right, on all counts.

The presidential campaign had just begun when an open letter was handed to the secretary general of the PAR. It was signed by ten prominent PAR members. Among them were the men who would later constitute the Secretariat of the Communist Party of Guatemala: José Manuel Fortuny, Alfredo Guerra Borges, Bernardo Alvarado Monzón, Mario Silva Jonama, and José Luis Ramos. In their letter, they announced their "irrevocable resignation" from the PAR and intimated their intention to create "a vanguard party, a party of the proletariat based on Marxism-Leninism."[18] One month later, on June 21, 1950, *Octubre* was launched. Edited by Fortuny, it carried on its masthead: "For a Great Communist Party, Vanguard of the Workers, the Peasants and the People." Would a communist party soon emerge, in open defiance of Arévalo?

The party already existed. The first attempt to reconstitute a communist party after its destruction by Ubico had been foiled by the police in September 1947, but no informer alerted the authorities two years later when a clandestine congress was held. To avoid suspicion, recalls Guerra Borges, "We only met on weekends and, occasionally, on weekday evenings."[19] No wonder, then, that the congress lasted from September 28 to December 18, 1949.

In numbers, the congress was not an impressive affair. The participants were less than fifty; most likely they were forty-three. No foreign party was represented, and none played a role in the creation of the Communist Party of Guatemala (PCG). "We met without any formalities," recalls Carlos Manuel Pellecer, "and we didn't give any thought to foreign delegates."[20] At age thirty-three, Fortuny, who was elected secretary general, seemed almost avun-

---

de Miguel Ydígoras Fuentes," *El I*, Feb. 2, 1950, p. 12; "Texto de la renuncia del general Ydígoras," *El I*, Mar. 29, 1950, p. 1; "El gran partido unificación anticomunista 'PUA': salvación con Ydígoras," *La Hora*, Nov. 3, 1950, p. 7.

[17] "Los ricos con el agua al cuello," *Impacto*, May 31, 1952, p. 1.

[18] For the full text of the six-page letter, dated May 20, see *GT*, Box 7, quoted pp. 1, 6. See also, "Diez izquierdistas renuncian del PAR," *El I*, May 27, 1950, p. 1.

[19] Interview with Guerra Borges.

[20] My major sources for the PCG in the Arévalo years are (1) interviews with Pellecer (quoted), Fortuny, and Guerra Borges; (2) Alvarado Arellano, *Apuntes*, pp. 11–28 and *Esbozo histórico*, pp. 6–18; Gutiérrez, *Apuntes*, pp. 20–27 and *Breve historia*, pp. 27–46. See also Fortuny's testimony in Cáceres, *Aproximación*, pp. 140–56, and Schneider, *Communism*, pp. 55–73.

cular. The other leaders were in their mid-twenties. They all shared urban lower-middle-class or middle-class backgrounds. Most were teachers or university students, who until 1944 had never lived outside Guatemala.[21]

Some, like twenty-four-year old Guerra Borges, had been totally apolitical when Ubico fell. Others, like Fortuny, had belonged to that restless youth that began the struggle against the dictator in late 1942. Not one had been a Marxist, let alone a Marxist-Leninist—not even Carlos Manuel Pellecer, who had lived in Mexico from 1940 to 1944 after a stint in Ubico's jails. (He had criticized army discipline while a cadet at the Escuela Politécnica.) In Mexico Pellecer had been preoccupied with earning a living, not with Marxism. "My love affair with communism," he later wrote, "began in Paris in 1947, when I read *Report from the Gallows* by [Czech communist writer Julius] Fucik."[22]

The "old communists" who emerged from the dictator's jails in 1944 played only a marginal role in the creation of the PCG. After twelve years of harsh imprisonment, "they had forgotten what little they had known of Marxism."[23] More influential were several exiles who had returned to Guatemala in 1944. But their effectiveness was hampered by the fact that they were Marxists, not Marxist-Leninists like the new leaders, and by their arrogance—their wisdom, they believed, gave them the right to lead. This was particularly true of the writer Luis Cardoza y Aragón.

Foreigners, particularly a handful of Salvadoran communists, were the major formative influence on the future leaders of the PCG. These men and women had not been sent by their party or by the Kremlin to spread the credo

[21] The hierarchy of the party was formalized at the second congress (Dec. 1952) as follows: (1) a 5-member Secretariat, led by the secretary general, which met daily; (2) a Political Commission of eleven members (including the Secretariat), which met once a week; (3) a 25-member Central Committee (including the Political Commission), which met every three months. The Secretariat was officially created at the second congress, but its members had constituted the inner core of the party from the outset. The next most important leaders were Víctor Manuel Gutiérrez, Carlos Manuel Pellecer, and José Alberto Cardoza. All were Guatemalans. See Partido Guatemalteco del Trabajo, *Estatutos*, pp. 18–25. For the composition of the Central Committee elected at the 1st Congress, see Alvarado Arellano, *Apuntes*, p. 18. Particularly useful were interviews with Fortuny, Guerra Borges, Pellecer, and Alejandro, the Cuban communist who served as adviser to the Guatemalan Communist Party in 1951–1954. For biographical sketches of the senior party leaders see Schneider, *Communism*, pp. 89–97.

[22] Pellecer, *Renuncia al comunismo*, p. 85. For Pellecer's version of his tribulations from his arrest in Guatemala to his return from Mexico, see his *Memoria en dos geografías*, pp. 111–499. On Fortuny as a student leader in 1942–1944, see Galich, *Del pánico al ataque*, pp. 84, 85, 134–35, 164, 185.

[23] Quoted from interview with Fortuny. Obando Sánchez, the only "old communist" who played more than a marginal role, refers to the 1944–1954 period in his *Memorias*, pp. 114–36. For insights on the "old communists" after 1944, see also Alfonso Solorzano in Quan Rossell, *Guatemala*, 1:245–46.

to Guatemala. They were exiles fleeing persecution; at home their party was in full disarray. In a cruel twist, just one day after Ponce surrendered in Guatemala, a military coup closed the democratic parenthesis in El Salvador that had been ushered in by the fall of Martínez: just as El Salvador had been a haven for Guatemalans between May and October 1944, so Guatemala became a refuge for Salvadorans. Among those who arrived in late 1944 were Miguel Mármol, Graciela García, Matilde Elena López, and Virgilio Guerra—communist party members of many years' standing, well-versed in clandestine work and familiar with Marxist-Leninist theory. They went into action at once, helping to mold the labor movement, working tirelessly, often unable to buy themselves a square meal: "The trade unions didn't have the money to pay their activists, let alone feed them. So I just ate whatever I could, whenever I could, and wherever I could," recalls Mármol.[24]

These Salvadorans were instrumental in the creation, in July 1945, of the labor school Escuela Claridad, which taught both labor organization and Marxism-Leninism. (The school, which had more than sixty students, was closed by Arévalo in January 1946.)[25] In the course of their work (public as union organizers, more discreet as Marxist proselytizers), they were harassed, and some were jailed for brief periods or deported. Yet their efforts bore fruit in the quality if not the quantity of their disciples. The Guatemalans who assembled at the founding congress in September 1949 could boast of impressive credentials: prominent journalists, congressmen, labor leaders, senior members of the PAR. They brought to the party a combination of dynamism, intellect, and integrity that was and would remain unequaled in Guatemalan politics. Two men, in particular, stood out: a twenty-six-year old teacher, Víctor Manuel Gutiérrez, who was a congressman and the secretary general of the CTG;[26] and Fortuny, also a member of Congress, a brilliant journalist and, until March 1949, the secretary general of the PAR.

[24] Dalton, *Miguel Mármol*, pp. 502–3. Two of these Salvadorans have written about their experiences in Guatemala: ibid., pp. 495–521, and García, *Páginas*, pp. 155–212, and *Las luchas revolucionarias*, pp. 57–131.

[25] In addition to the sources listed in nn. 20 and 24 above, see Bishop, "Guatemalan Labor," pp. 16–20, 26, and FBI, Hoover to Lyon, Nov. 23, 1945, NA 814.00.

[26] Gutiérrez resigned from the PCG in November 1949, even before the congress had ended, because of sincerely felt tactical differences. He created, in June 1950, the small Partido Revolucionario Obrero de Guatemala (PROG), which included both communists like Gutiérrez and others, mainly trade unionists, who were drawn by his personality or by the prospect of exploiting his prestige, but did not share his political views.

By 1951 the differences between Gutiérrez and the PCG had decreased markedly, and he was increasingly at odds with many leaders of his own party. Finally, in Feb. 1952, he was able to bring about the dissolution of the PROG. (He had tried in the previous months, but a majority of the leadership had refused to cooperate.) He im-

These may seem bold judgments—yet they parallel the conclusions that were reached by the U.S. embassy in the early 1950s, and they echo the conclusions of U.S. journalists and others whose anti-communist credentials are above suspicion, including those few, particularly Ronald Schneider, who have probed the vast documentary evidence in the *Guatemalan Transcripts*.[27] Schneider presents Gutiérrez as "the honest, humble and soft-spoken Gutiérrez, the revered leader of Guatemalan workers. . . . nicknamed the 'Franciscan' for his ascetic manner of living." Gutiérrez used his scarce free time to study and gave the bulk of his salary as a congressman to the party and the labor confederation, keeping only the bare minimum for himself. He neither sought nor accepted personal favors or privileges.[28] Of course, not all the communist leaders were pillars of virtue like Gutiérrez. Schneider points to Fortuny. "In spite of his obvious talents as a writer, speaker and theoretician," he states, "Fortuny's effectiveness was hampered by an unpleasant personality and the lack of morality in his private life. While Fortuny's contributions to the Guatemalan communist movement cannot be underestimated, he, less than any other leader, fits the image of the selfless, dedicated champion of the people."[29] Fortuny could indeed be abrasive; sure of his moral and intellectual superiority, he lacked Gutiérrez's modesty. His occasional extramarital flings contrast with Gutiérrez's impeccable private life. But not even the U.S. embassy, which devoted many hours to Fortuny, so much as hinted at an instance of corruption on his part. (Nor, for that matter, does Schneider.) One year after the fall of Arbenz, the *New York Times* noted that the communist leaders, unlike the other politicians, had not grown rich on their careers. Fortuny, in particular, "owned only a $200 share in the Communist daily *Tribuna Popular*"[30]—a remarkable feat for a man who had been one of Guatemala's

---

mediately rejoined the PCG and urged the members of the defunct PROG to follow his example. (Many did not.) He was elected forthwith to the Political Commission of the PCG.

For the PROG, and Gutiérrez's early differences with the PCG, see esp. Gutiérrez, *Apuntes*, pp. 25–26, and Alvarado Arellano, *Apuntes*, pp. 17–20, 24–26. The *GT*, Box 9, includes a folder of documents of the PROG. Schneider, *Communism*, pp. 61–68, is useful, but his conclusion, "the influence of the international Communist movement was used to induce Gutiérrez to submit to Communist Party discipline" (p. 68), overlooks the looseness of the Guatemalans' ties to other communist parties. (See below, pp. 183–89.) For a biographical sketch of Gutiérrez, see Thelma de Gutiérrez's testimony in Cáceres, *Aproximación*, pp. 59–76.

[27] See esp. Schneider, *Communism*, chs. 6–8.

[28] Ibid., pp. 94–95. For similar comments by other anticommunist writers, see Bishop, "Guatemalan Labor," p. 25; Suslow, "Social Security," p. 47; James, *Red Design*, p. 112.

[29] Schneider, *Communism*, p. 90.

[30] "Guatemala Reds Lose Properties," *NYT*, May 1, 1955, p. 17. Pellecer, who is

most influential politicians and the president's closest friend. And if Fortuny was scrupulously honest, he was equally gifted, hard-working, and devoted to the party that he has continued to serve, often under the most dangerous circumstances.[31] Marroquín Rojas first crossed swords with him during the 1945 Constituent Assembly. Fortuny is, he wrote, "rebellious, invincible . . . a courageous Congressman, indefatigable, astute and audacious. . . . Fortuny . . . is passionate and vigorous. He is an extremist."[32]

Some PCG leaders were temperamentally similar to Fortuny; others were more like Gutiérrez. They shared, however, honesty and dedication, setting their world far apart from that of Guatemala's other political groups. This was to be a great asset to the party and one of the sources of the ever growing attraction it held for Jacobo Arbenz.

Fortuny began considering himself a Marxist-Leninist in 1948, after joining Guerra Borges, Silva Jonama, Alvarado Monzón, and other PAR members in the Marxist circle Vanguardia Democrática. Together, they tried to lead the PAR toward Marxist positions. Their growing radicalism placed them in a minority within the party's councils; increasingly, they clashed with the anti-communist factions led by Charnaud MacDonald and Humberto González Juárez. At the PAR's convention of March 1949, they were decisively defeated—"We were massacred"—by a 382-to-120 vote.[33] In the name of party unity, they were given posts within the leadership, but they could no longer hope to sway the PAR's course. Aware that a communist party would be able to operate freely once Arbenz had assumed the presidency, they created the PCG in late 1949. A few months later, writes a PCG leader, "We decided that it was time for some of us to go public, while the others stayed underground to protect the party in case Arévalo struck."[34]

On May 20, 1950, Fortuny and his nine friends resigned from the PAR and intimated in their open letter their intention to create a communist party. Then on June 21 the first issue of *Octubre* appeared, and on September 8 the Jacobo

---

now a fervent anticommunist (see below p. 389) and no friend of Fortuny, asserts: "Fortuny was an honest man—an extremely honest man. He hated anything with even a whiff of corruption. This was typical of the leaders of the Communist party. It impressed and attracted me." (Interview with Pellecer.)

[31] See below, p. 389.

[32] Marroquín Rojas, *Crónicas*, pp. 61, 73, and 150.

[33] Interviews with Guerra Borges (quoted), Fortuny, Pellecer, and Charnaud. On the convention, see "Puñetazos y pistolas relucen en la sesión," *El I*, Mar. 16, 1949, p. 1; "Cambio de directiva," *DCA*, Mar. 16, 1949, p. 1; "Principios del Partido Acción Revolucionaria," *DCA*, Mar. 19, 1949, p. 1; Wells to SecState, no. 152, Mar. 22, 1949, NA 814.00; "Segunda convención nacional del PAR," *El Libertador*, Mar. 26, 1949, p. 1; "Nuevos principios de nuestro partido," *El Libertador*, Apr. 2, 1949, p. 1.

[34] Alvarado Arellano, *Apuntes*, p. 19.

Sánchez labor school was inaugurated. The school, explained *Octubre*, would offer "a short and basic course on Marxism."[35]

It was more than the government could tolerate. On September 13, the police closed *Octubre*—the communists had the right to express their views privately, but not to proselytize, explained Arévalo.[36] Two weeks later, the police closed the Jacobo Sánchez school, "and arrested those who were found on the premises—forty in all. . . . They also confiscated all written material, and even the paintings on the walls." Through Arbenz's personal intervention with the chief of police, those who had been detained were set free within a few hours.[37]

Octubre reappeared in November. The Jacobo Sánchez school was closed for two years,[38] at first to assuage anticommunist sensitivities during the electoral campaign, later because the communists had reassessed their priorities. They had too few qualified persons for too many tasks, a problem that would persist throughout the Arbenz years. As labor leaders, members of Congress, journalists, and members of Arbenz's inner circle, they were very busy with the electoral campaign, in addition to their tasks within the PCG. Fortuny, in particular, had a delicate assignment: at Arbenz's request, he wrote his campaign speeches, seeking to put a moderate spin on the issues that Arbenz wanted to address.[39] Unwitting praise for Fortuny's skill came from an exacting source: the Office of Intelligence and Research of the U.S. State Department noted, in late October, that Arbenz's speeches "have been essentially moderate in tone, containing few statements which could be construed as communist-inspired."[40]

While Arbenz was campaigning, Lt. Colonel Castillo Armas, the former *Aranista* commander, was plotting. His escapades would hardly deserve a foot-

[35] "Una escuela para la clase obrera," *Octubre*, Sept. 6, 1950, p. 3. See also "Un éxito la inauguración de la escuela 'Jacobo Sánchez,' " *Octubre*, Sept. 13, 1950, p. 2.

[36] "Cierre de Octubre ante el Congreso," *El I*, Sept. 14, 1950, p. 1; Arévalo to Fortuny, Sept. 20, 1950, *GT*, Box 8. See also Sierra Roldán, *Diálogos*, pp. 30–31. For *Octubre*'s absence in late July and August, see "Octubre de nuevo en la trinchera de lucha" (edit.), *Octubre*, Sept. 6, 1950, p. 1, and "Como vemos la situación actual," ibid., p. 3.

[37] "Escuela comunista 'Jacobo Sánchez' cierra Gobernación," *DCA*, Sept. 29, 1950, p. 1; "40 alumnos de la escuela comunista Jacobo Sánchez estuvieron detenidos," *El I*, Sept. 30, 1950, p. 1 (quoted); Fisher to DOS, no. 368, Oct. 5, 1950, NA 714.001. On Arbenz's role, interviews with Guerra Borges and Fortuny were useful.

[38] See "Segunda reaparición de Octubre," *Octubre*, Nov. 10, 1950, p. 1; "Actividad del partido," *Octubre*, Feb. 19, 1953, p. 7; *JW* 9, Feb. 27, 1953, I:3.

[39] Interviews with Fortuny, Guerra Borges, and María de Arbenz.

[40] "Guatemala: Communist Influence," report no. 5123, Oct. 23, 1950, p. 24, NA.

note were it not that in 1953 he was selected by the CIA to lead the "liberation" of Guatemala.

Castillo Armas and his plotters were united by their opposition to Arbenz and by their lack of realism. Some were former *Aranista* officers; like Castillo Armas, they had been dismissed from the army after the failure of the July uprising and were now bent on avenging their dead leader and their own disgrace. Others belonged to the landed elite. One was the former chief of Ubico's secret police, the notorious José Bernabé Linares, fresh out of jail.[41]

With the landowner Juan Córdova Cerna acting as intermediary, Castillo Armas approached General Ydígoras Fuentes. This was the first in a series of attempts at collaboration between these two intensely ambitious men. Ydígoras did indeed welcome the prospect of a military coup, but only if he lost the elections, that is (as he put it), if the government refused to honor his victory. A coup, he stressed, should be undertaken only to secure his claim to the presidency.[42]

This was not an attitude Castillo Armas could appreciate. His contacts with Ydígoras dragged on in growing acrimony as he continued to hatch his own plot. He struck on November 5, five days before the polls opened. With seventy men he attacked the Base Militar in the capital, confident that the element of surprise and the complicity of a few junior officers within the barracks would guarantee his success. (Castillo Armas, Marroquín Rojas later wrote, was "sure that the Base Militar would be his, as if it were a seat he had reserved at the theater."[43]) His initial victory, he believed, would spark a revolt in the army—a most bizarre proposition, since loyalist officers were in command of the troops.

---

[41] My main sources on the plot are: (1) CIA reports: "Col. Carlos Castillo Armas in Initial Stage of Organizing Armed Coup Against Guatemalan Government," no. deleted, Jan. 19, 1950; "Growing Opposition to Arbenz in Guatemalan Army Groups," no. S036757, Mar. 9, 1950; "Plans of Colonel Carlos Castillo Armas for Armed Revolt Against the Government," no. deleted, Aug. 24, 1950; "Plans of Colonel Carlos Castillo Armas to Overthrow Guatemalan Government," no. deleted, Nov. 3, 1950—while speaking highly of Castillo Armas, the reports were skeptical of his chances of success; (2) Clemente Marroquín Rojas, "Lo que fué el asalto a la Base Militar," *La Hora*, Sept. 18, 1953, p. 1, and "Temor a la verdad, virtud guatemalteca," *La Hora*, Sept. 21, 1953, p. 1; Pinto Recinos, "La rebelión," July 3, 1985, p. 2 and July 4, 1985, p. 2; Castillo Armas, "Organización del ataque"; (3) Interviews with Castillo Armas' supporters Taracena and Montenegro.

After Castillo Armas seized power in 1954, Linares resumed his old job. (See "J. Bernabé Linares tomó posesión de la Guardia Judicial," *El I*, Aug. 12, 1954, p. 1.)

[42] Interview with Taracena, who was involved in the plot.

[43] Marroquín Rojas, "Lo que fué el asalto a la Base Militar," *La Hora*, Sept. 18, 1953, p. 1.

As late as November 4, Lieutenant Montenegro, one of Castillo Armas' followers, had tried "to reason with him." The revolt, he argued, was hopeless even if they could seize the Base Militar.[44] But Castillo Armas didn't even seize the base. One of his accomplices betrayed him; the attackers were met with heavy fire and swiftly routed. Castillo Armas was wounded and captured; after spending some weeks in the military hospital, he was sent to the penitentiary to await trial.

"Nine Escape Like the Count of Montecristo," blared *El Imparcial* on June 12, 1951.[45] Castillo Armas, helped by other prisoners, had dug a long tunnel under the outer wall—or so he and his admirers have claimed, despite the fact that this would have required the guards to have been blind as well as deaf.[46] A less stirring but more plausible explanation is that some prison officials had been bribed, and the tunnel had been dug with their connivance in order to mask the true circumstances of the escape.[47]

Whatever the truth, Castillo Armas went straight from the penitentiary to the embassy of Colombia, where he sought asylum. On July 3, he left for Bogotá. He was the last of the *Aranistas*, a brave man who had failed to join the revolt of his friends on July 18, 1949, and who had now vindicated himself through his hopeless rebellion.

Castillo Armas was still in jail when on March 15, 1951, Arbenz was inaugurated president of Guatemala. Arbenz's victory at the polls, on November 10–12, 1950, had been massive: 258,987 out of 404,739 ballots cast. Ydígoras had come second, with 72,796 votes, while García Granados trailed as a distant third, followed by Giordani, in a field of ten candidates.[48]

Arbenz's victory had been assured. Ydígoras was the landowners' choice, but he lacked personal appeal and military support. García Granados and Giordani, two distinguished civilians who tempered their support for the revolution with pleas for moderation, had neither charisma nor political base. Arbenz, on the other hand, had the fervent backing of the country's two major political parties and of organized labor, which worked tirelessly on his behalf.[49] He

[44] Interview with Montenegro.

[45] "Nueve evadidos a lo Edmundo Dantés," *El I*, June 12, 1951, p. 1.

[46] For Castillo Armas' highly romanticized version of the escape, see L.A.H.A., *Así se gestó la Liberación*, pp. 10–17 and 51–54, and "Fuga de la Penitenciaria," *El Espectador*, July 3, 1955, p. 4.

[47] Some believe that Castillo Armas owed his freedom to Arbenz, who respected his courage and engineered his escape to avoid creating an unnecessary martyr. (See Cehelsky, "Guatemala's Frustrated Revolution," p. 43.) Arbenz's widow and two of his closest friends firmly reject this theory. (Interviews with María de Arbenz, Fortuny, and Guerra Borges.)

[48] For a breakdown of the vote, see Silvert, *Study in Government*, pp. 59–60.

[49] For two graphic examples, see Comité Político Nacional de los Trabajadores, "In-

would have won even had the elections been completely free, but in the Guatemala of 1950 elections could not be genuinely free. The 1945 constitution gave illiterate males only a public vote and disenfranchised illiterate women. It is naive to imagine that many Indians would have dared vote against the authorities' candidate—be it Ubico, Arana, Arbenz, or Ydígoras. Centuries of oppression had taught them the proper behavior. In the past, the army and the landowners had usually proceeded hand-in-hand; now they were divided. The military's influence reached farther than that of the landowners, and Arbenz was the military's candidate. But Arbenz also won a majority of the secret vote, conceded Marroquín Rojas, himself a defeated candidate. Despite a few incidents, he added, "the campaign was fair," and the elections were free, "as free as they could be in Guatemala."[50]

---

strucciones urgentes para las votaciones," Oct. 1950, *GT*, Box 15, and Comité Político Nacional de los Trabajadores, "Resolución adoptada por la Asamblea de Comités Políticos del departamento de Guatemala en su sesión de el 1o. de noviembre de 1950," ibid. See also Bishop, "Guatemalan Labor," pp. 121–29.

[50] Marroquín Rojas, "Comienzan las alegres elecciones," *La Hora*, Nov. 10, 1950 (quoted from pp. 1, 4); David Goliat (i.e., Marroquín Rojas), "Ya lo ves Chuchín Silva," *La Hora*, Dec. 8, 1950, p. 1; Marroquín Rojas, "Los analfabetos y las elecciones del Coronel Arbenz," *La Hora*, July 13, 1954, p. 4. Only the most partisan critics will find too mild the conclusion of Schneider: the government left "nothing . . . to chance," but "Arbenz was probably the choice of more voters than any of the opposition candidates." (*Communism*, p. 33.) See also Handy, "The Guatemalan Revolution and Civil Rights," esp. pp. 7–11.

CHAPTER 5

The United States and Arévalo: Arévalo's Sins

IN 1944, the United States had believed that Guatemala, with or without Ubico, would remain the docile little neighbor it had been for decades. Washington's confidence was soon shaken. Arévalo refused to show the customary deference to the State Department's "friendly representations."[1] This disquieting departure could be explained, many Americans believed, only by immaturity and the thrall of communism. During the previous half century, only one regime in all of Central America had offended Washington's sensibilities more: that of President José Santos Zelaya in Nicaragua, forced out by the United States in 1909. Washington's reaction to the Arévalo administration must be analyzed against this background of the past servility of Guatemala and the present servility of the other banana republics. While minor problems heightened tensions, the Guatemalans' major sins were two: their "persecution"[2] of American companies and their irresponsible attitude toward communism.

In the eyes of most Americans, it was self-evident that the country of Jefferson was not, and had never been, an imperialist power. The threat to the well-being and the sovereignty of the banana republics came from across the Atlantic. Monroe had been the first to challenge the ambitions of the European powers. Wilson had turned them back, nearly a century later, with his "Protective Imperialism" (strong medicine, perhaps, but administered for generous motives).[3] If at times the United States had been overbearing toward its Latin neighbors, the Good Neighbor Policy of Franklin Delano Roosevelt had removed all reasonable grounds for complaint.[4] Now, in the late 1940s, a new

[1] MemoTel, Aug. 2, 1949, *FRUS*, 1949, 2:659.

[2] The State Department used this term repeatedly, beginning in mid-1947.

[3] In 1940, Samuel Bemis wrote in his influential *The Latin American Policy of the United States*: "Wilson and Bryan . . . strove to strengthen [U.S.] influence and control in these regions in order to remove further than ever justification for any European intervention. All this they covered with a sincere Wilsonian zeal for saving the people from bad government, tyranny, and economic exploitation in order that they might be made fit and stable for self-government, liberty and the pursuit of happiness under protection of the United States. . . . All this the missionaries of Democracy desired in order that 'benighted' peoples might be saved from themselves by themselves" (p. 185).

[4] "Anti-American feeling has seldom been unknown in most countries south of us. A generation ago there was often good reason for it. That it should still exist in spite

enemy threatened the banana republics: Soviet imperialism, as barbarous as German nazism, but even more dangerous. Once again, America called her little sisters to a crusade against a common foe.

But Guatemala's new leaders failed to respond with proper enthusiasm, despite the fact that most of them were anticommunists. They acknowledged that the Soviet Union was an imperialist power, and they proclaimed their solidarity with the United States. But they lacked the zeal of a Somoza or a Trujillo. While Soviet armies threatened European countries, Europe was far away, and it was difficult to blame Russia for the trampled dignity of a banana republic. And the distinguishing mark of the middle-class leaders who came to sudden prominence after the fall of Ubico was their sense of national dignity. Many would discard their idealism as the rewards of power drew them from their roots, but few would discard their nationalism. The United States may have been the champion of the free world, but it was the United States that interfered in Guatemala's internal affairs, and it was American companies that held a stranglehold over the country's economy.

AMERICAN COMPANIES IN GUATEMALA

Total U.S. investment in Guatemala in 1944 was about $93 million,[5] concentrated in three companies: the Empresa Eléctrica de Guatemala, a subsidiary of Electric Bond and Share; the International Railways of Central America; and the United Fruit Company.

Empresa Eléctrica, originally a German company, had been seized by the Guatemalan government during World War I. The Wilson administration was as eager to pry this thriving concern from its new owners as the Guatemalans were reluctant to relinquish it. President Manuel Estrada Cabrera refused to sell the company to the Americans. He was overthrown in April 1920. His successor, Carlos Herrera, proved equally obtuse. In December 1921, he too was toppled. Herrera's successor eagerly agreed to the sale.[6] Nationalistic Guatemalans did not forget this story. Nor did they forget the paltry price that

---

of our Good Neighbor policy is baffling.'' (''The Guatemalan Incident,'' edit., *NYT*, Apr. 8, 1950, p. 12.)

[5] United States Treasury Department, *Census*, p. 70, table 2; CIA, ''Guatemala,'' SR-46, July 27, 1950, p. 32, Truman Papers, President's Secretary's File, Intelligence File, Box 261, TL.

[6] As Munro argues, the Wilson administration had not plotted against Estrada Cabrera; yet ''the erroneous belief that the United States had turned against the President seems to have been an important factor in the rapid growth of the opposition movement.'' The same belief contributed to the fall of Herrera. (*Intervention and Dollar Diplomacy*, p. 460.) See also Pitti, ''Ubico,'' pp. 20–38, 48–61, 68–72, 83, 88–104; Baker, ''Woodrow Wilson Administration''; Dinwoodie, ''Expedient Diplomacy,'' pp. 146–78.

the Americans had paid. Nor were they blind to the privileges the U.S. company had received. Resentment was fueled by the high rates charged by Empresa Eléctrica, which exploited its position of virtual monopoly (it supplied about 80 percent of the country's electricity) and by the poor service it provided. In 1944 the company was using the same equipment it had used in the 1920s.[7]

Unlike Empresa Eléctrica, the International Railways of Central America (IRCA) did not owe its status to direct U.S. pressure. President Estrada Cabrera was responsible for its monopoly and its privileges. Except for the state-owned 29.5 mile Verapaz Railway (seized from German owners during World War II) and the 207.1 miles of rail owned by United Fruit on its plantations, Guatemala's railways belonged to IRCA: 580.7 miles of single-track rail.[8] The absence of an adequate road system reinforced IRCA's monopoly. In particular, no road connected the capital with the Caribbean harbor of Puerto Barrios—an "inexplicable failure," the World Bank noted in 1951, since Puerto Barrios was Guatemala's only deep water port and accounted for over 60 percent of the country's foreign trade.[9] Not only did IRCA control the rail link between Puerto Barrios and the capital, it also owned Puerto Barrios' only pier.

Two ports on Guatemala's Pacific coast (San José and Champerico) played a minor role in the country's foreign trade; IRCA owned the pier at San José, and that of Champerico belonged to a subsidiary of the Grace Line. In other words, the three ports of any significance in Guatemala's foreign trade belonged to U.S. companies. Guatemala was not alone. As the United Nations observed in 1953, only three of the major ports of Central America were controlled by nationals; the others were in the hands of American companies. "Thus, there is a virtual monopoly of the foreign trade of the Central American countries, and it is impossible for them to control the port fees which are frequently excessive and discriminatory." This was the case, the report stated, at Puerto Barrios.[10]

As long as Ubico ruled, no criticism of IRCA had been permitted in Guatemala. After his ouster, Guatemalans complained loudly that IRCA's rates

[7] For a detailed analysis of Empresa Eléctrica see IBRD, *Economic Development*, pp. 218–43. The report focused on 1950, but its comments are also valid for 1945, since there were no significant changes in the intervening years. Bush, "Organized Labor," part 2, pp. 97–102, discusses the company's labor relations under Arévalo.

[8] IBRD, *Economic Development*, pp. 132–210, is the best analysis of transportation in Guatemala in the late 1940s. Also important is United Nations, *El transporte*. For background on IRCA, see Solis, *Los ferrocarriles*.

[9] Quoted from IBRD, *Economic Development*, p. 184. For the percentages see LaBarge, "Impact of the United Fruit," pp. 16–17, table 4.

[10] United Nations, *El transporte*, p. 218. For San José and Champerico, see de León Aragón, *Los contratos*, pp. 195–231.

were exorbitant; with equal fervor, the company proclaimed its innocence. In 1951, the World Bank concluded that while IRCA's rates for passenger traffic were reasonable, its average freight rates "exceed[ed] those of many other countries." They were higher, for instance, than comparable rates in the United States although, the report pointed out, the reverse should have been true. "It is quite possible," the bank observed with customary caution, "that they are higher than they should be," and it went on to stress "the absence of effective competition" and "the lack of any governmental control over IRCA's rates."[11]

To one customer, however, IRCA charged a bargain basement price: United Fruit, which owned 42.68 percent of IRCA's shares, paid about half the normal rate. (The rate was, a New York court later found, "unfair and unconscionable.")[12] Special treatment extended beyond price setting. In 1953, the United Nations observed:

> The community of interest between the railroad company . . . and the banana company has created a situation that does not always benefit the economy of the country. . . . The trains that carry bananas are given absolute priority; when they are running, all other trains must wait in a siding. Furthermore, they receive special treatment in the ports and have priority in loading and unloading. Therefore the trains and ships that do not carry bananas are forced to wait. In fact, the loading and unloading of other goods is interrupted in order to attend to the bananas.[13]

The World Bank flatly concluded: "to all intents and purposes, [Puerto Barrios] . . . is under the complete control of the United Fruit Company and the International Railways Company. That control extends over the movement of practically all import and export cargo through the Atlantic area."[14]

If IRCA was powerful, United Fruit was a colossus. It had been created in 1899, the result of a merger between the personal empire of Minor Keith, who

---

[11] IBRD, *Economic Development*, p. 172.

[12] Quoted from "United Fruit Loses $4,500,000 Rail Suit," *NYT*, June 29, 1959, p. 17. In 1949, minority stockholders of IRCA sued United Fruit, claiming that the freight rates paid by the latter were excessively low. In a series of judgments between 1957 and 1960, the court ordered United Fruit to pay IRCA $4.5 million plus interest, to pay higher freight rates for future shipments, and to divest itself of all shares of IRCA. See the coverage in the *NYT*: "Damage Suit Lost by United Fruit Co.," July 2, 1957, p. 44; "Award Put At $5,519,000," July 16, 1957, p. 37; "United Fruit Debt to Railroad Set," Dec. 19, 1957, p. 49; "Appeal is Argued in United Fruit Suit," Feb. 11, 1959, p. 77; "United Fruit Loses $4,500,000 Rail Suit," June 24, 1959, p. 17; "65 Million Claim Is Filed in Court," Mar. 25, 1960, p. 37; "State Appeals Court Upholds the Award," Dec. 2, 1960, p. 41. See also "Resumen seleccionado," *Economía*, pp. 31–32, 37–42, and 51–52.

[13] United Nations, *El transporte*, p. 13.

[14] IBRD, *Economic Development*, p. 185.

built railroads in Central America, and the Boston Fruit Company, which imported bananas from the Caribbean islands. Managed with ruthlessness, skill, and ambition, UFCO earned its sobriquet: the Octopus. As Arévalo ascended to the presidency, it was the world's greatest grower and exporter of bananas.

The heart of its empire was in Guatemala, Honduras, and Costa Rica, where it owned well over 1 million acres of banana plantations; but it also had plantations in Panama, Colombia, Ecuador, Jamaica, Cuba, and the Dominican Republic.[15] The Great White Fleet—eighty-five ships—carried UFCO's bananas to North America and Europe, making the company the largest carrier of the fruit.[16] The ships also carried a significant percentage of the foreign trade of many of the smaller republics in which UFCO operated, as well as some passenger traffic. The fleet was "more than a source of income: it was a symbol of the company's dominions—at home, in the tropics, and on the seven seas."[17] Still another tentacle had been added to UFCO in 1913, when the Tropical Radio Telegraph Company was incorporated to assure communications between the field and UFCO's Boston headquarters. By 1945, it controlled an important part of the international radio and cable traffic of Central America. The last major component of this well-integrated empire was the railroad. UFCO itself owned 1,400 miles of rail, mostly within its plantations. It also owned 42.6 percent of IRCA, whose 794 miles of railroad constituted "the most extensive rail network between Mexico and Panama."[18]

UFCO's annual budget was larger than those of the Central American countries in which it operated. Although by U.S. standards the largest company in Central America was not a giant, it was a well respected and well connected company, particularly in Massachusetts. This was evident in the Massachu-

---

[15] See UFCO's Annual Reports for 1944 and 1945, and Pollan, *United Fruit Company*. There is a large and highly partisan literature on United Fruit. The most sophisticated apologists are LaBarge, "A Study of United Fruit"; May and Plaza, *United Fruit*. Two classic studies, critical and well-documented, are Kepner, *Social Aspects of the Banana Industry* and Kepner and Soothill, *Banana Empire*. On Minor Keith, see Stewart, *Keith and Costa Rica*. For studies focusing specifically on UFCO and Guatemala, see LaBarge, "Impact of the United Fruit," and Bauer Paiz, *Como opera el capital yanqui*; both studies are highly partisan, but interesting.

[16] There were eighty-five ships in UFCO's fleet in 1940, before the losses caused by World War II. As soon as the conflict ended, "replacements were rushed down the ways. . . . The new recruits are better and faster." ("Banana Split—a la Zemurray," *Business Week*, May 4, 1946, p. 42.) For the modernization of the fleet in the immediate postwar period, see also "Great White Fleet," *Unifruitco*, Aug.–Sept. 1948, pp. 14–21.

[17] McCann, *American Company*, p. 24.

[18] United Nations, *El transporte*, p. 9. "From a practical standpoint," a U.S. official explained, "the United Fruit Company probably may be said to control IRCA. However, to our knowledge, this has never been admitted." (Ballentine to Wells, enclosed in Wells to Clark, Apr. 10, 1951, NA 714.00.)

setts delegation to the U.S. Congress. UFCO's shareholders included the venerable Cabots—Thomas was briefly the company's president in 1948, and his brother, John Moors, was assistant secretary of state for inter-American affairs in 1953.

Several high-powered lobbyists were on call to remind the State Department and influential Americans that United Fruit deserved their affection and their support. These included the former senator, Robert La Follette, who could boast impressive liberal credentials, and the prominent Washington lawyer, Thomas Corcoran. In the early 1940s, UFCO had hired yet another liberal, Edward Bernays, "the father of public relations" and "the biggest name in his field." [19] A battery of lawyers from America's most prominent law firms complemented the lobbyists' efforts. Indeed, as many authors have stressed, when the prestigious law firm of Sullivan and Cromwell negotiated UFCO's contract with Ubico in 1936, one of the firm's senior associates was John Foster Dulles. [20]

UFCO had expanded swiftly and efficiently in Guatemala. In a 1924 agreement with President Orellana, it consolidated and enlarged its holdings on the Caribbean coast, creating the immense division of Bananera; in 1930 it moved onto Guatemala's Pacific shore, receiving an expansive tract at Tiquisate. By 1945, it was the country's largest private landowner and biggest employer, dwarfing all others with its 566,000 acres of land and more than 15,000 workers. (The second largest private employer was IRCA, which employed approximately five thousand.)

For years, apologists and critics of United Fruit have engaged in fierce debate. After diplomatically conceding that the record is not untarnished, the apologists point out that UFCO was not forced on Guatemala by gunboat diplomacy; they add that it played a very positive role in the development of the country's resources and paid millions of dollars in taxes. It centered its activities in undeveloped areas "that otherwise might have remained closed to settlement and productive use for many decades," [21] and it introduced medical and sanitation services. The company's workers, they stress, were better paid, better fed, and better housed than those who toiled for other landowners.

There is some truth to these claims. Until the presidency of Arévalo, the State Department never intervened formally on behalf of UFCO: the company had never required such assistance. Yet there are more subtle forms of pressure. During the negotiations that led to the 1930 contract with President Chacón (the only time the company did not blithely get its way) the dispatches of the U.S. embassy to Washington expressed warm sympathy for UFCO's de-

[19] McCann, *American Company*, p. 45.

[20] On Dulles in the interwar period, see Pruessen, *Dulles*, chs. 4–7.

[21] May and Plaza, *United Fruit*, p. 230.

mands,[22] and it is inconceivable that the embassy hid this sympathy from the Guatemalan authorities.

Although UFCO developed previously neglected regions, it did so in return for immense privileges. Indeed, after the fall of Ubico, an internal State Department document acknowledged, "Foreign companies, through arrangements favorable to the dictator in power at the moment, have been able to obtain large concessions and large privileges." Among these privileges were the tax breaks granted to UFCO, IRCA, and Empresa Eléctrica—which were in no way modified under Arévalo. In a detailed 1950 study, three U.S. financial experts concluded, "A careful estimate indicates that in all three cases the tax liability is in the neighborhood of one-half of what it would be in the absence of the contracts."[23]

But Empresa Eléctrica and UFCO (evidence is lacking in the case of IRCA) evaded even their paltry fiscal obligations. As the Guatemalan government discovered when it audited the company in 1953, Empresa Eléctrica had consistently resorted to creative accounting.[24] And UFCO—like all large landowners in Guatemala—regularly undervalued its land in its tax declarations. Going beyond such elementary cheating, it also used methods that local landowners could not imitate. When UFCO shipped bananas to subsidiaries in North America and Europe, it recorded the sales at below market prices.[25] The fraud was exposed by the Canadian Trade Commissioner in a 1949 article:

> In total trade with Canada, Guatemala achieved [in 1948] a balance in her favor of $499,969, according to Guatemalan statistics. Canadian statistics show this balance to be much larger. This is due to the fact that the United Fruit Company, in its intercompany trading between Guatemala and the United States, only places a small nominal value on banana exports. On entry into Canada, they are recorded at their proper value which is some 700 percent higher than recorded in the Guatemalan export returns.[26]

Had UFCO declared the true value of the bananas, stated a 1950 CIA report, "bananas will be seen to contribute at least 39 percent of the total exports (by value) and coffee 47 percent or less," rather than the official averages of 20 percent and 60 percent respectively.[27] Reminiscing in 1976, a former United Fruit vice president cited other ways the company evaded its taxes. These gimmicks, he said, had become more sophisticated since the 1950s, but no

[22] See Pitti, "Ubico," p. 388.

[23] Quotations from "Current Relations with Guatemala," May 1950, *FRUS*, 1950, 2:898, and Adler, Schlesinger, and Olson, *Public Finance*, p. 124.

[24] See the well-documented analysis in Bauer Paiz, "La Electric Bond and Share Company," esp. pp. 31–34.

[25] Adler, Schlesinger, and Olson, *Public Finance*, p. 34.

[26] Birkett, "Confidence in Guatemala," p. 1010.

[27] CIA (see n. 5 above), p. 24.

one ever resorted to the "shell game" with "one shred more enthusiasm . . . than United Fruit demonstrated in those simpler days, starting with its very beginning."[28]

Until the fall of Ubico, the Guatemalan state allowed UFCO to operate as a private fiefdom, never interfering on behalf of the workers. While Guatemalan employers were similarly protected, UFCO had a special advantage: because of its power and the power of the American flag, it was spared the dictators' whims. Neither Estrada Cabrera (1898–1920) nor Ubico tolerated any show of disrespect toward United Fruit. Only in the 1920s, between dictators, did UFCO experience minor annoyances. Some criticism was voiced in the Guatemalan Congress and press, and there were uncharacteristic delays when the company requested more concessions.[29] Worse, in 1923 UFCO faced an assault from an unlikely quarter; its laborers went on strike. "The work is so well paid that . . . certain hidden motives" must be behind the strike, company officials told the U.S. embassy; agitators were "intimidating peaceful employees, and . . . spreading all kinds of Bolsheviki propaganda." The Guatemalan government promptly sent in the troops, but the company was not satisfied. The Minister of Development had urged UFCO to recognize the labor union, an attitude that was "nothing short of Bolshevism."[30]

Once Ubico assumed power, there were no more wayward ministers or ungrateful laborers, and UFCO remained undisturbed until 1944, an aloof feudal lord entrenched in its outlying domains and respected by the weak sovereign of the land. Dictatorship had served UFCO well in Guatemala—so well, in fact, that the company had become complacent and was unruffled at Ubico's fall.

UFCO's record on labor relations was indeed superior to that of the coffee elite. UFCO's workers were treated harshly by their white overlords,[31] but the coffee barons paid wages that were even more miserable and their brutality was seldom tempered by their much vaunted paternalism. Second to none in the virulence of their racism, they considered their Indian workers savages.[32]

[28] McCann, *American Company*, p. 41.

[29] See Pitti, "Ubico," pp. 286, 360–61, 386–90, 489.

[30] Quotations from R. K. Thomas, "Memorandum," Feb. 24, 1923, p. 3, and Thomas, "Memorandum re: Strike United Fruit Company Laborers," Mar. 4, 1923, pp. 4, 7, both enclosed in Thomas to Geissler, Mar. 7, 1923, RG165 RF, Box 1562, NA-S.

[31] See Williams, "Rise of the Banana Industry," pp. 111–22. Williams's account of UFCO's racism is particularly telling because he is generally sympathetic to UFCO.

[32] The extent to which UFCO's real wages were higher than those paid by the coffee elite has been the subject of fierce debate. The best study is Kepner, *Social Aspects of the Banana Industry*, pp. 109–59. Kepner concludes that UFCO's real wages were higher than those paid by other landowners, but that the difference was relatively small.

Judged by these standards, UFCO was a fair employer. For the company, its squalid record was a source of pride.

UNITED FRUIT AND THE ARÉVALO ADMINISTRATION

UFCO entered the Arévalo period confident of its power, its legal rights, and its position as Guatemala's model employer. It extended the hand of friendship to the new authorities, ready to entertain with them the same warm relations it had enjoyed with Ubico. It would not be long, however, before the company felt betrayed and persecuted. These feelings were shared by Empresa Eléctrica and IRCA, but UFCO would lead the struggle against the new government and, later, against Arbenz.

One of UFCO's grievances had some validity. The Arévalo administration was more vigorous in its protection of UFCO's workers than of other rural laborers. It may seem peculiar that a government so timid toward the native elite dared to disturb the American giant. In part, the paradox is explained by the nationalism of the revolutionary leaders. More disturbing than the plight of the peasants was the presence in their midst of an imperial enclave.[33] Another consideration was equally significant: unlike those who tilled the land of the coffee elite, UFCO's 15,000 workers had begun to organize in the summer of 1944, they had actively supported the candidacy of Arévalo, and they were closely connected with the urban labor movement.[34]

How grave were the sins of the Guatemalan government against United Fruit? Beyond offering some legal protection to the company's workers, Arévalo did not disturb UFCO's privileges. The day would come when, reeling under Arbenz's blows, United Fruit would remember Arévalo's "extremism" with something akin to nostalgia. At the time, however, the company was outraged by the Guatemalans' "aggressions."

While minor disputes between U.S. companies and the government had surfaced soon after Ponce's overthrow,[35] organized labor posed no serious

[33] For a vivid expression of this frustrated nationalism, see Bauer Paiz, *Como opera el capital yanqui*, and de León Aragón, *Los contratos*.

[34] For an eloquent statement to this effect by the Guatemalan ambassador in Washington, see MemoConv (García Granados, Braden), May 29, 1947, p. 1, NA 814.504. For the most comprehensive discussion of United Fruit's labor unions, see Bush, "Organized Labor," part 2, pp. 13–39.

[35] The first such dispute (the Denby affair) had pitted the Guatemalan government against Pan American Airways and Alfred Denby, an American citizen who had been a close associate of Ubico. The dispute, which provoked the intervention of the State Department, was settled in 1947 on terms that were satisfactory to the U.S. (For a good summary, see Immerman, *CIA in Guatemala*, pp. 86–87, and the *NYT*: "Guatemalan Line Set Up," Mar. 18, 1945, III-7; "Airline Seizure Approved," Nov. 25, 1945, p.

challenge to UFCO until 1947. The strike that broke out at Bananera in early October 1946 was only an annoyance. The strikers demanded higher wages and "an improvement in living conditions and treatment." It was the first strike in two decades, and it spread rapidly through the plantation. Even "the maids working for Americans have quit," noted the conservative *El Imparcial*. For the first time in the history of Bananera, white American women "are doing all their own housework—running errands and even cleaning their houses."[36] UFCO refused to negotiate. *El Imparcial* itself contrasted the intransigence of the company with the good behavior of the strikers and the moderate nature of their demands. Intransigence triumphed: when work resumed at the end of October, the company's only concession was to promise that it would take no reprisals. The settlement galled many Guatemalans.[37]

In May 1947, the Labor Code was enacted. For the remainder of the Arévalo presidency, this Labor Code was, to UFCO, the symbol of its persecution. While the list of the offending articles was long, one principle particularly riled UFCO. This principle established different degrees of protection and benefits for workers in industrial, commercial, or agricultural enterprises. Agricultural laborers employed in estates of five hundred or more permanent workers were granted many of the rights of industrial workers. While several Fincas Nacionales and at least four Guatemalan landowners fell into this category, so too did UFCO. The principle was blatantly discriminatory, UFCO charged; the offending articles had to be modified or removed.[38] The company turned to the State Department for support.

22; "Guatemala to Pay for Airline," May 22, 1947, p. 8; "Guatemala Paying Airline Claim," Dec. 22, 1947, p. 17.)

[36] "Toda Bananera está en huelga," *El I*, Oct. 16, 1946, p. 1 (quoted from p. 11). Writing in the late 1950s, LaBarge observed that in UFCO's plantations "the grievances that cause the most bitter conflicts are those which reflect upon the workers' status as human beings. . . . The attitude that 'these people' are an insensitive, inferior and stupid species for whom the most common courtesies are not required probably costs the Company more in strikes, in slowdowns, and in general bad relations and publicity than the entire battle against the banana diseases." ("A Study of United Fruit," p. 276.)

[37] *El I* provided the best coverage of this 1946 strike; see "A 60 fincas y 1,600 muelleros abarca el tremendo paro," Oct. 17, p. 1; "Junta en el Ministerio de Economía," Oct. 24, p. 1; "No acepta condiciones la Frutera," Oct. 25, p. 1; "El gobierno da fin a la huelga," Oct. 26, p. 1; "Terminada en firme la huelga," Oct. 30, p. 1; "Reanudada hoy la labor en el Atlantico," Oct. 31, p. 1. See also the reports for Oct. and Nov. 1946 by the Governor of Izabal, nos. 5568 and 5948, IMJP:G, Leg. 32721, AGCA.

[38] For representative statements by the company, listing the "discriminatory" articles, see La Follette to Braden, June 23, 1947, enclosed in La Follette to Newbegin, July 15, 1947; DOS, "Guatemalan Labor Code—Possible Discrimination against United Fruit Company," July 17, 1947; Corcoran to Newbegin, Aug. 1, 1947 (enclos-

The details of UFCO's interaction with the U.S. government during the presidencies of Arévalo and Arbenz will be known only when the company's archives are opened, and this, one of its lobbyists has delicately noted, "may take a very long time, since they [UFCO's successors at United Brands] may consider the record damning."[39] The available evidence indicates that the American Republics Area (ARA) of the State Department showed an "immediate grasp of the problem presented to the United Fruit Company by the . . . labor code," as an appreciative lobbyist wrote to Assistant Secretary Spruille Braden.[40] Braden's grasp was indeed so acute that he began to upbraid the Guatemalan ambassador without bothering to wait for the Legal Office of the State Department to determine whether the Labor Code was in fact discriminatory.[41] In mid-July, the legal adviser submitted his report. After conceding that two minor articles *might* be discriminatory, he categorically rejected the crux of UFCO's case: the State Department, he warned, "could hardly maintain" that the code's distinction between larger and smaller agricultural enterprises was discriminatory, since this same principle was recognized "in labor laws in the United States as well as in foreign countries."[42]

ARA was not perturbed. In late July, a senior ARA official left Washington for Guatemala. UFCO had requested that the State Department send "a good strong man" to press the company's case on the Guatemalan authorities.[43] Ever obliging, UFCO had even selected the ideal envoy, Raymond Geist, a Foreign Service officer stationed in Mexico. Braden, however, believed that it would be better if the special envoy spoke Spanish—not one of Geist's talents. He suggested the chief of ARA's Division of Central America and Panama Affairs, Robert Newbegin, "a person of backbone and initiative," who, he assured lobbyist La Follette, could be relied on "to present our case forcefully."[44]

---

ing copy of the memo of same date by William Taillon, UFCO manager in Guatemala, to Arévalo); La Follette to Newbegin, Aug. 12, 1947. All NA 814.504. For a list of employers with a permanent work force of more than five hundred, see Taillon to UFCO's Vice President S. G. Baggett, Nov. 29, 1948, NA 814.00.

[39] Interview with Robert Corrigan, a representative for United Brands, Washington, D.C., Sept. 15, 1981.

[40] La Follette to Braden, May 23, 1947, NA 814.504.

[41] MemoConv (García Granados, Braden), May 24, 1947, NA 814.504.

[42] MemoConv ("Guatemalan Labor Code and Possible Discrimination against United Fruit Company"), July 22, 1947, p. 1, NA 814.504. See also MemoConv (La Follette, Newbegin), July 18, 1947, NA 814.504.

[43] La Follette to Braden, May 23, 1947, NA 814.504.

[44] MemoConv ("Guatemalan Labor Code"), June 2, 1947 (quoted from p. 2); see also La Follette to Braden, June 23, 1947, enclosed in La Follette to Newbegin, July 15, 1947; MemoConv ("Effect of Guatemalan Labor Law on United Fruit Company"), July 10, 1947; Corcoran to Newbegin, July 21, 1947. All NA 814.504.

And so, Newbegin descended on Guatemala, as did several UFCO lobbyists and officials offering moral support and guidance. Newbegin was, indeed, a man of backbone and initiative. He began by informing the Guatemalan foreign minister that the purpose of his trip was "solely" to discuss the Labor Code and to urge the government to rewrite the offending articles "so that the Company could operate with sufficient guarantees and assurances."[45] While he resisted UFCO's suggestion that he file "an immediate protest," he sternly warned the Guatemalans that their treatment of UFCO "might well have a serious effect upon relations between the two countries."[46] It was a performance, concluded La Follette, that "impressed the Guatemalan authorities."[47]

Nevertheless, the Guatemalan government did not remove the offending articles, and UFCO's labor unions began to demand that the company comply with the code. While pressure mounted, UFCO officials and lobbyists flooded the State Department and the embassy with complaints and prognostications. At times they contended that the economic burden of compliance would be intolerable.[48] More often, they argued from a loftier height. It was not the cost that troubled them, but the injustice: UFCO was being penalized because it was owned by Americans. "The history of the Labor Code," explained lobbyist Corcoran, "indicated clearly that it had been adopted in order to discriminate against the United Fruit Company."[49] Where would appeasement lead? More than the survival of American investment in Guatemala was at stake; surrender in Guatemala would encourage "legal and pseudo-legal assaults on foreign enterprises in many places of Latin America."[50]

The discriminatory nature of the Labor Code was the result, UFCO asserted, of more than the greed of the labor leaders and the chauvinism of the Guatemalan authorities. Far more dangerous forces were at work: the Arévalo administration "was subjected to communistic influences emanating from outside Guatemala."[51] Addressing this accusation squarely, in June 1947 a junior official at the embassy in Guatemala introduced a note of caution:

[45] MemoConv, July 30, 1947, *FRUS*, 1947, 8:708–10, quoted from pp. 708, 709.

[46] Quotations from MemoConv ("United Fruit Company and Guatemalan Labor Code"), Aug. 4, 1947, p. 1, NA 814.504/7–2447, and MemoConv, July 30, 1947, *FRUS*, 1947, 8:709.

[47] MemoConv (La Follette, Newbegin), Aug. 7, 1947, NA 814.504.

[48] MemoConv ("Effect of Guatemalan Labor Law on United Fruit Company"), July 10, 1947, NA 814.504. ("Mr. Corcoran declared that the company might find it necessary to reduce its personnel now from 17,000 to less than 500 in order to avoid the penalties of the present law," p. 1.)

[49] MemoConv ("Guatemalan Labor Code and Possible Discrimination against United Fruit Company"), July 22, 1947, p. 2, NA 814.504.

[50] "Labor Pact Likely in Guatemala Now," *NYT*, Feb. 26, 1949, p. 5.

[51] MemoConv ("Effect of Guatemalan Labor Law on United Fruit Company"), July 10, 1947, p. 1, NA 814.504.

In its opening paragraph the United Fruit Company memorandum states that "foreign influence has evidently been very effective" in the preparation of the Code. This is of course true, since one of the principal drafters of the Code was Licenciado Oscar Barahona Streber, a Costa Rican. Most of the Code is modeled on the similar Costa Rican document. . . . The Labor Commission of the Guatemalan Legislature appears to have made every effort to take into consideration the observations of all sectors affected by the Code, and apparently took the advice of the United Fruit Company and the International Railways of Central America in many cases. The final document cannot be considered radical or revolutionary in any sense, except that no coordinated labor legislation existed in this country previously.[52]

No one else in the embassy expressed such iconoclastic views, not even the amiable Edwin Kyle, who served as U.S. ambassador from May 1945 to August 1948. Kyle was not unsympathetic to the Guatemalan government, and he believed that the suspicions of communist influence "were without foundation, at least in so far as President Arévalo is concerned." (He had misgivings, however, about Foreign Minister Enrique Muñoz Meany, "especially on the communist charge," and did not consider Arbenz as "dependable" as Arana.) Judiciously, Kyle pointed out that "a great deal" of the criticism directed at the Arévalo administration "came from the country's wealthy property owners and that it reminded him of opinions expressed by some of his wealthy fellow Texans relative to President Roosevelt."[53] It apparently never occurred to him that UFCO might also be a biased critic. On the contrary, he had only praise for the company. In June 1947, the same month that one of his subordinates challenged UFCO's assessment of the Labor Code, Kyle wrote, "I have every possible confidence in the United Fruit Company. As I told the [Guatemalan] Foreign Minister, I am convinced that next to what the Standard Oil Company is doing for the people and Government of Venezuela, that the United Fruit Company comes next in all of the Central and South American countries as doing the most for the territory in which it operates." His views did not change in the following year when the conflict between the company and the host government deepened. UFCO, he told the State Department as he returned to private life in the summer of 1948, "was doing a really constructive job in its Latin American relations."[54]

No one should accuse the unflappable Kyle of opportunism. He was an elderly dean of agriculture from Texas who had not sought to be an ambassa-

---

[52] Stines to Ives, June 6, 1947, quoted from p. 1, enclosed in Donovan to SecState, June 10, 1947, NA 814.504.

[53] MemoConv ("Final Remarks of Ambassador Edwin J. Kyle Relative to Guatemala"), Aug. 30 and Sept. 1, 1948, pp. 1, 2, NA 814.00. Muñoz Meany was foreign minister between June 1948 and August 1949.

[54] Quotations from Kyle to Newbegin, June 26, 1947, pp. 1–2, NA 814.504 and "Final Remarks" (see n. 53 above), p. 2.

dor and who looked forward to retirement.[55] Like a great many Americans, he believed in the virtues of big business and in the positive role it played in backward countries. He saw no contradiction between his exuberant praise of UFCO and his goodwill toward the Arévalo administration. He failed to realize that this praise lent credibility to UFCO's claim that sinister forces were at work in the Guatemalan government.

THE COMMUNIST THREAT

In July 1948, the legal adviser to the State Department intervened a second time, urging that "until we can establish that the United Fruit Company is, in practice, being discriminated against, we should take some steps to have the Embassy diminish its vigorous pressure on the Guatemalan Government."[56]

Such qualms did not trouble the officials at ARA. What concerned them was the communist threat. Nor was the new ambassador, Richard Patterson, who replaced Kyle in the summer of 1948, given to legalistic caution. Patterson was as arrogant as Kyle had been courteous; he was devoid of sympathy for the Guatemalan government and highly receptive to allegations of communist influence. He was, in short, in tune with United Fruit, as well as with the senior embassy staff and ARA officials in Washington.[57]

Initially the U.S. had viewed neither the revolution nor Arévalo with suspicion. There was some uneasiness, however, about the region as a whole. An August 1945 intelligence analysis had remarked that in Latin America "mass discontent is more acute than at any time in the past century," and it had listed Guatemala as one of the countries "where the old forms of society and government have completely broken down and new forms are in process of emergence." The assessment of the Arévalo administration was favorable; the only reservation was whether it would have the ability to direct the difficult transition.[58] Such concerns about the future of Latin America were amorphous and fleeting. A December 1946 intelligence report on Soviet objectives in the Western Hemisphere, for example, expressed no anxiety about communism in Central America, except in Costa Rica. In the other four republics, the report

[55] Interview with Woodward. For background on Kyle, see the Kyle Papers, Cornell University.

[56] MemoConv ("Section 130 of the Guatemalan Labor Code"), July 21, 1948, p. 2, NA 814.504.

[57] The Truman Library has two boxes of Patterson's personal papers that complement his dispatches from Guatemala and illuminate his personality.

[58] Office of Strategic Services, Research and Analysis Branch, "Estimate of the Situation in Central and South America," R&A no. 3356, Aug. 28, 1945, quoted from pp. 1 and 2, NA.

noted, the Communist party was banned, and "there is no indication that if any real communists exist, they have an appreciable influence."[59]

It was United Fruit that first raised the specter of serious communist infiltration in Guatemala, and it was the introduction of the Labor Code that provoked it to do so. In the months that followed, the company's accusations fell on fertile ground. It was evident that several labor leaders and politicians had veered sharply to the left. (The FBI had been collecting information on rogues such as Fortuny and Gutiérrez for over two years.)[60] Moreover, the Labor Code encouraged the fledgling labor movement and exasperated the upper class, which began to brandish charges of communist infiltration with even greater gusto than did UFCO.

Meanwhile the Cold War deepened. In 1945 and 1946 the Truman administration had shown antipathy toward dictatorial rule and sympathy for democratic regimes in its Latin American policy. By 1948, this stance had changed into appreciation for dictators as the strongest defense against communism. (Dictators, moreover, tended to be more friendly to American companies than were popularly elected presidents.)

Many U.S. officials accepted that social reforms were long overdue in Latin America, and some even intimated that such reforms could be the best antidote to communism. But reforms were acceptable only if they did not enhance the prestige of men whom Washington distrusted, such as Guatemala's labor leaders. Furthermore, these reforms must respect established American economic interests, and they must not antagonize the elites, those stalwart friends of the United States who benefited from the injustice of the status quo.

Although U.S. officials conceded that American firms abroad were at times persecuted simply because of the host governments naïveté, greed, and chauvinism, they were also on guard to the ever present danger of communism; very close scrutiny of the reformers was in order. The standards against which the Arévalo administration was judged were Ubico's Guatemala and the undemocratic regimes of El Salvador, Honduras, and Nicaragua.

U.S. officials were ill-equipped to assess the men who led Guatemala. They also lacked accurate information. They had been accustomed to a country where even in the moments of political opening (as in the 1920s) the relevant actors were few, well-known, and predictable: the upper class and aspiring military *caudillos*. Information was gathered in the beautiful houses of the

[59] DOS, Intelligence Research Report, "Soviet Policy and Objectives in the Other American Republics," OCL-4185, Dec. 31, 1946, quoted from p. 10, NA.

[60] See Hoover to Lyon, Jan. 14, 1946; Hoover to Lyon, Mar. 13, 1946; Lyon to Hoover, Apr. 5, 1946; Hoover to Lyon, Apr. 19, 1946; Hoover to Lyon, May 16, 1946; "José Manuel Fortuny," May 28, 1946; Hoover to Lyon et al., July 9, 1946; Hoover to Lyon et al., July 15, 1946; "Víctor Manuel Gutiérrez," Sept. 30, 1946; Hoover to Neal et al., Dec. 17, 1946. All NA 814.00B. In 1947, responsibility for intelligence gathering in Latin America passed from the FBI to the CIA.

upper class or by summoning the protagonists to the embassy. At other times, the relevant actors were even fewer: in Ubico's thirteen years, only one man mattered.

With the fall of Ponce, the United States faced a whirlwind of new groups, such as organized labor and the political parties of the middle class; groups that talked of changing Guatemalan society, although their rhetoric tended to be far more ardent than their actions; groups that were led by men with whom embassy officials were usually ill at ease; groups that were motivated by a nationalism that stood in sharp contrast to the accommodating greed of the leaders of happier days. "No one of the former governing class of old 'good families' was or has since been a member of this government," a U.S. diplomat lamented in 1949.[61]

To penetrate this strange new world of young revolutionary leaders, the embassy turned to those Guatemalans who appeared unswervingly pro-American; those who would be honest enough to acknowledge that the Labor Code was discriminatory, and that UFCO and its sister companies were being victimized; those who were sensitive to the communist threat. Not surprisingly, these worthies were found among Arévalo's enemies and particularly among the genteel upper class. These were the men who were eager to convince the Americans of the burgeoning communist threat. To be sure, Washington was not unaware that these men had their own agenda. But their warnings, U.S. officials believed, contained elements of truth; the more dangerous seemed the Arévalo regime, the less shrill seemed its critics. Governments hostile to Guatemala added damning information. Again, Washington did not uncritically accept these reports, but the accusations reinforced the mood of distrust.[62]

The Truman administration, and in particular the embassy in Guatemala, had another source of information, the one they valued most highly: those Americans who had long lived in the country. These men were the representatives of U.S. companies in Guatemala; foremost among them were two in-

[61] Siracusa, "Summary of Statements Made by Mr. Siracusa in Presentation of Guatemalan Situation," p. 3, enclosed in Siracusa to Patterson, Aug. 22, 1949, RG84 GR, Box 216, NA-S.

[62] For information from other governments, see AmEm Madrid, Moffitt to SecState, no. 141, Mar. 5, 1948, NA 814.00B, enclosing a five-page report "given the Embassy informally and voluntarily, by the Chief of the American Section of the Spanish Foreign Office"; HQs Panama Canal Department, "Weekly Intelligence Summary" no. 257, June 4, 1947, RG319 ID 373808, NA-S; Marshall to SecState, no. 1074, Oct. 23, 1947, NA 814.00B; Wells to DOS, no. 248, Sept. 6, 1950, NA 714.00. Alarmed by the Arévalo administration's insistent claims on British Honduras, British officials embarked on a campaign to impugn the Guatemalan government as communist. (Meers, "Pebble on the Beach," pp. 22–29.) For a revealing selection of British reports, see "Extract from Annual Review" and "Extract from Guatemala Report," RG84 CF, Box 15, NA-S.

telligent, persuasive and outspoken individuals, William Taillon, general manager of UFCO, and Thomas Bradshaw, president of IRCA. Milton Wells, the Foreign Service officer who essentially ran the embassy under both Kyle and Patterson, "entertained close ties with Taillon and Bradshaw," recalls an embassy official.[63]

Thus by the late 1940s, the Truman administration saw Guatemala as a nightmarish world infested not only by communists, but also by ill-defined yet dangerous species such as procommunists, fellow travelers, extreme leftists, and radical leftists. There was some truth to these fears; that Gutiérrez, for example, had become a communist was a fact that he himself hardly sought to hide. The same was true of a handful of labor leaders close to him.

But U.S. officials also branded as communists or communist sympathizers men who were at most mild leftists or even right of center. The prominent PAR leader Charnaud was not considered "a *proven* communist in the card-carrying sense," yet his strong procommunist orientation was flagrant, "since 1944 at least."[64] In fact Charnaud, who hardly knew who Marx was in 1944, was, by the end of Arévalo's term, an eloquent populist with slight leftist proclivities. The same virulent Red virus allegedly contaminated Foreign Minister Muñoz Meany, another moderate leftist whose major sins were strong hostility to dictatorship and sincere nationalism.[65] Other cases were still more farfetched. U.S. officials were not sure whether Jorge García Granados, a moderate candidate in the 1950 presidential elections, was a card-carrying communist—but he was certainly a communist sympathizer and a dangerous man.[66] The Honduran exile Medardo Mejía, who held mid-level positions in the Guatemalan bureaucracy and wrote in the progovernment press, was correctly identified as a "close friend of Arévalo." It was the Honduran Minister in Guatemala who had revealed Mejía's secret to the American embassy: he

[63] Interview with Steins.

[64] OIR, "Guatemala: Communist Influence," Oct. 23, 1950, p. 95, NA. An earlier in-depth report had noted that "there is good circumstantial evidence of party affiliation." (AmEmG, "Communism in Guatemala," p. 17, enclosed in Wells to SecState, no. 217, May 6, 1948, NA 814.00B.)

[65] For the U.S. view of Muñoz Meany, see HQs Panama Canal Department, "Weekly Intelligence Summary" no. 270, Sept. 3, 1947, p. 13, RG319 ID 397212, NA-S; "Communism in Guatemala" (see n. 64 above), p. 17; Wells to DOS, no. 794, June 27, 1950, NA 714.13; "Guatemala: Communist Influence" (see n. 64 above), pp. 43, 64.

[66] See Col. Devine, "Possible Russian and Communist Influence in Guatemala," Report 142-6, May 3, 1946, RG84 CF, Box 14, NA-S; HQs Panama Canal Department, "Weekly Intelligence Summary" no. 262, July 9, 1947, p. 11, RG319 ID 382208, NA-S; "Communism in Guatemala" (see n. 64 above), p. 10. By the end of the Arévalo administration, the U.S. perception of García Granados began to soften: see "Guatemala: Communist Influence" (see n. 64 above), p. 71, n. 1.

was "one of the principal agents" of communist penetration in Guatemala;[67] this information was accepted by U.S. officials even though it came from an obviously partisan source. Mejía, who shared the confused populist views of Arévalo, became, for the Americans, a dangerous character and was placed in the same gallery of scoundrels as Graciela García, a Salvadoran communist of many years' standing whom Arévalo had deported in 1947.[68]

Even Clemente Marroquín Rojas, a prominent right-wing intellectual, aroused the suspicions of U.S. officials. His nationalism, which was tinged with criticism of the United States, confused them, for they were accustomed to Guatemalan conservatives who loudly sang the praises of all things American. His daily *La Hora*, which had attacked Arévalo and his policies as extremist since late 1947, was branded as leftist.[69]

Given this hypersensitivity, it is hardly surprising that U.S. officials saw the revolutionary parties as ravaged by the Red virus. Once again, a distorted assessment grew around a grain of truth: the PAR had harbored communists—Fortuny and his friends. But even after their resignation, U.S. officials believed that communist influence in the PAR was significant,[70] not an unreasonable conclusion, given that they considered the party's major leader, the anticommunist Charnaud, to be at least a fellow traveler. U.S. officials also concluded that the infection had spread to RN, albeit to a "less pronounced" degree, and suspicions were even raised about the docile FPL.[71]

With hindsight, the embassy concluded that "demagogic incitement of the masses against the status quo [had] marked the first three years of the Arévalo Administration"[72]—a bold assessment that was not consonant with the embassy's own reporting in 1945 and 1946. The same hindsight colored the embassy's interpretation of the Labor Code. In 1947, U.S. officials had condemned merely its discriminatory nature, while UFCO had warned that it bore the signs of communist influence; by 1948, the embassy had discovered that the code was a "drastic document which, if enforced literally, would greatly facilitate the communist objective of state or worker control of industry." It warned that the social policies of the Arévalo administration were "motivated in part by a calculated effort to further class warfare, rather than being limited in scope to a sincere effort to bring about much needed social and economic adjustments."[73]

[67] "Guatemala: Communist Influence" (see n. 64 above), p. 41.

[68] Ibid., pp. 41–42. See also Comité Salvadoreño de Liberación Nacional, "Memorial dirigido por la emigración centroamericana al Presidente de la República de Guatemala," July 21, 1947, CPR, AGCA.

[69] "Guatemala: Communist Influence" (see n. 64 above), p. 74.

[70] Ibid., p. 22.

[71] See ibid., pp. 3, 22 (quoted), 80, and "Communism in Guatemala" (see n. 64 above), p. 5.

[72] "Communism in Guatemala" (see n. 64 above), p. 17.

[73] Ibid., pp. 18, 14.

The State Department and UFCO

While Washington's preoccupation with communism in Guatemala grew, American companies locked into an increasingly bitter conflict with the host government and organized labor. Once again, United Fruit led the way, resisting the demands of its labor unions that the Labor Code be implemented and that wages be increased.

The company remained firm: the code was discriminatory, and UFCO's wages were already the highest paid to agricultural workers in Guatemala. In a still-recent past, UFCO would have fired the insubordinate workers, and the government would have readily enforced the company's will. But now the Labor Code stipulated that workers could not be summarily dismissed and provided for inspectors to verify the unions' complaints. Furthermore, United Fruit was expected to use the mechanisms of conciliation and arbitration established by the new legislation.

The government's "persecution" of UFCO, however, should not be exaggerated. Between the summer of 1947 and early 1949, when the smoldering conflict erupted into a dangerous crisis, labor inspectors repeatedly found UFCO guilty of violations of the Labor Code, yet the total amount of the fines levied against the company was $690.[74] What exasperated UFCO, sure of its moral superiority and jealous of its autonomy, was the idea of any outside interference, even if this interference came from the sovereign government of the land.

Egged on by UFCO, the State Department exerted unrelenting pressure on the Arévalo administration to modify the Labor Code and to halt its "persecution" of American companies. In late July 1948, the legal adviser of the State Department had criticized ARA's stance, arguing that the discriminatory nature of the code had not yet been proven. ARA eventually conceded the point, and on November 2 it instructed the embassy to ascertain, "in as discreet a manner as possible," whether UFCO was indeed a victim of discrimination.[75] The nature of the debate, and its swift conclusion, were well summarized in a December 1948 memorandum to Robert Lovett, the undersecretary of state:

> In February 1947 there was enacted in Guatemala a labor code of more than 400 articles. In four of these . . . special benefits are conferred on employees of agricultural enterprises with more than 500 workers. In the specific Guatemalan setting it appeared clear that these articles were intended to place a special burden on the United Fruit Company. Consequently, the American Embassy, with the Depart-

[74] Bauer Paiz, *La Frutera*, p. 16. Bauer Paiz was the finance minister. For a vivid description of the travails of a labor inspector, see "Expediente relacionado con los conflictos tratados por el inspector de trabajo urbano Salvador Ruano Pimentel en la zona de Tiquisate," June 16, 1947, IGT, Leg. 48750, AGCA.

[75] Lovett to AmEmG, no. A-210, Nov. 2, 1948, NA 814.504/9-348.

ment's backing, in due course protested the seemingly discriminatory articles. . . . Later . . . doubts arose within the Department as to whether our government could, in view of much of its own legislation and the jurisprudence built up around it, properly represent that the four disputed articles were *prima facie* discriminatory in a legal sense. The views first expressed by our ambassador to the Guatemalan government were never retracted, but these doubts . . . were discussed by the Department with counsel and officers of the United Fruit Company. It was agreed between the Department and the Company that the Company would gather and present evidence to the Department as to whether there were enterprises besides the United Fruit Company covered by the articles in question, and, if so, whether such enterprises were complying with the law. These enterprises would possibly include a number of large farms operated by the Guatemalan government itself.

The Department could not and did not require of the United Fruit Company that it present clear and incontrovertible evidence on these points before proceeding further. In the nature of things Guatemalan it would be practically impossible for the Company and our Embassy to develop such evidence. It was only on December 9, 1948, that the company was able to present to the Department sufficient information to enable it to take a further step. On December 10, by telegram, the Department transmitted this information to the new Ambassador in Guatemala, Richard C. Patterson, Jr., and instructed him to verify it and then to renew representations in protection of the United Fruit Company's interests.

Representations were in the first instance begun by our Embassy as soon as the position in which the Guatemalan Labor Code placed the United Fruit Company had become clear and these representations were vigorously pushed by Ambassador Kyle. Our Government's stand has never been altered and with the new information at hand the case of the United Fruit Company will be vigorously pressed.[76]

Thus ended the ineffectual debate, in which United Fruit had been its own prosecutor, and the jury had been a most sympathetic embassy. A more serious investigation would have shown, as the Guatemalan government contended, that there were several agricultural enterprises with more than five hundred permanent workers, and that in some of these (Herrera y Cía and a few Fincas Nacionales), some provisions of the Labor Code were enforced.[77] The analysis would also have shown that the impetus to implement the code came from UFCO's labor unions, not from the Arévalo administration; as the Guatemalan

[76] Humelsine to Connelly, Dec. 15, 1948, pp. 1–2, enclosed in Connelly to Lovett, Dec 4 [sic], 1948. On the debate, see also Barber to Metzger, Sept. 3, 1948; MemoConv ("Article 130 of Guatemala Labor Code"), Sept. 27, 1948; Daniels to Barber and de Zengotita, Dec. 3, 1948, and enclosed Tate to Daniels of same date; Daniels to Acting Sec., Dec. 6, 1948; Brown to Daniels, Dec. 6, 1948. All NA 814.504.

[77] For the Fincas Nacionales and Herrera y Cía, see Taillon to Baggett, Nov. 29, 1948, NA 814.00.

ambassador had pointed out, agricultural workers elsewhere were far less combative.

The conclusion of the debate within the State Department came at a most opportune moment: less than a month later, United Fruit declared war on the Guatemalan government. Ordered by the government to submit its dispute with the labor unions to arbitration in the labor courts, UFCO responded by firing a large number of workers and stopping all shipping at Puerto Barrios. The impasse continued throughout February, while Arévalo threatened to sequester the company's properties and Ambassador Patterson, implementing Washington's orders with gusto, made it clear to Arévalo that the United States held his administration responsible for the conflict. "Recent developments [are] of deepest concern [to] U.S. Government and business circles," he warned, "and [are] being watched as testability and even willingness . . . [of the Guatemalan] Government to give American enterprises [in] this country the fair deal which certainly has been denied them during [the] past three years."[78]

It was an unequal contest. In March, a compromise was reached that reestablished normal relations between the company and the host government— that is, relations of extreme distrust. United Fruit had made good its refusal to submit to arbitration, and the unions had obtained only modest concessions, principally a wage increase of less than 10 percent. "It is clear," concluded *El Imparcial*, "that our country is too weak to challenge powerful American business interests."[79]

For the remainder of the Arévalo presidency, embassy reports and State Department communications referred repeatedly to Guatemala's "victimization" of American companies; "persecution" was the monotonous refrain. With rising irritation, Patterson lectured Arévalo about Guatemala's sins, and State Department officials administered the same medicine to the hapless Guatemalan ambassador in Washington.

And yet, in 1950, reviewing the record of many years of "persecution," the State Department concluded that American companies in Guatemala

[78] Patterson to SecState, no. 44, Feb. 1, 1949, p. 2, NA 814.504. For the origins of the conflict, see Juzgado de Trabajo y Previsión Social, Zona Sexta, Unión Sindical de Trabajadores de Puerto Barrios vs United Fruit Company, Leg. 2B, Pieza 84, Juzgado 1° de Trabajo de Izabal, OJR, AGCA.

[79] "Arreglo frutero," *El I*, Mar. 9, 1949, p. 1. For the terms of the agreement, see "Resuelto el conflicto frutero," *El I*, Mar. 5, 1949, p. 1, and "Suscrito el convenio entre la UFCO y los laborantes," *El I*, Mar. 7, 1949, p. 1. The 1949 contract was renegotiated the next year, in what was "actually a one-year extension of the old contract with a few modifications." (Steins to DOS, no. 474, Apr. 20, 1950, p. 2, NA 814.062.) For the continuing struggle between UFCO and its workers, see the "Inventarios del Juzgado de Trabajo y Previsión Social de la Sexta Zona Económica de los Juicios Laborales," Juzgado de Trabajo de Puerto Barrios, 1947–1958, OJR, AGCA.

"have suffered no serious harm."[80] This relatively happy situation, U.S. officials believed, had been possible only because of their spirited defense of the companies, and they had a point. In spite of UFCO's economic power, it is unlikely that Arévalo would have been as forgiving had it not been for the heckling of the State Department.

After December 1948, the record indicates only one instance when a U.S. official dared to suggest that the Guatemalan government was anything less than the villain of the piece. In a comprehensive memorandum, the labor officer of the Office of Regional American Affairs, John Fishburn, boldly stated that the State Department's embrace of UFCO was wrong. With only one exception, Fishburn argued, the "discriminatory" articles of the Labor Code were in fact "legitimate in terms of modern thinking." Noting UFCO's claim that it treated its Guatemalan workers generously, Fishburn responded: "The company will have to learn that labor often does not appreciate paternalism, but wishes to share in determining its fate. This trend to extend democracy in industrial relations is very powerful." Presciently, he warned: if UFCO "should attempt, with or without Embassy assistance, to fight this inevitable trend, . . . it will probably lead to the same conclusion experienced by the American and British oil companies in Mexico." That is, expropriation. He concluded:

> With respect to this Government's relations to the case, it would appear most unwise for us to be tied to the company's position, without regard for Guatemala's aspirations or sovereign feelings. It is my judgment that our unfortunate and necessarily ineffectual attempts to help the company have permitted the communists to pose as champions of labor and of national sovereignty, and have thereby aided them in achieving control over organized labor in Guatemala.[81]

The embassy in Guatemala shot off a sharply worded six-page rebuttal.[82] Edward W. Clark, of the Office of Middle American Affairs (MID), wrote to Milton Wells, the U.S. chargé in Guatemala: "All of us here in MID think Fishburn is way off the beam in his thinking on this matter and have told him so." A few days earlier, continued Clark, at the weekly meeting of assistant secretaries "the situation relating to our relations with Guatemala was discussed thoroughly and full approval was given . . . to the policy which we are presently following."[83]

U.S. officials did not dispute Fishburn's assertion that the communists were

---

[80] "Current Relations with Guatemala," May 1950, *FRUS*, 1950, 2:900.

[81] Fishburn to Miller, Apr. 10, 1950, ibid., pp. 880–84.

[82] See Wells to DOS, May 17, 1950, ibid., pp. 889–91, and the enclosed "Memorandum," ibid., pp. 891–96.

[83] Clark to Wells, June 6, 1950, ibid., p. 903. For the meeting of assistant secretaries mentioned by Clark, see ibid., pp. 901–2.

profiting from the labor conflicts and discrediting both UFCO and the U.S. government. But they believed that Fishburn's analysis was naive: any concessions on UFCO's part would have encouraged the communist bosses to raise new demands and enhanced their prestige among the workers. At fault was not the State Department's support of UFCO, but the Guatemalan government's tolerance, and even encouragement, of these communists. This connivance added an ominous dimension to the labor conflict and heightened U.S. suspicions about Arévalo.

The Caribbean Legion

Not only did Arévalo persecute American companies and show a disquieting tenderness toward communist agitators, his foreign policy was equally reckless. Guatemala, the State Department asserted in 1950, was "one of the principal causes of unrest and instability in the Caribbean."[84] The accusation was not baseless; no government helped the semimythical Caribbean Legion more than that of Arévalo. Arévalo's involvement with the Caribbean Legion illuminates both his personality and the struggles that stirred the Caribbean in the late 1940s. Further, it highlights the paranoia that had seized the Truman administration. In a less distorted world, Arévalo's support for the Caribbean Legion would have been proof that the president was an anticommunist or at least that he was not a communist; instead it was added to the indictment as evidence of his communist proclivities.

Indeed, it was partly this worldview that made the Caribbean Legion seem more powerful to Washington than it ever was. As a structured, formal organization, the Caribbean Legion never existed. (The name was coined by U.S. journalists in 1948.) What did exist were nuclei of exiled leaders from various countries who were, at times, able to coordinate their activities and mobilize "foot-soldiers"—exiles living throughout the region.[85]

---

[84] "Current Relations with Guatemala," ibid., p. 899.

[85] There is no definitive study of the Caribbean Legion. The best treatment is Ameringer, *Democratic Left*, pp. 59–110. Useful material is included in Corominas, *In the Caribbean Political Areas*; Vega, *Los Estados Unidos*; Unión Panamericana, *Tratado interamericano*, 1:33–149. The most important accounts by participants are Arvelo, *Cayo Confite*; Ornes, *Desembarco*; Henríquez Vásquez, "Cayo Confites"; Bosch, "Cayo Confites"; Wangüemert y Máiquez, "El diario de Cayo Confites"; Argüello, *Quiénes*; Bayo, *Tempestad*; Silfa, *Guerra*, 1:175–299; Figueres, *El espíritu del 48*; Morazán, "Los siete primeros." U.S. documents shed light not only on U.S. perceptions and policies but occasionally on the activities of the exiles and the governments concerned. Particularly helpful were interviews with the Dominican participants Ramírez Alcantara, Arvelo, Martínez Bonilla (a "foot soldier"); with the Guatemalans Fortuny, Arévalo, María de Arbenz, Barrios Peña, Charnaud; with the Costa Rican Figueres; and with the Nicaraguan Torres Espinoza.

In the twilight of the Second World War, the sudden emergence of democracy in Cuba, Guatemala, and Venezuela had swelled the hopes of exiles from the less fortunate republics in the region. No longer lonely outcasts, they could now count on the assistance of friendly governments. Freedom was contagious, they believed, and resistance to dictatorship was growing in their own countries. Among the dictators, Trujillo and Somoza were the pillars of tyranny. Should they be toppled, the wind of democracy in the Caribbean would prove irresistible.

While others plotted, the Dominican exiles acted. In the summer of 1947, with the complicity of President Ramón Grau San Martin and other high Cuban officials, they assembled the largest exile force that had ever congregated in the Caribbean. A potpourri of approximately 1,200 armed men, mainly Cuban volunteers and Dominicans with a sprinkling of Hondurans and other exiles, gathered in Cuba at Cayo Confites. The leaders of the expedition were confident of their own strength and that of the underground that awaited their arrival in the Dominican Republic. The underground did indeed exist, although they exaggerated its power. Had the exiles invaded, Trujillo would have been the likely victor. Had they invaded. Secrecy was a virtue that the exiles and their Cuban protectors had spurned; the preparations for the invasion were public knowledge, and Cuban complicity was flagrant. While Trujillo's complaints grew, the United States pressed Grau to desist, as did Cuban opposition politicians and even government officials (including the chief of staff of the army). Grau capitulated; in late September the Cuban military detained the entire expeditionary force.

In a matter of days the exiles were set free, but their hopes had been shattered. The chastened Cuban government was no longer willing to offer its country as a base for future expeditions. Worse, it confiscated the weapons that the exiles had accumulated so laboriously.[86]

It was at this juncture that Arévalo assumed center stage. The previous summer, while the Dominicans had been organizing in Cuba under Grau's protection, Arévalo had acted as their intermediary to buy weapons in Argentina, using his good contacts with the Buenos Aires government and claiming that the arms were for Guatemala.[87] He had also broken diplomatic relations with Trujillo in July 1947. It had been a useful, though secondary, role. But now that Grau had abandoned the exiles, Arévalo stepped forward as the champion of the Caribbean Legion; he was to retain this role for two years, and he acted with far more discretion than had Grau. In Guatemala, Arévalo's policy,

[86] For two vivid accounts of the Dominicans' efforts to recover the weapons from the Cuban government, see Arvelo, *Cayo Confite*, pp. 120–22, and Henríquez Vásquez, "Cayo Confites," Jan. 17, 1984, p. 10.

[87] See especially Silfa, *Guerra*, 1:180–82, and Bosch, "Cayo Confites," pp. 3, 8, 13.

which was never discussed publicly, was endorsed by leaders of the revolutionary parties. Within the military, Arbenz was sympathetic, and Arana grumbled. ("It's just adolescent bravado," he confided to friends.) Yet he went along, as was his wont.[88]

Sincere hostility to dictators only partially explains Arévalo's daring role between 1947 and 1949.[89] A dream that had deep roots in Central American history moved him to risk a confrontation with Trujillo and Somoza and to incur Washington's anger. It was a passionate longing that Arévalo had expressed in two essays written in his youth and that he reiterated in his inaugural address:

> There is no Guatemalan who does not dream of the Greater Motherland of Central America. . . . We feel impotent whenever we pause to consider the fact that we are still five small republics, exposed to the machinations of any adventurer and the exploitation of the powerful. Terrible enemies keep us apart. These enemies are our very own governments. The Federation of Central America would exist now if our governments had renounced their selfish interests. . . . The Federation is not an illusion: it could become a reality in the near future. We need only to unite . . . in order to resurrect this Central American nation as a great democracy, with a powerful economy and a modern army.[90]

Upon becoming President, Arévalo sought to achieve his goal by diplomatic means, expounding the idea of a gradual but steady federative process for the five Central American republics. His efforts led, in 1945 and again in 1946, to two highly publicized meetings with General Salvador Castañeda Castro, the strongman who ruled El Salvador. Florid treaties for the progressive unification of the two countries were signed. Meanwhile, the other three Central

[88] Quoted from interview with Arana's close associate, Barrios Peña. Some exiles have written accounts, published after Arana's death, that distort Arana's position into one of active opposition and even slander him as an accomplice of Trujillo. (See Ornes, *Desembarco*, pp. 90, 119, and Silfa, *Guerra*, 1:280–89.) Interviews with Fortuny, Charnaud, María de Arbenz, Cruz Salazar, Lorenzana, and Torres Espinoza were instructive.

[89] This hostility was not limited to the dictatorships of the Caribbean. At both the Rio Conference (1947) and at Bogotá (1948), Guatemala advocated a policy of nonrecognition of regimes in the hemisphere that had come to power through force, particularly those that had overthrown democracies. The proposal was rejected, but Arévalo adopted it unilaterally. Guatemala was also a vocal critic of Franco. See Frankel, "Political Development," pp. 50–68, 87–91.

[90] "Al asumir la presidencia," Mar. 15, 1945, in Arévalo, *Discursos en la presidencia*, pp. 7–21, quoted from pp. 12–13. The two essays are "Istmania (tierras del Istmo)," written in 1935, and "Cultura y posibilidades de cultura en la América Central," written in 1939; both were first published in Arévalo's *Escritos políticos*, pp. 12–28, 57–69.

American governments remained aloof. By 1947 it was clear that the treaties were worthless. In the words of a sympathetic scholar, Arévalo had become "completely disillusioned as far as the possibility of a successful unification effort was concerned."[91]

Yet his zeal was unquenched. The failure of his diplomatic efforts merely led him to conclude that the dictators themselves were the obstacle to Central American unification and that with their overthrow Central America would be one and democratic. It was this conviction that moved him, in the wake of the Cuban fiasco, to respond to the Dominicans' appeal for help. On their behalf, he urged his friend, President Grau, to release the weapons of Cayo Confites. Grau surrendered some of the weapons; he gave them, however, not to the exiles but to the Guatemalan government.[92]

Thus Guatemala became Mecca, and Arévalo the prophet. Dominicans, Hondurans, and leaders of rival Nicaraguan exile factions flocked to him. Also present was an eloquent Costa Rican, José Figueres. To be sure, Figueres could hardly qualify as an exile. Deported from Costa Rica in 1942, he had returned in 1944. Since then he had indulged unmolested in one of his fondest occupations: inveighing in scathing and scurrilous public denunciations of the administrations of Presidents Rafael Angel Calderón Guardia (1940–1944) and Teodoro Picado (1944–1948). More discreetly, Figueres was busy plotting against the government.[93]

Within that cacophony, Arévalo arbitrated with the assurance of the man who holds all the cards. Under his firm guidance the exiles were forced to patch up their differences and to sign, on December 17, 1947, a most extraordinary document, the *Pacto del Caribe*. The pact established an alliance "of the groups representing the Dominican Republic, Nicaragua, and Costa Rica. . . . As we overthrow each of these dictators, the resources of the liberated countries will be used to reinforce our common endeavor."

While explicitly targeting only Costa Rica, the Dominican Republic, and Nicaragua, the *Pacto del Caribe* had a more ambitious scope: "All groups representing the oppressed peoples of the Caribbean are invited to join this pact, so that they too—with our help—can liberate their own countries." The ultimate aim, so dear to Arévalo, was powerfully stated:

[91] Bishop, "Arévalo and Central American Unification," p. 108.

[92] See esp. Henríquez Vásquez, "Cayo Confites," Jan. 17, 1984, p. 10. U.S. intelligence was anxious to follow the movement of the weapons: see Kyle to SecState, no. 32, Jan. 21, 1948; Feinberg, Paraphrase no. P-10, Jan. 22, 1948; Neruob to SecState, no. 55, Jan. 22, 1948; Siracusa to Wells, Feb. 4, 1948; Kyle to SecState, no. 62, Feb. 5, 1948. All RG84 GR, Box 193, NA-S.

[93] Two superb, well documented and dispassionate books that deal with the regimes of Calderón and Picado, as well as with Figueres's role, are Aguilar Bulgarelli, *Costa Rica*, and Bell, *Crisis*.

We, the undersigned, declare that the immediate reestablishment of the Republic of Central America is necessary for this continent; this principle will be affirmed in the new constitutions of the liberated countries, and each new government will immediately work to implement it with all the resources at its disposal.

The liberated countries pledge to establish a Democratic Alliance of the Caribbean, which will be open to all the democracies of the Caribbean, as well as to El Salvador and Ecuador. . . .

The Democratic Alliance of the Caribbean will constitute an indivisible bloc in all international crises. Its fundamental aims will be: to strengthen democracy in the region; to demand the respect of the international community for each of its members; to liberate the European colonies that still exist in the Caribbean; to promote the creation of the Republic of the Lesser Antilles; to act as one in defense of our common economic, military and political interests.

Discreetly, Arévalo refrained from signing the document, yet his hand was evident in the flowery language that was his trademark. "All differences in the interpretation and implementation of this pact," the document concluded, "will be submitted to the irrevocable decision of President Juan José Arévalo, in whose ability, honesty and impartiality we place full trust. We are confident that he will not withhold the invaluable gift of his wisdom."[94]

Of course, to brand the governments of Calderón and Picado as dictatorships—as the *Pacto del Caribe* did—was hyperbole and to lump Costa Rica with Trujillo's Dominican Republic and Somoza's Nicaragua was sheer nonsense. Costa Rica had a hybrid system where electoral fraud (as in 1944) alternated with clean elections (as those for Congress, in 1946). Under President Calderón, and "above all" under Picado, the foremost authority on the period points out, the opposition "could act almost freely"; it was rarely cowed and responded in kind to the government's excesses."[95] By Costa Rica's previous standards, democracy did not fare badly under Calderón and Picado. It was comparable to that of Cuba under Grau. Furthermore, the administrations of Calderón and Picado contrasted with those of their predecessors in their advocacy of social reforms and in their alliance with the Communist party, which had polled 10 percent of the votes in the 1940 elections. It was this strong reformist bent, and the alliance with the communists, that exasperated the Costa Rican upper class, which had blithely overlooked the brazen electoral fraud and high-handed practices of Calderón's predecessor, León Cortés (1936–1940). Figueres shared the upper class's hostility toward Calderón and Picado, not because he opposed social reform, but because he wanted power.

Costa Rica's domestic politics were of little concern to the Caribbean exiles, even though many disapproved of Calderón's and Picado's association with

[94] For the text of the *Pacto del Caribe*, see Aguilar Bulgarelli, *Costa Rica*, pp. 307–12.

[95] Ibid., p. 300.

the communists. However, in the eyes of many exiles, Calderón and Picado were guilty of a particularly heinous crime: intent on domestic reforms and aware of the military weakness of their country, they remained aloof from the struggle against dictatorship in the Caribbean, and they strove to maintain proper relations with the powerful Somoza.[96] This policy led a faction of Nicaraguan exiles to strike an alliance with Figueres in 1943. With their help, Figueres eventually won over Edelberto Torres Espinoza and Roberto Brenes Mesen, two prominent Nicaraguan intellectuals who were friends of Arévalo. With them, and then with Arévalo in late 1947, Figueres argued a case that was as simple as it was straightforward: given its border with Nicaragua, Costa Rica was the ideal base from which to launch an attack against Somoza; should he, Figueres, seize power, he would offer his country and its resources to assist in the liberation of Nicaragua. With its risible army of three hundred men, the Costa Rican regime would be easily toppled.[97]

Figueres was eloquent, and Torres and Brenes were venerable figures. Although the *Pacto del Caribe* had established no sequence among the three regimes that were explicitly targeted for destruction, Arévalo had made his choice: Costa Rica would be first, followed by Nicaragua. Then, in ever stronger waves, other targets would be hit, until no dictator remained in the Caribbean. The Dominican exiles, the rightful owners of the weapons they no longer controlled, had no alternative but to accept this decision, which delayed their hour, but at least held out a promise of liberation for their country.

On March 1, 1948, the Costa Rican government annulled the February presidential elections, which had been won by the opposition, and thereby handed a welcome pretext to those who had already decreed its destruction. When, on March 12, the uprising that Figueres had been preparing for six years finally broke out, Arévalo promptly sent the weapons of Cayo Confites to the rebels.[98] Without this aid, a successful revolt could hardly have been staged, for Figueres had no arms. A handful of well-trained Caribbean exiles accompanied the weapons from Guatemala; they supplied "critical military skills that the traditionally pacific Costa Ricans lacked," and provided the insurgents

[96] See Schifter, *Las alianzas*, pp. 229–49.

[97] In a 1972 interview, Arévalo stated: "It's strange. I knew almost nothing about Figueres. I was first visited in my presidential office by Roberto Brenes Mesen, that great philosopher and writer who inspired the youth of our country. This was in 1947. He asked for help in his struggle against the government of Costa Rica that was infiltrated by communists." ("No sé si la ayuda que dimos a Figueres en 1948 fué para bien.")

[98] U.S. Intelligence had considerable difficulty in ascertaining Guatemala's role in this episode. See Kyle to SecState, no. 159, Mar. 23, 1948; Kyle to SecState, no. 162, Mar. 24, 1948; Wells to SecState, no. 177, Apr. 13, 1948; Wells to SecState, no. 206, Apr. 29, 1948 (all RG84 GR, Box 191, NA-S); Wells to Daniels, Sept. 1, 1948, RG84 GR, Box 190, NA-S.

with a "technical military advantage over the regular forces of the Costa Rican army"—an army whose officers demonstrated neither the ability nor the will to resist.[99]

Arévalo had honored his pledge to Figueres. Now it was Figueres' turn. Yet once in power, the Costa Rican was unable, and probably unwilling, to fulfill his promises. Granted, the Nicaraguan exiles who flocked to the country after Figueres's victory did not help their own cause. They were more interested in San José's bars than in military training. Their indiscreet, boisterous behavior alienated not only the Costa Rican public but also Figueres's supporters, who had not been privy to the commitments undertaken by their leader in the *Pacto del Caribe* and who had little desire to court unnecessary danger by challenging the mighty Somoza. In vain did Arévalo try to stiffen the resolve of the elusive Figueres; in vain did he beseech his erstwhile protegé to honor the *Pacto del Caribe*, "a pact," he pleaded, "signed in good conscience and that even included an oath to be loyal and disciplined until the fall of the last dictator."[100]

Months of inactivity were followed, in December 1948, by a small invasion of Costa Rica launched from Nicaragua by supporters of former President Calderón. At Figueres's urgent request, the Organization of American States intervened and swiftly rendered its predictable verdict: both Nicaragua and Costa Rica were guilty—Nicaragua of actual aggression, Costa Rica of potential aggression; they should desist at once and adhere strictly to the policy of nonintervention. Both governments happily complied: Somoza, who had intended merely to frighten Figueres, urged the invaders to withdraw to Nicaragua; Figueres, to the great joy of his supporters, told the Nicaraguan exiles to leave Costa Rica. Once again, it was to Guatemala that the leaders of Nicaraguan, Dominican, and other exile groups flocked, and it was to Guatemala that Figueres returned the bulk of the weapons that he had received from Arévalo.

Arévalo was prepared to make a final effort. This time, rather than to the

---

[99] Bell, *Crisis*, p. 138. The CIA also concluded, "The Caribbean Legion . . . was decisive" in Figueres's victory. (CIA, "The Caribbean Legion," ORE 11–49, Mar. 17, 1949, p. 2, Truman Papers, President's Secretary's File, Intelligence File, Box 256, TL.) In addition to Bell's *Crisis*, pp. 131–54, the best accounts of the uprising are Aguilar Bulgarelli, *Costa Rica*, pp. 317–98 and Acuña, *El 48*. Schifter's *Las alianzas* is a well-researched study of U.S. policy toward Costa Rica from 1940 to Figueres' victory. The "Diary (San José) 1948–1949" of U.S. Ambassador Nathaniel Davis is informative, insightful and entertaining. (Davis Papers, Box 1, TL.)

[100] Letter from Arévalo to Figueres, May 27, 1948, in Aguilar Bulgarelli, *Costa Rica*, pp. 414–15. For a scathing denunciation of Figueres' conduct, see Argüello, *Quiénes*—a biased but informative account. For a more balanced version by another participant, see Bayo, *Tempestad*, pp. 83–158. Among secondary sources, see esp. Aguilar Bulgarelli, *Costa Rica*, pp. 398–432.

discredited and faction-ridden Nicaraguans, his support went to the more co-hesive Dominicans. "Basically," one of these Dominicans has written, "our plan was the following: several groups of rebels with weapons for 500 or 600 men would be flown to the Dominican Republic. Unlike Cayo Confites, this would not be a full-fledged invasion, and we would not immediately confront Trujillo's army. . . . We had decided to land in three different places, and we would arrive by air, not by sea like in Cayo Confites."[101] About sixty men would participate in the invasion.

At Arévalo's behest, the Dominican exiles were trained at Guatemalan mil-itary facilities and were given the well-traveled weapons of Cayo Confites. Since President Prío, who replaced Grau in 1948, would not allow the rebels' planes to refuel in Cuba while en route to the Dominican Republic, Arévalo helped to persuade senior Mexican officials to permit refueling at the military airport of Cozumel in Yucatán.[102] Thus, while Figueres apparently contributed a small amount of money, and Prío a lame expression of sympathy, Arévalo was the only president to give active assistance to those fighting against the dictators. (The democratic government of Venezuela had been overthrown in November 1948.)

The Dominicans' plan was as foolhardy as it was brave. Due to bad weather and poor coordination at Cozumel, only one of the six planes of the invading squadron reached the Dominican Republic, landing near the town of Luperón on June 19, 1949, with fifteen men aboard, including the pilots. Had ten times their number arrived, disaster would have been inevitable. The underground no longer existed; some of its members had been killed, others were in jail, and those who had escaped detection were trying to forget that they had ever dared to plot against Trujillo.

The rebels who landed near Luperón were desperately alone. Within a few hours, ten had been killed. The others became Trujillo's prisoners; their public trial would expose the machinations of "international communism" (and of Moscow's puppet, Arévalo) against the peace-loving democracy of *Generali-simo* Trujillo.[103] The tragedy of Luperón closed the parenthesis of hope that had opened in 1944. The Caribbean Legion had fought its last battle.

Washington welcomed its demise. By the late 1940s the Truman administra-tion considered Trujillo and Somoza to be stalwart members of the inter-American family. Their anticommunism and their loyalty to the United States were above reproach, something that could be said neither of Arévalo nor,

---

[101] Arvelo, *Cayo Confite*, pp. 122–23; see also Ornes, *Desembarco*, pp. 30–31.

[102] See Arvelo, *Cayo Confite*, pp. 130, 133, and Ornes, *Desembarco*, pp. 152–55. Confirmed by interviews with Fortuny, Charnaud and María de Arbenz.

[103] In addition to many of the sources listed above in n. 85, see Crassweller, *Trujillo*, pp. 241–42; Dominican Republic, *White Book*, pp. 105–49; Rodríguez Loeche, "Por qué fracasó."

Washington believed, of the exiles of the Caribbean Legion. These "political malcontents"[104] threatened the *Pax Americana* with their plots and counterplots. They had sown division among the countries of the area, distracting them from the all-consuming East-West confrontation. The turmoil provoked by the Caribbean exiles, lamented Secretary of State Dean Acheson in a September 1949 address, had created a "situation . . . repugnant to the entire fabric of the inter-American system." The sacred principle of nonintervention had been violated, and the "United States could not be faithful to its international obligations if it did not condemn it in the strongest terms."[105]

Repeatedly in 1948 and 1949, the U.S. embassy had urged Arévalo to renounce his support of the Caribbean Legion; repeatedly, he had denied all involvement. Washington knew these denials to be untrue. In calmer times, U.S. officials would have explained Guatemala's behavior in the same way that they had explained Cuba's involvement in the Cayo Confites expedition: a mixture of adventurism, naïveté, and hostility to the tropical dictators. But this was not 1947, and Arévalo was not Grau. Moreover, Washington harbored new doubts about the Caribbean Legion: it was in the communists' interest, the argument ran, to create turmoil and dissension in the region. Might not, then, communist agents be at work in the Caribbean Legion?

This was, noted a major intelligence report, another ambiguous situation in which Guatemalan foreign policy could be explained either by antidictatorial inclinations or by communist proclivities.[106] (This was also the case, for instance, with Guatemala's opposition to Franco.) And the latter possibility was particularly credible because Foreign Minister Muñoz Meany, whose communist sympathies were beyond doubt, was, reported Ambassador Patterson, " 'up to his neck' in Caribbean Legion affairs." [107] It was, recalls a CIA analyst, "one of those areas where there was disagreement within the intelligence community."[108] At times, however, the tension between the different interpretations gave way to a less complicated conclusion: the communists "have influenced the [Guatemalan] Government to support the so-called 'Caribbean Legion,' " asserted the undersecretary of state in a September 1950 memorandum to Truman.[109] (The Communist Party of Guatemala begged to differ: it considered Arévalo's "support for the reactionary Figueres in Costa Rica" to be one of his major sins.)[110]

[104] "Current Relations with Guatemala," May 1950, *FRUS*, 1950, 2:899.

[105] "Waging Peace in the Americas," Sept. 10, 1949, *State Department Bulletin*, 21:462–66, quoted from p. 463. For a stinging rejoinder, see Bosch, "Errores."

[106] "Guatemala: Communist Influence," (see n. 64 above), pp. 63–65.

[107] Patterson to SecState, May 12, 1949, *FRUS*, 1949, 2:445.

[108] Interview with Dillon.

[109] Webb to Truman, Sept. 9. 1950, *FRUS*, 1950, 2:912.

[110] "Arévalo, presidente demócrata," *Octubre*, Mar. 7, 1951, p. 1. See also Alvarado Arellano, *Apuntes*, p. 15.

In its indignation with those who dared violate the principle of nonintervention without U.S. permission, and blinded by its bias, Washington failed to see that Arévalo had helped the anticommunist and pro-American Figueres to overthrow the only government in the hemisphere that still accepted the Communist party as an ally; it also failed to see that the leaders of the Caribbean Legion opposed communism and would side with the United States against Soviet imperialism. Indeed, the secret *Pacto del Caribe* had stated, with Arévalo's approval, that the members of the future Democratic Alliance of the Caribbean would "ally themselves in perpetuity with the United States and Mexico for the common defense."[111]

[111] Art. 9 of the *Pacto del Caribe*.

CHAPTER 6

The United States and Arévalo: The U.S. Response

BEING a sincere nationalist, Arévalo could never have been the malleable friend that the United States expected the president of a banana republic to be. Yet he had hoped to maintain cordial relations with Washington. The rhetoric of Spiritual Socialism notwithstanding, ideology did not separate Arévalo from the Americans, for he believed in capitalism and sharply condemned communism. His opposition to Soviet imperialism made him all the more ready to accept the geopolitical reality that Guatemala was in the U.S. sphere of influence. Arévalo asked only that his country begin to develop from satellite to ally, and he sought to restrain the American companies that dominated Guatemala's economy.

But imperial attitudes are long in dying. Perhaps the most striking aspect of U.S. behavior toward the Arévalo regime was its self-righteousness. U.S. officials were convinced that legitimate American interests were being victimized. While they readily conceded that Ubico had been "one of the most ruthless of all Guatemalan dictators,"[1] they held up their relations with Ubico as exemplary. Given this model, Assistant Secretary of State Edward Miller was correct in emphasizing the "growing lack of concern of the Guatemalan Government for the traditional good relations between the two countries"; nor was Undersecretary James Webb wrong when he stated that "Guatemala currently was not following its traditional policy of cooperation with the U.S."[2] Washington's conviction that it had observed a "policy of patience and forbearance" vis-à-vis Guatemala[3] was sincere, as was its indignation when, in March 1950, Arévalo requested the recall of Ambassador Patterson because of his persistent meddling in Guatemala's internal affairs. This unprecedented demand was seen as one more example of Guatemala's hostility, patently inspired by the communists. Patterson was clearly innocent. He had merely executed his superiors' policy to "support the legitimate aspirations of the Guatemalan people"[4] and to respect that country's sovereignty. The *New York Times* joined the chorus of critics:

> The present Guatemalan Government arose out of a revolt against a particularly unsavory dictator. This revolt had at first some promising features. Now it seems fairly

[1] "Current Relations with Guatemala," May 1950, *FRUS*, 1950, 2:898.

[2] Quotations from MemoTel, Aug. 2, 1949, *FRUS*, 1949, 2:659, and MemoConv, Sept. 16, 1949, ibid., p. 665.

[3] Wells to DOS, no. 89, July 22, 1950, p. 3, NA 714.00.

[4] SecState to President, Oct. 19, 1950, *FRUS*, 1950, 2:918.

obvious that the present leaders of the Guatemalan Government are permitting themselves to be manipulated by Communist revolutionaries. They fail to realize—or for political purposes refuse to admit—that the United States is not trying to block social and economic progress, but is interested rather in seeing that Guatemala becomes a liberal democracy and not a totalitarian slave state. We want to be friends with the Guatemalan people, but we do not believe the road to friendship lies through the uncomplaining acceptance of insults and discriminations. We applaud the State Department for its categorical rejection of such a policy.[5]

Unable to discern the blessings of traditional U.S.-Guatemalan relations, Arévalo saw in the behavior of the Truman administration neither generosity nor forbearance, but intolerance and contempt. If Arévalo had never been the Americans' friend by Washington's standards, by the time he left the presidency he was not their friend by any standard.[6] The same evolution marked the leaders of the revolutionary parties. Their bitter frustration, fueled by their impotence vis à vis their generous neighbor to the north, explains their occasional acts of defiance. At the Central American and Caribbean games in Guatemala City in February 1950, the Puerto Rican athletes were honored with a white flag bearing the Puerto Rican shield rather than the Stars and Stripes, and a military band played "La Borinqueña" instead of the "Star Spangled Banner."[7] The cooperative education program established in 1945 with the U.S. Institute of Inter-American Affairs was not renewed in 1950,[8] and the Guatemalan Congress postponed the ratification of the 1947 Rio Treaty until September 1950, a delay that was harshly criticized by Truman and was explained by ARA as "a pertinent example of the influence on government thinking by communist-minded individuals."[9] (In a recent study, Richard Im-

[5] "The Guatemalan Incident" (edit.), Apr. 8, 1950, p. 12. A rare exception to the condemnation of Guatemala in the American press was the *Nation*. ("The Shape of Things," edit., Apr. 22, 1950, pp. 358–59.)

[6] See Arévalo's speech on the day of Arbenz's inauguration, *DCA*, Mar. 15, 1951, pp. 3, 6.

[7] See "No se espera ninguna protesta de Patterson," *El I*, Feb. 27, 1950, p. 1; "Especulación sobre la ejecución de 'El Borinqueño,' " *DCA*, Feb. 27, 1950, p. 8; "Guatemala Snubs U.S. with Music," *NYT*, Feb. 27, 1950, p. 1; "Guatemalan Band Sounds Note of Harmony for U.S.," *NYT*, Feb. 28, 1950, p. 19; "Pulling Uncle's Whiskers," *Newsweek*, Mar. 13, 1950, p. 46; "Musical Disharmony," *Senior Scholastic*, Mar. 18, 1950, p. 8. La Borinqueña is a popular Puerto Rican song.

[8] For the Guatemalan decision, see Inman, *A New Day*, pp. 53–54, and González Orellana, *Historia de la educación*, p. 420. For the U.S. reaction, see Bennett, "Some Aspects of Communist Penetration in Guatemala," Mar. 23, 1950, pp. 17–19. On the program itself, see Griffith, "A Recent Attempt"; Casey, "Indigenismo," pp. 323–38; González Orellana, *Historia de la educación*, pp. 414–22.

[9] "Some Aspects of Communist Penetration" (see n. 8 above), p. 13. See also

merman argues that "Guatemala's opposition to the Rio Pact stemmed from its longstanding controversy over control of Belize," then a British colony. As he correctly notes, when Guatemala finally ratified the pact, it reserved its right to liberate the territory by any means. This amendment was rejected, and therefore the ratification was withheld.[10] But the delay had had nothing to do with Belize. In fact, Mario Fuentes Peruccini, chairman of the Foreign Relations Committee of the Guatemalan Congress, did not even mention Belize when explaining the delay; he stated merely that the committee had been preoccupied with more urgent matters. The Belize issue was raised only on the day before the final vote on the ratification.)[11]

To wary U.S. officials, these actions were further proof of communist influence. But to what extent was the Guatemalan government dominated by the communists? To those who sought to unravel the mysteries of Guatemalan politics, "the biggest enigma" was Arévalo.[12] "On occasion," U.S. officials conceded, he had adopted repressive measures against "overt manifestations of communist tendencies,"[13] but as U.S. suspicions waxed, the significance given to these measures waned. Arévalo deported very few communists relative to the number Washington had branded as Reds. (And on one occasion— "significantly"—he gave $100 "out of his private funds" to two Salvadoran communists prior to their deportation, which he had ordered.)[14]

Arévalo did condemn communism in his speeches and writings, but "these protestations of devotion to purely democratic principles," noted Chargé Wells, were "more and more . . . difficult to reconcile" with his friendship with "international communists" such as the Chilean Pablo Neruda. Neruda had not only been allowed to visit Guatemala, but he had been treated "virtually as a state guest."[15]

Two different views of democracy were clashing. In the United States the anticommunist witch-hunt was well under way. Not only was the party per-

---

FRUS, 1950, 2:866, 909, 920, 925–27. For Truman's remarks, see DOS, *Press Releases*, no. 29, Jan. 11, 1950.

[10] Immerman, *CIA in Guatemala*, p. 94.

[11] For Fuentes Peruccini's declaration, see "Pacto de Rio será suscrito próximamente," *El I*, Feb. 20, 1950, p. 1. The best coverage of the congressional debate on the ratification is by *El I*: "En brillante jornada ratifícase el tratado de Rio de Janeiro," Sept. 20, 1950, p. 1; "Reserva sobre Belice y Tratado de Rio debaten hoy finalmente en el Congreso," Sept. 21, 1950, p. 1; "Tratado de Rio sobre ruedas," Sept. 22, 1950, p. 1.

[12] Wells to SecState, no. 170, Mar. 31, 1949, p. 2, NA 814.00B.

[13] OIR, "Guatemala: Communist Influence," Oct. 23, 1950, p. 51, NA.

[14] Ibid., p. 39.

[15] Wells to DOS, Nov. 15, 1950, *FRUS*, 1950, 2:922. See also MemoConv, May 12, 1950, ibid., p. 886, and "Guatemala: Communist Influence" (see n. 13 above), p. 37.

secuted, but so too were individual communists and fellow travelers of every shade; no true American could have any ties, personal or professional, with them. McCarthyism antedated the notoriety of the man and continued well after him. But Arévalo, the obscure president of a banana republic, refused to humor Washington's paranoia. Anticommunism did not blind him, nor did it blind most of the revolutionary leaders. They believed a communist could be an honest and honorable person; he could even be a friend, as the Chilean communist César Godoy was Arévalo's friend. In Neruda they saw genius, not depravity.[16]

It was difficult for Arévalo and the revolutionary leaders to take the Red threat seriously when there were so few communists in Guatemala. Had the communists conspired against the country's first democratic government, Arévalo would have moved against them. "Their identities are known," he told Wells. "Come a crisis, they would be rounded up in twenty-four hours."[17] The communists, however, were not the plotters; the plotters were the pillars of the upper class.

American officials could not imagine that the president of a banana republic might hold a broader view of political democracy than did they; they also believed that communist influence in Guatemala was more pervasive than Arévalo claimed. His lofty anticommunist rhetoric rang hollow to them and did not mask the truth: "Arévalo and company . . . are responsible for inviting, yielding to, and instigating the move toward communism."[18]

While the indictment appeared devastating, the verdict was not yet in. "There was a lot of debate at all levels in the U.S. embassy as to whether

[16] Even *El I*, ever sensitive to the communist threat, was not critical of Neruda's visits to Guatemala in 1949 and 1950. See "Neruda viene al país," July 12, 1949, p. 1; "Pablo Neruda se reunió con la gente de prensa," Apr. 16, 1950, p. 1; "Homenaje de normalistas para Neruda," Apr. 21, 1950, p. 1.

Godoy had been a close friend of Arévalo since 1928. He was then a fervent anticommunist, something that he continued to be for many years. In 1944, Arévalo writes, Godoy told him that he was about to join the Communist party—"It is your business, César: these are personal matters." Godoy first visited Guatemala in 1945 to attend Arévalo's inauguration. He returned on two or three occasions in the late 1940s as Arévalo's guest. (He came from Mexico where he was living in exile following the anticommunist persecution unleashed by President Gabriel González Videla in Chile.) (Arévalo, *La Argentina*, quoted from p. 506. See also ibid., pp. 73, 76–77, 80, 82, and Arévalo, *El candidato*, pp. 60, 65, 638.) For U.S. indignation at Arévalo's friendship with Godoy, see Wells, "Cesar Godoy Urrutia, Chilean Communist," July 5, 1949, RG84 GR, Box 217, NA-S; Wells to Wise, Oct. 7, 1949, p. 2, NA 814.00B; Wells to DOS, Nov. 15, 1950, *FRUS*, 1950, 2:922.

[17] Wells to DOS, July 7, 1950, *FRUS*, 1950, 2:906.

[18] Siracusa, "Summary of Statements Made by Mr. Siracusa in Presentation of Guatemalan Situation," p. 17, enclosed in Siracusa to Patterson, Aug. 22, 1949, RG84 GR, Box 216, NA-S.

Arévalo and his government were communist, crypto-communist, under communist influence or not communist at all,'' recalls an embassy official.[19] The embassy's views were not always consistent. An extreme mood was reflected in a November 3, 1949, report by the Guatemala desk officer of the State Department:

> Many sources allege that the present Government of Guatemala is Communist (Moscow)-directed. When I visited there recently our Embassy did not go so far as that but did characterize the Guatemalan government as ''almost'' in that category and certainly as a menace to Inter-American unity and defense. Furthermore, some Embassy officers maintained that the present Guatemalan government is so far involved with international Communism that there is no possibility of its disentanglement.[20]

At other times more sober counsel prevailed. The embassy's most influential official, Milton Wells, pointed out in May 1948 that ''the saying 'one is known by the company he keeps' definitely adds to the case against Arévalo'' and compiled a long list of Arévalo's sins. And yet, his conclusion was equivocal: ''On balance, the writer is convinced that, despite these disturbing circumstances, the record does not make a closed case against Arévalo for alleged Communism. It is felt that he is more of a political opportunist of the extreme left.''[21]

With abrupt swings toward greater pessimism, this ''centrist'' view prevailed, both in the embassy and in Washington, for the remaining two years of the Arévalo presidency. Despite their fears and their irritation, U.S. officials conceded occasionally in 1949 and 1950 that Arévalo and his government could act in a constructive manner. In 1949, Guatemala renewed the agreement allowing two U.S. military missions (air force and army) to operate in the country. And in September 1950, the Guatemalan Congress finally ratified the Rio Treaty by an overwhelming majority ''over stubborn communist opposition.'' Furthermore after the Korean War broke out in June 1950, a July 14 memo stated, ''while equivocal at first, Guatemala has since given evidence of support for the United Nations and for the United States.''[22] In the following weeks, at the UN General Assembly, the Guatemalan Foreign Minister condemned ''the aggression perpetrated upon the Republic of Korea'' and reiterated that Guatemala ''fully supports the Security Council's timely and vigorous action'' (the dispatch of troops to Korea), while on Arévalo's behalf the Guatemalan ambassador informed the State Department that his

[19] Interview with Steins.

[20] Oakley to Miller, Nov. 3, 1949, p. 1, NA 814.00B.

[21] AmEmG, ''Communism in Guatemala,'' pp. 15–16, enclosed in Wells to SecState, no. 217, May 6, 1948, NA 814.00B.

[22] Quotations from Wells to DOS, Oct. 19, 1950, *FRUS*, 1950, 2:920, and Mann to Barber, July 14, 1950, ibid., pp. 908–9.

country, "was one hundred percent behind the United States and the United Nations, that if the United States needed bases in Guatemala it could have them and that Guatemala was prepared to make available to the United Nations men for the armed forces if needed. . . . He had been authorized to put the President's offer in the form of a note if the Department so desired."[23]

These developments should have reassured U.S. officials; instead they confused them and strengthened their belief that, whatever his precise ideology, Arévalo was "a master at intrigue despite his protestations of being 'just a simple school teacher.' "[24] This, at least, was an accurate perception.

Amid their confusion and their suspicions, U.S. officials acknowledged that the communists faced formidable obstacles in Guatemala. While "influential both within the Government and without, especially in the labor unions," the communists were fewer than five hundred, and their influence rested on "the personal patronage of Arévalo or members of his immediate official family."[25] They faced countervailing forces, including the Church, the upper class, and, above all, the Guatemalan armed forces—"the key to the situation," stressed the embassy.[26]

U.S. reporting on the Guatemalan military was bizarre—yet consistent with the Americans' confused analysis of the country. This is illustrated by the two major U.S. reports on communism in Guatemala in the Arévalo years: a 28-page study written by a senior embassy official in 1948, and a 120-page analysis prepared by the State Department's Office of Intelligence and Research in 1950. In both reports, the reader frequently has the feeling that the communists are in control of Guatemala, or at least that the threat is severe and accelerating. Pages are devoted to minor aspects of communist infiltration, such as the possible emigration to Guatemala of Spanish exiles who, U.S. officials suspect, would include a goodly number of Reds.[27] There follows a

[23] Quotations from speech by Foreign Minister Ismael González Arévalo to the UN General Assembly, Sept. 21, 1950, p. 2 (Truman Papers, OF, Box 1287/439, TL), and MemoConv (Goubaud, Mann, Clark), Aug. 14, 1950, p. 2, NA 714.00. See also "Guatemalan Chief Ties Nation to U.S.," *NYT*, July 18, 1950, p. 6, and "Declaraciones de nuestro canciller en Washington," *El I*, Sept. 22, 1950.

[24] "Some Aspects of Communist Penetration" (see n. 8 above), p. 8.

[25] Quotations from "Current Relations With Guatemala," May 1950, *FRUS*, 1950, 2:900, and Wells to DOS, Nov. 15, 1950, ibid., p. 922. For the figure of less than five hundred communists, see "Guatemala: Communist Influence" (see n. 13 above), p. 81.

[26] Kyle to SecState, no. 189, Apr. 21, 1948, p. 3, NA 814.00.

[27] "Communism in Guatemala" (see n. 21 above), pp. 11–12; "Guatemala: Communist Influence" (see n. 13 above), pp. 42–45. Concerning the suspect Spaniards, the Guatemalan official in Paris who dealt with them has written: "Our Finance Minister, Charnaud MacDonald, wanted to develop Guatemala's fishing industry, so we

brief treatment of the Guatemalan armed forces: less than half a page in the 1948 study, less than three in the lengthier 1950 report.[28] Suddenly, we enter the realm of objectivity.

While the Guatemalan upper class claimed that the army was deeply infiltrated by the communists, U.S. officials disagreed: "There is better reason to believe that Communist infiltration is nonconsequential," argued the May 1948 report, not a mean concession from an embassy so prone to see communists everywhere. Infiltration was "virtually non-existent at present," concluded the 1950 study.[29]

Throughout the Arévalo presidency, no U.S. report even raised the possibility that the communists had infiltrated the military; rather, the army was "a keystone of stability." The military, the embassy noted, occupies "a relatively privileged position: officers are well-paid, and many have handsomely profited since the 1944 Revolution."[30] Unlike labor unions and middle class politicians, the army was, for U.S. officials, a familiar institution, and one they had dealt with for decades. Their reports indicate a dearth of information about the internal politics of the military, but the Americans believed they understood the Guatemalan officer. He might be opportunistic and corrupt, but he was fundamentally anticommunist. And he would never risk his privileged status in suicidal adventures in the heart of the American sphere of influence. It was, as events would demonstrate, a sound assessment.

It was Arana, U.S. officials believed, who controlled the military, and he was the soul of moderation. "If anyone within the present Government is well disposed towards the United States, it is Arana." His anticommunism was "above question." Embassy reports consistently stressed "that his concern regarding communist infiltration in this country is genuine," praised his sympathetic stance in favor of American companies, and noted how "on more than one occasion . . . [he had] demonstrated undisguised antipathy toward certain Government policies and toward certain individuals (described as ex-

---

were told to get fishermen from among the Spanish refugees in France. After several meetings with officials of the Spanish government-in-exile, Spaniards began to arrive at our embassy. . . . Every single one claimed to be a fisherman. Frequently, they were accompanied by children and very beautiful women. They knew nothing about fish except how to eat them." (Pellecer, "Crónica," p. 84.) "All in all, about fifty Spaniards emigrated to Guatemala. Not one was a communist, or even a fisherman—except for the López family, who now own a fishmarket in Guatemala City called La Catalana." (Interview with Pellecer.)

[28] "Communism in Guatemala" (see n. 21 above), p. 20; "Guatemala: Communist Influence" (see n. 13 above), pp. 55, 71–72.

[29] Quotations from "Communism in Guatemala" (see n. 21 above), p. 20, and "Guatemala: Communist Influence" (see n. 13 above), p. 55.

[30] Quotations from Wells to SecState, no. 175, Apr. 1, 1949, p. 1, NA 814.00, and Kyle to SecState, no. 189, Apr. 21, 1948, p. 3, NA 814.00.

tremists or communist suspects) closely identified with Arévalo and his Government."[31] Arana had actively cultivated the embassy's goodwill, informing U.S. officials of his devotion to American ideals and his sympathy for American companies, yet he did not mention his schemes and plots. The evidence persuasively indicates that the United States was unaware of his bid for power in the weeks that preceded his death; indeed, in early June 1949 an embassy dispatch had indicated that Arana and Arbenz had "composed their differences."[32]

Arana's death and the defeat of his followers alarmed U.S. officials. Arana "has always represented [the] only positive conservative element in [the] Arévalo Administration and was determined [to] run for the Presidency," a senior ARA official lamented on July 19. "Regardless responsibility [for] assassination," cabled Patterson on July 20, "end result eliminates important moderate elements Government and strengthens Leftist materially"; the following day he warned: "Consensus . . . [is] that developments forecast sharp leftist trend within [the] government."[33]

Arbenz was now the strongest man in the military. U.S. officials did not know him well, but their initial sympathy for this "highly idealistic" officer had given way, as Arbenz had moved to the left, to wariness and distrust.[34] No one suggested that he was a communist or a communist sympathizer but, cabled Patterson on July 22, 1949, "Arbenz is associated politically with Par-

[31] Quotations from: Wells to de Zengotita, Nov. 15, 1948, RG84 GR, Box 192, NA-S; "Communism in Guatemala" (see n. 21 above), p. 20; Wells to SecState, no. 2757, Dec. 12, 1947, NA 814.00B; Wells to SecState, no. 175, Apr. 1, 1949, p. 1, NA 814.00. See also Col. Devine, "Intelligence Report" no. 52–46, Feb. 6, 1946, RG319 GF, Box 1582, NA-S; Donovan to SecState, no. 1538, July 10, 1946, RG84 CF, Box 14, NA-S; HQs Panama Canal Department, "Weekly Intelligence Summary" no. 262, July 9, 1947, RG319 ID 382208, NA-S; HQs Panama Canal Department, "Weekly Intelligence Summary" no. 265, July 30, 1947, RG319 ID 388826, NA-S; Donovan to SecState, no. 2601, Aug. 12, 1947, RG84 GR, Box 177, NA-S; Wells to de Zengotita, Nov. 19, 1948, RG84 GR, Box 192, NA-S.

[32] Wells to SecState, no. 267, June 3, 1949, p. 2, NA 814.00.

[33] Quotations from: Siracusa, "Guatemala Situation," July 19, 1949; Patterson to SecState, no. 324, July 20, 1949; Patterson to SecState, no. 327, July 21, 1949. All NA 814.00.

[34] Quoted from Affeld, "Confidential Biographic Data: Francisco Javier Arana," Apr. 4, 1945, p. 2, RG84 GR, Box 217, NA-S. See also: Woodward to SecState, no. 2426, Apr. 24, 1945, RG84 GR, Box 134, NA-S; Col. Devine, "Alleged Communist Penetrations," no. 104–46, Mar. 29, 1946, RG84 CF, Box 14, NA-S; Donovan to Newbegin, Aug. 1, 1946, NA 814.00; Enclosure no. 1 in Donovan to SecState, no. 2075, Jan. 2, 1947, NA 814.00; AmEmG, "Re: Guatemala Political," Feb. 26, 1947, p. 6, RG84 GR, Box 176, NA-S; HQs Panama Canal Department, "Weekly Intelligence Summary" no. 262, July 9, 1947, RG319 ID 382208, NA-S.

tido Acción Revolucionaria and is identified with the more radical fringe of the Arévalo regime.''[35] These were not good references.

U.S. fears quickly subsided. As early as July 29, 1949, an ARA official, Ernest Siracusa, who had a ''close association with the situation in Guatemala,''[36] struck a far more positive note. While not excluding the possibility that ''Arbenz may decide to string along with Arévalo, thereby making the possibility of further leftism very real,'' Siracusa outlined a more comforting scenario, based on his conclusion that Arbenz was dishonest and shallow:

> Arbenz is not, in my opinion, a person with any deep seated intellectual alliance to the leftist cause, and, as such, no real sympathy for the lower classes or for the many outside communists who have infiltrated Guatemala.
>
> Arbenz is, in my opinion, essentially an opportunist who has strung along with the Arévalo bandwagon principally as a means of accumulating personal wealth and of giving ascendancy to his own political star. He has no admixtures of Indian blood, and is basically of an autocratic character.
>
> . . . Arbenz seems strongly to want to be president and he has a wife, with strong ideas, who wants to be first lady.
>
> The conclusion is this: Arbenz . . . might effect a coup d'état, using as his excuse the necessity of saving Guatemala from Communism.
>
> Not being an intellectual nor an honest leftist, Arbenz would make of himself a strong dictator, a necessary thing if he is to rid Guatemala of its leftist penetration. He will also have to be a strong dictator in order to remove from Guatemala some of the truly liberal gains of the revolution.
>
> My estimation of Arbenz is that he is the type of man who could and might do just this, and who could be truly ruthless if necessary.
>
> My judgment of him is that I don't and never have liked him, as a man. He has appeared to me to be shifty and not trustworthy.
>
> Such an eventuality would probably mean the end of the coercion of U.S. capital, a return of Guatemala to cooperation with the United States, and the end of any personal freedom in Guatemala.[37]

The thrust of the argument was clear: Arbenz was an unsavory character with whom the United States could work well. Siracusa's assessment was echoed within the State Department, where another ''Guatemala watcher'' argued two weeks later: ''If Arbenz continues to ally himself with the leftists, this will probably be only a temporary move in the interests of expediency. . . .

[35] Patterson to SecState, no. 385, July 22, 1949, p. 1, NA 711.14.

[36] Wise to Miller, July 29, 1949. Siracusa had been second secretary of the U.S. embassy in Guatemala until Mar. 14, 1949. In July 1949, he was the Guatemala desk officer.

[37] Siracusa to Wise, July 29, 1949, NA 814.00. See also Siracusa to Patterson, Aug. 3, 1949, RG84 GR, Box 216, NA-S.

(My long run guess is that Arbenz no longer has anything to gain by alliance with leftists, that a clash will occur from his pressure to contain them, and that he will, sooner or later, use this as a pretext for overt action in his own interests.)"[38]

Abandoning his earlier pessimism, Patterson heartily concurred. After the defeat of the *Aranistas*, he wrote to UFCO's president:

> The first inclination of most people here was that it forecast a sharper leftward move in the Government. All along I have felt that this is not necessarily the case because of the kind of man I believe Arbenz to be. He is an opportunist with no deep seated leftist convictions. . . . Since he wants to be President and is clever, his best bet is an alliance with the United States. Therefore, if he remains in the saddle it means better results for American interests and the possible eradication of the foreign Communist element. In any event, I believe that United Fruit and other interests will not suffer because of the Revolution.[39]

Over the ensuing months, through the presidential elections of November 1950 and into the first weeks of the Arbenz presidency, this became the dominant view of U.S. officials, although a slight feeling of uneasiness persisted. From Guatemala, the State Department received comforting reports of conversations that senior embassy officials held with Arbenz between August 1949 and March 1951.[40] It is difficult to determine what most deluded U.S. officials in these conversations. Was it what Arbenz said, though judging from the embassy's reports he seldom ventured beyond banalities? Or was it, as his wife suggests, the polite silence with which he listened to the Americans' diatribes about developments in Guatemala?[41] In any case, U.S. officials were certainly led astray by their own bias. They had already decided that Arbenz was a man devoid of strong political beliefs. Moreover, he was a military officer: a left-wing colonel was an unknown species in Central America.

In August 1949, Milton Wells provided a rare glimpse of a different Arbenz:

> With obvious sincerity and clarity of language Colonel Arbenz spoke at length on the basic aims of the 1944 Revolution and the Arévalo regime—which, in simple

---

[38] Bennett to Barber and Miller, Aug. 9, 1949, p. 1, NA 711.14.

[39] Patterson to Zemurray (president of United Fruit), Aug. 11, 1949, Patterson Papers, Box 5, TL. See also Patterson to Miller and Patterson to Siracusa, both Aug. 12, 1949, RG84 GR, Box 216, NA-S.

[40] See esp. Patterson to SecState, no. 385, July 22, 1949, NA 711.14; Patterson to SecState, no. 417, Aug. 3, 1949, NA 711.14; Wells to SecState, no 433, Aug. 11, 1949, NA 814.00; Wells to SecState, no. 435, Aug. 12, 1949, NA 711.14; Wells to DOS, no. 395, Mar. 31, 1950, NA 611.14; CIA, "Guatemala," SR-46, July 27, 1950, pp. 45–46, Truman Papers, President's Secretary's File, Intelligence File, Box 261, TL; Wells to DOS, Nov. 15, 1950, *FRUS*, 1950, 2:922–25; Wells to Clark, Jan. 22, 1951, NA 714.00.

[41] Interview with María de Arbenz; also interviews with Fortuny and Guerra Borges.

terms, are to bring social and economic betterment to the people, and to establish a decent, democratic way of life, which will make impossible the old-style military coups d'etat and personal dictatorships under which the people have suffered for generations. It must be understood, he argued . . . that the laws of the land are general, affecting Guatemalan and United States firms and persons alike.[42]

This image of a compassionate man was utterly overlooked. Questions were raised neither by Wells who wrote the report, nor by those who read it. Arbenz's opportunism had become an article of faith for U.S. officials. This opportunist would have few qualms, they argued, at betraying his friends from the PAR and organized labor (including the communists) after he had used them to win the elections. He would sacrifice them in order to curry the favor of the dominant player—the United States. The military would welcome the reversal of Arévalo's radical policies: "The Army is going to back Arbenz in a determined anti-Communist policy," reported Wells. Thus, the embassy welcomed Arbenz's presidential victory with "restrained optimism."[43] On February 16, 1951, the embassy informed the State Department that the communists "are probably seeking to strengthen themselves against the possibility of finding themselves in disfavor with the future [Arbenz] administration."[44]

Thus, the Truman administration reassured itself that under Arbenz the Guatemalan army would remain a formidable bulwark against communism. Arbenz was a dishonest and unsavory character, but self-interest would drive him into the familiar embrace of Washington. Arana's death, which had initially unnerved the Americans, was not as disruptive as they had feared. The military, Guatemala's most powerful institution, was still healthy—that is, anti-communist.

It is this conviction, held before Arana's death and reestablished soon after it, that explains why, their indignation and their concern notwithstanding, U.S. officials did not plot to overthrow Arévalo. But short of that, they exerted whatever diplomatic, economic, and psychological pressure they could on the Guatemalan regime. They were hampered by two constraints. They wanted to avoid causing undue damage to the inter-American system and the most obvious sanction—the denial of economic aid—was hardly an option, given the minimal amount of aid offered to Latin America at the time. "Fortunately or

[42] MemoConv (Arbenz, Kielhauer, Patterson, Wells), Aug. 9, 1949, quoted from pp. 1–2, enclosed in Wells to SecState, no. 435, Aug. 12, 1949, NA 711.14.

[43] Wells to DOS, Nov. 15, 1950, *FRUS*, 1950, 2:923, 925. It was "the firm belief of the American Embassy . . . that he [Arbenz] would move to the Right," the British Legation reported. ("Extract from Guatemala Report dated 4th May, 1951," RG84 CF, Box 15, NA-S.)

[44] Wardlaw to DOS, no. 839, Feb. 16, 1951, p. 2, NA 714.00.

unfortunately," an embassy official moaned, "our most obvious weapons are useless."[45]

ARA officials briefly considered arraigning Guatemala before the Organization of American States, but they dismissed the idea because even they realized that none but the most servile of banana republics would have endorsed the proposition that Arévalo was the aggressor against the United States and a threat to inter-American security. In State Department parlance, this was translated into the bizarre observation that "even though Latin American states might feel a deep concern with developments in Guatemala, there would doubtless be many which would censor any United States act or policy which was or appeared to be interventionist."[46] Obviously, it had not occurred to U.S. officials that their relentless diplomatic pressure on the Arévalo regime might already be considered interventionist. Until 1950, the Truman administration provided only insignificant amounts of aid to Latin America; a termination of the tiny U.S. program of technical assistance to Guatemala, the State Department concluded, would have little practical effect on that country, while supplying potent fodder for leftist propaganda. Hence, a policy of "selective withholding of cooperation" was adopted by default.[47] This policy was extended to military affairs. Beginning in 1949, the United States imposed a systematic embargo on arms sales to Guatemala.[48]

Greater opportunities to punish the Arévalo administration arose in 1950, after Congress had approved Truman's Point Four foreign aid program. "Until such time as the overall situation in Guatemala changes," Secretary Acheson decreed, no Point Four money would be given to it.[49] In 1950 the World Bank,

[45] Siracusa (see n. 18 above), p. 20.

[46] MemoConv, Dec. 29, 1950, *FRUS*, 1950, 2:930 (quoted), and "Current Relations with Guatemala," May 1950, ibid., p. 900.

[47] Clark to Wise, Oct. 6, 1949, NA 711.14. See also de Zengotita to Barber, Woodward and Daniels, June 7, 1949, NA 711.14; MemoConv (Patterson, Daniels, Barber, de Zengotita), June 8, 1949, NA 814.00; Wise to Barber and Miller, Aug. 1, 1949, NA 814.00; "Current Relations with Guatemala," May 1950, *FRUS*, 1950, 2:901. For a detailed example of the thinking behind this policy, see Siracusa (see n. 18 above), pp. 20–23.

[48] For the arms' embargo, which was not made public at the time, see Clark to Bennett, Feb. 6, 1950, NA 714.5; Clark to Mann, Sept. 13, 1950, NA 714.56; MemoConv (Mara, Clark), Oct. 25, 1950, NA Lot 57D95, Box 2. For a telling exchange, see Col. Deerwester to Ambassador, July 10, 1951, RG84 CF, Box 15, NA-S, and DOS, "Guatemalan Request for Defence Order Priority for Five Hundred 38 Calibre Revolvers," July 23, 1951, NA 714.5614. In the former, the U.S. air attaché "recommends, from the standpoint of necessity for law enforcement, that favorable consideration be given this request [for 500 pistols for the police force]"; in the latter, the powers that be in Washington and Ambassador Schoenfeld in Guatemala deny the request.

[49] SecState to AmEmG, Oct. 11, 1950, *FRUS*, 1950, 2:918.

in which U.S. influence was decisive, refused "a much-needed loan to Guatemala." As Assistant Secretary Miller later explained to Congress, the World Bank "sent a mission down there . . . to make some recommendations for loans. We asked [them] . . . not to do that, that we . . . would exercise the veto power against such loans."[50]

There was only one significant deviation from this pattern of niggardly aid. Between 1945 and 1951, Washington contributed $6 million to the construction of the Guatemalan portion of the Inter-American Highway, which would link Texas to Panama. The project was beneficial to Guatemala—but also to the United States, as Miller stressed in his forceful May 1950 congressional testimony.[51]

While there is no evidence that U.S. officials urged Arana to overthrow Arévalo, the tenor of U.S. reports in 1948 and 1949 (including those reports dealing with the possibility that Arana might seize power) indicates that such a move would not have been unwelcome; this was in stark contrast to U.S. reports in 1945 and 1946, which had expressed frank opposition to any military coup. It is evident that, at least after 1947, Arana was restrained by his own scruples and hopes, not by Washington. And when he finally acted in July 1949, he did so without informing the United States.

In May 1950, several months after Arana's death, UFCO's lobbyist Corcoran paid a visit to Thomas Mann, director of the State Department's Office of Middle American Affairs. "He had been turning over in his mind the possibility that the American companies might agree between themselves on some method to bring moderate elements into power in Guatemala," and he wanted to know whether the State Department "had any program for bringing about the election of a middle-of-the-road candidate" in the November presidential contest. His overture was rebuffed by Mann, who argued that any attempt to interfere in the elections would become known, causing a backlash in Guatemala and throughout Latin America, and that it would, in any case, prove ineffectual. U.S. policy, Corcoran was told, was to wait and see. "Although," Mann went on, "I would not like to try to guess what the policy in the future might be if it were definitively determined that the Guatemalan Government and people had fallen under the totalitarian control of communist elements."[52]

By the time this exchange took place, some U.S. officials had been advo-

[50] Quotations from "Red Shadow in Elections," *Newsweek*, Nov. 13, 1950, p. 52, and U.S. Congress, *HCFA*, p. 399. See also MemoConv (Consolo, Waterson, Miller, Cady, Wise), Dec. 14, 1949, RG84 GR, Box 217, NA-S.

[51] See Miller's testimony before the Senate Committee on Public Works, May 25, 1950, Miller Papers, Box 2, TL, and Patterson's testimony before the same committee, May 25, 1950, Patterson Papers, Box 5, TL. See also United Nations, *El transporte*, pp. 17–18.

[52] MemoConv, May 15, 1950, *FRUS*, 1950, 2:888–89.

cating another form of punishment for the wayward Guatemalans: "We should encourage outstanding newspapers and magazines to take an interest in happenings in Guatemala, to study them on the spot, and to report them forthrightly." In an August 1949 cable to the State Department, Ambassador Patterson welcomed the appearance of a highly critical article in the *Wall Street Journal*. (A few months later, in a letter to UFCO President Samuel Zemurray, Patterson also urged that there be "an all-out barrage in the United States Senate on the bad treatment of American capital in Guatemala.")[53] In the same vein, in the fall of 1950, UFCO's consultant Edward Bernays proposed that the company engage in a public relations offensive on the communist threat in Guatemala. UFCO executives, Bernays complains in his memoirs, were slow to appreciate the wisdom of his suggestions; and the offensive began in earnest only two years later; this delay, he concludes philosophically, "was not unusual in corporate life, where do-nothing is rather safer than taking a chance."[54] Apparently UFCO, though having lost none of its arrogance, was no longer the risk-taking company it once had been; it preferred to rely on the exertions of the State Department and on its own economic muscle in its dealings with Arévalo. "Companies, like people," an UFCO executive has remarked, "have most of their energy when they are young, and as they age they lose their potency. . . . When I joined United Fruit in 1952 . . . the company was already well into middle age and its arteries had started to harden."[55]

Still, whether on their own initiative or prodded by the State Department, the conservative *New York Herald Tribune* and the liberal *New York Times* decided to probe developments in Guatemala. The results were strikingly similar. In February 1950, the *Herald Tribune* published a five-part series by Fitzburgh Turner entitled "Communism in the Caribbean," which was followed in June by Will Lissner's *New York Times* series on the same subject, both front page news.[56] The two series closely echoed the views of the State Department, with shrill cries about the communist threat and unabashed praise of UFCO. Turner and Lissner were instant experts who hid their ignorance behind glibness. Reading their articles, one had the impression that Guatemala's communist agents (both foreign and native) had trooped into the journalists' hotel rooms to confess their dastardly schemes. More likely, however, the revelations came from more respectable sources: embassy officials, represen-

[53] Quotations from Siracusa (see n. 18 above), p. 22 and Patterson to Zemurray, Jan. 11, 1950, Patterson Papers, Box 5, TL. See also Wise to Barber and Miller, Aug. 1, 1949, RG84 GR, Box 216, NA-S; "Things in Guatemala," *WSJ*, Aug. 10, 1949, p. 1; Patterson to SecState, no. 445, Aug. 18, 1949, NA 711.14.

[54] Bernays, *Biography of an Idea*, p. 760.

[55] McCann, *American Company*, p. 14.

[56] Turner, "Communism in the Caribbean," *New York Herald Tribune*, Feb. 8–13, 1950, and Lissner, "Soviet Agents Plotting to Ruin Unity, Defenses of Americas," *NYT*, June 22–27, 1950.

tatives of the American companies, and upper-class Guatemalans. Lurid details laced the stories: "communist goons resembling New York mobsters bullied students, workers, intellectuals. . . . democrats lived in terror for their lives," and so on. And the moral: as a result of the persecution of American companies, the Guatemalan people suffered while, thanks to Truman's Point Four, business was booming elsewhere in Central America; while Arévalo connived with the communists, rulers like Somoza were looking after the welfare of their people. It was yellow journalism in the style of the 1890s, and it was also typical of American journalists dealing with banana republics in the late 1940s. Cold war paranoia and sheer ignorance were more powerful than all the manipulations of Edward Bernays and other skillful minions in the pay of United Fruit.

A systematic press campaign against Guatemala was not under way. To be sure, by 1949 and 1950 friendly references to the Arévalo regime were extremely rare; the most conspicuous example was an article in *The Nation* in January 1950.[57] Communist penetration of Guatemala and Guatemala's persecution of American companies were generally treated in tandem; even the liberal *Hispanic American Report*—the voice of Stanford University on Latin American affairs—heaped scorn on the "Red-stained" Arévalo, the "unmistakable party-line nature of many of his policies," and the "communist tendencies" of his government.[58] Guatemala, however, did not loom large in the American press. Between Lissner's diatribe and the end of Arévalo's term, only four major stories appeared. In *The Reporter*, Theodore Draper presented the Guatemalan government as naughty and inept, but not communist; compared to the other stories, this was restraint. The *Reader's Digest* exposed Guatemala's role in the communists' "global master-plan against the United States." The *Saturday Evening Post* revealed that *Arevalismo* was a "systematic effort to make the Guatemalan revolution follow the course of the October Revolution in Russia." And *Life* ran a five-page spread, replete with photographs, on "Sam the Banana Man," the generous, misunderstood Samuel Zemurray, president of UFCO.[59]

[57] Ovidio Gondi, "Chaos on Our Doorstep," Jan. 28, 1950, pp. 81–83. Gondi's article evoked a stern response from UFCO's President Zemurray. (See "La Frutera's Record," *The Nation*, Mar. 25, 1950, pp. 287–89.) On March 18, *The Nation* had published an article that combined a contemptuous critique of the Arévalo administration with an even harsher assessment of Turner's series in the *New York Herald Tribune*. (Ellis Ogle, "Communism in the Caribbean?" pp. 246–47.)

[58] Quotations from *Hispanic American Report*: Dec. 1950, p. 13; Mar. 1950, p. 12; Aug. 1950, p. 12.

[59] Draper, "The Minutemen of Guatemala," *The Reporter*, Oct. 24, 1950, pp. 32–35 and "How Red is Guatemala?" *The Reporter*, Nov. 7, 1950, pp. 23–27; J. P. McEvoy, "Trouble in Our Own Back Yard," *Reader's Digest*, Aug. 11, 1950, pp. 7–11 (quoted p. 10); Leigh White, "Red Threat on Our Tropic Frontier," *Saturday Eve-*

The Congress of the United States occasionally turned its attention to Arévalo's Guatemala. The august body first noticed the tiny country in February 1949. Two issues sparked the congressmen's interest: UFCO's travails and Truman's Point Four. Not surprisingly, the Massachusetts delegation led the attack. Senator Henry Cabot Lodge delivered the first broadside on February 14: UFCO was being persecuted in Guatemala "through actions which, I am informed, can be directly traced to Communist influences"; aid was a two-way street, conditioned on the principle of just and equal treatment— Guatemala had disqualified itself from the benefits of Point Four.[60] Within the month two other senators and three representatives shared their wisdom on Guatemalan affairs with Congress: UFCO was being persecuted, the company's record deserved strong praise, and the communists were scheming.[61]

After the congressional outburst of February 1949 and the settlement between UFCO and the unions in March, Congress was silent on Guatemala for the rest of the year. There was a lone exception: Senator Francis Myers, noting the *Diario de Centro América*'s (Guatemala's government daily) tribute to George Washington on the Fourth of July, placed a tribute to Guatemalan and Central American independence in the *Congressional Record*.[62] In 1950, only two congressmen spoke out in Congress about Guatemala. Spurred by the Patterson incident, Alexander Wiley, a prominent member of the Senate Foreign Relations Committee, warned that while "redder pastures appear in the distance in Europe and in China . . . right on this continent we have a red pasture." The same warning had been given in the House a few days earlier by Representative John McCormack, who combined his scathing attacks on the Arévalo administration with unabashed praise of United Fruit.[63]

For a Congress that was busy unmasking traitors at home and debating the "loss" of China, entanglement in Europe, and war in Korea, Guatemala was a minor and unglamorous issue, an issue, moreover, that could not be exploited for partisan purposes. The Republicans had no quarrel with the administration's handling of Guatemalan matters: even crusty Senator Wiley—at first suspicious that the State Department might not be 100 percent behind Patterson after the ambassador had been "booted out" of Guatemala "by a

---

ning Post, Oct. 28, 1950, pp. 24–25, 146, 148–49 (quoted from p. 148); John Kobler, "Sam The Banana Man," *Life*, Feb. 19, 1951, pp. 83–84, 87–88, 91–92, 94.

[60] Lodge (R-Mass), Feb. 14, 1949, *CR*-Senate, p. 1172.

[61] Claude Pepper (D-Fla), Feb. 17, 1949, ibid., pp. 1353–54; Lister Hill (D-Ala), Feb. 14, 1949, ibid., p. 1353; John McCormack (D-Mass), Feb. 21, 1949, *CR*-House, pp. 1463–64; Christian Herter (R-Mass), Feb. 24, 1949, ibid., p. 1496; Mike Mansfield (D-Mont), Feb. 21, 1949, ibid., p. 1498.

[62] Myers (D-Pa), Sept. 15, 1949, *CR*-Senate, p. 12936. For the article in *DCA*, see "Nuestro saludo a la patria de Washington y Roosevelt," July 2, 1949, p. 1.

[63] Wiley (R-Wisc), Apr. 27, 1950, *CR*-Senate, pp. 5879–81 (quoted from p. 5879); McCormack, Apr. 3, 1950, *CR*-House, pp. A2538–41.

Red controlled government''—was mollified by the visit of a State Department delegation to the office of his legislative assistant.[64]

Guatemala was not yet perceived as the Soviet beachhead in the Western Hemisphere. It remained *terra incognita* for the immense majority of Americans. To President Truman and the senior members of his administration, Guatemala was but an eddy in a sea of worries. Washington was willing to give the unsavory Arbenz a chance. But American patience was not infinite: ''If the Arbenz Administration fails to take a positive stand, public opinion in the United States and elsewhere in the Hemisphere would probably support a more direct approach to the problem,'' the State Department concluded.[65] The words were not vehement, but the implications were ominous.

[64] Wiley to Miller, Aug. 26, 1950, Truman Papers, OF, Box 1352/558, TL.
[65] MemoConv, Dec. 29, 1950, *FRUS*, 1950, 2:930.

CHAPTER 7

The World of Jacobo Arbenz

JACOBO ARBENZ betrayed the hopes of the Truman administration. Had he been the opportunist the Americans anticipated, had he been the cynic they expected, he would have used the power of the presidency to court the Americans. Had he chosen this path, it is difficult to see who could have stopped him. The officer corps was loyal and had no desire for more reforms; urban labor was weak and unarmed; the countryside was quiet. Arbenz could easily have imposed a pause in the revolution. Instead he advanced along an unprecedented and increasingly dangerous road. His presidency would be marked by three departures: agrarian reform, close ties with the Communist party, stubborn defiance of the United States. As he pressed forward, he lost touch with his original power base, the military. He became a lonely man who had to act on two levels: the private Arbenz who confided only in his wife and the leaders of the Communist party, and the public Arbenz who hid his true beliefs. This secretive and increasingly harried man accomplished a unique feat: the first true agrarian reform of Central America. As in a Greek tragedy, the more he accomplished, the closer he came to his destruction and the destruction of his dream. When he fell, in June 1954, he was mentally and physically exhausted.

Many explanations have been offered for the fate of this enigmatic man. Conservative critics have seen in him a man driven by ambition and greed. Liberal analysts have seen in him a well-intentioned reformer who became to some degree a prisoner of the communists' embrace. Radical authors have spurned him as a petty bourgeois who was either unwilling or unable to deepen the revolution.[1]

A major influence on Jacobo Arbenz, friends and foes agree, was his Salvadoran wife, María Vilanova. Indeed, some have described her husband as putty in her hands. Jacobo and María were, in fact, partners in a process of radicalization that began slowly and became increasingly rapid. They shared the same evolution, the same beliefs, and the same friends.

They met in 1938, while María was spending a few weeks in Guatemala, her mother's country. She was immediately attracted to the good-looking and se-

---

[1] See for instance Martz, *Communist Infiltration*; James, *Red Design*; Immerman, *CIA in Guatemala*; Schlesinger and Kinzer, *Bitter Fruit*; Cardoza y Aragón, *La Revolución Guatemalteca*; Jonas and Tobis, *Guatemala*.

rious young officer, who spoke and laughed little, but had, at times, "a smile that made me fall in love."[2]

And yet they seemed very different. From a rich Salvadoran family, María had studied in the United States, was relatively well read, liked classical music and painting, and combined a deep intellectual curiosity with a gregarious personality. Jacobo had never left Guatemala, showed little interest in the arts, and found it difficult to express his feelings. María recalls of their courtship:

> At times, I would ask him, "Do you like Beethoven?" There would be a silence. Then, very seriously, he would answer, "I have never heard Beethoven." I would ask him, "Do you like this book?" Again, silence, and then, always very serious, he would answer, "I have never read this book," and I would despair, and wonder, "Why am I falling in love with this man, so different from me, with whom I share so few interests?" But then, once, I asked him, "What would you like to be?" And very seriously he answered, "I would like to be a reformer," and then I thought, "Yes. We do have something very important in common."[3]

Neither could have explained what it meant to be a reformer or how and what one should reform. They simply shared a feeling that something was wrong, deeply wrong, in the society that surrounded them. They were married a few months later, in early 1939, without the permission of María's parents, who bitterly disapproved of their daughter's match with a penniless lieutenant. ("My family was furious and refused to have anything to do with us," recalls María.)[4] Jacobo was twenty-six and his bride twenty-four years old.

Two people who would deeply influence one another had joined together. María had enjoyed a comfortable youth, untroubled by family dramas. Her father, a rich landowner, sent her to the College of Notre Dame in Belmont, California, but at the onset of the Great Depression she had returned to El Salvador. The family was rich, but not rich enough to afford the luxury of maintaining a daughter in the United States during an economic crisis. In a few years she would marry, and a woman of her class would have no need to work. It was, on the face of it, a most banal story.[5]

Less banal was that María, who spent her summers on her father's estates, became uneasy about the desperate plight of the peasants. Her father's participation in the peasants' massacre of 1932 troubled her. ("He spoke of it in

---

[2] Interview with María de Arbenz.

[3] Interview with María de Arbenz.

[4] Interview with María de Arbenz. "Jacobo was slow to propose. At last, when I was just about to return to El Salvador, he asked me, 'Will you come back to Guatemala? I would like to marry you. But I can't right now because I don't earn enough.' I left for El Salvador. But once back home, I thought: 'Why wait? What do I care about money? Let's get married right away!' I went back to Guatemala and we got married without my family's approval."

[5] Interview with María de Arbenz.

such a matter of fact way . . . 'We killed so many.' '') And her grandmother's piety failed to reassure her. ("She went in her beautiful car to hand out old clothes and food to destitute peasants.") Something was terribly wrong, even though she hardly knew what and why.[6] These were just doubts, shadows of questions that a conventional marriage might well have stifled. Instead she met Arbenz.

Arbenz's youth had been far less comfortable and was scarred by personal tragedy. His father, a Swiss German, had come to Guatemala in 1901 and had settled in Quetzaltenango, the country's second city. There he had opened a pharmacy and married a middle-class Ladino woman. Born in 1913, Jacobo grew up in comfortable circumstances, with the cachet of a European father whose Nordic complexion he inherited. (He was, a 1950 CIA study noted, "of upper-class European ancestry.")[7] Then disaster struck: Jacobo's father became addicted to morphine. He neglected his business. The pharmacy went bankrupt and the family was forced to retire to a small estate in the vicinity of Quetzaltenango that a German friend put at their disposal "out of charity." This was a trauma the young Jacobo never forgot.[8]

The family's financial disaster meant that Jacobo could no longer hope to go to the university. "He would have liked to have been an economist or an engineer." He had no desire to enter the military, but if he won a scholarship he could get a free education at the Escuela Politécnica.[9] He applied, passed the entrance examinations, and in 1932 entered the academy as a cadet. Two years later, his father committed suicide.

In the Escuela Politécnica, Jacobo Arbenz was occasionally rebellious and always reserved. He was also "an exceptional student," in the words of a 1971 history published by the Guatemalan armed forces.[10] Excelling both in athletics and in academics, he became first sergeant, the highest honor to which a cadet could aspire and a distinction that only six other cadets achieved between 1924 and 1944.[11] Indeed, notes a fellow officer, "his abilities were such that the officers treated him with a respect which was rarely granted to a

[6] Interview with María de Arbenz.

[7] CIA, "Guatemala," SR-46, July 27, 1950, p. 39, Truman Papers, President's Secretary's File, Intelligence File, Box 261, TL.

[8] Interviews with María de Arbenz (quoted), Fortuny, and Rolz Bennett, a childhood friend of Arbenz. For a biographical sketch of Arbenz, see Zea Carrascosa, *Semblanzas*, pp. 283–86. García Añoveros, *Jacobo Arbenz*, is the only biography of Arbenz, but it is disappointing and perfunctory.

[9] Interviews with María de Arbenz (quoted), Fortuny, Rolz Bennett, and Guerra Borges.

[10] Zea Carrascosa, *Semblanzas*, p. 284.

[11] On Arbenz as a cadet, see ibid., pp. 283–84; Samayoa Coronado, *La Escuela Politécnica*, 2:96, 98; Morazán, "Apuntes," pp. 248–57, 466–73, 522–33. For a list of the first sergeants between 1924 and 1944, see Escuela Politécnica, *Centenario*.

cadet.'' This respect was shared by Major John Considine, the American director of the Escuela Politécnica, and the other U.S. officers who served in the academy.[12]

Arbenz graduated in December 1935, having so impressed his superiors that they had him transferred back to the academy in early 1937, when a position became vacant. In the interval Arbenz experienced the squalid life of a junior officer in Ubico's army, serving first at Fort San José in the capital and then in the tiny army garrison in the small town of San Juan Sacatepéquez "under an illiterate colonel."[13] While at San José, he, like the other officers, had to lead squads of soldiers who escorted chain gangs of convicts (including political prisoners) to perform forced labor. For Arbenz, "it was yet another trauma; he felt like a *capataz*." It was then that he first met Arana, who was stationed at Fort Matamoros, also in the capital. They met while watching their convicts, jailers performing a degrading task.[14]

From March 1937 until the fall of Ubico, Arbenz was stationed at the Escuela Politécnica, an oasis in the grim world of the Guatemalan armed forces. "In a dismal lethargic Army," the U.S. military attaché reported, "it is the only alert unit."[15] Instead of supervising convicts and serving under illiterate colonels, he was in daily contact with competent military officers—the Americans on loan to the academy. In addition to his other duties, he became a professor, teaching cadets a wide range of courses (from military subjects to history and physics) and, in the process, broadening his own limited education. In 1943 he was promoted to captain and placed in command of the entire corps of cadets. It was the third highest position in the academy and "one of the most prestigious posts to which a young officer could aspire."[16]

The brilliant cadet had grown into a superb officer. Even colleagues who later turned against him remember his "magnetism," and readily acknowledge that he was "a born leader"[17]—characteristics that helped him, in later

[12] Interviews with Maj. Paz Tejada (quoted), Lt. Col. Mendizabal, and Cols. Guillén, Lorenzana, Mendoza, and González Siguí.

[13] Quoted from interview with Fortuny. See also Zea Carrascosa, *Semblanzas*, p. 283, and Samayoa Coronado, *La Escuela Politécnica*, 2:99.

[14] Interviews with Fortuny (quoted) and María de Arbenz. See also Lt. Enrique de León Aragón, "Situaciones sobre el origen de la Revolución del Veinte de Octubre," *El Libertador*, Oct. 23, 1945, p. 10.

[15] Marsh, "National Military Academy," no. 414, May 18, 1942, p. 3, RG165 RF, Box 1572, NA-S.

[16] Quoted from interview with Paz Tejada. Zea Carrascosa, *Semblanzas*, p. 284, lists the courses taught by Arbenz: military history of Central America, world history, military reporting, communications and fortifications, physics, mechanics, the art of war, geometry, and tactics.

[17] Quotations from interviews with Lt. Montenegro and Col. Lorenzana. All the Guatemalan officers interviewed by the author concurred with this assessment.

years, to retain the respect, if not the loyalty, of the Guatemalan officer corps. His keen intelligence was nourished by a growing interest in books that his wife helped to stimulate.

Arbenz could be affable, but he remained inscrutable. "It was difficult to know what he thought";[18] he had many acquaintances but few friends. "He lived in his own world, thinking his own thoughts," recalls a cadet who served under him; "he was a reformer who encouraged some of us to read books that other officers considered subversive."[19] A professor at the academy remembers Arbenz as an officer whose "grasp of civilian and military matters was unusually broad for a man of his age and surroundings, and whose concern for the future of his country was intense."[20]

One night when Arbenz was on duty, "he saw me arrive among those who were to be punished," writes Carlos Manuel Pellecer, who was then a cadet.

> He called me to his office and poured me a strong coffee. He gave me a copy of the *Essays* of Emerson. . . . Yes, the *Essays* of the North American philosopher Ralph Waldo Emerson, and he told me: "This will be more useful than punishment. Read it." Two hours later, he came and asked: "What have you learned?" I responded by quoting from the book: "As a plant upon the earth, so a man rests upon the bosom of God; he is nourished by unfailing fountains, and draws, at his need, inexhaustible power. Who can set bounds to the possibilities of man? Once inhale the upper air, being admitted to behold the absolute natures of justice and truth, and we learn that man has access to the entire mind of the Creator, is himself the creator in the finite." . . . Arbenz smiled and gave me permission to leave.[21]

Pellecer was an unusual cadet, highly intelligent, rebellious and full of intellectual curiosity; he was eventually expelled from the Escuela Politécnica and later became a leader of the Communist party. But in 1964, when he wrote of this encounter with Arbenz, he had renounced his past and was courting Arbenz's foes.[22] He had nothing to gain, and something to lose, from portraying Arbenz in a favorable light.

The world of Jacobo Arbenz and his wife, in those last years of Ubico's rule, was not that of the Guatemalan upper class. "But what did we care?" María muses. "They were parasites—like in El Salvador. I wanted to broaden my horizons. I hadn't come to Guatemala to be a socialite and play bridge or golf."[23] But if Arbenz did not belong to the upper class, neither was he the pauper that some have portrayed. His position at the Escuela Politécnica gave

[18] Interview with Col. Lorenzana.
[19] Interview with Lt. Col. Mendizabal.
[20] Interview with Arriola.
[21] Pellecer, *Memoria en dos geografías*, p. 140.
[22] For Pellecer after 1954, see below, p. 389.
[23] Interview with María de Arbenz.

him a degree of social prestige and a salary that, while modest, was three times that of an officer of similar rank who did not serve at the academy.[24] Nor were he and his wife outcasts. They had a number of upper-class acquaintances (particularly from Quetzaltenango, Arbenz's hometown), and one of Arbenz's sisters had married into one of Guatemala's most prominent families, the Aparicios. Upon the birth of their first child, nine months after the marriage, María's parents forgave the couple. (Yet the initial rejection had deeply hurt Arbenz.)[25] It was hardly a period of frustrations. "We were young; we were in love. Together we were learning and growing."[26] María indulged in one of her great passions, painting, as she still does today. One of their closest friends was Enrique Muñoz Meany, a civilian who taught at the Escuela Politécnica, an intellectual with progressive leanings who helped Jacobo Arbenz to imagine a world beyond Guatemala's narrow confines.[27]

They were, then, an attractive couple, both good-looking, both white (socially an important factor), he withdrawn but with "an imposing personality that inspired respect,"[28] she full of verve and *joie de vivre*. An interesting couple, of some social status, and an intellectual couple, especially by the abysmal standards of their milieu. But in no way were they, or did they appear to be, revolutionaries.

The first hint of revolt came in early 1944 when Arbenz and a small group of officers and civilian professors from the Escuela Politécnica began to plot against Ubico. Their plans, however, never got off the drawing board.[29]

The first act of revolt came in July 1944, in the wake of Ubico's resignation. On July 3, with several friends, Arbenz went in civilian clothes to the special session of Congress called to elect the provisional president of the republic. He was present, therefore, when troops occupied the building to remind the legislators that the man they wanted was General Ponce. "Jacobo," María wrote a few days later to her parents, "left the Congress seething. . . . He came home choking with rage." That same week he resigned from the army

[24] "The salary of a lieutenant was $30 per month. In the Escuela Politécnica, Arbenz earned $90." (Interview with Paz Tejada.)

[25] Interviews with María de Arbenz, Fortuny, and Rolz Bennett. The child, Arabella, was María's parents' first grandchild.

[26] Interview with María de Arbenz. See also María Vilanova de Arbenz, "Aclaración."

[27] Interview with María de Arbenz. On Muñoz Meany, see Saker-Ti, *Enrique Muñoz Meany*; "Enrique Muñoz Meany muere en Paris," *El I*, Dec. 22, 1951, p. 1; "Homenaje a Muñoz Meany," *DCA*, Dec. 9, 1953, p. 1.

[28] Interview with Col. Mendoza.

[29] Interview with Arriola, a civilian professor at the academy who joined the plot (as did Arbenz's friend Muñoz Meany). Confirmed by interview with María de Arbenz. See also de León Aragón, "Situaciones" (see n. 14 above), p. 8.

to protest the imposition of Ponce. He was the only Guatemalan officer to do so.[30]

Arbenz began plotting. He and Major Aldana Sandoval were the military leaders of the conspiracy that eventually overthrew Ponce. "It was Arbenz," muses Aldana Sandoval, "who insisted that civilians be included. At the Guardia de Honor, our position was: 'No civilians, military men only.' So all contact with the civilians was through Arbenz—only Arbenz."[31]

On October 4, Arbenz wrote to his wife, who was with her parents in El Salvador:

> All the players will soon be in place. The civilians have confidence in me; they support us. I think that you are going to enjoy what is in store. . . . We are almost ready and we will strike decisively. I have been authorized to form a *de facto* government. . . . We will call elections for a Constituent Assembly and then presidential elections, both of which will be completely free. Therefore, Arévalo will win. If we succeed, we will have written a brilliant and patriotic page in our history.[32]

Ponce fell, and Arbenz kept his promise. Overcoming Arana's resistance, he and Jorge Toriello made sure that president-elect Arévalo was inaugurated on schedule. Unlike Arana and Toriello, he never plotted against Arévalo.

Jacobo Arbenz and his wife knew nothing of Marxism when the Arévalo presidency began. They shared, however, "a love of books" and "restlessness and sensitivity to social problems."[33] In a Guatemala suddenly exposed to new ideas, their questions were becoming more urgent, as they searched for explanations of Guatemala's underdevelopment and of the plight of the lower classes. ("How can the country progress when its people don't have enough to eat? . . . I often thought of this and felt ashamed.") Their nationalism, too, was assuming more definite contours, and Arbenz, who had been so appreciated by his American superiors at the Escuela Politécnica, began to question the U.S. role in Guatemala. Muñoz Meany, a staunch nationalist and a *bête noire* of the U.S. embassy, remained a close friend, and relationships that were based on respect rather than warmth developed between Arbenz and some young leftist leaders, notably Charnaud MacDonald.[34]

[30] Quoted from María de Arbenz, letter to her parents, July 7, 1944; Arévalo Martínez, *Ubico*, pp. 299–300; de León Aragón, "Situaciones" (see n. 14 above), pp. 8, 10; Krehm, *Democracies and Tyrannies*, p. 52; Wardlaw to DOS, no. 617, Dec. 21, 1950, NA 714.11.

[31] Interview with Aldana Sandoval. Confirmed by interview with Rolz Bennett, a civilian plotter.

[32] Jacobo Arbenz, letter to his wife, Oct. 4, 1944. María had been sent by Arbenz to her parents' house in San Salvador to shield her from danger. Arbenz's letters to his wife are warm and affectionate. (María de Arbenz asked the author not to quote any personal passages.)

[33] Interview with Charnaud, who knew Arbenz well at the time.

[34] Interview with Charnaud, quoting Arbenz. Also helpful were interviews with

The first Marxist work came by chance into Jacobo's and María's hands. It was the *Communist Manifesto*, which María received at a women's congress, read, and placed on Jacobo's bedside table before leaving for a brief vacation. "When I returned," she recalls, "he asked me: 'What is this that you left for me?' He too had been moved. Together we talked about the *Manifesto*. It seemed to us that it explained what we had been feeling."[35] Increasingly, Arbenz read about history and economics; he also began to develop a taste for philosophy. Increasingly, his reading included Marxist writings, among them works by Marx, Lenin, and Stalin. "Marxist theory," María observes, "offered Jacobo explanations that weren't available in other theories. What other theory can one use to analyze our country's past? Marx is not perfect, but he comes closest to explaining the history of Guatemala."[36]

As U.S. relations with Arévalo soured and the conflict with American companies grew ever more bitter, Arbenz's frustrated nationalism stimulated first his curiosity, then his sympathy, for the Soviet Union. In the words of Charnaud MacDonald, for Arbenz the Soviet Union represented "something new in the world—rising in opposition to the old world. Three basic facts attracted Arbenz: it was governed by a class which had been ruthlessly exploited; it had defeated illiteracy and raised the standard of living in a very short time; it had never harmed Guatemala." As an officer, Arbenz was also deeply impressed by the Soviet triumph over Hitler; increasingly he attributed this triumph not only to the Russian people, but to their social system.[37]

This political radicalization went hand in hand with Arbenz's growing disenchantment with the revolutionary parties, which seemed to lack both the ability to conceptualize the radical changes that he believed Guatemala needed and the will to implement them.

Friends also played a role in his radicalization. By the late 1940s, Arbenz was growing closer to a group of young Guatemalan communists—the future leaders of the PGT[38]—men like Alfredo Guerra Borges, Víctor Manuel Gutiérrez, Mario Silva Jonama, Bernardo Alvarado Monzón. These were warm relationships, grounded both in politics and in friendship. But of all his friends, none would be as close as José Manuel Fortuny, who in 1948 became

---

María de Arbenz, Fortuny, Guerra Borges, Paz Tejada. Initially, Arbenz had discussed broadening the role of the U.S. military missions in Guatemala with embassy officials. See Woodward to SecState, no. 2426, Apr. 24, 1945, p. 2, RG84 GR, Box 134, NA-S.

[35] Interview with María de Arbenz.

[36] Interview with María de Arbenz. For a revealing report of a conversation between María de Arbenz and an embassy official, see MemoConv (Mrs. Arbenz, Wardlaw), Aug. 3, 1951, RG84 CF, Box 15, NA-S.

[37] Interviews with Charnaud (quoted), María de Arbenz, Fortuny, Guerra Borges.

[38] *Partido Guatemalteco del Trabajo*, the new name adopted by the Guatemalan Communist party in Dec. 1952.

the secretary general of Vanguardia Democrática, the clandestine forerunner of the Guatemalan Communist party.[39]

Arbenz and Fortuny had starkly different personalities. Fortuny, like María, was extroverted. He was full of wit, vivacious, interested in everything from movies to politics; he could talk for hours, without ever becoming boring (a quality he has retained).[40] Like Arbenz, he was moved by fierce nationalism and an ardent desire to improve the lot of the Guatemalan people; like Arbenz, he searched for answers in Marxist theory.

In Fortuny, Arbenz found the brother he had never had, the complement of himself, a man with whom he felt totally at ease, "without having to wear a mask, relaxed," sharing the most intimate thoughts, both personal and political. It was a relationship he would never have with anyone else, except María.[41]

Their friendship began in the fall of 1947, after Arbenz stood up in the cabinet and forcefully opposed the move to deport several labor leaders accused of being communists. Fortuny, who had seen no difference between Arbenz and Arana until then, paid a visit to the defense minister, intrigued by his unexpected behavior.[42]

He discovered a man unlike the stereotype of the military, a man who, with his wife, had "a burning desire" to learn more and to grapple with every issue that he considered vital to the future of Guatemala. "There was almost a competition between them to see who would learn more. . . . Soon Jacobo began to overtake María."[43] In 1950, the CIA paid Arbenz a handsome compliment: he was, a lengthy study noted, "brilliant . . . cultured."[44]

A first, rather formal encounter between Arbenz and Fortuny was followed by others that became increasingly frank. Arbenz began inviting Fortuny to his house; "the conversations would last until late in the night."[45] Jacobo and his wife had begun exploring Marxism (and the Soviet Union) before their relations with Fortuny grew close. In Fortuny, they found someone who had embarked along the same road, although he frankly acknowledged that he was still a novice. (Thus, recalls Fortuny, he was reading books by Soviet generals about the Russian front in the Second World War, notably one that focused on the battle of Kursk. Arbenz asked him: " 'What do you think is the cause of

[39] Interviews with María de Arbenz, Guerra Borges, and Fortuny. There is no evidence to support the oft-repeated assertion that Salvadoran and other foreign communists played a key role in the radicalization of Doña María. She herself denies it.

[40] Based on extended conversations with Fortuny between 1978 and 1988.

[41] Interviews with María de Arbenz (quoted), Fortuny, Pellecer, and Guerra Borges.

[42] Interview with Fortuny. See also above, pp. 58–59.

[43] Interview with Fortuny.

[44] CIA (see n. 7 above), p. 39.

[45] Interviews with Fortuny (quoted) and María de Arbenz.

the Soviet victory over the Germans?' I answered: 'I am not quite sure, but the laws of dialectic. . . . look, I don't really get it yet, but I think . . .' ")[46]

There were other friends too. Some belonged to the middle and the upper classes, people whom Arbenz and his wife had known for years. They danced together, they drank together, but they did not talk about politics. María enjoyed the company of artists. Arbenz, for his part, was genuinely fond of several young officers who had been his colleagues or students at the Escuela Politécnica, men such as Alfonso Martínez, Terencio Guillén, Amadeo García, Carlos Bracamonte, Carlos Enrique Díaz. With them, too, he remained reticent about what most preoccupied him. And he shared fewer and fewer of his political thoughts with earlier confidants like Muñoz Meany and Charnaud MacDonald. By the late 1940s, recalls his wife, "Of all the political leaders, the only ones with whom we had informal, relaxed conversations were those from the PGT, Fortuny above all."[47]

In 1950, when the presidential contest began, Arbenz asked Fortuny to write his campaign speeches. With Fortuny, and to a lesser degree with the other leaders of the fledgling Communist party, he explored the future of Guatemala; increasingly his thoughts turned to the necessity of agrarian reform, the battle cry of the Communist party. In Fortuny's words, "1950 was a decisive year in the ideological evolution of Jacobo Arbenz."[48]

After Arbenz became president, the leaders of the revolutionary parties besieged him in their incessant quest for personal gain, quarreling among themselves for his favor. More and more Arbenz appreciated the honesty and discipline of his communist friends, who sought advantage not for themselves, but for their cause; alone among the government's supporters, they had a program that was specific, at least by Guatemalan standards. Arbenz was increasingly attracted to this as the best hope for the Guatemalan people and nation. Ronald Schneider, whose *Communism in Guatemala* is not known for its sympathy for Arbenz, suggests how the president grew closer to the communists in the first eighteen months of his term:

> The Communists . . . impressed Arbenz as the most honest and trustworthy, as well as the hardest working of his supporters.
>
> . . . As the politicians of the other revolutionary parties lapsed into opportunism and concentrated upon getting the lion's share of the spoils of office, the Communists' stock rose in the President's eyes.
>
> The Communists worked hardest in support of the President's pet project, agrarian reform, and were able to provide the background studies, technical advice, mass

[46] Interview with Fortuny.

[47] Interview with María de Arbenz. Interviews with Rolz Bennett, Lt. García, and Col. Guillén were useful in developing this portrait of Arbenz.

[48] Interview with Fortuny.

support and enthusiasm which the project required. The struggle for the enactment of agrarian reform became a dividing line in the eyes of Arbenz; those who opposed it were his enemies and those whose support was only lukewarm dropped in his esteem. . . . In contrast to the other politicians, the Communists brought him answers and plans rather than problems and constant demands for the spoils of office.[49]

Agrarian reform was, indeed, Arbenz's "pet project." This passionate interest was "an aberration"[50] for a middle-class Ladino, an aberration that only a deep urge for social justice can explain. The revolutionary leaders showed little enthusiasm for comprehensive agrarian reform. Radical change, they feared, might trigger economic chaos and, worse, unleash forces that they might be unable to control. The awakening of the rural masses—largely Indians—alarmed revolutionary leaders content with the rewards of political life. These leaders were also preoccupied, one of their number concedes, with more immediate tasks: "When Arbenz became president," notes Charnaud MacDonald, "the revolutionary parties were fighting among themselves over who got what posts. What help could Arbenz expect from them in his struggle for agrarian reform? Their program was opportunistic; that of the PGT was honest."[51]

Nor was there strong pressure for reform from the countryside. Apart from UFCO's plantations, rural Guatemala had been largely untouched by the Arévalo years. The labor confederations had been calling for land reform, but they were impotent without the active support of the state. Under Arévalo the central government had provided no such support, and its representatives in the countryside, including the army and the police, had sided with the landowners.

While most of Guatemala's politicians considered that the revolution had peaked, Arbenz became ever more committed to the revolution which, in his view, had only begun. Agrarian reform would forge the political basis for the eventual radicalization of the Guatemalan revolution.[52]

Before becoming president Arbenz had been reading about agriculture, Guatemala's in particular. He profited from lengthy conversations with María's brother, Tonio, who was an agricultural expert, and in 1950 with a Mexican economist, Manuel Germán Parra. He also learned from his own finca, El Cajón, which he had bought in the late 1940s with money borrowed from his in-laws and turned into an experimental farm run by modern methods.[53] No higher compliment could be paid to Arbenz's grasp of agricultural affairs

---

[49] Schneider, *Communism*, pp. 195, 196 and 197.

[50] Silvert, *Study in Government*, p. 12.

[51] Interview with Charnaud.

[52] Interviews with María de Arbenz, Alejandro, Fortuny, and Guerra Borges.

[53] Interviews with Fortuny, María de Arbenz, Guerra Borges, Guillén (who became El Cajón's resident administrator), and Zachrisson (wife of Tonio Vilanova).

than that proffered by an eminent Guatemalan intellectual, Mario Monteforte Toledo, whose sympathy for Arbenz was, at best, tenuous. Monteforte writes, "In the meetings that President Arbenz had with the representatives of AGA to discuss agrarian reform [in May 1952], he knew more about the country's agrarian problems than they did."[54]

In late 1951, while public discussion about agrarian reform proceeded in dilatory fashion, Arbenz prepared to act. He secretly summoned three communist leaders: Fortuny, Gutiérrez, and Silva Jonama. In the following weeks they met informally to discuss "the basic structure of the agrarian reform."[55] After several meetings, Arbenz asked Fortuny to prepare the first draft of the law. As Fortuny proceeded article by article, each was reviewed by the PGT's Political Commission. (Some articles relating to the mode of compensation of expropriated landowners were first drafted by a noncommunist, the economist Guillermo Noriega Morales.) The complete draft was then presented to Arbenz. After introducing several modifications, Arbenz called a second working group, which included three PGT leaders—Fortuny, Gutiérrez, and Pellecer—and one noncommunist, the CNCG's secretary general, Leonardo Castillo Flores. After several more meetings, the draft acquired its final form, the brainchild of the PGT "with the extremely active participation of Jacobo Arbenz."[56]

In March 1952 Arbenz announced, "The first draft of an agrarian reform law will be sent this year to the Congress." These words, he noted a year later, "received little attention, except among the workers. . . . Perhaps so many promises had been made to the Guatemalan people in the past that this promise, too, seemed to be empty rhetoric."[57]

But in late April 1952 Arbenz presented an unsuspecting cabinet with a fait accompli: a fully developed program of agrarian reform. ("I can't tell you who prepared the document," remarks a minister. "It was handed to us, and we were asked for our reactions.") On May 10, after a few days of cursory discussion in the cabinet, the draft was formally introduced in Congress.[58]

Throughout the country passions rose, fear spread, and hope surged. The

[54] Monteforte Toledo, *Guatemala*, p. 435, n. 2.

[55] Interviews with Fortuny (quoted), María de Arbenz, and Guerra Borges.

[56] Interviews with Guerra Borges (quoted), María de Arbenz, Alejandro, Fortuny, and Pellecer. (Pellecer claims that he was included in the deliberations from the beginning and that he drafted several articles.) Interview with Noriega Morales confirmed the others' accounts of his participation.

[57] Arbenz, *Informe del ciudadano presidente*, pp. viii–ix.

[58] See "Proyecto entrega el Ejecutivo al Congreso," *El I*, May 10, 1952, p. 1, and "Proyecto de reforma agraria al Congreso," *DCA*, May 10, 1952, p. 1. For the full text of the draft see "Ley de reforma agraria," *DCA*, May 12, 14, 15, 16, 1952 (all p. 4). For the discussions in the cabinet, interviews with ministers Arriola (quoted), Charnaud, and Galich were helpful.

landed elite, represented by the Asociación General de Agricultores (AGA), responded with cries of pain and anger, pressing Arbenz to withdraw his bill and to accept instead its own hastily prepared project of agrarian reform, which emphasized generous government credits for its own members.[59] AGA inveighed against "a totalitarian law" that constituted "the most monstrous act of robbery ever perpetrated by any ruler in our history," and claimed that "the immense majority of the Guatemalan people . . . rejects categorically the communist origins of this law and its nefarious consequences for our motherland." Guatemala, AGA warned, was entering "the most dramatic and decisive days of its history."[60] The Church and most of the press supported AGA.[61] It was all to no avail. Jacobo Arbenz would not budge.

The leaders of the revolutionary parties were uneasy about a document they considered premature and radical, and they were taken aback by Arbenz's methods; they had been neither informed nor consulted about the preparation of the draft. They had, however, little choice but to support the president. Arbenz was more than the leader of the government coalition: he was a military caudillo and a formidable personality. By his actions, and through private and public remarks, he had made it clear that agrarian reform had become "the heart of his program, almost an obsession."[62] He had never been, the U.S. embassy reported, "so obstinate about any particular thing."[63] Open defiance would have created a dangerous crisis. Under intense presidential pressure and amid public demonstrations of support organized in the capital by the labor confederations, the bill was approved in Congress in the early hours of June 17, 1952. That same day, Arbenz signed it into law as Decree 900.[64] After

---

[59] See Asociación General de Agricultores, *Proyecto de ley agraria*. For the government's response see Guatemala, *Crítica al proyecto de ley agraria*.

[60] Quotations from "La AGA al pueblo de Guatemala," *La Hora*, June 18, 1952, p. 10, and from "La AGA ante la conciencia honrada del pueblo de Guatemala rechaza temerosas imputaciones," *La Hora*, June 19, 1952, p. 10. These are only two of an avalanche of communiqués published by the association. Some titles are particularly evocative, for instance: "The Wolves Cast Off Their Sheep's Clothing" (*La Hora*, May 30, 1952, p. 10), and "Selling the Leather Before Killing the Cow" (*La Hora*, June 3, 1952, p. 10).

[61] See below, pp. 210–15.

[62] Particularly useful were interviews with the following politicians: Galich (quoted), Charnaud, Morgan, and Capuano.

[63] Miller to Krieg and Larsen, May 27, 1952, p. 1, RG84 CF, Box 15, NA-S.

[64] For the debates in Congress, see Actas del Congreso, *Primer periodo ordinario de sesiones, 28 de febrero al 30 de mayo 1952* (Libro no. 15, 1952), and *Sesiones extraordinarias, 12 de junio a 3 de julio, 1952* (Libro no. 16, 1952). For the changes introduced in Congress to the government's bill, see Paredes Moreira, *Reforma agraria*, pp. 50–51. Of the press, *DCA* and the opposition dailies *El I* and *La Hora* are particularly useful.

years of sterile discussions, the country had a comprehensive agrarian reform law, thanks to Jacobo Arbenz and the PGT. If a revolution began in Guatemala, the date was not October 20, 1944, but June 17, 1952.

It was the preparation and the enactment of the agrarian reform bill that finally brought Arbenz over to the communists' side. By late 1952, President Arbenz had chosen the stand from which he would not deviate. His closest political friend was the PGT, and his closest personal friends were its leaders. Arbenz continued to read. "He read books on the Russian revolution, the history of the USSR, the military strategy of the Soviet generals in WWII. All this molded his way of looking at the world," observes Fortuny.[65] By 1952, "through all this reading," adds his wife, "Jacobo was convinced that the triumph of communism in the world was inevitable and desirable. The march of history was toward communism. Capitalism was doomed."[66]

Arbenz did not become a member of the PGT until 1957, three years after he had been overthrown; had he joined while president, he would have had to submit to party discipline. This could have created unnecessary conflicts and disturbed the close cooperation between him and the party. But in the last two years of his administration he considered himself a communist, and with his few confidants, he spoke like one. The PGT leaders formed his "kitchen cabinet," and with them he took his most important decisions; the only major disagreement between the president and the party occurred in the last two days of his presidency and concerned his eventual resignation. Perhaps Arbenz should not formally be called a communist, yet fellow traveler fails to convey the intensity of his commitment.[67]

Arbenz and the PGT did not think that a communist state, however desirable, could be established in Guatemala in the near future.[68] Guatemala, they believed, was a semifeudal country; therefore, it must first pass through a capitalist stage in which the material conditions for socialism would be developed by means of an agrarian reform program that would eventually lead to industrialization and the growth of a proletariat. This was the view of the international Communist movement toward semifeudal countries (as all Latin American Communist parties, at the time, saw their respective countries), and this is what Lenin had argued in his *Development of Capitalism in Russia*, a treatise that became a textbook for the Political Commission of the PGT. Only a

---

[65] Interview with Fortuny.

[66] Interview with María de Arbenz. (I had asked for her response to Fortuny's statement quoted immediately above.)

[67] Interviews with Fortuny, María de Arbenz, Guerra Borges, Alejandro, and Charnaud, who became a close friend of Arbenz after his overthrow.

[68] The remainder of this chapter is based primarily on interviews with María de Arbenz, Fortuny, Alejandro, and Guerra Borges.

country favored by geography could afford to skip the capitalist stage and move directly toward socialism: Mongolia, which had the good fortune "to border the Soviet Union," and the "tiny great nation of Albania."[69] Pragmatic considerations reinforced the theory. Guatemala was in the heart of the American empire. While Arbenz and the PGT underestimated the American threat, they were, nevertheless, convinced that in the foreseeable future Washington would not tolerate the emergence of a communist Guatemala. Thus, theory provided the welcome reassurance that the impossible need not be attempted. As a result, recalls Guerra Borges, the PGT "enthusiastically endorsed the thesis that Guatemala must first go through a capitalist stage. When we stated this we were not trying to hoodwink anyone. We were convinced of it."[70] This capitalist phase, the president and the party believed, had to be planned and executed carefully. Capitalist development under a government as corrupt and conservative as that of President Miguel Alemán in Mexico would be very different from that which would occur in Guatemala under a government led by Jacobo Arbenz. Moreover, while progressing into this capitalist stage, "the idea was to do nothing that would make the introduction of socialism more difficult, but rather to take steps that would make it easier."[71]

Arbenz, his wife, and the leaders of the PGT were convinced that the entire world would eventually become a socialist community. "Communism was inevitable, we thought,"[72] and it might come to Guatemala before it came to the United States. For this to happen, however, there had to be a change in the correlation of forces, both at the international level and within Guatemala itself. How long this would require they did not know. On those few occasions when they touched on the subject, the length of the delay (many years, a few decades) varied according to their optimism at the moment. Someday, they concluded, Guatemala would be Marxist-Leninist. But for the time being it was far more important to devote their energy to the tasks at hand than to indulge in idle speculation. Of the tasks at hand, none was more compelling than agrarian reform.

[69] Quotations from interview with Guerra Borges, and from Fortuny, *Informe sobre la actividad del Comité Central*, p. 35.

[70] Quoted from interview with Guerra Borges.

[71] Quoted from interview with María de Arbenz.

[72] María de Arbenz, letter to the author, Dec. 11, 1987, p. 10.

Jacobo Arbenz and his wife María, shortly after their marriage in 1939.

Jacobo and María, September 1945. Arbenz was the minister of defense. María Vilanova was an upper-class Salvadoran. Together they could have led a charmed, upper-class life.

The civilian, Jorge Toriello, flanked by Francisco Arana on his right and Jacobo Arbenz on his left. This triumvirate assumed power after the fall of the dictator Ponce. (On the left is Aldana Sandoval, who helped plan the revolt, but lacked the courage to participate in it.) After the uprising, the civilians handed back their weapons, and effective power resided in the army.

Guatemalan soldiers being greeted by Jorge Toriello, October 22, 1944.

Juan José Arévalo returned to Guatemala from Argentina to become the first president of the Guatemalan revolution. A charismatic, honest, and self-confident man, he declared that his doctrine of Spiritual Socialism was "a true innovation for Latin America . . . which until now has been grappling with only conservatives, liberals and Marxists."

Francisco Arana, chief of the armed forces under Arévalo, was arguably the most powerful man in Guatemala. In 1949, he was poised to become the next president, but he was killed in a shootout near Guatemala City. His killers were never apprehended.

Arévalo "had the physique of a very big man," a U.S. diplomat recalls. "And his opinion of himself was also very big."

Arana courted U.S. officials. They considered him "the only positive, conservative element in the Arévalo administration" and were alarmed by his death.

Arana and Arévalo. It was not the army that prevented Arévalo from enacting an agrarian reform program: Arévalo was a middle-class Ladino; the world of the Indian was distant and fearsome.

Carlos Paz Tejada and Arévalo. Paz Tejada became chief of the armed forces after the death of Arana. As the U.S. air attaché reported, he was "intelligent . . . gracious . . . a good organizer and administrator."

President Arbenz on his inauguration day. Arbenz, U.S. officials believed, was "an opportunist"; his presidency would mean "a return of Guatemala to cooperation with the United States, and the end of any personal freedom in Guatemala." In fact, his presidency was to be marked by agrarian reform, close ties with the Communist party, and stubborn defiance of the United States.

María de Arbenz on inauguration day. Some have described her husband as putty in her hands, but she was actually his partner in a process of radicalization that became increasingly rapid. They shared the same evolution, the same beliefs, and the same friends.

Arbenz in exile, painted by his wife in 1965.

Arbenz in Havana, 1962. ''The Cubans were very condescending,''
recalls María. ''They made Jacobo feel useless.''

CHAPTER 8

The Agrarian Reform

IN HIS INAUGURAL address, Arbenz set forth the goals of his economic program: "to transform Guatemala from a dependent nation with a semi-colonial economy into a country that is economically independent; to transform Guatemala from a backward country with a semifeudal economy into a modern capitalist country; to proceed in a way that will ensure the greatest possible improvement in the standard of living of the great masses of our people."[1]

Agrarian reform was the heart of Arbenz's program, but he also emphasized the need to modernize the country's physical infrastructure. Both were essential to the economic development of Guatemala and to the transformation of its rural population from serfs into citizens. In tackling these two fronts—agrarian reform and public works—Arbenz faced an added challenge: he would not rely on foreign capital. He had little choice. In view of the reputation of his administration, it was most unlikely that Americans would lend money to Guatemala, and the United States was, at the time, virtually the only source of foreign private capital available to a Central American country. Nor could the World Bank be relied upon. It had refused a "much needed loan" to Arévalo in 1950 at Washington's behest, and there was no reason to expect it to be more forthcoming. (In 1951, the World Bank asked the State Department's permission before showing its report on Guatemala to the Guatemalan authorities.)[2]

In the absence of foreign loans, Guatemala could undertake a program of public works only if the agrarian reform did not deplete the country's resources and decrease agricultural output. Good luck would also be necessary; the high international price of coffee that had blessed the Arévalo presidency would have to be maintained.

This, then, defined Arbenz's economic program: self-sustained economic development based on agrarian reform and public works. Together, they would provide the foundation for a more distant aim, the light industrialization of Guatemala. Industrialization, Arbenz stated, could not begin in earnest in the short span of his presidency, but he would support existing industries and look favorably on new ones.

[1] Arévalo, *Discursos del doctor Juan José Arévalo y del teniente coronel Jacobo Arbenz*, p. 26.

[2] For the 1950 incident, see above, pp. 128–29. For that of 1951, see MemoConv ("Mr. Lopéz-Herrarte's impressions of the situation in Guatemala"), Jan. 18, 1951, NA 714.00.

Arbenz was about to embark on the first comprehensive development plan in the history of Guatemala, whereas his predecessor had not even outlined such a plan. In his first speeches as president, Arbenz frankly acknowledged that he could only offer a blueprint and that much planning remained. He pledged, however, that he would transform his words into deeds. And he stressed, with a passion that many dismissed as empty rhetoric, the centrality of social justice:

> I grant great importance to economic policy, but only as a means to achieve our social goals. All the riches of Guatemala are not as important as the life, the freedom, the dignity, the health and the happiness of the most humble of its people. How wrong we would be if—mistaking the means for the end—we were to set financial stability and economic growth as the supreme goals of our policy, sacrificing to them the well being of our masses. . . . Our task is to work together in order to produce more wealth. . . . But we must distribute these riches so that those who have less—and they are the immense majority—benefit more, while those who have more—and they are so few—also benefit, but to a lesser extent. How could it be otherwise, given the poverty, the poor health, and the lack of education of our people?[3]

Arbenz spoke these words in April 1951. For the next twelve months the land tenure system remained unchanged, and no major public works were begun. Then the tempo accelerated, as Arbenz presented his draft of the agrarian reform law to a stunned Congress. Five weeks later, on June 17, 1952, Decree 900 was approved.

DECREE 900

The law, a senior FAO official reported, "was constructive and democratic in its aims. . . . It would bring about a land structure and a system of land tenure largely centering around the needs and aspirations of the individual peasant families."[4] It stipulated that all uncultivated land in private estates of more than 672 acres would be expropriated; idle land in estates of between 224 and 672 acres would be expropriated only if less than two thirds of the estate was under cultivation; estates of less than 224 acres would not be affected. By contrast, the government-owned Fincas Nacionales would be entirely parcelled out.[5]

---

[3] Arbenz, *Exposición*, pp. 8–9.

[4] AmEm Rome, Hayes, "Report of Director, Agriculture Division, FAO [Food and Agriculture Organization], on Land Reform Situation in Guatemala," Oct. 22, 1952, p. 2, RG84 CF, Box 15, NA-S.

[5] Arts. 9–12. For the text of Decree 900, see *El Guatemalteco*, June 17, 1952, 135:86, pp. 957–62.

Land expropriated from private estates would be given in private ownership or in lifetime tenure according to the recipient's wishes; in the latter case, upon the death of the beneficiary, his family would receive preferential consideration to rent the same land.[6] The Fincas Nacionales would be distributed in lifetime tenure only. For twenty-five years, every beneficiary would pay the government 3 percent of the annual value of the crop if he had received the land in lifetime tenure and 5 percent if he had received the land in outright ownership.

The former owners would be compensated with 3 percent agrarian bonds maturing in twenty-five years; the value of the expropriated land would be that declared by the owners on their tax returns prior to May 10, 1952, the day the agrarian reform bill had been presented to Congress.[7]

The introduction of the lifetime tenure system, the government claimed, would prevent large landowners from quickly recovering the parcels given to the peasants.[8] For Arbenz and the PGT, there was another, unstated rationale: "to introduce a progressive element into a capitalist reform." In Fortuny's words, "It was the PGT that proposed that land be given in lifetime tenure. Arbenz agreed."[9]

Decree 900 established a hierarchical system to implement the reform. At the bottom were the local agrarian committees (*comités agrarios locales* or CALs). Each CAL had five members, one appointed by the governor of the department in which the CAL was located, one by the municipality, and three by the local labor union. Where there was no labor organization or where there was more than one, the peasants and the agricultural workers would elect their representatives in popular assemblies.[10] Any people who thought they were entitled could petition the CAL for land that they considered eligible for expropriation. The CAL would assess the validity of the request and forward its recommendation to the departmental agrarian committee (*comité agrario departamental* or CAD).

The CADs, too, had five members: one chosen by the landowners' association (AGA), one each by the country's two labor confederations, one by the department's governor, and one by the newly created National Agrarian Department (*Departamento Agrario Nacional* or DAN). The CADs would supervise the work of the CALs and report to the DAN in the capital; the DAN

---

[6] Art. 39.

[7] Art. 6.

[8] See "Contestación a la AGA," *DCA*, June 3, 1952, p. 1, and "No hay contradicciones en el proyecto de ley de reforma agraria del Ejecutivo ni la AGA quiere hacer más 'propietarios,' " *DCA*, June 6, 1952, p. 8.

[9] Quotations from interviews with María de Arbenz and Fortuny. By June 1954, only 27.5 percent of the land had been given in freehold. (Paredes Moreira, "Aspectos y resultados," p. 59.)

[10] Art. 57.

would review the CADs' decisions. At the apex stood the president of the republic who "would serve as the final arbiter of all disputes raised by the implementation of the law." Thus, while the principle of administrative review was established throughout the expropriation process, the courts were expressly excluded.[11]

Many analysts portray Decree 900 as a moderate law cast in a capitalist mold. In particular, they note, only uncultivated land could be expropriated, and that only from large estates.[12] However, not only did Decree 900 introduce the lifetime tenure system, but it stipulated that the expropriation process would have to be completed in six weeks—a dramatic change in a country "accustomed to red tape and bureaucracy, where 'wait and see' is a way of life, where social legislation in the past had always been circumvented."[13] Moreover, through the CADs and the CALs, Decree 900 sought to stimulate the participation of the peasants and the labor organizations, rather than to impose the reform from the top alone. In Fortuny's words,

> We [the PGT] proposed the creation of peasant committees [CALs] in order to lay the groundwork for the eventual radicalization of the peasantry. We talked to Arbenz about this, and he agreed with us. What we wanted was to foster the control of the reform from below. This would give the peasants a strong sense of their common needs. And if, from the system of lifetime tenure, cooperatives developed, the seeds of a more collective society would have been sown.[14]

The Office of Intelligence Research (OIR) of the State Department had little criticism of the technical aspects of Decree 900. "If the Agrarian Law is fully implemented," it noted, "the impact upon private landholders would be borne chiefly by a minority. . . . Of 341,191 private agricultural holdings only 1,710 would be affected. These 1,710 holdings, however, comprise more than half of the total private acreage." The OIR went on to voice its deep concern: successful implementation of Decree 900 would strengthen the government's influence in the countryside and would provide the communists with "an excellent opportunity to extend their influence over the rural population."[15]

The months that followed the enactment of Decree 900 were, on all sides, a time of preparation. While the government began to establish the machinery

---

[11] Arts. 52, 54–56, 59 (quoted), and 60.

[12] Even the U.S. embassy concluded that the law was "relatively moderate in form." ("Economic and Financial Review—1953," no. 953, May 19, 1954, p. 21, NA 814.00.)

[13] Melville and Melville, *Guatemala: The Politics of Land Ownership*, p. 54. For the expropriation process, see arts. 63–83 of Decree 900.

[14] Interviews with Fortuny (quoted), María de Arbenz, and Guerra Borges.

[15] OIR, "Agrarian Reform in Guatemala," no. 6001, Mar. 5, 1953, pp. 7, 4, 5, NA.

for the administration of the agrarian reform, "representatives of labor and farm workers' unions toured the countryside instructing workers in the operation of the law and distributing forms for petitioning land."[16] Seeking to shield their workers from this plague, landowners closed the roads running through their plantations. "When one farm covered several thousand acres of land and straddled main highways," an authority has observed, "they could prevent people from travelling." In response, the government announced that all private roads would become public property on August 1, 1952; failure to open a road would result in fines of up to $2,000 per day.[17] The threat proved effective.

Strongly supported by the government, the labor confederations organized rural unions and helped to establish networks of CALs. They also began an intensive campaign to overcome the peasants' fears, spawned by landowners and priests, that the agrarian reform would lead to the collectivization of their wives and children, economic ruin, and eternal damnation. "It wasn't easy for the peasants to withstand the manipulations of the feudal landlords," noted the secretary general of the national peasant confederation (CNCG), Castillo Flores, in his report to its February 1954 Congress. "The propaganda unleashed by the landowners was hard-hitting. . . . And it met with some success. . . . The landowners also coopted some workers with good wages and bribes. . . . They offered many of the peasant leaders special privileges, and more than a few surrendered to temptation."[18] In the same vein, the PGT's secretary general, Fortuny, noted in August 1953 that "months of patient labor" had been necessary to convince the laborers of Concepción, one of the largest Fincas Nacionales, of the benefits of the agrarian reform.[19]

The distribution of land from the Fincas Nacionales began in August 1952. On January 5, 1953, Arbenz signed the first four decrees expropriating private land.[20] For the next eighteen months, the agrarian reform proceeded at a swift pace.

There is no question that mistakes and excesses marred the implementation of Decree 900. Arbitrary seizures took place at the hands of CALs that were

[16] AmEmG, "Monthly Economic Report—August 1952," no. 212, Aug. 28, 1952, p. 1, NA 814.00.

[17] Pearson, *"Confederación,"* p. 174 (quoted); "Guatemala Opens Roads," *NYT*, July 24, 1952, p. 2.

[18] Castillo Flores, "Informe del Secretario General a el III Congreso Nacional Campesino," Feb. 19, 1954, pp. 1–2, *GT*, Box 11.

[19] Fortuny, "Sobre la parcelación de 'Concepción,' " *Tribuna Popular*, Aug. 26, 1953, p. 1 (quoted) and Aug. 27, 1953, p. 3.

[20] See "Positiva realidad el Decreto 900," *DCA*, Aug. 7, 1952, p. 1; *JW* 42, Oct. 16, 1952, I:4; *JW* 47, Nov. 20, 1952, I:2; "Acuerdase expropiación de las primeras fincas particulares," *DCA*, Jan. 6, 1953, p. 1; "Expropiadas las primeras fincas de particulares" (edit.), *DCA*, Jan. 7, 1953, p. 3.

strongly biased against landowners. At times, acts of violence were perpetrated against owners of large and middle-sized estates; on other occasions, landless peasants seized the holdings of their marginally better-off neighbors. Disputes erupted among peasants coveting the same land and between members of unions associated with different government parties. With the rapid pace of the agrarian reform, ancient tensions between neighboring peasant communities surfaced. On occasion, conflicts divided a single community.[21]

In his March 1954 message to Congress, Arbenz acknowledged, "There have been excesses [in the implementation of the law], such as the illegal occupation of estates and the seizure of land by some peasants to the detriment of others."[22] Castillo Flores struck the same note in his report to the third congress of the CNCG.[23] Letters written to Castillo Flores include poignant appeals. From Tecpán, in the department of Chimaltenango, a group of peasants complained: "Peasant Union of Chuatzunuj is full of greedy men. It has stolen our land"; from Senahú, in the department of Alta Verapaz, the peasants wrote: "Our neighbors have taken over our fields. . . . Please send a telegram on our behalf to the governor."[24] Other letters, telegrams, and reports addressed to the president of the republic, the DAN, members of Congress, and governors of departments tell of similar incidents.[25] Clashes between groups of peasants left several dead and wounded at San Pedro Ayampuc, at San Vicente Pacaya, at San Pedro Yepocapa, and at San Juan La Ermita.[26]

[21] The major primary sources on the implementation of the agrarian reform are (1) the reports of the U.S. embassy, particularly the *JW*, the Labor Reports (NA 814.06), and the Economic Reports (NA 814.00); (2) the Guatemalan press, esp. the official *DCA*, the PGT's *Octubre* and *Tribuna Popular*, and the opposition dailies *La Hora* and *El I*; (3) the *GT*.

The most important secondary sources on the implementation of the reform are by Paredes Moreira, *Reforma agraria*, *Aplicación*, and "Aspectos y resultados." On agricultural credit, see esp. Comité Interamericano de Desarrollo Agrícola, *Tenencia de la tierra*, pp. 31–54. On other aspects of the agrarian reform, see Pearson, "*Confederación*" and "Guatemala"; Aybar de Soto, *Dependency*; García Añoveros, "El 'caso Guatemala' "; Wasserstrom, "Revolution in Guatemala"; Handy, *Class and Community* and " 'The Most Precious Fruit' "; Whetten, *Guatemala* and "Land Reform."

[22] Arbenz, "Informe del ciudadano presidente," p. 3.

[23] Castillo Flores (see n. 18 above).

[24] Quotations from Diego Lares Bocal to Castillo Flores, Tecpán, Mar. 31, 1954, *GT*, Box 43, and Marcelino Tux, Secretario General Unión Campesina San Juan, to Castillo Flores, Senahú, May 23, 1954, *GT* Box 44.

[25] See *GT*, Boxes 11, 12, 42, and 43, and CO:G, AGCA for the relevant period.

[26] The incidents at San Pedro Ayampuc and San Vicente Pacaya occurred on Feb. 12 and 14, 1953; at San Pedro Yepocapa on Aug. 26, 1953; at San Juan La Ermita on Apr. 30, 1954. See esp. *DCA*, *El I*, *La Hora*, and *Tribuna Popular*.

The opposition press claimed that a wave of violence was engulfing the countryside, and many in Guatemala and the United States wept for the poor dispossessed landowners. Not only were they to be compensated in bonds rather than cash, but the amount of the compensation would be nugatory: it was common knowledge that the landowners had consistently and grossly understated the value of their estates on their tax returns.

In February 1953, yet another blow provoked howls of indignation from the opposition in Guatemala and struck many in the United States as definitive proof of the regime's totalitarian character. In two split decisions, the Supreme Court declared that Decree 900's exclusion of judicial review was unconstitutional, and it ordered the agrarian reform suspended until the lower courts could investigate charges that private lands were being expropriated illegally. This meant, as the *New York Times* pointed out, that "Guatemala's Land Law [was] halted."[27] Arbenz's response was swift: he summoned an extraordinary session of Congress. "You must decide," he told the deputies, "whether the Supreme Court can hear appeals on cases related to the agrarian reform, or whether, to the contrary, it must abide by . . . Decree 900 and refuse to hear them."[28] The message was couched in terms that were, conceded an opposition daily, "temperate,"[29] yet Arbenz's position was unmistakable.

Congress acted immediately. After a few hours of tumultuous debate, it impeached the errant judges by a 41 to 9 vote on grounds of "ignorance of the law which shows unfitness and manifest incapacity to administer justice," and replaced them with more sympathetic individuals. The new judges reversed their predecessors' rulings, and the agrarian reform continued free from judicial restraint.[30]

The difficulties associated with the implementation of the agrarian reform must be weighed against its results. Although the analysis is hampered by two constraints—the reform ran only until June 1954, when Arbenz was ousted, and many relevant documents were destroyed in the wake of his fall—enough data exist to assess its impact.

By June 1954, over 1.4 million acres had been expropriated (that is, one quarter of the total arable land of Guatemala). This represented "about half the acreage that the government contemplated would be affected by the law," the U.S. embassy noted. "Those persons who lost land owned extremely large quantities of it," an expert later wrote. "In many, if not most of these cases,

[27] "Guatemala's Land Law Halted," *NYT*, Feb. 6, 1953, p. 20.
[28] Arbenz's Feb. 5 message to Congress quoted in "Destituida hoy la corte," *El I*, Feb. 6, 1953, p. 9.
[29] "Destitución de la corte" (edit.), *El I*, Feb. 6, 1953, p. 1.
[30] The episode can be followed in *DCA*, *El I*, and *Prensa Libre*. For the Feb. 5 session of Congress, see "Actas de la séptima sesión extraordinaria," in *Sesiones extraordinarias, enero–febrero 1953*, (Libro no. 12, 1953), unpaginated.

the finqueros were absentee land-owners."[31] There is no agreement as to the exact number of beneficiaries. Some scholars believe that as many as 138,000 families received land; others accept the figures of eighty to ninety thousand given by the government of Castillo Armas, who overthrew Arbenz. But on one occasion Castillo Armas's director of agrarian affairs, who was certainly in a position to know, assessed the total number at "100,000 heads of families." This assessment is endorsed by some of the leading authorities on Arbenz's agrarian reform.[32] A simple calculation based on the 1950 census translates this figure to five hundred thousand Guatemalans.

From the moment of his inauguration, Arbenz had stressed that access to credit was crucial to any agrarian reform. For peasants in Guatemala, loans were a rare and costly privilege. "Agricultural credit for the Indian is practically nonexistent," concluded the World Bank in 1951.[33] Enlarging on the same point, former State Department official Nathan Whetten wrote:

> Scarcity of rural credit facilities has made loans difficult to get and resulted in exorbitant rates of interest. A study of rural credit facilities in 37 *municipios* made in 1950–51 . . . estimated that 10 per cent of the Indian farmers of these *municipios* had obtained loans of some kind during the previous year. Usually these loans were small, ranging from 5 to 100 dollars per recipient and extended over short periods of time, ordinarily not more than a few months. The rates of interest, however, were generally extremely high and computed on a monthly basis. In the 37 *municipios* studied the average rate of interest varied from 3.2 per cent per month to 12.6 per cent per month. The average for the 37 *municipios* combined was 7.9 per cent per month. This is equivalent to a yearly rate of interest amounting to 94.8 per cent.[34]

Decree 900 stipulated that the provision of credit would be an integral part of the agrarian reform. In February 1953, the government presented a bill to Congress that established the National Agrarian Bank (*Banco Nacional Agrario* or BNA), whose sole purpose would be to provide credit to the beneficiaries of the agrarian reform and to other small farmers. The bill was accompanied by Arbenz's request that it be approved before the Congress adjourned on March 1.[35] In the meantime, credit would be granted through an established government agency, the Crédito Hypotecario Nacional (CHN).

---

[31] Quotations from Krieg to DOS, no. 818, Mar. 29, 1954, p. 3, NA 814.20, and Pearson, "*Confederación*," p. 171. For statistical data see Paredes Moreira, *Reforma agraria* and *Aplicación*.

[32] Montenegro, "El capitán Montenegro defiende"; see also Paredes Moreira, *Aplicación*, pp. 76–77, and Comité Interamericano de Desarrollo Agrícola, *Tenencia de la tierra*, p. 42.

[33] IBRD, *Economic Development*, p. 26.

[34] Whetten, *Guatemala*, p. 156.

[35] See *DCA*: "Aprobado el anteproyecto del Banco Agrario," Feb. 3, 1953, p. 1; "El Banco Agrario Nacional" (edit.), Feb. 4, 1953, p. 3; "Ultimos toques a la ley del

After months of delay, Congress bowed to strong executive pressure and approved the creation of the BNA on July 7, 1953. With the creation of this "new type of financial institution for Guatemala," reported the U.S. embassy, "the basic agrarian reform legislation was completed."[36] Between March 1953 and June 1954, the CHN and the BNA approved $11,881,432 in loans, of which $9 million was disbursed before the overthrow of Arbenz. An average of $225 was given to each of the 53,829 applicants—a sum that was almost twice Guatemala's annual per capita income in 1950 ($137) and well over twice per capita income in the countryside ($89).[37] In a dramatic break with the past, interest rates were fixed at 4 percent annually for loans of up to twelve months, and 6 percent for longer term loans (three to six years). To facilitate the procedure, the country was divided into six regions, and the BNA opened offices in each. Competently staffed, the bank earned its reputation as the most efficient government bureaucracy. (Even the U.S. embassy, which was deeply concerned by leftist influence within the BNA, offered no criticism of its structure or performance.)[38] The bank's director, Alfonso Bauer Paiz, was unusual among revolutionary politicians for his expertise and his honesty.

Of course, there were problems. As a senior BNA official recalls, "some borrowers used their loans to buy things like bikes, radios, etc. . . . You can't change everything at once. It takes time to educate the people. But these were isolated cases: most borrowers used their loans responsibly." In fact, of the $3,371,185 in loans granted by the CHN between March and November 1953, $3,049,092 had been repaid by June 1954, as had some of the loans given by the BNA, which began operations only in November 1953. This was crucial: "the BNA had limited resources, loans had to be turned over rapidly."[39] It was also proof that the beneficiaries were making good use of the opportunities created by the land reform.

Banco Agrario," Feb. 11, 1953, p. 1; "Proyecto del Banco Agrario fue enviado al Congreso," Feb. 12, 1953, p. 1; "Proyecto del Banco Agrario fué enviado ya al Congreso," Feb. 13, 1953, p. 1. For the draft, see "Texto del proyecto de creación del Banco Nacional Agrario," *DCA*, Feb. 16, 17, and 18, 1953 (all p. 8).

[36] *JW* 28, July 9, 1953, II:3. See also "Ley orgánica del Banco Agrario, aprobada," *DCA*, July 8, 1953, p. 1; " 'Publíquese y cúmplase' a la ley del Banco Nac. Agrario," *DCA*, July 9, 1953, p. 1; "El Banco Nacional Agrario" (edit.), *DCA*, July 11, 1953, p. 3.

[37] Comité Interamericano de Desarrollo Agrícola, *Tenencia de la tierra*, p. 43. (Paredes Moreira, *Reforma agraria*, p. 139, gives slightly different figures: $11,772,400 in loans and 53,950 successful applicants.) For per capita income in 1950, see Palacios, "Formas de redistribución," p. 430.

[38] Based on a reading of the embassy's reports. For the bank's organization, see *Informe mensual del Banco Nacional Agrario*, no. 1, May 1954, pp. 1–4.

[39] Quoted from interview with Noriega Morales, who was a senior official of the BNA. For the figures, see Comité Interamericano de Desarrollo Agrícola, *Tenencia de la tierra*, p. 42.

Some exacting critics point out that the government's efforts "to provide capital at low interest to *campesinos* needing farm equipment fell short of meeting the needs of the new landowners, with the result that many *campesinos* found themselves with land but with little or no capital to cultivate it profitably."[40] Arbenz was president, however, of poor and backward Guatemala, not of Sweden. The significance of the $12 million in loans approved by the government can be appreciated if one considers that in 1954 the total amount of loans processed by Guatemalan banks, excluding the BNA, was $45,292,000.[41] Similarly, it might be noted that the loans granted represented one sixth of the government's total expenditure for the 1953–1954 fiscal year.

In view of Guatemala's history, and of the severe economic and technical constraints faced by the government, the amount of credit provided by the CHN and the BNA is remarkable. A 1965 report sponsored by the Organization of American States—not a radical group—concluded, "The success of the agrarian credit policy was no less impressive than that of the land redistribution policy."[42] Indeed, Guatemala's experience was unprecedented in Latin America, where significant land redistribution was extremely rare and provision of credit to poor peasants even rarer.

Contrary to the hopes of the government's detractors, Decree 900 did not result in the collapse of agricultural output. Rather, notes an American scholar, the existing data, "seem to indicate that agrarian reform . . . unleashed new productive energies from both the peasants and those *finqueros* whose previously idle land was put into use."[43] Nor did the U.S. embassy, which closely monitored the country's economy, claim that agricultural production was declining. On the contrary, in August 1953 the embassy reported a 15 percent increase in the production of corn. Corn, it added, "is the chief crop of small landholders in Guatemala and is cultivated by the majority of persons who have received land under the Agrarian Reform Law."[44] Almost a year later, the embassy concluded that "production of food crops in 1953 was satisfactory." The corn harvest was "about 10 percent higher than 1952," rice and wheat production had increased by 74 percent and 21 percent respectively over 1952, and bean production had remained the same. In 1952–1953 coffee production did decrease slightly, but this was "due principally to weather conditions."[45] Furthermore, recovery was swift. The 1953–1954 coffee crop was

[40] LaCharite, *Case Study in Insurgency*, p. 60.

[41] See Aybar de Soto, *Dependency*, p. 195, n. 98.

[42] Comité Interamericano de Desarrollo Agrícola, *Tenencia de la tierra*, p. 42.

[43] Pearson, "*Confederación*," pp. 187–88.

[44] *JW* 34, Aug. 21, 1953, II:1.

[45] Quoted from "Economic and Financial Review—1953" (see n. 12 above), p. 6. See also McKnight to DOS, no. 238, Oct. 15, 1953, NA 814.231, and Paredes Moreira, *Reforma agraria*, p. 61, table 15.

the second highest in Guatemala's history.[46] In late 1954, in its postmortem of Decree 900, the embassy conceded, "The impact of agrarian reform during the Arbenz regime was principally political and did not greatly affect agricultural production."[47]

These results are particularly significant in light of the fact that agricultural production tends to decrease, often steeply, in the first years of a swift land reform. Such was the case in Bolivia in the 1950s, Cuba in the 1960s, Peru in the early 1970s, and Nicaragua in the early 1980s.

It would seem, moreover, that the reform led to an increase of the area under cultivation. Almost all of the private land expropriated (or otherwise seized) had not been cultivated. The landed elite, though cursing Decree 900 and the "communist" government, did not retaliate by reducing agricultural production. Some authorities even suggest that, fearing expropriation, many landowners hastened to cultivate land they had not previously tilled. In any case, production of rice and cotton, two crops grown mainly by large landowners, rose markedly during the life of Decree 900. Purchase of farm equipment by large landowners, which had dropped sharply after the enactment of the Agrarian Reform Law, was increasing by early 1954.[48] And not even U.S. officials, despite their dire prognostications, argued that Decree 900 was affecting the coffee crop of the landed elite.

About a quarter of Guatemala's coffee crop had been grown on the Fincas Nacionales. Their dismemberment, a chorus of Cassandras had warned, would prove disastrous. "The workers," they claimed, "knew nothing about coffee culture except performance of routine tasks. . . . coffee production would decline and . . . there would be a reversion to the mere subsistence crops of corn and beans."[49] In fact, Decree 900 had stipulated that in the Fincas Nacionales the beneficiaries could not change the existing crops without the permission of the agrarian authorities, and there is no indication that the acreage devoted to coffee in the Fincas Nacionales, or its productivity, decreased. The former workers, now acting as independent producers, proved at least as efficient as the administrators who had overseen the Fincas Nacionales under Arévalo.[50]

[46] United Nations, FAO, *World Coffee Economy*, Table 1A.

[47] McKnight to DOS, no. 309, Oct. 14, 1954, p. 5, NA 814.231.

[48] AmEmG: "Economic Summary—March 1954," no. 851, Apr. 12, 1954, p. 1; "Economic Summary—April 1954," no. 919, May 7, 1954, p. 1; "Economic Summary—May 1954," no. 995, June 9, 1954, p. 1. All NA 814.00.

[49] Whetten, *Guatemala*, p. 154 (quoting landowners).

[50] The U.S. agricultural attaché kept an eagle eye out for any loss of productivity in the cultivation of coffee due to the agrarian reform, but he was forced repeatedly to admit that he had no bad news to report. See McKnight to DOS: no. 748, Feb. 27, 1953; no. 902, Apr. 14, 1953; no. 304, Oct. 8, 1953; no. 854, Apr. 9, 1954; no. 308, Oct. 13, 1954. All NA 814.2333.

The Arbenz government sought to provide technical assistance to the beneficiaries of the agrarian reform through the newly created Oficina de Programas de Producción Agrícola and through special publications such as *El Campesino*, which explained in straightforward language how to increase productivity and fight blight; these educational efforts were made more effective by the development of the network of local agrarian committees and rural unions.[51]

Furthermore, contrary to what Fidel Castro later did in Cuba, Arbenz and his communist advisers did not attempt to impose a land tenancy system that went against the wishes of the rural population. Collectivization, they had concluded, was politically impossible in Guatemala and would remain so for a long time.[52]

Finally, the government did not turn the internal terms of trade against the rural producers in order to court the urban populace. As the U.S. embassy noted, it adopted a "policy of setting support prices for certain basic crops as a means of stimulating agricultural production."[53]

It is hardly surprising, then, that "many thousands of peasant families lived much better than ever before."[54] Decree 900 even benefited many of those who had not received land. By decreasing the labor pool, it pushed up real wages for agricultural workers, as did the growing unionization of rural labor and the government's sustained efforts on its behalf.[55]

Nor were the benefits simply material. What an anthropologist wrote of Guatemala in the early 1930s still held true in the fifties: "The land is for the Indian the symbol of his right to live, the connecting link between the material life with the divine existence."[56] For the first time since the Spanish conquest, the government returned land to the Indians. In the words of an unsympathetic U.S. official, "The Indians are not only to receive land, but they are in the process educated to regard it as a right."[57] For the first time, also, the rural workers and small peasants participated in trade union activities, even though their role was confined to the local level. The status of many landless agricultural workers was also enhanced by articles 13 and 14 of Decree 900, which stipulated that, on private estates, all settlements of agricultural workers con-

---

[51] One issue of *El Campesino* (Jan.–Mar. 1954) is in the *GT*, Box 7.

[52] Interviews with María de Arbenz, Fortuny, Guerra Borges, and Alejandro.

[53] *JW* 42, Oct. 16, 1953, II:2.

[54] Pearson, "Guatemala," p. 326. A glimpse of life in the countryside is provided by the voluminous documentation in CSC:DAT, AGCA for 1952 (which includes items for 1951 and 1953), 1953, and 1954.

[55] An examination of the labor contracts for the relevant period indicates an average of 35¢–50¢ per day in 1950 and 80¢ per day in 1953. (See CT:DAT, 1950–1953, AGCA.)

[56] Moisés Saenz, quoted in Reina, "Chinautla," p. 98.

[57] Hill to Ambassador, Oct. 2, 1952, p. 2, RG84 CF, Box 15, NA-S.

sisting of more than fifteen families would be designated urban centers, and private roads connecting these settlements with the outside world would be nationalized. This facilitated "state control" over the agricultural workers, lamented a State Department report.[58] Perhaps so, but only insofar as it weakened the landowner's grip over his workers' lives.

In early 1954, as a companion measure to Decree 900, the government began a literacy campaign in the rural areas. Although Arbenz, like Arévalo before him, was hampered by scarce resources, his campaign promised to be far more effective than the efforts of his predecessor. A network of support now existed in the countryside: the CNCG and the CGTG with their labor unions. These two labor confederations prodded their rural affiliates "to seize this magnificent opportunity." Literacy, land, and credit were, they stressed, intimately connected: the peasants needed to read and write in order to "present their demands [for land], transact their business with the agrarian authorities, and deal with other problems such as writing to the Agrarian Committees, asking for credit from the Agrarian Bank, buying and selling their crops, etc."[59]

This pragmatic approach was evident at the third congress of the CNCG in February 1954. As president of Guatemala, Arévalo had extolled the virtues of literacy for the rural masses, but he had offered them neither land nor credit and had thus robbed literacy of practical value. Now, at the congress of the CNCG, the impassioned appeal of a semiliterate peasant leader from the Indian department of Huehuetenango explained the importance of literacy with a clarity the eminent professor had lacked: "We must be able to read and write so that we can take advantage of the agrarian reform and take charge of our lives."[60]

Change was stirring in the countryside. In a study conducted in the summer of 1954 among peasants jailed after the overthrow of Arbenz, Richard Adams noted:

An awakening of profound import did take place for many . . . but it was not what usually has come under the rubric of "ideological." It could better be called a "sociological awakening," for it amounted to a realization that certain of the previously accepted roles and statuses within the social system were no longer bounded by the same rules, and that new channels were suddenly opened for the expression of and satisfaction of needs. The heretofore established series of relationships between political leader and countryman, between employer and laborer, between Indian and

[58] OIR, "Agrarian Reform in Guatemala," no. 6001, Mar. 5, 1953, p. 5, NA.

[59] Quotations from Castillo Flores to the Secretarios de Uniones Campesinas del Departamento de Izabal, June 2, 1954, *GT*, Box 12, and from CNCG, Circular, Feb. 15, 1954, p. 1, *GT*, Box 11. For other relevant documents, see ibid., Boxes 10–12.

[60] "Exposición de la federación campesina de Huehuetenango ante el Tercero Congreso Nacional Campesino," *GT*, Box 12.

Ladino, were not suddenly changed, but it abruptly became possible to introduce some change into them.[61]

The injustices of some arbitrary land seizures must be weighed against the massive injustices corrected by the implementation of Decree 900. The acts of violence among peasants struggling for the same land and those committed by peasants against landowners are regrettable, but such incidents were few, both in actual numbers and relative to the magnitude of the transformation taking place.

The reports of the Guatemalan opposition press were sensational, but they cited very few concrete cases of illegal land occupations or acts of violence against property or persons.[62] Equally instructive are the reports of the U.S. embassy. In February 1953, the embassy stated that "incidents" associated with the agrarian reform had been "local in scale and sporadic"; there were reports of "several minor clashes in rural areas," but "in general, the Administration moved forward without serious incident in its accelerated Agrarian Reform program."[63] On March 27, the embassy noted that "instances of violence in rural areas continued to be reported," but added that "in some cases" the local authorities had taken steps to restore order. "The pace of these lawless acts [has] diminished," it concluded at the end of April. And indeed a reader of U.S. reports will find little on the subject for the rest of the year.[64] In March 1954, reporting on land seizures in the department of Escuintla, the embassy stated: "Last year when the planting season got underway in March there was a marked decrease in such agrarian disturbances."[65]

It was only in the last weeks of the Arbenz regime that violence in the countryside increased—a time, that is, when fear of an attack abetted by the United States was mounting. Even so, the conclusion of Neale Pearson, the foremost American authority on Decree 900, is unimpeachable. There were cases, he wrote, "in which the peasants illegally occupied lands and a few in which they burned pastures or crops in order to have land declared uncultivated and subject to expropriation. But these cases were isolated and limited in numbers."[66] Moreover, the peasants' attacks against landowners were often acts of self-defense: "in a number of instances the plantation owner burned the shacks of the workers and drove them off the plantation," writes Whetten, a former State Department official.[67]

[61] Adams, "Receptivity," p. 361.

[62] Based on a thorough reading of *El I* and *La Hora* and a selective reading of *El Espectador* and *Prensa Libre*.

[63] Quotations from *JW* 8, Feb. 20, 1953, I:2 and *JW* 9, Feb. 27, 1953, I:2.

[64] Quotations from *JW* 13, Mar. 27, 1953, I:1 and *JW* 17, Apr. 24, 1953, I:3.

[65] *JW* 10, Mar. 12, 1954, p. 3.

[66] Pearson, "*Confederación*," p. 180.

[67] Whetten, *Guatemala*, p. 158. Reports of such incidents can be found in the *GT*,

On several occasions, particularly in the early months of Decree 900, the landowners' violence was condoned by the local authorities. Police officers, other officials and even some governors of departments found it difficult to curb their sympathy for the "genteel" elite that knew how to reward favors.[68] This was the time-honored response of a world that Arévalo had hardly disturbed. But now, under Arbenz, unprecedented orders emanated from the capital. A lengthy February 1953 circular from the national chief of the police is revealing. Noting that "lately peasants have voiced complaints against the police," he admonished the police chiefs of all the departments of the republic:

> Put an end to such abuses immediately. It is of utmost importance to avoid friction between the policemen and the peasants; otherwise the latter will think of the police . . . with the same revulsion they felt for them during the dictatorships of Ubico and Ponce. There have already been occasions when the peasants have asserted that today's policemen are the same as the bloodthirsty individuals from that nefarious past. Therefore I urge you, if you want to retain my trust, do not stuff these orders in a drawer without first being sure that your subordinates understand that they must absolutely avoid insulting or abusing the peasants.[69]

Abuses against the peasants by the local authorities continued, but they were sharply reduced because of pressure from the capital and the removal of some particularly obnoxious local policemen. Abandoned, therefore, to their own devices, and fearing the government's retribution, the landowners moderated their behavior.[70] As a result, violence in the countryside decreased, at least until the last weeks of the regime. In comparison with the land reform that occurred at roughly the same time in Bolivia, the Guatemalan reform was a model of order. Had the level of violence been significant, agricultural output would have suffered, as it did in Bolivia.

Indeed, some of the excesses were indispensible to the success of the agrarian reform. The impeachment of the four Supreme Court justices in February 1953 was the only illegal act committed by the Guatemalan Congress during the

---

esp. Boxes 10 and 12, in the government press and even, at times, in *La Hora*, whose owner, Marroquín Rojas, was the maverick of the Guatemalan right. (See, for instance: "CNC denuncia varios asesinatos," Jan. 3, 1953, p. 1; "Se incendiaron terrenos que habían entregado a los agraristas," Mar. 4, 1953, p. 1; "Cinco asesinatos cometidos en la laguna de Retana motivan protesta renovada de dirigentes campesinos," June 10, 1953, p. 1.)

[68] See *GT*, Boxes 1, 5, 12, and 20.

[69] "Rogelio Cruz Wer a señor jefe de la guardia civil departamental," Feb. 25, 1953, *GT*, Box 14. The circular was leaked to *El I*. (See "Curiosa circular," *El I*, Aug. 7, 1953, p. 1; "Circular de la Guardia Civil," *El I*, Aug. 8, 1953, p. 1.)

[70] See *GT*, Boxes 10 and 12.

entire Arbenz period, and it was done solely so that the agrarian reform would not be paralyzed. It is striking that those Americans who showed the most indulgence for the "pecadillos" of men like Somoza and Trujillo were the most outraged by this transgression by Arbenz and the Guatemalan Congress.

And was the system of compensation for expropriated lands as unjust as many claimed? Guatemala was, after all, following America's example: the U.S.-directed agrarian reform in Formosa and Japan had also stipulated payment in bonds over a twenty-to-twenty-five-year period with annual interest rates of 3 percent. Moreover, if the amount of compensation offered by Decree 900 was nugatory, who could be faulted but the "victimized" landowners? No one had forced them to cheat on their tax returns. Among these landowners was United Fruit. From May 1951 to March 1952, the company had been locked in an increasingly bitter conflict with its workers over the renewal of labor contracts. Throughout those months, the company proved that it had lost none of its arrogance and intransigence, as it laid off 3,746 workers without pay and resisted the government's attempts to mediate. In the final settlement, the workers largely accepted UFCO's conditions.[71] But the company had little time to celebrate. In June 1952, the Agrarian Reform Law was enacted. The following March President Arbenz upheld the DAN's decision to expropriate 234,000 acres of uncultivated land at UFCO's 295,000 acre plantation at Tiquisate. In February 1954 UFCO lost 173,000 acres of uncultivated land at Bananera, a plantation of 253,000 acres. The Guatemalan government assessed the value of the expropriated land at $1,185,000—that is, the amount declared by UFCO for tax purposes prior to May 10, 1952. UFCO immediately protested that the land was really worth $19,355,000, a claim that was steadfastly endorsed by the State Department.[72]

Champions of United Fruit have argued that the Arbenz administration acted in a discriminatory manner by expropriating such a high percentage of the company's land. UFCO, they contend, needed to keep most of its land fallow as a precaution in case of Panama disease (a blight that attacks banana plantations), as well as other natural disasters. The highly technical debate as to the exact amount of land UFCO needed to hold in reserve has never been resolved satisfactorily, but it is likely that the claims of both sides were exaggerated.[73]

[71] The crisis can best be followed in *DCA* and *El I*, and in embassy despatches filed in NA 814.062 (esp. despatches nos. 348, 454, 500, 697). See also the fifty-second and the fifty-third annual reports of United Fruit.

[72] On UFCO's claim and the State Department's response, see NA, Lot 57D618, Boxes 2 and 3; *Department of State Bulletin*, no. 29 (July–Dec. 1953), pp. 357–60, and no. 30 (Jan.–June 1954), pp. 678–79; *JW* 9 (Feb. 27, 1953), 10 (Mar. 6, 1953), 12 (Mar. 19, 1953), 33 (Aug. 14, 1953), 8 (Mar. 1, 1954).

[73] See the excellent discussion in Aybar de Soto, *Dependency*, pp. 200–204.

THE PUBLIC WORKS PROGRAM

Arbenz was seeking more than land. He intended to break the power of a foreign enclave that threatened the country's sovereignty. In this pursuit, he faced more than UFCO and would have to initiate more than agrarian reform. Vital sectors of the country's infrastructure were controlled by American companies that enjoyed immense privileges. Determined to loosen their grip on his country's economy, Arbenz moved forward with his public works program. This program would displace the Americans through competition rather than expropriation and call on foreign expertise, but not foreign capital. Largely following the blueprint suggested by a 1951 World Bank report on Guatemala, it had three major components.[74]

The first was the contruction of a large road network. "The inadequacy of present facilities for transportation," the World Bank had stated, "probably constitutes the greatest single barrier to the economic development and the cultural integration of the Republic." Particularly critical was a road linking the capital with the Caribbean coast; such a road would supplement the railway to Puerto Barrios, which was inadequate, expensive, and American. "Without this road—or at least positive proof that it will be constructed in the immediate future—there is no real indication that the Government is vitally interested in expediting or cheapening the movement of international freight," the World Bank had concluded.[75]

The second component was the construction of a port in the bay of Santo Tomás on the Caribbean coast, a few miles from Puerto Barrios—"a dream that had persisted for three and a half centuries."[76] Here, too, economic and political considerations went hand in hand. The inadequate facilities at Puerto Barrios created costly bottlenecks in the handling of foreign trade and were controlled by an American company. The third component of the program was the construction of a hydroelectric plant. The country's production of electricity was insufficient, uneconomical, and controlled by a U.S. company.

In April 1953 the government unveiled its road building plan. It proposed the construction of 750 miles of paved roads in the remaining four years of Arbenz's term. Except for its ambitious deadlines, the plan basically followed the 1951 World Bank report.[77]

Had the Guatemalan authorities attempted to accomplish so much in only

[74] For Arbenz's public works program, interviews with María de Arbenz, Fortuny, Guerra Borges, Paz Tejada, Charnaud, Bauer Paiz, and Capuano were particularly helpful. For the World Bank report, see IBRD, *Economic Development*.

[75] IBRD, *Economic Development*, pp. 132–210. Quoted from pp. 132 and 201.

[76] Griffith, "Santo Tomás," p. 40.

[77] From Apr. 10 to Apr. 28, 1953, *DCA* ran a series of articles on the plan, which presented the government's views. For comments by the U.S. embassy, see *JW* 16–18, Apr. 17–May 1, 1953.

four years, they would have courted disaster, for the country's technical and financial resources were inadequate. Fortunately, they followed a more pragmatic approach: they concentrated their efforts on the all-important 193-mile Atlantic Highway, which would connect the capital with the port of Santo Tomás. The necessary heavy equipment had been imported from the United States in 1952, and actual work began in earnest in the last months of that year. The U.S. embassy reported in mid-1953: "The Highway has continued to receive top priority among Guatemalan public works projects and has gained widening public support as results have been demonstrated."[78] The steady progress seemed to justify the government's promise that the highway would be completed by mid- or late-1955. (Arbenz's overthrow delayed the work, and the highway was not opened until mid-1957. As Arbenz and the World Bank had predicted, its existence forced the railway to lower its rates.)[79]

On July 2, 1953, Guatemala signed a contract with a subsidiary of the Morrison-Knudsen Company of San Francisco for the construction of the port of Santo Tomás, the future terminus of the Atlantic Highway. The contract stipulated that the port be completed within twenty-four months at a cost of $4.8 million. The government deposited this sum in foreign exchange in the United States as guarantee of payment, and the company posted a performance bond.[80] While the Guatemalan Congress, at Arbenz's request, declared the project to be one of public necessity (which insured certain priorities and immunities),[81] company representatives told the U.S. embassy that "they were satisfied with the contract." It was, the embassy concluded with little enthusiasm, "a major step in the Government's four-year economic development program."[82]

A few months earlier, in April 1953, Guatemala had contracted another U.S. firm, Westinghouse, to study the feasibility of a 28,000-kilowatt hydroelectric plant at Jurún in the department of Escuintla. This study would serve as the basis for the opening of competitive bidding for the construction of the plant, which would take approximately four years and cost $6 million.[83]

[78] *JW* 21, May 22, 1953, II:2.

[79] See Piedra-Santa, "La construcción de ferrocarriles," pp. 26–28.

[80] See "Firmado contrato con la Morrison," *DCA*, July 3, 1953, p. 1. The text of the contract was published in *DCA*, July 3, 6, 8, 9, 10, and 11, 1953.

[81] "Declaración de utilidad y necesidad públicas construcción del muelle de Santo Tomás," *DCA*, June 15, 1953, p. 1, and "Declarada de utilidad pública la expropiación de terrenos en donde se construirá puerto Santo Tomás," *DCA*, July 8, 1953, p. 1.

[82] *JW* 28, July 9, 1953, II:1–2. The port began operations in September 1955. (See "Decreto inaugural del puerto de Santo Tomás," *El I*, Sept. 13, 1955, p. 1.)

[83] See "Estudios técnicos para la construcción de la planta hidroeléctrica de Marinalá," *DCA*, June 1, 1953, p. 1; Government Information Bureau, *Guatemala*, no. 7,

A "Basically Prosperous" Economy

"The present Government . . . promises to leave a record of real accomplishments in the field of public works," conceded the U.S. embassy in May 1954.[84] In fact, both aspects of the government's economic program were proceeding successfully. The embassy had originally assumed that the agrarian reform would fail. Now it reserved its judgment. After listing Arbenz's claims of success in his March 1954 message to Congress, it concluded: "A preliminary analysis of the President's report left little doubt, as long as coffee prices are at their present high level, that the Guatemalan economy was basically prosperous."[85]

Despite UFCO's furious complaints that the government was strangling it and would force it to leave the country, 1953 saw the highest level of banana exports since 1948, thanks mainly to favorable weather conditions and to a diminution of labor conflicts.[86] Decree 900 had precipitated capital flight, but this loss was amply offset by the high coffee prices—in this regard, luck truly blessed Arbenz. As a result, the government's foreign currency reserves were sound: $39.4 million on December 31, 1950; $44 million two years later; $42.4 at the end of 1953.[87] Indeed, the U.S. embassy, after noting the $1.6 million drop in reserves between December 1952 and December 1953, explained,

---

Aug. 1, 1953, pp. 1–2; MemoConv (Schoenfeld, Whitbeck), Sept. 3, 1952, RG84 CF, Box 15, NA-S; MemoConv (Ford, Dyktor, Leddy), May 15, 1953, NA 814.2614; MemoConv (Schoenfeld, Dyktor), May 25, 1953, enclosed in Schoenfeld to Leddy, June 12, 1953, NA 814.2614; MemoConv (Partridge, Attwood, Leddy), Apr. 5, 1954, NA 814.2614.

[84] "Economic and Financial Review—1953" (see n. 12 above), p. 22.

[85] *JW* 9, Mar. 5, 1954, pp. 4–5. See also John Peurifoy, U.S. Congress, *HCFA*, Jan. 26, 1954, p. 463.

[86] See McKnight to DOS, no. 349, Oct. 23, 1953, NA 814.2376; McKnight to DOS, no. 875, Apr. 26, 1954, NA 814.2376; "Economic and Financial Review—1953" (see n. 12 above), pp. 6–7, 9–10.

[87] See "Economic and Financial Review—1953" (see n. 12 above), p. 10, and AmEmG, "Balance of Payments, Guatemala, 1953," no. 918, May 7, 1954, NA 814.10. Because of higher prices, the value of Guatemala's coffee exports soared from $33,670,000 in 1949 to $68,229,000 in 1953 and $71,380,000 in 1954. The effect was dramatic: Guatemala's balance of trade showed a small surplus in 1946 ($475,000); a deficit from 1947 to 1951 (1947, −$5,286,000; 1948, −$18,184,000; 1949, −$15,757,000; 1950, −$3,616,000; 1951, −$4,761,000). It showed a surplus in 1952 ($11,741,000) and in 1953 ($9,384,000). This surplus was achieved despite considerable increases in the cost of the imports. See Guatemala's *Anuario de comercio exterior* and the annual economic reports of the U.S. embassy (NA 814.00) for the relevant years.

not only were these [December 1953] totals much more than adequate for the requirements of the Guatemalan monetary laws, but they were higher than they had stood at the end of 1949, 1950 or 1951. Furthermore, the abnormally late coffee season in 1953 delayed the inflow of foreign exchange from the sale of the new coffee crop so that the drop below the mark of the year end of 1952 was of no significance, and in fact, with the heavy movements of the crop in January, February and March 1954, the Monetary Stabilization Fund and official international monetary reserves reached all-time highs.[88]

The funds needed for the agricultural credits provided by the government and for the public works program came mainly through indirect taxation. The rising value of Guatemala's foreign trade brought higher receipts from existing import and export duties. The authorities also sought to tighten collection and began, in late 1952, to raise taxes and duties. These measures hit the well-off hardest, but the urban poor were not unaffected.[89]

The emphasis on agrarian reform and public works meant, moreover, that Arbenz had been unable to focus on the needs of the urban population. Real income in urban areas did not rise during his presidency, as wage increases were offset by higher indirect taxes and inflation.[90] Nor did the government alleviate the housing crisis in the cities. In November 1953, Congress passed a rent control law, but, as *Diario de Centro América* noted, it did "not solve the housing problem. . . . The solution is to build more low cost housing, but this would take time and money that we do not have."[91] While the law brought some respite to the urban lower class, it also aggravated the slump in private sector housing construction.

Furthermore, the government was hampered by the graft and incompetence of many of its officials. (On both counts, the most striking example was the October 1953 Fair, a notorious fiasco that cost the state close to $1 million.)[92]

[88] "Economic and Financial Review—1953" (see n. 12 above), p. 16; see also the embassy's economic summaries for Feb.–June 1954 (NA 814.00).

[89] For the beginnings of the policy, see AmEmG, "Monthly Financial Statement—June 1951," no. 78, July 20, 1951, NA 814.10; for a useful summary see "Economic and Financial Review—1953" (see n. 12 above), pp. 14–15.

[90] While there is no study on this subject, there is a wealth of material in the Guatemalan press and in the economic and labor reports of the U.S. embassy. A series of articles in *DCA* about Guatemala's first Conference on the High Cost of Living is particularly instructive; see esp. "Llamamiento a la Conferencia Contra el Alto Costo de la Vida," July 30, 1953, p. 1; " El alto costo de la vida" (edit.), Aug. 7 and 21, 1953, both p. 3; "Ministro Fanjul inauguró la conferencia," Aug. 28, 1953, p. 1; "Clausurada la Conferencia del Alto Costo de la Vida," Aug. 29, 1953, p. 1; "Importantes resoluciones aprobadas," Aug. 31, 1953, p. 1; "Resoluciones de la Conferencia Contra el Alto Costo de la Vida," Sept. 4, 8, 10, 11, 12, and 17, 1953 (all p. 4).

[91] "La Ley de Inquilinato," *DCA*, Nov. 18, 1953, p. 3.

[92] See "La Feria de Octubre" (edit.), *DCA*, Aug. 3, 1953, p. 3; "Propaganda y

But Arbenz wisely concentrated his small pool of efficient bureaucrats in the most critical programs. He also sought technical assistance from international agencies. "Government cooperation in technical assistance programs has generally been fairly good," noted the U.S. embassy.[93] He did not hesitate to seek the services of U.S. companies for the construction of the port of Santo Tomás and the hydroelectric plant at Jurún.

Yet the government was unable to balance the 1953–1954 budget, the largest in the country's history. This failure led to a more realistic budget for the following year and to the determination to enact the first income tax in Guatemala's history. The tax would increase the government's receipts and democratize what U.S. experts justly considered a most regressive fiscal system.[94] Noted *Diario de Centro América*:

> Our poor millionaires yell bloody murder whenever the government touches their pocketbooks. . . . But whether they like it or not, the Revolution cannot go forward given the present tax system. It has become increasingly difficult for the State to develop its progressive programs under our feudal fiscal system that has barely changed since 1944. The time has come to correct this situation. Our unfortunate millionaires will have to pay taxes appropriate to our new circumstances, that is, to the capitalist development of our country. . . . The meaning of income tax is simple: the rich man pays as a rich man, and the poor man pays as a poor man. If there are differences in wealth and income, then there must also be in taxes.[95]

In December 1953, the government presented an income tax bill to Congress. During the next months the draft was revised first by a congressional committee and then by the executive. On May 28, the bill was approved by Congress in the first of three required readings;[96] the second reading was postponed to allow Congress to consider the government's budget for 1954-1955,

---

contrapropaganda a la Feria de Octubre en Estados Unidos" (edit.), *DCA*, Sept. 22, 1953, p. 3; "La Feria de Octubre culminará en éxito" (edit.), *DCA*, Oct. 14, 1953, p. 3; "La mala organización del coso originó el desorden de la Feria," *Tribuna Popular*, Oct. 22, 1953, p. 8; "La Feria que quisimos conocer" and "Una tarde en la Feria," *DCA*, Nov. 12, 1953, pp. 2 and 4; "Lo recaudado en la Feria no es ni la 10a. parte de lo invertido," *La Hora*, Nov. 18, 1953, p. 1. See also *JW* 43, Oct. 23, 1953, II.

[93] "Economic Development in Guatemala," no. 793, Mar. 13, 1953, p. 6, NA 814.00. The State Department had toyed with the idea of pressuring the UN to cut off its technical assistance to Guatemala but decided against it "since it was impossible to keep anything confidential in the United Nations." (MemoConv, "U.N. Technical Assistance to Guatemala," May 3, 1951, NA Lot 58D18 & 58D78, Box 3.)

[94] See Adler, Schlesinger, and Olson, *Public Finance*, pp. 41–66. See also United Nations, ECLA, *La política tributaria*, p. 123.

[95] "Desfeudalización de los impuestos," *DCA*, Jan. 4, 1954, p. 1.

[96] "Ley de impuesto sobre la renta conocida en primera lectura," *DCA*, May 29, 1954, p. 1; "Las leyes a toda maquina," *El I*, May 29, 1954, p. 1.

which was approved on June 7.[97] In a few more days, Guatemala would have had its first income tax law.

On the surface, the healthy state of the economy was matched by equally satisfactory developments in the political realm: the administration was popular, Arbenz's control of the government coalition appeared firm, and the opposition was in disarray. In the shadows, disaster loomed.

[97] "Aprobado ayer el presupuesto," *DCA*, June 8, 1954, p. 1. At $70,094,000, the FY 1954–1955 budget was $4,496,000 lower than that of the previous year. As the U.S. embassy noted, it made "no provision for some of the grandiose highway plans previously publicized by the government" and was realistic in its estimate of government income. (*JW* 14, Apr. 9, 1954, p. 4 [quoted], and Wardlaw to DOS, no. 1027, June 29, 1954, NA 814.10.)

CHAPTER 9

The Revolutionary Forces

ON DECEMBER 18, 1953, a squad of gun-toting braves stormed the headquarters of Renovación Nacional (RN), the party created by a group of teachers in July 1944. In the ensuing fistfight, the leader of the attackers, Jaime Díaz Rozzotto, pistol-whipped one of the defenders, an RN congressman. Before things got worse, the police intervened.

The affray at RN was not the prelude to an attack on the government. Díaz Rozzotto was not a right-wing plotter; he was, or rather had been, RN's secretary general. He was merely out to wrest the party headquarters—and his post—from his rivals, who had expelled him the previous day.

The Guatemalan Congress immediately censured Díaz Rozzotto. Undeterred, he proceeded to expel his adversaries from RN, and he was in turn expelled again. And so it continued, to the delight of the opposition press. The developments in RN, remarked the U.S. embassy, were "of the type which adds to the disciplined Guatemalan Communist Party's carefully cultivated reputation as the 'most honest' of the leftist parties supporting the Arbenz administration."[1]

Eventually, the warring factions convened a "Unity Congress"; it opened at noon, March 20, 1954, and closed a few hours later, amid gunshots, leaving one policeman dead and two delegates wounded. By the time Arbenz fell, there were four tiny "RNs" locked in fierce competition for the official party name and the government's patronage.[2]

[1] Krieg to DOS, no. 533, Dec. 21, 1953, p. 1, NA 714.00. For the battle and its immediate aftermath, see "Sucesos de ayer en Renovación Nacional," *DCA*, Dec. 19, 1953, p. 1; "Gangsterismo político sancionado" and "El escandalo de Renovación," *El I*, Dec. 19, 1953, p. 1; "Dos fracciones pugnan por la legitimidad en Renovación," *El I*, Dec. 21, 1953, p. 1. See also the series of interviews with the protagonists in *Tribuna Popular*: "Divergencias conmueven al Partido Renovación Nacional," Dec. 19, 1953, p. 1; "De las divergencias en Renovación Nacional," Dec. 20, 1953, p. 1; "Divergencias en Renovación Nacional," Dec. 22, 1953, p. 1; "De las divergencias en Renovación Nacional," Dec. 23, 1953, p. 1.

[2] The best press coverage of the congress is by *El I*: "Alas renovacionistas citan a consejo general," Mar. 17, 1954, p. 1; "Díaz Rozzotto o Fión Garma; convención RN empieza," Mar. 20, 1954, p. 1; "Alas RN rotas en sangre" and "Sucesos trágicos del Gimnasio Olímpico," Mar. 22, 1954, p. 1. For later developments in RN, see "Ultimatum a Renovación vence viernes," *El I*, Apr. 27, 1954, p. 1; "El partido RN en estertores de agonía," *La Hora*, Apr. 30, 1954, p. 1; "Directiva unitaria en el PRN,"

THE REVOLUTIONARY PARTIES

The schisms of RN notwithstanding, the coalition that supported Arbenz continued practically unchanged from the 1950 campaign to his fall. It included the revolutionary parties, the Communist party and the country's two labor confederations, the CGTG and the CNCG. Together, they formed the Frente Democrático Nacional (FDN), an advisory body chaired by Arbenz.[3]

To be sure, the names and the number of the revolutionary parties changed in the Arbenz years. They had been four as Arbenz became president—the PAR, RN, the FPL, and the PIN. They became five in July 1951, as a split in the PAR gave birth to the Partido Socialista (PS). (The PS, a judicious observer remarked, had "neither ideology nor platform.")[4] Eleven months later, the five suddenly merged and became one, the Partido de la Revolución Guatemalteca (PRG).[5] Within six weeks, most PAR and RN leaders had withdrawn to re-create their old parties amid a flurry of recriminations. Yet the PRG survived; it included the PS, the moribund FPL, the minuscule PIN, and former members of the PAR and RN.

Despite this tendency to split, reunite, and rename, the revolutionary parties scored massive victories in the congressional and municipal elections, and it was their leaders whom Arbenz chose as his ministers and senior officials. They had a powerful ally in the country's largest labor confederation, the peasant-based CNCG, whose leaders had little sympathy for communism and the PGT. By February 1954, the CNCG had 1,500 local unions and 150,000 to 190,000 members.[6] Its impressive growth—it had claimed only twenty-five local unions in May 1950—was due to Arbenz's unwavering support and to the dynamism unleashed in the countryside by the agrarian reform.

Tribuna Popular, May 7, 1954, p. 8; "No existe todavía unidad en Renovación Nacional," *DCA*, May 10, 1954, p. 1; "Cuatro alas renovacionistas," *El I*, May 17, 1954, p. 1; "Al morir Renovación, dejó huérfanos a siete diputados," *La Hora*, May 18, 1954, p. 1; "No inscriben planilla de Renovación," *DCA*, June 1, 1954, p. 1. See also *JW* 12, Mar. 26, 1954, p. 3, and *JW* 19, May 14, 1954, p. 2.

[3] The FDN was not Arbenz's "kitchen cabinet." It met irregularly, was not privy to the president's secret decisions, and dealt mainly with minor issues. Its significance is comparable to that of the cabinet: not an irrelevant body, but not one of great importance either. (Interviews with Charnaud, Guerra Borges, Capuano, Bauer Paiz, María de Arbenz; see also Gutiérrez, *Breve historia*, p. 70, and Unión Patriótica Gualtemalteca, *Guatemala*, p. 21.)

[4] Pearson, "*Confederación*," p. 102.

[5] See: "Fusión del PAR y PS, de gran importancia para la revolución," *DCA*, June 11, 1952, p. 1; "A toda la nación: Hacia un partido único de la Revolución de Octubre," *DCA*, June 12, 1952, p. 6; "Manifiesto del FPL," ibid., p. 1; "Manifiesto del Partido de la Revolución Guatemalteca," *DCA*, July 1, 1952, p. 6; *Boletín informativo del PRG*, no. 1, Aug. 9, 1952, *GT*, Box 9.

[6] See Pearson, "*Confederación*," pp. 40–43.

While careful to maintain its independence, the CNCG was solidly encamped within the fold of the revolutionary parties. Secretary General Castillo Flores was a PAR deputy when he had helped found the CNCG in May 1950. After joining the PS in July 1951 and the PRG one month later, he returned to the PAR in August 1952.[7] Throughout his wanderings, he retained firm—though not absolute—control of the CNCG, purging rivals when necessary. Most CNCG leaders followed him back to the PAR; others stayed with the PRG. The official line of the CNCG was that it was not a political organization; therefore its members could "belong to whatever party treats the peasants best."[8] In practice each leader told the peasants, more or less discreetly, which party to join. This resulted in a massive turnout for the PAR and, to a lesser degree, for the PRG.

While the CNCG was quite united under Castillo Flores, the revolutionary parties were plagued by infighting that acquired at times the character of a B western. Díaz Rozzotto's December exploit was not unprecedented. Two months earlier, on October 13, 1953, the recently ousted secretary general of the PAR, Francisco Fernández Foncea, had stormed the headquarters of his party with a band of armed associates. His motivation was as selfless as that of Díaz Rozzotto: to save the PAR from the grip of the newly installed Executive Committee, which had just expelled him. Mutual excommunications succeeded one another at a rapid clip, while telegrams from each faction poured into the offices of bemused party officials admonishing them, in peremptory terms, to reject the rival leadership. "These episodes in the PAR," reported U.S. Ambassador Schoenfeld, "once again illustrate the lack of ideological firmness and the opportunism which prevail in the leftist administration parties and the consequent improbability of the crystallization of a vigorous anticommunist left at the present juncture in Guatemalan politics."[9] Unlike RN, however, the PAR was able to regain some cohesion as one faction gained control and reestablished discipline.[10]

[7] Castillo Flores's peregrinations are well described by Pearson, ibid., pp. 101–10, and Schneider, *Communism*, pp. 158–63.

[8] Castillo Flores to López Fernández, Sept. 10, 1951, *GT*, Box 12.

[9] Schoenfeld to DOS, no. 333, Oct. 16, 1953, p. 2, NA 714.00.

[10] For the October affray and its aftermath, see "Consejo Nacional del PAR en sesión," *DCA*, Oct. 10, 1953, p. 1; "Nueva directiva del PAR," *Tribuna Popular*, Oct. 11, 1953, p. 1; "Fernández Foncea asumió hoy la dirección general del PAR," *DCA*, Oct. 13, 1953, p. 1; "Inscrita la planilla del PAR que encabeza Julio Estrada de la Hoz," *DCA*, Oct. 14, 1953, p. 1; "Decisión del Registro esperan hoy en el PAR," *Tribuna Popular*, Oct. 14, 1953, p. 1; "Al frente de cien marcha a las oficinas," *El I*, Oct. 15, 1953, p. 1; "Acuérdase no otorgar el amparo pedido por Fernández Foncea," *DCA*, Oct. 24, 1953, p. 1; "Manifiesto del grupo de diputados del PAR," *Tribuna Popular*, Nov. 11, 1953, p. 5; "Recurso de Fernández Foncea fué denegado," *DCA*, Nov. 20, 1953, p. 1; "Paristas del ala de Fernández Foncea retornaron al partido,"

Only the PRG escaped the indignity of having former secretaries general invade party headquarters. In its first year, its co–secretaries general, Roberto Alvarado Fuentes and Augusto Charnaud MacDonald, coexisted uneasily while each maneuvered to oust the other. Then, after a purge in August 1953, Alvarado Fuentes was dispatched into genteel exile as Guatemala's Ambassador to Mexico. Charnaud was in command; he was a highly intelligent and competent man, but he was distracted by ambition. In the months that followed his victory, he maintained unity in the PRG by purges and by the postponement of the party's first congress, which was not held until January 1954. Carefully orchestrated, the congress proceeded uneventfully, ratifying the existing leadership despite muted grumblings.[11]

The infighting that bedeviled the revolutionary parties owed little to ideological considerations; in fact, no faction had a coherent ideology or strategy. It was the ambitions of too many leaders that caused the dissension. Their squabbles and lack of direction reinforced the authority of Arbenz, a president with a program. One such squabble, and Arbenz's reaction to it, are described in the diary of a revolutionary politician. It was the fall of 1952, in a meeting in the presidential palace between Arbenz and the leaders of the administration parties.

"At our last meeting," Arbenz began, "we spent seven hours determining the slate of candidates for the upcoming [congressional] elections. I had assumed that we had been proceeding on the basis of revolutionary unity and loyalty, but I have just now learned that one of the parties here has been scheming against another. . . .

"Gentlemen, I am shocked and deeply worried." While saying this, his face was suffused with anger. "What kind of revolutionary unity is this? What do you think

---

DCA, Dec. 9, 1953, p. 1. For telegrams by the rival factions to local party officials, see *GT*, Boxes 1 and 6.

[11] For the PRG's congress and the infighting that preceded it, see "A todos los hombres y mujeres del Partido de la Revolución Guatemalteca," June 1953, *GT*, Box 8; "Comunicado de prensa," Aug. 8, 1953, *GT*, Box 9; "Fracción parlamentaria del PRG retiran del Frente Democrático," *DCA*, Sept. 25, 1953, p. 1; "Divergencias entre los diputados y la Comisión Política del PRG," *Tribuna Popular*, Sept. 26, 1953, p. 1; "Se reunirá bloque de diputados del PRG," *Tribuna Popular*, Sept. 27, 1953, p. 1; "Bloque de diputados del PRG por la unidad del partido," *DCA*, Sept. 29, 1953, p. 1; "Reafirman unidad en el PRG," *DCA*, Oct. 1, 1953, p. 1; "Fracción parlamentaria del PRG debe actuar conforme estatutos," *DCA*, Oct. 2, 1953, p. 1; "Texto de renuncias de 6 PRG," *El I*, Oct. 15, 1953, p. 1; "Sesiones de la Comisión Política y del Comité Ejecutivo Nacional," Dec. 23, 1953 (internal PRG document), *GT*, Box 9; "Instalada la Convención del PRG," *DCA*, Jan. 16, 1954, p. 1; "Directivo del PRG electo ayer," *DCA*, Jan. 18, 1954, p. 1; *Diario del Pueblo*, issues of Jan. 15, 16, 18, and 19, 1954. For the full text of Charnaud's speech at the congress, see "Informe a la Primera Convención Nacional del Partido de la Revolución Guatemalteca," Jan. 15, 1954, *GT*, Box 9. See also Krieg to DOS, no. 613, Jan. 19, 1954, NA 714.00.

we will achieve if we proceed like this? We are acting like spoiled brats without any sense of our responsibility toward the people. We quarrel among ourselves, and we betray each other without a backward glance. . . .

"God damm it!" He slammed his fist on the table. "There is only one president of the republic, one president of the Congress, one president of the judiciary, but everyone wants to be a president. Every jerk wants a seat in the Congress! Gentlemen, leave this farce behind. . . .

"Do you think that we will be able to sustain the revolution if we act like this? The political parties cannot be groups of village gossips. They must be strongly organized on the basis of a clear revolutionary ideology. Otherwise, what will happen?

"There are times, gentlemen, when I deeply regret that I am an officer. At times, I think that you believe that because I am an officer the army will always be behind us and we are sitting on foundations of granite. But you are completely wrong: the army may tire when we least expect it. And the only way to make sure that this does not happen is to remain united, honorable, and consistent in everything we do. Our task is to consolidate the revolution that began in 1944. We have to take momentous strides forward. We must leave behind our petty ambitions, our rancor, our greed.

"I am sorry that I have had to talk to you like this in the presidential office, but imagine that Jacobo Arbenz was talking to you in your party's offices. I am used to speaking the truth bluntly, and I want you to answer me in the same manner: honestly, without evasion."[12]

The revolutionary politicians endorsed Arbenz's vision of an industrialized Guatemala, but their support for his agrarian reform was lukewarm. They concentrated on garnering peasant support for their own parties and factions, rather than on implementing the reform. As a result, party rivalries deepened. As RN was paralyzed by its internal struggle, the rivalry between the PAR and the PRG intensified.[13]

The model of the revolutionary leaders, insofar as they had one, was Mexico's ruling Partido Revolucionario Institucional (PRI). Their desire to have a similar party in Guatemala led to the creation of the PRG in June 1952. A

[12] Zea González, *El espejismo*, pp. 333–35. I would like to thank José Antonio Montes, who sent me a copy of this privately published book.

[13] For a particularly sharp exchange, see "Manifiesto del Partido de la Revolución Guatemalteca (PRG) a toda la nación," *DCA*, Jan. 14, 1954, p. 4, and "El Partido Acción Revolucionaria—PAR," *DCA*, Jan. 25, 1954, p. 8. A series of documents in the *GT*—Box 13 in particular—illuminates the squabbling among revolutionary parties seeking to steal campesinos from each other and indicates that this concern was more important than the implementation of the agrarian reform. The documents also reveal that several leaders of the revolutionary parties in rural areas flirted with latifundistas— while in other instances latifundistas joined the local branch of a revolutionary party in order to protect their interests and subvert the agrarian reform.

united party would be in a stronger position vis-à-vis the president and his communist friends.[14] Arbenz's antipathy for the project contributed to its swift demise, but it would have failed in any case.[15] Too many self-proclaimed *caudillos* bloated the PRG; unity was impossible.

Many revolutionary leaders were not corrupt. Integrity and selfless commitment to his work characterized Alfonso Bauer Paiz, a senior member of the PRG. Under Arbenz he occupied several key positions with great distinction, notably as the director of the Banco Nacional Agrario. But there were many who took liberties with the country's monies. At times, scandals became public: some exposed or fabricated by the opposition press, others by revolutionary politicians bent on slandering their rivals. Thus the opposition *El Espectador* accused PAR Congressman José Felipe Dardón of attempting to extort $5,000 from auto-parts dealers by threatening to introduce a bill that would have limited their profits to 10 percent. In the course of a tumultuous congressional debate on Dardon's business practices, PAR and PRG deputies swapped insults and charges of corruption, while PGT deputy Pellecer vainly warned that it was a mistake "to stage such a demeaning spectacle for the benefit of the reactionaries." The PGT, Pellecer added drily, was the only party free of such scandals. ("A Mr. Galeano was recently expelled from our party for stealing 40 cents from the receipts of our paper, *Tribuna Popular*," he pointed out.)[16] The U.S. embassy concluded: "The scene in Congress fur-

[14] See de Wiche, "El comunismo en Guatemala," and Guerra Borges, "Apuntes," p. 117. Interviews with Charnaud, Galich, Capuano, and Bauer Paiz were helpful.

[15] Arbenz's opposition, voiced behind the scene, was adamant. (Interviews with María de Arbenz, Fortuny, Guerra Borges.) The PGT expressed its hostility in a four-part series in *Octubre*, which argued that the aim of the "petty bourgeois leaders" of the new party was to isolate the communists in order to stall "the growth of the labor movement and of the Communist party." (Fortuny, "Elementos para analizar la unificación de los partidos democráticos del Gobierno Arbenz," *Octubre*, July 3 [quoted], 10, 17 and 24, 1952.) See also Fortuny, "La ruptura del PRG," *Octubre*, July 31, 1952, p. 6, and letters from Pinto Usaga to Fortuny (Mexico, July 30, 1952, *GT*, Box 8) and from Cuenca, a senior PRG leader, to Fortuny (Aug. 1952, *GT.*, Box 9). Significantly, after delivering a bitter attack on Fortuny's *Octubre* articles (an attack in which Arbenz's name was not even mentioned), Cuenca felt the need to add, "N.B.: Even though it is clear from the text, I want to put in writing that this letter is not an attack on the president of the republic, Colonel Jacobo Arbenz Guzmán." Cuenca understood that Fortuny had expressed Arbenz's sentiments.

[16] Guatemala, *Diario de las sesiones del Congreso*, Nov. 27, 1953, vol. 16, no. 26, pp. 6–21, quoted from p. 16. For the most extensive press coverage of the session, see "Comisión especial investigará las denuncias," *DCA*, Nov. 28, 1953, p. 1, and "Se fijan en un pan y no en los ladrones de la revolución, dijo Fernández Foncea," *El I*, Nov. 28, 1953, p. 1. For the original accusation against Dardón, see "Chantaje usando el nombre del Congreso?" *El Espectador*, Nov. 17, 1953, p. 1.

Schneider provides ample support for Pellecer's statement about Galeano, and adds

ther lowered the prestige of the Administration politicians and gave the Communists an opportunity to claim superior dedication and honesty.''[17]

If venality characterized many revolutionary politicians, self-indulgence was even more widespread. Their penchant for soft desk jobs and perks stood in sharp contrast to the integrity of the PGT, which, the U.S. embassy lamented in late 1953, ''is now the only administration party that has not been shaken by a major scandal in many months.'' (The embassy had never reported any scandal, major or minor, involving the PGT.)[18]

Thus, the revolutionary leaders were not pure and hardy revolutionaries. On the contrary, they combined an increasingly hollow social conscience with a growing empathy for the ''sweet sorrows'' of the bourgeoisie. And their concern about their enigmatic president, whose communist proclivities (and communist friends) were ever more in evidence, deepened. They supported Arbenz with misgivings and looked forward to the 1956 presidential elections.

They compensated for their lack of revolutionary fervor with a fierce nationalism that had blossomed during the Arévalo years and was fanned by the arrogance of the U.S. government and the intransigence of the American companies. This nationalism was coddled, until late 1953, by a false sense of security. The revolutionary leaders believed that the United States might holler, threaten, and even impose limited sanctions on Guatemala. They did not believe, however, that the United States would overthrow the government. Arbenz and the PGT shared this illusion.

---

another example: ''Abel Mazariegos was expelled from the party for drinking, sleeping on the job of selling the Communist newspaper *Tribuna Popular*, as well as for following the usual bureaucratic practice of putting the 'bite' on those who fell under his jurisdiction as an Inspector of the Public Sanitation. . . . Jesús Galeano, a rising young Communist militant . . . was expelled as 'unworthy to be a Communist' for embezzling in excess of 63¢ from *Tribuna Popular*. Expelled by his cell, Galeano appealed to higher organs, but they upheld his expulsion. Galeano attempted to prove himself worthy of readmittance by working long and faithfully for the Third Congress of the CNCG, the peasant labor confederation under Communist influence, the Second Congress of the CGTG, and the Organizing Committee of the Festival of Friendship. He spread Communist propaganda . . . and used his job as Labor Inspector to the advantage of the party. Finally he humbly sought to be readmitted to the party, but the leadership ruled that his request was 'very premature' and that he would have to continue proving that he was worthy of the honor of being Communist.'' (Schneider, *Communism*, p. 112.) On Galeano, see also *GT*, Box 8.

[17] *JW* 49, Dec. 4, 1953, I:2. See also Krieg to DOS, no. 460, Nov. 30, 1953, NA 714.00. When the Guatemalan Congress legislated a pay raise of $200 a month for its members, the communist deputies handed the full amount to the PGT. (Schoenfeld to DOS, no. 1334, June 28, 1952, NA 714.2.)

[18] For the embassy's statement, see Krieg to DOS, no. 533, Dec. 21, 1953, p. 2, NA 714.00. Neither embassy's dispatches for the relevant period nor Schneider in his authoritative *Communism* implicate the PGT in any scandal.

The combination of frustrated nationalism and a heady sense of impunity helps to explain the strident rhetoric of most revolutionary leaders. Hostility to Washington easily translated into verbal support for the Soviet Union, according to the formula enunciated by a Mexican general in the early 1920s: "We are all Bolsheviks! . . . I don't know what Socialism is; but I am a Bolshevik, like all patriotic Mexicans. . . . The Yankees do not like the Bolsheviks; the Yankees are our enemies; therefore, the Bolsheviks must be our friends, and we must be their friends. We are all Bolsheviks!"[19] Radical rhetoric also polished the tarnished revolutionary credentials of its authors; above all, it might please Arbenz, whose patronage they all courted.

For Arbenz's sympathies were unmistakable. While the Guatemalan Foreign Ministry maintained a neutral line in international affairs, the government daily, *Diario de Centro América (DCA)*, did not always disguise its preference for the Soviet bloc. A faithful reader of *DCA* was bound to develop respect for communist Czechoslovakia. In 1953 alone, fifty-three articles described life there, always in sympathetic terms; no other country received such attention. Some titles speak for themselves: "Czechoslovakia and Peace"; "Workers Visit Czechoslovakia: Impressed by Culture of Fellow Workers"; "The Victorious Path of the Slovak People"; "The High Standard of Living of the Czech Workers"; "Job Security in Czechoslovakia"; "All Czech Workers Enjoy Annual Vacations."[20] The following description of a visitor's encounter with Czechoslovakia epitomizes the general tone:

[19] Quoted by Roy, *Memoirs*, p. 154.

[20] DCA: Jan. 8, 1953, p. 6; Aug. 11, 1953, p. 8; Sept. 24, 1953, p. 8; Nov. 19, 1953, p. 4; ibid., p. 1; Dec. 30, 1953, p. 4. The other articles on Czechoslovakia that appeared in *DCA* in 1953 are "La historia del teatro checoslovaco de marionetas," Jan. 5, p. 2; "Interesante exposición en Praga," Jan. 10, p. 6; "Estudios superiores para los trabajadores checos," Jan. 12, p. 2; "Una nueva población surge en Karvina," Feb. 11, p. 8; "El prof. Zdenek Mejedly cumple sus 75 años," ibid.; "Dos mil representaciones de 'La Novia Vendida,' " Feb. 12, p. 6; "El pueblo checoslovaco recuerda al héroe nacional Julio Fucik," Mar. 4, p. 6; "Las fundiciones 'Klement Gottwald' la mayor obra que se realiza en Checoslovaquia," ibid.; "Condecoración del académico Zdenek Nejedly," ibid.; "Dos grandes películas checas," Mar. 13, p. 2; "La primera película para ciegos," Apr. 9, p. 2; "Estreno del drama 'Los de Stalingrado,' " Apr. 14, p. 6; "Mikolas Ales, el gran pintor del pueblo checo," Apr. 16, p. 2; "Una película sobre la vida de Julio Fucik," Apr. 21, p. 4; "Exito de las artes gráficas en Checoslovaquia," Apr. 22, p. 3; "Jaroslav Hasek, maestro del humor satírico," Apr. 24, p. 2; "Aumenta la producción en Checoslovaquia," May 15, p. 4; "Iniciase la televisión checa," May 19, p. 4; "Manifestación de paz en Terezin," May 29, p. 8; "Decreto de amnistía en Checoslovaquia," ibid.; "El deporte en Checoslovaquia," ibid., p. 5; "Nueva ley escolar en Checoslovaquia," June 11, p. 4; "Monumento a la literatura nacional en Praga," ibid., p. 8; "Sesión plenaria del Comité Checoeslovaco de Mujeres," ibid., p. 8; "Sesión plenaria del Comité Checoeslovaco de Defensores de la Paz," ibid.; "Reformarán la ley monetaria en Checoslovaquia," June 13, p. 8;

The sky of Czechoslovakia extends its blue hands to welcome all the youths who gather in the train stations along the border. We meet a youth of steel and hope, we meet a youth of fire and joy; workers step forward with music and bread, with accordions and apples, and join this celebration that even the dead applaud from the depths of the earth. It is a foretaste of the great victory, the victory that will return to man what is rightfully his. . . . Already Prague shimmers in the new light, it is the embodiment of our dreams. It is a flower that cannot be crushed. In the streets of Prague there are soldiers, there are girls, there are flowers, there are apples, there are prams with babies that the mothers push toward home and toward the future. Throughout the city one breathes an atmosphere of civic struggle. . . . Here in Czechoslovakia the new world has established one more pillar, whose granite foundations have deep roots in the heart of man. Here man begins to be man; he begins to rise from the swamp into which he has been thrown by the false prophets of fatalism and resignation, by the existentialists of all times, the bitter painters, the failed poets, the kings, the bankers, the businessmen.[21]

DCA did not consistently adopt a procommunist line in international affairs; its articles tended to be neutralist and only occasionally veered to a warm procommunist stance. Still, one can imagine the reaction of U.S. embassy officials when they saw in the cultural section of *DCA* a poem in honor of the "Canal Volga-Don"[22] or when they read fulsome praise of Communist China in "We embrace the women of China."[23]

While the coverage of the Korean War generally avoided editorial comment

---

"Ludvik Kuba, el gran pintor del pueblo checoeslovaco," June 16, p. 3; "Noticias de Checoeslovaquia," July 1, p. 8; "La 'Primavera de Praga—1953,' " July 23, p. 8; "Nuevo éxito de la televisión checoeslovaca," ibid.; "Intercambio de mercancías entre Checoeslovaquia y Austria," ibid.; "Campos de entrenamiento para deportistas en Checoeslovaquia," Sept. 1, p. 5; "Hace diez años fué ejecutado por el nazismo el gran Julio Fucik," Sept. 8, p. 8; "En el noveno aniversario de la insurrección nacional eslovaca," Sept. 24, p. 3; "Comienzo del año escolar en Checoeslovaquia," Sept. 28, p. 8; "Homenaje a Julio Fucik rindió el pueblo de Checoeslovaquia," Oct. 26, p. 4; "Desarrollo de la aviación en la república checoeslovaca," Nov. 7, p. 8; "Films checoeslovacos en el extranjero," Nov. 13, p. 2; "Primera exposición en México de productos industriales checoeslovacos," ibid., p. 8; "Vida cultural de los extranjeros que residen en Checoeslovaquia," Nov. 14, p. 8; "Inauguración de la exposición de productos industriales checoeslovacos," Nov. 19, p. 4; "Leos Janacek en el 25 aniversario de su muerte," Nov. 20, p. 2; "Los mercados campesinos en la república checoeslovaca," Nov. 21, p. 4; "Varios artistas ingleses opinan sobre la situación checoslovaca," Dec. 15, p. 1; "Escuelas cooperativistas del trabajo están funcionando en Checoeslovaquia," Dec. 28, p. 2; "Exposición de Nicolas Copernico exhibiéndose en Checoeslovaquia," ibid., p. 8.

[21] Carlos Castro Saavedra, "El mundo nuevo," *DCA*, May 21, 1953, p. 2.

[22] *DCA*, Jan. 8, 1953, p. 2.

[23] Atala Valenzuela, *DCA*, Mar. 7, 1953, p. 8.

on the nature of the conflict, there were significant exceptions, as if the editors had suddenly tired of restraint. When a January 2, 1953, editorial pointedly referred to "the unjustifiable origins" of the war,[24] the meaning could have escaped only the most obtuse readers; nor could there have been much confusion when another editorial argued that the United Nations Charter had been "abused in the Korean case by an interested party."[25] Perhaps the editorial which greeted the armistice at Panmunjom best conveys the *DCA*'s stance: "Mankind is tired of war. We have learned that for Big Business war is profit, but we have also learned that the World Peace Movement is not a futile and weak movement. It is strong and heroic."[26] The Departamento Agrario Nacional, a government agency, felt less compelled to be diplomatic; it firmly praised "the iron will of the people [of North Korea] . . . who proved the greatness of their ideals in their struggle to create a truly democratic government" and lambasted "the cynicism of the arms merchants."[27]

The government broadcasting network (whose director, Carlos Alvarado Jérez, was an alternate member of the PGT's Central Committee) followed a line on international affairs similar to that of *DCA*. And Arbenz himself, while generally cautious in his public statements, often sent messages of support to front organizations and at times provided government assistance to their meetings. When the Second Continental Congress of Democratic Lawyers was held in Guatemala in October 1953, it met in the Salón de Vistas of the Supreme Court, and the Guatemalan government provided $10,000. Arbenz sent Interior Minister Charnaud to convey his greetings, and the entire Supreme Court attended.[28]

It is hardly surprising that the revolutionary politicians declaimed speeches with a marked pro-Soviet bent—speeches that were usually couched in rudimentary Marxist jargon. The reaction to the armistice in Korea is a case in point. *Nuestro Diario*, which was controlled by the PAR, celebrated the ar-

---

[24] "Las posibilidades de este año," *DCA*, Jan. 2, 1953, p. 2.

[25] "Guatemala y la paz," *DCA*, July 28, 1953, p. 3.

[26] "La paz en Corea," *DCA*, July 27, 1953, p. 3.

[27] *Boletín Agrario*, no. 1, Aug. 1953, p. 2.

[28] For the 1953 coverage by *DCA* see esp. "Delegado al congreso jurídico de esta capital," Sept. 5, p. 1; "Adesiones a la Conferencia Continental de Juristas," Sept. 29, p. 1; "Convocada II Conferencia Continental de Juristas," Oct. 7, p. 1; "Repercusión americana del II Congreso de Juristas," Oct. 9, p. 1; "Brillante inauguración," Oct. 17, p. 1; "Clausurada la Conferencia de Juristas, ayer," Oct. 22, p. 1; "Resonancias del II Congreso Continental de Juristas," ibid., p. 3; "Resoluciones aprobadas en la Segunda Conferencia Continental de Juristas," in five parts, Nov. 2–6 (always p. 8). For two enthusiastic articles in the PGT's daily *Tribuna Popular*, see "II Conferencia Continental de Juristas iniciada anoche entre ovaciones," Oct. 17, p. 1, and "Soberanía, paz y democracia," Oct. 22, p. 8. Less warm was the coverage by the U.S. embassy: see *JW* 42, Oct. 16, I:3–4, and *JW* 43, Oct. 23, I:1, 3.

mistice as a triumph of the world peace movement over the "warlike appetite of a great power" and praised "the Korean people who have endured horrible crimes at the hands of the western aggressor."[29] In Congress, the revolutionary majority applauded enthusiastically when a PGT deputy extolled the victory of the peace-loving forces led by the Soviet Union over U.S. imperialism in Korea.[30] The president of the Congress, PAR Deputy Guillermo Ovando Arriola, gave free rein to his oratory. "The warmongers," he asserted, had provoked the war in order to foster their own economic interests and had sent the youth of their countries to die for a sordid cause, "turning them into butchers of a people whose only crime was their unquenchable yearning to be free."[31] A few days later, at a massive rally to honor the armistice, the leaders of the PAR, the PRG, and RN pilloried the United States. Charnaud, who was both Arbenz's minister of the interior and the leader of the PRG, paid homage "to the brave people of Korea who fought against the foreign aggressor"; PAR's Secretary General Fernández Foncea "condemned the 'insane warmongers' who had caused the Korean conflict"; Díaz Rozzotto, the unsavory secretary general of RN, pointed out that the Korean people "taught the imperialists an eloquent lesson."[32] It was, Ambassador Schoenfeld observed, "a public demonstration of the Arbenz administration's cooperation with the local communist group. President Arbenz," he added, "did not attend the meeting or publicly endorse it. But since the rally was attended by ranking administration officials, political leaders and army officers subject to his discipline and dependent on his goodwill, it was evident that there was more than official tolerance for it."[33] The logic was unimpeachable.

Nationalism and a longing to see the world impelled many revolutionary politicians to attend youth festivals, peace congresses and similar pro-Soviet gatherings in Western and Eastern Europe. (Their propensity to travel was invigorated by their hosts' willingness to defray their expenses.) To wary U.S. officials, these junkets appeared sinister.[34]

On March 12, 1953, thirty deputies of the Guatemalan Congress introduced a resolution asking for a minute of silence "to honor the memory of the great statesman and leader of the Soviet Union, Joseph Vissarionovish Stalin, whose passing is mourned by all progressive men." Following a violent three-

[29] Quoted from "Firmase la paz en Corea," *Nuestro Diario*, July 27, 1953, p. 1, and "Jubilo por el armisticio," *Nuestro Diario*, July 31, 1953, p. 3.

[30] "Gutiérrez aplaudido en el Congreso," *Nuestro Diario*, July 28, 1953, p. 1; Guatemala, *Diario de las sesiones del Congreso*, July 27, 1953, vol. 27, no. 18, p. 4.

[31] "Duramente condenada la guerra," *DCA*, July 27, 1953, p. 1, quoted from p. 6.

[32] "Triunfo de las fuerzas pacifistas celebrado anoche en un gran mitin," *DCA*, Aug. 1, 1953, p. 1 (quoted from p. 6) and "Grandioso mitin de la paz," *Nuestro Diario*, Aug. 1, 1953, p. 1 (quoted from p. 6).

[33] *JW* 32, Aug. 8, 1953, I:1.

[34] See *JW* 12, Mar. 26, 1954, pp. 2–3.

hour debate with the handful of opposition deputies, all but two members of the majority voted in favor of the resolution and the Guatemalan Congress rose in silent homage to the late leader. It was, as a U.S. official pointed out, "the only government body in the Western Hemisphere to do so."[35]

The desire "to give a slap to the Yankees"[36] explains the overwhelming vote. (Few deputies failed to realize, moreover, that a negative vote would have offended Arbenz.) The roots of this desire were vividly expressed during the debate by PAR Deputy Julio Estrada de la Hoz in his reply to a deputy who had claimed that the Soviet Union was imperialistic. "I want to ask the opposition: is United Fruit a Soviet company? Who killed Sandino? Who stole the piers in our harbors?"[37] The debate occurred several months before fear of Yankee retribution would moderate the rhetoric of many revolutionary leaders. "Had Stalin died a year later, very few in Congress would have voted for the minute of silence," remarked the secretary general of the PGT three decades later.[38]

THE PARTIDO GUATEMALTECO DEL TRABAJO (PGT)

In the January 1953 congressional elections, the revolutionary parties increased their majority. In a Congress of fifty-six members, the PAR now held twenty-two seats, the PRG sixteen and RN seven. By contrast, the PGT had only four deputies, the opposition had five, and there were two progovernment independents. No one sympathetic to the PGT sat in Arbenz's cabinet, and very few senior government officials were close to the party; the two highest posts held by the PGT in the administration were those of director of national broadcasting (Carlos Alvarado Jérez) and deputy director of the Departamento Agrario Nacional (Waldemar Barrios Klée).

But Guatemala had a presidential system, and Arbenz was a strong president. With his backing, the communists gained influence far beyond their numbers. The PGT leaders—Fortuny foremost—were Arbenz's closest advisers and constituted his kitchen cabinet, which discussed all major decisions. This was true of the agrarian reform as well as of the purchase of weapons from Czechoslovakia; when Arbenz decided to resign, on June 26, 1954, he consulted only the PGT. By contrast, the official cabinet and the revolutionary leaders learned that weapons from Europe had reached Guatemala's shores only after the State Department loudly denounced their arrival; and when Ar-

[35] Leddy to Cabot, May 21, 1953, *FRUS, 1952–1954*, 4:1072. For the session of Congress, see "*1er periodo ordinario de sesiones, 22 febrero–29 mayo 1953* (Libro no. 13, 1953).

[36] Interview with a former member of Congress who asked to remain anonymous.

[37] "Minuto de silencio de Stalin al rojo," *El I*, Mar. 13, 1953, p. 1, quoted from p. 2.

[38] Interview with Fortuny.

benz told his assembled ministers of his decision to step down, Fortuny was already at work writing his resignation speech.

The first public documents signed by the Communist Party of Guatemala appeared in April 1951, one month after Arbenz's inauguration. On June 21, the first anniversary of the party's weekly *Octubre* was openly celebrated. "It is most interesting," the U.S. embassy reported, "that the Minister of Education . . . made an official request . . . that the theater be made available for this 'cultural activity.' "[39] The PGT had fewer than one hundred members, and it was still illegal, although it was obvious that its legalization was just a matter of time. That time came in December 1952, when the party held its second congress. It was a public affair, well advertised in the press and attended by high-ranking guests from the revolutionary parties, the labor confederations and the government. The congress changed the party's name to Partido Guatemalteco del Trabajo (PGT), since "the name Communist Party, however dear to us, makes it harder for us to reach the masses. . . . We must place the task of developing the party before any sentimental attachment to a name."[40] A few days later, the PGT was registered as a legal party despite the outcry of the opposition.[41] As a member of the recently created Frente Democrático Electoral, it was allied with the PAR, PRG, and RN in the January 1953 congressional elections.

The second congress had affirmed the PGT's status within the country, but the communist parties of only Cuba, Mexico, and Costa Rica had sent dele-

[39] *JW* 25, June 22, 1951, I:2. See also "Movimiento comunista sale sin mascara a la luz," *El I*, June 22, 1951, p. 1; "Mitin de aniversario de 'Octubre,' " *Octubre*, June 29, 1951, p. 1; "Communists in Guatemala" (edit.), *NYT*, July 14, 1951, p. 12.

[40] Partido Guatemalteco del Trabajo, *Estatutos*, p. 4. See also "Desarrollo del histórico II Congreso del PGT," *Octubre*, Dec. 18, 1952, p. 1, and Guerra Borges, "No sé por qué se hacen bolas," ibid., p. 3. This issue of *Octubre* is devoted to the congress; several relevant articles are also included in the issues of Dec. 26, 1952, and Jan. 9, 1953.

[41] "El PC cambia de montera," *La Hora*, Dec. 15, 1952, p. 1; "Partido Guatemalteco del Trabajo surge," *El I*, Dec. 15, 1952, p. 1; "Maniobras comunistas," *El I*, Dec. 16, 1952, p. 1; "Partido Guatemalteco del Trabajo queda inscrito," *El I*, Dec. 20, 1952, p. 1; "Doquiera que estéis, como quiera que os presentéis, siempre os reconoceremos," *La Hora* (edit.), Dec. 22, 1952, p. 1; "La flagrante violación incurrida por las autoridades electorales," *La Hora* (edit.), Dec. 24, 1952, p. 1; "CEUA pide la copia del acta de inscripción del PGT," *El I*, Dec. 24, 1952, p. 12; "Una gran victoria popular," *Octubre*, Dec. 26, 1952, p. 4; "Que la inscripción del PGT se cancele por ser completamente ilegal pide el PUA," *El I*, Dec. 29, 1952, p. 1; "La Junta Nacional Electoral busca salida," *La Hora* (edit.), Jan. 3, 1953, p. 1; "Cuando el pez por su boca muere," *La Hora* (edit.), Jan. 5, 1953, p. 1; "Puede la Junta Electoral apegarse con exclusividad a un procedimiento legalista?" *La Hora* (edit.), Jan. 13, 1953, p. 1.

gates.[42] This meager attendance from fraternal parties was not a ploy to disguise the fact that the PGT was part of the international communist movement; on the contrary, the PGT proclaimed this connection proudly. It merely reflected the party's low status and limited contacts.

The PGT had developed practically in isolation. In the late 1940s, no foreign party had made any effort to assist in the creation of a Guatemalan Communist party. Guatemala was too backward a country and its communists were too few to attract the attention of a Latin American communist movement that was reeling under the blows of the Cold War. Some Latin American communists who visited Guatemala were asked for advice and provided it, but these were sporadic and superficial contacts.[43]

It has been argued that the Chilean communist Deputy César Godoy was "of particular help to the Guatemalan Communists from 1947 to 1950."[44] Godoy visited Guatemala on two or three occasions in the late 1940s as Arévalo's guest.[45] The extent of his participation in the creation of the PGT is highlighted by one of the party's founders, Alfredo Guerra Borges:

> Godoy happened to be in Guatemala when we held the founding congress of the party. We invited him to the session in which we discussed the report on international affairs. He said that we were not paying enough attention to the Chinese revolution, which he considered as important as the Russian revolution. (We had only referred to it in passing, because of our lack of information.) This was Godoy's entire contribution to the creation of the party.[46]

Even later, in the Arbenz years, the PGT remained isolated in Latin America. Weakened by the Cold War and the attendant repression, the South American communist parties had little time for a fledgling organization in faraway Guatemala. Closer to home, Costa Rica's once powerful Vanguardia Popular was in disarray after its defeat in the 1948 civil war. The communist parties of Nicaragua and El Salvador were weak and persecuted. In the Dominican Republic, the communist Partido Socialista Popular had been destroyed by Trujillo in the late 1940s; no communist parties existed in Honduras and Haiti. The PGT and Arbenz could offer a safe haven to persecuted communists from the region, but they lacked the wherewithall to provide any active support to communist groups in neighboring countries.

The PGT maintained regular contacts with only two communist parties, those of Mexico and Cuba. The Partido Comunista Mexicano (PCM), minuscule and torn by internal strife, showed little interest in the PGT. The latter, in

---

[42] Interviews with Fortuny, Pellecer, and Guerra Borges.

[43] Interviews with Fortuny, Pellecer, and Guerra Borges.

[44] Schneider, *Communism*, p. 281.

[45] On Godoy and Arévalo, see above, p. 120, n. 16.

[46] Interview with Guerra Borges; confirmed by Fortuny.

turn, felt little respect for the PCM and its leaders; it never sought and never received any guidance.[47] This was not the case with the Cuban Communist Party (Partido Socialista Popular or PSP). In the words of Guerra Borges, "The PSP was our window on the world, and from time to time we gazed through it." The Guatemalan communists looked up to the PSP as an older, wiser brother. "We were very small in comparison to them," recalls Fortuny. "For us, the PSP was a mature party, fully developed; we considered ourselves a minor party, not only because of our small numbers, but also because of our lack of experience and our limited knowledge of Marxist theory."[48] In 1950, the Guatemalan communists approached the PSP for assistance, and the PSP, which had helped other fledgling parties from the region, responded positively. "The Cuban communists were the only party to truly help us. Not with money, but they sent us a member of their Central Committee (Alejandro) who stayed with us to help us strengthen our party. The PSP was the only Communist party that had the vision to see that a strong Communist party could be created in Guatemala."[49]

Alejandro arrived in Guatemala in mid-1951. PGT leaders remember him as "a wise comrade; he had a good grasp of theory and a lot of practical experience." He was "very good at dealing with people; he wasn't arrogant or dominating, and he was very discreet."[50] Yet his influence and that of his party should not be exaggerated. Batista's coup in Cuba in March 1952 made contacts between the two parties precarious, and Alejandro, who remained in Guatemala until the fall of Arbenz, failed to save the PGT from its mistakes and did not guide it to its successes. Until early 1954, the PGT's leadership was united behind the strong personality of Fortuny. Alejandro was in a country of which he had no previous knowledge, and during his stay he met few of its political leaders; few Guatemalans knew of his presence, and even fewer of his role. His strength may have been his understanding of the limits of this role.

On occasion PGT leaders did travel to the Soviet bloc. To wary U.S. officials, these trips were further proof of the growing international communist

[47] Interviews with Fortuny, Pellecer, and Guerra Borges. Tenuous contacts with the American Communist Party (CP) were maintained through infrequent correspondence with CP member A. B. Magil. (Interviews with Fortuny and Guerra Borges.) In the spring of 1954, Magil wrote a short book about Guatemala: Travis and Magil, *The Truth About Guatemala*.

[48] Quotations from interviews with Guerra Borges and Fortuny.

[49] Interviews with Guerra Borges (quoted), Fortuny and Alejandro.

[50] Quotation from interviews with Fortuny and Guerra Borges. This paragraph is based on interviews with Guerra Borges, Fortuny, Pellecer, and Alejandro. (Alejandro, who secretly returned to Cuba after the overthrow of Arbenz, has occupied several important official posts since 1959, notably as Cuba's ambassador to the Soviet Union.)

conspiracy against Guatemala. At times they recorded trips that had never taken place—thus they believed that Fortuny had been in Moscow in 1949 and 1953, when in fact he had not gone beyond Czechoslovakia, the only communist country he had visited before Arbenz fell. (Fortuny first went to the Soviet Union in 1957.) Actually, only one member of the PGT's Secretariat traveled to the Soviet Union before Arbenz's overthrow; en route to the Asian and Pacific Peace Conference in mid-1952, Mario Silva Jonama stopped briefly in Moscow, saw some low level Soviet officials ("they didn't pay much attention to him"), and resumed his journey.[51]

The evidence in the *Guatemalan Transcripts* (*GT*) supports the testimony of PGT leaders that their contacts with West European and Soviet bloc communist parties were very limited. The PGT was invited to attend meetings organized by front organizations such as the World Federation of Trade Unions and the World Peace Council, frequently at their own expense. Relations with the Soviet Union meant occasional visits to the Soviet embassy in Mexico by PGT leaders who happened to be there. "We only saw minor officials. They would ask us a few questions about the party, etc. They never offered us any advice. They never invited us to Moscow." The PGT was not even invited to the nineteenth congress of the Communist Party of the Soviet Union (PCUS), held in October 1952, and the first PGT leader to visit the Soviet Union on party business was Guerra Borges, who represented the PGT at the twentieth congress of the PCUS in October 1956. "We were knocking on the Soviets' door," explains Pellecer, "but they didn't answer."[52]

On two or three occasions, the PGT leaders told Soviet officials in Mexico that they, and Arbenz, would like the Soviet Union to open at least a consulate in their country. "We were told that they would pass on our request and that was always the end of it."[53] Fortunately so, one might add, for such a step would have had only one tangible byproduct, to supply ammunition to those

[51] Interviews with Fortuny (quoted), Alejandro, Pellecer, and Guerra Borges. For Fortuny's 1953 trip to Czechoslovakia, see below, pp. 279–81. For a brief account by Fortuny of his 1949 trip to Czechoslovakia, see Cáceres, *Aproximación*, pp. 145–48. For Silva Jonama's trip, see Krieg to DOS, no. 341, Oct. 14, 1952, NA 714.001.

[52] Interviews with Fortuny (quoted), Pellecer (quoted), Guerra Borges, and Alejandro. Some leading PGT members, including Gutiérrez, visited the Soviet Union in the Arévalo and Arbenz years, but only as guests of front organizations.

[53] Interviews with Guerra Borges (quoted), Fortuny, Pellecer, and Alejandro. Guatemala had established diplomatic relations with the USSR in April 1945, and the prominent writer Luis Cardoza y Aragón had been sent as minister to Moscow. But the Soviets failed to open a legation in Guatemala, and Arévalo took advantage of this lack of reciprocity to close the legation in May 1946. The two countries did not formally break diplomatic relations. In *Retorno al futuro*, Cardoza y Aragón describes his stay in the Soviet Union.

who charged that Guatemala was the Soviet bridgehead in the Western Hemisphere.

There is evidence of financial transactions between the Soviet Union and the PGT: the notorious "Moscow Gold" to which some Americans referred at the time. The PGT ordered a few books and magazines from the Soviet Union, and the *GT* include two letters from Moscow's *Mezhdunarodnaja Kniga*; these letters express impatience at the PGT's failure to settle its outstanding accounts of $12.35 and $10.60 and firmly demand that the debt be paid "as soon as possible."[54] Chastened, the PGT complied. With only slight exaggeration, Guerra Borges later protested, "We paid them religiously. We were the only ones in Latin America who paid them. People from the Mexican Communist Party told me: 'You people are crazy; we haven't paid them a cent for at least 10 years.' As for the 'Moscow Gold,' Moscow got money from us, not the other way around."[55] The PGT never received any financial assistance other than occasional travel expenses from foreign communist parties or front organizations.

Only on one occasion did the Soviet Union indicate an interest in developing ties with Guatemala. In late October 1953, Mikhail Samoilov, the Soviet commercial attaché in Mexico, visited Guatemala for three days. (Never before had a Soviet official come to the country.) He spoke with Arbenz and Fortuny and expressed his government's desire to establish commercial ties with Guatemala, something that both Arbenz and the PGT desired.[56] The Soviet Union, Samoilov stated, was willing to buy a very large quantity of Guatemalan bananas (more than the country actually produced); it offered agricultural equipment in exchange; since the Soviet Union did not have refrigerator ships, Guatemala would have to supply the transport. Arbenz and Fortuny explained that Guatemala had no ships; its bananas were exported in the bottoms of United Fruit, and it was unlikely that UFCO would hand over its ships to foster Soviet-Guatemalan friendship. However, they noted, Guatemala could sell coffee to the Soviet Union.

Samoilov was not impressed. The Soviet Union already had many long-term agreements to buy coffee abroad and could not purchase Guatemalan coffee in the near future. On this note, the conversation closed, "and that was

[54] Mezhdunarodnaja Kniga to Alfredo Mendoza, Apr. 17 and July 24, 1953, *GT*, Box 8. The expression is used in both letters.

[55] Interviews with Guerra Borges (quoted), Alejandro, Fortuny, and Pellecer.

[56] The account of Samoilov's conversation with Arbenz is based on interviews with Fortuny (who was present), María de Arbenz (who was told by Arbenz), and Guerra Borges and Alejandro (who were told by Fortuny). On Samoilov's visit to Guatemala see also: *JW* 44, Oct. 29, 1953, I:1, 3–4, and II:1–2; "Delegado del Soviet está en Guatemala," *El I*, Oct. 24, 1953, p. 1; "Competencia soviética tenemos en propia casa," *La Hora*, Oct. 24, 1953, p. 1; Col. McCormick, "Intelligence Report" no. R-8-54, Jan. 8, 1954, RG84 G&C, Box 4, NA-S.

that.''[57] It had been an exploratory mission that had revealed, above all, Moscow's ignorance of Guatemala, for it was no secret that Guatemala had no fleet, much less its own refrigerator ships.

One may speculate about the reasons for Moscow's lack of interest in the PGT and Guatemala. In Stalin's last years, mistrust characterized the Soviets' attitude toward Third World countries. Their attention was riveted on relations with the United States and on developments in Europe and Asia. Latin America was far from their preoccupations.[58] Within that inhospitable continent, Guatemala was a tiny and backward land thrust into the heart of the American empire. Arbenz was a military man, and the Soviet leaders dismissed Third World officers as imperialism's stooges. The PGT was a small group that lacked the traditions and international contacts of older Latin American communist parties.

Following Stalin's death, indications of greater flexibility began to appear in Moscow's attitude to the Third World. Samoilov's visit reflects the limits of this incipient change. Another reflection of the change was the Soviet decision, in December 1953, to allow Guatemala to buy weapons from Czechoslovakia. "If Stalin had been alive," remarks Fortuny, "they wouldn't have sold them to us."[59]

In the spring of 1954, Soviet journals expressed a growing optimism that Latin American countries might be willing and able to lessen their dependence on the United States.[60] Eventually, this new appraisal might have led the Soviet Union to show greater interest in Guatemala, had Arbenz not been overthrown. But in the first six months of 1954 only one tangible change occurred: the PGT began receiving (gratis!) some issues of *Pravda*. In Guatemala, however, not even the most devout communist could read Russian.[61]

Yet the PGT was perturbed neither by Moscow's indifference nor by the paucity of its international contacts. "We were a provincial party; we didn't look beyond our village; we didn't even have an international committee." The party's leaders were very busy: "We were overwhelmed with work. We were preoccupied with the development of the PGT and with Guatemalan domestic politics."[62] They sent delegates to the international congresses to which the PGT was invited, but usually the leaders stayed home;[63] they were content

[57] Interview with Fortuny.

[58] See Clissold, *Soviet Relations with Latin America*; Hough, *The Struggle for the Third World*; Kanet, *The Soviet Union and the Developing World*, ch. 1; Donaldson, *Soviet Policy toward India*, ch. 3.

[59] Interview with Fortuny.

[60] See Dinerstein, *The Making of a Missile Crisis*, pp. 10–14.

[61] Interviews with Fortuny and Guerra Borges.

[62] Quotations from interviews with Guerra Borges and Fortuny.

[63] The only senior party member to travel with relative frequency was Gutiérrez in his capacity as secretary general of the CGTG.

to applaud the Soviet Union and its policies from afar, with genuine enthusiasm. Other communist parties, small sects unable to influence events in their own countries, sought in endless congresses abroad and the occasional nods of minor Soviet officials the legitimacy they lacked at home. The PGT, however, unlike every other Communist party in the hemisphere, was gaining strength. If its leaders needed expert advice, they had Alejandro. He was well versed in Marxism and more familiar with Guatemala than party officials from distant lands. Success reinforced the provincial spirit of the PGT and might have led, over time, to a more sober assessment of the Soviet bloc.

Without Arbenz, the PGT would have been utterly isolated. Most revolutionary leaders felt little sympathy for the party. Left to their own devices, they would have spurned cooperation with the PGT and have barely tolerated its legalization. Instead, Arbenz's control of the government's purse and patronage, and his forceful personality, stirred politicians and bureaucrats to court the party that basked in the president's favor.

Arbenz was influential in the October 1951 merger of the two main labor confederations of the Arévalo period—the FSG and the CTG—into the communist-led CGTG.[64] In the spring of 1954, he helped the communists take control of the railway union (SAMF), the only important urban labor union that still opposed them.[65]

Even more critical was the president's impact on the peasant-based CNCG, created in May 1950 by a group of noncommunist and anticommunist labor leaders. Throughout the Arbenz years, these leaders resented the PGT's and the CGTG's efforts to gain influence in the countryside. But the CNCG was always penniless, and it needed the government's financial assistance.[66] Thus, its leaders spouted pro-Soviet rhetoric and even joined, after much hesitation, the Soviet-dominated World Federation of Trade Unions.[67] Above all, they sought a modus vivendi with the PGT and the CGTG. Verbal skirmishes in

[64] For the CGTG, see *GT*, Boxes 24, 27, 30–38. Among secondary sources, see esp. Bishop, "Guatemalan Labor," pp. 130–50; Schneider, *Communism*, pp. 141–55; Ramos Guzmán de Schmoock, "El movimiento sindical," pp. 118–69.

[65] The episode is well described by Schneider, *Communism*, pp. 176–84. Of the many boxes in the *GT* that deal with the SAMF (20, 21, 45–52, 80, 86, 87), particularly relevant are boxes 50–52.

[66] For the financial straits of the CNCG, see Pearson, "*Confederación*," pp. 47–54. For the government's assistance, see the following note signed by Castillo Flores on May 28, 1953: "I received $25,000 from the government to cover expenses related to the CNCG." (*GT*, Box 23.)

[67] For an excellent discussion of the CNCG's pro-Soviet rhetoric, see Pearson, "*Confederación*," pp. 81–83 and 88–95. For a thoughtful discussion of Castillo Flores's and of the CNCG's dilemma by a visiting American scholar, see MemoConv (Krieg, Alexander), Apr. 1, 1954, RG84 G&C, Box 4, NA-S.

1950 and 1951 gave way to tentative cooperation. Behind this friendly facade, tensions simmered. Years later, Gutiérrez lamented about "the lack of a true alliance between workers and peasants" under Arbenz and "the failure of the Coordinating Committee of the two labor confederations to foster closer ties between them."[68] Had the CNCG not needed Arbenz's support, its distrust of the communists would have turned into open hostility.

And yet, the men who led the PGT did not owe everything to Arbenz. They had acquired a leading role in the CTG in the Arévalo years. Their success was their own and not, as U.S. officials had believed, due to the patronage of Arévalo (who mistrusted the CTG and preferred the more moderate FSG). And if in 1951 Arbenz was instrumental in the unification of the FSG and the CTG under communist leadership, of equal or greater importance was the growing personal prestige of the CTG leaders among the rank and file of both labor confederations. As a U.S. scholar, Edwin Bishop, has pointed out, on one side stood the "opportunistic, corruptible anticommunist leaders"; on the other, "the dedicated, incorruptible Communist leaders like Gutiérrez." (Therefore, concludes the anticommunist Bishop, "it was the misfortune of the rank and file that they had but small choice.")[69]

This was at least as important as the role of Arbenz in determining the outcome of the conflict that rent the railway union, SAMF, in the spring of 1953. The anticommunist group that was decisively defeated in the June union elections was led by the prominent PRG labor leader Arturo Morales Cubas. Even the U.S. embassy, so sympathetic to any effort to weaken PGT influence, conceded that Morales Cubas was "unscrupulous," and that his management of the SAMF's Consumer Cooperative had been marred by serious financial irregularities.[70] Those SAMF leaders who supported Morales Cubas tended to

[68] Gutiérrez, *Breve historia*, pp. 71, 55.

[69] Bishop, "Guatemalan Labor," p. 148.

[70] *JW* 21, May 22, 1953, I:1. Morales Cubas, the embassy had earlier reported, "had been 'lending' himself and his friends large sums of Cooperative funds on no more than nominal security (e.g., $16,615 against an $85 deposit)." (*JW* 39, Sept. 25, 1952, I:3–4; see also: "Morales Cubas en la balanza," *El I*, Oct. 3, 1952, p. 1; Krieg to DOS, no. 379, Oct. 24, 1952, NA 814.062; "La cooperativa: Sección de préstamos en eso se ha convertido," *El I*, Dec. 23, 1952, p. 1; "En entredicho el estado financiero de la cooperativa de consumo del SAMF," *La Hora*, Feb. 2, 1953, p. 1.)

The embassy followed the denouement of the struggle within SAMF closely. See *JW* 21–24, 26 of 1953, and Schoenfeld to DOS: no. 1055, May 30, 1953; no. 1097, June 12, 1953; no. 1143, June 24, 1953; all NA 814.062. Press coverage was extensive. See esp. "El SAMF se sacudirá de los comunistas," *La Hora*, May 11, 1953, p. 1; "Mañana habrá tormenta en el SAMF," *La Hora*, May 14, 1953, p. 1; "Llamamiento de la CGTG," *DCA*, May 15, 1953, p. 1; "Golpe Cubista en el SAMF," *La Hora*, May 16, 1953, p. 1; "Triunfo rotundo," *DCA*, May 16, 1953, p. 1; "El PRG no puede enjuiciar a un lider," *La Hora*, May 23, 1953, p. 1; "Llamamiento de la

share his shortcomings. As Schneider has pointed out in his analysis of the SAMF elections:

> The moderate leaders themselves must bear partial responsibility for their failure and hence for the success of the Communists. The tragedy is that Morales Cubas and his followers discredited themselves, by taking advantage of their positions for personal gain at the workers' expense. Even when there were no sins of commission on the records of the opponents of Communism, they partially defaulted to the Communists and their allies. Many of the moderate leaders were too interested in their own economic well-being and job advancement to devote as much time to union affairs as did the extremists. Some moderate leaders stagnated once they tasted the better things of life and others gave up the fight and resigned to care for their personal or family interests. These actions and attitudes lost them the support of such dedicated leaders as José Luis Caceres R., who began to see in the Communist labor leaders a model more worthy of emulation.[71]

The PGT, however, never controlled the labor confederation. Its influence depended on Arbenz's support and on the personal prestige of a handful of CGTG leaders who belonged to the party, such as the CGTG's secretary general, Gutiérrez, and his deputy, José Alberto Cardoza. Within the CGTG, individual unions retained a large degree of autonomy, and only a few were led by PGT members. With the exception of union elections, the great majority of the hundred thousand CGTG members voted for the revolutionary parties and not for the PGT.[72]

A few revolutionary leaders were sincerely attracted to the PGT. Unable to forget their youthful dreams, they were distressed by the evolution of their own parties. To these men, the PGT appeared more and more as a model; weakness or ideology might keep them from joining this austere party but did

---

CGTG al SAMF hacia la unidad," *DCA*, May 23, 1953, p. 1; "Sosistas y Cubistas se disputarán en firme la directiva del SAMF," *La Hora*, May 25, 1953, p. 1; "El DAT manda al SAMF a convocar a elecciones," *DCA*, May 28, 1953, p. 1; "Comunicado sobre la situación actual del movimiento obrero," *DCA*, June 2, 1953, p. 1; "PRG ante el conflicto en el SAMF," *DCA*, June 18, 1953, p. 1; "Violenta pugna samfista," *El I*, June 19, 1953, p. 1; "Los votos samfistas en la capital," *La Hora*, June 22, 1953, p. 1; "Empezó escrutinio," *Nuestro Diario*, June 22, 1953, p. 13; "Planilla que encabeza Jaime Zabala triunfó en el SAMF," *DCA*, June 23, 1953, p. 1; "Rotundo triunfo," *Nuestro Diario*, June 23, 1953, p. 11; "Gran jubilo entre ferroviarios," *Nuestro Diario*, June 25, 1953, p. 8; "Posesionó la nueva directiva del SAMF," *DCA*, July 7, 1953, p. 1. See also above, n. 65.

[71] Schneider, *Communism*, p. 184.

[72] According to Gutiérrez, the CGTG had 104,000 members in late January 1954. (Gutiérrez, *Breve historia*, pp. 51–52.) "Convocatoria al Segundo Congreso Nacional Sindical de la C.G.T.G.," *DCA*, Dec. 12, 1953, p. 4, refers to 109,829 members.

not dampen their admiration. Their number, however, must not be over-stated—they were just a handful. Only a careless observer would include among them PAR Secretary General Fernández Foncea, who burst out in an October 5, 1953, session in Congress, "I endorse most of all the Communist party, the party of Pellecer, Cardoza and Gutiérrez, which is the most patriotic, decent, honest and consistent in the country. The PAR is only a temporary party, like the other parties of the revolution that are destined to disappear and be absorbed in the World Communist Party." This bold statement surprised the PGT, which had no inkling that Fernández Foncea might harbor such thoughts; predictably, it provoked an uproar in the PAR, which swiftly expelled him. The declaration, however, was not the public confession of a closet communist. On the contrary, Fernández Foncea fought tooth and nail to remain the PAR's secretary general. The explanation was more mundane: the man had been drinking.[73]

Had the PGT sought to impose its exacting standards on the revolutionary parties, it would have aroused fear and resentment. As it was, those within the government who resented the PGT's mounting influence and access to Arbenz were gratified that the party was indulgent of their peccadillos. The PGT also demonstrated welcome restraint in the division of bureaucratic spoils: its members let their noncommunist allies grow rich in soft jobs while they were content with less prestigious positions in which they soon became indispensable. In short, concluded a *New York Times* correspondent, they did very little that was "sensational or extraordinary. They merely organized closely where others organized loosely. They worked devotedly for their group's interests where others worked for their own personal interest. They did the dreary, menial jobs while others sought the glamorous jobs. . . . They were a highly disciplined group."[74]

These dangerous qualities were acknowledged by the U.S. embassy and by some Guatemalans who loathed the PGT. "Licenciado Silva Peña," the embassy reported in December 1953, "said that the Communists made their influence felt a great deal through hard work. For instance, once last year he was on a committee which had been unable to settle a question in a certain meeting. Everyone except the Communists had gone off that evening to see the 'Ice Festival' which was in town. The Communists had worked all night and came

---

[73] "Fernández Foncea preconiza el triunfo total de los comunistas en Guatemala," *Prensa Libre*, Oct. 6, 1953, p. 3. For Fernández Foncea's speech, see also "Fernández F. vociferó en favor del comunismo," *El I*, Oct. 6, 1953, p. 1; "Francisco Fernández Foncea ratifica sus conceptos," *DCA*, Oct. 8, 1953, p. 1; Guatemala, *Diario de las sesiones del Congreso*, Oct. 5, 1953, vol. 16, no. 10, pp. 29–30. For the PGT's reaction: interviews with Fortuny and Guerra Borges; and Fortuny, *Por un frente único*, pp. 32–34. For Fernández Foncea's attempts to hold onto power, see above, p. 173.

[74] Flora Lewis, "Communism in Guatemala: A Case History," *NYT*, Feb. 21, 1954, D11.

in the next day with a completely new set of proposals which carried the day.''[75] In a similar vein, an embassy dispatch reported a few weeks later:

> In a graphic illustration of the local Communists' ability quickly to exploit situations to their advantage, Carlos Manuel Pellecer . . . began to organize a relief committee for local market women within a few hours after a major fire in Guatemala City's No. 2 market burned down over 500 wooden shops and stalls. The Alianza Femenina Guatemalteca . . . , the Communist-front women's organization, also stepped in quickly with offers of aid, but the anti-Communist organizations apparently did nothing, although the market women have been among their strongest supporters.[76]

Thirty years later Bill Krieg, the embassy's deputy chief (DCM) in the Arbenz years, highlighted the contrast between the PGT and the other administration parties:

> The revolutionary parties were groups of bums of first order; lazy, ambitious, they wanted money, were palace hangers-on. Those who could work, had a sense of direction, ideas, knew where they wanted to go, were Fortuny and his PGT friends; they were very honest, very committed. This was the tragedy: the only people who were committed to hard work were those who were, by definition, our worst enemies.[77]

The communists' abilities, rather than merely Arbenz's favor, explain why the four PGT deputies acquired such influence in the National Congress. The PGT was represented in all fourteen committees elected by Congress in March 1954. PGT deputies chaired two committees of particular importance: Agrarian Reform (Gutiérrez), and Reform of the Labor Code (Cardoza).[78]

The PGT was moderate in its public statements. Although it acknowledged that its ultimate objective was the creation of a Marxist-Leninist Guatemala it stressed that this was a distant prospect. For the present, and for a long time to come, the party's task would be to assist in the creation of a modern, capitalist and fully independent Guatemala. No revolutionary politician could object. Lingering fears were assuaged by the comforting thought that in March 1957 Arbenz's presidency would end and the communists would lose their champion.

In the meantime, the PGT was growing. Profiting from the new climate of

[75] MemoConv (Hill, Silva Peña), Dec. 28, 1953, p. 2 enclosed in Krieg to Fisher, Dec. 29, 1953, NA 714.00.

[76] *JW* 4, Feb. 1, 1954, p. 4. For the fire, see " 'La Placita' reducida a cenizas,'' *DCA*, Jan. 25, 1954, p. 1, and several articles in *El I* of the same date.

[77] Interview with Krieg.

[78] For a list of the committees and their members, see "Comisiones del Congreso para el ciclo 1954–55," *GT*, Box 1. See also "Dirigente comunista por primera vez en directiva del Congreso," *El I*, Feb. 18, 1954, p. 1, and "Monopolizadas comisiones en el Congreso," *El I*, May 7, 1954, p. 1.

freedom, it sought to become a full-fledged party, able to compete in national elections. This led it to change its name and, shortly thereafter, to loosen the requirements for party membership. Secretariat member Bernardo Alvarado Monzón described the new approach:

> Our workers, our peasants and our middle class are very backward because of the semifeudal conditions in our country and because of the tyrants who oppressed us for so long. But these are our people, in whose midst we must forge our party. . . . This is why we are critical of those comrades who look down on our new members and welcome only those who are already "well-prepared." They forget that communists are molded within the party. . . . The belief that the party should be small, that it should be primarily a school of Marxist theory, and that its prospective members should arrive well-qualified . . . has isolated us from the masses and restricted the party's growth.
>
> There are comrades who cross themselves devoutly before entering a meeting, but they enter and listen to the party's teachings. These are the people whom the party must attract in order to enlist the best and transform them into good communists. . . .
>
> "Won't this weaken the party?" the most sectarian of our comrades will ask in fear. But . . . what weakens the party is to be cut off from the masses. . . . It would be worse if these honest peasants, after making the sign of the cross, went off to hear a venomous anticommunist diatribe.[79]

This approach differed sharply from the classic Leninist conception of a Bolshevik party, but the results seemed to vindicate the leaders' tactics. In particular, through the agrarian reform, the PGT began penetrating the countryside.

The communists and their sympathizers filled only a minority of the posts in the bureaucracies established by Decree 900, but to assess the PGT's role by a head count is misleading.[80] Schneider's assertion that the communists "sought and received virtual control of the machinery" implementing the agrarian reform is not without foundation.[81] Leaving abundant opportunities

[79] "Informe presentado por el camarada Bernardo Alvarado M. a nombre de la comisión de organización del comité central en la conferencia nacional de organización del Partido Guatemalteco del Trabajo—8 y 9 de agosto de 1953," *Organización*, no. 7, Sept. 1953, pp. 7–8.

[80] The most important positions held by PGT members in the Departamento Agrario Nacional were Waldemar Barrios Klée, deputy director, and Mario Sosa, chief inspector. Many agrarian inspectors belonged to the PGT. "There are communists in the DAN, but they are the best workers and the most honest," Arbenz told a group of officers in early June 1954. (*GT*, Box 11. See below, p. 307.) See also Pearson, "*Confederación*," pp. 170–71.

[81] Quoted from Schneider, *Communism*, p. 205. For a careful assessment of the

for graft to the revolutionary politicians, the PGT concentrated on garnering support in those areas of the countryside where the land redistribution process was gathering momentum, with the rich department of Escuintla as its first priority.

Of course, the party faced formidable obstacles: the relentless hostility of the Church; the deep suspicion of the Indians of anything that was Ladino and of the peasantry as a whole of all that was urban. The PGT was, after all, an urban-based Ladino party led by middle-class intellectuals, and the very word communist evoked fears inculcated by decades of state and Church propaganda.

Yet, the party's progress was real and afforded a reasonable hope that in a few years the PGT could develop a solid base of support in the countryside. By June 1954 the PGT had over five thousand members—a not insignificant number in a country of 3 million inhabitants and for a party that three years earlier had claimed less than a hundred. Many of the new members were agricultural workers, including Indians. "The PGT," notes Guerra Borges, "grew in the countryside because of the agrarian reform, even among the Indians, but our true strength was among the agricultural workers."[82]

Lenin would have been appalled: the inevitable result of a rapidly expanding membership in a backward society was that "the immense majority" of the PGT members "knew nothing of Marxism-Leninism." The number of *cuadros*—skilled activists who possessed a basic knowledge of Marxism-Leninism—was extremely small. "The good *cuadros*, well-prepared, who could think and organize, probably were no more than forty," recalls Fortuny. "And when I say forty, perhaps I am exaggerating." This was part of the legacy of underdevelopment and tyranny. And the frenetic activity of the party leaders had left them little time for anything but the most immediate tasks. "Had we been in the opposition [in the Arbenz period] we would have had more time

---

number of PGT members involved in the administration of the agrarian reform program, see Krieg to DOS, no. 818, Mar. 29, 1954, pp. 6–8, NA 814.20.

[82] Interviews with Fortuny and Guerra Borges (quoted). The PGT had close to five thousand members according to Fortuny, close to six thousand according to Guerra Borges. (Schneider's figure of four thousand is overly conservative [*Communism*, p. 101].)

According to the official party figures (which have been broadly confirmed in interviews with Fortuny and Guerra Borges), the membership of the PGT in Aug. 1953 included: 50 percent agricultural and industrial workers; 29 percent peasants; 21 percent members of the middle class. ("Informe presentado por el camarada Bernardo Alvarado M." [see n. 79 above], pp. 1–9; see also Fortuny, *Informe*, Dec. 11, 1952, p. 53.) The agricultural workers who joined the PGT were mainly from the departments of Escuintla, San Marcos, and Rhetaluleu. They usually belonged to peasant unions affiliated to the CGTG rather than to the CNCG. (See also Pearson, "*Confederación*," p. 134.)

to prepare *cuadros*," notes Fortuny. "But when you are in the government, there isn't enough time."[83]

The growth in membership was paralleled by success at the polls. In the January 1953 congressional elections, the PGT was the weakest of the four government parties. But the elections had been held only one month after the PGT's legalization, before it had launched its drive to transform itself into a broad-based organization, and before the agrarian reform had gained momentum. Less than a year later, in the November 1953 municipal elections, the PGT's progress was unmistakable. "It was the first time," remarked the U.S. embassy, "that the PGT had run as an independent party and it made an impressive showing."[84] Of the four provincial towns in which it fielded candidates, three elected communist mayors. Among them was Escuintla, capital of the important department of the same name, where the PGT's candidate won 40 percent of the vote in a four-way race.[85] By the following spring, knowledgeable observers predicted that in the November 1954 congressional elections, the PGT would gain an additional two or three seats.[86]

Given the president's support, the agrarian reform, the dissension of the other government parties—and its own cohesion and dedication—the PGT stood an excellent chance of increasing its strength in the November 1956 congressional elections, perhaps having close to a fifth of the seats in Congress by the time Arbenz's successor was inaugurated in March 1957. Was this a prospect that justified fears of a communist takeover, or at least of a controlling communist influence in Guatemala?

THE GUATEMALAN ARMED FORCES

It is striking that those who emphasize the "Red Threat" in Arbenz's Guatemala say so little about communist subversion in the armed forces. Those few American observers who did not mince words offered no corroboration.

---

[83] Interviews with Fortuny (quoted) and Guerra Borges.

[84] *JW* 48, Nov. 27, 1953, I:1–2.

[85] The administration parties won an overwhelming number of the 310 municipalities at stake, with the PAR, once again, the strongest, followed at a distance by the PRG. For press coverage, see esp. "Elecciones municipales," *El I*, Nov. 20, 1953, p. 1; "A vencer votando," *Tribuna Popular*, Nov. 21, 1953, p. 1; "Los candidatos del PGT y de unidad van a la cabeza," *Tribuna Popular*, Nov. 22, 1953, p. 1; "En la mayoría de los municipios triunfaron las fuerzas revolucionarias," *DCA*, Nov. 23, 1953, p. 1; "Rotunda victoria en las municipales," *Tribuna Popular*, Nov. 24, 1953, p. 1; "Confirman más triunfos de las fuerzas revolucionarias," *DCA*, Nov. 24, 1953, p. 1; "En los diversos departamentos mayoría para los revolucionarios," *El I*, Nov. 25, 1953, p. 1.

[86] See "Frente Democrático Nacional somete a consideración el reparto de curules," *El I*, May 24, 1954, p. 1; "Los comunistas van a tener más curules en el congreso," *La Hora*, May 24, 1954, p. 1; Schneider, *Communism*, p. 235.

"Russian sympathizers have top posts in the army," revealed *U.S. News and World Report* in early June 1954, but it said no more.[87] Daniel James, a respected journalist who was considered an authority on Guatemalan affairs, was equally blunt. "Even the army was infiltrated by the Red Virus," he stated boldly in his well-received *Red Design for the Americas*, the first retrospective of the Arbenz regime by a U.S. author. Colonel Arbenz was a traitor, and so was the chief of the armed forces, Colonel Carlos Enrique Díaz, who, after Arbenz's fall, "tried to save Guatemala for Communism." Many other members of the officer corps and of the ranks were "either communists or staunch sympathizers."[88] But in vain does the anxious reader wait for more details, the names of at least a few of the "many" communists and fellow travelers within the military, or a more precise estimate of the degree of infiltration of the Red virus. James's imagination failed him. After this one paragraph, he abandoned the topic. In a book of over three hundred pages about the communist threat in Guatemala, he never again mentioned the crucial subject of communist subversion in the armed forces.

James's assessment was not shared by U.S. officials. In May 1954, a lengthy State Department study noted that the PGT had "established its dominion over the key institutions in Guatemalan political life, with the exception of the armed forces, which, however, have not opposed Communism." In a fifteen-page description of the party's "Levers of Power," the document never once referred to the military. The armed forces were only briefly mentioned in a later section on the "Weaknesses of the PGT Position": "The PGT has yet made no palpable inroads on the Guatemalan army"[89]—a conclusion that was consistent with the reams of reports on Guatemala written by U.S. officials in the Arbenz years.

Ronald Schneider, who had access to an impressive array of Guatemalan primary sources, discusses communist infiltration in the different sectors of Guatemalan society at great length. To the military he devotes only two pages, roughly the same space allotted to the relatively marginal Alianza Femenina Guatemalteca, and much less than that reserved for the Comité Nacional de la Paz, a communist front organization of secondary significance.[90] His conclusions are undramatic:

[87] "Red Plan for War in the Americas," *U.S. News and World Report*, June 4, 1954, p. 30.

[88] James, *Red Design*, p. 19. On James' book, see Gillin and Silvert, "Ambiguities in Guatemala," p. 471, n. 1. Even these authorities on Guatemala described the book as "carefully written."

[89] "The Partido Guatemalteco del Trabajo: A Basic Study," in DOS, *Penetration of the Political Institutions*, quoted from pp. iii, 32. On the bizarre transformation of this document, see Wood, "Self-Plagiarism."

[90] See Schneider, *Communism*, pp. 214–16 for the army; pp. 110–11, 263–65 for the Alianza Femenina Guatemalteca; pp. 253–58 for the Comité Nacional de la Paz.

Communist infiltration of the army was perhaps less successful than in any other area of the government; that the army tolerated the Communists as long as it did was largely out of loyalty to the President. This is not to say that the Communists did not try, nor that they did not have success with some of the younger politically ambitious officers. (The greatest success of the Communists was of course with Arbenz himself.) The Communists did not have time to infiltrate the army from below; and with the exception of Arbenz and perhaps Paz Tejada and Aldana Sandoval, their wooing of the top officers proved to be far less effective than they had hoped.[91]

It is a sober assessment—and yet it still overstates reality.

An army of approximately 6,200 men, poorly-trained and badly equipped; an insignificant navy of 150 men; an air force of a few decrepit planes and 350 men: these were the Guatemalan armed forces under Arbenz. Hardly an impressive war machine, even though stronger than the other rag-tag armies of Central America. While the 1944 revolution had abolished the rank of general, colonels abounded: there were more than two hundred in the army alone. The officer corps numbered nine hundred: one officer for every six enlisted men. The officers were Ladinos. The enlisted men were mostly illiterate Indians, drafted for two years; they were treated less harshly than in the Ubico era, yet a chasm separated their world from that of the officers.[92]

Arbenz's military credentials were impressive: an outstanding cadet, a highly regarded professor at the Escuela Politécnica, and a hero of the 1944 revolution. As defense minister under Arévalo, he had led the anti-Arana faction; during the *Aranista* uprising he had displayed, even his foes acknowledge, outstanding bravery and skill. Many officers were drawn to him by a sense of loyalty or friendship. He elicited respect from his friends and fear from his enemies. When he succeeded Arévalo, in March 1951, many officers saw Arbenz as *their* president; others were indifferent but not hostile; only a minority secretly opposed him.

"I do not recall any doubts about Arbenz's political orientation prior to his winning the election," a U.S. military attaché has written. The Guatemalan officers "stated that he [Arbenz] had courted the labor groups to assure his election but in no way did they think that these leftist and labor groups would be permitted to influence him."[93] But in 1951, Arbenz knew what only a few officers had begun to suspect: the soldier was undergoing a process of political radicalization. This set him apart from the army whose leader he had become.

[91] Ibid., p. 214.

[92] The literature on the Guatemalan military in the revolutionary period is spare. The most useful studies are Adams, *Crucifixion*, pp. 238–77; Monteforte Toledo, *Guatemala*, pp. 359–74; Frankel, "Political Development," pp. 122–68; LaCharite, *Case Study in Insurgency*, pp. 81–97. All the Guatemalan officers interviewed for this book were asked about the issues examined in this section.

[93] Lt. Col. Manuel Chavez, letter to the author, June 11, 1989, p. 2.

Arbenz knew that this was potentially dangerous and that it could imperil his ability to lead. This knowledge shaped his policies toward the army.

The story of Major Carlos Paz Tejada is a case in point. Paz Tejada had distinguished himself in the October 1944 uprising against Ponce and again in July 1949 when the *Aranistas* rose in revolt. He was able, honest, efficient. His performance as chief of the armed forces after Arana's death had been, by all accounts, outstanding. As the U.S. air attaché reported, he was "intelligent . . . gracious . . . a good organizer and administrator." He was a superb candidate for a top military position in the Arbenz administration, such as chief of the armed forces or minister of defense.[94] Arbenz, who deeply respected Paz Tejada, carefully considered him for such a post.[95]

But Paz Tejada was flawed: not only was he anticommunist, he had a strong personality, and he could be neither bought nor seduced. He could become very dangerous, Arbenz concluded: he could lead the army in a revolt against a president who was too close to the Communist party. The key positions in the armed forces had to be held by officers who would be loyal and pliant. Military competence and personal integrity could not be the primary considerations.[96]

Arbenz appointed Paz Tejada minister of public works, removing him from active duty. As chief of the armed forces, he chose instead a gregarious, hard-drinking colonel, thirty-seven-year-old Carlos Enrique Díaz. Díaz was an unexceptional officer, but Arbenz believed he was loyal. As defense minister, he chose Colonel José Angel Sánchez, a man whom the U.S. embassy described as "ineffectual; heavy drinker . . . Loyal to Arbenz."[97] Arbenz had found the

[94] Maj. Chavez, "Intelligence Report" no. 11–53, Jan. 18, 1953, p. 2, RG84 G&C, Box 4, NA-S. See also Col. Lewis, "Intelligence Report" no. IR-80-49, Aug. 6, 1949, RG319 ID 591102, NA-S, and Wardlaw to DOS, no. 941, Mar. 27, 1951, NA 714.13.

Even three decades later, in conversations with the author, both former officers and civilians (including political adversaries) proved unstinting in their praise of Paz Tejada. For Paz Tejada during the uprising against Ponce, see Zamora Alvarez, *Las memorias de Andrés*, p. 116.

[95] Interviews with María de Arbenz and Col. Guillén, who was present once when Arbenz considered this matter. "I never heard Arbenz speak ill of Paz Tejada; on the contrary, he respected him." (Interview with Fortuny.)

[96] Interviews with María de Arbenz and Fortuny. Carlos Paz Tejada never curried the favor of Arbenz's enemies, and he opposed the overthrow of Arbenz. In 1960, it was Paz Tejada who first denounced—and from Guatemala—the training of Cuban exiles in his country for the Bay of Pigs. (Paz Tejada, "Aclaración y denuncia," *Prensa Libre*, Oct. 5, 1960, p. 19.) In 1962, he led one of the first guerrilla groups in an abortive attack against the undemocratic government of President Ydígoras. Thereafter, Paz Tejada has lived in exile, with quiet and impressive dignity.

[97] Confidential report (no name or date), p. 2, enclosed in Pearson to Attwood and Burrows, May 21, 1954, NA Lot 58D18 & 58D78, Box 2. See also Maj. Chavez, "Intelligence Report" no. 11–53, Jan. 18, 1953, RG84 G&C, Box 4, NA-S. For Ar-

malleable men he had sought, but he overestimated their loyalty, their nationalism and their competence.

Arbenz could have been an unchallenged military *caudillo*, but by being true to his political beliefs he weakened his support among the military. His charisma, the fear and the respect he inspired—and the sincere attachment some officers felt to him—would delay this process of erosion. But he was embarking on a most daring endeavor: he would govern the country with a kitchen cabinet of communists while the army was firmly anticommunist; he would impose unprecedented social reforms while the great majority of his officers were unsympathetic to social change and feared the power of organized labor. He knew, moreover, that even among dedicated *Arbencista* officers, revolutionary fervor had severe limits, and their loyalty, which was never unconditional, was to Arbenz the colonel, not to Arbenz the communists' friend.

Arbenz had intended, when he became president, to address the officers on a regular basis. He had hoped to educate them politically and to cultivate their loyalty.[98] He gave one such talk, and then a second—"and he did not return."[99] An indifferent public speaker, Arbenz was uncomfortable addressing large groups. There was, however, a more compelling reason to discontinue the talks. The gulf between him and the officer corps was too wide. He had wanted to educate them, but he had to hide his true political beliefs, and this rendered communication particularly awkward. Arbenz has been criticized for giving up the attempt, yet it is highly unlikely that mere words would have achieved much. Thus, in mid-1953, when he spoke at length about the benefits of the agrarian reform, the officers listened respectfully, but afterward they commented among themselves: "Look, the president thinks that he can fool us. These are all lies. The truth is that he's in bed with the communists."[100]

Arbenz tried to find other ways to retain the loyalty of his officers. He treated them "with kid gloves," and his wife was enlisted to help: "I had pages and pages of names of the officers, their children and their wives and all their birth dates so that I could send them presents (watches, etc.). I had a secretary who spent all her time doing this."[101]

It was a genteel touch, but more tangible signs of appreciation were required. Indeed, the claim that "the army never had it as good as under

---

benz's view of Díaz, particularly helpful were interviews with María de Arbenz and Fortuny. Sánchez, like Arbenz, was from Quetzaltenango. "The three of us had been friends since childhood," Rolz Bennett remembers. (Interview with Rolz Bennett.)

[98] Interviews with María de Arbenz and Fortuny.

[99] Interview with Col. González Siguí.

[100] Interview with Col. Guillén, who attended the meeting.

[101] Interview with María de Arbenz.

Arbenz''[102] is not exaggerated—if the comparison refers to previous regimes, rather than to those that followed. As had been true since the fall of Ponce, the officers' salaries increased far more rapidly than those of civil servants and blue collar workers. Arbenz expanded the commissaries established by Arévalo, where officers could buy imported goods at reduced prices.[103] Predictably, many officers purchased more than they needed and sold the surplus at a profit. Generous travel allowances and lucrative positions in the bureaucracy—all the governors of the country's twenty-two departments were colonels—helped to boost the morale of the officer corps. Attentive to the officers' needs, the Arbenz administration also began to build houses for them in preferred districts of the capital. The program was financed "with loans obtained from the Production Development Institute (INFOP)—a government agency. . . . Although the terms of these loans were easy, in most cases payments were in arrears. It was reported that INFOP employees were told not to press for payment.''[104] This, then, was the first prong of Arbenz's military policy: "coddling of the army to retain its loyalty," as the U.S. embassy put it.[105] It was a policy that had begun under Arévalo, the effects of which an officer aptly characterized years later: "Under Arévalo and Arbenz the officer corps was mollified with high salaries, elegant uniforms, expensive cars, beautiful country clubs, long vacations and readily available scholarships to study abroad.''[106]

These emoluments help to explain the military's acceptance of Decree 900. "The Army has swung completely behind President Arbenz and his Agrarian reform law," the U.S. air attaché reported in late May 1952.[107] Most officers disliked a measure that they thought would strengthen the labor unions in the countryside. The instinctive distrust and the contempt most officers felt for the "Indios" and the fear that agrarian reform would foster communist influence among them reinforced the army's uneasiness.[108]

Yet the officers failed even to express their misgivings to the strong-willed president who showered them with benefits and whose anger they feared. In

[102] "When Communists Take Over," *U.S. News and World Report*, Feb. 20, 1953, p. 15.

[103] See esp. "Dos decretos aprobados ayer por el h. Congreso," *DCA*, p. 1; "Las concesiones al ejército" (edit.), *La Hora*, p. 1; *JW* 37, I:4. All Sept. 11, 1953.

[104] LaCharite, *Case Study in Insurgency*, p. 96.

[105] *JW* 34, Aug. 21, 1953, I:1.

[106] Col. Silva Girón, *La batalla de Gualán*, p. 27.

[107] Col. Deerwester, "Intelligence Report" no. 106-52, May 29, 1952, p. 2, RG84 CF, Box 15, NA-S.

[108] On the officers' view of the Indians, see Monteforte Toledo, *Guatemala*, pp. 364–71. On land ownership among officers (and their reaction to Decree 900), see ibid., as well as Frankel, "Political Development," p. 139, and Sierra Roldán, *Diálogos*, pp. 72–73.

July 1952, the U.S. embassy predicted that the Guatemalan army would not take a strong stand against the agrarian reform. "During his term in office," it pointed out, "President Arbenz has made every effort to retain the goodwill and support of the armed forces. Army and Air officers have enjoyed preferred positions in the Guatemalan government and opportunities to engage in lucrative enterprises have been better than ever before. In general, Army and Air Force officers appear to be satisfied with their conditions. The majority take little interest in government policies which do not affect them directly." [109]

The agrarian reform did not affect the officers' economic interests. They were mainly of middle-class extraction. While many owned fincas, these were generally of small or middle size; in any case, they were carefully spared the pain of expropriation. A few officers even profited from the reform. Through a little-used article of Decree 900, a handful of them received parcels of land in lifetime tenure;[110] the transaction was legal, yet clearly contrary to the intent of the law. On other occasions, some profited through outright graft. Decree 900 stipulated that cultivated land could not be expropriated but failed to provide precise guidelines to determine whether land was, in fact, under cultivation. This enlarged the role of the local agrarian authorities, over whom the governors (all colonels) exerted a modicum of influence. In some instances, governors were swayed by the pleas of latifundistas who were eager to reward goodwill with tangible tokens of gratitude.

The opportunities for graft were deliberately limited, as were the perquisites that Arbenz bestowed on his officers. He saw material rewards as necessary to secure the officers' loyalty to a regime that sought radical change, but these rewards must not jeopardize his larger aims.

Economic rewards alone could not assure the army's loyalty. There were two further conditions, never openly stated but understood by all: the army had to retain the monopoly of weapons and it could not be the target of subversive infiltration—let the communists proselytize among the civilians, if such was the president's will; the military must remain inviolate. (As Doña María put it, "Don't corrupt our little soldiers.")[111]

Even officers who opposed the regime have emphatically stressed that under Arbenz "there was absolutely no communist influence in the armed forces." Indeed, "there was not even any sympathy."[112] The two senior officers men-

---

[109] *JW* 30, July 25, 1952, I:3.

[110] See: "Jefes y oficiales del ejército reciben tierra," *DCA*, May 9, 1953, p. 1; McKnight to DOS, no. 1009, May 15, 1953, NA 814.20; "Tierras para seis miembros del Ejército Nac. de la Revolución," *DCA*, Jan. 8, 1954, p. 1. (The relevant article of Decree 900 was 106.)

[111] Interview with María de Arbenz.

[112] Quotations from interviews with Col. Lorenzana and Lt. Col. Cruz Salazar. All the officers and other participants interviewed for this book have supported this conclusion.

tioned by Schneider as possible communist sympathizers (Paz Tejada and Aldana Sandoval) were no exception. Major Paz Tejada was distrusted by Arbenz because of his unusual combination of integrity, professional ability, and anticommunism. Colonel Aldana Sandoval, who possessed only the last of these attributes, was, until January 1952, ambassador to Washington, where he voiced his concern about his government's leftist tendencies to U.S. officials.[113] He then replaced Paz Tejada as minister of public works, and he later won the dubious distinction of being the first cabinet member to seek asylum—on June 26, 1954, the day before Arbenz resigned.[114]

"Communists have devoted little effort to military," Ambassador Schoenfeld cabled Secretary Dulles. "Communist influence within . . . armed forces is extremely slight. . . . No (rpt no) Guatemalan officer on active service is known to be a Communist. . . . There is thus no (rpt no) evidence of Communist indoctrination among military."[115] The PGT had indeed made no attempt to infiltrate the military. Both Arbenz and the party recognized the risks of such an undertaking ("it would have been like waving a red flag in front of a bull") and its difficulties ("the army was arcane and hostile territory; it would have been as hard to infiltrate as the Church").[116] Lacking both knowledge and resources, its few *cuadros* overextended and ignorant of military politics, the PGT concentrated on more promising domains. Arbenz, his wife recalls, "saw the army more or less as his preserve and did not discuss it much with the PGT. He had great confidence in Fortuny, and great respect for his political skill, but he thought that he knew much more than Fortuny and the PGT about military matters, and so he didn't consult the party about these things."[117] Arbenz, however, was steadily losing touch with military politics, and he relied increasingly on Armed Forces Chief Díaz and Defense Minister Sánchez, fair-weather friends of limited abilities.

This, then, was the ransom: perks, the monopoly of weapons, and the absence of communists in the ranks. In return, the officer corps remained loyal, or at least quiescent, while regretting that "Jacobo had changed so much."[118] A few malcontents banded together in loosely organized cliques—first the "Grupo de los Brujos" and then the "Club del Libro." Under the pretext of social gatherings, they met every one or two weeks, usually on a Saturday, "elaborating plans from late in the evening until five in the morning."[119] Their

---

[113] See MemoConv (Aldana Sandoval, López Herrarte, Nufer), June 12, 1951, and Nufer to Miller, July 31, 1951, both NA 714.00.

[114] See below, p. 346.

[115] Schoenfeld to SecState, no. 342, Feb. 28, 1953, p.1, NA 714.001.

[116] Quotations from interviews with María de Arbenz and Fortuny.

[117] Interview with María de Arbenz. Confirmed by Fortuny and Guerra Borges.

[118] These words were repeated by many of the military officers interviewed.

[119] Interview with Lt. Col. Cruz Salazar. Nothing has been written about these two

plotting never progressed beyond the venting of frustrations among friends fortified by strong drink. "We knew that we had to do something, but we didn't know what," recalls one of them.[120] Few of the would-be plotters occupied positions of any importance, and self-interest was sobering medicine. After all, life under Arbenz was not unpleasant even for disgruntled officers, and very few were willing to risk dismissal. They also lacked a leader. In the words of a lieutenant who eventually found the courage to rebel: "The opposition to Arbenz within the army never crystallized. Arana's death put an end to what could have been a serious, strong opposition to Arbenz in the officer corps." The Guatemalan army, the U.S. embassy noted as early as June 1951, "continues almost devoid of strong leaders and spokesmen."[121] Paz Tejada could have been such a leader, but Paz Tejada was no longer on active duty.

In March 1953, the U.S. army attaché had written, "It can be expected that the military leaders will hold fast to their present position of supporting President Arbenz . . . providing Arbenz continues to pursue his present policy of keeping the military contented."[122] By early 1954, however, a new situation had developed. Danger from the United States was undermining the army's toleration of Arbenz. Guatemalan officers, especially the younger ones, were not immune to nationalism.[123] Many did not resent, and some even welcomed, the president's firmness vis-à-vis the United States, but only as long as Washington's anger did not threaten them. For the Guatemalan military was above all prudent, and this led Arbenz to a contradictory policy. On the one hand, relations with the United States grew increasingly hostile. On the other hand, a U.S. army mission of four officers and an air force mission of three officers were stationed in Guatemala; when the 1945 agreement sanctioning their presence expired in early 1953, they continued their work "on the basis of the lapsed contracts with no difficulties."[124] This Arbenz conceded to assuage the sensitivities of his officers.

---

groups, whose importance was truly modest. My major sources are interviews with Cruz Salazar, Lt. Montenegro, and Col. Mendoza.

[120] Interview with Lt. Col. Cruz Salazar. Cruz Salazar was "hostile to Arbenz but unwilling to take any risks," a U.S. military attaché observed. (Interview with Col. McCormick.)

[121] Quotations from interview with Lt. Montenegro and from *JW* 26, June 28, 1951, I:3. Montenegro is one of the few officers who plotted with Castillo Armas.

[122] Col. McCormick, "Intelligence Report" no. R-18-53, Mar. 2, 1953, p.2, RG84 G&C, Box 4, NA-S.

[123] U.S. reports during the Arbenz years consistently noted the existence of this budding nationalism. See also Monteforte Toledo, *Guatemala*, p. 369, and Frankel, "Political Development," p. 143.

[124] *JW* 48, Nov. 27, 1953, I:3. See also MemoConv ("The Guatemalan Situation"), Feb. 5, 1953, NA 714.00, and "Second Progress Report on NSC 144/1," Nov. 20, 1953, *FRUS*, 1952–1954, 4:40–41.

These same sensitivities explain the cordial "social as well as business relations" that existed between "leading Guatemalan army officers and the American service attachés," as the *New York Times* noted in mid-1953.[125] Indeed, the chief of staff of the Guatemalan army, Colonel Enrique Parinello de León, proudly recalled, some twenty-five years later, "The American officers really liked me a lot. . . . On my birthday, the members of the military mission always gave me a party."[126] Like Parinello, a great many Guatemalan officers were eager to display their goodwill toward the United States. After a forty-eight-hour visit to Guatemala, U.S. General R. G. Partridge expressed his surprise at his conversation with Colonel Sánchez, Arbenz's defense minister. Sánchez, Partridge noted, spoke "almost exclusively . . . of his three children being educated in the United States and brought out pictures of them and his wife and talked at some length about his visits to the U.S. and his children's lives there. I considered this a rather striking attempt to impress me with his closeness to and friendly feelings for the United States."[127]

By demonstrating their pro-American feelings, the Guatemalan officers were trying to mitigate the danger of their government's bitter conflict with Washington. By early 1954, the exercise had become precarious, and cold fear haunted the officer corps. The threat of U.S. military aggression made the old rules obsolete. The time had come for Arbenz to distance himself from the communists; this was the only way to appease Washington. Arbenz stubbornly refused, yet he realized, albeit imperfectly, that the price could be the forfeiture of the army's loyalty.

COMMUNIST INFLUENCE AND THE 1956 ELECTIONS

The absence of communist sympathizers in the armed forces is of cardinal importance in examining the prospects for communist influence in Guatemala. Had Arbenz not been overthrown, the PGT's influence would have continued to increase through the remaining years of his presidency. Influence would not have become control because of the anticommunism of the military.

Arbenz's presidency was scheduled to end on March 15, 1957; the 1945 constitution forbade a second consecutive term; indeed, the constitution obliged the armed forces to overthrow a president who sought to succeed himself.

One might argue that Arbenz, urged on by his communist friends, would have tried to prolong his tenure. The president would have had few moral qualms about setting the bourgeois constitution aside, but this action, tanta-

---

[125] "Guatemalan Army Apathetic to Reds," *NYT*, Aug. 5, 1953, p. 5.

[126] Interview with Parinello.

[127] Partridge to Cabot, "Notes on Visit to Four Central American Countries," May 20, 1953, p. 2, NA 714.00/3-2053.

mount to a coup d'état, would have been possible only with the army's support. And why should the military cooperate? Loyalty to Arbenz was not unconditional even among *Arbencista* officers, and it was progressively weakened by the mounting evidence of the president's ties to the PGT. Nor would opportunism lead the officer corps to close ranks behind Jacobo Arbenz, the communists' friend. The military did not need Arbenz's protection; if anything, its privileges would have increased under a less forceful president. Arbenz's coup d'état would bring only danger: it would strengthen the PGT and provoke the wrath of the United States; it would undermine the regime's legitimacy in Latin America. Growing radicalization at home and decreasing support from Latin American governments would heighten the danger of U.S. aggression. And if the United States decided to remove Arbenz, what would be the fate of those officers who had been his accomplices? Dare they hope for indulgence, or would they face professional and economic ruin—even prison and death?

Another, more mundane concern would have led a number of senior officers and administration politicians to uphold the constitution: many of them nurtured presidential ambitions. By the spring of 1954 there were already a dozen presidential hopefuls, including Interior Minister Charnaud, Armed Forces Chief Díaz, and Defense Minister Sánchez. As Doña María would later remark, "Presidentitis is a very common illness in Latin America. Every man with a B.A. thinks he should be president." In 1954, Guatemala could ill afford these pretensions; they distracted the attention of administration politicians at the very moment that they should have been focusing on the international threat to Guatemala.[128]

The leaders of the PGT looked uneasily at the crowded field of presidential candidates. The most they could hope, they concluded, was that Arbenz's successor would not be actively hostile to the party. Arbenz had reached the same conclusion. He told his PGT friends that, under the circumstances, the best candidate would be Colonel Díaz. He had no illusions about Díaz's political leanings—the colonel was not a man of the left, much less a man sympathetic to the PGT, even though "to please Arbenz he smiled broadly on the party." But Arbenz believed that Díaz was loyal to him, that he had the support of the officer corps, and that he harbored no particular hostility to the communists.[129]

---

[128] Quoted from interview with Maria de Arbenz. For a list of prospective candidates, see "Los grupos revolucionarios temen nuevas divisiones," *La Hora*, Jan. 2, 1954, p. 1. See also Ramón Blanco, "Galera," *El I*, Jan. 6, 1954, p. 2, and "Primera lucha con vista a las elecciones de presidente," *El I*, Apr. 19, 1954, p. 1.

[129] Quoted from interview with Fortuny. Other sources for the paragraph include interviews with María de Arbenz, Alejandro, and Guerra Borges; Fortuny, *Por un frente único*, p. 31; entry of Nov. 5, 1953, in the diary of Secretariat member Silva Jonama; "Análisis de la situación," *Tribuna Popular*, Feb. 9, 1954, p. 1. For com-

The PGT leaders had made no formal decision—there was still time—but "deep down we thought of Díaz as the candidate." They knew that under Díaz they would no longer be the president's favorites; but neither, they hoped, would they become pariahs. In the meantime, what was crucial was to strengthen the party.[130]

ments by the U.S. embassy on Díaz's presidential ambitions, see *JW* 11, Mar. 19, 1954, pp. 2–3.

[130] Interviews with Guerra Borges (quoted), Alejandro, and Fortuny. Díaz was confident of his chances. Thus he told a fellow colonel: "Look, it's really possible—in fact I think it's going to happen—that I'll be the next president. You will be my right hand man." (Interview with Col. Guillén.)

CHAPTER 10

The "Christian" Opposition

AT 1 A.M. SUNDAY, March 29, 1953, one hundred rebels stormed the town of Salamá and the nearby village of San Jeronimo. At 6 p.m., a hundred government soldiers from the military base at Cobán regained possession of both towns "with little fighting." Only a few rebels escaped. There were fewer than twenty casualties.[1]

This was no valiant attempt of freedom-loving Guatemalans to overthrow a communist dictatorship. "The political opposition has been left to the lunatic fringe," a respected American scholar wrote, "which . . . is really against not only Communism and the Administration, but against the Revolution and all it implies: social security, trade unionism, agrarian reform, political democracy."[2] Sidney Gruson of the *New York Times* offered an equally unflattering assessment: "During his recent visit to Guatemala this correspondent could find out easily enough what these [opposition] groups were against. But they never showed they stood in favor of something."[3] A similar judgment was reached by Theodore Geiger in his influential *Communism Versus Progress in Guatemala*. Decrying the mounting communist conspiracy "against the people of Guatemala," Geiger asserted: "By far the most important reason for the failure of the opposition is its lack of a positive and constructive program for the country."[4] The State Department concurred: "The opposition groups . . . have no positive program of their own."[5]

By the time of the Salamá revolt, the Guatemalan upper class was in despair. In 1950 many members of the elite had hoped that as president, Arbenz would

---

[1] Quoted from CIA, "Revolt in Salamá," cs-6591, Apr. 6, 1953. For press coverage of the Salamá incident, see esp. *El I* and *DCA*, Mar. 30–Apr. 21, 1953. See also "Breve reseña de los acontecimientos surgidos a raíz del movimiento subversivo del 29 de marzo de 1953," Salamá, Apr. 15, 1953, *GT*, Box 22. See also below nn. 52–54.

[2] Alexander, "Revolution in Guatemala," p. 8.

[3] "Foes' Disunity Aids Guatemalan Reds," *NYT*, Feb. 24, 1953, p. 9.

[4] Geiger, *Communism versus Progress*, p. 28. Geiger's study was well received. (See "Red Grip Detailed within Guatemala," *NYT*, p. 27; "Reds in Guatemala Reported Extending," *WP*, p. 4; "Guatemala Faces Likely Conquest by Reds, Analysts Find," *Washington Star*, p. 13; "Guatemalan Communists Held Hemisphere Peril," *CSM*, p. 4. All Dec. 14, 1953.)

[5] DOS, *Intervention of International Communism*, pp. 85–86.

reverse Arévalo's "communistic" policies. A year later this hope had faded as Arbenz encouraged organized labor and the Communist party. Then came Decree 900, and doubt settled into hatred.

While the Asociación General de Agricultores (AGA) was intransigent in its opposition to the regime, the country's few industrialists were less cohesive. Some belonged to the small Cámara de Comercio e Industria de Guatemala (CCIG); others to the even smaller Asociación General de Industriales de Guatemala (AGIG). The former tended to be members of the landed elite, the latter were the nouveaux riches. Both opposed Decree 900, assailed the government's communist proclivities, and worried about the growing assertiveness of labor. But AGIG appreciated Arbenz's effort to assist Guatemala's fledgling industries through tariff adjustments; hence it was torn between limited collaboration with the regime and intransigent opposition to it.[6] For the CCIG, by contrast, collaboration was anathema. In December 1952, the two associations clashed openly. They had been invited by the government to participate in talks on the development of a national industrial policy. Only dupes or knaves would negotiate with a communist-dominated government, proclaimed the CCIG. To refuse to attend was unpatriotic, countered the AGIG, adding that it was ready to talk to anyone, "even the communists."[7] And so the bickering continued, until Arbenz was overthrown.

Those few members of the upper class who supported the government were almost all from Quetzaltenango, Arbenz's hometown. In 1949 they had founded the Partido Integridad Nacional (PIN) to back the candidacy of their friend Jacobo. This party of the "progressive bourgeoisie" was a small and dwindling group. It was led by Nicolás Brol and Roberto Fanjul, the former a rich landowner, the latter a successful businessman. In March 1951, Brol's appointment as minister of agriculture had been welcomed by the upper class. Then, after a year of heightening frustration, the elite was relieved when Fanjul joined Brol in the cabinet as minister of economy. "Señor Fanjul," noted the U.S. embassy, was "a successful and reputedly anti-communist businessman"; his appointment "raised hopes that relations between government and private capital might be improved."[8] But Fanjul and Brol remained in the

[6] AGIG's attitude was well summarized by the U.S. embassy: "The [Arbenz] administration has always been willing to aid domestic industry as long as the assistance does not adversely affect organized labor, small farmers, or the Government itself. Although the Association of Guatemalan Industrialists (AGIG) officially is pleased with such concessions, individual members privately doubt that there will be substantial private industrial expansion without a more responsible labor force, more realistic labor and financial legislation, and an improvement in the political atmosphere." (*JW* 52, Dec. 23, 1953, II:3; see also *JW* 47, Nov. 21, 1952, II:1–2.)

[7] *JW* 50, Dec. 12, 1952, II:3. The clash can be followed in the Guatemalan press of that month, esp. *El I*.

[8] Quotations from *JW* 13, Mar. 28, 1952, I:3 and *JW* 14, Apr. 4, 1952, II:1. See

cabinet even after the enactment of Decree 900. Indeed, at Arbenz's request, it was Fanjul who introduced the bill in Congress; he thus found himself, the *New York Times* observed, "in the odd situation of being attacked by the very people who hailed his recent appointment as an indication that President Arbenz was shaking off an asserted influence of Communists."[9]

Brol and Fanjul remained loyal to Arbenz. They believed that his policies favored the emergence of capitalism in Guatemala, but they were branded imbeciles or traitors by their former friends from the upper class. "The position of Minister Brol defies understanding," wrote Marroquín Rojas. "And Fanjul? Poor Fanjul! He will be a casualty of communism because a landowner . . . a captain of industry . . . can never be a socialist. When he received his ministerial portfolio he took leave of his senses: he imagines he is a 'comrade' of Víctor Manuel Gutiérrez! Tomorrow, when they no longer need him, they will throw him to the dogs."[10] Marroquín Rojas accepted the need for some social reforms, and he was a nationalist who resented Guatemala's status as a banana republic. Hence U.S. officials had labeled him leftist in the late 1940s. But he abhorred communism. If the choice was between social reforms with the slightest whiff of communism and the status quo, he opted for the latter. There were also idealists within the opposition, men like the student leader Eduardo Taracena de la Cerda, men who fought for what they believed to be the country's true interests,[11] but they were the exceptions. The overriding motivation of the men who led the opposition, as Marroquín Rojas at times intimated and U.S. reports freely conceded, was the implacable defense of privilege.

Waving the banner of anticommunism, these men engaged in a relentless campaign of opposition. Assisted by the country's major newspapers and radio stations, they sought to raise the specter of Armageddon among a people largely lacking political sophistication. Posing as champions of a Catholic faith threatened by Red hordes, they strove to inflame religious passions, and they received the full backing of the Church.

In 1950 Archbishop Rossell y Arellano had believed that Arbenz would purge the communists. How could it be otherwise, he had reasoned, when Arbenz "was married to a woman from a very rich family, was a military officer, lived in a house in Zone 10 of the capital (where the rich lived), and had the look of an aristocrat: white, distinguished."[12] Decree 900 persuaded

---

also Wells to SecState, no. 333, Mar. 15, 1951, NA 714.11; Wardlaw to DOS, no. 941, Mar. 27, 1951, NA 714.13; Krieg to DOS, no. 971, Mar. 26, 1952, NA 714.13.

[9] Gruson, "Guatemalan Foes Talk of Civil War," *NYT*, May 18, 1952, p. 10.

[10] "Los ricos con el agua al cuello," *Impacto*, May 31, 1952, p. 1.

[11] My view of Taracena is based on my conversations with him as well as with people who knew him well, both friends and enemies.

[12] Interview with Fr. Bendaña Perdomo.

Rossell y Arellano that he had been betrayed: the government was communist. Immediately, the archbishop lent his support, and the dignity of his office, to Arbenz's most bitter foes.[13]

Verbum, the mouthpiece of the Church, and the Catholic weekly *Acción Social Cristiana* assailed the government as fiercely as did AGA. There might be an agrarian problem in Guatemala, *Verbum* conceded, but it had been "provoked almost artificially by all the governments, especially by those called revolutionary, in order to gain the vote of the illiterates on behalf of their partisan interests. . . . If there really is a problem, it is not as flagrant or as grave as they have tried to make us believe."[14] Meanwhile, in the countryside, the clergy urged peasants and agricultural workers to resist a communist law that would bring them material and spiritual ruin.

In January 1953, Rossell y Arellano was the prime mover behind the creation of the Partido Anticomunista Demócrata Cristiano, which, he hoped, would become the political arm of the Church; but the party failed to thrive.[15] That same month he embarked on yet another undertaking, sending a reproduction of the statue of the "Black Christ" of Esquipulas on an extended perambulation through the country. It was, argued the official *Diario de Centro América*, a "bizarre pilgrimage," one that caused a near riot in the village of Esquipulas.[16] Rossell y Arellano, however, believed that he was countering

[13] On the Church in the Arbenz years, see Bendaña Perdomo, "Historia general," and Frankel, "Political Development." For Rossell y Arellano's collaboration with the plotters, interviews with Bendaña Perdomo and Taracena were helpful.

[14] "El ante-proyecto de ley agraria formulado por el Ejecutivo" (edit.), *Verbum*, May 25, 1952, p. 1. Decree 900 transformed Arbenz into an "agrarian dictator" and crudely violated "our sacred constitution," admonished *Acción Social Cristiana*, adding: "No reform is called for." ("La dictadura agraria," May 15, 1952, pp. 1–2.) *Acción Social Cristiana* was at least consistent. In 1947, it had warned, "Nothing would disrupt productivity more than agrarian reform." ("El comunismo y la reforma agraria," May 29, 1947, p. 1.) See also Frankel's excellent discussion, "Political Development," pp. 224–30.

[15] For the creation of the party see "Un Partido Demócrata Cristiano," *El I*, Jan. 24, 1953, p. 1; "Partido anticomunista cristiano," *La Hora*, Jan. 24, 1953, p. 1; *JW 5*, Jan. 30, 1953, I:3–4.

[16] "Miles de personas a Esquipulas," Jan. 3, 1953, p. 1. The population of Esquipulas loudly protested the archbishop's decision to send the statue through the country. It would have been the first time in three centuries that the statue had left the village. The uproar forced Rossell y Arellano to compromise: he sent a copy instead. For articles in the opposition press about the pilgrimage, see "Cristo de Esquipulas saldrá en peregrinación," *El I*, Dec. 22, 1952, p. 1; "El Cristo de Esquipulas recorrerá el país," *La Hora*, Dec. 22, 1952, p. 1; "Cristo de Esquipulas ingresará en la capital," *El I*, Dec. 29, 1952, p. 1; "No será movida de su sitial la imagen del Cristo de Esquipulas," *El I*, Dec. 31, 1952, p. 1; "Amenazado el parroco de Esquipulas," *La Hora*, Jan. 3, 1953, p. 1; "El Cristo de Esquipulas sale a peregrinación," *La Hora*, Jan. 16, 1953,

a challenge: the devil "was stalking the countryside" disguised as an agrarian reformer and "Christ would sally forth from Esquipulas to give him battle."[17]

Within the Church, one man opposed Rossell y Arellano's extremism. The papal nuncio, Genaro Verolino, did not believe that Decree 900 threatened Catholic Guatemala; there was an agrarian problem, he argued, and the decree had positive aspects. Communists did influence the government, and the communists' main champion was Arbenz, but Arbenz was not attacking the Church, and the military opposed communism. Therefore, Verolino concluded, the communists were not in control, and they would be greatly weakened when Arbenz left the presidency in 1957. In the meantime, he urged, the Church should bear with the government.[18]

A relationship marked by respect and some cordiality developed between Arbenz and the nuncio. This led to concessions on several issues important to the Church. In 1953, the government allowed a religious program ("The Voice of the Sacred Heart of Jesus") to be broadcast on the state radio; never before had such permission been granted in Guatemala. Acceding to the nuncio's request, the authorities also permitted an unprecedented number of foreign priests to work in Guatemala.[19]

They did, however, deport one priest, the American Sebastian Buccellato. Buccellato denied that he had ever advocated the overthrow of the government, as the authorities had intimated, but had merely done his duty as a Christian and as a priest. "The . . . agrarian reform Law . . . [was] a ruthless political tool that accomplished a bloodless Red revolution," he explained.

> I viewed the whole diabolical scheme with horror. . . . Those parish members who were offered land . . . asked my opinion. Naturally I told them that Communism and Christianity are irreconcilable. A few peasants, of course, accepted [the offer of land] . . . and left the parish. But with the help of 35 lay catechists, who toured the countryside, most of the members remained true and turned down the Communist

---

p. 1; "Abierta la inscripción para llevar en hombros al Cristo de Esquipulas," *La Hora*, Jan. 21, 1953, p. 1; "Imponente recibimiento al Cristo de Esquipulas," *La Hora*, Jan. 26, 1953, p. 1; "Multitudes desbordantes de fé," *El I*, Jan. 26, 1953, p. 1; "Una semana estará el Cristo de Esquipulas en Catedral," *La Hora*, Jan. 27, 1953, p. 1; "El Cristo de Esquipulas saldrá el próximo domingo para la Antigua," *La Hora*, Jan. 29, 1953, p. 1; "Desbordan de fé en Cristo la capital y Antigua," *El I*, Feb. 2, 1953, p. 1. See also "Memorial de los católicos de Esquipulas," no. 28, Feb. 27, 1953, Correspondencia, AHA.

[17] Interview with Bendaña Perdomo.

[18] Interview with Bendaña Perdomo; see also Bendaña Perdomo, "Historia general," p. 51, and Richard and Meléndez, *La iglesia*, p. 199.

[19] Interviews with Bendaña Perdomo and María de Arbenz. See also Bendaña Perdomo, "Historia general," p. 59; Calder, *Crecimiento*, p. 52; Alonso and Garrido, *La iglesia*, p. 191.

offer. . . . I left the country by plane on February 3 [1954], but not until I had broadcast the truth to the people over the anti-Communist radio in Guatemala City.[20]

Had the government been willing to risk a confrontation with the Church, many foreign priests would have shared Buccellato's fate, for many spoke the same inflammatory language and brazenly interfered in Guatemala's internal affairs. But the government did not openly attack the Church. It remonstrated, instead, that Decree 900 was in accordance with Catholic teachings.[21]

Arbenz's concessions and Verolino's arguments were to no avail. The clergy, from bishop to village priest, rallied behind Rossell y Arellano. Some were moved by chauvinism; the nuncio was a foreigner. But not even the foreign clergy supported Verolino, not even those priests who had come to Guatemala courtesy of his intercession. Deaf to the nuncio's subtle reasoning, they embraced the archbishop's simple and effective message: the government was communist and Christian virtue demanded opposition. "There is no indication," a Guatemalan Jesuit later remarked, "that a single priest opposed either the stance or the methods of Rossell y Arellano against Arbenz; nor do I know of any priest who had any sympathy for the government. In his conciliatory policy the nuncio was completely alone."[22]

The Church lent a veneer of legitimacy to the invectives of the upper class. It sparked the opposition's most combative battalion: "the outspoken market women of Guatemala City."[23] These women, wrote the *New York Times*, "were the only militants the opposition could put forward. Highly religious, and with a tough independence of spirit, [they were] willing not only to leave their sidewalk stalls and march to Government buildings in protests but also to use their scanty financial resources in their campaigns whether their wealthy

[20] Sebastian Buccellato, "I Saw the Reds Taking Over!" *This Week Magazine*, June 27, 1954, quoted from pp. 7, 18, 19. The government expelled Buccellato on a technicality; he had failed to renew his residence permit: see "Caso del Padre Buccellato," *El I*, Feb. 3, 1954, p. 1; "Buccellato estaba ilegalmente en el país," *DCA*, Feb. 4, 1954, p. 1; "Guatemalan Assures Press," *NYT*, Feb. 4, 1954, p. 2; "Foreign Minister of Guatemala Explains Ouster of Cleric," *NYT*, Feb. 5, 1954, p. 6. For background on Buccellato, see Federico Juarez Rodas to Ministro de Gobernación, May 26, 1954, CO:G, May 1954, p. 472, AGCA.

[21] See Frankel's authoritative discussion, "Political Development," pp. 233–35. Benites, *Meditaciones*, attempts to refute the Church's charges against Decree 900 point by point.

[22] Interview with Bendaña Perdomo. A possible exception is Fr. Augusto Herrera, parish priest of San Juan Sacátepequez. (See Augusto Herrera to Mgr. Gilberto Solorzano B., Feb. 1, 1952, no. 36, Correspondencia, AHA and Herrera to Carlos Alvarado Jérez, ibid.

[23] "Anti-Red Rifts Held Guatemala Threat," *CSM*, Jan. 24, 1953, p. 13.

compatriots support[ed] them or not."[24] Few among the lower classes shared the market women's selfless devotion to the political teachings of the Guatemalan Catholic Church. Three quarters of a century of anticlerical regimes, the U.S. embassy pointed out with regret, had weakened the clergy's hold over the people.[25] With its sparse ranks, the Church was unable to proselytize effectively, particularly in the rural areas. Even though the total number of priests rose from 114 in 1944 to 195 in 1954, Guatemala remained the country with the lowest priest-per-inhabitant ratio of Latin America.[26] Moreover, the message of the Guatemalan Church was not rousing: "To exorcise the communist demon, he [Rossell y Arellano] preached more charity from the rich and more humility from the poor." But the rich had little taste for charity, and the poor were weary of humility. The CIA's analysis was concise: "The Church has been handicapped by the small number of priests and by a lack of a constructive social program."[27]

The Church's attacks on Arbenz's agrarian reform in 1952 heightened many peasants' suspicions about the decree. As its implementation brought benefits rather than misery, the impact of the clergy's diatribes diminished. "In general, land reform has been popular with the masses," a December 1953 CIA report conceded,[28] while the following April a State Department study pointed out, "The large Guatemalan landowners and United Fruit Company have been the major targets of the reform. Neither has elicited any sympathy in Guatemalan public opinion. . . . The net internal political result of the implementation of [Decree 900] . . . has been to strengthen the Arbenz Administration."[29] The clergy had failed to generate widespread opposition to the regime, and the upper class was unable to garner enough popular support to warrant any hope of winning power through elections.

The opposition parties claimed that it was the government's repression that had rendered them impotent. Their shrill complaints were echoed by an op-

---

[24] "Foes' Disunity Aids Guatemalan Reds," *NYT*, Feb. 24, 1953, p. 9.

[25] *JW* 46, Nov. 13, 1953, I:4.

[26] Alonso and Garrido, *La iglesia*, p. 271, and Turner, *Catholicism*, pp. 135–36, 184, table 4. In 1954 Guatemala had one priest for every 14,611 inhabitants; ranked next was Honduras with one for every 12,103 inhabitants.

[27] Quotations from Frankel, "Political Development," p. 212 and CIA, "Present Political Situation In Guatemala and Possible Developments during 1952," NIE-62, Mar. 11, 1952, p. 3, Truman Papers, President's Secretary's File, Intelligence File, Box 254, TL. Frankel provides the best overall treatment of Rossell y Arellano. More sympathetic but less persuasive is Turner, *Catholicism*, pp. 131–40. Pike, "Catholic Church," is an apology; see esp. pp. 92, 102, 111–12.

[28] CIA, "Evaluation of Recent Political and Economic Developments," number deleted, Dec. 3, 1953, p. 2.

[29] "Political Developments in Guatemala since May 1953," IR-6579, quoted from pp. 1, 2, enclosed in Burgin to Leddy, Apr. 22, 1954, NA 714.00.

position press that was remarkably outspoken. The following titles of editorials from *La Hora* are illustrative: "Guerra Borges incites a massacre" (Guerra Borges was a member of the PGT's Secretariat); "The duplicity of Poncho Bauer" (Bauer Paiz was the director of the Banco Nacional Agrario); "The stupidity of our leaders"; "Blood is still flowing, Colonel Arbenz."[30] *El Imparcial* and *Prensa Libre*, the other major opposition dailies, were equally intemperate; some publications virtually advocated the overthrow of the regime.[31] The government did not intervene. Freedom of the press in Arbenz's Guatemala greatly surpassed that of neighboring Mexico; in Latin America, it was equaled only by Uruguay and, perhaps, by Chile and Costa Rica.

Even unsympathetic American journalists were struck by the degree of freedom that existed in Guatemala. In an essay that applauded the overthrow of Arbenz, one such journalist, Keith Monroe, wrote that in a 1953 visit to Guatemala he had found that "anti-communist and pro-American newspapers were still in business. They attacked the government as hotly as Hearst used to attack the New Deal, yet their editors walked the streets unharmed. Fences and adobe walls were daubed with damn-the-Communists slogans. Shops and homes displayed cards in their windows: 'THERE IS NO COMMUNISM IN THIS HOUSE.' "[32] By West European standards, political democracy in Guatemala was limited, in part because the Indians traditionally voted as the local authorities wished. But the reports of the U.S. embassy highlighted the lack of violence in the elections that were held under Arbenz; these reports include no allegations of government pressure on the people or of restrictions on the opposition's freedom to campaign in the rural areas.[33] The January 1953 congressional elections were praised by Marroquín Rojas: "Now that this most recent election is behind us, we can state with confidence that democracy has taken root."[34]

When several dozen people were detained in the wake of Salamá, the opposition press lambasted the regime. Several months later, however, the U.S.

---

[30] *La Hora*: Jan. 18, 1954, p. 3; Feb. 26, 1954, p. 3; Mar. 3, 1954, p. 3; Mar. 18, 1954, p. 3.

[31] See, for example, the daily *El Espectador* and the many leaflets and bulletins of the often ephemeral anticommunist committees. For a compilation of articles from *El I*, see Blanco, *25 galeras*, a collection of twenty-five of this prominent journalist's columns written between Sept. 30, 1953, and June 1, 1954. *25 galeras* conveys the intensity of his hostility for the Arbenz regime and provides graphic proof of the freedom of the press in that time.

[32] Monroe, "Guatemala: What the Reds Left Behind," p. 61.

[33] On the Jan. 1953 elections, see *JW* 1–5 (Jan. 1–30, 1953). See also Schoenfeld to DOS, no. 490, Jan. 8, 1953; Schoenfeld to DOS, no. 621, Jan. 21, 1953; Schoenfeld to DOS, no. 660, Jan. 30, 1953. All NA 714.2. On the Nov. 1953 elections, see *JW* 48, Nov. 27, 1953.

[34] "Lo que puede salir de la experiencia electoral que acaba de sucederse," *La Hora*, Jan. 20, 1953, p. 1.

embassy observed: "Most of the people arrested subsequent to the [Salamá] uprising were actually involved in the group seeking to overthrow the Government."[35] The following January, in a second wave of arrests, two dozen were detained; again the opposition press vented its indignation, and again the embassy reported that the "victims" had been plotting the overthrow of the regime. Repression in Arbenz's Guatemala began only in late May 1954, in dramatic circumstances brought about by the United States.

It was neither political repression nor electoral fraud that robbed Arbenz's foes of victory at the polls. Bitter, petty divisions sapped their strength. In October 1952, the U.S. embassy noted "the ineffectiveness of the Guatemalan anti-communist movement"; complained about the "multiplicity of anti-communist organizations, their frictions and jealousies"; and lamented the resulting "wave of disillusionments . . . in the anti-administration sector."[36] That same month, a prominent opposition journalist pushed the analysis further:

> Anticommunist activities have achieved to date the most complete failure. . . . The explanation is very simple: in the first place, they lack a leader. . . . In the second place, they lack what Clemente [Marroquín Rojas] calls "guts." . . . In the third place, they lack the will to sacrifice. . . . The communists are prominent because of their intellectual abilities. . . . The anticommunists move without organization, discipline, or cooperation. Many "anticommunists at heart" don't even reach into their pockets to give a small donation when a committee or group asks for a few cents to aid at least in the propaganda campaign. . . . The so-called "leaders" incite the fray from their homes and vanish from even the telephone directory at the first sign of a clash.[37]

They lacked guts, and they lacked popular support. Both a Guatemalan protagonist and an American scholar, neither swayed by sympathy for the regime, came to similar conclusions. In a February 1954 editorial, the Guatemalan, Marroquín Rojas, frankly acknowledged that the rural masses backed the government:

> The peasants do not support the opposition. They support the government, for they have been seduced by the agrarian reform and other promises. True, there are smart peasants who have understood how hollow are the government's words. But there are just a few. . . . In the present circumstances, it is the rich—the landowners and the landlords—who would have to fight in the streets, and they will never do it. The members of AGA are good marksmen, but they only know how to shoot ducks and other defenseless birds; they couldn't shoot a man holding a gun. . . . Somoza has

---

[35] Wardlaw to Peurifoy ("Conversation Regarding Possibility of Attempt against Guatemalan Government"), Dec. 29, 1953, p. 1, NA 714.00/1-454.

[36] Krieg to DOS, no. 334, Oct. 10, 1952, quoted from pp. 1, 3, NA 714.00.

[37] Alvaro Contreras Velez, "Cacto," *Prensa Libre*, Oct. 2, 1952, p. 3.

told them: "I'll give you the weapons, the ammunition and the money; you find the men." But neither Ydígoras, nor Castillo Armas, nor Córdova Cerna, nor Coronado Lira has been able to find ten men willing to fight.[38]

The scholar, Ronald Schneider, concluded in 1958:

> Most Guatemalans . . . were greatly concerned about the preservation of the fruits of the Revolution of 1944, and there was little in the attitudes or actions of the opposition to indicate sincere support for that goal. . . . The working class had particular reason to feel loyal to the revolutionary regime. . . . The lower classes enjoyed the novelty of living in a new atmosphere, officially fostered, in which they were treated with a measure of respect and dignity.[39]

Lacking popular support, the scions of the upper class had little alternative but to seek a foreign patron. The pilgrimages to U.S. embassies of would-be liberators eager to oust Arbenz began even before his inauguration. General Ydígoras Fuentes, the unsavory presidential candidate of November 1950, appeared at the U.S. embassy in San Salvador on January 10, 1951. He presented Chargé d'Affaires William Wieland with a dramatic revelation and a bold offer. "He asked," Wieland wrote, "if I would have time to listen to his story concerning Arévalo. Without waiting for an answer," Ydígoras proceeded to reveal how, at a gathering in London in 1946, he had met a Chilean professor whose name he couldn't quite recall. Mistaking Ydígoras for a communist, the professor had immediately confided that both he and Arévalo were Soviet agents and that Arévalo had been sent to Guatemala "to take over the country" on the Kremlin's behalf. Arévalo, the garrulous professor had continued, "had done a masterful job in applying his Communist orders in Guatemala."

Ydígoras explained that he was ready and eager to defend his homeland. He would need, however, assistance. Wieland politely "thanked the general for his very pleasant and informative visit." Not for the last time, Ydígoras had made a dismal impression on an American whose support he had courted.[40]

A few weeks later, two of Ydígoras's men visited Somoza. "They claimed," the U.S. embassy reported, "that they had all the military assistance they needed, that their plans were laid and the coup would take place February 28, but that they needed money." Somoza assured them of his high regard for Ydígoras and sent them packing; he did not believe that the Guatemalan army would support a coup.[41]

Throughout Arbenz's first year, Ydígoras and other exiles pursued their

[38] "El caso del diputado José Luis Arenas R.," *La Hora*, Feb. 27, 1954, p. 3.

[39] Schneider, *Communism*, pp. 302–3.

[40] AmEm San Salvador, Wieland to DOS, no. 518, Jan. 11, 1951, quoted from pp. 1–4, NA 714.00.

[41] AmEm Managua, Waynick to DOS, no. 759, Feb. 25, 1951, NA 714.00.

quest for a foreign patron. In Guatemala a few hotheads engaged in sporadic acts of violence,[42] but most opposition leaders, acutely aware of their own weakness and still hopeful that Arbenz would move to the right, were content with rhetorical outbursts, upbraiding the government for its dalliance with the communists and urging the populace to give no quarter to the Reds. "The communist in the department of Quetzaltenango is outlawed," warned the Partido Independiente Anti-Comunista Occidental. "He will not be allowed to buy or sell anything, he will not be given work, and he will be despised as though he were a rabid dog."[43]

The opposition occasionally organized demonstrations to demand that the authorities wipe out communism. After a series of particularly noisy rallies in the capital and other towns, the U.S. embassy reported that the demonstrators, who were "mostly fairly well-dressed," had been neither attacked nor harassed; the government's willingness to allow the opposition forces "to express their feelings," noted the *New York Times*, suggested to many Guatemalans and Americans that Arbenz's commitment to the Reds might be superficial.[44]

Decree 900 plunged the upper class into despair. Marroquín Rojas, in a May 31, 1952 editorial, castigated his conservative friends:

> Many of the rich were *Arbencistas* [in the 1950 election]. Asturias Beltranena and many others were sure that Colonel Arbenz was a man of the right; that he couldn't be a Marxist because he was a military man, because he was associated with capitalists, and "because he liked the good life." I, on the other hand, had become acquainted with the true Arbenz in the Council of Ministers, and notwithstanding my personal regard for him, I understood . . . that he would never be parted from his extremist inclinations. . . . For this reason, I always said that he would turn either to the right or to the left. The proposed agrarian reform has shown it to be the

[42] Taracena recalls: "In 1951, I participated in some terrorist acts—against property, not people. I was found out, and I had to go into exile." (Interview with Taracena.) In January 1952, there were two bomb attacks against the PGT. (See "Bomba misteriosa estalla," *El I*, Jan. 19, 1952, p. 1; "Deben ser castigados," *Octubre*, Jan. 24, 1952, p. 1; "Atentado terrorista con bomba nylon," *El I*, Jan. 28, 1952, p. 1; "Desesperados ante auge de la lucha popular los anticomunistas arrojaron otra bomba," *Octubre*, Jan. 31, 1952, p. 1.) For additional examples, see L.A.H.A., *Así se gestó la Liberación*, pp. 57–58; MemoConv (Schoenfeld, Whitbeck), June 9, 1952, RG84 CF, Box 15, NA-S; Schoenfeld to DOS, no. 1288, June 17, 1952, NA 714.52.

[43] "ALERTA PUEBLO!!" Partido Independiente Anti-Comunista Occidental, Quetzaltenango, Aug. 1951.

[44] Quotations from *JW* 13, Mar. 28, 1952, I:1 and "Guatemalans Firm in Anti-Red Effort," *NYT*, Mar. 24, 1952, p. 5. See also "Guatemalan Ban on Reds Is Sought," *NYT*, Mar. 22, 1952, p. 4; "Anti-Red Meeting Stirs Guatemala," *NYT*, Mar. 23, 1952, p. 26; "Rallies Are Peaceful in Rural Guatemala," *NYT*, Mar. 25, 1952, p. 10; "Anti-Reds' Views Asked," *NYT*, Mar. 30, 1952, p. 27.

latter. There now can be neither hope nor doubt. . . . Arbenz will be true to his beliefs until he is brought down. . . . But . . . the rich still hope for compromise. . . . That is their mistake.[45]

This was a call to war, because—as Marroquín Rojas well knew—the opposition would not gain power through elections. Spurred on by the agrarian reform, the number of plotters increased. So did the frequency of the plotters' visits to U.S. embassies in Guatemala and other Central American republics. (Some went directly to the State Department in Washington.) As always, they wanted U.S. support, particularly dollars. As always, each poured scorn on the other plotters—the competition for favor was ruthless. Overestimating American credulity, some inflated their own importance to the point of absurdity. Colonel (ret.) Roberto Barrios Peña, who appeared in May 1952 at the State Department unbidden and "extremely agitated about the agrarian reform law," claimed that he was "the leader of the anti-communist movement in Guatemala which . . . had some 300,000 followers."[46] The figure must have been charmed: a year later, Guillermo Putzeys, who belonged to a rival and equally insignificant group, announced to U.S. officials that "his movement had 300,000 members."[47] This out of a total population of 3 million.

U.S. officials gave a courteous hearing to all and, until the summer of 1953, gave them all the same answer: the United States was concerned about communist influence in Guatemala, but it was not prepared to back a coup. From Guatemala, Ambassador Schoenfeld, who was aware of the weakness of the would-be rebels, warned the State Department of "the constant danger that confronts the anti-communist movement in this country from intemperate elements who undertake premature subversive action."[48]

Though the plotters' words were bold, their actions were cautious. The saga of Lt. Colonel Castillo Armas is representative. After his failed November 1950 uprising, he escaped from jail in July 1951 and left within a few days for exile in Colombia. Upon arriving in Bogotá, he predicted with bland assurance "that before the end of the year, the armed forces and the anti-communist civilian forces will have overthrown the government."[49] In late 1951, he

---

[45] "Los ricos con el agua al cuello," *Impacto*, May 31, 1952, p. 1.

[46] MemoConv (Barrios Peña, Siracusa, Clark), May 27, 1952, p. 1, NA 714.00. See also MemoConv (Barrios Peña, Mann, Clark), May 28, 1952, NA 714.00.

[47] MemoConv (Putzeys, Padilla, Fisher), May 14, 1953, p. 1, NA 714.00.

[48] Schoenfeld to DOS, no. 1075, Apr. 25, 1952, p. 2, NA 714.00. He was referring to the activities of a Comité Ejecutivo de la Liberación Nacional, which had initiated a series of chain letters "calling in thinly veiled terms for a rising" against Arbenz (p. 1).

[49] CIA, "Colonel Castillo Armas, Guatemalan Exile," number deleted, Aug. 2, 1951, quote p. 2. See also above, pp. 81–83.

moved to Tegucigalpa. He intended to enter Guatemala from El Salvador on January 25, 1952, a CIA report noted. He would be met at the border by one of his most loyal followers, the student leader Mario Sandoval Alarcón. The revolt would begin that night.[50]

Castillo Armas did not cross the border, and the uprising was postponed until late February—when, once again, nothing happened. In June, rebel sources informed the CIA that the bellicose colonel would invade Guatemala within a few days, this time from Honduras; as soon as he crossed the border, most of the Guatemalan army would rise in revolt, and in the capital a "civilian large scale uprising" would begin. (The CIA report ended with a note of caution: "Time and possible success highly unpredictable. Will primarily depend on degree of army support, principally in Guatemala City, of which we have no reliable information.")[51] Again, nothing happened. Castillo Armas lacked organization, popular support, and influence in the military. Prudently, he, like the rest of the plotters, refrained from launching an uprising.

The one exception to this pattern of caution was the ill-fated attack on Salamá. This "premature and poorly planned attempt by a small group," as a CIA report called it, took the agency by surprise. Swamped by warnings of uprisings that never materialized, it had ignored rumors that a revolt "will be attempted in Guatemala during Holy Week."[52]

The leaders of the revolt were César Izaguirre, an inveterate plotter, and Carlos Simmons. Simmons, the U.S. embassy reported, "was until recently employed by the Tropical Radio Company, a subsidiary of the United Fruit Company." Izaguirre and Simmons had received a large sum of money and,

---

[50] CIA, number and day deleted, Jan. 1952. Forty years later, upon hearing this report, a close aide of Castillo Armas exclaimed, "Ah! The inexperience of youth! Yes, we thought there were six or seven officers on our side in the military zone of Jutiapa. And we imagined that with them, we'd be able to take control of the zone, and that then Castillo Armas could arrive from El Salvador." (Interview with Taracena.)

[51] CIA, IN 75738, June 23, 1952, quoted from pp. 1, 2. See also CIA, "Possible Revolution in Guatemala," SO 90855, June 25, 1952; CIA, "Plot to Overthrow Arbenz Government," 00-B-53060, July 1, 1952; Smith to Undersec. of State, Dec. 12, 1952, *FRUS*, 1952-54, 4:1055–56.

[52] Quotations from CIA, "Revolutionary Activity in Guatemala," CS-9229, May 1, 1953 and AmEm Managua, Whelan to SecState, no. 152, Mar. 4, 1953, NA 714.00. See also CIA, "Revolt in Salamá," CS-6591, Apr. 6, 1953; CIA, CS-9934, May 14, 1953; CIA, "Attitude of the Guatemalan Army toward Current Political Developments," CS-10050, May 14, 1953.

Following the fashion to see the CIA behind every tree, some authors assert that the agency sponsored Salamá, despite the fact that all the evidence indicates that it was surprised by it. One of the most inventive is Higgins (*Perfect Failure*, p. 19), who flashes two sources (one of which is *FRUS*) to support his claim. One source does indeed mention Salamá, but not the CIA; the other mentions neither.

apparently, weapons from Trujillo and United Fruit. Emboldened, these "hotheaded anti-Communists" had acted without seeking the support of other groups of plotters, hoping to preempt the competition and savor the rewards of success alone.[53]

After the inevitable debacle, Izaguirre and Simmons escaped to foreign embassies and soon left the country. Their motley band of followers, who had been assured that they were but the vanguard, was left to reflect on their credulity in jail. Meanwhile, rival plotters hastened to express their disapproval of the untimely undertaking to U.S. officials. Throughout, the Guatemalan army had shown no disloyalty to the government, and the garrison of Cobán had acted "promptly and efficiently to put down the revolt," the U.S. embassy reported. This confirmed Arbenz in his belief that he could rely on his officers. "Jacobo," his wife recalls, "was not unduly disturbed. He felt that the army was loyal. The outcome of Salamá gave him a sense of security."[54]

This was the Guatemala that the Eisenhower administration faced in the summer of 1953 when it decided to engineer the overthrow of Arbenz. Within the country the opposition was weak and ineffectual. Small groups of bickering exiles hovered on Guatemala's borders, particularly in Honduras and El Salvador. They included "democrats" who had left the country rather than submit to a "communist" regime, and "democrats" who, having engaged in subversive activities, had fled to escape arrest or had been deported. By mid-1953, a majority of those who had congregated in Honduras acknowledged Castillo Armas as their leader; he enjoyed Somoza's protection and was the favorite of Archbishop Rossell y Arellano. Most of those who lived in El Sal-

[53] Quotations from *JW* 16, Apr. 17, 1953, I:3, and Krieg to Ambassador, Apr. 20, 1953, p. 1, RG84 G&C, Box 3, NA-S. On Izaguirre, see Krieg to SecState, no. 392, Mar. 30, 1953, NA 714.00. On UFCO's role, the following memo is suggestive: "Mr. Orray Taft, Jr., Office of Munitions Control, called me at 5 p.m., to tell me that he had just received a call from Mr. Emerick, Deputy Commissioner of Customs in Charge of Investigations, who told him that his agents in New York were investigating acquisitions of arms by [UFCO President] Zemurray for the overthrow of the Guatemalan government, and that he would supply Mr. Taft with a copy of the report on the investigation." (Fisher to Mann, May 19, 1953, NA 714.00.)

[54] Quotations from Krieg to SecState, no. 393, Mar. 31, 1953, NA 714.00, and from interview with María de Arbenz. In addition to those cited in nn. 1, 52, and 53 above, useful U.S. documents on Salamá are: *JW* 14, Apr. 3, 1953, I; *JW* 15, Apr. 10, 1953, I; *JW* 18, May 1, 1953, I; *JW* 23, June 5, 1953, I; Krieg to SecState, no. 390, Mar. 30, 1953, NA 714.00; Maj. Chavez, "Intelligence Report" no. IR-49-53, Apr. 9, 1953, RG84 G&C, Box 3, NA-S; Schoenfeld to DOS, no. 905, Apr. 15, 1953, NA 714.00; Schoenfeld to DOS, no. 1002, May 13, 1953, NA 714.00; MemoConv (Barrios Peña, Leddy, Fisher), Apr. 28, 1953, NA 714.00.

vador followed Ydígoras Fuentes, who competed for Trujillo's favor with Colonel Roberto Barrios Peña.[55]

Castillo Armas and Ydígoras did try to unite. On March 31, 1952, they signed the *Pacto de los Caballeros* in San Salvador, but the pact was stillborn. It was "ratified" in August 1953, again to no avail.[56] Intense rivalry drove these two champions apart. Each wanted to be the "supreme savior" of Guatemala, and each wanted to replace Arbenz. Relations between the two remained "acrimonious."[57] Without U.S. support, Ydígoras and Castillo Armas would have been insignificant even had they united; divided, they were pathetic.

[55] According to the well-informed Cehelsky, Barrios Peña was Trujillo's chosen man, and Ydígoras was his second choice. ("Guatemala's Frustrated Revolution," pp. 53–54.) Confirmed by interview with Taracena.

[56] For the text of the pact, see Guatemala, *La democracia amenazada*, pp. 8–31.

[57] Quoted from interview with Taracena. Both Taracena and Barrios Peña, another Castillo Armas supporter, waxed eloquent on Ydígoras' perfidy. Ydígoras, for his part, pilloried Castillo Armas. (Interviews with Taracena, Barrios Peña and Ydígoras.)

CHAPTER 11

The International Conspiracy against Guatemala

WHEN ARÉVALO became president in March 1945, democracy was on the rise in the Caribbean; the dictators were on the defensive. Somoza and Trujillo were kept at arm's length by the Truman administration, and the fledgling democracies of Cuba, Venezuela, and Guatemala symbolized the new era.

When Arévalo stepped down six years later, Trujillo and Somoza were more powerful than ever. The Truman administration now praised the tropical dictators as steadfast allies in the war against communism. Venezuela's young democracy had ended in November 1948, as a military coup ushered in the dictatorship of Marcos Pérez Jiménez. Then, in March 1952, Fulgencio Batista seized power in Cuba. Only two democracies remained in the Caribbean: Guatemala and Costa Rica.

Three countries bordered on Guatemala: Mexico, El Salvador and Honduras. The Mexican authorities accepted that Central America was Washington's backyard. Their relations with Guatemala—strained under Ubico, cordial under Arévalo—grew distant as Arbenz moved to the left and Mexican President Adolfo Ruiz Cortines (1952–1958) moved to the right.

In El Salvador a young officer, Major Oscar Osorio, had won carefully staged elections in 1950. Osorio spouted populism, occasionally comparing his "revolution" to that of Guatemala. He granted some political freedom, as long as it did not threaten his rule, and enacted highly circumscribed social reforms in the cities, where a minority of Salvadorans lived. In the countryside, where the land tenure structure was as unjust as in pre-1952 Guatemala, agrarian reform remained taboo, and unionization was strictly forbidden. In foreign policy, while willing to follow Washington's lead, he tried to retain a degree of independence. The limited amount of U.S. investment in the country minimized the possible flashpoints.

Whereas El Salvador grew no bananas, Honduras was the country in which UFCO's plantations were the most extensive; it was the quintessential banana republic. After fifteen years of iron rule, General Tiburcio Carías had stepped down in 1948 in favor of his protegé, Secretary of War Juan Manuel Gálvez, a civilian who had long been United Fruit's lawyer. Gálvez carefully cultivated his ties with the United States and UFCO. Like Osorio, he allowed some freedom in the cities and firmly opposed change in the countryside. As elsewhere in the region the Communist party was illegal.

When Arbenz became president, Guatemala was isolated. Arévalo's support for the Caribbean Legion had aroused the wrath of Trujillo and Somoza and the suspicion of the ruling elites of El Salvador and Honduras. In 1947, Guatemala had broken diplomatic relations with Nicaragua and the Dominican Republic; in 1948, it had severed ties with Venezuela.

But by 1950, for all practical purposes, the Caribbean Legion had ceased to exist, and, keenly aware of his country's isolation, Arbenz sought to reassure his Central American neighbors. In September 1951, he reestablished diplomatic relations with Nicaragua, and, setting aside Arévalo's practice, he did not break relations with Cuba despite Batista's coup. At the prompting of Foreign Minister Manuel Galich, Guatemala became a moving force behind the creation, in October 1951, of the Organización de Estados Centroamericanos (ODECA), which included the five republics of Central America. Arévalo had believed that unification would be possible only when all the Central American countries were democracies. The theory underlying ODECA was that steps toward unification should be undertaken immediately despite the diversity of regimes. This position was unrealistic, but useful to Guatemala: through ODECA, Arbenz tried to calm his suspicious neighbors. In this, he was reminiscent of Calderón Guardia (1940–1944) and Picado (1944–1948) of Costa Rica, both of whom had implemented significant social reforms and collaborated with the Communist party, but had avoided all interference in Nicaragua's affairs; in return, Somoza had left them alone.[1]

But in Guatemala the pace of social change was frighteningly rapid, and the communists wielded far more influence than they had in Costa Rica. The Guatemalan example was too dangerous to ignore, as even Osorio of El Salvador made clear. Osorio had been the Central American president most sympathetic to Arbenz. Both were military officers, Osorio liked to consider himself a revolutionary, and the fact that Arbenz's wife was an upper-class Salvadoran

[1] On the reestablishment of diplomatic relations with Nicaragua and the creation of ODECA, see AmEm San Salvador, Shaw to DOS, May 29, 1951, RG84 CF, Box 15, NA-S; AmEm Managua, Ellis to DOS, no. 172, Aug. 31, 1951, NA 713.00; AmEm San José, Cohen to DOS, no. 274, Sept. 5, 1951, NA 713.00; AmEm Managua, Ellis to DOS, no. 202, Sept. 10, 1951, NA 713.00; AmEm Managua, Ellis to DOS, Sept. 15, 1951, RG84 CF, Box 15, NA-S; AmEm San Salvador, Silberstein to DOS, no. 359, Oct. 16, 1951, NA 713.00; MemoConv (Schoenfeld, Galich), Oct. 30, 1951, RG84 CF, Box 15, NA-S; DOS, "Monthly Political Summary—Central America and Panama," Oct. 31, 1951, pp. 2–3, NA 713.00. An interesting, though not always reliable account of Guatemala and ODECA is Galich, *Por qué lucha Guatemala?*, pp. 240–57. Interviews with Galich, Fortuny, María de Arbenz, and Sol were helpful.

Arbenz was also less provocative vis-à-vis British Honduras than his predecessor had been. Arévalo had pursued Guatemala's claims on the territory with robust energy, earning in the process the hostility of the British government. (See above, p. 100, n. 62.) Under Arbenz, Guatemala's demands on British Honduras softened—as did the British allegations of communist influence in Guatemala. (Meers, "Pebble on the Beach," pp. 23, 33–35, 72.)

added a gentle touch to the relationship. Nevertheless, in August 1952—two months after the enactment of Decree 900—El Salvador introduced a resolution urging that ODECA adopt a policy against the "subversive actions of International Communism in Central America."[2] The resolution was not formally directed against Guatemala. As a member of ODECA, Guatemala was actually asked to join in the anticommunist crusade. Agreement was, of course, impossible for Arbenz. An impasse ensued, paralyzing the organization. Then, in late September, Osorio unearthed a nonexistent communist plot in his country and unleashed a wave of repression against the Salvadoran labor movement. This, noted the U.S. embassy in Guatemala, was Osorio's response to Decree 900. While the Arbenz administration maintained an uneasy silence, the Guatemalan opposition loudly praised Osorio. Stressing that the communists also threatened Guatemala, they pointed out "how right the Salvadoran foreign minister had been in proposing that the five Central American states unite against the communist advance in the region." Returning the compliment, Osorio praised his Guatemalan admirers as good patriots—"an action," the U.S. embassy remarked, "which is little likely to endear him to the Guatemalan authorities."[3]

Bitterness and distrust had replaced the tentative cordiality that had marked relations between the two countries in Arbenz's first year. Relations with Honduras and Costa Rica were equally strained, and Nicaragua was openly hostile. ODECA was doomed. In April 1953 Guatemala withdrew from the organization.[4]

[2] "Ponencia contra infiltración comunista," *El I*, Aug. 12, 1952, p. 1.

[3] Quotations from "Sucesos de El Salvador," *El I*, Sept. 29, 1952, p. 2 and from *JW* 41, Oct. 9, 1952, I:2. See also: "Redada de rojos bajo el estado de sitio," *El I*, Sept. 27, 1952, p. 1; "Salvador Charges a Communist Plot," *NYT*, Sept. 27, 1952, p. 6; "Celulas se adiestraban para acción subversiva," *El I*, Sept. 29, 1952, p. 1; "Cinco comités solidarios con Osorio" and "Sucesos de El Salvador," *El I*, Oct. 3, 1952, p. 1; "El Salvador Protests," *NYT*, Oct. 5, 1952, p. 27; DOS, "Monthly Political Summary—Central America and Panama," Oct. 28, 1952, pp. 1, 3, NA 713.00; "Sigue la tragicomedia en El Salvador," *Octubre*, Feb. 19, 1953, p. 3. For a haunting account by one of Osorio's victims, see Carpio, *Secuestro y capucha*. Particularly useful on the relations between Osorio and Arbenz were interviews with María de Arbenz, Sol, Fortuny, and Galich.

[4] On the protracted demise of ODECA, see AmEm San Salvador, Duke to DOS, no. 45, July 23, 1952, NA 713.00; Clark to Duke, Aug. 4, 1952, NA 713.00; MemoConv (Krieg, Tattenbach), Oct. 8, 1952, RG84 CF, Box 15, NA-S; AmEm San José, MemoConv (Cohen, Canessa), Feb. 4, 1953, enclosed in Fleming to DOS, no. 743, Feb. 5, 1953, NA 713.00; AmEm San Salvador, Donovan to DOS, no. 642, Apr. 9, 1953, NA 713.00. For the government's communiqué announcing the withdrawal, see "Guatemala denuncia la Carta de San Salvador," *DCA*, Apr. 7, 1953, p. 1. See also the editorial of the same title in *DCA*, Apr. 8, 1953, p. 3; "Repercusiones de nuestra salida de la ODECA" (edit.), *DCA*, Apr. 9, 1953, p. 3; "Razones de Guatemala para

By that time Trujillo and United Fruit were busy plotting against Arbenz, and so was Somoza. Indeed in the summer of 1952, Somoza had enlisted Truman's help.

Washington's hopes that Arbenz would reverse Arévalo's extremist policies had soured before the introduction of the Agrarian Reform Bill. In March 1951, Assistant Secretary Miller had stated that "Arbenz is a much less woolly-headed man than the previous president. . . . The situation is going to improve in our favor." By July, the State Department's Office of Intelligence and Research (OIR) observed dryly, "The reverse seems to have happened." The following April the same agency, whose reports were among the most professional of the U.S. government, remarked, "other Latin American governments . . . have in the past worked with Communists, generally because of their influence in labor unions. In no other Latin American country, however, has the ruling group in power accepted the Communists with such cordiality into a political partnership including the frequent support of the Communist line by administration media."[5]

Similar concerns were being heard in Congress. "Vociferous anti-American people [are] in the saddle [in Guatemala]," Secretary of State Acheson testified. "The Guatemalan situation is a very troublesome one. . . . The Communists . . . have gotten into the Government and they are causing a great deal of trouble and concern to us."[6] The same shift from hope to hostility was seen in the American press. As early as June 1951, the *New York Times* had warned: "Despite the hope that President Arbenz would curb their activities and purge the Government and labor unions of their influence, the power of the Communists has grown at an alarming rate. Regardless of good intentions, President Arbenz has been able to accomplish little and his dismissal of the question by saying that there is no Communist Party in Guatemala and his pointing to the register of political parties to prove it, does not represent reality." Three days later, a *New York Times* editorial concluded: "It is time to register a sense of deep disappointment and disillusionment over the trend of Guatemalan politics in the two months since Colonel Arbenz became President. . . . the Communist trend, far from being reversed, has been strengthened."[7]

---

retirarse de la ODECA," ibid., p. 1; "Centroamericanismo de Guatemala en evidencia," *DCA*, Apr. 10, 1953, p. 3; "Hacia la dignificación," *DCA*, Apr. 14, 1953, p. 2.

[5] Quotations from: Miller, Mar. 16, 1951, U.S. Congress, HCFA, p. 393; OIR, "Communism in the other American Republics: Quarterly Survey, April–June 1951," No. 5180.6, July 19, 1951, p. 10, NA; OIR, "Communism in the other American Republics: Quarterly Survey, January–March 1952," No. 5180.9, Apr. 18, 1952, p. 6, NA.

[6] U.S. Congress, SCFR, vol. 4, 1952, p. 28. (Acheson testified on Jan. 14, 1952.)

[7] Quotations from "Guatemalan Reds Trade on Old Ills," June 5, 1951, p. 6, and "The Guatemalan Cancer" (edit.), June 8, 1951, p. 26.

Yet throughout Arbenz's first year, the concern of U.S. officials and journalists lacked urgency. Congressional speeches about Guatemala, while critical, were few and brief; press coverage was infrequent. The hope lingered that Arbenz was "essentially an opportunist" who would ultimately betray his leftist friends. In the words of Bill Krieg, the DCM at the U.S. embassy in Guatemala, "incident after incident accumulated and we became increasingly concerned and pessimistic, but no irrevocable line had been crossed."[8] Arbenz had not yet enacted any legislation that would have caused an irreparable break with the upper class. Relations with the American companies were strained, but no worse than they had been under Arévalo. And the Communist party, although enjoying the president's favor, was not yet legal. This indicated, many hoped, that Arbenz could still turn to the right.

Until the spring of 1952, Truman's policy toward Arbenz was similar to that adopted toward Arévalo in the late 1940s. Diplomatic pressure was accompanied by the denial of economic aid. Washington continued to refuse to sell weapons to Guatemala and began a successful effort to prevent Arbenz from acquiring arms in other Western countries. In June 1951, the United States halted financial assistance for the construction of the Guatemalan segment of the Inter-American Highway.[9]

[8] Quotations from CIA, "Present Political Situation in Guatemala and Possible Developments During 1952," NIE-62, Mar. 11, 1952, p. 2, Truman Papers, President's Secretary's File, Intelligence File, Box 254, TL, and from interview with Krieg. Between Mar. 1951 and Apr. 11, 1952, Guatemala was attacked ten times in the House of Representatives and once in the Senate. See *CR*-House, 1951, pp. 3803–5, 9808–9; *CR*-House, 1952, pp. 1336, 1338, 2975–78, A1316, A1426, A1449, A1714; *CR*-Senate, 1952, pp. 2278–81. For a representative sample of the press during the same period, see: "A Round for the Reds," *Time*, May 7, 1951, p. 42; "The Reds and the President," *Newsweek*, July 16, 1951, p. 40; "Anti-Red Outburst," *Newsweek*, July 23, 1951, p. 46; "Under Western Eyes," *Time*, July 23, 1951, p. 24; "There's More Than Meets the Eye," *Business Week*, Oct. 13, 1951, p. 168; "Harassed United Fruit," *The Commonweal*, Nov. 9, 1951, p. 108; "Showdown in Guatemala," *Business Week*, Dec. 8, 1951, pp. 177–78; "Fruit Trade Rift Widens in Guatemala," *CSM*, Dec. 18, 1951, p. 9; "Bananas and Politics," *New Republic*, Jan. 28, 1952, p. 7; "Economic Suicide in Guatemala," *Washington Daily News*, Feb. 14, 1952, p. 8; "Red Front Tightens Grip on Guatemala," *WP*, Feb. 17, 1952, p. 2; "Red Cell in Guatemala," *WP*, Mar. 4, 1952, p. 12; "Red Footprints Get Bigger in Guatemala," *CSM*, Mar. 4, 1952, p. 10; "Communists Are Making Inroads in U.S. 'Back Yard,' " *U.S. News and World Report*, Mar. 7, 1952, pp. 38–41; "Operations in Guatemala Resumed by United Fruit," *CSM*, Mar. 15, 1952, p. 1; "The Reds Lose a Round," *Time*, Mar. 17, 1952, p. 36; "Banana Bonanza," *Newsweek*, Mar. 24, 1952, p. 62; "Guatemala's Distrust of U.S. Feeds Communist Cauldron," *NYT*, Mar. 27, 1952, p. 15; "United Fruit Becomes Victim of Guatemala's Awakening," *NYT*, Mar. 28, 1952, p. 5; "Guatemalan Reds Are Strong but They Don't Run Country," *NYT*, Mar. 29, 1952, p. 4.

[9] On the arms embargo by third parties, see Col. McCormick, "Intelligence Report"

Then, in May 1952, the Agrarian Reform Bill burst upon the scene. In the weeks that followed, embassy officials witnessed the prominent role played by the communist deputies in the congressional debates that led to the enactment of Decree 900, and they understood that the bill's champions were the president and the PGT. The canard that Arbenz was an opportunist who would betray his friends was finally discarded. Some U.S. officials condemned Decree 900 because they were clearly sympathetic to the landed elite and United Fruit. Others were less biased. But on one point they all agreed: "the law opened the way for a further extension of Communist influence."[10]

It was at this juncture that Somoza approached the United States with a proposal to overthrow Arbenz. Only the outlines of the plan are known. The major protagonists have long since died, and the main source is *New York Times* correspondent Herbert Matthews, who has related what Assistant Secretary Miller told him a year after the scheme was hatched.[11] Additional information is provided by the written report of a March 1953 conversation between Rolland Welch, first secretary of the U.S. embassy in Managua, and Somoza's son Tachito. Tachito, noted Welch, claimed that "the 'Guatemalan matter' was first proposed in a conversation between his father and an attorney for the United Fruit Company."[12]

---

no. R-22-52, Nov. 13, 1952, RG84 CF, Box 15, NA-S; Schoenfeld to DOS, no. 68, July 24, 1953, NA 714.56; *JW* 45, Nov. 6, 1953, I:4–5; Krieg to DOS, no. 443, Nov. 23, 1953, p. 3, NA 714.00; AmEm Stockholm, Abbott to SecState, no. 776, Mar. 19, 1954, NA 714.56; AmEm Stockholm, Abbott to SecState, no. 788, Mar. 24, 1954, NA 714.56; Fisher to Holland, May 18, 1954, NA Lot 58D18 & 58D78, Box 2; Holland to SecState, May 25, 1954, ibid.; AmEm Stockholm, Cabot to SecState, no. 1040, June 2, 1954, NA 714.5614; Hanford, "Communist Beachhead," pp. 20, 35–36; Meers, "Pebble on the Beach," pp. 37–38, 40–41.

For Guatemala's repeated requests for aid for the Inter-American Highway and for the repeated U.S. refusals, see Ballentine to DOS, no. 223, Aug. 29, 1951, NA 814.2612; Siracusa to Schoenfeld, Sept. 13, 1951, NA 814.2612; U.S. Congress, HCFA, Feb. 29, 1952, pp. 399–400; *JW* 24, June 13, 1952, II:2; MemoConv (Schoenfeld, Arbenz), Sept. 25, 1952, *FRUS*, 1952–1954, 4:1039–40; "Truman no ha dicho la verdad," *La Hora*, Jan. 14, 1953, p. 1; "Guatemala ha iniciado gestiones para que se reanude colaboración norteamericana," *DCA*, Apr. 20, 1953, p. 1; Minutes of Cabinet Meeting, Mar. 5, 1954, p. 2, WF, Cabinet Series, Box 3, EL.

[10] Quoted from *JW* 25, June 20, 1952, I:2. See also Siracusa to Nufer et al., May 22, 1952, NA 714.34; *JW* 23, June 6, 1952; *JW* 24, June 13, 1952; Schoenfeld to DOS, no. 1261, June 10, 1952, NA 714.00. Interviews with DCM Krieg, Second Secretary Wardlaw, and OIR analyst Hyman were particularly helpful.

[11] Matthews, *World in Revolution*, pp. 262–64.

[12] AmEm Managua, Welch to Ohmans, Mar. 11, 1953, NA 714.00 (quoted) and enclosed MemoConv (Somoza, Welch), Mar. 9, 1953. Also useful are papers of Truman's assistant military aide, Col. Cornelius Mara, Truman Papers, OF, esp. Boxes

Somoza had arrived in the United States on April 28, 1952, on a private trip. His visit was marked by great cordiality on both sides. The Nicaraguan dictator was duly effusive in his praise of the United States as the champion of democracy—democracy that he had crushed at home. He was honored with New York City's Medal of Honor and responded appropriately: the Nicaraguan people, he pledged, were and would always be the best friends of the United States in Latin America. "We appreciate the kindness, protection and help you have given us"; the United States was a "big brother, always willing to help small countries."[13]

Somoza stressed his personal ties to America. Not only had he, his wife, and his three children been educated in the United States, but his daughter's six children had been born there, and one of his sons was graduating from the University of Maryland, and the other from West Point. "I have always considered the United States my second country," he said time and again.[14]

Beyond these pleasantries, Somoza had a serious message. "Just give me the arms, and I'll clean up Guatemala for you in no time," he promised Truman, Acheson, and other U.S. officials. The offer was laughed off as a good joke. There the matter rested until early July when Somoza left for Managua aboard a U.S. military plane.[15]

With him flew Colonel Cornelius Mara, assistant military aide to Truman and a close associate of General Harry Vaughan, Truman's trusted friend. Mara had met Somoza previously on trips that he and Vaughan had taken to Central America. His presence on the plane was intended as mere protocol— a mark of respect for a loyal dictator—but it turned out to be much more. By the time they landed in Managua, Somoza had persuaded Mara that if the United States provided the arms, he could engineer Arbenz's overthrow; together, they had decided what weapons would be needed.[16] Back in Washington, Mara became Somoza's champion. His report to Truman must have been truly eloquent; so eloquent, in fact, that Truman immediately "initialed the report" and instructed General Walter Bedell Smith, the CIA Director, "to

---

1286/432 and 1287/439, TL. Schlesinger and Kinzer, *Bitter Fruit*, pp. 92, 102, contribute additional data based on their interviews with lobbyist Tom Corcoran and on an unpublished manuscript by Richard Harris Smith about Allen Dulles.

[13] "Head of Nicaragua Gets City's Medal," *NYT*, June 21, 1952, p. 6 (quoted) and "General Somoza Honored," *NYT*, June 19, 1952, p. 10.

[14] "Somoza in Washington," *NYT*, May 2, 1952, p. 2 (quoted), and "Head of Nicaragua Gets City's Medal," p. 6.

[15] Quoted from Matthews, *World in Revolution*, p. 262.

[16] Ibid., p. 263. See also "Cornelius J. Mara," Truman Papers, OF, Box 1663/1420, TL; Waynick to Truman, Jan. 20, 1951, ibid., Box 1286/432; Somoza to Vaughan, June 23, 1952, ibid.; Vaughan to Somoza, June 25, 1952, ibid.; Cross Reference Sheet ("Somoza"), Apr. 28 [sic.], 1952, ibid., Box 1287/439.

put it into effect.'' Truman did not inform Acheson or any other State Department official.[17]

And so Smith unleashed his cowboys from the CIA's Directorate of Plans. The plot, code named OPERATION FORTUNE, took shape over the next few weeks. State Department officials ''were at all times ignorant of what was brewing''; the CIA, United Fruit, and Somoza were the schemers. Trujillo and Venezuela's Pérez Jiménez were contacted; they responded enthusiastically and apparently contributed money. OPERATION FORTUNE did not contemplate direct intervention by a foreign power: the job would be done by Somoza's protegé, Castillo Armas. The plan depended on one crucial assumption—that ''important officers of the Guatemalan army'' would rise in revolt, as Castillo Armas had promised, as soon as he had crossed the border with his band of exiles.[18]

It was not the first time that Castillo Armas had proffered such bold assurances, and as late as June 1952, the CIA had responded with a healthy dose of skepticism. Now, under Somoza's spell, skepticism turned into credulity.

As summer faded into autumn, the plotters pressed forward with their preparations. ''The arms were gathered. A representative of the United Fruit in Nicaragua was assigned to receive them. The United Fruit turned over one of its freighters which it had specially refitted for this purpose. Two leaders of the stevedores in New Orleans had to be told about it. The arms were loaded into the ship as 'agricultural machinery' in cases, and the ship sailed for Nicaragua.'' The ship was still en route when Acheson learned of the plot: ''A CIA representative went to Miller and asked him to initial a paper on behalf of the Munitions Department of the State Department. . . . Miller refused and showed the document to [Deputy Undersecretary] Doc Freeman Matthews and David Bruce, Undersecretary of State, both of whom hit the ceiling, went to Acheson, who went to Truman and a message was sent redirecting the ship to Panama, where the arms were unloaded.''[19]

Thus ended the first U.S. conspiracy against Arbenz. Castillo Armas was utterly deflated. ''Always at the last minute difficulties arose,'' he grumbled. Whereas a few weeks earlier he had been ''full of the almost certain success in the future,'' an informant reported in late October, ''his attitude has distinctly changed. He had certainly managed to get hold of some money . . .

[17] Matthews, *World in Revolution*, p. 263. See also Mara, memo for the President, July 11, 1952, Truman Papers, OF, Box 1286/432, TL.

[18] Quotations from Matthews, *World in Revolution*, p. 263, and from AmEm Managua, MemoConv (Somoza, Welch), (see n. 12 above), p. 1. (Matthews misidentifies Castillo Armas as a ''Castillo Moreno'' and calls Mara ''Marrow.'') See also Schlesinger and Kinzer, *Bitter Fruit*, p. 92. It was probably on this occasion that Trujillo provided $60,000 for Castillo Armas. (See Crassweller, *Trujillo*, p. 335, and Paniagua to Trujillo, Tegucigalpa, May 14, 1953, Vega File.)

[19] Matthews, *World in Revolution*, p. 264.

[but] he was losing hope.''[20] It was just as well. The plan was madness. The Guatemalan military had not yet been subjected to months of psychological warfare by the United States, and its support for Arbenz was still firm. Had Castillo Armas invaded, he would have been defeated as easily as were the Salamá rebels a few months later.

The most likely explanation for the abrupt termination of OPERATION FORTUNE is that Acheson had convinced Truman that it would fail. Perhaps he had also argued that Guatemala's sins were not yet so grevious as to justify an attempt to overthrow Arbenz. But Acheson's thinking, and the entire operation, remain mysterious. Years later, in the wake of the Bay of Pigs, he wrote to Truman: "Why we ever engaged in this asinine Cuban adventure, I cannot imagine. Before I left [for Europe] it was mentioned to me and I told my informants how you and I had turned down similar suggestions for Iran and Guatemala and why." Unfortunately, he did not elaborate.[21]

In the weeks that followed the demise of OPERATION FORTUNE, events that were bound to heighten U.S. anxieties occurred in Guatemala.

On December 11, 1952, the Communist party opened its second congress; senior government officials and administration politicians were present. Eight days later, the party was legalized. That same month, noted the State Department's Office of Intelligence and Research (OIR), the PGT scored ''the outstanding political victory of the quarter'' when it was formally included in the administration's electoral coalition for the January 1953 congressional elections.[22] These were striking developments. Since 1948, no other Latin American government had collaborated with the Communist party; communists were persecuted in most Latin American countries.

In January 1953, the implementation of Decree 900 began in earnest. The PGT, reported OIR, ''continued in the forefront of agrarian reform agitation and Communist propagandists were especially active in rural areas.''[23] In the weeks that followed, UFCO land at Tiquisate was expropriated, and the four Supreme Court justices were dismissed by the Guatemalan Congress.

By April 1953, when OIR's next quarterly report appeared, Arbenz's Guatemala had committed even more damnable crimes:

In Guatemala, now the only country in the world outside the Soviet orbit (except San Marino) where the Communist Party has formal membership in a government

[20] Letter to Col. Sawyer, U.S. army attaché, Tegucigalpa, Oct. 27, 1952, RG84 CF, Box 15, NA-S.
[21] Acheson to Truman, May 3, 1961, in McLellan and Acheson, *Among Friends*, pp. 206–7.
[22] OIR, "Communism in the other American Republics: Quarterly Survey, October–December 1952," no. 5180.12, Jan. 28, 1953, p. ii, NA.
[23] Ibid., p.11.

coalition, official and pro-administration channels continued to be freely available for Communist propaganda. The administration press featured reports of the Guatemalans who had recently made the grand tour of "the popular republics of the Soviet Union and New China," serialized Jean Paul Sartre on the subject of the December 1952 Vienna peace front congress, and played up Communist youth front preparations for a Vienna meeting in March 1953. The Guatemalan Congress paid a "minute of silence" tribute to Stalin. Communist *Octubre*, in an impressive 12-page special edition commemorating Stalin, carried eulogies by leaders of the administration parties as well as by Communist leaders.[24]

The American press followed developments in Guatemala with growing concern. In mid-1952, the Agrarian Reform Law had provoked a spate of articles, some very sympathetic to UFCO and the Guatemalan landed elite, others stressing the need for land reform and highlighting the plight of the Indians. There was a common thread running through all these articles: fear of the spread of communist influence in the countryside. Some journalists expressed this fear in lurid terms. Others were more restrained. All sensed that the established order was crumbling in rural Guatemala, and all feared for the future.

The legalization of the PGT, its participation in the electoral alliance, and the January 1953 expropriations of private land triggered a fresh flurry of articles. In mid-January, *U.S. News and World Report* pointed out that Arbenz was a weak executive who, while not a communist himself, "usually does what the Communists want him to do." The following month, it warned: "What Guatemala is getting in the way of Government, and land reform, is a startling example of Russian-type action in the Western Hemisphere"; the country was moving into a period of "widespread strife, maybe revolution"; its airfields were but two hours from the Panama Canal, and less than three from vital oil and chemical industries in Texas.[25]

Newsweek announced that the PGT had "armed shock troopers in every town, village, and hamlet," and that "hordes of armed Indians" had been invading plantations "all over the republic"[26]—gross distortion that echoed tales spun in the fashionable cafés of Guatemala City. With even richer imagination, *American Mercury* stated that in Guatemala "a great espionage, sabotage, and propaganda organization works day and night for the Soviet Union"; there was "documentary proof" that the country's labor and agrarian

[24] "OIR, Communism in the other American Republics: Quarterly Survey, January–March 1953," no. 5180.13, Apr. 23, 1953, p. 1, NA.

[25] "Communists Get New Toe Holds," *U.S. News and World Report*, Jan. 16, 1953, pp. 31–32, and "When Communists Take Over," *U.S. News and World Report*, Feb. 20, 1953, pp. 14–16.

[26] "Reds at the Polls," *Newsweek*, Jan. 26, 1953, p. 59, and "The Fog Lifts," *Newsweek*, Feb. 9, 1953, p. 46.

legislation had been "consciously planned [by the communists] to bring about slow strangulation of the economy . . . [and] to create economic chaos."[27]

Agrarian reform was necessary, but Decree 900 had given the communists "their greatest opportunity to supplement their tough city cadres with peasant battalions," Sidney Gruson, the *New York Times*' Guatemala expert, warned on February 23. A few days later, the *Times* ran another article by Gruson, entitled "How Communists Won Control of Guatemala." Accompanying the article was "Moscow Samba" a cartoon of a Guatemalan dancing to Stalin's tune. Unlike many of his colleagues, Gruson told no lurid tales of Indian hordes running amok or Soviet agents manipulating Guatemala from smoke-filled rooms; he merely stressed the "superior organization" of the Guatemalan communists, their "missionary zeal and devotion to party causes rather than self-enrichment." Their influence was growing, he asserted, but they

Moscow Samba. (From *The San Diego Union*, February 18, 1953. Reprinted with permission from *The San Diego Union*.)

[27] Ralph de Toledano, "The Soft UNDERBELLY of the U.S.A.," *American Mercury*, Feb. 1953, pp. 114–28, quoted from pp. 114, 115.

were not yet in control. A similar conclusion had been reached by Robert Hallett, another outstanding journalist, in a long article in the *Christian Science Monitor*: because the communists were more honest, hardworking, and devoted than any other political group in Guatemala, they were gaining ground.[28]

A series by Daniel James in the *New York Herald Tribune* contributed the alarming information that Guatemala was but five hours from New Orleans. James agreed that the communists did not control Guatemala, but he was disturbed by their growing influence. After comparing the tactics of the PGT with those of Mao Zedong and the Yenan Way (communist wolves in agrarian reformers' clothing), he ended by stating ominously that Guatemala had recently quit ODECA because it objected to El Salvador's proposed united front against communism.[29]

When James' series appeared, the Eisenhower Administration had been in power for two months. The Republicans had triumphed in the November 1952 elections after a campaign waged under the shadow of McCarthyism. Relentlessly, they had charged that the Democrats had embarked on a road to surrender that had led to Yalta, the loss of China, and disaster in Korea—"twenty years of treason," in the words of Eisenhower's running mate. Containment, the Republicans charged, was negative, futile, immoral. To the American people, they now offered a credo of victory: rollback. Under Eisenhower, they pledged, the United States would seize the initiative and liberate the captive nations of Europe. More important still, they promised that the hero of World War II would end the war in Korea. Furthermore, they would reduce Truman's military budget, and hence taxes. It mattered little that the new crusaders failed to explain how this would be achieved; their vagueness was rewarded at the polls.[30] The Democrats were chased from the White House and lost (if barely) the control of the Congress. Eisenhower became president, and John Foster Dulles secretary of state.

The conventional wisdom that Eisenhower gave "an unparallelled gift of authority"[31] to Dulles, amiably following his secretary's lead in foreign pol-

---

[28] Gruson, "Guatemalan Reds Seek Full Power," *NYT*, Feb. 23, 1953, p. 4; Gruson, "How Communists Won Control of Guatemala," *NYT*, Mar. 1, 1953, D6; Hallett, "Communists Move Cautiously to Safeguard Gains Chalked Up in Guatemala," *CSM*, Jan. 15, 1953, p. 7.

[29] "The Truth About Guatemala," *New York Herald Tribune*, Apr. 7–9, 1953, always p. 22.

[30] On the 1952 campaign, see Bernstein, "Election of 1952"; Divine, *Foreign Policy*, pp. 3–85; Parmet, *Eisenhower*, pp. 83–149; Ambrose, *Eisenhower*, 1:529–72.

[31] Quoted in Reichard, "Eisenhower as President," p. 273.

icy, has been debunked as documents have been declassified.[32] As Stephen Rabe writes, "Few still doubt that Eisenhower was a strong, decisive, and intelligent leader."[33] He was in charge of his administration's foreign policy, and this foreign policy was in many respects a continuation of Truman's. Like his predecessor, he followed a policy of containment vis-à-vis the Soviet Union. Like his predecessor, the linchpin of his policy was Europe, where he continued and developed Truman's work. Like Truman, he knew very little of the Third World; he was aware that emerging nationalism and rising expectations confronted the United States with challenges that required innovative responses, but he, too, was distracted by other problems and crippled by bias and by narrow anticommunism. He tended to gloss over Latin America—until the late 1950s, when Castro forced a wrenching reassessment. Until then, Eisenhower believed, he had faced only one significant challenge in the hemisphere, the Guatemalan revolution. And in his memoirs, while by no means revealing the full extent of his administration's role in the overthrow of Arbenz, he listed it as one of his proudest accomplishments.[34]

But if Eisenhower presided over the overthrow of Arbenz, other men executed his orders. Within the high councils of the new administration, three men, other than the president, were to be instrumental in the fall of Arbenz: John Foster Dulles, his brother Allen, and General Bedell Smith.

Eisenhower actually liked John Foster Dulles. In this he was virtually unique, notes Stephen Ambrose, the president's foremost biographer. "Nearly everyone else found Dulles impossibly pompous, a prig, and unbearably dull."[35] Behind an unpleasant exterior lay, however, a mind of "considerable breadth . . . notable depth as well."[36] By 1952, at age sixty-four, Dulles had proven his abilities as a very successful corporate lawyer, as a diplomat, and to a lesser extent as a writer. But as he attained his lifelong ambition to be secretary of state, "much of the subtlety and sophistication of vision that Dulles had possessed was lost." He had grappled intellectually with the problems of war and decolonization, "but when it came to working for, or adjusting to, some new global order, he . . . fell back on a very traditional pursuit of national interest. . . . He increasingly camouflaged this pur-

---

[32] For the conventional view, see Childs, *Eisenhower*, and Hughes, *Ordeal of Power*. For the revisionist view, see Immerman, "Eisenhower and Dulles"; Divine, *Eisenhower and the Cold War*; Cook, *Declassified Eisenhower*; Greenstein, *Hidden-Hand Presidency*; Ambrose, *Eisenhower*, vol. 2. For review essays, see De Santis, "Eisenhower Revisionism"; Reichard, "Eisenhower as President"; McAuliffe, "Eisenhower, the President"; Schlesinger, "Ike Age Revisited"; Joes, "Eisenhower Revisionism"; McMahon, "Eisenhower and Third World Nationalism."

[33] Rabe, *Eisenhower and Latin America*, p. 5.

[34] Eisenhower, *Mandate*, pp. 421–27 and 573–75.

[35] Ambrose, *Eisenhower*, 2:21

[36] Pruessen, *Dulles*, p. 500.

suit with a series of facile assumptions about the profundity of his proposals, the benefits that would prevail for mankind, and the divine approval which seemed manifest."[37]

Dulles hailed from the international wing of the Republican party and had supported Truman's policy of containment until the Republican defeat in the 1948 presidential elections and the "loss" of China made it politically expedient to abandon bipartisanship in foreign policy. In the 1952 presidential campaign, few had waved the flag of liberation with more enthusiasm than had John Foster Dulles. This had been Dulles the campaigner. As secretary of state, however, "he understood that the Eisenhower administration could not *act* much more forcefully than its predecessor; the facts of nuclear life dictated caution. But the administration could, and through Dulles it would, *speak* more forcefully."[38]

Like his predecessor, Dean Acheson, Dulles knew very little of Latin America; his meager exposure had been gained in the interwar years as a corporate lawyer. (He had, for instance, represented Electric Bond and Share in Guatemala in the early 1920s.)[39] He, like Acheson, had no interest in inter-American questions, "except peripherally as a side issue in his anticommunist crusade."[40] He knew, however, who his country's best friends in the region were. "His instructions are flat," remarked an aide. "Do nothing to offend the dictators; they are the only people we can depend on."[41] The Truman administration had also embraced the dictators, but never as warmly as did Dulles.

Unlike his elder brother, CIA Director Allen Dulles had an engaging personality. He deferred to Foster, who in turn trusted him implicitly. He too had been a highly successful lawyer—until the United States entered World War II and his great adventure began. As head of the Bern office of the Office of Strategic Services, he had directed American espionage in Europe. He had found his true calling. He had returned from Europe after the war's end with an impressive reputation and a consuming passion for the secret world of covert operations. Under Truman, he became deputy director of the CIA. Eisenhower promoted him to director.

In government, as before, the two brothers were in constant, easy commu-

[37] Ibid., p. 508.

[38] Brands, *Cold Warriors*, p. 14.

[39] See Pruessen, *Dulles*, chs. 4–7 (esp. p. 64), and Pitti, "Ubico," p. 100. Contrary to a persistent allegation (see, for instance, Treverton, *Covert Action*, p. 53), Dulles never represented United Fruit.

[40] Cabot, *First Line*, p. 90. In 1953, Cabot was assistant secretary for inter-American affairs.

[41] Robert Woodward (who was deputy assistant secretary for inter-American affairs in 1953), quoted in the diary of Adolph Berle, Feb. 8, 1955, Berle Papers. Berle and Jacobs, *Navigating the Rapids*, is an abridged version of the original diaries. It omits much that is important.

nication. Often, after a day's work, Allen would drop by Foster's house to go over unfinished business.[42] Never have a secretary of state and a CIA director enjoyed so close a relationship—so close, in fact, that it bothered some. "It is a relationship that it would be better not have to exist," remarked the chairman of a committee appointed by Eisenhower to investigate the agency. Eisenhower disagreed: "Part of CIA's work is extension of work of State Department."[43]

As Eisenhower's chief of staff during World War II, General Walter Bedell Smith had earned the trust and the respect of the future president. He was, according to Eisenhower, "a godsend—a master of detail with clear comprehension of the main issues."[44] He was also a "formidable personality"[45] who was quick to anger. His years as ambassador in Moscow after the war may not have mellowed his temper, but they sharpened his anticommunist sensitivities. "He had come away with a deep suspicion of Marxist philosophy, a hatred of Soviet cruelty, deception, and hostility, and a contempt for any 'parlor pinks,' as he called them, in the United States. . . . He was a rabid enemy of the Soviet system abroad and *any* form of socialism at home. . . . He was once, for instance, reputed to have called Nelson D. Rockfeller a 'red' for a lukewarm statement in favor of the unions."[46] In the wake of the outbreak of the Korean War and the CIA's failure to predict North Korea's attack, Truman made him DCI, director of the CIA. And a dynamic director he was. "He was the boss," Kim Philby wrote later, "and a boss of outstanding intellect and character."[47] As DCI, General Smith had been the frustrated patron of OPERATION FORTUNE. A champion of covert operations, he had chafed under the Truman-Acheson refusal to move against Mohammed Mossadegh. Kim Roosevelt, who eventually directed the CIA plot in Iran, relates a conversation with the general in early 1953. Eisenhower had not yet been inaugurated, but Smith was raring to go: " 'When is our goddam operation going to get underway?' [Smith asked] in his usual aggressive fashion."[48]

Smith was not to oversee the fall of Mossadegh from the CIA: Eisenhower shifted him to the State Department's number two slot, the undersecretary. Within a few weeks, the proud Smith had developed a hearty dislike for Foster

---

[42] See DP, *passim*, e.g. TelConv (JFD, AWD), Mar. 18, 1954, 2:11 p.m., JFD:CS, Box 7, EL; TelConv (JFD, AWD), Mar. 23, 1954, 5:45 p.m., ibid.; TelConv (JFD, AWD), Apr. 5, 1954, 6:10 p.m., ibid.; MemoTel (JFD, AWD), June 5, 1954, 12:50 p.m., ibid., Box 8.

[43] Gen. Doolittle and DDE, Oct. 19, 1954, WF, Adm. Series, Box 13, EL.

[44] Ambrose, *Eisenhower*, 1:187.

[45] Kirkpatrick, *The Real CIA*, p. 91. Kirkpatrick was Smith's executive assistant.

[46] Mosley, *Dulles*, pp. 269–70; see also Ambrose, *Eisenhower*, 2:56.

[47] Philby, quoted in Mosley, *Dulles*, p. 270.

[48] Roosevelt, *Countercoup*, p. 115.

Dulles.[49] Concerning Guatemala, however, he had no differences with the secretary.

By appointing the Dulles brothers and Smith to these key posts, Eisenhower assured that the State Department and the CIA would act in concert. Under his leadership, the CIA was given increased latitude, and its covert operations were emphasized.

As soon as Eisenhower became president, the CIA began plotting the overthrow of Mossadegh; OPERATION AJAX was formally approved on June 25 in a session chaired by Foster Dulles.[50] Eisenhower stayed in the wings, but he was very much in control.

Before going into operation, AJAX had to have the approval of the President. Eisenhower participated in none of the meetings that set up AJAX; he received only oral reports on the plan; and he did not discuss it with his Cabinet or the NSC. Establishing a pattern he would hold to throughout his Presidency, he kept his distance and left no documents behind that could implicate the President in any projected coup. But in the privacy of the Oval Office, over cocktails, he was kept informed by Foster Dulles, and he maintained a tight control over the activities of the CIA.[51]

While preparing to overthrow Mossadegh, the administration was also under pressure to move against Arbenz. The prestigious Council on Foreign Relations urged Eisenhower to be bold. "The Guatemalan situation," its confidential report stressed, "is quite simply the penetration of Central America by a frankly Russian-dominated Communist group. . . . There should be no hesitation . . . in quite overtly working with the forces opposed to Communism, and eventually backing a political tide which will force the Guatemalan government either to exclude its Communists or to change."[52] Among the council's members was Adolph Berle, a distinguished former diplomat, an intellectual activist well-connected with both parties. Berle considered himself a liberal; he had been a member of Roosevelt's brain trust, and he would later be, under Kennedy, one of the fathers of the Alliance for Progress. He was also something of an expert on Latin America, a rarity among prominent Americans. However, as his diary attests, he knew very little about Central America, but this did not stop him from sharing his wisdom about it.

Guatemala worried him. On October 17, 1952, he jotted down what a high Salvadoran official, Miguel Magaña, had just told him. Magaña's tale, which Berle soon relayed to senior CIA officials, ran as follows:

[49] See Jackson Papers, Aug. 18, 1953, Box 56, EL, and Hanes, memo, Aug. 17, 1953, DP, Subject Series, Box 6, EL.

[50] Roosevelt, *Countercoup*, pp. 1–19.

[51] Ambrose, *Eisenhower*, 2:111.

[52] Quoted by Immerman, *CIA in Guatemala*, p. 128. See also Shoup and Minter, *Imperial Brain Trust*, pp. 195–99.

He said that the government of El Salvador is thoroughly worried and unhappy about the situation in Guatemala. This is a Communist government, net: hardly even disguised. They captured on the border the documents shipped in from Moscow and headed for El Salvador via Guatemala, setting up organization to eventually seize El Salvador's government. They have likewise been intercepting steady shipment of arms into Guatemala; these arms were all Czechoslovak.[53]

In March 1953, Berle spent five days in Nicaragua; from there, on an impulse, he went to Costa Rica for a day. He wanted to assess José Figueres, who was branded a communist by U.S. officials in Managua; he also wanted to discuss Arbenz with Figueres.[54] Two liberals—the prominent American and the leading Costa Rican politician—were about to meet.

It had been in Costa Rica, in early 1948, that Arévalo had scored the one success of his Caribbean policy: he had helped Figueres to overthrow the communist-supported government of Picado. After Picado's fall, Figueres ruled the country with semidictatorial powers and a harsh hand toward his defeated foes. In late 1949, he was succeeded by a conservative president, Otilio Ulate. By the time Berle arrived in Costa Rica, Ulate's term was coming to an end; elections were scheduled for July 1953, and it was common knowledge that Figueres would win.

Figueres combined an obvious lust for power with a frank hostility for the dictators of the region—above all, Somoza. He favored moderate social change; timely reforms, he argued, would strengthen the capitalist system. To the Central American upper class, this was heresy. To Somoza, the issue was clear: Figueres was a communist. Others were more open-minded: Figueres was probably not a party member, but he was a fellow traveler. "President Figueres," *El Diario de Hoy* warned from San Salvador in 1954, "is still playing the same wily trick he played in 1948—he talks tough to the communists, but in fact he supports them and their program."[55] He baffled U.S. officials. Assistant Secretary Miller told Congress in 1952, "I am a little worried

[53] Berle Diary, Oct. 17, 1952, Berle Papers; see also entries of June 18, Dec. 2, and Dec. 8, 1952.

[54] See ibid., Apr. 1, 1953. This entry includes Berle's account of his Mar. 19–26 Central American trip.

[55] "Conjeturas sobre la abstención de Costa Rica," *El Diario de Hoy*, San Salvador, Mar. 1, 1954, p. 7. While the Guatemalan upper class generally shared Somoza's view, *La Hora* was less consistent. At times it castigated Figueres "as an underhanded communist . . . who embraced subversives from everywhere"; on other occasions, it merely branded him an unsavory rogue with dangerous Red proclivities. See "Incógnita electoral en Costa Rica," July 25, 1953, p. 1; "Contradicciones de quien viaja en hombros soviéticos," Sept. 12, 1953, p. 1; "La reunión de Caracas puede fracasar," Nov. 17, 1953, p. 1; "Parece que le llega el turno a Figueres," July 12, 1954, p. 1 (quoted).

about Figueres because you can be a demagogue without being a Communist." Miller's successor was no less confused: "It is one of those never never situations that could only happen in a Latin American country. . . . The Communists are ostensibly supporting . . . Figueres' opponent, [but] Figueres is receiving considerable wads of dough from official sources in Guatemala. It does not make any sense but that is the way it is." Eisenhower's ambassador to Costa Rica described Figueres as "an extreme socialist . . . a very strange personality . . . who is supposed to be anti-communist, but is probably as dangerous a man as there is in all of the Latin American countries."[56]

Of one thing U.S. officials were certain: Figueres' gestures of independence betrayed his leftist leanings. The March 1954 Inter-American Conference was a case in point. Withstanding U.S. pressure, Costa Rica, alone among its sister republics, refused to attend because the conference was held in Caracas, the seat of one of the most ferocious dictatorships of the hemisphere. Although Figueres immediately endorsed the anticommunist resolution sponsored by the United States, Dulles was not mollified.[57]

Only men blinded by anticommunist paranoia and imperial hubris could have failed to realize that Figueres was a fervent anticommunist who readily embraced the principle of U.S. hegemony in the Caribbean. "I was one of the first to recognize the menace of communism in our hemisphere," he countered his critics, "and I defeated communism in my country in 1948 at a time when many still failed to recognize the threat." Had he not overthrown a communist-supported regime? Had he not outlawed the Communist party, which had been legal since the early 1930s?[58] From Guatemala, the PGT vigorously confirmed Figueres' anticommunist credentials. Figueres, wrote *Octubre*, "established a regime of terror. He is a fawning servant of U.S. imperialism."[59] These accusations, however exaggerated, underlined a basic truth: there could be no friendship between José Figueres and Jacobo Arbenz. As Berle was to discover in Costa Rica, Figueres was very much Arbenz's foe.

Figueres, Berle recorded in his diary, "said that he and all his friends fully recognized that a Kremlin-Communist government in this hemisphere was impossible." Years later, recalling this encounter with Berle, Figueres was

---

[56] Miller, Feb. 29, 1952, U.S. Congress, *HCFA*, p. 406; Cabot, May 22, 1953, ibid., pp. 418–19; Hill, Jan. 26, 1954, ibid., p. 477.

[57] See Ameringer, *Don Pepe*, pp. 117–19. For Washington's reaction, see also Figueres, "Oral History Interview," pp. 33–35; Davis to Figueres, Feb. 22, 1954, Davis Papers, Box 1, TL; Hill to Davis, Mar. 1, 1954, ibid.; TelConv (JFD, Pearson), Mar. 24, 1954, 10:25 a.m., DP, JFD:CS, Box 7, EL; Berle Diary, Feb. 8, 1955, Berle Papers.

[58] "En la emergencia de Guatemala estamos cooperando con otros miembros del sistema americano," *La Prensa Libre*, San José, June 1, 1954, p. 1 (quoted from p. 14).

[59] "La elección de Figueres," *Octubre*, Aug. 6, 1953, p. 3.

straightforward: "Berle asked me whether I was ready to cooperate in a plan to overthrow Arbenz, and I answered that I had no moral qualms. In fact, I was all for overthrowing Arbenz, who was a communist, but on one condition: that Somoza not be involved."[60]

Spurred by his conversations with Figueres, Berle went to work as soon as he had returned to the United States. On March 31, he presented the fruit of his labor—a sixteen-page memorandum—to C. D. Jackson, a senior White House official. "The United States cannot tolerate a Kremlin-controlled Communist government in this hemisphere," the memorandum began. U.S. military intervention should be ruled out, however, "except as an extremely bad last resort, because of the immense complications which it would raise all over the hemisphere." An alternative was to organize a "counter-movement, capable of using force if necessary," and led by Nicaragua. But Somoza was an unsavory and discredited dictator. He should not be allowed to lead the movement against Arbenz, yet he could not be completely excluded, since "it is difficult to expect that anything effective could be done from the Central American side without Nicaragua in the picture." Berle saw a way out of this dilemma:

The course of action I should recommend is . . . to work out a Central American "Political Defense" action, using . . . Salvador, Nicaragua and Costa Rica as chief elements, with what help can be obtained from Honduras. . . . The key to such action . . . seems to be Costa Rica. There . . . the summer's elections will result in putting in as President José Figueres. . . . Of the men who have . . . popular support in Central America, Figueres is easily the most dynamic, and I should think the fairest-minded. As between betting on him and betting on a senescent dictatorship in Nicaragua, I should immensely prefer the one democracy which has made its way. . . . A theatre commander for a job like the Guatemalan operation does not, apparently, exist in Central America. So, the *first* job is to get a theatre commander for the operation. . . . Guatemala is an unfriendly country and our own people—or Costa Ricans or Salvadorians friendly to us—ought to go in and organize in the country. This would have to be sub-rosa. In other countries whose governments will be brought to cooperate, the organization can be in the open and it should be done by nationals of those countries.

. . . A quiet understanding should be reached between the governments of Costa Rica, Salvador, Honduras and at least some powerful elements in Nicaragua. This last, I think, can be done.

. . . Some powerful Central American figure—I suggest Figueres—should be encouraged to take leadership and deal with the problem, all-out.

The result ought to be an organization of a party of Democratic Defense in the five

[60] Quotations from Berle Diary, Apr. 1, 1953, Berle Papers, and from interview with Figueres.

Central American republics, taking as its first job the clearing out of the Communists in Guatemala.[61]

A few days later Berle met with C. D. Jackson.[62] He was thanked—and heard no more.

Even if his plan had been sound, it would have found little favor in an administration which, in Foster Dulles' words, saw Figueres as a "pretty rotten fellow"[63] and praised Somoza as a pillar of virtue. But Berle's plan was naive. How could one expect the governments of Honduras and El Salvador to participate in an enterprise led by Figueres, a man they loathed? Similarly, it was preposterous to imagine that Somoza would assist such an undertaking, or to believe that "some powerful elements in Nicaragua" would dare participate without the dictator's permission. Berle also overlooked the fact that the leaders of the Guatemalan opposition fought not for political democracy, but against social reform; they were, in other words, Somoza's natural allies and Figueres's foes. There was no liberal way to overthrow Arbenz—the road to Guatemala City passed through Managua, not through San José.

In May 1953, a senior Pentagon official, General Richard Partridge, spent forty-eight hours in Guatemala while on an official trip to Central America. Upon his return he wrote a memorandum on the Guatemalan question that was more brief and more cogent than that penned by Berle:

> It appears to me that right now we are holding a middle position between two definite policies, one of which we should choose and start implementing. One policy would be to support Arbenz in making his reforms and insist that in return for our support he use some moderation and eliminate the known Communists from power in his regime. The other policy is to oppose Arbenz seriously with the intention of knocking him and his regime out of power. . . . Acting as we are in between these policies without coming out strongly either one way or another, we are providing Arbenz good propaganda to justify his extreme acts. We are not moving either in the direction of controlling him or of getting rid of him but are simply accepting his activity on his own terms. There is no question but what these drastic reforms which he is implementing do affect the neighboring countries which are only slightly less overdue for reforms of a similar nature. That explains the great concern of the neighboring countries over his activities.[64]

[61] Memo to the Jackson Committee, Mar. 31, 1953, Berle Diary, Apr. 1, 1953, Berle Papers.

[62] Berle Diary, Apr. 1, 1953, ibid.

[63] TelConv (DDE, JFD), Oct. 7, 1953, WF, DDE:DS, Box 5, EL.

[64] Partridge, "Notes On Visit to Four Central American Countries," p. 3, enclosed in Partridge to Cabot, May 20, 1953, NA 714.00/3-2053.

The first policy outlined by General Partridge was out of the question. Even the Truman administration had contemplated a modus vivendi with Arbenz only if he first adopted an anticommunist and pro-American course. The only choice, then, was whether to continue Truman's policy of cold hostility and limited sanctions, or to seek to overthrow Arbenz. In the spring of 1953, Eisenhower's "passivity" vis-à-vis Guatemala was due to very prosaic and transient considerations: the new administration was just settling in after two decades of Democratic presidents, it was preoccupied with ending the Korean War and defining a policy toward the Soviet Union, and it had already embarked on a major covert operation in Iran.

But if the judges were temporarily busy elsewhere, they had already decided that the accused was guilty, and the hour for sentencing was fast approaching. In September 1953, writes John Moors Cabot, Miller's successor as assistant secretary for inter-American affairs, "I went to Bedell Smith and said that I thought that a CIA-organized coup was the only solution [in Guatemala]. He nodded and smiled, and I got the impression that the plan was already underway."[65] Cabot was right: Operation Success—PBSUCCESS—had begun.[66]

The precise date and the exact circumstances of the birth of PBSUCCESS are unknown. It was in the late summer of 1953—most likely in August, when AJAX was either on the verge of fruition, or in the immediate aftermath of its success.[67] The decision was taken with little internal debate and a heartening unanimity among the few policymakers involved. Eisenhower reserved the right to grant or deny final approval before H-hour, but this was a standard procedure for operations of this nature.

The planning of PBSUCCESS "took place with the utmost stealth. Only Eisenhower, the Dulles brothers, and a few other top-level members of the White House, State Department, and Central Intelligence Agency knew that an operation was even being considered, let alone were privy to its details."[68] The Pentagon, which later played a limited but not insignificant role in the Bay of Pigs, was involved neither at the policy nor the operational level; its contribution consisted at most of "some military personnel who were on loan to the CIA—but this was a constant practice."[69]

[65] Cabot, *First Line*, p. 90.

[66] "PB doesn't mean anything. The names of most covert operations have a two letter prefix that is arbitrary." (Interview with Bissell.)

[67] See Immerman, *CIA in Guatemala*, pp. 134–36, and Schlesinger and Kinzer, *Bitter Fruit*, p. 108.

[68] Immerman, *CIA in Guatemala*, p. 133.

[69] Interviews with Bissell (quoted) and Kirkpatrick. In 1963, Thruston Morton, who had been assistant secretary for congressional relations in 1954, was the first Eisenhower administration official to make a public statement confirming U.S. involvement in the overthrow of Arbenz. In his brief account, he exaggerated the role of the Pentagon. ("History: Damn Good and Sure," *Newsweek*.)

The conduct of PBSUCCESS was placed in the hands of the CIA's Directorate of Plans (DDP), which was in charge of covert operations. Within the DDP, "typically, the operation was closely held." A special unit was set up, with "its own communication facilities, financial officers, support people, covert agents, and special authority to requisition confidential funds."[70] The DDP's Western Hemisphere chief, Colonel J. C. King, was "shunted aside," because the Deputy Director of Plans, Frank Wisner, "wanted to run the show. King was very upset."[71] Wisner assumed the direction of PBSUCCESS under the overall control of Allen Dulles. Throughout the life of the operation, approximately ten months, Wisner focused on it with such intensity that he left his deputy, Richard Helms, "more or less in charge of all other things. PBSUCCESS became Wisner's project."[72]

The other side of the CIA, the Directorate of Intelligence, was not involved in PBSUCCESS, "absolutely not." Robert Amory, who as deputy director of intelligence was Wisner's counterpart, was never briefed. He sensed something was afoot, but he knew no details, no timetables. "If I had been captured by Arbenz and tortured to death," he has observed, "I would not have been able to tell them anything that could have done me any good." During PBSUCCESS, the CIA station in Guatemala did report to the Directorate of Intelligence about developments in the country—"but to the exclusion of anything dealing with or referring to the plot to overthrow Arbenz."[73] This was a crippling limitation, as Richard Bissell, who participated in PBSUCCESS and later rose to be deputy director of plans, admits. "With hindsight, one of the major mistakes of my career was my failure to include people from the analytical side in covert operations."[74]

If the analysts of the CIA lacked the "union cards"[75] to work for PBSUCCESS, so did State Department officials, with two major exceptions: Secretary Dulles and Undersecretary Smith. Foster Dulles was, with his brother Allen, a prime mover and enthusiastic supporter of PBSUCCESS, just as he had been of AJAX. As in the case of AJAX, he paid relatively little attention to the operation once the decision to act had been taken.[76] Distracted by his many duties and confident that the undertaking was in good hands (Allen's), he saw his role as briefing Eisenhower and ensuring that the CIA avoided doing anything that might embarrass the government. More intimately involved in PBSUCCESS was

[70] Quotations from Powers, *The Man Who Kept the Secrets*, p. 108, and Immerman, *CIA in Guatemala*, pp. 138–39.

[71] Interviews with Roettinger (quoted), Bissell, and Helms.

[72] Interviews with Bissell (quoted) and Helms.

[73] Interview with Amory.

[74] Interview with Bissell.

[75] "The intelligence people of the CIA are not operators; they don't have the union cards, so to speak." (Interview with Amory.)

[76] Interviews with Bissell and Amory.

Undersecretary Smith. "He was, at high level, the immediate contact of the CIA with the State Department; Wisner dealt with him on many issues without the need to go up all the way to Foster Dulles."[77]

The rest of the State Department was kept in the dark. The department's senior official for Latin America, John Moors Cabot, knew of the plot but played no active role. "An officer in ARA," he writes, "was designated liaison with other agencies involved in developing the plans. For the rest of my tour as Assistant Secretary I was in constant touch with this officer, but I never knew the details of the planned operation, nor did I want to know them; my principal concern was to keep secret any United States involvement in the projected coup."[78] The official in question, Raymond Leddy, "could clam up very well," remembers a colleague. Leddy, who was the officer in charge of Central American and Panamanian affairs, acted as the CIA's day-to-day contact in the State Department; "they dealt with him on those issues that did not require the immediate attention of Beedle Smith or Foster Dulles."[79]

In March 1954 Cabot was replaced by Henry Holland, a well-connected Texas lawyer. "Cabot," notes Deputy Assistant Secretary Robert Woodward, "left his job without ever telling me anything about PBSUCCESS, though he was fully aware of it since August or September 1953. All I was told by Cabot was that Leddy was working on something confidential (something pertaining to Central America and Guatemala), and that I should not bother with it."

In the first week of April, Holland went to Woodward. " 'Bob,' Holland said to me, 'I've just been told about a plan to overthrow Arbenz. I'm tempted to resign. Take two or three hours to think it over, and come back and tell me what you think I should do.' A few hours later, I urged Holland: 'Don't resign. Try to buck it. This CIA plot will destroy our nonintervention policy and throw us back to 1931–32, before Roosevelt's Good Neighbor Policy.' I doubted that the plan would succeed, and that, if successful, the U.S. role could be hidden; I also questioned whether the extent of the communist threat in Guatemala justified taking the risk. The next day Holland told me: 'I spoke with [Foster] Dulles; he's given me until the end of the year to come up with other ways to take care of the communist problem in Guatemala.' "[80]

Woodward had been tested, found wanting and fed a lie. Years later, when told of the incident, Bissell remarked: "This is common practice when an officer is opposed to this kind of plan, in order to avoid leaks. Although in Woodward's case, he was an honorable man and would have kept silent."[81]

On one point Holland had spoken the truth: he was opposed to the CIA plot

[77] Interview with Bissell.
[78] Cabot, *First Line*, pp. 90–91.
[79] Quotations from interviews with Jamison and Bissell.
[80] Interview with Woodward.
[81] Interview with Bissell.

against Arbenz. PBSUCCESS, notes Bissell, "was Holland's first encounter with a major covert operation, and he thought it was not the way to proceed. As a result, he was regarded by Wisner and others in the Directorate of Plans as one of our opponents within the State Department." After Arbenz fell, "Holland changed completely and became a very strong supporter of the CIA and of covert operations. This has happened to quite a lot of men in the State Department."[82] Holland's initial opposition meant, however, that he was excluded from the closeknit group who oversaw PBSUCCESS.

The planners of PBSUCCESS had no delusions about the Guatemalan opposition. Their attention was riveted on the army. "The Army is the key to the stability of the Arbenz regime," an intelligence report had underlined in June 1953,

> and could effect a rapid and decisive change in the Guatemalan political situation if it were to take concerted action. Although a quick change of attitude is always possible, there is no present reason to doubt the continued loyalty of the Army high command and of most of the Army officer corps to Arbenz. The Army would be unlikely to take revolutionary action [against Arbenz] unless the high command or a substantial body of unit commanders became convinced that their personal security and well-being were threatened. . . . The Communists have little power of their own.[83]

From its inception, PBSUCCESS was based on one premise: only the Guatemalan army could overthrow Arbenz. Psychological warfare would be the CIA's main weapon to convince the Guatemalan officers that their security and well-being were at stake, and thus prod them toward treason. As part of this effort, the United States would attempt to isolate Guatemala and wave the specter of multilateral sanctions. In the process, the civilian forces loyal to the regime would be demoralized and the civilian opposition would gather strength.

The Guatemalan exiles were to serve as the spark[84] if the army failed to rise against Arbenz on its own. At no moment did PBSUCCESS assume that the exiles would be able to defeat the Guatemalan army. The purpose of the invasion—coming after months of psychological destabilization and supported, it was hoped, by an active fifth column organized by the CIA—was to confront the Guatemalan officers with the stark choice: they could defeat the rebels and face the wrath of the United States, or they could turn against Arbenz and save themselves. The threat would be credible only if Washington had persuaded

[82] Interview with Bissell.

[83] Division of Research for Latin America, "Effect upon Guatemala of Arms Procurement by El Salvador, Honduras, and Nicaragua," Special Paper no. 21, June 12, 1953, pp. 2 and 4, enclosed in Armstrong to Cabot, June 16, 1953, NA 714.00.

[84] The term *spark* was used in separate interviews by DCM Krieg and by Taracena.

the officers that the exiles were U.S. proxies whose defeat would trigger a U.S. invasion.

President Eisenhower and Secretary Dulles wanted to protect the image of the United States abroad, particularly in Latin America. Just a few weeks before Eisenhower assumed the presidency, a CIA National Intelligence Estimate had stressed that Latin America was threatened by "the pressure of exaggerated nationalism," and that this trend might eventually "affect Hemispheric solidarity and U.S. security interests"; the same warning was repeated by Allen Dulles at a February 18, 1953, meeting of the National Security Council (NSC), and in mid-March, NSC 144/1 stated that the United States must "avoid the appearance of unilateral action" in the internal affairs of the Latin American republics.[85]

Thus, there was "a paradox at the heart of PBSUCCESS," a paradox that was resolved by a figleaf. "The figleaf was designed to deny U.S. involvement," muses Bissell, "yet the success of the operation hinged on convincing the Guatemalans that the U.S. was indeed involved."[86] This concern for appearances is evident in the handling of the president's press conference that was held the day before the exiles were set to invade Guatemala. Prior to the conference, Allen Dulles sent the press secretary, James Hagerty, a "Draft of Possible Press Conference Statement on Guatemala" that was couched in very harsh language. In response, Holland fired off an angry memo: "I most vigorously oppose the use of this statement." Holland feared that the use of such language by the president just before D-Day would strip away the figleaf. "I have reiterated . . . again and again to every Latin American Ambassador," he noted, "that the United States is undertaking to solve the problem [of communism in Guatemala] without unilateral intervention, whether political or economic, in Guatemalan affairs." Secretary Dulles decided in Holland's favor. Eisenhower, he reminded Allen, must not give the impression that he was issuing "an open call for revolution." Allen agreed and the secretary told Hagerty the following day "to avoid the implication we were seeking a revolution there."[87]

[85] Quotations from: "Conditions and Trends in Latin America Affecting U.S. Security," NIE-70, Dec. 12, 1952, p. 9, Truman Papers, President's Secretary's File, Intelligence File, Box 254, TL; "Discussion at the 132 Meeting of the National Security Council on Wednesday, February 18, 1953," Feb. 19, 1953, WF, NSC Series, Box 4, EL; "United States Objectives and Courses of Action with Respect to Latin America," NSC 144/1, Mar. 18, 1953, *FRUS*, 1952–1954, 4:7.

[86] Interview with Bissell. In 1952, a U.S. official had posed the dilemma starkly: "We must be careful in our own minds to distinguish between intervention and being caught at it." (Hill to Ambassador, Oct. 2, 1952, p. 3, RG84 CF, Box 15, NA-S.)

[87] Quotations from: Holland to JFD, June 15, 1954, *FRUS*, 1952–1954, 4:1168; TelConv (JFD, AWD), June 15, 1954, 6:24 p.m., DP: TCS, Box 2, EL; TelConv (JFD, Hagerty), June 16, 1954, 9:37 a.m., DP, JFD:CS, Box 8, EL. AWD, "Draft of

As would become clear as PBSUCCESS gathered momentum, it was not difficult to maintain the fiction. The governments of Western Europe and Latin America were willing to overlook U.S. violations of international law, as long as a pretense of compliance was maintained. In the United States, ignorance, anticommunism, and self-righteousness blended seamlessly to generate the comforting conviction in the political and intellectual elites, in the press, in the Congress, and in the public at large that Guatemala was the aggressor and the United States, the long-suffering victim.

PBSUCCESS was hatched at a time when the Guatemalan opposition was particularly weak. The arrests that followed the Salamá uprising had dealt a heavy blow to the various cliques of plotters; the agrarian reform was strengthening the government in the countryside; the military showed no signs of disloyalty. *New York Times* correspondent Sidney Gruson wrote in late July:

> To an observer revisiting Guatemala after six months, the overriding factor in the political situation is the disintegration that has occurred among the organized opposition. . . . What remains of it has lost what little confidence it once may have had. The accepted thing seems to be . . . to hope that somehow from somewhere something will happen to salvage the cause. This wishful thinking that someone else will eventually do the job of opposing the Communists is an old fault of the Guatemalan opposition.[88]

The exiles were still plotting, and United Fruit still gave them encouragement and, apparently, some material assistance.[89] But the region's strongmen were tiring of the exiles' incompetence, their perennial squabbles, and the gulf between their wild promises and pitiful performances. Trujillo now rebuffed his protegé, Colonel Roberto Barrios, complaining that ''every time something started there were twenty people who wanted to be president after the uprising, and none who would cooperate with the other nineteen.'' Trujillo had concluded that ''the only way the [Guatemalan] government would be overthrown was if the United States did it.'' This was also Somoza's view.[90] ''When the United States decided to help us, in the fall of 1953, we were isolated,'' recalls a close aide of Castillo Armas. ''Somoza was helping us very little. He would never have dared to act on his own. He needed the OK

Possible Press Conference Statement on Guatemala'' is enclosed in Holland to JFD, June 15, 1954, *FRUS*, 1952–1954, 4:1168. See also Hagerty Diary, June 14–16, 1954, EL.

[88] ''Anti-Reds Give Up Guatemalan Role,'' *NYT*, Aug. 1, 1953, p. 3.

[89] See Fisher to Mann, ''Alleged Implication of Mr. Samuel Zemurray in Illicit Arms Traffic,'' May 22, 1953, NA 714.00, and Keay to Belmont, ''Possible Anti-Communist Revolution in Guatemala,'' June 2, 1953.

[90] Hill, Memo, Nov. 3, 1953 (quoted) and MemoConv (Montenegro, Peurifoy, Krieg), Nov. 6, 1953. Both enclosed in Krieg to Leddy, Nov. 10, 1953, NA 714.00.

and the participation of the United States. And Honduras had done nothing for us."[91]

Washington's decision to move against Arbenz raised Somoza's spirits. PBSUCCESS called for a small Liberation army to be organized and trained in Nicaragua. It would eventually move into Honduras, which would serve as the springboard for the invasion. A fifth column of saboteurs, also trained in Nicaragua, would be infiltrated into Guatemala before D-Day. The invasion would begin no later than June 1954, that is, before the onset of the rainy season. Trujillo was left on the sidelines. Lacking a border with Guatemala, the Dominican Republic had little to contribute to PBSUCCESS. It is doubtful that the Dominican dictator was even informed of the plot.

In August 1953, Washington asked the embassy in Guatemala to suggest someone to lead a movement against Arbenz. (The question was framed in hypothetical terms.) "We decided," recalls DCM Krieg, "that among poor starters Castillo Armas was probably the best."[92]

Years later, in his autobiography, Castillo Armas's main rival, General Ydígoras Fuentes, sought to explain why the Eisenhower administration had spurned a man of his ability:

> A former executive of the United Fruit Company, now retired, Mr. Walter Turnbull, came to see me with two gentlemen whom he introduced as agents of the CIA. They said that I was a popular figure in Guatemala and that they wanted to lend their assistance to overthrow Arbenz. When I asked their conditions for the assistance I found them unacceptable. Among other things, I was to promise to favor the United Fruit Company and the International Railways of Central America; to destroy the railroad workers labor union; to suspend claims against Great Britain for the Belize territory; to establish a strong-arm government, on the style of Ubico. Further, I was to pay back every cent that was invested in the undertaking on the basis of accounts that would be presented to me afterwards. I told them that I would have to be given time to prepare my conditions, as theirs seemed to me to be unfavorable to Guatemala. They withdrew, promising to return; I never saw them again.[93]

Ydígoras' explanation is straightforward: he was passed over because of his unbending nationalism; Castillo Armas must have been more pliant.

Many writers have accepted Ydígoras's words at face value. Yet as president of Guatemala (1958–1963), Ydígoras was subservient to American companies, undemocratic, and corrupt.[94] Why then believe a self-serving state-

---

[91] Interview with Taracena.

[92] Interview with Krieg.

[93] Ydígoras Fuentes, *My War with Communism*, pp. 49–50.

[94] Jonas calls Ydígoras "a corrupt *ubiquista* with close ties to Dominican dictator Trujillo" yet accepts his claim that he refused the CIA/UFCO offer. ("Guatemala," p. 195. See also Jonas and Tobis, *Guatemala*, p. 68, and Schlesinger and Kinzer, *Bitter Fruit*, pp. 120–21.)

ment so out of character with the man? His autobiography—a rambling apologia remarkable only for its distortions and lies—is hardly a reliable source. His entire record indicates that, had he been offered the leadership of the crusade, Ydígoras would have accepted any conditions.

Castillo Armas was a more attractive candidate. He had been an excellent cadet and a highly competent officer, whereas Ydígoras was notorious as one of Ubico's subservient generals. In Arbenz's words, Castillo Armas "performed with great bravery" in the 1944 uprising against Ponce; Ydígoras's role, noted a U.S. official, had been "ambiguous and odd."[95] On July 18, 1949, a demoralized Castillo Armas failed to join the revolt of his *Aranista* friends, but his lonely uprising of November 1950 and his dramatic escape from prison restored his reputation for bravery.

Ydígoras had never risked his life, for any cause. He was a *bon vivant* and, in the words of a U.S. official who knew him well, "as crooked as they come."[96] Castillo Armas, on the other hand, was a fanatic. He sought to avenge Arana's death and to atone for his failure to fight in July 1949. Ambition, anticommunism, and the frustrations of exile propelled him forward. He was ready to side with anyone who wanted to overthrow Arbenz: the landed elite, the "tropical dictators," the United States—anyone, as long as they would anoint him Arbenz's successor. He was not distracted by a social conscience. As president he would tolerate corruption and champion the status quo. And yet he was courageous, not unintelligent, honest, and able to command the devotion of a small band of followers.

Furthermore, Castillo Armas was the favorite of Archbishop Rossell y Arellano and of Somoza. Ydígoras was merely one of Trujillo's protegés, and PBSUCCESS had cast the Dominican dictator in a supporting role, giving Somoza the lead. Thus, between the two aspiring and pliant *caudillos*, Washington's choice was eminently sensible.[97]

---

[95] Quotations from Arbenz, "Habla Arbenz," p. 122, and AmEm Tegucigalpa, Erwin to DOS, no. 181, Nov. 5, 1953, p. 3, NA 714.00.

[96] Interview with Jamison.

[97] According to Immerman, many CIA officials preferred the lawyer Juan Córdova Cerna, a prominent member of the landed elite, to Castillo Armas, but a routine medical examination revealed that Córdova Cerna had cancer. (*CIA in Guatemala*, p. 142; see also Phillips, *Night Watch*, p. 53.) This is highly questionable on several grounds: (1) Immerman's only source is the entertaining but unreliable Howard Hunt; (2) Córdova Cerna was active and in good health when the CIA chose Castillo Armas and remained active throughout the following year; U.S. reports attest to his vitality and ambition, and say nothing of his health (see for instance *FRUS*, 1952–1954, 4:1219, 1223–24); (3) Córdova Cerna was a civilian while the focus of PBSUCCESS was the military; (4) Córdova Cerna had been an attorney for United Fruit, and the U.S. government had no desire to hand ammunition to those who claimed that its quarrel with

On September 20, 1953, Castillo Armas wrote to Somoza from Teguci-galpa: "I have been informed by our friends here that the government of the North . . . has decided to let us develop our plans. Because of the importance of this decision, I immediately sent confidential messages so that it could be confirmed to me directly. Nevertheless up to now I have not received any reply which apparently can be interpreted as confirming the foregoing."[98]

A few days later, recalls his aide, Taracena de la Cerda, the CIA told Castillo Armas that he was the chosen one.[99] On October 15, in a letter to Somoza's son Tachito, Castillo Armas exulted: "Our work with our friends from the North has ended in our complete triumph. . . . We will soon enter into a very active phase which will lead inevitably to the victory that we all desire." The letter ended with warm thanks for the "generous support that we have received from those men who understand the nature of our struggle, especially from your Dad and you, who have been our true protectors in this difficult crusade."[100]

The selection of Castillo Armas to be the future liberator of Guatemala did not stop his rivals from importuning U.S. officials. Some were unaware of PBSUCCESS; others knew that something was afoot and that Castillo Armas was the anointed, but found it difficult to bow to the inevitable. Reports by U.S. officials make for amusing reading. José Luis Arenas, a member of the Guatemalan Congress, told DCM Krieg that he had a scheme to overthrow Arbenz that was "sure to work." Wasting no time on details, Arenas "inquired without ambiguity" if the embassy would provide him with $200,000 "to do the job." Upon being politely turned down, he asked whether he could not receive at least a "down payment."[101]

Even Ponce, Ubico's unlucky successor, surfaced from obscurity to press his claims. In January 1954, he appeared twice at the U.S. embassy in Managua. He was, he explained, "still the legal president of Guatemala," the only one, he insisted, with "legal and moral rights to the Presidency." The Guatemalan people and the Guatemalan army "would follow no one but him." His plans were ready, though he preferred not to discuss them in detail "at this time." If the United States would provide money to buy weapons, he would return to Guatemala "among the cheers of the multitude" and oust Arbenz.[102]

Guatemala was rooted in bananas. On Córdova Cerna, see also Villagrán Kramer, "Los pactos," July 12, 1987, p. 11.

[98] Guatemala, *La democracia amenazada*, pp. 92–93.

[99] Interview with Taracena.

[100] Guatemala, *La democracia amenazada*, p. 46.

[101] Quotations from Krieg to Fisher, Nov. 24, 1953, p. 1, NA 714.00, and from the enclosed MemoConv (Arenas, Ocaña, Krieg), Nov. 18, 1953, p. 2. See also Leddy to Fisher, Jan. 5, 1954.

[102] AmEm Managua, Welch to DOS, no. 272, Jan. 12, 1954, p. 1, NA 714.00.

None of the supplicants was as persistent as Ydígoras. To the very end, he harassed U.S. officials, waxing eloquent about Castillo Armas's sins and his own virtues; his followers did the same. Ydígoras's "henchmen," a June 1, 1954, State Department memo noted, "frequently call at the Department pleading for U.S. support, the latest being one Cesar Lanuza . . . on May 17. The *Ydigoristas* claim to have a large underground organization in Guatemala with good army connections, but they have thus far shown themselves totally ineffective in opposition to the present government and with the passage of time their prestige has steadily declined."[103] Ydígoras was indefatigable in his efforts to unseat Castillo Armas, but the other aspiring *caudillos* gradually fell in line, with more or less grace, behind Washington's man.

While searching for a Liberator, in the summer of 1953 the planners of PBSUCCESS also sought a new U.S. ambassador for Guatemala—a team player. They found him in John Peurifoy. Peurifoy's predecessor, Rudolph Schoenfeld, was a career official who had become a harsh critic of the Arbenz administration. ("The Communist power-drive in Guatemala has reached an advanced state of infiltration," he asserted in his debriefing.) Schoenfeld, however, lacked the inclination and the training to participate effectively in a major covert operation. He was, Eleanor Lansing Dulles told her brother Foster, "first class . . . intelligent, intellectual . . . but . . . a bit cautious."[104]

In October 1953, as Peurifoy arrived in Guatemala, the local CIA station began to expand rapidly.[105] The rest of the embassy staff was not informed about a covert operation against Arbenz. It was only in February or March 1954 that Peurifoy told DCM Krieg and a few other embassy officials (including the military attachés and members of the military missions) that a plot was underway.[106]

Peurifoy told them that he knew only the broadest outlines of PBSUCCESS. In fact, he was "very involved."[107] Before he left for Guatemala, the CIA

[103] Burr to Holland, June 1, 1954. For Lanuza's May 17 visit, see MemoConv (Lanuza, Woodward, Fisher), May 17, 1954, NA 714.00. After claiming that Castillo Armas was revealing the names of army officers who favored Ydígoras to Arbenz, Lanuza ended with a parting shot: "It was obvious" that in his 1951 escape from jail, Castillo Armas "had bought his way out and not dug a tunnel as alleged"—an irrelevant detail to his American audience.

[104] Quotations from "Debriefing of Ambassador Rudolph E. Schoenfeld, October 28, 1953," *FRUS*, 1952–1954, 4:1087, and TelConv (JFD, Eleanor L. Dulles), Aug. 1, 1953, 4:35 p.m., DP, JFD:CS, Box 4, EL. Schoenfeld had presented his credentials to Arbenz on Apr. 24, 1951. Since the Patterson incident, the United States had been represented by a chargé.

[105] Interview with Bissell.

[106] Interview with Krieg; confirmed by interview with Bissell.

[107] Interview with Bissell.

"made certain that it would have a direct line to him at all times"; to avoid leaks, the agency communicated with Peurifoy through " 'back channels.' Once received by the CIA Guatemala station, the messages would be hand-carried or conveyed verbally to the Ambassador by Birch O'Neil, the CIA station chief."[108]

He was no suave diplomat, the "pistol packing" Peurifoy.[109] Indeed, wrote an admiring journalist, Flora Lewis, it was "jarringly wrong" to call him a diplomat at all. His loud checkered shirts, and his preference for a "jaunty, bright-green Borsalino . . . in place of the diplomat's black homburg," matched his ideas of diplomatic intercourse. "He is much more the politician than the diplomat," Lewis remarked, "but he is striking at it because he goes politicking around foreign countries instead of at home among the voters."[110]

Peurifoy came to Guatemala from Greece, where at age forty-three he had landed his first ambassadorial appointment. His colorful career had included stints as a Capitol Hill elevator operator and as a salesperson at Woodward and Lothrop. Once in the State Department, he demonstrated that he was an effective organizer and administrator.[111] In 1950 he was sent to Greece, where the civil war had just ended with the communists' defeat, to shore up the corrupt conservative government and to prevent even a hint of communist resurgence. He began in characteristic fashion: "He told dignified old Sophocles Venizelos, then foreign minister and deputy premier, 'Look Soph, you call me Jack. Let's talk frankly about all this.' "[112] He intervened so brazenly in the country's internal affairs that even the meek Greek government felt compelled, on one occasion, to complain publicly that decisions in purely domestic matters should be left "to the Greek people and government."[113] Throughout his tenure in Greece, Peurifoy worked closely with the embassy's CIA station, "proving himself a most willing and able ally."[114]

This was the ambassador whom the planners of PBSUCCESS had chosen for

---

[108] Schlesinger and Kinzer, *Bitter Fruit*, p. 135.

[109] The expression is from a poem that Peurifoy's wife, Betty Jane, composed to celebrate the overthrow of Arbenz. See *Time*, July 26, 1954, p. 34.

[110] Flora Lewis, "Ambassador Extraordinary: John Peurifoy," *NYT Magazine*, July 18, 1954, p. 9. Lewis's piece is a model of good taste when compared with other feature articles on Peurifoy that appeared in the U.S. press after Arbenz's overthrow. See, for instance, Donald Grant, "Ambassador John E. Peurifoy," *St. Louis Post-Dispatch*, July 11, 1954, C1, and Ralph de Toledano, "Unconventional Ambassador," *American Mercury*, Oct. 1954, pp. 28–32.

[111] For Peurifoy's background, in addition to the sources cited in n. 110 above, see Schlesinger and Kinzer, *Bitter Fruit*, pp. 132–35; Immerman, *CIA in Guatemala*, pp. 137–38; Eisenhower Records Central File, OF, Box 163, EL.

[112] Lewis, "Ambassador Extraordinary" (see n. 110 above), p. 26.

[113] Couloumbis, *Greek Political Reaction*, pp. 53–68, quoted from p. 55.

[114] Immerman, *CIA in Guatemala*, p. 137.

Guatemala: a man used to upbraiding the officials of a client government, a doer rather than a thinker, a militant anticommunist, an ambitious career officer. His loud, aggressive personality, so different from the aloof politeness of Schoenfeld, was an asset. He was sent to frighten. In the words of a Guatemalan colonel who turned against Arbenz, Peurifoy was "an abusive, arrogant ambassador—but this was very effective: he scared a lot of officers."[115]

Peurifoy was preceded by his reputation as the high-handed proconsul who had presided over the anticommunist witch hunt in Greece. Sidney Gruson, the well-informed *New York Times* correspondent, reported: "It is generally expected in Guatemala that his advent means a change in the asserted passivity with which the United States has watched the growth of the Communists' influence to the point where, at least to the outsider, they seem to be masters of the country in all but name."[116] Peurifoy immediately vindicated these expectations. On the very day of his arrival, he had a long interview with Foreign Minister Raúl Osegueda. He did not suggest, as he had done with old Venizelos in Greece, that they be on a first-name basis. Rather, he immediately raised the issue of communist influence and all but called Osegueda a liar to his face. For his performance he was warmly praised from Washington by Leddy, the PBSUCCESS man at the State Department.[117] In a different vein, the PGT's daily *Tribuna Popular* wrote:

> The new U.S. ambassador, Señor Peurifoy, has arrived; like the ancient gods, he has been preceded by flashes of lightning and the rumbling of thunder. It is easy to divine why a man who has been in Greece—more as the mastermind of its struggle against the communists and Greek patriots than as an ambassador—has been sent to our country. The State Department does not need men like Peurifoy in Honduras, El Salvador or Nicaragua. These countries are led by men who are the lap dogs of Yankee monopolies.[118]

The embassy closely monitored the impact of Peurifoy's arrival. He presented his credentials on November 4 "amid a flurry of press and official speculation concerning United States intentions toward Guatemala." Two weeks later, Peurifoy himself observed: "I have psychological advantage of being new and government feels I have come to Guatemala to use the big stick. We have been letting them stew." The mere arrival of Peurifoy, stressed DCM Krieg, had

> provided a milepost for the smaller politically-conscious element of Guatemala to reassess the internal situation and set off the greatest wave of press and public spec-

[115] Interview with González Siguí.

[116] "U.S. To Re-Examine Guatemalan Role," *NYT*, Nov. 8, 1953, p. 9.

[117] See Peurifoy to Leddy, Oct. 30, 1953; Krieg to DOS, no. 378, Nov. 2, 1953, NA 611.14, and enclosed MemoConv (Osegueda, Peurifoy, Krieg), Oct. 29, 1953; Leddy to Peurifoy, Nov. 6, 1953, NA 611.14.

[118] "El nuevo embajador yanqui" (edit.), *Tribuna Popular*, Nov. 11, 1953, p. 5.

ulation in recent times as to what the U.S. would do about Communist influences in Guatemala. . . . The more conservative elements naturally seized upon the change of Chief of Mission as a portent that forceful action by the United States was imminent, as they had previously done when President Eisenhower succeeded President Truman. But on this occasion persons formerly sympathetic to the [Arbenz] Administration joined in by privately complaining that unbridled Communism was imperiling the country. In the past two weeks . . . this embassy has heard from . . . informed sources . . . that many Administration politicians are dissatisfied with the situation. . . . the non Communist politicians feel . . . that they are on a roller coaster over which they have no control but from which it would be dangerous to jump.[119]

Peurifoy had one serious conversation with Arbenz, a six-hour dinner on December 16, 1953. Only the ambassador, the president and their wives were present. Since Peurifoy knew only two Spanish words ("muchos [sic] gracias"), Doña María served as interpreter. (Arbenz, she notes, "understood English pretty well, but it gave him more time if I translated.")[120] Peurifoy played the role of the inquisitor, besieging his host with precise questions about communist influence in Guatemala; Arbenz, on the defensive, offered lame responses.

Two days later, Peurifoy sent Secretary Dulles a five-page report about the dinner. "I am definitely convinced that if the President is not a Communist, he will certainly do until one comes along," he concluded.[121] Thereafter, Peurifoy's contacts with Arbenz were purely formal, as were his contacts with the foreign ministry. Relations between the embassy and Guatemalan officials, already cold under Schoenfeld, were now icy.[122]

There was, however, one exception. U.S. officials intensified their contacts with the Guatemalan army. The State Department had decided in early 1953 to maintain the military missions in Guatemala unless Arbenz asked for their removal. Peurifoy endorsed this decision. The "army is anti-Communist . . . day may not be too far off when we will need friends where it will count," he wrote in a November 19 dispatch to the State Department. Despite occasional complaints by naive congressmen, who could not understand why such a favor should be bestowed on a procommunist regime, the military missions re-

[119] Quotations from: *JW* 45, Nov. 6, 1953, I:1–2; Peurifoy to SecState, no. 124, Nov. 19, 1953, NA 611.14; Krieg to DOS, no. 427, Nov. 18, 1953, pp. 1–2, NA 714.00.

[120] Interview with María de Arbenz. (Peurifoy's ignorance of Spanish was confirmed by interviews with the following embassy officials: Krieg, Wardlaw, and Wright.) For a discussion of the meeting between Arbenz and Peurifoy, see below, pp. 363–64.

[121] MemoConv (Pres. Arbenz, Mrs. Arbenz, Amb. Peurifoy, Mrs. Peurifoy), Dec. 17, 1953, p. 5, enclosed in Peurifoy to DOS, no. 522, Dec. 18, 1953, NA 611.14. An edited version of this document appears in *FRUS*, 1952–1954, 4:1091–93.

[122] Interviews with María de Arbenz, Krieg, Wardlaw, Osegueda, and Toriello.

mained in the country; they were "in constant touch with the Guatemalan officers," whom they urged to betray Arbenz.[123]

In the same month that Peurifoy arrived in Guatemala, two major developments added to the foreboding atmosphere. On October 6, the State Department suddenly asked the Council of the Organization of American States to include a new item, "Intervention of International Communism in the American Republics," in the agenda of the Tenth Inter-American Conference, to be held in March 1954.[124] Guatemala, the only country to vote against this request, was the target, as everyone understood.[125]

Also in October, U.S. officials began a sustained campaign of public denunciations of the Arbenz administraton. Assistant Secretary Cabot launched the first broadside. He assailed the Guatemalan authorities for "openly playing the Communist game," and asked ominously whether the "activities of the international Communist conspiracy to destroy free governments are prejudicing the independence" of Guatemala and its neighbors. Senator Wiley, chairman of the Senate Foreign Affairs Committee, added his own fulminations to the growing chorus.[126] There had been earlier attacks by the U.S. press, the Congress, and the State Department, but they had not been as systematic and virulent as they were from October 1953 until Arbenz fell.

It was all part of PBSUCCESS. The United States Information Agency (USIA) and the CIA helped to write and disseminate articles attacking the Arbenz regime.[127] Many of these articles were reprinted in the Guatemalan opposition press as proof that U.S. patience was fast coming to an end. "These . . . outstanding, courageous newspapers . . . will reprint anything against the Government," Peurifoy explained to the House Committee on Foreign Affairs

[123] Quotations from Peurifoy to SecState, no. 124, Nov. 19, 1953, NA 611.14, and from interview with Col. González Siguí. Peurifoy vacillated on this issue: see Peurifoy to SecState, Dec. 23, 1953, *FRUS*, 1952–1954, 4:1094; and Peurifoy to Fisher, May 24, 1954, NA 714.58.

[124] OAS, *Annals*, pp. 293–302.

[125] The vote came on Nov. 10. For the position of the Guatemalan government, see "Defensa de la soberanía," *DCA*, Nov. 12, 1953, p. 1; "Democracia e intervención" (edit.), *DCA*, Nov. 13, 1953, p. 3; "Pueblo y gobierno solidamente únidos en defensa de la soberanía," *DCA*, Nov. 30, 1953, p. 4; Guerra Borges, "El voto de Guatemala en la OEA," *Tribuna Popular*, Nov. 14, Nov. 17, and Nov. 18, 1953, p. 5.

[126] See Cabot, *Toward Our Common American Destiny*, pp. 41–60, 82–121 (quoted from p. 88), and "Wiley Scores Guatemala," *NYT*, Oct. 17, 1953, p. 13. For a more detailed account of Wiley's speech, see "Reds Gaining in Guatemala," *Milwaukee Journal*, Oct. 16, 1953, p. 4.

[127] On USIA, see "Report on Actions Taken by the United States Information Agency in the Guatemalan Situation," July 27, 1954, *FRUS*, 1952–1954, 4:1212–17.

in January 1954 as he urged the congressmen to make more speeches lambasting the Arbenz administration.[128]

In the same month, Peurifoy intensified the scare campaign. "Public opinion in the U.S.," he told *Time*, "might force us to take some measures to prevent Guatemala from falling into the lap of international Communism. We cannot permit a Soviet republic to be established between Texas and the Panama Canal."[129] In Guatemala, Peurifoy's statement was understood by all as a threat of military intervention. ("If the situation in Guatemala continues to deteriorate, the ultimate possibility of unilateral U.S. action cannot be ruled out," *Time* had added.)[130] The fears were hardly assuaged, or the hopes dimmed, by Peurifoy's half-hearted claim that he had been misquoted. "The statements attributed by *Time* to Ambassador Peurifoy," an embassy note stated, "were taken out of context and without authorization. They are not a fair representation of the ambassador's point of view. . . . The ambassador did not mean to imply that the Pan-American concern about communism in Guatemala need necessarily precipitate unilateral action by the United States."[131]

As Gruson later reported, the incident "only confirmed the worst fears of Guatemalan officials that Mr. Peurifoy's appointment was the forerunner of energetic United States action against them."[132] Marroquín Rojas patiently drove the point home:

> Our foreign minister has officially accepted Ambassador Peurifoy's explanation of his interview in *Time*. But Dr. Osegueda knows that a magazine like *Time*, published in a country where lies are severely punished, would not falsify the words that it put so emphatically in Peurifoy's mouth. There is no doubt that Peurifoy said what *Time* printed, and there is no doubt that he was expressing the opinion of the White House, the Congress, and the Pentagon. How could the leaders of Guatemala imagine that the United States would tolerate a nest of enemies on its very doorstep? It would be absurd; indeed another country . . . would already have sent in the troops. To argue otherwise, and to spout about our "sovereignty" is childish. It is naive. Germany, powerful even though defeated, is still occupied, and so is Japan—and we will be too, we poor fools who don't even produce fireworks, much less the ammunition for a token resistance.[133]

[128] U.S. Congress, *HCFA*, pp. 481 (quoted), 468, 477.

[129] "The Problem of Guatemala," *Time*, Jan. 11, 1954, p. 27.

[130] Ibid.

[131] "Nota del Embajador Peurifoy," *La Hora*, Jan. 13, 1954, p. 1.

[132] "Guatemala Story of Plot Scouted," *NYT*, Jan. 31, 1954, p. 13. See also Osegueda, *Operación Guatemala*, pp. 202–12.

[133] Marroquín Rojas, "Y usted: ¿Qué deduce, señor ministro?" *La Hora*, Jan. 14, 1954, pp. 1, 10.

In the following weeks, Marroquín Rojas hammered away at the same theme. The principle of nonintervention would not inhibit the United States; the Americans did not hesitate to intervene militarily when they deemed it necessary; legal niceties would not restrain them.[134] As if in confirmation, two weeks after Peurifoy's *Time* interview, the Arbenz administration exposed a plot against it abetted by the United States.

In late September 1953, a man by the name of Isaac Delgado had approached Francisco Morazán, an aide of Arbenz. Delgado, who was Panama's commercial attaché in Managua, moonlighted as a secret courier for Castillo Armas. Was the Guatemalan government interested, he inquired, in his services?

Indeed, the government was very interested. Over the next few months, Delgado performed well as a double agent; among the many documents he sold were Castillo Armas's September 20 and October 15 letters to the Somozas, with their damning references to the government and friends from the North.[135]

But in January 1954, Delgado's lucrative career abruptly ended, as the Guatemalan government decided to publish the documents he had stolen. It was time, Arbenz and his advisers had concluded, to seize the initiative. "This decision," recalls PGT leader Guerra Borges, "was connected to our strategy for the Caracas conference." The publication of Delgado's incriminating material would unmask the aggressor and provoke indignation throughout Latin America. At Caracas, Washington's attempt to impose sanctions on Guatemala would be blocked.[136]

On January 21, the Guatemalan police arrested a former army major, Enrique Trinidad Oliva. This was a "severe blow," opposition sources told the U.S. embassy, since Oliva was a "key figure" of the Castillo Armas group in the country.[137] Over the next five days, two dozen plotters were detained. On

[134] See esp. *La Hora* articles: "El perrito del señor embajador," Jan. 16, 1954, p. 3; "Pues ni la realidad los convence," Jan. 19, 1954, p. 3; "Un comunista que invoca a Dios," Mar. 15, 1954, p. 1.

[135] Interviews with Fortuny, Guerra Borges, and Toriello. Delgado's role was first described in "125 hombres iniciaron la invasión a Guatemala," *La Nación*, San José, July 7, 1954, p. 1, and "Vivo o muerto se busca al nica Isaac Delgado," *La Hora*, July 22, 1954, p. 1. See also: Krieg to SecState, no. 250, Jan. 26, 1954, NA 714.00; Krieg to DOS, no. 643, Jan. 27, 1954, NA 714.00; L.A.H.A., *Así se gestó la Liberación*, p. 166; Selser, *El Guatemalazo*, pp. 101–3.

[136] Interviews with Guerra Borges (quoted), Fortuny, and Toriello. Toriello, who became foreign minister in January 1954, was involved in the decision to publish the documents.

[137] Krieg to SecState, no. 234, NA 714.00 (quoted); "Jeep que transportaba granadas de mano capturado," *DCA*, p. 1; "Exhibición personal del mayor Enrique Oliva," *El I*, p. 1. All Jan. 22, 1954.

January 28, the government announced that a press conference would be held the following day, at 10 a.m.; telegrams had already been sent to invite foreign journalists.[138]

"COUNTERREVOLUTIONARY PLOT," was the title splashed across the front page of the government daily on January 29. Below were several of Delgado's documents, including Castillo Armas's September 20 and October 15 letters to the Somozas.[139] The authorities did not identify the "Government of the North" that had pledged to assist Castillo Armas, but among Mexico, Canada, and the United States it was not difficult to choose.

The leaders of the opposition responded to the January arrests with impotent rage. Those who had been detained, they claimed, were the innocent victims of a repressive state. Loudly supported by the opposition press, they sought to arouse public indignation—"without much success," lamented the U.S. embassy. Aware that the innocent victims were in fact inveterate plotters, the embassy urged USIA "promptest press, radio coverage. . . . Imply arrests made arbitrarily and form part of campaign to intimidate anti-Communist opposition to Communist-influenced Arbenz administration."[140]

From Washington, Undersecretary Smith joined the fray. He urged that Serafino Romualdi, the representative for Latin America of the American Federation of Labor (AFL), persuade the AFL-sponsored Inter-American Organization of Labor (ORIT) to denounce Arbenz's persecution of labor. (Four of the arrested plotters were members of a very small antigovernment trade union.) But ORIT's Secretary General Luis Monge (a future president of Costa Rica and a close associate of Figueres) refused to comply. Monge's hostility

[138] "Mañana se emitirá comunicado," *DCA*, Jan. 28, 1954, p. 1. The best source on the arrests (Jan. 21–26) is the U.S. embassy. See: Krieg to SecState, nos. 233 and 234, Jan. 22, 1954; Krieg to SecState, no. 246, Jan. 25, 1954; Krieg to SecState, nos. 247, 250, and 252, Jan. 26, 1954; Krieg to DOS, no. 643, Jan. 27, 1954; Krieg to SecState, no. 264, Jan. 28, 1954; Krieg to DOS, no. 663, Feb. 3, 1954; Wardlaw to DOS, no. 664, Feb. 3, 1954. All NA 714.00. For an official Guatemalan perspective on the arrests, see Charnaud to Jefe de la Guardia Judicial, and Charnaud to Director General de la Guardia Civil, both Jan. 25, 1954, CO:G, Jan. 1954, unpag., AGCA. For press reports, see esp. "Enrique Oliva nada sabe de complot," *El I*, Jan. 23, 1954, p. 1; "La policía no está obligada a informar, dice Charnaud M.," *La Hora*, Jan. 26, 1954, p. 1; "El tráfico de la alarma" (edit.), *DCA*, Jan. 27, 1954, p. 3; "Guatemala Aide Explains Arrests," *NYT*, Jan. 27, 1954, p. 10; "Situación de zozobra," *El I*, Jan. 27, 1954, p. 1.

[139] The official communiqué, the press conference of the secretario de propaganda y divulgación, and several incriminating letters can be found in the major Guatemalan newspapers of Jan. 29 and 30, 1954. More documents were later published by the government in *La democracia amenazada*.

[140] Quotations from Krieg to SecState, no. 263, Jan. 28, 1954, and Krieg to USIA, TOUSI 26, Jan. 26, 1954. Both NA 714.00. For the embassy's cognizance that those arrested had been plotting, see the documents cited in n. 138 above.

to the Arbenz regime was not in question, but in South America, he argued, "the public and labor are quite ignorant of the true conditions [in Guatemala]." Any statement from him condemning Arbenz would "redound to the benefit of Guatemala rather than the free world." And so ORIT remained silent, and the AFL was left to write an open letter expressing great anxiety over "the growing influence of the Communist elements in Guatemala."[141]

In the United States, the revelations and the January arrests provoked contempt and anger. The State Department set the tone. An official press release began ritualistically, "it is the policy of the United States not to intervene in the internal affairs of other nations." It then dissected Guatemala's behavior: the detention of innocent opposition leaders and the slanderous charges against the United States, "coming as the climax of an increasingly mendacious propaganda campaign," were typical communist techniques. The timing of the accusations—"immediately prior" to the Caracas Conference—betrayed their purpose. They were "a Communist effort to disrupt the work of this conference and the Inter-American solidarity which is so vital to all the nations of the Hemisphere."[142]

The U.S. media were not likely to credit the wild charges of a procommunist banana republic over the lofty denials of the State Department. Their mistrust of the Guatemalans was heightened by two untimely actions. On February 3, the Arbenz administration deported Father Buccellato, that relentless foe of Decree 900; Buccellato was a priest and an American. The previous day, in an unprecedented move, Guatemala had expelled two journalists: Marshall Bannell of the National Broadcasting Company and Sydney Gruson of the *New York Times*.[143]

Gruson was, with Robert Hallett of the *Christian Science Monitor*, the most insightful of the American journalists covering Guatemala. Unlike most of his colleagues, he rarely resorted to sensationalism. In a sober style, he repeatedly acknowledged that the Arbenz government enjoyed popular support, that its

[141] Smith to AmEm San José, no. 69, Jan. 27, 1954, NA 714.00; AmEm San José, Stewart to SecState, no. 72, Jan. 28, 1954, NA 714.00; Krieg to SecState, no. 268, Jan. 29, 1954, NA 714.00; AmEm San José, Cohen to DOS, no. 613, Feb. 9, 1954, NA 714.00 (quoted); "Guatemalans Get Plea from A.F.L.," *NYT*, Feb. 7, 1954, p. 1 (quoted); Schlesinger and Kinzer, *Bitter Fruit*, pp. 141–42; Immerman, *CIA in Guatemala*, p. 105, p. 232, n. 14.

[142] Press release, Jan. 30, 1954, *Department of State Bulletin*, Jan. 25–31, 1954, pp. 251–52.

[143] See "Sydney Gruson expulsado del país," *DCA*, Feb. 2, 1954, p. 1 (includes the official communiqué); "Bannell se dedicó a actividades que no le estaban permitidas en el país," *El I*, Feb. 3, 1954, p. 1; "Rechazo a protesta de la SIP" and "El periodista no es un difamador público," *DCA*, Feb. 4, 1954, p. 1; "Guatemala Ousts Two U.S. Newsmen," *NYT*, Feb. 3, 1954, p. 7.

The government rescinded the orders against Gruson and Bannell a few weeks later.

social reforms were necessary, and that the opposition lacked a constructive program. But in a widely quoted November 1953 article he announced that Arbenz had become "a prisoner of the embrace he so long ago gave the Communists."[144] And he heaped scorn on the January plot revelations in an article that he wrote in Mexico City, where he was based.[145] As the article appeared in the *New York Times*, he landed in Guatemala—only to be expelled. Sydney Gruson, charged the official communiqué, "has systematically defamed and slandered this republic." The Guatemalan government may have hoped that irrefutable evidence of a plot abetted by Washington would dampen the American reaction to the deportation of three particularly nettlesome individuals. Or perhaps it merely acted impulsively, in a spasm of exasperation. To American eyes, however, the arrests and the plot revelations fit into the same pattern as the deportations of Buccellato, Bannell, and Gruson. "It all seemed to add up," concluded *Newsweek* in a mid-February article that closely paralleled the State Department's line. "The immediate object" of these fresh outrages was to provoke "some kind of drastic action by the United States. This could be built up into the standard charge of 'yanqui imperialism' with a consequent strain on hemispheric solidarity—all to the greater glory of World Communism."[146] *Time* also endorsed the State Department's "coolly reasoned explanation." The Guatemalan plot revelations were "a sort of Reichstag fire in reverse, masterminded in Moscow" on behalf of the "Red-wired" Arbenz government; their aim was to disrupt the upcoming Caracas Conference.[147]

In April 1953, Daniel James, an influential editor of the *New Leader*, had argued that the communists, though gaining ground, were far from controlling Guatemala.[148] In February 1954, he no longer entertained such hopes. The plot revelations, he charged, were only "the most disturbing of a series of unfortunate events." Until the late spring of 1953, "there was a possibility that the Guatemalan Communists would slow down their drive toward power. . . . There was also a possibility that Arbenz might decide to jettison the Communists or that the Army might do so. . . . Those possibilities apparently no longer exist." Within the last year, "rumors of Communist infiltration of the Army have increased, and its chief, Colonel Diaz, is now reported to be a fellow-traveler."[149]

The *Saturday Evening Post*, *The Atlantic*, and even the *Christian Science Monitor* (which had provided some of the best reporting on Guatemala) pub-

[144] "Guatemala Reds Increase Powers," *NYT*, Nov. 6, 1953, p. 3.

[145] "Guatemala Story of Plot Scouted," *NYT*, Jan. 31, 1954, p. 13.

[146] "Guatemala: Made in Moscow," *Newsweek*, Feb. 15, 1954, p. 54.

[147] "Plot Within A Plot," *Time*, Feb. 8, 1954, p. 36.

[148] "Is Guatemala Communist?" *New Leader*, Apr. 13, 1953, pp. 3–5; "The Truth about Guatemala," *New York Herald Tribune*, Apr. 7–9, 1953, always p. 22.

[149] "Showdown in Guatemala?" *New Leader*, Feb. 15, 1954, pp. 6–8 (quoted from pp. 6, 7).

lished articles along similar lines, while the scholarly *Hispanic American Report* derided the Guatemalan charges as "fantastic." More conservative publications, such as *American Mercury* and *Reader's Digest*, had long been preaching that Guatemala was a Soviet colony: Soviet agents crowded Guatemala City and were busy establishing military bases from which to threaten not only Guatemala's unfortunate neighbors but also the United States.[150]

Every American publication within the liberal-conservative arc blithely dismissed the charge that the United States was plotting against Arbenz. *The Nation*, which generally offered the most balanced coverage of Guatemalan matters, remained silent.[151] True, the *New York Times*, after harshly condemning the expulsion of Gruson and Bannell,[152] introduced a sober note: "The swiftness with which events appear to be moving in Guatemala is probably deceptive," a February 9 editorial told the Cassandras. "As in almost all Latin-American countries the ultimate power rests with the military, who are not Communists in Guatemala." But the *Times* was not naive. The plot charges were, of course, sheer fabrication, and the editorial lectured the mendacious Guatemalans: "The Guatemalan Government could help itself and the whole hemisphere by being less sensitive and less prone to carrying a chip on its shoulder. In railing against 'Yankee Imperialism' it is fighting a ghost of the dead past, resurrected only in the imagination of extreme nationalists and Communists. Guatemalans have no right to accuse North Americans of misunderstanding them when their own misunderstandings are so colossal."[153]

The Congress of the United States was not as restrained as the *New York Times*. On January 14, Senator Wiley had offered twenty-two proofs that Guatemala had become "a serious beachhead for international communism in this hemisphere." Following the plot revelations, a more intelligent man, Senator William Fulbright, rose to fulminate against the "vicious propaganda attack" of the "Communist-dominated Government of Guatemala." Meanwhile, Wiley added to his catalogue proof number twenty-three. The plot charges and the expulsion of two American correspondents, he explained, were just "the latest sickening demonstration of the Communist octopus at work"; the "ten-

---

[150] "The Reds Must Get No American Beachhead," *Saturday Evening Post* (edit.), Mar. 20, 1954, p. 10; "Guatemala," *Atlantic*, Apr. 1954, pp. 4, 6; Hallett, "Guatemalan Turmoil Linked to Communism," *CSM*, Feb. 3, 1954, p. 4; *Hispanic American Report*, Feb. 1954, p. 1 (quoted); Ralph de Toledano, "The Soft UNDERBELLY of the U.S.A.," *American Mercury*, Feb. 1953, pp. 114–28; Michael Scully, "Red Ruin for Guatemala?" *Reader's Digest*, Dec. 1953, pp. 25–30.

[151] Flora Lewis, "The Peril Is Not Red," merely noted that Guatemala "recently charged that the United States was involved in an 'invasion plot' against it." (*The Nation*, Feb. 13, 1954, pp. 127–29, quoted from p. 127.)

[152] "Censors in Guatemala" (edit.), *NYT*, Feb. 3, 1954, p. 22, and "Guatemala's Explanation" (edit.), *NYT*, Feb. 4, 1954, p. 24.

[153] "Guatemalan Reforms" (edit.), *NYT*, Feb. 9, 1954, p. 26.

tacles [of the] dangerous Communist octopus,'' he repeated, ''are tightening around every segment'' of Guatemala. This was blatant communist aggression against the people of Guatemala and against the Western Hemisphere.[154]

Representative Frances Bolton had never before addressed Congress on matters Guatemalan; her specialty was the Middle East. But it required no great expertise, she asserted, to understand what was occurring in Guatemala. Though her language was less colorful than Wiley's, the gentlewoman from Ohio was every bit as inflamed. The expulsion of Gruson and Bannell was ''one more fact in evidence that the Government of Guatemala is Communist.'' Guatemala, she reminded her fellow representatives, ''is about four hours' flight from New Orleans and considerably less than that from the Panama Canal. We can only interpret the recent actions by the Guatemalan Government as an open threat to the way of life we in this country—and most of our neighbors—hold dear.''[155]

Representative Donald Jackson, chairman of the House Subcommittee on Inter-American Affairs, considered himself an expert on Latin America. He now rose to denounce a grave error: two U.S. military missions were still operating in Guatemala. Unaware that his protest would make the planners of PBSUCCESS shudder, he demanded that the missions be withdrawn at once:

> The obvious purpose of such training missions in any country is to strengthen the ability of a nation to withstand aggression from without and generally to contribute to the overall defenses of the free world. Obviously, in the instance of Guatemala, there is no further purpose to be served in the training of the armed services to withstand outside aggression in light of the fact that the principal forces of world slavery and confusion are already at work within the country and in the rear of the military establishment. . . . The military leaders of the nation approve and support the actions of the Red-dominated government.[156]

Other members of Congress advocated economic sanctions. On February 8, Senator Margaret Chase Smith introduced Senate Resolution 211. The resolution stated the apparently twin points that the price of Guatemalan coffee was exorbitant and that the communists dominated the economic and political affairs of Guatemala. Eisenhower should ''take such action as may be required to exclude from importation into the United States all coffee originating in the Republic of Guatemala until such time as he is satisfied that (1) the economic and political affairs of that country no longer are dominated and controlled by

[154] Wiley, Jan. 14, 1954, *CR*-Senate, pp. 248–50 (quoted from p. 248); Fulbright (D-Ark), Feb. 1, 1954, ibid., p. 1073; Wiley, Feb. 4, 1954, ibid., pp. 1321–23 (quoted from p. 1322).

[155] Bolton (R-Ohio), Feb. 3, 1954, *CR*-House, p. 1258.

[156] Jackson (R-Cal), Feb. 25, 1954, ibid., pp. 2305–7 (quoted from p. 2306).

the Communist movement, and (2) the unjustified prices of coffee imposed by producers in that country have been undercut to reasonable levels.''[157]

In Guatemala, the resolution was attacked bitterly in both the administration and the opposition press, while the landed elite vehemently rejected any insinuation that the high price of coffee might be due to communist manipulations.[158] Throughout Latin America, the response was indignation. The prospect of U.S. economic sanctions rekindled deep fears. The Coffee Committee of the OAS's Inter-American Economic and Social Council immediately adopted a resolution condemning a coffee boycott. On February 11, the council voted to give this resolution the ''widest dissemination''; foes as bitter as Trujillo's Dominican Republic and Arbenz's Guatemala voted as one, while the lone dissenting vote was cast by the United States.[159]

Nor was Smith's resolution welcomed by the Eisenhower administration. The State Department had earlier considered and rejected a coffee embargo. It would be difficult to enforce, they reckoned, and in a seller's market (as was coffee at the time), Guatemala would find alternative buyers—whereas the political costs for the United States would be high. It might hurt the present regime in Guatemala a little economically, but it would give that regime a good weapon to attack our economic imperialism throughout the hemisphere,'' Assistant Secretary Cabot had noted.[160]

The planners of PBSUCCESS were equally unenthusiastic: Senator Smith was not the first, nor would she be the last, to suggest that the administration adopt economic sanctions against Guatemala, and these suggestions they consistently rejected. In a Janus-faced approach, they sought to frighten the Guatemalans with the specter of sanctions and yet to assure the Latin Americans that the United States would not impose unilateral sanctions.[161] Furthermore, ''the

[157] Smith (R-Maine), Feb. 8, 1954, *CR*-Senate, p. 1475.

[158] ''Boycot al café de Guatemala sería 'inoperante,' '' *El I*, Feb. 9, 1954, p. 1; ''El boycot al café perjudica no solo América, sino a los EU,'' *DCA*, Feb. 10, 1954, p. 8; ''La propuesta de la senadora Smith,'' *Prensa Libre*, Feb. 10, 1954, p. 2; ''La senadora Smith desconoce las realidades económicas,'' *La Hora*, Feb. 9, 1954, p. 1; *JW* 6, Feb. 12, 1954, pp. 1, 3–4; Wardlaw to DOS, no. 706, Feb. 15, 1954, NA 814.2333. The editor of the opposition paper *Prensa Libre* became ''excited and irrational over the . . . proposed boycott,'' a U.S. official reported. ''He was absolutely furious.'' (MemoConv [Urist, Pedro Julio García], Feb. 26, 1954, RG84 G&C, Box 4, NA-S.)

[159] ''Americas Issue Coffee Warning,'' *NYT*, Feb. 12, 1954, p. 1.

[160] Cabot to McDermott, Sept. 12, 1953, *FRUS*, 1952–1954, 4:1009; see also MemoConv (''Guatemalan Coffee''), Nov. 25, 1953, ibid., pp. 1088–91. For a thorough exposition of the arguments against coffee sanctions, see Department of Commerce to Wiley, [Mar. 1954], filed in NA 714.001, and Department of Agriculture to Wiley, enclosed in Hyde to Brown, Apr. 7, 1954, NA Lot 58D18 & 58D78, Box 1.

[161] When Peurifoy urged the abrogation of the trade treaty with Guatemala, Dulles cabled: ''Department desires avoid action suggestive of unilateral economic sanc-

intelligence community was very skeptical of the efficacy of economic sanctions."[162]

Senator Smith's proposal was particularly untimely, a confidential State Department memorandum noted. "On the eve of the Caracas conference, the Communist-influenced Government of Guatemala is thus served the most perfectly tailor-made issue it could seek in order to disrupt the conference."[163] On behalf of the State Department, Thruston Morton, assistant secretary for congressional affairs, hastened to explain to Congress that the high price of Guatemalan coffee was due not to communist machinations, but to the worldwide coffee shortage; the exclusion of Guatemalan coffee would be likely to further inflate coffee prices in the United States. "I do not feel," he concluded, "that the proposed measure would be advisable at the present time."[164] The Smith resolution did not resurface.

Congressman Jackson, perhaps enlightened by the CIA, dropped the subject of U.S. military missions in Guatemala. He seized instead on another idea. It was true, he conceded in a February 25 speech, that a coffee embargo would violate the 1936 Reciprocal Trade Agreement with Guatemala. But no one could rob the American people of their right to express their opposition to the Red plague. American companies should refuse to sell oil and gasoline to Soviet Guatemala; America's housewives should refuse to buy Guatemalan coffee; and the nations of the OAS, too, should demonstrate their love of freedom. Within a few days they would assemble at Caracas. There, they must adopt strong measures against the Arbenz regime, lest Caracas become "the Munich of our hemisphere." Let no one deny the truth: "The Soviet threat in Guatemala is aggression and as surely so as if it were backed by the bayonets of the Red army."[165]

While in the United States, the victim was branded as the aggressor, in Managua, Somoza responded to the publication of Delgado's incriminating documents with furious denials and *macho* defiance. For many years, he claimed, he had been the target of plots abetted by Guatemala, "but I don't complain because I have prepared a welcoming committee for those who

---

tions." (Dulles to AmEmG, no. 1194, June 8, 1954, NA 714.00. See also Peurifoy to SecState, June 2, 1954, *FRUS*, 1952–1954, 4:1156.)

[162] Interview with Hyman of the OIR who adds: "In 1953, the question was put to us as to what economic sanctions against Guatemala would be available and feasible (coffee, etc.). We decided in the negative." The attitude of the intelligence community toward economic sanctions, and particularly toward their usefulness in Guatemala, was confirmed in interviews with Kirkpatrick and Bissell. For the special case of oil, see below, p. 376.

[163] "The Coffee Problem as It Affects Communist Plans in Guatemala," p. 2, NA Lot 57D95, Box 5.

[164] Morton to Sen. Potter, Feb. 12, 1954, *CR*-Senate, Feb. 17, 1954, pp. 1896–97.

[165] Feb. 25, 1954, *CR*-House, pp. 2305–7 (quoted from p. 2307).

threaten the peace and security of Nicaragua. I am ready for them."[166] Undersecretary Smith hastened to soothe the ruffled dictator: "Inform President," he cabled the U.S. embassy in Managua, "this Government . . . applauds Somoza's . . . strong rejection of false Guatemalan accusations." In Costa Rica, the prestigious *La Nación* ridiculed the alleged plot: "Anyone who has followed developments in Guatemala over the last month will appreciate the true meaning of these accusations."[167]

Few in Guatemala had *La Nación*'s insight. The evidence presented by the Arbenz administration seemed highly persuasive, and the State Department's denials sounded even more hollow than had those of Peurifoy a few weeks earlier. The Guatemalan government scored a moral victory—for Washington's lies were transparent—but it had also suffered a severe defeat. By exposing U.S. plotting, it had exacerbated the fears of many military officers and administration politicians. Worse, the threats and the abuse of the United States press and Congress in response to the plot revelations dashed the hope that American public opinion might restrain Eisenhower's hand.

Arbenz reacted with defiance, pledging that his administration would not retreat one step.[168] Meanwhile, *Diario de Centro América* assailed the State Department's hypocrisy and lambasted the ignorance and the arrogance of American journalists and congressmen alike. "The Success of Our Revolution Has Aroused the Imperialists' Anger," "The Imperialists Distrust Any Manifestation of Patriotism," "The U.S. Spouts a Language That Befits a Master": these are the titles of the articles that filled the pages of *DCA* in those tense days.[169]

It was a dignified response. But should the weak challenge the mighty, particularly when the latter is stalking? For many of his supporters, Arbenz's defiance inspired not pride but anxiety.[170] This anxiety was heightened by the fear of what might happen at Caracas, where the Tenth Inter-American Conference was about to begin.

[166] "Embajador nica lleva la respuesta," *La Prensa*, Managua, Jan. 31, 1954, p. 1 (quoted from p. 2). See also AmEm Managua, Welch to SecState, no. 80, Feb. 2, 1954, NA 714.00; and AmEm Managua, Welch to DOS, no. 306, Feb. 9, 1954.

[167] Smith to AmEm Managua, no. 72, Feb. 1, 1954, NA 714.00; "Los complots internacionales contra Guatemala" (edit.), *La Nación*, San José, Feb. 2, 1954, p. 6.

[168] "Arbenz afirma su fé en la victoria contra traidores," *DCA*, Feb. 2, 1954, p. 1; "Guatemala Chief Hits Critics in U.S.," *NYT*, Feb. 5, 1954, p. 6; Krieg to DOS, no. 677, Feb. 8, 1954, NA 714.00.

[169] *DCA*: Feb. 5, 8, and 9, 1954, always p. 1.

[170] Confirmed by the testimonies of virtually all the Guatemalans interviewed by the author.

CHAPTER 12

The Caracas Conference

Two VIEWS clashed at Caracas. The Latin American governments sought U.S. aid in the form of development loans, higher prices for their raw materials, and easier access to the U.S. market. These had been their demands since the end of the Second World War. They had been repeatedly rebuffed by the Truman administration, which gave less aid to the twenty Latin American countries combined than to Belgium and Luxembourg. Privately, U.S. officials derided the Latin Americans' "deplorable tendency to extend their empty palms collectively in our direction";[1] publicly, they stated that what these countries needed was private investment, not U.S. loans. The Latin Americans were told to create a suitable climate for foreign investment. Economic nationalism was counterproductive, and any laws that violated free trade and investment principles must be expunged.

Predictably, the niggardliness and the haughtiness of the Truman administration stirred resentment in Latin America. In the 1952 presidential campaign, Eisenhower chided the Truman administration for its failed Latin American policy. He promised change.[2]

In the first year of the Eisenhower administration, a new development added to the Latin Americans' plight. The region's postwar economic growth "had ended abruptly."[3] Overall GNP had declined in real terms in 1952 and barely returned to the 1951 level in 1953. Meanwhile, the population continued to increase by 2.5 percent each year. Caracas was the Latin Americans' hope; from the unsavory dictators of the Caribbean to the democratic government of Uruguay, all agreed that, this time, the United States had to address their grievances.

Hope was edged with fear. The Latin Americans were convinced that Washington was preparing to violate the principle of nonintervention. To American journalists, these fears were patently anachronistic: couldn't the Latins see that since FDR, the United States had forsworn interference in the affairs of its sisters? But the Latin Americans saw instead the rising fury of the United States toward Guatemala and the documents released by Arbenz that pointed

---

[1] Assistant Secretary Miller to his father, Mar. 30, 1951, Miller Papers, Box 5, TL.

[2] For an excellent analysis of the economic relations between the Truman administration and Latin America, see Rabe, "Elusive Conference." For Eisenhower's criticism of Truman, see Rabe, *Eisenhower and Latin America*, p. 6.

[3] NSC 5407, Feb. 17, 1954, *FRUS*, 1952–1954, 4:209.

to a U.S. conspiracy. At Caracas, they expected Foster Dulles to try to loosen the legal knots that had been woven in the inter-American fabric in order to restrain the United States. To some Latin American governments, this would have been an acceptable price for Arbenz's fall, but a majority sharply disagreed, more in dread of a dangerous precedent than in sympathy with the Guatemalans.

At its outset, the Eisenhower administration sensed that all was not well in Latin America. In March 1953, the National Security Council warned that there was a "drift in the area toward radical and nationalistic regimes" (NSC 144/1). Its recommendations, however, differed little from those of the past. The United States should encourage "Latin American governments to recognize that the bulk of the capital required for their economic development can best be supplied by private enterprise and that their own self-interest requires the creation of a climate which will attract private investment." The United States should refrain "from overt unilateral intervention in the internal political affairs of the other American states." This prescription, however, was not unconditional. NSC 144/1 included a sentence that is still routinely deleted from the public record: should the inter-American system "fail to protect vital United States national interests in this hemisphere, it is recognized that unilateral action by the United States may be necessary."[4] Eisenhower was "extremely pleased" with the document. "Let us all look for a new approach" to Latin America, he exhorted his cabinet.[5]

To this end, the president sent his brother and highly trusted adviser, Milton, on a well-publicized visit to ten South American republics in the summer of 1953. But Milton Eisenhower, despite his genuine sympathy for Latin America, failed to come up with any bold or imaginative ideas in the report he submitted to the president on his return. "Economic cooperation," he stressed, "is without question the key to better relations between the United States and the nations to the South." Economic aid should be granted in par-

---

[4] "United States Objectives and Courses of Action with Respect to Latin America," NSC 144/1, Mar. 18, 1953, ibid., pp. 6–10, quotations from pp. 6, 8, and 7. The sentence on unilateral intervention has been deleted from the copy of NSC 144/1 deposited at the Eisenhower Library and from *FRUS* (see ibid., p. 7) but can be found in "Discussion at the 137th Meeting of the National Security Council on Wednesday, Mar. 18, 1953," Mar. 19, 1953, p. 12, WF, NSC Series, Box 4, EL. This document states unequivocally that NSC 144 was adopted by the NSC "subject to the following changes," which include the sentence on unilateral action. The document concludes with the statement: "NSC 144 as amended subsequently circulated as NSC 144/1" (ibid.). See also "Minutes of the 137th Meeting of the National Security Council," p. 4, White House Office, Special Assistant for National Security Affairs: Records 1952–61, NSC Series, Administration Subseries, Box 1, EL.

[5] See "Discussion at the 137th Meeting," *FRUS*, 1952–1954, 4:3, and Eisenhower, Handwritten Minutes of the July 3, 1953 Cabinet Meeting, unpaginated, White House Office, Staff Secretary: Records, 1952–1961, Cabinet Series, Box 1, EL.

ticular circumstances, and U.S. trade policy must respect the legitimate interests of the Latin Americans. The emphasis, however, was on private capital. U.S. companies, Milton Eisenhower noted, were already playing "an important role in promoting better understanding and friendship among the peoples of the American republics." Unfortunately, most Latin American governments were not yet reciprocating with fair treatment of American capital.[6]

Dr. Eisenhower's analysis was not such as to stir U.S. policymakers into action. The true difficulty in U.S. relations with Latin America, he argued, lay not in the policies of the United States, but in the Latin Americans' "misunderstanding and lack of information" about U.S. economic policy. "Fortunately," he stated, "the misunderstandings we found with respect to economic affairs are not matched in other areas. We were delighted to find a growing understanding of the United States as a nation and as a people . . . [and a] genuine pride in the Inter-American system." With one exception, the Latin American republics "share our desire for peace, freedom, and independence, and continue to cooperate effectively in the political councils of the world." The exception was Guatemala, which "has succumbed to Communist infiltration."[7]

More instrumental than Dr. Eisenhower in shaping the administration's economic policy toward Latin America was Secretary of the Treasury George Humphrey. "One of Eisenhower's closest and most trusted advisers," Humphrey was a rock of conservative orthodoxy and a champion of economic retrenchment. "On fiscal matters he was even more conservative than the president."[8] His formula for assisting the region was straightforward: "If we could find a few first-rate business men and send them as our ambassadors to the key Latin American nations, it would do far more good than any amount of money we could dole out."[9] Both President Eisenhower and Secretary Dulles tended to share Humphrey's views. "I want you to devise an imaginative policy for Latin America—but don't spend any money," Dulles warned Assistant Secretary Cabot in early 1953.[10] Foreign aid, the president explained to his brother, was appropriate only for those countries directly threatened by "the Communist menace."[11] Other than in Guatemala, however, the communist

---

[6] "Report to the President: United States–Latin American Relations," Nov. 18, 1953, pp. 17 and 29, DP:SS, Box 4, EL.

[7] Ibid., pp. 15, 14, 16, and 6.

[8] Kaufman, *Trade and Aid*, p. 30. This is the best study of Eisenhower's foreign aid policy. See also Rostow, *Eisenhower, Kennedy, and Foreign Aid*, pp. 75–151. On aid to Latin America during the Eisenhower administration, see Rabe, *Eisenhower and Latin America*, and Zoumaras, "Eisenhower's Foreign Economic Policy."

[9] "Discussion at the 137th Meeting," *FRUS*, 1952–1954, 4:4.

[10] Cabot, *First Line*, p. 87.

[11] DDE to Milton, Dec. 1, 1954, quoted in Rabe, *Eisenhower and Latin America*, p. 65.

threat in the hemisphere seemed too remote to require medicine, and in Guatemala, by contrast, the threat had progressed too far for anything but surgery.

It is not surprising, then, that Foster Dulles traveled to Caracas bereft of economic concessions or proposals. His one concern was his anticommunist resolution, the attack on Guatemala. In February 1954, a State Department memorandum had posited: "The minimum United States objective at Caracas with respect to the Communist item is to achieve adoption of a resolution which will lay ground work for subsequent positive action against Guatemala by the Organization of American States. Our maximum objective would be the adoption, should conditions permit, of effective multilateral measures against Guatemala."[12] By the time the conference convened, U.S. policymakers, aware of the Latin Americans' suspicions, had decided to focus on the minimum objective outlined in the February memo: the "adoption of a resolution which, without mentioning Guatemala by name, . . . would in effect express the serious concern of the OAS over the penetration of Communism in Guatemala and would lay the necessary ground work for subsequent positive multilateral action."[13] The mere prospect of collective sanctions, they reasoned, would demoralize Arbenz's supporters in Guatemala. It was only fitting that Secretary Dulles, in preparing his keynote speech for Caracas, sought the assistance of his brother Allen, the director of the CIA.[14]

As the seat of one of the most repressive dictatorships of the hemisphere, Caracas was not the most appropriate venue for a meeting of the OAS, an organization that boasted about its devotion to democracy. In Latin America several legislative assemblies, labor and political organizations, and major newspapers had demanded that if Pérez Jiménez wanted to host the conference, he must first free his political prisoners and restore basic political freedoms. President Figueres was blunt: Costa Rica would not send a delegation to Caracas.[15]

Few in the United States had shared these scruples. The U.S. Congress, vociferous on behalf of Guatemalan democracy, was apparently unaware that Pérez Jiménez was a dictator. The State Department firmly supported meeting in the Venezuelan capital and denounced any contrary view as interference in the internal affairs of a sister republic.

To many Latin Americans, this lofty stance was a poor disguise: Washing-

---

[12] "Guatemala and the Discussion of Communism at the Tenth Inter-American Conference," Feb. 10, 1954, *FRUS*, 1952–1954, 4:290.

[13] Ibid., p. 292.

[14] TelConv (JFD, AWD), Feb. 25, 1954, 11:10 a.m., John Foster Dulles Files, ML.

[15] See Figueres et al. to the Secretary of the OAS, enclosed in AmEm San José, Cohen to DOS, no. 639, Feb. 19, 1954, RG84 G&C, Box 2, NA-S; Betancourt, "La opinión continental"; Inman, *Inter-American Conferences*, pp. 257, 259; Kolb, *Democracy and Dictatorship*, pp. 127–28 and 135–39.

ton's best friends in the hemisphere were the dictators, men like Pérez Jiménez. Their cynicism was well founded. "I was glad we were meeting in Venezuela," Secretary Dulles told a House committee. "Venezuela is a country which has adopted the kind of policies which we think that the other countries of South America should adopt. Namely, they have adopted policies which provide in Venezuela a climate which is attractive to foreign capital to come in." If all Latin America followed suit, the danger of communism and social disorder would disappear.[16] President Eisenhower had honored the dictator with the Legion of Merit for his "spirit of collaboration and friendship toward the United States," his encouragement of the "expansion of foreign investments . . . his constant concern toward the problem of Communist infiltration," and his recognition of the "similarity of interests of the United States and Venezuela."[17]

The jails of Venezuela were still packed with political prisoners, and the ruthless repression continued as the delegations of the United States and nineteen Latin American republics assembled in the magnificent Aula Magna of the University of Caracas. At 4 p.m. on March 1, 1954, as Pérez Jiménez welcomed his illustrious guests, the Tenth Inter-American Conference opened. The battle would now begin.

The Guatemalan delegation had left for Caracas optimistic. "We were confident," recalls Foreign Minister Guillermo Toriello, "that the countries of Latin America would rally around us and reject Dulles' proposal because that was the only way to preserve the inter-American system." Mexico, Argentina, Chile, Uruguay, and probably Bolivia would vote with Guatemala; several other countries would abstain, and Dulles' resolution would fall short of the required two-thirds majority.[18] This was also the thinking of Arbenz and most leaders of his administration, including those of the PGT. This confidence had sustained them through the first two months of 1954, as the press, the Congress, and the administration of the United States intensified their verbal onslaught, and the pressure became "brutal." Caracas would demonstrate to the Americans, and to those Guatemalans whose loyalty was increasingly frayed, that Latin America stood behind Guatemala, firm in defense of the principle of nonintervention.[19] For weeks now, *Diario de Centro América* had been delivering this message of hope to a population that heard only dire warnings from the opposition press. "Today it is Guatemala," wrote *DCA*. "Who

---

[16] Quotations from U.S. Congress, *HCFA*, p. 516, and Smith, *The United States and Cuba*, p. 184.

[17] Kolb, *Democracy and Dictatorship*, pp. 142–43.

[18] Interviews with Toriello (quoted) and Noriega Morales, another member of the delegation.

[19] Interviews with María de Arbenz, Guerra Borges (quoted), Fortuny, and Charnaud.

knows what country will be next? This is the burning question on the minds of all Latin American officials, while their people are demanding that they resist anything that smacks of aggression against Guatemala." At Caracas, Dulles would be defeated.[20]

On March 4, Foster Dulles addressed the conference. He quoted Bolívar, stressed Eisenhower's deep concern for the economic well-being of Latin America and assailed the international communist conspiracy that threatened the hemisphere. "The danger mounts," he warned, and he proffered his anti-communist resolution.[21] Its key passage read: "The domination or control of the political institutions of any American state by the international Communist movement . . . would constitute a threat to the sovereignty and political independence of the American states, endangering the peace of America, and would call for appropriate action in accordance with existing treaties."[22] Among these existing treaties was that of Rio, which stipulated that diplomatic and economic sanctions were mandatory when supported by a two-thirds majority.

Toriello rose to respond. Never before had a banana republic dared to challenge the United States in an international forum. Dulles had spoken of the menace of communism—but Toriello spoke of the menace of the United States. Dulles had sought to enrobe his country in the PanAmerican mantle, but Toriello assailed the arrogant meddling of the United States in the internal affairs of the Latin American republics. Dulles's resolution, he argued, was not aimed at a threat from across the seas: it was aimed at Guatemala. It sought to legitimize aggression. Guatemala's only sin, Toriello concluded, was its attempt to assert its sovereignty.[23]

[20] "La intervención: Amenaza para todos los gobiernos," *DCA*, Feb. 11, 1954, p. 1. The following is a representative sample of articles from *DCA*: "México está con Guatemala," Dec. 17, 1953, p. 4; "Pueblo haitiano concede a Arbenz la más alta prueba de amistad," Dec. 28, 1953, p. 8; "Chile solidario con Guatemala," Jan. 8, 1954, p. 1; "Defensa de nuestra revolución," Jan. 18, 1954, p. 1; "Trabajadores bolivianos con Guatemala," Feb. 1, 1954, p. 1; "Buena impresión dejó en Haiti nuestra delegación especial," ibid., p. 8; "Solidaridad continental con la democracia guatemalteca," Feb. 5, 1954, p. 1; "Sociedad de amigos de Guatemala en Bolivia," ibid.; "Personalidades chilenas repudian la intervención," ibid.; "Responden los parlamentarios de Ecuador y de Costa Rica," ibid.; "Solidaridad del continente con Guatemala," ibid., p. 3; "Senadores chilenos pronuncianse en favor de Guatemala," Feb. 10, 1954, p. 1; "Cárdenas está con Guatemala," Feb. 11, 1954, p. 1; "Costa Rica contra la intervención," Feb. 13, 1954, p. 1; "Bolivia solidaria con Guatemala," Feb. 16, 1954, p. 1; "Caluroso recibimiento tributado al Dr Arévalo," ibid.; "Rechazo a moción contra Guatemala," Feb. 17, 1954, p. 4.

[21] "Address by the Secretary of State at the Second Plenary Session," Mar. 4, 1954, in DOS, *Tenth Inter-American Conference*, pp. 43–51, quoted from p. 45.

[22] Ibid., p. 157.

[23] See "Address by His Excellency Guillermo Toriello Garrido, Minister of Foreign

The applause that greeted Toriello's speech, wrote the *New York Times*, was almost twice as long as that received by Dulles.[24] "He said many of the things some of the rest of us would like to say if we dared," observed a South American delegate.[25]

At Caracas, Toriello became a hero—but he had been dragged to glory. For he spoke words that he had not intended to speak. At Arbenz's request, a few weeks before the conference convened, the Foreign Ministry and the PGT had each presented a draft of the address that Toriello would deliver at Caracas. One was prepared by José Luis Mendoza, a senior Foreign Ministry official; the other was written for the PGT by Guerra Borges, a man of evident literary talents.[26] Mendoza sought to avoid a direct challenge to the United States and wrote in sober, legalistic terms. Over Toriello's objections, Arbenz chose Guerra Borges's draft, more passionate, more direct, openly crying out the bitterness of Guatemala's wounded nationalism and its abhorrence of U.S. arrogance.

As the Guatemalan delegation left for Caracas, Arbenz was uneasy. Would Toriello, who did not belong to his inner circle, spurn his instructions and deliver Mendoza's speech?[27] When Julio Estrada de la Hoz, secretary general of the PAR, left Guatemala to join the delegation at Caracas, he received an urgent message from Arbenz: he must make sure that Toriello obeyed his orders.

In Caracas, Estrada de la Hoz found the delegation in turmoil. Two of its members, Carlos González Orellana and Julio Gómez Padilla, were preparing to return to Guatemala in protest; Toriello had decided to use Mendoza's draft. But on March 5, when Toriello addressed the conference, his speech was that of Guerra Borges. Estrada de la Hoz's intervention had succeeded.

In 1944, Toriello had been one of the most impassioned speakers of the youth that had challenged Ubico. As ambassador to Washington from 1952 to January 1954, however, he had sought to assuage the Americans' growing anger. Now at Caracas, listening to the thunderous applause that greeted his speech, he reverted to the young man of 1944. Eagerly assuming, then and forever, full credit for a speech he had been loath to deliver, he spoke, throughout the conference, with passion and daring. "The brilliant Toriello,"

Affairs of Guatemala, in the Third Plenary Session, March 5, 1954," in OAS, *Tenth Inter-American Conference*, Document 95.

[24] "Guatemala Lays Plotting to U.S.," *NYT*, Mar. 6, 1954, p. 1, quoted from p. 6.

[25] "Keeping Communists Out," *Time*, Mar. 15, 1954, p. 30.

[26] For the genesis of Toriello's speech: interviews with Fortuny, Guerra Borges, María de Arbenz, and Noriega Morales; another member of the delegation, Julio Gómez Padilla, refers to the episode in Quan Rossell, *Guatemala*, 1:375–77. Toriello's own account of the Caracas conference does not mention the origins of his speech. (*La batalla de Guatemala*, pp. 59–94.) For Guerra Borges's literary talents, see his articles in *Tribuna Popular*.

[27] Interviews with María de Arbenz, Fortuny, and Guerra Borges.

praised a Mexican magazine, "played the music we love and attacked the things we hate."[28]

The duel between Toriello and the American secretary of state dominated the first half of the conference. Foster Dulles, Eisenhower had noted in his diary, "is not particularly persuasive in presentation and, at times, seems to have a curious lack of understanding as to how his words and manner may affect another personality."[29] To most Latin Americans and to a handful of sensitive U.S. observers, these traits were very much in evidence at Caracas.

After days of debate, it was clear that the democratic and semidemocratic governments of Latin America—notably Uruguay, Chile, Mexico, and Argentina—were unimpressed with Dulles's arguments. Among Washington's staunchest supporters were Trujillo, Somoza, Pérez Jiménez, and Batista. "It was embarrassing to see all the minor dictatorships of Latin America rush to support the United States," complained *Hispanic American Report*.[30] From Montevideo, *Marcha* expressed the same truth more sardonically: "It is in Caracas, once the proud city of Bolívar, now the domain of Pérez Jiménez, that a conference to promote peace and assail dictatorship is being held. The representatives of Trujillo, Batista and Odría are leading the democratic wave."[31] Even Dulles conceded to a closed congressional hearing that "the support of the so-called dictator countries . . . was sometimes a bit embarrassing."[32]

After rejecting wide-ranging amendments submitted by Mexico, Argentina, and Uruguay, Dulles consented to an insignificant change proposed by Colombia. Henceforth, the last sentence of his key paragraph (". . . and would call for appropriate action in accordance with existing treaties") would read ". . . and would call for *a meeting of consultation* [of OAS foreign ministers] *to consider the adoption of* appropriate action in accordance with existing treaties." He also tacked a final paragraph onto the resolution: "This declaration of foreign policy made by the American Republics in relation to dangers originating outside this Hemisphere is designed to protect and not to impair the inalienable right of each American State freely to choose its own form of government and economic system and to live its own social and cultural life."[33]

On March 13, the resolution was approved. Seventeen countries voted in

[28] "Guatemala en Caracas," *Humanismo*, Mexico City, Mar.–May 1954, pp. 11–16, quoted from pp. 13, 15.

[29] Ferrell, *Eisenhower Diaries*, p. 237, entry of May 14, 1953.

[30] *Hispanic American Report*, Apr. 1954, p. 1.

[31] "La farsa continúa," *Marcha*, Montevideo, Mar. 12, 1954, p. 1.

[32] U.S. Congress, *HCFA*, p. 502. Dulles's testimony to the House committee upon his return from Caracas is on pp. 499–505. (See also pp. 521–36 for the testimony of Assistant Secretary Holland.)

[33] DOS, *Tenth Inter-American Conference*, pp. 156–58.

favor. Argentina and Mexico abstained. Costa Rica was absent, but Figueres immediately endorsed the resolution. Guatemala cast the lone negative vote.

The additional paragraph, remarks an American scholar, made the resolution "either inconsistent or meaningless."[34] This was not the view of the U.S. press, however, which hailed the vote as "a triumph for Secretary Dulles, for the United States and for common sense in the Western Hemisphere."[35] Nor was it the view of Dulles and his delegation: "We didn't see it [the additional paragraph] as a major qualifier; it was primarily Latin American window dressing—somehow they have to stress their independence."[36] And it was certainly not the view of the Latin Americans themselves: "We contributed our approval without enthusiasm, without optimism, and without feeling that we were contributing to the adoption of a constructive measure," averred a Uruguayan delegate.[37]

Caracas, lamented the prominent Mexican jurist Isidro Fabela, "marks a deplorable assault on the principle of nonintervention which is the keystone of PanAmericanism." How could the qualifier be significant when everyone knew that the people and the government of the United States believed that no communist regime could ever be established with the consent of the governed, and the mere possibility of such a regime, to paraphrase Congressman Jackson, was considered evidence of aggression as flagrant as if it had been perpetrated by Soviet bayonets? The Caracas resolution did not specify how to determine if a country was dominated by international communism. Today against Guatemala, later against another wayward country, the United States could invoke the resolution to summon a meeting of OAS foreign ministers and demand the imposition of multilateral sanctions. And if the Latin Ameri-

[34] Slater, *The OAS*, p. 120.

[35] "Victory at Caracas" (edit.), *NYT*, Mar. 14, 1954, p. E10. It was a "striking victory for freedom and self-government in this part of the world." ("Declaration of Caracas," edit., *WP*, Mar. 15, 1954, p. 10.)

[36] Interview with Jamison. See also Dulles' testimony in U.S. Congress, *HCFA*, p. 503, and in "Memorandum of Discussion at the 189th Meeting of the National Security Council on Thursday, Mar. 18, 1954," *FRUS*, 1952–1954, 4:306. See also "Third Progress Report on NSC 144/1," May 25, 1954, ibid., p.45: "The United States achieved its primary objective of obtaining a clear-cut policy statement against Communism." For a rare expression of dissent by a U.S. official, see a May 28, 1954, memorandum by Louis Halle, of the State Department's Policy Planning Staff: "The 17 votes for our anti-Communist resolution at Caracas were granted only after the resolution had been watered down to the point of saying virtually nothing, and then grudgingly" (ibid., p. 1148). Halle's point was accurate, but narrow; this was not the way the Guatemalans saw it (see below, pp. 277–78)—and perception was paramount.

[37] "Guatemala reafirma su actitud frente al voto anticomunista," *El I*, Mar. 16, 1954, p. 1 (quoted from p. 2).

cans had failed to restrain the United States at Caracas, asked Fabela, what guarantee was there that they could mount a more effective resistance at a later date? "It would not be impossible for the United States to get the necessary two thirds majority: there are dictators in our Latin America who are beholden to Washington."[38]

The imposing majority that voted for the Caracas resolution had not been swayed by, as *Time* patriotically averred, the "intellectual force of Dulles' arguments."[39] They had surrendered, instead, to "very severe arm twisting." Foster Dulles, recalls a senior U.S. official, "spared no effort and spared no blandishment to get this Caracas Resolution through."[40] Decades of submission and "sordid calculations . . . [based on] the hope of receiving a *quid pro quo* on economic issues"[41] ensured the pitiful capitulation.

Those Latin Americans who had sold Guatemala for the lure of U.S. dollars were robbed of the payment. One hour after his resolution had been approved, Dulles boarded the plane back to Washington. His abrupt departure, comments a member of his delegation, was seen by the Latin Americans as "one more example of callous U.S. indifference to their economic problems."[42] Manners aside, the secretary's continued presence would have served no purpose; the U.S. delegation had nothing to offer on economic matters. It made only one concession: a special meeting of the Economic and Social Council of the OAS would be held to address the Latin Americans' concerns in Rio de Janeiro in late 1954. (The Rio meeting, notes a Dulles aide, proved to be "one of the worst failures of any conference that we've ever had. It was just a completely negative thing from the beginning.")[43]

It was with deep frustration that the Latin American delegates left Caracas at the end of March. "Caracas was a fiasco," blurted the foreign minister of El Salvador with uncharacteristic boldness. "Nothing was achieved in economic matters. . . . The resolution should have been accompanied by con-

---

[38] Fabela, "La conferencia de Caracas," pp. 32, 12.

[39] "Keeping Communists Out," *Time*, Mar. 15, 1954, p. 30.

[40] Rubottom, "Oral History Interview," p. 9.

[41] *Hispanic American Report*, Apr. 1954, p. 1.

[42] Interview with Jamison.

[43] Rubottom "Oral History Interview," p. 29. See also Rabe, *Eisenhower and Latin America*, pp. 70–77. For Milton Eisenhower's critique of the U.S. position for the Rio Conference and the president's response, see Milton to DDE, Sept. 7, 1954, WF, Name Series, Box 12; Milton to DDE, Oct. 22, 1954, ibid.; DDE to Milton, Oct. 25, 1954, WF, DDE:DS, Box 8; MemoTel, Oct. 30, 1954, ibid., Box 7; MemoTel, Nov. 9, 1954, ibid.; MemoTel, Nov. 20, 1954, ibid.; Milton to DDE, Monday [n.d.], WF, Name Series, Box 12; DDE to Milton, Nov. 23, 1954, WF, DDE:DS, Box 8; Milton to DDE, Nov. 30, 1954, WF, Name Series, Box 12. See also TelConv (JFD, Milton), Oct. 27, 1954, 1:11 p.m., DP:TCS, Box 3; TelConv (Holland, JFD), Oct. 29, 12:40 p.m., ibid. All EL.

structive agreements on economic matters. What we need is better prices for our raw materials. . . . Only with better prices will we be able to give a better life to our people."[44]

In Guatemala, tens of thousands greeted Toriello as he marched from the airport to the presidential palace, a flag in his hand. "Our delegates bring us a great moral victory," stated Arbenz in his welcoming speech. Even "many anti-Government Guatemalans," reported DCM Krieg, "got a feeling of perverse national pride from the spectacle of Willy Toriello standing up to Mr. Dulles."[45]

As with the January plot revelations, moral victory was overshadowed by a psychological defeat. At Caracas, the delegates of Mexico and Argentina had spoken with passion against Dulles's resolution, but they had abstained from voting against it. Other delegations, like that of Uruguay, had openly expressed their displeasure, yet they had voted with Dulles. Seventeen votes in favor, one against—it was a crushing defeat. While Arbenz stressed that "at Caracas not only did we not surrender our independence, but we voiced the hopes of all the peoples of Latin America,"[46] many of his supporters, civilians as well as military, somberly reflected that moral victories and the applause of spectators are of little help against a powerful aggressor. "At Caracas, our delegates were courageous, and we applauded them," recalls a Guatemalan officer, "but the net effect of the conference on most Guatemalans was fear. It was all part of the psychological warfare against Guatemala. Our moral victory was pyrrhic."[47]

For all his brave words, for all his efforts to inspire confidence, Arbenz himself was deeply shaken by the vote. The whoops of triumph in the United States, and the expressions of regret and fear in Latin America provided the Greek chorus: Guatemala, standing alone, was being led inexorably to her fate. "Our ship had been crippled; we were slipping with dignity beneath the waves," María de Arbenz remembers. "Yes, this is the way the bell tolls."[48]

The fact that Dulles succeeded despite his rude behavior made the situation

[44] "Conferencia de Caracas fué un fracaso," *La Prensa Libre*, San José, Mar. 30, 1954, pp. 1, 14.

[45] Quotations from "Recepción triunfal se ofreció a Toriello," *El I*, Mar. 30, 1954, p. 1 (quoted from p. 6) and from Krieg to Peurifoy, "Considerations Regarding U.S. Policy towards Guatemala," Apr. 27, 1954, p. 2, RG84 G&C, Box 3, NA-S.

[46] "Texto del discurso pronunciado por el ciudadano Presidente de la República," *DCA*, May 3, 1954, p. 1 (quoted from p. 8). On the government's efforts to present Caracas as a success, see also *JW* 11, Mar. 19, 1954, pp. 1–2; *JW* 12, Mar. 26, 1954, p. 1; *JW* 13, Apr. 2, 1954, pp. 1–2.

[47] Interview with Paz Tejada. His analysis and conclusions have been confirmed by the overwhelming majority of the Guatemalans I have interviewed, both civilian and military, friends and foes of the regime.

[48] Interview with María de Arbenz.

seem even more hopeless to Arbenz's supporters. American brazenness had not rallied the Latin American delegates. If an emboldened Eisenhower should strike Guatemala, what would the sister republics do? They would lament the aggression, certainly, but their lamentations would be of little comfort. The Guatemalans would pay the price of their loyalty to President Arbenz.

Some revolutionary politicians responded to the rising American threat with spasms of nationalism. Many more rued Arbenz's defiant stance. The president's ties with the PGT, always distasteful, were now dangerous. Inchoate ideas floated among many administration politicians: the revolution must take a step backward in order to pacify Washington; Arbenz should loosen his ties with the communists; some PGT leaders should leave the country for an extended "period of study"; others should renounce their positions in the bureaucracy; the agrarian reform should be slowed, if not altogether halted.

Few dared broach these ideas with Arbenz; when they did, the reaction was so negative as to paralyze any further attempt.[49] Deep malaise descended over the revolutionary camp. Without openly breaking with the regime, many politicians began to distance themselves from it. Meanwhile, unbeknownst to them and to most of his government, Arbenz had a daring plan.

[49] Interviews with María de Arbenz, Fortuny, Charnaud, Galich, and Guerra Borges.

CHAPTER 13

The Agony of the Regime

THE UNITED STATES had refused to sell weapons from Guatemala since 1949. In 1951 it began to frustrate the attempts of the Arbenz administration to buy weapons from other countries, to the dismay of the Guatemalan officer corps. This dismay, however, was not shared by Jacobo Arbenz, his public protestations notwithstanding. "Jacobo was not eager to buy weapons for the army," recalls his wife. "He was afraid that the officers would become overconfident and use them against him or the people."[1]

Nevertheless, in October 1953, when Arbenz learned from the documents delivered by Delgado that the United States was plotting his overthrow, he and the Secretariat of the PGT responded with a desperate gamble. Secretly, they would import weapons from Czechoslovakia, and secretly, some of these weapons would be given to the PGT to arm workers' militias should the need arise. It would be the first time that Arbenz had breached the army's monopoly of weapons and the first time that a Soviet bloc country had sent arms to the Western Hemisphere. The project was dangerous, for its discovery could trigger a military coup. But Arbenz felt he had little choice. Fear of the United States threatened to undermine the army's loyalty.[2]

Strict secrecy would be maintained. The military would learn that the weapons had reached Guatemala only after the arms earmarked for the PGT had been spirited away; it would not be told the true origin of the shipment. No cabinet member would be informed.[3] The PGT alone knew of the operation.

On November 16, an opposition paper reported that Fortuny had been spotted a week earlier in Mexico City boarding a plane for Vienna. He had been

[1] Interview with María de Arbenz; confirmed by Fortuny.

[2] Interviews with Fortuny, María de Arbenz, Guerra Borges, and Alejandro. Arbenz stated in a 1968 interview: "Because the threat was growing, I decided to get weapons from Czechoslovakia, so that I could arm the workers if necessary. . . . I did not inform the army." (Arbenz, "Habla Arbenz," p. 122.) As Fortuny notes, the PGT "had a great deal of influence among the dockers of Puerto Barrios." (Interview with Fortuny.) There is no agreement among my sources as to the exact percentage of weapons to be set aside for the civilians; their recollections vary from 25 percent to 50 percent of the total. In any case, these weapons were to be rifles and a few machine guns; the army would also receive heavier equipment such as mortars. The weapons set aside would be hidden in Arbenz's finca and in PGT safe houses.

[3] Confirmed by interviews with Interior Minister Charnaud and Army Chief of Staff Parinello.

on his way to Moscow to participate in the November 7 celebrations of the thirty-sixth anniversary of the Bolshevik revolution, responded the PGT daily, *Tribuna Popular*.[4] The U.S. embassy in Guatemala conscientiously relayed the information to Washington; it became an article of faith for U.S. officials that in November 1953 Fortuny had gone to the Soviet Union. And yet, as Ronald Schneider has pointed out, *Tribuna Popular* "did not explain how he [Fortuny] could be in Mexico on the 9th and get to Moscow by the 7th," that is, in time for the celebrations.[5] In fact, Fortuny was headed for Prague.

Soon after his arrival, Fortuny was received by Antonín Novotný, first secretary of the Communist Party of Czechoslovakia. "I told Novotný," he recalls, "about the dangers that Guatemala was facing, and I asked him if Czechoslovakia would sell weapons to us." Fortuny also explained that the weapons were not destined for the army alone, "but that we would keep some of them in case it became necessary to arm the people." If Novotný agreed, a Guatemalan military expert would arrange the details of the transaction later.[6]

Novotný was profuse in his expressions of sympathy for the struggle of the Guatemalan people; his government would study Fortuny's request. "He told me that he could not make any promises, but that I should trust him, and he assured me, 'You will not leave empty-handed.' " Fortuny waited: "I thought that they would reply in a week or two at most, but after more than fifteen days had gone by, I decided that the Czechs must be consulting the Soviets, and I asked them to arrange a trip to Moscow for me. I didn't tell them, but I had decided that it would be better if I talked directly to the Russians." The Czechs were noncommittal; they would transmit his request, they said. A few days later, a curt answer arrived: "They told me that it was not necessary to go to Moscow."

Ten more days passed before Fortuny was finally informed that Czechoslovakia would sell weapons to Guatemala. On January 8, 1954, he was back home after an absence of more than two months.[7] The unexpected length of

---

[4] "Rodeandose de completo misterio José Manuel Fortuny salió el 5 hacia Viena," *Prensa Libre*, Nov. 16, 1953, p. 2; "El viaje de José Manuel Fortuny," *Tribuna Popular*, Nov. 17, 1953, p. 5.

[5] Schneider, *Communism*, p. 100, n. 6.

[6] The account of Fortuny's stay in Prague and the quotations in this and the subsequent paragraphs are from interviews with Fortuny. Guerra Borges, Alejandro, and María de Arbenz confirmed Fortuny's account.

[7] "Fortuny regresó ayer," *Tribuna Popular*, Jan. 9, 1954, p. 1. In reporting Fortuny's return, the U.S. embassy concluded, "His trip to Moscow was thus of over two months duration." (Krieg to DOS, no. 583, Jan. 11, 1954, NA 714.001. See also *JW* 2, Jan. 15, 1954, p. 2.) The embassy was more successful in keeping tabs on Fortuny after his return. On January 21, an embassy official reported to Peurifoy: "A source told me today that Arbenz and Fortuny spent the weekend of January 8–10 alone at Arbenz's 'El Cajón' finca. The source said this information was absolutely reliable as

his stay in Prague, Fortuny believes, was due to the fact that his hosts consulted Moscow, that both they and the Russians knew little of Guatemala, had
only loose ties with the PGT, and had more pressing concerns than the plight
of Jacobo Arbenz.

On January 19, 1954, a few days after Fortuny's return, an incident surprised
Guatemalan and foreign observers alike: the "mysterious departure" (to quote
the U.S. embassy) of retired army major Alfonso Martínez, the head of the
National Agrarian Department.[8] Martínez had boarded a plane for Mexico,
explaining that his final destination was Switzerland. "No family members or
government officials accompanied him to the airport," noted *La Hora*; his
departure, stressed *El Imparcial*, "took government officials by surprise."[9]

Rumors spread. In view of Martínez's prominence and of the well-known
fact that he was a close friend and protegé of Arbenz, the incident attracted
attention in Guatemala and abroad. Some believed that Martínez, who had
never fully recovered from a serious wound received at the Puente de la Gloria
on July 18, 1949, had left for medical reasons. (He had gone to Switzerland
for a check-up, a government communiqué stated flatly on January 23.) Many
more, including the U.S. embassy and the *New York Times*, were suspicious.[10]
It was no secret that Martínez resented the growing influence of the communists in "his" department of agrarian reform. It was also common knowledge
that on January 18, the day before he left, Martínez had had lunch with Arbenz
in a fashionable restaurant on the outskirts of the capital. No one had over-
heard their conversation, but they had appeared tense, agitated; they seemed
to be quarreling. The explanation was obvious: they had been arguing, *La
Hora* stated, about "matters related to the agrarian reform" and, in particular,
the role of the PGT. Arbenz had sided with the communists. The next day,
Martínez had left Guatemala.[11] "Lively rumors," reported the U.S. embassy
on February 1, ". . . continued to circulate in the press and among the public
throughout the week and those gaining the widest credence held that Martínez

---

he had obtained it from a personal employee of Arbenz." (Hill to Ambassador, Jan.
21, 1954, NA Lot 58D18 & 58D78, Box 1.) This information was correct. (Interviews
with Fortuny and María de Arbenz.)

[8] *JW* 4, Feb. 1, 1954, p. 1.

[9] "No dan importancia política al viaje del jefe del DAN a Suiza," *La Hora*, Jan.
20, 1954, p. 4; "Alfonso Martínez a México y de allí a Europa y a Suiza," *El I*, Jan.
19, 1954, p. 1.

[10] See esp. *JW* 3, Jan. 22, 1954, pp. 1, 2; *JW* 4, Feb. 1, 1954, pp. 1, 3–4; Krieg,
"Political Situation in Guatemala," Mar. 17, 1954, RG84 G&C, Box 3, NA-S; "Top
Arbenz Aide Quits Guatemala," *NYT*, Feb. 8, 1954, p. 7.

[11] "No dan importancia política al viaje del jefe del DAN a Suiza," *La Hora*, Jan.
20, 1954, p. 4.

had clashed with President Arbenz's pro-Communist views and had decided or been told to get out of the country."[12]

No one told the story with more flair than the influential *Diario de Hoy* in neighboring El Salvador. Like so many other politicians in Guatemala, Alfonso Martínez had "flirted with the communists: he cynically encouraged them, naively believing that it would always be possible to control them. He, like many others, ignored the fact that the Reds are Frankensteins who destroy those who help them." A disgraced Martínez had now fled Guatemala, "to seek refuge in democratic Switzerland." *Diario de Hoy* saw it as a cautionary tale: "Martínez was able to escape from the communists' clutches, but few have been so lucky. All those Central American 'leaders' who flirt with the Reds should be forewarned."[13]

On February 20, however, Martínez returned to Guatemala. "Smiling and relaxed" at a press conference, he explained that he had been in a Swiss sanatorium attending to a heart problem; "I didn't even visit Rome or Paris."[14] In fact, he was returning from Prague, the one and only destination of his trip.

Arbenz had asked Martínez to handle the technical aspects of the arms sale. The selection of Martínez, who had pressing and important duties as head of the agrarian reform, illustrates the extent of Arbenz's alienation from the officer corps. The thirty-one-year old Martínez was his friend. He was not a man of the left, but he owed his high position to Arbenz alone. The bond between them had been sealed by the death of Arana; it had been Martínez whom Arbenz had sent to arrest the rebel colonel on July 18, 1949. His loyalty and discretion were proven. Keenly intelligent, he would conduct the sensitive mission with skill. Arbenz believed that no other officer had comparable credentials.[15]

The secret of the mission would be best guarded, Arbenz concluded, if it were thought that Martínez had left Guatemala because of a rift with him. Hence the circumstances of Martínez's departure. He left without informing his closest aides; no government official went to the airport to see him off; once he had gone, the authorities remained silent for several days as rumors spread—only belatedly did they issue a brief communiqué. Extraneous events

---

[12] *JW* 4, Feb. 1, 1954, p. 3.

[13] "El caso del coronel Martínez y las maniobras rojas en Centro América," *Diario de Hoy*, San Salvador, Jan. 30, 1954, p. 7.

[14] Quotations from "Guatemala Aide Back, Denies Rift," *NYT*, Feb. 24, 1954, p. 12, and "Alfonso Martínez asumió nuevamente la jefatura del DAN," *El I*, Feb. 23, 1954, p. 1 (quoted from p. 2).

[15] Interviews with María de Arbenz and Fortuny were particularly helpful for the story of Arbenz and Martínez. On Martínez, see Rose, Military Attaché Report no. 1224, June 9, 1944, RG165 RF, Box 1574, NA-S; Schoenfeld to Miller, Aug. 13, 1951, NA Lot 53D26, Box 7; Hill, "Alfonso Martínez Estevez," Aug. 12, 1952, RG84 CF, Box 15, NA-S.

facilitated the deception. Martínez's relations with the PGT were indeed strained. Moreover, Guatemala City was tense. On January 11, Peurifoy's *Time* interview had appeared; in late January (just a few days after Martínez's departure) several plotters were arrested, and then the conspiracy abetted by the "Government of the North" was revealed. Even implausible rumors became credible.

Arbenz added a personal touch to the ploy. He and Martínez were not quarreling when they lunched together on January 18. They were acting, and Arbenz had purposefully chosen one of the most fashionable restaurants as the stage. The following day, after Martínez had boarded his plane, the luncheon quarrel and the departure would be linked.

What was not faked, however, was Martínez's satisfaction when he returned to Guatemala. Not only had the secret been maintained, but he brought back the news that Prague would soon send two thousand tons of light weapons seized from the Germans in the Second World War. Captured German equipment was common in Europe and would mask the identity of the supplier.[16] The Czechs would arrange the transportation. "Payment," Martínez later explained, "was made directly from the Banco de Guatemala to a secret account at the Union des Banques Suisses in Zurich." The first dispatch of weapons from the Soviet Bloc to Latin America was neither a gift nor a loan. It was a sale, to be paid, at once, in cash.[17]

Meanwhile, a debate was unfolding within the Secretariat of the PGT. It had begun in early 1954, and it reached its climax in the weeks following Caracas. Guatemala was besieged; how should the party respond?[18]

For Alfredo Guerra Borges, for Bernardo Alvarado Monzón, for Mario Silva Jonama, for José Luis Ramos—and for Alejandro, the Secretariat's nonvoting Cuban adviser—only one answer was possible: the revolution must accelerate. Too much effort had been spent; too many successes had been achieved; time and again the forces of reaction had been defeated; Guatemala could not capitulate to U.S. imperialism; the revolutionaries could not retreat. They drew comfort from the weakness of the domestic opposition and from their faith in the population's growing revolutionary fervor.

[16] The weapons were in satisfactory condition. (Interviews with Col. Parinello, Lt. Cols. Hernández and Mendizabal, and Maj. Paz Tejada.) For a list of the weapons, see Hanford, "Communist Beachhead," appendix 6.

[17] Alfonso Martínez, "En México se pelea duro el Arevalismo y Martínez Estévez," *La Hora*, Mar. 4, 1963, p. 7. The payment was made with funds from the budget of the Atlantic Highway. There is disagreement as to the exact amount paid. The most likely figure is $1 million. See also Hill to DOS, no. 269, Oct. 4, 1954, NA 714.00; Wardlaw to DOS, no. 328, Oct. 19, 1954, NA 714.00.

[18] My main sources for this debate are interviews with Fortuny, Guerra Borges, and Alejandro, as well as Fortuny, "Autocrítica."

And so the revolutionary process surged forward. The pace of the agrarian reform was accelerated in January 1954, particularly in the important department of Escuintla, where the PGT had considerable influence. While their eyes scanned the horizon for the ship with its secret cargo, these leaders of the PGT intended, with Arbenz's support, to create as many *faits accomplis* as possible and to stiffen the will of the people.

Fortuny found himself isolated within the Secretariat that he had once dominated. He had fully supported the decision to buy weapons from Czechoslovakia. Yet, as the weeks passed, he felt that his friends were failing to grasp the gravity of the threat facing Guatemala. He agreed with them that the regime could handily repel the forthcoming invasion led by Castillo Armas, but this, he believed, was only the overture. Washington would respond to Castillo Armas's defeat by intensifying its aggression—even, if necessary, by sending in the troops.

There was no way that Guatemala alone could defeat a U.S. invasion, and Guatemala was alone. Caracas had exposed her isolation, and the messages of support that had poured in from politicians, intellectuals, and trade unionists of several Latin American countries were of little solace.[19] Searching for a viable policy, Fortuny decided that the party should "exercise self-restraint": the pace of the agrarian reform should not be accelerated; those communists in highly visible government positions should resign for "reasons of health"; and the government and the PGT should moderate their rhetoric. He hoped that such steps would give pause to the United States so that after the defeat of Castillo Armas, Eisenhower would hesitate before ordering more extreme measures.

The lines of the debate were confused. Fortuny was hesitant. He was afraid that he might appear defeatist, and he was afraid that his policy had very little chance of success—that it was too little, too late. In the past, his self-assurance had been a powerful weapon; now it was shaken, and the other members of the Secretariat argued with the fervor of desperation. In his "Autocrítica," written a year after Arbenz fell, Fortuny bares the doubts that enfeebled his warnings: "I was aware that my influence in the Secretariat was waning. . . . I was also worried that my views might be considered cowardly and that they would split the Political Commission at a time when unity was essential. But also, I was not sure of myself; I was not sure that I was right. These were my inner thoughts, and I made the mistake of not voicing them."[20]

Sickness also sapped Fortuny's strength,[21] but more debilitating was his growing sense of impotence. His calls for "self-restraint" were spurned. On

---

[19] Many of these messages were published in *DCA*; still others can be found in the *GT*, esp. Box 5.

[20] Fortuny, "Autocrítica," pp. 2–3.

[21] Ibid., p. 1.

May 1, there was the traditional workers' parade, purportedly organized by the labor confederations, but directed in fact by the PGT. A gigantic portrait of Ho Chi Minh opened the march and set the tone.[22] This was a flagrant rejection of Fortuny's advice that the government should moderate its tone, a rejection made more painful by the fact that he had not even been consulted.

For some time, Fortuny recalls, he had been considering stepping down, at least temporarily, from the leadership of a Secretariat he no longer led. The only alternative was to bring the disagreements within the Secretariat to the attention of the Political Commission and the Central Committee (CC) of the PGT. This, he believed, would have been divisive precisely when unity was imperative; the move would have been particularly unjustified, he may have felt, since he was not confident that he had a viable policy to offer. He was also aware that most members of the CC and the Political Commission supported the stance of the majority of the Secretariat.

Fortuny, Alejandro counters, "did not resign of his own accord. He was asked to resign."[23] The other members of the Secretariat considered him "burnt out."[24] His poor health provided a convenient pretext. In two sessions of the Secretariat—one in late April, the other in early May—Fortuny repeated his reservations: "I was worried that the party might go beyond what was realistically possible, and no longer take into account the objective conditions of the struggle, the political level of the people, or the constraints on the government." Then he and the other Secretariat members agreed on the immediate solution: "I would be temporarily relieved of my post as secretary general for medical reasons."[25] He would remain, however, as the link between the party and Arbenz. The decision was relayed to the Political Commission and the CC of the PGT. The explanation focused on Fortuny's poor health and only alluded to political differences.[26] On May 27, the PGT publicly announced Fortuny's temporary withdrawal; Bernardo Alvarado Monzón would be secretary general *ad interim*.[27]

---

[22] See "Gigantesco desfile," *DCA*, May 3, p. 1; "El 1° de mayo: Una respuesta," ibid., p. 4; "Guatemalan Fete Is Anti-U.S. Affair," *NYT*, May 2, p. 32; "60 mil desfilaron," *Tribuna Popular*, May 4, p. 1; "Orden, júbilo marcan ritmo con carrozas en profusión," *El I*, May 3, p. 1. All 1954.

[23] Interview with Alejandro.

[24] Interview with Guerra Borges.

[25] Fortuny, "Autocrítica," pp. 2, 3.

[26] Ibid., pp. 3–4.

[27] "Reunión del Comité Central del PGT," *Tribuna Popular*, May 27, 1954, p. 1. For the views of the U.S. embassy, which was confounded by Fortuny's resignation, see Wardlaw to DOS, no. 994, June 9, 1954, NA 714.001. For the views of the opposition, which was equally confused, see "Resoluciones que, según los afiliados, pueden aliviar la posición del gobierno," *La Hora*, May 28, 1954, p. 1, and "Profunda escisión dentro del Partido Comunista trasciende," *El Espectador*, June 7, 1954, p. 1.

Arbenz was not aware of the debate within the Secretariat. "It is true," Fortuny stressed in his "Autocrítica," that "President Arbenz and I were very close friends . . . that we talked of very personal matters, but I did not discuss internal party business with him."[28] Fortuny's resignation was a blow to Arbenz. "Jacobo knew Fortuny wasn't telling him the whole truth," recalls Doña María, "but he respected Fortuny's discretion, and he didn't pursue the matter. But it did bother him."[29]

One may wonder whether Fortuny's silence was due solely to discretion. Had Fortuny been more sure that he had an alternative to offer, he might have been less reticent. As it was, until mid-June—roughly until Castillo Armas attacked—the two friends maintained a mutual silence about their worst fears, each perhaps wary of demoralizing the other, each perhaps afraid that had he voiced his deepest fears they would have become more real.[30]

Arbenz, like the PGT, believed that the army would remain loyal if faced with Castillo Armas. Like Fortuny, he looked beyond the exiles' attack. What would the United States do after Castillo's Armas's defeat? Caracas had shaken him. "Now we are truly in danger," he confided in a rare moment of openness to an old friend, Colonel Terencio Guillén, governor of the department of Escuintla. "We must press on with the agrarian reform. We have to get tangible benefits for the people, benefits that it will be very hard to take away. Please help me. We must do as much as we can."[31]

One suspects that had Arbenz sat on the Secretariat of the PGT, he would have sided against Fortuny, not because he did not share his fears, but because he saw no salvation in retreat. "We cannot relent," he told Guillén. "It is better to remain at our posts until we are overwhelmed than to retreat; if we must, let us die fighting. If we waver, we will be routed."[32]

In public and in private, Arbenz sought to strengthen the morale of the population and to rally administration politicians who fervently hoped for a step backward. In his March 1 annual message to Congress, in his address welcoming the return of the Caracas delegation, in his May 1 speech, he spoke as a man who was self-assured and in control. The revolution faced external difficulties, he conceded, but these could be overcome—through firmness, not retreat. He stood by his policies, he warned, and there would be no "step backward." (Privately, to the leaders of the PGT he pledged: "I will be by

[28] Fortuny, "Autocrítica," p. 6.

[29] Interview with María de Arbenz; interview with Fortuny confirmed Arbenz's reticence in asking questions about the internal affairs of the PGT.

[30] Interviews with María de Arbenz and Fortuny.

[31] Interview with Guillén. Interviews with María de Arbenz and Fortuny were very useful.

[32] Interview with Guillén.

your side until the end.'')[33] The U.S. embassy found him ''defiant,'' but neither shrill nor petulant.[34]

Yet Arbenz was anxious. He alternated between waves of deep pessimism and surges of optimism. His optimism, notes his wife, who was his closest confidante through those harrowing weeks, ''was a means of self-defense: it was better to grasp at straws than to be defeated psychologically before the final battle.''[35] In fact, Arbenz lived in a private world fraught with ghosts and contradictions, and nowhere were these contradictions more apparent than in the decision to import arms from Czechoslovakia. The weapons would build the morale of an army that had long been frustrated in its desire for new materiel. They would also increase its capacity to defeat a U.S. sponsored invasion of Guatemala. Yet the decision to set aside some of the weapons derived from mistrust of the very institution that would be strengthened by the remainder. In one stroke, Arbenz and the PGT were providing for a workers' militia they knew the army would never countenance, and they were giving the army weapons to crush it should it appear.

Arbenz, Fortuny, and the other members of the PGT's Secretariat were groping tensely and awkwardly for a way to save the revolution, but their political instincts had been dulled by the relentless pressure from Washington. And their enemies were circling.

Among them was Archbishop Rossell y Arellano, the highest Catholic authority in the land. On April 9, he issued a pastoral letter. Read in every church and echoed in the opposition press and radio stations, the pastoral was, in effect, a call to rebellion:

> We again raise our voice to alert Catholics that anti-Christian communism—the worst atheist doctrine of all time—is stalking our country under the cloak of social justice. We warn you that those whom the communists help today, they will condemn to forced labor and terrible suffering tomorrow. Everyone who loves his country must fight against those who—loyal to no country, the scum of the earth—have repaid Guatemala's generous hospitality by fomenting class hatred, in preparation for the day of destruction and slaughter which they anticipate with such enthusiasm. . . . Guatemala must rise as one against this enemy of God and country.[36]

[33] Interviews with María de Arbenz (quoted), Fortuny, and Guerra Borges.

[34] See for instance JW 9, Mar. 5, 1954, pp. 1–2; JW 10, Mar. 12, 1954, p. 1 (quoted); JW 18, May 7, 1954, pp. 1–2.

[35] Interview with María de Arbenz.

[36] Carta Pastoral ''Sobre los avances del comunismo,'' El I, Apr. 9, 1954, pp. 1, 6 (quoted). The archbishop's words, the U.S. embassy remarked, gave ''sanction to activities outside of the confining limits of 'legal and constitutional' opposition.'' They constituted, ''his strongest anti-communist pronouncement to date.'' (Quotations from

In vain did the nuncio, who had not been consulted about the pastoral, urge Rossell y Arellano to soften his rhetoric. Months of tension between the two clergymen culminated in "a very violent clash."[37] Rossell y Arellano pressed forward with the attack: "Any relationship between the Church and the government of Guatemala has ceased to exist," he told the *New York Times*.[38] He failed to mention that his attack was part of a larger effort; the timing and the venom of the pastoral were weapons in the rising war of nerves orchestrated by the planners of PBSUCCESS.[39]

While Rossell y Arellano's pastoral resonated through the churches of the republic, other Guatemalans were training in CIA camps in Nicaragua and Honduras, and still others were the guests of the CIA at Opa Locka, a semi-abandoned air force base near Miami.

In command at Opa Locka was Al Haney, a "handsome, rugged six-footer," with a pugnacious personality.[40] In October 1953, Allen Dulles had summoned Haney from Seoul, where he was CIA station chief, to take charge of the day-to-day conduct of PBSUCCESS. Under his vigorous leadership, Opa Locka became the nerve center of the operation. "He got all the funds," recalls an agent who was on the scene. Closely supervising and directing the work of the CIA stations in Central America, Haney steadily increased his autonomy, to the rising irritation of Frank Wisner, who was in charge of PBSUCCESS in Washington. "It was," explains Richard Bissell, "a system of double headquarters that led to a lot of squabbling. It was a mistake that we

---

Krieg to DOS, no. 852, Apr. 12, 1954, p. 2, NA 814.413, and *JW* 15, Apr. 14, 1954, p. 1.)

[37] Interview with Fr. Bendaña Perdomo. See also: Bendaña Perdomo, "Historia general," p. 52; "Si non e Vero-Lino e ven trovatino," *La Hora*, July 14, 1954, p. 1; "Si non Vero-lino e ven trovato," *La Hora*, July 21, 1954, p. 1; "Varios católicos protestan por una alusión al Excelentísimo Nuncio Apostólico," *La Hora*, July 27, 1954, p. 1; "El Nuncio Verolino negó que haya diferencia alguna con el Arzobispo," *El I*, Feb. 4, 1956, p. 1.

[38] "Guatemala Cleric Vows War on Reds," *NYT*, Apr. 18, 1954, p. 12.

[39] Interviews with Bendaña Perdomo and Taracena. For the role played by the Catholic press (*Acción Social Cristiana* and *Verbum*) in the spring of 1954, see L.A.H.A., *Así se gestó la Liberación*, pp. 139, 148, 151, 153, 155–57, 160, 165. Following the publication of the pastoral, and as part of PBSUCCESS's psychological offensive, the rumor was spread that "the government is considering the expulsion of the Archbishop and of all foreign priests." (Ibid., p. 158.)

According to some sources, Cardinal Francis Spellman of New York helped the CIA to establish contact with Rossell y Arellano. (See Schlesinger and Kinzer, *Bitter Fruit*, p. 155, and Frankel, "Political Development," p. 235.) It should be noted, however, that the archbishop was plotting with Castillo Armas before PBSUCCESS began.

[40] Schlesinger and Kinzer, *Bitter Fruit*, p. 109. "I didn't know anyone who liked Haney." (Interview with Roettinger who was based at Opa Loca from February to April 1954.)

avoided in the Bay of Pigs operation; Opa Locka was used again, but there was only one headquarters—Washington, period!''[41]

Among the CIA officials who worked under Haney was Howard Hunt. Hunt, who enjoyed modest fame as a writer of spy thrillers, later gained notoriety when he was arrested in the Democratic Party Headquarters in the Watergate.[42] During PBSUCCESS, he served as political action officer. He was flamboyant, intelligent, and articulate. He also had, notes a colleague, ''a penchant for the devious [that] was apparent in almost every conversation. For example, most propaganda undertaken covertly is handled in this fashion only because it cannot be handled overtly, but Howard was inclined to consider the option of using the Department of State only if the effort was not possible by CIA stealth.''[43]

The propaganda put out by the CIA during PBSUCCESS had more than a touch of the melodrama that characterized Hunt's thrillers. And it is to the misfortune of historians that Hunt, certainly the most loquacious of the CIA agents who participated in the operation, demonstrated the same penchant for the devious and love of the melodramatic in his accounts of the plot.[44]

The planners of PBSUCCESS had counted on the collaboration of Honduras and Nicaragua. Honduras was key, as it would serve as the launching pad of the invasion, but President Gálvez and his associates lacked the requisite zeal and backbone. They required constant prodding. Not to worry: Whiting Willauer was there.

In February 1954, just as a handful of CIA instructors began training a few dozen exiles in a finca near Tegucigalpa, Willauer arrived at his post.[45] He had learned about communism at first hand. As General Claire Chennault's right-hand man in the Civil Air Transport Company, he had worked with the CIA and the Chinese Nationalists in the late 1940s; in the process he had witnessed the communist triumph in China.[46]

Entries in the log of C. D. Jackson, a senior White House aide who worked very closely with the CIA, suggest that in the spring of 1953 Willauer was a leading contender for the post of ambassador to Guatemala; they also indicate that Frank Wisner was deeply involved in the selection process. As late as July

---

[41] Quotations from interviews with Roettinger and Bissell; see also Schlesinger and Kinzer, *Bitter Fruit*, pp. 109–10 and Immerman, *CIA in Guatemala*, pp. 139–40. Until the late spring of 1954, ''It was really Opa Locka that was giving directions and making policy. Then Washington stepped in and took control. By that time, headquarters at Opa Locka had grown to about 100 people.'' (Interview with Bissell.)

[42] For a biography of Hunt, see Szulc, *Compulsive Spy*.

[43] Phillips, *Night Watch*, p. 36.

[44] See esp. Hunt, *Undercover*, pp. 83–101.

[45] Interview with Roettinger who joined the group in April.

[46] See Leary, *Perilous Missions*. See also Eisenhower Records Central File, OF, Box 165 OF8-F, Willauer, EL, and U.S. Congress, *Communist Threat*, pp. 861–88.

18, the log noted: "Lunch—Willauer-Wisner—on Guatemalan ambassador-ship. . . . Looks good right now, but you never know."[47]

In the end, Willauer lost out to Peurifoy and landed as ambassador in Hon-duras.[48] He had gone to his new job, he later told a congressional committee, as part of a "team"—activist ambassadors who worked closely with the CIA to implement PBSUCCESS. This team, he added, also included Ambassador Tom Whelan in Nicaragua and, of course, Jack Peurifoy.[49]

[47] Entries of Apr. 15, May 2, and July 18 (quoted), 1953, Jackson Papers, Box 56, EL.

[48] See entry of Sept. 22, 1953, ibid.; Hanes to Undersecretary of State, Nov. 20, 1953, DP:SACS, Box 4; MemoTel (JFD, Saltonstall), Jan. 19, 1954, DP, JFD:CS, Box 6. All EL.

Some authors suggest that Willauer, who was a Republican, lost to Peurifoy, a Dem-ocrat, because the administration preferred to have a member of the opposition party on the front line should PBSUCCESS fail. (See Immerman, *CIA in Guatemala*, pp. 136–37, and Schlesinger and Kinzer, *Bitter Fruit*, p. 132.) While Willauer was being con-sidered as ambassador to Guatemala, Peurifoy was the leading candidate to be ambas-sador to Honduras. (See SecState, "Memorandum for the President," n.d., DP:SS, Box 6, EL.) Given the importance of the operation, it is more likely that the Admin-istration chose Peurifoy because he was considered the better man.

[49] See U.S. Congress, *Communist Threat*, p. 866. Whelan, who had developed close personal ties to Somoza, was one of the handful of Truman's political appointees who survived Dulles's 1953 purge of the State Department.

In his testimony, Willauer included Robert Hill, the ambassador to Costa Rica from late 1953 to late 1954, in the "team." Hill himself declined the honor. (Immerman, *CIA in Guatemala*, p. 141.) Immerman, the only scholar to have examined this issue, notes that "documents refer to him [Hill] in connection with the Guatemalan project." He cites an Apr. 11, 1958 letter by C. D. Jackson, who was well informed about PBSUCCESS: "Dear Ambassador Hill was the character," wrote Jackson, "who made so much trouble for us in his previous post." Immerman's other major item of evidence is an Apr. 21, 1958 memo, again by Jackson, that mentions "all the trouble we had with Hill when he was in Guatemala." (Ibid.)

The following points must, however, be borne in mind:

1. PBSUCCESS assigned no active role to Costa Rica.
2. Hill's appointment was not engineered by the CIA. It was due, rather, to Styles Bridges, the powerful Republican senator from his home state of New Hampshire, who was friendly with Hill's family and respected Hill as a successful young businessman. (See: TelConv [JFD, Bridges], Oct. 19, 1953, 12:10 p.m., DP, JFD:CS, Box 5, EL; Hill, "Oral History Interview," 1964, pp. 1, 2, 18–19; and Hill, "Oral History Interview," 1973, pp. 7–13.)
3. Hill never served in Guatemala. While C. D. Jackson's Apr. 21, 1958, memo mentions "all the trouble we had with Hill when he was in Guatemala," the en-closures that Jackson attached to the memo indicate that he meant El Salvador. The "trouble" did not have to do with PBSUCCESS, but with an intemperate attack that Hill made in the Salvadoran press against *Time*'s critical reporting on Salva-doran affairs: " 'The unfortunate inaccuracy and often fraudulent articles written

"I suppose most of you have looked up Honduras on your maps before coming here," Willauer told a meeting of the World Affairs Council in 1960. "I must confess that I had to do so when it was first suggested that I should become ambassador."[50] Like Peurifoy, he had not set foot in Central America before he arrived as ambassador. But if his knowledge was faulty, his instincts were sure. By stealth and deception, the communists were preparing to reenact their Asian triumphs in the heart of the American Mediterranean. Should they consolidate their control of Guatemala, the infection would spread. Honduras would fall next, and then the other Central American republics.[51]

Willauer was proud to help reverse the tide. To be sure, he has acknowledged modestly that Peurifoy was "the principal man" in the ambassadorial team unleashed against Arbenz, but he, too, "was called upon to perform very important duties, particularly to keep the Honduran government . . . in line,

---

about the Latin American Republics make the work of our embassy much more difficult than it would be otherwise,' says the Ambassador." (*Prensa Gráfica*, Aug. 19, 1955, Jackson Papers, Box 49, EL. See also Dubois to Alexander, ibid.) After leaving the Eisenhower administration in 1954, Jackson had been a senior *Time* executive—hence his remarks on the trouble "we" had with Hill. In the same vein, when he mentioned Hill's "previous post" (where the trouble had occurred) in his Apr. 11, 1958, letter, he was not referring to Costa Rica. In 1958 Hill was ambassador to Mexico; his previous post, therefore, had been in El Salvador.

4. The only documents connecting Hill to Guatemala deal with diplomatic matters such as Hill's efforts to convince Figueres to participate in the Caracas conference and to endorse the U.S. preparations, in May–June 1954, for another OAS conference directed against Guatemala. With the one exception of Willauer's brief reference in his 1961 testimony, no document implicates Hill in PBSUCCESS.

Also not involved was Michael McDermott, who was appointed ambassador to El Salvador on May 21, 1953, that is, before PBSUCCESS was born. McDermott had been the State Department's press secretary since 1927. He was liked by State Department officials, including Secretary Dulles. Since he was nearing retirement, he was rewarded with an ambassadorship, the first and last of his life. No evidence links him to PBSUCCESS. (On McDermott's appointment, an interview with Deputy Assistant Secretary Woodward was particularly helpful. See also Purse to Willis, May 18, 1953, Eisenhower Records Central File, OF, Box 162, EL; Willis to Adams, July 28, 1954, ibid., Box 165; McDermott to Eisenhower, Aug. 13, 1954, ibid., Box 162. For a biographical sketch of McDermott see "Michael J. McDermott," ibid.)

To conclude, the CIA's "ambassadorial team" to Central America included only Peurifoy, Willauer, and Whelan, who served in the three countries that participated directly in the plot. Costa Rica and El Salvador were expected to provide only diplomatic support.

[50] Willauer, "Draft no. 1. Speech for World Affairs Council," Nov. 12, 1960, p. 1, Willauer Papers, ML.

[51] See ibid., esp. pp. 7–21. See also Willauer to Harrington, June 15, 1954, ibid., and Willauer to Sherry, June 9, 1954, ibid.

so they would allow this revolutionary activity [by Castillo Armas] to continue, based in Honduras.'' President Gálvez and his government were eager to see Arbenz overthrown, but they were afraid of what would happen if Castillo Armas failed. They feared the Guatemalans, and they feared their own people. In fact, explained Willauer, they were ''scared to death about the possibilities of themselves being overthrown.''[52] And so Willauer, flaunting the power of the United States and his own aggressive personality, did his best to cajole and bully his hosts and keep them in line. And in line they stood.[53]

There was no need to bully Somoza; the dictator was eager and enthusiastic. In February 1954, the CIA opened two training camps in Nicaragua: at Momotombito, an island in Lake Managua, and at El Tamarindo, a Somoza estate. Meanwhile, at an abandoned air strip near Puerto Cabezas, a handful of Guatemalan pilots was training for Castillo Armas's air force, while the CIA gathered the planes through dummy companies. Since the planners of PBSUCCESS were eager ''to give the impression that the rebels had bought the planes on the international market,'' the rebel airforce finally consisted of a motley assortment of a dozen or so World War II P-47s and C-47s.[54] Most of the pilots were Americans hired by the CIA—men like Jerry Fred DeLarm, ''a slim, short, hawk-featured man who liked to lay a 45 down on the table in front of him when talking to a stranger.''[55] Theatrics apart, these Americans were congenial fellows, gregarious and happy-going, just a mite too boisterous and indiscreet. ''Your pal will be in the middle of the blood and thunder . . . on June 18, 19 or 20,'' one of them wrote to a friend a week before D-Day.[56]

While the pilots were trained at Puerto Cabezas, a force of another kind was being organized at El Tamarindo and at Momotombito. PBSUCCESS called for

[52] Willauer testimony, in U.S. Congress, *Communist Threat*, p. 866. On U.S. concerns about domestic instability in Honduras, see Erwin to SecState, no. 50, Jan. 24, 1954; Erwin to DOS, no. 331, Feb. 2, 1954; Erwin to DOS, no. 339, Feb. 9, 1954; Erwin to SecState, no. 84, Feb. 21, 1954; Willauer to SecState, no. 154, Apr. 1, 1954; Willauer to DOS, no. 408, Apr. 2, 1954. All AmEm Tegucigalpa; all NA 715.00.

[53] ''The Gálvez regime in Honduras became generally frightened about the Castillo Armas movement, to the point where in February 1954 they forced him to bring his activities to a near standstill. Very fortunately, however, this loss of courage was short-lived and finally by April 1954 Castillo Armas was again permitted to continue with the preparations in Honduras.'' (Willauer, [see n. 50 above], p. 23.)

[54] Interview with Bissell (quoted). There is some disagreement as to the exact size and composition of Castillo Armas's air force. See Cline, *Secrets, Spies and Scholars*, p. 132; Phillips, *Night Watch*, p. 36; Willauer to Chennault, June 30, 1954, *FRUS, 1952–1954*, 4:1308. On the dummy companies, see Schlesinger and Kinzer, *Bitter Fruit*, pp. 115–16.

[55] Wise and Ross, *Invisible Government*, p. 186. For a creative and melodramatic account of Delarm's exploits, see Larsen, ''Sulfato.''

[56] ''U.S. Citizen Joins Anti-Red Rebels,'' *NYT*, June 22, 1954, p. 3 (quoted); FBI, report no. 1 from Havana, Cuba, June 8, 1954; FBI, Belmont to Boardman, June 10, 1954; FBI, Hoover to Olney, 2-14Oc-4, June 11, 1954.

two to three hundred men to invade Guatemala on D-Day. In the preceding weeks, 150 "hornets" would infiltrate the country.[57] With recruits from the "home front," they would organize a fifth column that would strike as soon as the invasion had begun. The would-be saboteurs learned their trade at El Tamarindo, whereas a couple hundred invaders were whipped into shape at Momotombito. "We trained for about six weeks," recalls Eduardo Taracena, a close aide of Castillo Armas who reached Momotombito in March. "Our instructors were taciturn, friendly Americans whom we knew only by first name. (They were all called Pepe or José.) They told us when we arrived that the invasion would begin in May."[58]

As the training progressed, the host, President Somoza, was very much in the news. Prominently featured with him was his nemesis, Figueres of Costa Rica. On April 5, the Nicaraguan government announced the discovery of an armed band of approximately twenty-five men who had been preparing an attack on Somoza; pursued by the National Guard, some had been killed, some had been captured, and others had escaped.[59] The plot was no CIA concoction to implicate Arbenz in an attack on his peaceful neighbor. The agency, in this case, was innocent, as was Somoza. Arbenz was equally innocent, and so were his communist friends, but it soon became evident that the plotters, who had entered Nicaragua from Costa Rica, had benefited from the complicity of high Costa Rican officials—even, perhaps, Figueres himself.[60]

Somoza was delighted to blame Arbenz for the plot, but he also wanted revenge against Figueres. His approach was straightforward: damn them both. Arbenz, he pointed out, was a communist, but then, so was Figueres, "who has been secretly conniving for many years with Soviet agents based in Guatemala and other Caribbean countries"; both belonged to the international communist conspiracy that had targeted him because he was the "foremost anticommunist leader of Central America."[61] Therefore, argued Somoza, a meeting of OAS foreign ministers should be convened to consider sanctions

[57] Tracy Barnes, a senior aide to Wisner, coined the term. (Interview with Roettinger.)

[58] Interviews with Taracena (quoted) and Bissell. See also L.A.H.A., *Así se gestó la Liberación*, pp. 181, 184; Wise and Ross, *Invisible Government*, pp. 185–86; Schlesinger and Kinzer, *Bitter Fruit*, p. 114.

[59] "Comunican el cierre de frontera sur," *La Prensa*, Managua, Apr. 6, 1954, p. 1; "Nicaragua Foils Assassins' Plot," *NYT*, Apr. 6, 1954, p. 7; "Frontier Is Closed," *NYT*, Apr. 7, 1954, p. 26; "6 Slain in Nicaragua," *NYT*, Apr. 8, 1954, p. 8; "3 Slain in Nicaragua," *NYT*, Apr. 9, 1954, p. 3; "Nicaraguan Rebel Chief Slain," *NYT*, Apr. 10, 1954, p. 6.

[60] For the plot, see Martz, *Central America*, pp. 186–93 and Ameringer, *Democratic Left*, pp. 205–12.

[61] "Memorandum confidencial sobre la infiltración comunista en Centro América," Managua, [May 1954], p. 2, Archives of the Nicaraguan embassy, Washington, D.C.

against both Costa Rica and Guatemala.[62] Without first consulting the United States, he approached Honduras and El Salvador to inquire whether they "would be willing to back the Nicaraguan request."[63]

Busy as they were cinching the noose around Arbenz, the planners of PBSUCCESS now had to placate the infuriated dictator. Gently, but firmly, Washington reminded Somoza that Arbenz was the target and that an OAS conference condemning both Guatemala and Costa Rica would deflect attention from this primary concern.[64] Reluctantly, Somoza relented.

On May 6 the Nicaraguan delivered another bombshell: a large cache of weapons had just been discovered on the country's Pacific coast; a few days earlier, he added, a mysterious submarine had been sighted in the area. For anyone who couldn't divine the source of the weapons and the nationality of the submarine, a clue was obligingly provided: the arms "were stamped with a hammer and sickle."[65] The weapons had, in fact, been planted by the CIA, with Somoza's enthusiastic complicity.[66] The ploy, however, was too crude to have much value as propaganda and received only limited attention at the time.

While Somoza spluttered, a small group of Guatemalans and their American adviser were setting up camp on a hillside near Managua.[67] The American, David Atlee Phillips, had been living in Chile, where he edited an English-language newspaper and moonlighted for the CIA.[68] In early March 1954, Phillips writes, he had been urgently summoned to the United States and offered a special assignment. A clandestine radio station, "which would pretend to be broadcasting from Guatemala," would be set up in Nicaragua. "A team of radio technicians, writers and announcers, including two women, was being recruited in Guatemala City. They would come to Florida for planning sessions before going off to the third country [Nicaragua] where the transmitter was now being erected. I was to act as an adviser to the team."[69] He was

[62] See Ministerio de relaciones exteriores, Managua, "Memorandum confidencial," May 24, 1954, Archives of the Nicaraguan Embassy, Washington, D.C.

[63] Foreign Minister Oscar Sevilla Sacasa to Amb. Guillermo Sevilla Sacasa, Managua, no. 232, May 24, 1954, Archives of the Nicaraguan Embassy, Washington, D.C.; see also Ministerio de Relaciones Exteriores, "Memorandum confidencial" (see n. 62 above), and AmEm Tegucigalpa, Willauer to SecState, no. 353, May 21, 1954, NA 714.00.

[64] See MemoConv (Dulles, Sevilla Sacasa), May 20, 1954, and MemoConv (Sevilla Sacasa, Holland), May 21, 1954. Both NA 714.00.

[65] "Armas en sacos impermeables hallan en costa del Pacifico," *La Prensa*, Managua, May 7, 1954, p. 1.

[66] See Schlesinger and Kinzer, *Bitter Fruit*, p. 150.

[67] Interview with Roettinger, who was there in late June.

[68] Phillips describes his Chilean days in *Night Watch*, pp. 4–29.

[69] Ibid., p. 36. For Phillips' account of his participation in PBSUCCESS, see pp. 30–54.

selected for the job, Phillips believes, because he possessed two skills unusual among CIA agents: he spoke flawless Spanish and had acting and broadcasting experience.[70] For the next few weeks he and his Guatemalan charges were guests of the CIA at Opa Locka. In late April they left for Managua.

The facilities were spartan: "the jungle transmitter was being set up in an old cow barn, and living quarters would be in a dilapidated shack."[71] Phillips knew that they had little time. Before leaving, he had been told that the radio had to start broadcasting on May 1 and that Castillo Armas's invasion would begin in mid-June;[72] his Guatemalans, writes Phillips, had "just six weeks to build toward the climax of their propaganda campaign."[73]

On May 1, *La Voz de la Liberación* broadcast its first message, announcing amid popular American songs that the hours of the "traitor Jacobo" were numbered.[74] The radio reception was excellent, and the country "was swept by speculation as to where the station was located and who was its sponsor."[75] The station, claimed its announcers and the Guatemalan opposition press, was operating from inside Guatemala, outwitting Arbenz's police.[76] The broadcasts were useful fodder in the war of nerves but by mid-May they had "lessened in effectiveness," noted the embassy, because of government jamming.[77]

The embassy's report was dated May 14. Three days later, tension in Guatemala reached a new high as the State Department announced that a Swedish ship, the *Alfhem*, had just landed at Puerto Barrios, loaded with arms from behind the Iron Curtain.[78]

It was true. The weapons promised by Novotný were aboard the ship in

[70] Interview with Phillips.

[71] Phillips, *Night Watch*, p. 38.

[72] Interview with Phillips.

[73] Phillips, *Night Watch*, p. 42.

[74] See, for example, the testimony of López Villatoro, one of the Guatemalan radio broadcasters, in U.S. Congress, *Communist Aggression*, pp. 97–111.

[75] *JW* 18, May 7, 1954, p. 3; see also Krieg to McCormick, et al., "Clandestine Radio Station in Guatemala," May 6, 1954, RG84 G&C, Box 3, NA-S, and Krieg to DOS, no. 915, May 6, 1954, NA 714.00.

[76] See, for instance: "Sigue la radioemisora clandestina" (edit.), *La Hora*, May 6, 1954, p. 4; "Vuela avión para localizar la radioemisora clandestina," *La Hora*, May 8, 1954, p. 1; "Radio Clandestina sigue siendo un fantasma," *El I*, May 8, 1954, p. 1; "Dónde se halla emplazada la radioemisora clandestina?" *La Hora*, May 14, 1954, p. 1.

[77] *JW* 19, May 14, 1954, p. 4. See also Marroquín Rojas, "Los cuatros entusiasmos de los últimos meses," *La Hora*, May 31, 1954, p. 4.

[78] "Communist Arms Unloaded in Guatemala by Vessel from Polish Port, U.S. Learns," *NYT*, May 18, 1954, p.1. For the text of the State Department's press release see *Department of State Bulletin*, May 31, 1954, p. 835.

crates labeled optical equipment. In April, the CIA had learned from an agent in the Polish port of Stettin (where the weapons had been loaded) that military equipment was on its way to a country "in the Western Hemisphere"[79]—obviously Guatemala. But the CIA lost track of the *Alfhem* as it proceeded along a circuitous route to Puerto Barrios. ("The deception . . . was excellent," Wisner later told Secretary Dulles.)[80] The ship was rediscovered only as it reached Guatemalan waters.[81] On May 16, a few hours after the *Alfhem*'s arrival, the State Department instructed its embassy in Stockholm to persuade the Swedish government "to order *Alfhem* sail from Puerto Barrios at once without unloading," while Peurifoy was told "to encourage IRCA to cause maximum delay" while investigating the cargo.[82]

U.S. officials were alarmed by the *Alfhem*. They feared that it would strengthen support for Arbenz among the officer corps that longed for new weapons.[83] Its arrival, some analysts have argued, triggered the decision to launch PBSUCCESS: "When the *Alfhem* docked in Puerto Barrios," writes Immerman, "Eisenhower and his advisers decided thay they could no longer delay the authorization to effect PBSUCCESS. Castillo Armas's invasion had to begin before Arbenz distributed the new supplies, either to the peasants or to his cohorts elsewhere in Central America."[84]

The evidence does not support this assertion. Taracena recalls that before the arrival of the *Alfhem*, "Castillo Armas had been told that the invasion would begin in May. The date was postponed because we were not ready."[85] David Phillips, the CIA operative in charge of the clandestine radio, writes in his memoirs that he was told in late April that there were "just six weeks" before the invasion was launched.[86] Assistant Secretary Holland wrote on

---

[79] Tully, *CIA*, p. 64.

[80] TelConv (JFD, Wisner), May 17, 1954, 4:32 p.m., DP:TCS, Box 2, EL.

[81] The most exhaustive account of the CIA and the *Alfhem* is Tully, *CIA*, pp. 62–65. See also Richard and Gladys Harkness, "America's Secret Agents: The Mysterious Doings of CIA," *Saturday Evening Post*, Oct. 30, 1954, pp. 19–20. (This article was submitted to Allen Dulles for approval and revised according to his suggestions. See Fuoss to Grogan, Aug. 9, 1954, and Harkness to AWD, rec'd Aug. 13, 1954, AWD Papers, Box 62, ML.)

[82] DOS, "Chronology of Events (Secret)," entry of May 16, 1954 (quoted), RG84 G&C, Box 3, NA-S, and Holland to SecState, "Action to Prevent Delivery of Czech Arms to Guatemala," May 18, 1954, NA Lot 58D18 & 58D78, Box 2.

[83] Both Peurifoy and the CIA soon concluded, however, that there was no evidence that the shipment had in fact improved Arbenz's position. See Peurifoy to SecState, no. 854, June 1, 1954, NA 714.00, and CIA, *Current Intelligence Digest*, June 3, 1954, p.16.

[84] Immerman, *CIA in Guatemala*, p. 160 (quoted); Higgins, *Perfect Failure*, p. 26; Ranelagh, *Agency*, p. 266.

[85] Interview with Taracena.

[86] Phillips, *Night Watch*, p. 42.

April 20, "There are possibilities of new developments in the Guatemalan situation between now and the end of June."[87] Holland was one of the few who knew about PBSUCCESS; "new developments" was, clearly, a guarded reference to the invasion. The evidence suggests that well before the *Alfhem* appeared on the scene, the invasion was planned for May or June. There is no indication that the arrival of the *Alfhem* accelerated its tempo.[88]

It did, however, present the planners of PBSUCCESS with an opportunity they were determined to exploit: violent condemnations of this flagrant act of aggression by the Soviet Union and its Guatemalan puppet were accompanied by ostentatious measures purportedly designed to protect Nicaragua and Honduras. The United States had signed a Mutual Security Treaty on April 23 with Nicaragua; it now hastened to conclude a similar pact with Honduras.[89] On May 24, the Pentagon airlifted fifty tons of weapons to Nicaragua and Honduras. The United States, wrote the *New York Times*, would be sending additional arms to these two countries that were threatened by "Guatemalan aggression or . . . Communist subversion."[90] Other highly publicized military measures were taken rapidly: on May 23, the U.S. navy dispatched two submarines from Key West, "saying only that they were going 'south.' "[91] Four days later, the air force sent three intercontinental bombers, B-36s, to partici-

[87] Holland to Acting Secretary, Apr. 20, 1954, *FRUS*, 1952–1954, 4:1101.

[88] Exactly when Eisenhower gave the final go-ahead for the operation is not known. Ambrose and Immerman offer no source for their claim that in the wake of the *Alfhem*, "at a secret, emergency session of the National Security Council . . . Eisenhower approved the program [Allen] Dulles outlined. The CIA-sponsored invasion of Guatemala was on." (*Ike's Spies*, pp. 216–17.) It is likely that, as he had done with AJAX, Eisenhower gave the final okay very shortly before the invasion was launched. (This was also Kennedy's procedure in the Bay of Pigs.) Therefore, while the final authorization was probably given after the arrival of the *Alfhem*, this does not prove any causal relationship between the two events.

[89] "U.S. and Honduras Sign Arms Accord," *NYT*, May 22, 1954, p. 4. In fact, the United States, Nicaragua, and Honduras had agreed on the military assistance pacts several months earlier; they had been waiting for an opportune moment to announce them. Peurifoy had urged that "unless other considerations are overriding, announcement be deferred until after Caracas meeting since prior announcement would doubtless be used there by Guatemalans to claim United States was preparing for armed intervention in Guatemala." (Peurifoy to SecState, no. 321, Feb. 12, 1954, NA 714.00. For background, see *FRUS*, 1952–1954, 4:144–46, 150–53, 168–69; MemoConv [McDermott, Canessa], Feb. 9, 1954, NA Lot 58D18 & 58D78, Box 3; Leddy to Peurifoy, Mar. 8, 1954, NA 611.14, and Peurifoy to Leddy, Mar. 2, 1954, [enclosed].)

[90] "U.S. Flying Arms to 2 Latin Lands near Guatemala," *NYT*, May 25, 1954, p. 1. See also "U.S. Tanks for Honduras," *NYT*, June 2, 1954, p. 12, and "U.S. Aid to Grow," *NYT*, June 3, 1954, p. 10.

[91] Schlesinger and Kinzer, *Bitter Fruit*, p. 160.

pate in the celebrations for Nicaragua's Army Day—which coincided with Mrs. Somoza's birthday. The B-36, the *New York Times* stated dryly, "is capable of delivering the atomic bomb." As the planes flew overhead, the Nicaraguan crowds cried: "Long live the United States! Long live Somoza!"[92] For Nicaragua, it was a singular distinction: "this is the first time," the *Times* pointed out, "that any of the big strategic bombers have taken part in a foreign holiday."[93] Those who sent the planes were not thinking, however, of Mrs. Somoza's birthday. The "goodwill mission," explained a prominent columnist, "is merely a maneuver reminiscent of the 1910 muscular diplomacy celebrated by Richard Harding Davis."[94] The bombers flew over Nicaragua; their shadow fell on Guatemala.

The State Department, meanwhile, warned that the arrival of Soviet-bloc weapons in Guatemala might be in contravention of the Rio Treaty and justify the adoption of sanctions.[95] Foster Dulles was eloquent: the "extension of Soviet Colonialism to this hemisphere would, in the words of the Caracas Resolution, endanger the peace of America." He elaborated, "No member of the Rio Pact gives up what the Charter of the United Nations calls the inherent right of individual or collective self-defense: that right is reserved. Nevertheless, it is contemplated that, if the circumstances permit, there should be an effort, a sincere effort, at collective action, and we would expect to comply with both the letter and the spirit of our country's obligations."[96]

Hysteria seized the U.S. Congress and the American press. "The threat of Communist imperialism is no longer academic; it has arrived," proclaimed the *Washington Post* in an editorial, which asserted that "the shipment of arms from . . . Stettin ought to remove any lingering doubts that Guatemala is the beachhead for active Communist designs in the Western Hemisphere."[97] The *Wall Street Journal* saw the arms as a means of spreading the germ of communism like "Typhoid Mary,"[98] while the *New York Times* speculated about

[92] Quotations from "U.S. Detains Ship for Arms Search," *NYT*, May 27, 1954, p. 6, and "Vuelan los aviones atómicos sobre la ciudad de Managua," *El I*, May 28, 1954, p. 1. See also "Aviones atómicos a Managua," *El I*, May 27, 1954, p. 1; "U.S. Bombers Visit Nicaragua," *NYT*, May 28, 1954, p. 7; "Día del Ejército," *La Prensa*, Managua, May 28, 1954, p. 1.

[93] "U.S. Detains Ship for Arms Search," *NYT*, May 27, 1954, p. 6.

[94] Arthur Krock, "A Communist Arms Depot in Central America?" *NYT*, May 27, 1954, p. 26.

[95] "U.S. Wants Rio Pact Inquiry on Arms Sent to Guatemala," *NYT*, May 19, 1954, p. 1; "Latin Arms Cargo Upsets President," *NYT*, May 20, 1954, p. 1.

[96] Quotations from "Communist Influence in Guatemala," May 25, 1954, *Department of State Bulletin*, June 7, 1954, p. 874, and "Dulles Cites Danger of Reds Near Canal," *NYT*, May 26, 1954, p. 12.

[97] "Communist Beachhead" (edit.), *WP*, May 21, 1954, p. 22.

[98] "Repeating History," *WSJ*, June 1, 1954, p. 12.

the "secret jungle paths" along which the *Alfhem*'s machine guns would travel on their way to communist groups in other Central American countries.[99] Only *The Nation* observed that it was Guatemala, rather than its neighbors, that was threatened.[100]

In newspaper articles and in congressional speeches, the Monroe Doctrine was unearthed and batted around. "We find that one of our most cherished basic doctrines, which we have long considered to be a protection for North and South American countries, is now under direct attack by the Communists," warned Senator George Smathers. "We must decide whether we are to stand on the principle of the Monroe Doctrine or are we to retreat from it and let it become a meaningless memory."[101]

Guatemala endangered the hemisphere. "This cargo of arms is like an atom bomb planted in the rear of our backyard," argued Congressman McCormack. "It is as if a Soviet ship brought an atom bomb in her hold and berthed at a slip in the New York harbor calmly confident that at any time it could blow up the City of New York." The bones of American history were rattled in the chambers: "If Paul Revere were living today," said Representative William Lantaff, "he would view the landing of Red arms in Guatemala as a signal to ride and warn the Americas of the present acute danger of Communist infiltration in Latin America." Representative Robert Sikes compared the arrival of the *Alfhem* to Italy's invasion of Ethiopia in 1935 and noted how the failure of the democracies to respond had led to World War II.[102] The storm raged on, as congressman after congressman rose to denounce the Guatemalan regime.

The arrival of the *Alfhem* reignited the issue of the U.S. military missions in Guatemala. On May 18, at 11:38 a.m., Senator William Knowland, one of the most powerful Republicans in Congress, phoned Foster Dulles. He was "confused," Knowland said. He had just realized that "we have a military

[99] Krock, "A Communist Arms Depot in Central America?" *NYT*, May 27, 1954, p. 26.

[100] "Again the Big Stick" (edit.), *The Nation*, May 29, 1954, p. 453. "The Administration has blown it up [the *Alfhem* episode] into an international incident of impressive magnitude, and by doing so has crudely revealed the town-bully attitude it tried so hard to hide at Caracas under a camouflage of pan-American 'unity.' But what kind of attitude is this? How does it differ from the attitude of Russia toward one of its lesser satellites? The State Department is angry at Guatemala for pursuing a left-wing policy. . . . It is also annoyed by Guatemala's stubborn, tough dealings with big American companies operating there. And so, obsessed with its role as boss-defender of the hemisphere, it [the State Department] refuses to sell arms to Guatemala, refuses to allow Guatemala to buy arms from friendly nations, and then denounces Guatemala as a threat to security when it gets arms where it can."

[101] Smathers (D-Fla), May 20, 1954, *CR*-Senate, p. 6916.

[102] McCormack (D-Mass), May 25, 1954, *CR*-House, p. 7092; Lantaff (D-Fla), May 24, 1954, ibid., p. 7016; Sikes (D-Fla), May 25, 1954, ibid., pp. 7091–92.

mission [in Guatemala].'' What consistency is there, he asked, in ''having a mission and at the same time being concerned about the shipment of arms for the army there?''[103]

Dulles sprang into action. First he phoned his brother. Allen was not in his office, and so by 11:42 a.m. he was on the phone with Allen's deputy, Wisner:

> The Secretary mentioned that he had talked with AWD re keeping the missions in Guatemala, and now thinks new thought could be given to it. AWD has thought up to now it is desirable to keep it there. . . . The Sec. referred to Knowland's call. . . . The Sec. said maybe we should pull them right out. W. said one of the Pentagon's thoughts and theirs is that the strongest single bulwark against the Communist-controlled government is the army, and this could be used for discussion with the Congressman. . . . The Sec. said he has to let his friends on the Hill know what to say. W. said they can say we don't know if the arms are for the army. The effect of this might be good as it might make the army mad. Confidentially the Sec. can say that the mission, like others we have behind the Iron Curtain, is used as eyes and ears for us.[104]

Dulles immediately reported the conversation to Knowland.[105] In the afternoon, Allen returned his brother's call. ''AWD said he is opposed to taking the fellows [the military missions] out of Guatemala. He will be glad to help on the Hill—talk to Knowland, etc. . . . The only hope [for PBSUCCESS] is defection there [among the Guatemalan officers].''[106] The CIA prevailed: the military missions were not mentioned in Congress.

The furor provoked by the *Alfhem* in the United States was heightened by the fact that a strike had broken out in early May among the forty thousand workers of United Fruit and Standard Fruit in Honduras, the two American giants that monopolized banana production there. By the time the *Alfhem* reached Guatemala, the entire northern region, the heart of Honduras's economy, was paralyzed. It was without precedent. Honduras, noted *Business Week*, had been ''an employers' paradise'': there were no unions for rural workers ''and little labor legislation beyond some paper government machinery for settling labor disputes.''[107]

From Tegucigalpa, Ambassador Willauer had cabled on May 9 that ''while the Honduran Government was likely to maintain control, he had important reservations.'' That day, the State Department had ''dèclined to predict de-

[103] TelConv (Knowland, JFD), May 18, 1954, 11:38 a.m., DP:TCS, Box 2, EL.

[104] TelConv (JFD, Wisner), May 18, 1954, 11:42 a.m., ibid.

[105] TelConv (JFD, Knowland), May 18, 1954, 11:46 a.m., ibid.

[106] TelConv (JFD, AWD), May 18, 1954, 5:10 p.m., ibid.

[107] ''Banana Battle,'' *Business Week*, May 22, 1954, p. 166. The best studies of the strike are Posas, *Luchas*, pp. 95–185, and Meza, *Historia*, pp. 67–98. See also La-Barge, ''A Study of United Fruit,'' pp. 294–304.

velopments.''[108] On May 13, the Dulles brothers commented, ''We may want to send forces [into Honduras] . . . but this is not yet necessary.'' They both hoped that the strike would be broken.[109] Instead, it spread to Tegucigalpa and other towns. On May 23, a panicky President Gálvez asked that two U.S. warships be stationed off the north coast, ready to land marines should the need arise.[110] The State Department agreed. The Pentagon had already drawn up plans.[111]

From the outset, the Hondurans had claimed that international communism lay behind the strike, and they had singled out Guatemala for blame. There was no proof, but none was needed: every major labor conflict was, by definition, communist inspired. The Hondurans also knew that the most effective way to discredit the strikers, and to elicit the support of the United States, was to brandish the Red threat and, in particular, the ''Guatemalan Connection.''

In fact, neither the Guatemalan government nor the PGT had fomented the strike. Their association with it was insignificant: *Diario de Centro América* expressed support for the strikers, and the CGTG collected a few hundred dollars for them and served as a conduit for a similar amount sent from Mexico by the *Confederación de Trabajadores de América Latina*.[112]

To the Americans—journalists, congressmen, officials—the strike was too

---

[108] Memorandum for the Chairman, Joint Chiefs of Staff, May 13, 1954, DDI-12-54, quoted p. 1.

[109] TelConv (JFD, AWD), May 13, 1954, 9:46 a.m., DP, JFD:CS, Box 7, EL.

[110] Secretaría de Relaciones Exteriores de la República de Honduras, Memorandum Confidencial, May 23, 1954, enclosed in AmEm Tegucigalpa, Coerr to DOS, no. 495, May 28, 1954, NA 714.001. See also Willauer to Holland, May 24, 1954, 1 a.m.

[111] JFD to President, ''Unsettled Labor and Political Conditions in Honduras,'' May 11, 1954, WF, Dulles/Herter Series, Box 2, EL. There is a wealth of documentary material on this matter. See, for instance, Hall, ''Assistant Secretary Henry Holland's Remarks on Latin America in the Planning Board Meeting on Monday, May 24, 1954,'' White House Office, Special Assistant for National Security Affairs: Records, 1952–61, NSC Series, Administrative SubSeries, Box 4, EL; Op-30 to Op-03, May 28, 1954, Op-303E/csv Ser. 000510P; Chief of Naval Operations to Joint Chiefs of Staff, May 29, 1954, Op-383/aas Ser. 0005-81; CINCLANTFLT no. 516, June 8, 1954. For relevant NSC documents, see: NSC 5419, May 24, 1954, *FRUS*, 1952–1954, 4:1129–31; ''Memorandum of Discussion at the 199th Meeting of the National Security Council, May 27, 1954,'' ibid., pp. 1131–35; NSC 5419/1, May 28, 1954, ibid., pp. 1135–36.

[112] See, for instance, *DCA*: ''En huelga contra la United Fruit trabajadores de la costa norte de Honduras,'' May 5, 1954, p. 8; ''Más mensajes de apoyo,'' May 17, 1954, p. 1; ''Jóvenes con trabajadores de Honduras'' and ''Primeros aportes para los huelguistas de Honduras,'' May 18, 1954, p. 1. See also Lombardo Toledano to Gutiérrez, June 4, 1954, *GT*, Box 24, and Gutiérrez to Lombardo Toledano, June 10, 1954, ibid. Boxes 25 and 44 of the *GT* include two folders dealing with the efforts of the CGTG and the CNCG to assist the Honduran strikers.

sudden, too well organized, too widespread not to reek of international communism. "This strike," proclaimed Senator Mike Mansfield on May 28, "has been conducted in the Communist manner, with workers thoroughly organized, disciplined and carrying out precise orders completely uncharacteristic of the natives of Honduras and Guatemala." And it would not stop there: "Reports now reach Washington," revealed Representative Hale Boggs, "that Guatemalan agents are now attempting to foment strikes in Panama. The canal itself may be threatened."[113]

Two incidents that had attracted little attention when they were first announced were reinterpreted in the light of the *Alfhem*. In the words of Representative Clark Fisher, "The Communist hand was shown last April . . . in the attempt to assassinate the vehement anti-Communist President Anastasio Somoza of Nicaragua. . . . About the same time Nicaraguan agents discovered Soviet marked guns, believed to have been smuggled in by submarines."[114] Even the *New York Times*, albeit more tentatively than Fisher, could not resist the temptation to see a grand Guatemalan conspiracy linking the *Alfhem*, the Honduran strike, the plot against Somoza, and the Nicaraguan arms cache.[115]

Many Congressmen and journalists were tired of the passivity of the Eisenhower administration. "With its head-in-the-sand attitude . . . [the State Department] has chosen to ignore the dangers of the situation," charged Representative Lantaff. "We might well do away with diplomatic niceties right away," urged Senator Margaret Chase Smith. The gentlewoman was bitter. The previous February she had introduced a resolution "toward placing a ban against importing Guatemalan coffee. . . . What happened? The State Department, playing the game of timidity and fear of offending someone—and a game dangerously close to appeasement of the Reds—expressed its opposition to my anti-Communist legislation against the Guatemalan Reds. By such op-

[113] Mansfield (D-Mont), May 28, 1954, *CR*-Senate, p. 7337; Boggs (D-La), May 25, 1954, *CR*-House, p. 7092. The first official U.S. statement implicating Guatemala in the Honduran strike was made by Secretary Dulles at his May 11 news conference. (See *The Department of State Bulletin*, May 24, 1954, p. 801.)

[114] Fisher (D-Texas), June 14, 1954, *CR*-House, p. 8193. But perhaps none said it as well as an article in *Harper's* one year later: "Evidence has been found that a razzle-dazzle triple play was planned for April and May 1954. In Nicaragua, Somoza was to be assassinated. The underground Communist organization would rise, and one-third of the *Alfhem* arms would give it a good chance of crushing all opposition. In Honduras, a general strike was starting, led by expert agitators from abroad. It was to be turned into a revolution by arming the strikers. . . . If Nicaragua, Honduras, and Guatemala were quickly welded together into a new Red dominion, then the United States would face the hard choice of fighting another Korean War close to home or letting Central America go the way of Indochina." (Monroe, "Guatemala: What the Reds Left Behind," p. 63.)

[115] "Arming of Guatemala Alarms Its Neighbors," *NYT*, May 23, 1954, D9.

position the State Department stymied action by the Senate Foreign Relations Committee."[116]

Representative Sikes sought guidance in America's past: "In other days, America has acted promptly and vigorously to protect her interests and her friends. The incident of the Barbary pirates, the campaign of Andrew Jackson, the courage of Teddy Roosevelt are all part of our glorious heritage. In those days we did not hesitate to act, we did not allow ourselves to become entangled in diplomatic red tape, we got results."[117]

Behind the scenes, the Eisenhower administration sought to restrain overzealous congressmen from pushing through measures that would openly violate the principle of nonintervention, while hinting to key congressmen that more discreet activities to eliminate the Guatemalan threat were underway. The administration did not discourage, however, the uproar in the Congress and the press. The tumult added to the psychological warfare of PBSUCCESS. For, as the *Christian Science Monitor* concluded, it sent a clear message: "The United States is determined that the pro-Communist government in Guatemala must go."[118] The morale of the Guatemalans could not fail to be shaken, particularly the morale of the institution on whom PBSUCCESS depended: the armed forces.

"Guatemala Has Not Bought Weapons From the Soviet Union or Poland," the Arbenz administration announced on May 21, after days of silence[119]—a moot point, since the arms had been bought in Czechoslovakia. While refusing to identify the source of the shipment, Foreign Minister Toriello and other officials stressed their government's right to acquire weapons wherever it wished, particularly in light of the American embargo.[120] "Guatemala is not a colony of the United States," stated *Diario de Centro América*.[121]

[116] Lantaff, May 24, 1954, *CR*-House, p. 7016; Smith, "It is Time to Stifle Guatemala's Reds," *Star Ledger* (Newark, N.J.), May 24, 1954, p. 10.

[117] Sikes, May 25, 1954, *CR*-House, p. 7092. See also Mansfield, May 20, 1954, *CR*-Senate, pp. 6915-18; Boggs, May 25, 1954, *CR*-House, p. 7092; McCormack, May 25, 1954, ibid.; Henry Reams (Ind.-Ohio), June 2, 1954, ibid., p. 7534; Patrick Hillings (R-Calif), June 10, 1954, *CR*-Senate, pp. 8018–19; Fisher, June 14, 1954, *CR*-House, pp. 8192–94; Bourke Hickenlooper (R-Iowa), June 17, 1954, *CR*-Senate, pp. 8442–44; Senate Minority Leader Lyndon Johnson (D-Texas), quoted in "Problem Is Communism," *Time*, June 7, 1954, p. 41.

[118] Hallett, "U.S. Views on Guatemala Find Latin America Wary," *CSM*, May 25, 1954, p. 1.

[119] For the text of the communiqué, see *DCA*, May 21, 1954, p. 8.

[120] See "Declaraciones de la cancillería," *DCA*, May 21, 1954, p. 1; "Guatemala Says U.S. Tried to Make Her Defenseless," *NYT*, May 22, 1954, p. 1; "Guatemala Hints U.N. Case on Arms," *NYT*, May 23, 1954, p. 1.

[121] "Guatemala no es una colonia norteamericana" (edit.), *DCA*, May 22, 1954, p. 3.

The brave words and half-truths could not change reality: the gamble had backfired. Not only had Arbenz and the PGT handed Washington an excuse to escalate its aggression, but their hope of secreting arms for workers' militias was dashed. Senior Guatemalan military officers who had been informed of the shipment by the United States appeared at the pier to take charge of the cargo. Arbenz had to approve. The weapons, he explained, were for the armed forces; their communist origins were due only to the American embargo.[122]

Under normal circumstances, the officers would not have objected to the fact that the shipment came from Czechoslovakia or even to the secrecy surrounding its arrival because they had wanted arms for so long. But the circumstances were not normal, and the price—the wrath of the United States—was staggering. Publicly, the military proclaimed its gratitude to Arbenz: the acquisition of weapons had been an "urgent necessity."[123] Privately, the officers were increasingly distressed by the president who was leading them to a head-on collision with Washington.

The loyalty of the officer corps had been faltering since the arrival of Peurifoy. On November 23, 1953, Bill Krieg, the DCM of the embassy, had written: "The officers may not yet be said to have abandoned their often-reported loyalty to Arbenz, but at the moment they are wondering and speculating more than hitherto about his actions."[124] In late December, Colonel Anselmo Getellá repeatedly conveyed his fears to sources close to the U.S. embassy: "If he [Arbenz] keeps on, he will bring us to ruin with him." Getellá, noted another report, "is frustrated, discontented and apparently has no faith that the country can go on much longer under the present circumstances." His malaise was particularly significant, Peurifoy remarked, because he was considered deeply loyal to Arbenz.[125] "Getellá will tell me the truth," Arbenz used to say.[126] (But if Getellá did not lie, he could also be silent. It was not until June 25, a week after the invasion had begun, that he expressed his fears to Arbenz. By then, it was too late.)

Getellá's complaints were quietly echoed by many of his colleagues. "A

---

[122] Interviews with Fortuny, María de Arbenz, and two senior Guatemalan officers who asked not to be identified.

[123] "Estamos prontos a sacrificar nuestras vidas, si fuera necesario, en defensa de los caros intereses de la patria," statement read over the radio by Army Chief of Staff Parinello, *DCA*, May 27, 1954, p. 1 (quoted from p. 12); see also "Voto de gratitud del Consejo de la Defensa al Presidente," *El I*, June 2, 1954, p. 1.

[124] Krieg to DOS, no. 443, Nov. 23, 1953, p. 3, NA 714.00.

[125] Quotations from Plihal and Herrera, "Report," Dec. 31, 1953, p. 2, and Plihal, "Report," Dec. 26, 1953, p. 2, both enclosed in Peurifoy to Leddy, Jan. 5, 1954, NA 714.00.

[126] Interviews with María de Arbenz and Fortuny. Getellá was a *Centenario* of Arbenz and was one of the very few officers who addressed him with the familiar "vos" form.

great number of officers are extremely unhappy about the Communists in the government and the poor U.S.-Guatemalan relations,'' reported the assistant air attaché at the U.S. embassy in mid-February; yet, he added, ''none dares to speak out for fear of jeopardizing his personal security.''[127] Two weeks later, as the Caracas conference opened, a CIA report pointed out the ambivalence of many officers, torn between their growing fear of the United States and their reluctance to plot against Arbenz: ''The loyalty of certain key officers . . . to President Arbenz apparently is wavering. . . . There is no conclusive evidence that the officers are yet prepared to oust Arbenz.''[128] Following the Caracas conference, reported Krieg, the officers were ''in a highly nervous state, anticipating U.S. action against Guatemala.''[129]

Guatemalan officers confirm these reports. Even before the conference opened, the psychological pressure was brutal. Caracas only heightened their fears: ''The army was in profound disarray''; it was ''a minefield.''[130] To the threats that rained from Washington were added threats from U.S. officials in Guatemala. ''Many officers,'' recalls Colonel Rubén González Siguí, ''were approached by the U.S. embassy and by the U.S. military mission.''[131] The message, be it explicit or implicit, was always the same: the United States could no longer tolerate Arbenz; should the Guatemalan army fail to act, Washington would resort to extreme measures. ''We were,'' laments Colonel Ernesto Paiz Novales, ''under enormous pressure. The U.S. military mission even hinted that the United States would invade.''[132] Bill Krieg concurs: the possibility of a direct military intervention was ''only hinted—but I'm sure that the Guatemalan officers got the point, and they inferred from it even more than was implied: they exaggerated everything we told them.''[133]

Fear spread among the Guatemalan officers and their families. Fear and confusion. Amid the growing demoralization, no one knew who could be trusted, who would betray. Many, indeed, no longer knew where they themselves stood. Arbenz's defense minister, Colonel José Angel Sánchez, was no

---

[127] Lt. Col. McAdam to Peurifoy, enclosed in Krieg to DOS, no. 722, Feb. 19, 1954, NA 714.00. See also Col. McCormick to Ambassador et al., Feb. 15, 1954, RG84 G&C, Box 3, NA-S.

[128] CIA report (title and number deleted), Mar. 5, 1954.

[129] Krieg to Peurifoy, Mar. 29, 1954.

[130] Quotations from interviews with Col. Parinello and Maj. Paz Tejada.

[131] Interview with Col. González Siguí, who claims that he refused to join in a plot against Arbenz—a statement that many officers dispute. In early June 1954, Arbenz dismissed González Siguí from the army. For González Siguí's account, see ''Battle of the Backyard,'' Time, June 28, 1954, pp. 43–44.

[132] Interview with Paiz Novales (who claims that he withstood the pressure). Also useful were interviews with the following officers: Parinello, Montenegro, Cruz Salazar, Paz Tejada, Mendoza.

[133] Interview with Krieg.

exception. An embassy official told Peurifoy of a conversation between the minister, his brother (Colonel Rodolfo Sánchez) and his cousin (Srta. Barrilla):

> Srta. Barrilla, who has much influence on the Minister, asked him if he did not realize what the situation was here and what would happen to the whole family in the event that Arbenz was overthrown. Colonel Rodolfo Sánchez asked if there was nothing the Minister could do to bring about a change in the situation here. Colonel José Angel Sánchez replied that there was nothing he could do. . . . [He] himself no longer had any idea of how the Army would react in the event of a move against the government. He imagined that some officers would stand by the government and others would be disposed to oppose it, but at present it was impossible to know which ones were which. It was, therefore, useless to try to do anything. Besides, he added, President Arbenz had told him that he would not leave the National Palace unless he were shot out of it.[134]

The men behind PBSUCCESS knew that fear was spreading through the Guatemalan officers, yet they were unable to assess its impact. They had drummed up only a few collaborators from the officer corps—none of whom held a key position—and they were not sure how the Guatemalan army would respond to Castillo Armas's invasion. Even three days after the invasion had begun, the CIA noted: "The controlling factor in the situation is . . . the position of the Guatemalan armed forces, and thus far this group has not given any clear indication of whether it will move, and if so, in which way."[135]

U.S. reports in the months preceding the invasion stressed that the Guatemalan officers were afraid of Arbenz. This was true. They feared dismissal; they feared disgrace. But there was more than fear. There was also, for many, a sense of nationalism and respect for Arbenz; several also felt gratitude for personal favors they had received. This respect, this gratitude, this warmth, were still evident thirty years later as Colonel González Siguí spoke of Arbenz. Arbenz, he remembered, was a magnificent officer, a charismatic military leader, a man of deep intelligence, a fervent nationalist who dared stand up to the Yankees and to Peurifoy, "the arrogant and abusive ambassador." The same respect for Arbenz was expressed by other officers who, like González Siguí, ultimately betrayed him.[136]

Until late May, Guatemalan officers had refrained from expressing their growing reservations to Arbenz. In the words of González Siguí, "No one said anything to Arbenz, but we all knew that things were going badly." Now,

[134] Hill to Peurifoy et al., Feb. 26, 1954.

[135] DCI to President, "The Situation in Guatemala as of 20 June," *FRUS*, 1952–1954, 4:1174–75. See also below, pp. 334–38.

[136] Particularly instructive were interviews with Cols. González Siguí (quoted), Mendoza, Parinello, and with Lt. Col. Paiz Novales.

under the avalanche of threats from the United States that followed the arrival of the *Alfhem*, fear of Washington overwhelmed them. "We could smell the invasion, and we knew that Castillo Armas was Washington's man."[137]

On the first of June, Arbenz called an officers' meeting, one of the very few he held during his presidency. He wanted to strengthen their morale. During the meeting, no one challenged Arbenz, but even he, who had lost touch with the officer corps, realized that his audience was uneasy, restless, unconvinced. Aware that he was not at his best addressing large groups, Arbenz thought that he would be able to reassure the officers through the power of the written word. He invited them to give him a list of questions expressing all their concerns; he would respond promptly.[138]

On June 5, the list, prepared by Army Chief of Staff Parinello and other senior officers, was presented to Arbenz.[139] It was a peculiar document. Cast in a very respectful tone, it began by stressing the army's loyalty to "Señor Presidente." The officers would obey him "absolutely and without reservation"; the questions were formulated only "to comply with the wishes of Señor Presidente." There followed twenty questions. They addressed one issue only: communism. Did the president not think that communist influence in Guatemala was excessive? Did the president agree that the communists, "who defame and insult foreign governments," were a threat to the country's well-being? "Might not Señor Presidente rely only and exclusively on his army—which is unconditionally loyal"—and eliminate the communists from the positions of influence they occupied? How did the president interpret article 32 of the constitution, which forbade organizations of an international character? Wouldn't the country's domestic and foreign policies be better served if the Communist party were marginalized?

Arbenz and the Secretariat of the PGT still failed to grasp the depth of the officers' dissatisfaction.[140] They believed that the officers were merely voicing doubts, doubts they could allay. Arbenz outlined the responses, and Fortuny fleshed them out. They reiterated what Arbenz had so often stated in public: "I am not now, nor will I be, a communist, but . . . neither am I, nor will I be, an anticommunist." Communist influence in the bureaucracy was extremely limited. "There are communists in the agrarian reform department," he conceded, "but they are the best workers and the most honest." Beyond

[137] Interview with González Siguí.

[138] Interviews with Parinello, González Siguí, and (for Arbenz's reactions) María de Arbenz and Fortuny. See also "El ocho de junio comenzó revolución interna," *La Hora*, July 26, 1954, p. 1.

[139] "Pliego de consultas de la oficialidad del Estado Mayor del Ejército, preparado por sugestión del señor Presidente de la República," June 5, 1954, *GT*, Box 11. Also useful were interviews with Col. Parinello, Lt. Col. Cruz Salazar, and Lt. Peralta Méndez.

[140] Interviews with María de Arbenz, Fortuny, Guerra Borges, Alejandro, Charnaud.

this refrain, Arbenz struck one theme: there would be no change in his policies. He considered the army's support decisive, but to rule "only and exclusively" with the army, as the officers had suggested, "is what is done by dictators like Pérez Jiménez and Somoza."[141]

There was no open break between the president and the officers; there was no further exchange of views. Arbenz and the Secretariat of the PGT thought they had reassured the officers. But only a pledge from Arbenz that he would immediately expel the PGT from the government could have satisfied the officers who cowered in the shadow of Washington's big stick. As it was, Arbenz's responses heightened the officers' exasperation with him and their fear of the United States.

While the army's morale was faltering, and while American journalists and congressmen demanded that Eisenhower halt Red aggression, only the blind and the gullible could have failed to notice that an armed attack on Guatemala was imminent. On May 19, Nicaragua had broken diplomatic relations with Guatemala. "This break," explained the *Washington Post*, "had been building up for some time because of the Guatemalan plotting against the Nicaraguan regime."[142] Encouraged by Washington, Somoza called for a meeting of OAS foreign ministers to discuss Guatemala's threat to the peace and security of the region. He was joined by Figueres; the foes united.[143] Meanwhile, Haiti declared the two ranking officials at the Guatemalan embassy in Port-au-Prince *persona non grata*, and in Havana, Batista ordered army, navy, police, and intelligence chiefs to be particularly alert to communist subversion emanating from Guatemala.[144] Given that Arbenz had made a special effort to cultivate good relations with Haiti and to maintain correct relations with the unsavory Batista, these diplomatic snubs were ominous.[145] Adding "to the

[141] A copy of Arbenz's written answers is in *GT*, Box 11. The document is undated, but it was delivered by June 10 at the latest. (Interviews with Fortuny and Parinello.)

Rumors about the officers' meeting with Arbenz spread, but the United States had no clear idea of what went on. See, for instance, TelConv (JFD, AWD), June 15, 1954, 10:17 a.m., DP, JFD:CS, Box 8, EL.

[142] "Communist Beachhead" (edit.), *WP*, May 21, 1954, p. 22.

[143] See MemoConv (Holland, Sevilla Sacasa), May 21, 1954, NA 714.00; "Gobiernos del Istmo consultan," *El I*, May 20, 1954, p. 1; "Consultas en el Caribe," *El I*, May 21, 1954, p. 1; "El embajador Sevilla Sacasa habla de consultas a la OEA," *La Hora*, May 21, 1954, p. 1; "Guatemala Hints U.N. Case on Arms," *NYT*, May 23, 1954, p. 1; "U.S. Detains Ship for Arms Search," *NYT*, May 27, 1954, p. 6; Herron and Wieland to Holland, Memo no. 208, June 9, 1954.

[144] See "Cuba Tightens Security," *NYT*, May 25, 1954, p. 12, and "Non grato encargado de negocios A.I. en Haiti," *El I*, May 25, 1954, p. 1.

[145] For Guatemala's overtures toward Haiti, see "Saludo y homenaje a Haiti," *DCA*, May 18, 1953, p. 4; "Pueblo haitiano concede a Arbenz la más alta prueba de amis-

impression that Guatemala was rapidly becoming isolated internationally,'' Panama and Costa Rica recalled their ambassadors for consultations.[146]

On May 25 the Honduran ambassador to Guatemala left abruptly, ''on the urgent instructions of his government.'' Guatemalan officials explained that the hasty departure did not presage a break in diplomatic relations, but the opposition *El Imparcial* was keen to dispel false illusions. ''Well-informed sources,'' it pointed out, ''note that Ambassador Duran will not return. . . . The Ambassador has left with everything, even his reserves of wine and alcohol. His baggage included five cases of champagne, four of whiskey, and five of French table wine.''[147] As the ambassador crated his wine, the press in the other Central American republics was sounding the tocsin: Guatemalan troops were massing at the Honduran border; equipped with the *Alfhem* weapons, Guatemala stood poised to attack peaceful, defenseless Honduras.[148]

In Guatemala, everyone knew that this was nonsense. Such an attack would have been suicidal, for it would have triggered the American response. What, then, lay behind these rumors? Pieced together ''with other reports that the United States was flying arms into Honduras and Nicaragua,'' there was, for the Guatemalans, only one possible explanation: Honduras was about to attack, this attack would be presented as Guatemalan aggression against Honduras, and U.S. military intervention would thereby be justified.[149]

On May 26, an unmarked C-47 flew over Guatemala City dropping leaflets that informed the Guatemalans that their liberation was at hand. ''If they had been napalm bombs and not leaflets, we wouldn't be here to talk about it,'' *El Imparcial* wrote for the benefit of the dim-witted.[150] On the succeeding days,

---

tad,'' *DCA*, Dec. 28, 1953, p. 8; ''Haiti condecora a Arbenz,'' *Tribuna Popular*, Dec. 30, 1953, p. 1; ''Buena impresión dejó en Haiti nuestra delegación especial,'' *DCA*, Feb. 1, 1954, p. 8.

[146] *JW* 21, May 28, 1954, p. 2.

[147] ''Embajador hondureño sale subito,'' *El I*, May 25, 1954, pp. 1, 5.

[148] For relevant articles, see ''Fuerzas militares a frontera con Honduras,'' *La Prensa*, Managua, May 23, 1954, p. 8; ''Inminente la guerra entre Honduras y Guatemala,'' *Diario de Costa Rica*, San José, May 25, 1954, p. 1; ''La guerra entre Honduras y Guatemala es inminente,'' *La Nación*, San José, May 25, 1954, p. 1. For a lucid critique of this war scare, see Alberto Quinteros, ''Serenidad y espíritu fraternal en estos momentos difíciles para Centro América,'' *El Diario de Hoy*, San Salvador, June 2, 1954, p. 6. (''Many Central American newspapers . . . have exacerbated the climate of fear by announcing the movement of Guatemalan troops to the Honduran border, by discussing the possibility of an attack on the Panama Canal from bases in Guatemala and by printing other alarming stories.'')

[149] Quoted from *JW* 21, May 28, 1954, p. 2. Meanwhile in Washington, ''It was agreed that there would be wide publicity in connection with the visit to the U.S. by the Honduran military man, Velasquez, in order to create further nervousness in Guatemala.'' (DOS, Meeting of Guatemalan Group, June 2, 1954, p. 2.)

[150] ''Avión desconocido voló dejando caer propaganda contra el comunismo,'' *El I*,

other "mystery planes" appeared over the capital in what seemed to be an "obvious rehearsal for the dropping of bombs."[151]

One of the commando groups trained by the CIA in Nicaragua had already sprung into action. On May 20, a train carrying the *Alfhem* weapons from Puerto Barrios to the capital "was almost blown up" (the explosion produced very little damage; unexploded sticks of dynamite were later found); there was a shootout; one soldier was killed, three were wounded; one of the saboteurs was also killed, and the others escaped. The attack was praised by the U.S.-controlled *Voz de la Liberación*. There were further attempts to sabotage trains linking Puerto Barrios with the capital on May 21 and May 25.[152] Both attempts failed, but another, less violent form of warfare was waged in the capital in the last week of May. At night, "leaflets were pushed under the doors . . . telling people to prepare lists of communists and known communist-sympathizers. Immediately after the government was overthrown, the leaflets said, the people were to take the lists to the new authorities, who would deal out 'justice.' "[153]

While journalists in the United States and Central America described Honduras as the innocent victim, it was an open secret that Castillo Armas was preparing to attack Guatemala from Honduras. By late May "his soldiers in uniform swaggered around the streets of Tegucigalpa," *U.S. News and World Report* later wrote. "Correspondents visited his headquarters and filed dispatches saying that the revolution was going to start."[154] And when Rodolfo Mendoza, formerly chief of the Guatemalan air force, fled Guatemala on June 4 aboard a private aircraft, everyone assumed that he had defected to join Castillo Armas. More ominously still, with him was an American citizen, Major (ret.) Ferdinand Schupp, who had been the deputy chief of the U.S. Air

---

May 27, 1954, p. 1, quoted from p. 5. For a less enthusiastic account, see "Avión extranjero provoca al gobierno de la revolución," *DCA*, May 27, 1954, p. 1.

[151] William Krehm, "A Victory for the West in Guatemala?" *International Journal*, Autumn 1954, p. 300.

[152] "Tren estuvo a punto de ser dinamitado," *El I*, May 21, 1954, p. 1 (quoted); "Ferrocarrileros indignados por el atentado dinamitero," *DCA*, May 21, 1954, p. 1; "Terrorismo dinamitero: Pieza de un engranaje," *DCA*, May 22, 1954, p. 1; "Investigase atentado dinamitero," ibid.; "Atentado a convoy con armamento," *El I*, May 22, 1954, p. 1; "Guatemala Says U.S. Tried to Make Her Defenseless," *NYT*, May 22, 1954, p. 1; "Radio clandestina felicitó a los terroristas el sabado," *DCA*, May 24, 1954, p. 1; "Nuevo acto de sabotaje a tren de Barrios," *El I*, May 26, 1954, p. 1. On the role of the CIA, see Schlesinger and Kinzer, *Bitter Fruit*, p. 151.

[153] Gruson, "Guatemala Grim as Tension Rises," *NYT*, May 30, 1954, p. 16.

[154] "A Revolt U.S. Couldn't Win," *U.S. News and World Report*, July 2, 1954, pp. 22, 24. For an admiring interview with Castillo Armas in Tegucigalpa by a prestigious Central American newspaper, see "Por la patria y por nuestra religión," *La Nación*, San José, June 9, 1954, p. 19.

Force Mission in Guatemala until 1952.[155] Mendoza was not just a retired colonel. He had been "the most experienced and capable pilot in the Guatemalan Air Force."[156] Nor was Schupp just a U.S. citizen. Because of his previous position, many Guatemalans saw him as an agent of the U.S. government. Mendoza and Schupp would be back in a few days, flying over the capital as part of Castillo Armas's air force.

Perhaps the dramatic departure of Mendoza and Schupp had been timed by the CIA to reap maximum psychological advantage; perhaps the timing was due to fear that their participation in PBSUCCESS had been discovered. In any case, they left when tension was at a peak. The mood in Guatemala City that week was captured by Sidney Gruson:

> The climax of the crisis in the immediate future is widely expected. There is talk of a possibility of an economic boycott or of an armed invasion by Guatemalan exiles, or even the possibility of a landing of United States troops to sweep the Communists from political power. . . . The nervousness is not confined to the ordinary people here. The government's concern is apparent. . . . Even more apparent are the jitters spreading among leaders of the non-Communist revolutionary parties. As a result of the crisis, the leaders, for the first time, are talking guardedly of the dangers . . . [of] having allowed the Communists to gain wide powers.[157]

In vain did the Arbenz administration seek to quell the storm. On May 27, Foreign Minister Toriello sent a cable to his Honduran counterpart urging the immediate conclusion of a pact of friendship and nonaggression. The cable had been sent, the *New York Times* pointed out, at 3:30 a.m., "about nine hours after an unidentified C-47 plane had showered the City of Guatemala with anti-government leaflets."[158]

Toriello's offer was spurned. In Tegucigalpa, officials explained to sympathetic journalists that "Guatemala was using an old communist trick: it was just trying to put the Honduran people off guard so that it would be easier to

---

[155] "Rodolfo Mendoza huyó por aire," *El I*, June 5, 1954, p. 1; "Coronel Mendoza desaparece en una avioneta particular," *DCA*, June 5, 1954, p. 1; "Rodolfo Mendoza obtuvo el asilo político en la república salvadoreña," *El I*, June 7, 1954, p. 1; "Quien es el incógnito personaje que voló con el coronel Mendoza," *La Hora*, June 7, 1954, p. 1; "Top Flyer Escapes," *NYT*, June 7, 1954, p. 6; "U.S. Ex-Officer Joins Guatemalan in Flight," *NYT*, June 8, 1954, p. 1; Peurifoy to SecState, no. 910, June 7, 1954, NA 714.00; *JW* 23, June 11, 1954, p. 4.

[156] HQs Panama Canal Department, "Weekly Intelligence Summary" no. 274, Oct. 2, 1947, p.8, RG319 ID 0402769, NA-S.

[157] "Guatemala Grim as Tension Rises," *NYT*, May 30, 1954, p. 16.

[158] "Guatemala Proposes Pact with Honduras," *NYT*, May 28, 1954, p. 1 (quoted); "Pacto de amistad y no agresión con Honduras propone el gobierno de Guatemala," *DCA*, May 27, 1954, p. 1; "Amistad y no agresión" (edit.), *DCA*, May 28, 1954, p. 1.

attack them later." In the U.S. Congress, Representative Ray Madden damned the offer as further proof of the true intentions of "the Communist conspirators in Guatemala." The Guatemalan proposal, he revealed, followed "exactly the same blueprint used to place Lithuania, Latvia, and Estonia, and other captive nations under Kremlin slavery."[159]

Guatemala called for talks with the United States to reduce tensions. Toriello declared his "well-founded hope" that the problems between the two countries would be settled "in the most amicable fashion" and even claimed that Peurifoy "has always behaved like a gentleman." Peurifoy's rejoinder was "No comment," while from Washington flowed further indications that the decision was irrevocable: Arbenz must go.[160]

"U.S. Detains Ship for Arms Search," announced the *New York Times* on May 27, as the State Department disclosed that a French merchant vessel was being searched by U.S. customs officials in the Canal Zone "with the knowledge and the approval of the French Government and the French line."[161] The Eisenhower administration had imposed a naval quarantine. No weapons and no ammunition would be allowed to reach Guatemala. "If it is necessary as a last resort to damage them [the suspect ships] to cause them to stop . . . that will be done," read the instructions to the task force that had been patrolling the Gulf of Honduras since May 24. Operation Hardrock had begun.[162]

[159] "La proposición de Guatemala a nuestro gobierno suscita conjeturas en Panama," *El Día*, Tegucigalpa, June 3, 1954, p. 1; Madden (D-Ind), June 8, 1954, *CR-House*, p. 7881.

[160] Quotations from "Embajador de EE.UU: Sostuvo conferencia con Toriello," *El I*, May 24, 1954, pp. 1, 2. See also "Guatemala Eases Stand toward U.S.," *NYT*, May 25, 1954, p. 12; "Guatemalans Fail to Grasp Concern of U.S. over Reds," *NYT*, May 26, 1954, p. 13; "Guatemala for Talks," *NYT*, May 29, 1954, p. 5; "Reunión personal con Eisenhower podría aliviar situación de C.A.," *DCA*, May 31, 1954, p. 1; "Guatemala Aide Meets U.S. Envoy," *NYT*, June 2, 1954, p. 10; *JW* 21, May 28, 1954, pp. 2–3; *JW* 22, June 4, 1954, pp. 1–3; Peurifoy to SecState, no. 860, June 1, 1954, NA 714.00; Peurifoy to SecState, June 2, 1954, *FRUS*, 1952–1954, 4:1155–56. Guatemala did not intend to make concessions on the communist issue. Furthermore, while Toriello expressed willingness to hold talks with United Fruit officials, he also stated "that his government would put . . . one limitation on negotiations with the company. The agrarian reform law . . . 'is not a subject for negotiation or discussion.' " ("Guatemala for Talks," *NYT*, May 29, 1954, p. 5.)

[161] "U.S. Detains Ship for Arms Search," *NYT*, May 27, 1954, p. 1. (The article includes the text of the State Department's communiqué.)

[162] U.S. Atlantic Fleet, Cdr. Honduras Patrol, no. 003-54, June 28, 1954, p. A4. On Operation Hardrock, see esp. DOD, Annual Report of the Cdr.-in-Chief U.S. Atlantic Fleet (Supplementary), Part 4; U.S. Atlantic Fleet, Cdr. Honduras Patrol, no. 001-54, May 24, 1954, report of Cdr. USS Fessenden, "Operation Hardrock Baker," June 1, 1954; U.S. Atlantic Fleet, Cdr. Honduras Patrol, no. 001-54, June 1, 1954; report of Cdr. Escort Squadron 10, "Operations of the Honduras Patrol Group," June 8, 1954; U.S. Atlantic Fleet, Cdr. Honduras Patrol, no. 002-54, June 12, 1954.

In London, the quarantine was considered particularly insulting. Accustomed to ruling the waves, and jealous of their "special relationship" with the United States, the British sought assurances that they would not be treated like mere Frenchmen—that British ships would not be boarded. Foster Dulles was unmoved. He could offer no promises, he told the British ambassador. The Foreign Office began to prepare a paper on the legality of the blockade, only to be told by Prime Minister Churchill, who did not consider the issue worth jeopardizing American goodwill, to forget it. Britain would comply.[163]

Secretary Dulles and his brother Allen, the prime movers behind the measure, knew that they were violating international law. The legal adviser of the State Department had said as much, and not one of the officials consulted had claimed otherwise.[164] None, however, had opposed the measure except Robert Murphy, deputy assistant secretary of state, who had not been consulted, but had learned of the decision "by a casual reference" at lunch. In a memo to Secretary Dulles, Murphy did not mince words. "Now that the President and you have decided on this action it must, of course, be seen through," he wrote, "but I would like you to know that I believe the philosophy back of the action is wrong and that it may be very expensive over the longer term. My instinct, and perhaps my ignorance of Guatemalan problems, tells me that to resort to this action confesses the bankruptcy of our political policy vis-à-vis that country. Instead of political action inside Guatemala, we are obliged to resort to heavy-handed military action on the periphery of the cause of trouble."[165]

During the quarantine, which ended only with the fall of Arbenz, U.S. warships found no weapons or ammunition destined for Guatemala. Yet Operation Hardrock was not mere bravado; it packed a psychological punch. To anxious Guatemalans, the spectacle of U.S. warships patrolling the Gulf of Honduras and openly flouting international law stirred disturbing memories of the marines landing on the shores of Central America.

More recent memories—those of Caracas—were rekindled by rumors that the United States was seeking a special OAS conference to vote sanctions against Guatemala. On June 1, the Guatemalan chargé d'affaires in Washing-

---

On the decision to establish the quarantine, see TelConv (JFD, AWD), May 18, 1954, 9:05 a.m., DP:TCS, Box 2, EL; TelConv (JFD, AWD), May 19, 1954, 8:56 a.m., DP, JFD:CS, Box 7, EL; MemoConv, May 22, 1954, *FRUS*, 1952–1954, 4:1122–23; "Memorandum of Discussion at the 199th Meeting of the National Security Council, May 27," ibid., pp. 1131–35.

[163] Meers, "Pebble on the Beach," pp. 44–49; Young, "Great Britain's Latin American Dilemma," pp. 577–79.

[164] See TelConv (JFD, Anderson), May 19, 1954, 9:00 a.m., DP, JFD:CS, Box 7, EL; TelConv (JFD, Holland), May 19, 1954, 9:05 a.m., ibid.; English to Holland, May 20, 1954, NA 714.00; Holland to Donnelly and Pawley, May 27, 1954, NA 714.00.

[165] Murphy to SecState, May 25, 1954, NA 611.14.

ton informed Toriello that the preparatory work "had progressed very far."[166] The conference, the *New York Times* stated a few days later, would be held at Montevideo on July 1. U.S. officials, it added, seemed "confident of support by a majority of other Latin American Republics."[167]

The *Times*' information was accurate. When the article appeared, on June 10, Washington could count on the required two-thirds majority to pass two types of sanctions: the prohibition of travel by agents of international communism to and from Guatemala and the prohibition of the importation of military equipment into Guatemala. A special task force within the State Department, the Guatemalan Group, had been at work since early May (that is, before the arrival of the *Alfhem*) coaxing and pressuring the Latin American republics to support these sanctions.[168]

Guatemala alone of the OAS members had been excluded from the prelim-

---

[166] Peurifoy to SecState, no. 870, June 2, 1954, NA 714.00, quoting Toriello.

[167] "Panama Favoring Guatemala Talks," *NYT*, June 10, 1954, p. 12.

[168] For the creation of the Task Force, see "OAS Action against Communism in Guatemala," May 10, 1954, *FRUS*, 1952–1954, 4:1102–5. For the draft resolution, see "The Secretary of State to Diplomatic Offices in the American Republics," June 5, 1954, ibid., pp. 1157–60.

Rabe writes, "In a straw vote, the State Department found it could count on only eleven Latin American votes." (*Eisenhower and Latin America*, p. 53.) This was two votes short of the required two-thirds majority. Other votes were, however, in the pipeline: on June 19, Panama pledged its vote. (MemoConv [Heurtematte, Holland], June 19, 1954, NA 714.00.) And, of course, there was Brazil: as Foster Dulles noted, Brazil had enthusiastically supported the U.S. position against Guatemala at Caracas (U.S. Congress, *HCFA*, p. 502), and had warmly endorsed the draft resolution against Guatemala prepared by the United States for the Montevideo conference. (MemoConv [Dulles, Muñiz, Holland] May 11, 1954; MemoConv [Dulles, Muñiz, Holland] May 24, 1954; MemoConv [Dulles, Muñiz, Holland] May 27, 1954; MemoConv [Muñiz, Holland] May 28, 1954. All NA 714.00.) That Brazil had not yet officially joined the co-sponsors of the draft resolution was not due to sudden scruples about the principle of nonintervention. It was because the foreign minister was "very irritated" with the State Department; he had asked that Brazil be granted the honor "to take the lead in approaching Uruguay, Paraguay, Bolivia and Chile" on behalf of the draft resolution, but the emissary he had appointed for the purpose had been delayed by illness, and the State Department proceeded without him. (Quotations from MemoConv [Muñiz, Holland] June 10, 1954, p. 1, and DOS, "OAS Action against Communism in Guatemala," May 29, 1954, p. 1. Both NA 714.00.) After he had vented his frustration, the foreign minister softened: if the State Department would accept two changes in the draft resolution, Brazil would not only endorse it, but also "try to get others" to support it. "These [two amendments] are acceptable to the U.S. . . . Brazil's joinder should bring in several waverers and give us more than the required fourteen votes." (Quotations from: TelConv [JFD, Holland] June 16, 1954, 11:29 a.m., DP, JFD:CS, Box 8, and from Holland to Undersecretary, June 16, 1954, NA Lot 58D18 & 58D78, Box 2.)

inaries. No Latin American government had informed the Arbenz administration of the nature of the sanctions under discussion. "It was a miracle," marveled Assistant Secretary Holland on June 10, "that the secrecy of the resolution had been preserved."[169] To the Guatemalans, Holland's miracle was a nightmare: they could only speculate about the gravity of the sanctions that were being hammered out even before the conference began, and they imagined the worst.[170] On June 9, Minor Keilhauer, an upper-class friend of Arbenz, appeared in desperation at the U.S. embassy. He and other prominent supporters of the administration, among them Foreign Minister Toriello, "were greatly disturbed over the possibility of sanctions. All of them," Peurifoy reported,

> realize that the government could not operate if sanctions were applied. He [Keil-hauer] stated that many of Arbenz's friends had been working on him to change the

These fourteen countries had accepted the draft resolution in its entirety *in advance of* the conference and it is very unlikely that all the other countries would have voted against the resolution. On June 17, an OIR report concluded, "There is no doubt that the substance of the anti-Guatemala resolution proposed for Montevideo will be approved by more than two-thirds of the OAS nations." (Intelligence Report, June 17, 1954, p. 1, NA 714.00.)

[169] MemoConv (Holland, Jara, Suarez, Barrell), June 10, 1954, p. 1, NA 714.00. Interviews with María de Arbenz, Fortuny, and Toriello confirm that the government did not know what sanctions were being planned.

Even democratic Uruguay, considered an ardent supporter of the principle of nonintervention, expressly excluded Guatemala—and included the United States—in its deliberations about the conference. Ambassador José Mora told Holland that his government would send a special ambassador to Guatemala before the conference "to investigate on the ground." This envoy, Holland noted, "would get in touch with our ambassador there, but would not report to the local government." Uruguay had earlier informed the State Department "that it would support the calling of the conference" and agreed to have it in Montevideo. (Quotations from MemoConv [Mora, Holland] June 10, 1954, and MemoConv [Mora, Holland] June 7, 1954. Both NA 714.00.) It was only after Castillo Armas's invasion had begun that Uruguay expressed "strong opposition to going ahead with the plans" for the conference and warned that it might "revoke permission to use Montevideo as a site." (CIA, *Current Intelligence Digest*, June 25, 1954, p. 16.)

[170] Confirmed by all the Guatemalans interviewed on this point. See also *JW* 21, May 28, 1954, p. 1. "Action by the [OAS] Foreign Ministers might include an agreement to stop all trade with Guatemala," opined *Newsweek*. ("U.S. Showdown on Guatemala?" June 14, 1954, p. 54.) While *DCA* barely mentioned the forthcoming conference, the opposition press speculated about it recklessly. See, for instance, *El I*: "Hacia consulta interamericana," May 27, 1954, p. 1; "El Salvador no admite el envio," May 28, 1954, p. 1; "Senador Johnson predijo planteamiento de las sanciones contra Guatemala," May 29, 1954, p. 1; "Canciller colombiano declara que debe convocarse junta de América," June 2, 1954, p. 1; "La ilusión de la solidaridad," June 3, 1954, p. 1; "Montevideo posible sede," June 8, 1954, p. 1.

government's attitude and actions. Keilhauer asked me if I would see the President [Arbenz] and attempt to bring about a change in the situation. . . . He said . . . time was running short in view of the proposed meeting of the OAS. He and his conferees knew this conference would vote economic sanctions against Guatemala, and that the government would not survive.[171]

Peurifoy, however, had neither the time nor the inclination to chat with Arbenz. He was too busy trying to convince Washington to do more to destabilize the government before Castillo Armas's invasion began.[172]

Three decades later, in a Georgetown sitting room, a man who had been a senior member of the Guatemalan Group looked back at the curious timing of the Montevideo conference. "I am beginning to think that the preparations for Montevideo were part of a cover-up and that there was never any intention of holding the conference," Deputy Assistant Secretary Woodward mused.[173] The conference was planned for early July, that is, after the date set for the invasion of Guatemala. If the invasion succeeded, it would have been unnecessary to have held the conference; if the invasion failed, it would have been foolhardy. Arbenz would have become a hero in Latin America, Dulles himself noted, and it would have been difficult to have held the Latin American governments in line.[174] Those State Department officials who, like Woodward, were not privy to PBSUCCESS and who, like Woodward, labored hard for a conference that would never take place, were unwitting pawns of PBSUCCESS.

In theory, the United States could have held the Montevideo conference before the invasion, used the sanctions to further weaken the Guatemalans' morale and then launched Castillo Armas's band. But there is no indication that this was considered.[175] Perhaps they reasoned that preparing for a paper conference would strengthen the figleaf: the United States was acting responsibly within the framework of the Organization of American States; it was not indulging in covert operations. Perhaps they reasoned that the threat of unspecified sanctions was, for the Guatemalans, more frightening than the imposition of the specific sanctions that were planned.

And the Guatemalans were indeed frightened. Tension and anguish escalated among the *Arbencistas*, and finally "something like hysteria took

[171] Peurifoy to SecState, no. 945, June 10, 1954, NA 714.00.

[172] See Peurifoy to SecState, June 2, 1954, *FRUS*, 1952–1954, 4:1155–56 and Peurifoy to SecState, no. 956, June 11, 1954, NA 714.00.

[173] Interview with Woodward.

[174] "The Secretary believed that on the assumption that [Castillo] Armas failed, Arbenz and Toriello would become heroes and we may not succeed in obtaining our resolution. Such a diplomatic defeat would be a great blow to the US prestige." (DOS, Meeting of Guatemalan Group, June 25, 1954, p. 1.)

[175] Interviews with Bissell and Kirkpatrick.

over.''[176] In despair and self-defense, the regime began to lash out at the only foe that it could reach—the internal opposition—in an attempt to destroy the fifth column before the invasion began. On June 8, constitutional guarantees were suspended.[177] Censorship was imposed, and the opposition media ceased their furious attacks on the regime. ''They had reported sensationally the developing political crisis in Guatemala'' until the day the decree was announced, reported the U.S. embassy.[178]

A wave of arrests had begun in the last days of May.[179] In the final four weeks of the regime several hundred suspects were detained. Among them were many plotters, but also many who were not involved in any conspiracy. ''Prisoners were tortured. At least seventy-five were killed and hastily buried in mass graves.''[180]

In the United States, the repression provoked an uproar. Congressmen and journalists inveighed against a ''tyrannical Communist minority'' that was trying ''to maintain itself against the will of the people.''[181] Secretary Dulles ''spoke out bluntly'' against the ''reign of terror,'' and President Eisenhower ''added the weight of his disapproval and deep regret.''[182]

The depth of the indignation that seized so many in the United States who

[176] Krehm (see n. 151 above), p. 300. This is an excellent article by a first-rate journalist.

[177] ''Restringidas las garantías,'' *DCA*, June 8, 1954, p. 1; ''Garantías restrictas un mes,'' *El I*, June 8, 1954, p. 1; ''Guatemala Calls Emergency and Suspends Civil Liberty,'' *NYT*, June 8, 1954, p. 1.

[178] *JW* 23, June 11, 1954, p. 3.

[179] See ''Tras cateos, cinco asilados,'' *El I*, May 31, 1954, p. 1; ''Capturas por complot siguen,'' *El I*, June 1, 1954, p. 1; ''Dos capturas más,'' *El I*, June 2, 1954, p. 1; ''Inseguridad de las personas'' (edit.), ibid.; ''Descubierto el más grande complot,'' *DCA*, June 3, 1954, p. 1; ''El aventurismo golpista'' (edit.), ibid., p. 3; ''No tardaré en el destierro, dijo Goicolea Villacorta,'' *El I*, June 4, 1954, p. 1; ''Nuevas capturas quedan en misterio,'' *El I*, June 5, 1954, p. 1; ''Salvoconductos a dos exilados más,'' *El I*, June 7, 1954, p. 1; Peurifoy to SecState, no. 873, June 2, 1954, NA 714.00; Peurifoy to SecState, no. 903, June 5, 1954, NA 714.00; ''Plot in Guatemala Charged as 5 Flee to Embassy Haven,'' *NYT*, June 1, 1954, p. 1; ''Plot Still Fought by Guatemalans,'' *NYT*, June 3, 1954, p. 1. For a letter that vividly conveys the tension of the time, see Charnaud to Toriello, June 15, 1954, CO:G, June 1954, pp. 408–10, AGCA.

[180] Krehm (see n. 151 above), p. 300. This is the most accurate estimate. After Arbenz's fall, the bodies of many ''communists'' executed by the *Liberacionistas* were displayed to foreign journalists as the victims of the defeated regime. See below, pp. 333–34.

[181] Hickenlooper, June 17, 1954, *CR*-Senate, p. 8843.

[182] Quotations from ''Dulles Pictures Guatemalan Fear,'' *NYT*, June 16, 1954, p. 8, and ''Guatemala, Battle in the Backyard,'' *Time*, June 28, 1954, p. 43. For the transcript of Eisenhower's press conference see *NYT*, June 17, 1954, p. 14.

were usually philosophical about violence in Latin America is somewhat surprising. Arbenz, however, was the enemy. For too long, his government had posed a disquieting paradox for the Americans: riddled with communists, it had nevertheless upheld political democracy and civil liberties to a degree that was highly unusual in Latin America.

In the words of Senators Wiley and Hickenlooper, the "Communist wolves" had finally shed their "sheep's clothing." Now, at last, the communists were moving "to crush the free spirit of the Guatemalan people." Representative Javits expressed the views of many when he proclaimed, "The suspension of constitutional guarantees by the Government of Guatemala is a final confirmation of the grave threat to the peace and security of the Americas due to the Communist-infiltrated government of that unhappy country."[183]

Many rushed to condemn the Arbenz administration to eternal opprobrium. If this required that history be rewritten, so be it. By claiming that the crimes perpetrated in the last weeks of the regime were unusually atrocious ("treatment I have never heard of before, nor imagined"), by claiming that these were "unLatin" acts,[184] they sought to convey the unprecedented nature of the threat: "For a suitable analogy [to these crimes] one must look behind the Iron Curtain."[185] Like the weapons on the *Alfhem*, they were stamped with a hammer and sickle.

[183] Wiley, June 16, 1954, *CR*-Senate, p. A4443; Hickenlooper, June 17, 1954, ibid, p. 8443; Javits, June 7, 1954, *CR*-House, p. 8107.

[184] Quotations from Monroe, "Guatemala: What the Reds Left Behind," p. 60, and Martz, *Communist Infiltration*, p. 101.

[185] James, *Red Design*, p. 263.

CHAPTER 14

The Fall of Arbenz

ON JUNE 18, 1954, the Tegucigalpa daily *El Cronista* published a statement issued by Eduardo Valenzuela, the foreign minister of Honduras. He had informed Lt. Colonel Castillo Armas that if he violated the neutrality of Honduras he would be expelled. "The Honduran public can be confident," Valenzuela pledged, "that the government is firm and will be firm in maintaining and honoring its neutrality."[1]

The *New York Times* told a different story. In a "virtual wide-open movement," it reported, Guatemalan exiles were being flown in Honduran planes to the Guatemalan border.[2] The story was out of date before it appeared; on June 17, the invasion of Guatemala had begun.[3]

For the next ten days the international press bandied about contradictory reports of the war, the Guatemalan army released confident communiqués, and Castillo Armas's American patrons began to fear the worst. On the twenty-sixth, an army bulletin announced that the rebels were on the run, and *Diario de Centro América* blared: "Government Triumphs!"[4]

On June 27, Arbenz resigned. A game of musical chairs began in Guatemala City. At each pause, Castillo Armas was closer to the throne. Meanwhile, hundreds of *Arbencistas*, and Arbenz himself, sought refuge in foreign embassies, and repression swept the country. "The years of spring in the land of eternal tyranny" had abruptly concluded.

Throughout his exile, Arbenz would be subjected to the reproaches of former supporters and to the thinly disguised contempt of a new generation of Latin American leftists who grew in the shadow of Fidel Castro. During his presidency, these critics argued, Jacobo Arbenz had proudly challenged the

---

[1] "Castillo Armas recibió la prevención en el despacho de nuestra cancillería," *El Cronista*, Tegucigalpa, June 18, 1954, p. 1. For a vehement apology of the official position of the Honduran government, see Moya Posas, *La jornada épica*.

[2] "Anti-Arbenz Men Move in Honduras," *NYT*, June 18, 1954, p. 7.

[3] American authors, following the *NYT*, regularly cite June 18 as the beginning of the invasion; Guatemalan authors, the Guatemalan press and Guatemalan participants assert that Castillo Armas's men crossed the border in the early hours of June 17 and occupied El Florido, Jocotán, and other hamlets along the road to Chiquimula later in the day.

[4] Quotations from "Persecución de los agresores ha continuado sin cuartel," *El I*, June 26, 1954, p. 1, and "Fuerzas de la revolución triunfantes," *DCA*, June 26, 1954, p. 1.

American colossus—only to surrender as if he were the abject president of a banana republic. For months on end, they asserted, that stubborn, enigmatic man had imposed a steady course on those who had wavered, but at the moment of crisis he had sought refuge in a foreign embassy. The marines had not been necessary; economic sanctions had not been necessary; a handful of exiles had sufficed. No major battles had been fought and on the two occasions when the rebels had met resistance, they had been defeated. Arbenz, the indictment ran, gave up without even going to the front, without even attempting to arm the people. He was a petty bourgeois, not a revolutionary, concluded those who sought wisdom in simplistic class analysis.[5] And yet Arbenz was not a coward: "Military attachés, diplomats and journalists who have met the Guatemalan President," *Time* reported on June 28, 1954, "are in striking agreement that the mainspring of his character is dogged, stubborn, self-willed courage."[6]

THE INVASION

Arbenz's initial response to the invasion was based on his belief that Castillo Armas posed no military threat. His informers in Honduras had assured him that there were only a few hundred rebels.[7] To defeat them would not be difficult.[8]

His assessment of the rebels' strength was correct. Castillo Armas's "rather ramshackle army" of *Liberacionistas* consisted of about 250 men: approximately 150 rebels crossed the border on June 17 and headed in the direction of Zacapa; the others attacked Puerto Barrios, to the north, a few days later.[9]

[5] See, for example, Cardoza y Aragón, *La Revolución Gualtemalteca*; Cardoza, "A treinta años," p. 92; and Góngora, *Introducción*, pp. 92–93.

[6] "Guatemala: Battle in the Backyard," *Time*, June 28, 1954, p. 38.

[7] See the numerous reports by Chargé d'Affaires Paredes Moreira, Military Attaché Col. Morales, and Amb. Chinchilla Orellana in *GT*, Boxes 7 and 72. These reports cover Oct. 1953 to June 1954.

[8] Interviews with María de Arbenz, Fortuny, Guerra Borges, Alejandro, Toriello, Charnaud, and Cols. Parinello and Guillén.

[9] Quoted from Allen W. Dulles, "My Answer to the Bay of Pigs," p. 16, AWD Papers, Box 138, ML. The figure usually given—150 to 200—does not include the hundred rebels who attacked Puerto Barrios. On the main force, see Putzeys Rojas, *Así se hizo la Liberación*; L.A.H.A., *Así se gestó la Liberación*; Santa Cruz Morales, "El Ejército de Liberación."

Liberacionista accounts of the invasion are rare, florid and fantastic. The most useful are Putzeys Rojas, *Así se hizo la Liberación* and L.A.H.A., *Así se gestó la Liberación*. See also Flores Avendaño, *Memorias*, 2:401–45; Guatemala, *Efemérides*; López Villatoro, *Por qué fué derrotado el comunismo en Guatemala?* pp. 47–53. Works that do not deal with the invasion but perpetuate the *Liberacionista* myth include López Vil-

Not only were the rebels a mere handful, but their weapons were of the same quality as those of the Guatemalan army, that is, World War II vintage—a nod to the figleaf that still rankles many who had expected to be given sophisticated arms.[10] Only in communications equipment and in aircraft did the rebels enjoy a marked advantage.

Arbenz's realistic assessment of the military insignificance of the rebel challenge had a perverse effect on his overall assessment of the invasion. Throughout the previous months, he had believed that the army would remain loyal if faced with an exile attack in which the United States did not directly participate. The military weakness of the invasion reinforced his illusions. Arbenz, his wife recalls, "believed that the army would defend the motherland. Our army would refuse to submit to Castillo Armas, a traitor who had been defeated in 1950 and who was leading a motley band of outlaws—not even soldiers. The army would not dishonor itself. The officers would not capitulate to a traitor."[11]

Thus, Arbenz concluded that an attempt to arm the population would be unnecessary and dangerous, unnecessary because the army would defeat Castillo Armas and dangerous because the officers might refuse to distribute the weapons. The very weakness of the rebel force aggravated this danger. Lacking any military justification, an order to arm the civilians would strike the officers as a blatant insult, or betrayal—that is, proof that Arbenz intended to establish workers' militias.[12]

On June 18, and again two or three days later, Armed Forces Chief Díaz told Arbenz and leading politicians that a decision to arm the civilians "would deeply disturb the army. It is their job to defeat Castillo Armas, and they can do it alone. Be confident," he urged. "The army will do its duty."[13] Díaz was sincere. But he failed to mention what everyone feared: if ordered to arm the population, the officers might rise in revolt—a boon to Castillo Armas.

Arbenz decided not to arm the civilians. The PGT and the other administration forces concurred. Until June 25, when the army's betrayal was flagrant, no political party or labor confederation asked for weapons. Consistently expressing their confidence in the army, they voiced their eagerness to assist in any way the military might deem useful. The workers were ready to act "under the direction of the army," declared Gutiérrez for the CGTG; "all the

latoro, *Por los fueros de la verdad histórica*; Comisión permanente, *El libro negro*; Nájera Farfán, *Cuando el árbol cae*; de la Guarda, *Castillo Armas*.

[10] Interview with Taracena.

[11] Interviews with María de Arbenz (quoted), Fortuny, Guerra Borges, Alejandro, Charnaud, Toriello, and Cols. Parinello and Guillén.

[12] Interviews with María de Arbenz, Fortuny, Guerra Borges, Alejandro, Charnaud, Toriello, and Col. Parinello.

[13] Interviews with Fortuny (quoting Díaz) and Charnaud, both of whom were at the meetings.

peasants are eager to be led by the army,'' Castillo Flores pledged on behalf of the CNCG.[14]

To all but a select few, Arbenz expressed only confidence that Castillo Armas would be defeated. To his wife and Fortuny, he confided his anguish. The thought that had haunted him since Caracas tormented him now. What would the United States do after the defeat of Castillo Armas? Would Eisenhower send in the marines? Or would Honduras attack on Washington's behalf, only to be followed by U.S. troops sent to punish the ''aggressor''? Or would the United States turn to economic strangulation? Eisenhower, Arbenz told Fortuny, ''could cut off our oil supplies.'' What would happen then? Guatemala imported all its oil. Mexico was not even self-sufficient in oil; would it dare defy the Americans? Oil-rich Venezuela was ruled by Pérez Jiménez.[15] On June 3, Arbenz had invited Roberto Saravia, the manager of Esso in Guatemala, to the presidential palace. Arbenz ''asked about stocks on hand, rate of consumption and expected deliveries . . . [and] whether it would be possible for the Guatemalan Government to purchase one million gallons of gasoline in barrels.'' Saravia told the president that it would not be possible and hastened to report the conversation to the U.S. embassy.[16] How long could Guatemala survive without oil? ''The economy could not withstand it, nor would the army,'' Arbenz told Fortuny.[17]

Fortuny and Doña María shared Arbenz's fears. Like him, they had no answers, only tenuous hopes: perhaps the United Nations would help; perhaps international pressure would restrain Eisenhower. Latin American public opinion was already responding with fury to an invasion that reeked of Washington. ''We had heard,'' recalls Toriello, ''about protest marches across the continent, rallies of 100,000 people in Mexico, huge demonstrations in Chile.''[18] These reports heartened Arbenz. The dispatch of U.S. troops to Guatemala, he believed, would do untold damage to Eisenhower's carefully cultivated international image: ''the hero of the Second World War pummeling

[14] Quoted from ''Inconmovible alianza de los obreros y campesinos,'' *Nuestro Diario*, June 22, 1954, p. 5. Communiqués by political parties echoed the same line; see, for instance, the PAR's statements in *Nuestro Diario*, June 23, 1954, p. 4 (''Unidos defenderemos Guatemala''), and June 25, 1954, p. 10 (''Comunicado del PAR a las bases del país''). See also the speech by Edelberto Torres Rivas, secretary general of the PGT's youth, ''Cuatrocientos jóvenes juraron fidelidad a la causa del pueblo,'' *Nuestro Diario*, June 26, 1954, p. 5.

[15] Interviews with Fortuny (quoted) and María de Arbenz.

[16] Wardlaw to Ambassador and Krieg, ''President Arbenz' Concern About Gasoline Supplies,'' June 4, 1954, pp. 1–2 (quoted), and Wardlaw to Ambassador and Krieg, ''Conversation with Roberto Saravia,'' June 9, 1954. Both RG84 G&C, Box 3, NA-S.

[17] Interview with Fortuny.

[18] Interview with Toriello.

a small and defenseless nation!'' Economic sanctions would provoke a wave of hatred throughout Latin America, shattering the myth of the Good Neighbor Policy and forcing even timid governments to adopt a firmer stance against the aggressor. Even Western Europe would not find it easy to remain aloof. Therefore, might not Eisenhower conclude after Castillo Armas's defeat that it was prudent to leave Guatemala alone?[19] Arbenz himself has recalled that he had hoped that "the formidable mobilization of the peoples of Latin America and the outcry of the whole world would stop the United States from intervening in an even more flagrant manner."[20]

As hope and despair spun in a debilitating vortex, Arbenz dismissed Castillo Armas's attack as a sideshow. The battlefront was the capital: it was from Guatemala City that the international effort to restrain Eisenhower would be launched. Why, then, should he leave to lead his troops against Castillo Armas's puny band? No one suggested that he do so: not Fortuny and his PGT friends, who were convinced that the army would crush the rebels; not the leaders of the revolutionary parties, who feared not Castillo Armas, but U.S. retribution after his defeat. Nor did Arbenz's senior military aides ever suggest that he go to the front—not Colonel Díaz, not Defense Minister Sánchez, and not Army Chief of Staff Parinello.[21]

Arbenz remained in the capital and asked Díaz to select the men who would lead the troops against the rebels. He approved Díaz's choices, for they seemed eminently reasonable. Díaz had selected three close friends. He placed in overall command Colonel Víctor M. León, the inspector general of the army, who was thought to be a loyal *Arbencista*. Colonels Pablo Díaz and José Barzanallana completed the trio. Pablo Díaz, who had held only desk jobs prior to his appointment as head of the Base Militar, was reputed to be a man of personal integrity. Barzanallana, the commander of the Guardia de Honor, had been in command of the Base Militar in 1950 when Castillo Armas had attacked it. He had routed the rebels and earned their hatred; Barzanallana, Castillo Armas had written, was a murderer who "had forsaken his honor as a soldier, and as a man." Self-preservation, Arbenz and Díaz believed, dictated that Barzanallana would be eager to defeat Castillo Armas again.[22]

On the night of June 19, most of the troops from the Guardia de Honor and the Base Militar left for Zacapa, a town thirty miles west of the Honduran border. Small army detachments from the departments of Quetzaltenango, Es-

[19] Interviews with María de Arbenz (quoted) and Fortuny.

[20] Arbenz, "Jacobo Arbenz relata detalles," p. 9.

[21] Interviews with María de Arbenz, Fortuny, Guerra Borges, Alejandro, Charnaud, Toriello, and Cols. Parinello and Guillén.

[22] Quoted from L.A.H.A., *Así se gestó la Liberación*, p. 53. Interviews with Parinello, Paz Tejada, and Peralta Méndez. The PGT had no say in these appointments, nor did it offer any suggestions "because we knew very little about the army." (Interview with Fortuny.)

cuintla, and Cobán followed suit. Zacapa, Arbenz had decided, would be the headquarters of the troops sent against Castillo Armas; from there, León and his colleagues would launch the counteroffensive against the rebels. But first they had to let Castillo Armas penetrate several miles deep into Guatemala: "This invasion is a farce," Arbenz told Fortuny. "We can shoo them away with our hats. What I'm afraid of—and this is why I ordered Díaz to let the mercenaries advance into our territory—what I'm afraid of is that if we defeat them right on the border, the Honduran government will manufacture a border incident, declare war on us, and the United States will invade."[23]

The countryside was rife with rumors that the fifth column was preparing to strike. Local peasant unions were flooding the national offices of the CGTG and the CNCG with requests for weapons. "We beg you to send guns for the defence of the government," pleaded the union of Santa Teresa; "Comrade, convince them to send us arms; we want to fight beside the army," urged the union from Catarina. All received the same reply: there was no need to arm the population; the "army is successfully defending our country"; the peasants should remain vigilant "day and night" against possible acts of sabotage and provide whatever assistance the army might require.[24]

The peasants did what they could. In late May and early June, saboteurs trained by the CIA had infiltrated into Guatemala; they would join hands with the "internal front" and weaken the regime's grip at home. But throughout the invasion, as the U.S. embassy pointed out, the fifth column failed to materialize and the only acts of sabotage were occasional disruptions of the telegraph lines between Zacapa and the capital.[25] Even before the invasion had begun, the peasants had started manning roadblocks. They were "polite but firm."[26] They searched for weapons that rebel planes had been dropping since June 14, and they dutifully handed them over to the local army and police

[23] Interviews with Fortuny (quoted), María de Arbenz, Col. Parinello, and Lt. Col. Mendizabal were particularly useful for this paragraph. See also Toriello, *La batalla de Guatemala*, p. 121. For the troops' departure from the capital, see Peurifoy to SecState, no. 1054, June 20, 1954, NA 714.00, and CIA, *Current Intelligence Digest*, June 24, 1954, p. 14.

[24] Quotations from: Moises Hernández to CGTG, Santa Teresa, June 20, 1954, *GT*, Box 5; Edrulfo Morales Arreaga to Castillo Flores, Catarina, June 20, 1954, *GT*, Box 11; Castillo Flores to Morales Arreaga, June 20, 1954, ibid.; Castillo Flores to the Secretaries General of the Federaciones Campesinas de la República, June 19, 1954, *GT*, Box 5. The *GT*, esp. Boxes 5, 11, and 71, include a wealth of documents that illuminate the response of local peasant unions to the invasion.

[25] *JW* 25, June 25, 1954, p. 3.

[26] Peurifoy to SecState, no. 1012, June 16, 1954, NA 714.00. See also Wardlaw to Ambassador et al., "Conditions in Pacific Coast Area," June 17, 1954, RG84 G&C, Box 3, NA-S; "Anti-Arbenz Men Move in Honduras," *NYT*, June 18, 1954, p. 7; *JW* 25, June 25, 1954, p. 3.

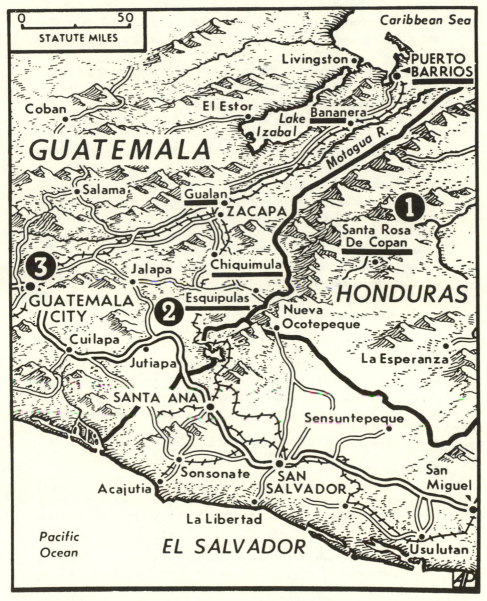

Guatemala Hotspots: A Map of the Invasion. (From the United States Information Service files in the National Archives, June 23, 1954.)

authorities.[27] "Travelers from the provinces," stated the *New York Times* on June 22, "reported that labor syndicate officials and agricultural committees were exercising control in the villages."[28] This remained true until Arbenz fell.

Eager to show its support for the army, the CGTG urged the population to donate blood for "our soldiers wounded in the line of duty," and to give cigarettes to the troops "as a gesture of gratitude to the Army of the Revolution."[29] Meanwhile rebel planes strafed the capital for a few minutes every day and occasionally dropped a bomb, causing little damage but unnerving the populace. "The last seven days," wrote a *New York Times* correspondent from Guatemala City on June 24, "have been filled with anxiety and confusion." Yet, he added, "the effect on normal living has been slight. A gasoline shortage was indicated last week, but this appears to have ended. Food prices have risen slightly, but the Government acted early to institute price controls."[30] The city was quiet but tense. The government radio and the *Voz de la Liberación* were broadcasting contradictory reports and rumors were rampant: had Castillo Armas been routed or were the rebels several thousand strong, advancing relentlessly?

In fact, very little was happening at the front. Between June 17 and June 19 the rebels advanced unopposed along a strip of territory five to fifteen miles deep and twenty to thirty miles wide in the general direction of Zacapa.[31] Then at Gualán, on June 20, they fought their first battle. Gualán, a small town fifteen miles west of the Honduran border, was defended by Lieutenant César Augusto Silva Girón and thirty soldiers. Receiving neither instructions nor assistance from Zacapa, the stubborn lieutenant fought for thirty-six hours— until the rebels withdrew in defeat.[32] The victory of an isolated and outnum-

[27] See *GT*, esp. Boxes 5, 11, and 71; see also CIA, "Current Unrest in Guatemala," CS-40-75, June 21, 1954, p. 1, and *JW* 24, June 18, 1954, pp. 3–4.

[28] "Battle for Port," *NYT*, June 22, 1954, p. 3.

[29] Quoted from CGTG, Circular, June 23, 1954, *GT*, Box 19. See also José Alberto Cardoza, no. 187, June 23, 1954, *GT*, Box 61; Cardoza to Estado Mayor del Ejército Nacional, June 25, 1954, *GT*, Box 71; Col. Víctor Quilo to Cardoza, June 26, 1954, ibid.

[30] "Capital near Normal," *NYT*, June 25, 1954, p. 3.

[31] See DOS, Circular 499, June 22, 1954, NA 714.00. *Liberacionista* accounts do not claim otherwise.

[32] Silva Girón provides a turgid but accurate account in his *La batalla de Gualán*. Understandably, *Liberacionista* sources are far more discreet. They either summarily explain the defeat by claiming that Silva Girón had "ten times more men" than they did (L.A.H.A., *Así se gestó la Liberación*, pp. 184 and 188 [quoted]), or they don't mention Gualán. Silva Girón's version was confirmed in interviews with Guatemalan officers of differing political sympathies, including González Siguí, Parinello, Mendizabal, and Paiz Novales.

bered outpost strengthened Arbenz in his belief that the army would trounce this band of traitors, just as it had defeated those who had attacked Salamá the year before.

On June 21, approximately one hundred rebels launched a surprise attack on Puerto Barrios. One third had come by sea on a Honduran vessel; the others had infiltrated from Honduras. Within a few hours the rebels were on the run, leaving behind twenty prisoners (including eleven Hondurans and one Salvadoran), several dead, their ship, and their weapons. They had been defeated by the police of Puerto Barrios and by hastily armed civilians, mainly labor union members.[33]

By the time the rebels had fled from Gualán and Puerto Barrios, over two thousand soldiers entrusted to Colonel León had assembled at Zacapa. Arbenz expected that they would now rout what was left of the rebel force, but León reported that his offensive would be delayed; a rebel plane had attacked a train bringing additional supplies and equipment to Zacapa. (The attack had indeed occurred, but the damage had been slight.) There was no reason to worry, he stressed. He would attack very soon; morale was good; Castillo Armas was doomed. In the capital, Colonel Carlos Enrique Díaz, who was in charge of communication with Zacapa, relayed these assurances to Arbenz. Díaz was confident: Víctor M. León, Pablo Díaz, and José Barzanallana were his friends.[34]

Arbenz, the PGT, and most government leaders believed these promises.[35] Others knew better—and said nothing. Army Chief of Staff Parinello was sent by Díaz to inspect the front on the twenty-third. He stayed only a few hours ("it was a whirlwind tour") and returned convinced that the army would not fight.[36] He did not, however, tell this to Arbenz or Díaz. It was not that he was

[33] For the names and nationalities of the prisoners, as well as a summary of their depositions and other useful information, see Jaime Rosenberg to Arbenz, June 23, 1954, *GT*, Box 1. See also Francisco Vásquez to Arbenz, *GT*, Box 71; T. Alvarado N., memo 564, ibid.; Cornelio Lone Mejía, memo 565, *GT*, Box 4. All June 21, 1954. For the size of the force that attacked Puerto Barrios, see also L.A.H.A., *Así se gestó la Liberación*, p. 188.

[34] Interviews with Cols. Parinello and Guillén, and with Fortuny, María de Arbenz, and Charnaud. For the attack on the train, see also Peurifoy to SecState, nos. 1060 and 1068, both June 21, 1954, NA 714.00.

[35] There were, of course, exceptions. On June 22, Marcos Antonio Franco Chacón, a PAR leader and the president of the Guatemalan Congress, told Major Paz Tejada "that he was very worried and did not believe Díaz's optimistic reports." (Interview with Paz Tejada.) But this was a minority viewpoint. (Interviews with María de Arbenz, Fortuny, Guerra Borges, Alejandro, Toriello, Charnaud, and Parinello; see also CIA, *Current Intelligence Digest*, June 28, 1954, p. 15.)

[36] Interview with Parinello. Parinello's trip to the front was recorded in the *Boletín* no. 6 of the *Alto Mando Militar*. (See *El I*, June 24, 1954, p. 1.)

afraid of Castillo Armas; he was afraid of the United States. Eisenhower, he believed, had decided that Arbenz had to go, and the Americans "would most likely send in the marines if Castillo Armas failed."[37] Parinello was not ready to join in any plot—not yet, at least—but neither was he willing to take any risks. He epitomized the "loyal" officer.

While professions of loyalty and promises of victory continued to flow from Zacapa, Arbenz focused on the diplomatic battle—Guatemala's only hope, he believed, against the United States.

The Guatemalan government asked El Salvador to lend its good offices with Honduras, but the Salvadoran ambassador merely leaked the request to Peurifoy, spicing it with spiteful comments about the Arbenz regime.[38] Guatemala's emissaries were dispatched to Mexico to seek its diplomatic support, but Mexico remained aloof.[39] Arbenz and Toriello placed their hopes, above

[37] Interview with Parinello, who related an episode that sheds light on his own attitude. In the spring of 1954, he was approached by a Guatemalan officer who told him: "Colonel, there are some people from the U.S. Secret Service who want to overthrow Arbenz. They want to meet you in Antigua for a very confidential lunch. Arbenz is going to fall." Parinello refused to go—but he did not denounce the officer. (Interview with Parinello.)

[38] See Peurifoy to SecState, no. 1102, June 24, 1954, 7 p.m., NA 714.00. The evidence suggests that President Osorio, while clearly wanting Arbenz overthrown, preferred to watch the spectacle from the sidelines and spare his country Honduras's demeaning role. (See AmEm San José, MemoConv [Canessa, Cohen], Feb. 4, 1953, enclosed in Fleming to DOS, no. 743, Feb. 5, 1953, NA 713.00; AmEm San Salvador, McDermott to Cabot, Oct. 2, 1953, NA Lot 58D18 & 58D78, Box 1; DOS, "Briefing on El Salvador," Apr. 23, 1954, NA 716.00. Also helpful was interview with Sol.)

[39] Interviews with Toriello, Fortuny, Guerra Borges, and Cardoza y Aragón (who had close contacts with high Mexican officials). Since its glorious revolution, Mexico's support for the principle of nonintervention has been exemplary; this, at least, is what Mexican officials assert. Their country, they note, provided a haven for Sandino. Their country was the only member of the OAS to refuse to impose sanctions against Castro's Cuba. And their country said no to Foster Dulles at Caracas in defense of Guatemala's sovereignty.

In fact, Mexico's support for the principle of nonintervention has been undermined by its fear of Washington and by the conservatism of its leaders. Mexico was a treacherous friend to Sandino, it colluded with the CIA against Cuba, and it turned against Arbenz's Guatemala. (On Mexico and Sandino, see Macaulay, *Sandino Affair*, pp. 146–50, 156–60. On Mexico and Cuba in the 1960s, see Pellicer de Brody, *México y la Revolución Cubana*.)

Mexico did abstain at Caracas and this abstention did contrast favorably with the spinelessness of the other Latin American countries, but in the weeks that followed, the Mexican authorities responded complacently to the State Department's preparations for another OAS conference to vote sanctions against Guatemala. On June 11, the

all, in the United Nations. Guatemala's case was so solid and the evidence of Honduras's and Nicaragua's complicity was so glaring that the United Nations would have to intervene.[40] On June 18, Toriello asked the UN Security Council "to take the measures necessary . . . to put a stop to the aggression," which he blamed on Nicaragua, Honduras, and "certain foreign monopolies whose interests have been affected by the progressive policy of my government."[41]

It seemed for a moment that the august body would consider Guatemala's plight. On June 20, the Security Council approved a French motion calling for "the immediate termination of any action likely to cause bloodshed" and requesting "all Members of the United Nations to abstain . . . from rendering assistance to any such action."[42] Publicly, the United States supported the motion, but Secretary Dulles was furious. The behavior of the French was

---

Mexican government announced that it would attend the Montevideo conference. "Mexico," U.S. Ambassador White was told, "had decided that it . . . would cooperate with the United States there, but that it would not commit itself in advance to any actions." Significantly, the Mexican authorities did not inform Guatemala of the contents of the draft resolution. (See MemoTel [White, Holland], June 1, 1954; MemoConv [Tello, Holland], June 7, 1954; MemoConv [White, Holland], June 7, 1954; MemoConv [White, Holland], June 9, 1954; MemoConv [White, Holland], June 10, 1954, quoted; MemoConv [Tello, Nieto, Holland], June 19, 1954; all NA 714.00. See also AmEm Mexico City, White to Holland, May 14, 1954, NA Lot 57D295, Box 4; AmEm Mexico City, White to Holland, May 26, 1954, NA 714.001; AmEm Mexico City, White to Holland, June 1, 1954, NA Lot 57D295, Box 4.)

When Washington's verbal assault on Guatemala reached unprecedented levels, the Mexican government was silent, and it maintained its "cautious reserve" after the invasion had begun. The government-controlled organizations and media were equally discreet—all the while loudly proclaiming their country's anticommunism. The press castigated former President Lázaro Cárdenas for voicing his solidarity "with the people and the government of Guatemala," and the First Congress against Soviet Intervention in Latin America heaped abuse on Arbenz. The congress, which opened in Mexico City in late May, was organized by the CIA with the financial assistance of the Mexican government. (Pellicer de Brody and Mancilla, *Historia de la Revolución Mexicana*, pp. 102–10, quoted from pp. 109, 104. This book provides the only scholarly discussion of Mexico's attitude toward Guatemala in the last months of the Arbenz administration. See also AmEm Mexico City, White to SecState, no. 1345, May 16, 1954; AmEm Mexico City, White to SecState, no. 1348, May 17, 1954; AmEm Mexico City, White to SecState, no. 1362, May 19, 1954; Hughes to Holland, "Monthly Summary—Mexico," June 29, 1954, NA 712.00; "Guatemala Issue Disturbs Mexico," *NYT*, June 14, 1954, p. 7; "Officials' Kin in Mexico," *NYT*, June 17, 1954, p. 8.)

[40] Interviews with María de Arbenz, Toriello, and Fortuny.

[41] "Guatemala's Note and U.N. Charter Articles Cited," *NYT*, June 20, 1954, p. 2.

[42] United Nations, Security Council Official Records, June 20, 1954, p. 38. For the debate, see pp. 1–41.

"shabby," he told Henry Cabot Lodge, the U.S. ambassador to the United Nations. "We have . . . held up putting Indochina in the UN in deference to their request. And then without prior understandings etc., they jump right in when another international body should have been used."[43] Dulles's position was that only the Organization of American States was competent to address the Guatemalan complaint. The United Nations must not interfere in the affairs of the Western Hemisphere. His stance was immediately endorsed by Honduras and Nicaragua. Indignantly, they asked that the Inter-American Peace Committee of the OAS investigate Guatemala's slanderous charges.[44] They knew, of course, that no OAS body would conduct any investigation against the will of the United States.

On June 21, Toriello turned again to the Security Council, asking it to take "whatever steps are necessary" to stave the flow of foreign assistance to the rebels.[45] Four days of frantic activity followed, as Dulles lined up the votes and instructed Lodge, the Council's president, to delay a meeting.[46] "Lodge Holds Off on Guatemala Bid," blared the *New York Times* on June 24.[47] "I will have to have a meeting, probably tomorrow," Lodge told Dulles at 9:55 a.m. that same morning.[48] Eisenhower was ready "to use the veto if necessary," Dulles informed the ambassador a few hours later. It would be the first U.S. veto in the history of the United Nations, and, as such, a severe propaganda defeat: "If they vote against us, that will raise 'hell,' " Dulles fumed.[49]

Dulles was referring to France and England. They wanted the Security Council to consider the Guatemalan matter and to dispatch UN observers to the area.[50] Both were concerned with the legal ramifications of the case, not

[43] TelConv (JFD, Lodge), June 22, 1954, 4:30 p.m., DP:TCS, Box 2, EL.

[44] "Inter-American Commission Defers Action on Guatemala," *NYT*, June 22, 1954, p. 1.

[45] "Guatemala Asks U.N. to Carry Out Cease-Fire Order," *NYT*, June 23, 1954, p. 1. For the text of the Guatemalan note, see p. 2.

[46] TelConv (Lodge, JFD), June 24, 1954, 9:11 a.m., DP:TCS, Box 2, EL; see also Lodge to SecState, no. 870, June 24, 1954, 11 a.m., NA 714.00.

[47] "Lodge Holds Off on Guatemala Bid," *NYT*, June 24, 1954, p. 1.

[48] MemoTel (Dulles, Lodge), 9:55 a.m., *FRUS*, 1952–1954, 4:1185.

[49] Quotations from TelConv (JFD, Lodge), June 24, 1954, 4:01 p.m., DP, JFD:CS, Box 8, EL, and TelConv (Hagerty, JFD), June 25, 1954, 10 a.m., DP:TCS, Box 10, EL. See also: MemoConv (Dulles, Bonnet, de Juniac, Key), June 24, 1954, NA Lot 58D18 & 58D78, Box 3; Minutes of Cabinet Meetings, July 9, 1954, WF, Cabinet Series, Box 3, EL; Hagerty Diary, June 24, 1954, EL.

[50] "Lodge informed Holland that the British and French representatives to the Security Council are prepared to go along with a Soviet proposal that the Council send peace observers to Central America." ("Notes of a Meeting of the Guatemalan Group," June 23, 1954, *FRUS*, 1952–1954, 4:1178.) See also Lodge to SecState, no. 870, June 24, 1954, 11 a.m., NA 714.00, and Lodge to SecState, June 24, 1954, 6 p.m., *FRUS*, 1952–1954, 4:1185.

with the fate of Arbenz. At issue was the jurisdiction of the United Nations. Their concern was shared by many other UN delegations and by the UN secretary general, Dag Hammarskjöld, who bitterly opposed the U.S. position and was subjected in turn to harsh and relentless pressure from Lodge to remain silent.[51]

"The president," Dulles told Lodge, "said he thinks you should let the British and French know that if they take [an] independent line backing [the] Guatemalan move in this matter . . . we would feel entirely free without regard to their position in relation to any such matters as any of their colonial problems in Egypt, Cyprus, etc."[52] The same threats were delivered by the American ambassadors in France and England, and by Dulles himself to Foreign Secretary Anthony Eden, who arrived in Washington with Churchill on June 25 for an untimely visit. In the limousine from the airport, Dulles upbraided the cornered Eden. "He said that if the first thing that happens after they [Eden and Churchill] arrive is that we split on this, they better pack up and go home."[53]

On the evening of June 25, after five hours of debate, the Security Council refused to consider the Guatemalan matter. Four countries—the Soviet Union, Denmark, Lebanon, and New Zealand—voted in favor. Among the five who voted against were the council's two Latin American members, Colombia and Brazil. England and France abstained.[54] The American position, Hammarskjöld later told the British delegate, "was the most serious blow so far aimed at the Organization."[55]

[51] "U.N. Bars Debate over Guatemala Pending Inquiry," *NYT*, June 26, 1954, p. 1. For Hammarskjöld's clash with Lodge, see Urquhart, *Hammarskjöld*, pp. 88–94.

[52] MemoTel (Dulles, Lodge), 9:55 a.m., June 24, 1954, *FRUS*, 1952–1954, 4:1184.

[53] TelConv (JFD, Lodge), June 25, 1954, 9:56 a.m., DP, JFD:CS, Box 8, EL. See also TelConv (Lodge, JFD), June 25, 1954, 9:11 a.m., ibid.; TelConv (JFD, Lodge), June 25, 1954, 11:22 a.m., ibid.; Lodge to SecState, no. 880, June 25, 1954, 7 p.m., NA 714.00; Shanley Diaries, Box 2, July 9, 1954, p. 1599, EL; Handwritten Minutes of Cabinet Meetings, July 9, 1954, p. 3, White House Office, Staff Secretary: Records, 1952–61, Cabinet Series, Box 2, EL; Hagerty Diaries, June 25–26, 1954, EL. For a sanitized version, see Eden, *Full Circle*, pp. 133–38.

For an excellent account of Anglo-American tensions focusing on the role of the Security Council in the resolution of the Guatemalan crisis, see Meers, "Pebble on the Beach," pp. 55–67. See also Young, "Great Britain's Latin America Dilemma," pp. 581–86.

[54] For the debate see United Nations, Security Council Official Records, June 25, 1954, pp. 1–34. See also "U.N. Bars Debate over Guatemala Pending Inquiry," *NYT*, June 26, 1954, p. 1; Munro, "Oral History Interview," pp. 5–7; Connell-Smith, *Inter-American System*, pp. 231–37.

[55] Quoted by Urquhart, *Hammarskjöld*, p. 92. Hammarskjöld considered lodging a formal complaint about the behavior of the United States but was dissuaded by the British delegate. (Meers, "Pebble on the Beach," pp. 71–72.)

For Arbenz, the council's decision was shattering. And yet how could a vote in New York have affected the fast-moving events in Guatemala? On June 25, as the Security Council was rejecting the Guatemalan case, other news reached Arbenz: the army at Zacapa had rebelled.

After the battles of Puerto Barrios and Gualán, the front had been quiet, except for occasional attacks by rebel planes. On June 23, Castillo Armas established a provisional government at Esquipulas, six miles from the Honduran border. León continued to send reassuring messages from Zacapa: he would move soon against Castillo Armas. Carlos Enrique Díaz remained confident. But as the promised offensive failed to materialize, Arbenz grew uneasy. León seemed overly cautious. Arbenz did not, however, suspect betrayal. His attention was elsewhere. During the first week of the invasion, "Jacobo was constantly on the phone with New York, wanting news about the Security Council: 'What's happening? How's it going? When are they going to meet?' We were grasping at straws," remarks his wife. "But what else could we do? How else could we hope to stop the United States?"[56]

It was the PGT that broke the spell. Many party leaders, like Guerra Borges, were wrapped "in irresponsible optimism." Others, though confident that the army would crush the rebels, wanted more information. On the evening of June 23, without consulting either Arbenz or the Secretariat, Acting Secretary General Alvarado Monzón sent Octavio Reyes, a member of the PGT's Central Committee, to Zacapa. Early on the twenty-fifth Reyes was back in Guatemala City, exhausted physically and emotionally. The officers at Zacapa, he reported, were demoralized, afraid, unwilling to fight; when he had chastised them, he had barely escaped arrest.[57]

Fortuny took Reyes to Arbenz. After listening to Reyes, the president turned to his friend: "Do you trust him?" he asked. "Absolutely," responded Fortuny.[58]

Stunned but not persuaded—Reyes was, after all, unfamiliar with military matters—Arbenz summoned Colonel Getellá, a trusted officer. He must leave for Zacapa at once and return with a detailed report.

Getellá left immediately, and he was back late that same night. He confirmed Reyes's account, and he brought a message from the officers at Zacapa: "*Centenario*, the high command asked me to tell you that you must resign. The situation is hopeless. The officers don't want to fight. They think that the Americans are threatening Guatemala just because of you and your communist

---

[56] Interviews with María de Arbenz (quoted), Fortuny, Parinello, Toriello, and Charnaud.

[57] Interviews with Guerra Borges (quoted), Pellecer, Alejandro, and Fortuny. See also Fortuny, "Observaciones," p. 68.

[58] Interview with Fortuny. See also Arbenz, "Jacobo Arbenz relata detalles," p. 9.

friends. If you don't resign, the army will march on the capital to depose you. They have already begun to arrest peasants."[59]

Getellá had not sought to reason with the mutinous officers. "He was known to be a brave man," recollects an eyewitness, "but in Zacapa I saw him shaking."[60] Getellá himself says: "I returned [to the capital] depressed and scared. Defeat was inevitable. There was no way to stop the gringos."[61]

Getellá did not actively betray Arbenz, but neither did he stay to support him. As he left the presidential palace, he had one piece of advice for Arbenz: "You must decide quickly. Otherwise the army will make a deal with Castillo Armas and move against the capital."[62] That same day, in grim confirmation of his words, came the news that Chiquimula had fallen to Castillo Armas on the twenty-fourth. Chiquimula, the first important town between the Honduran border and Zacapa, had been defended by several hundred well-armed soldiers led by Lt. Colonel Jorge Hernández, a loyal officer—or so Arbenz had believed.

Searching for tales of glory in a barren campaign, the *Liberacionistas* present the battle of Chiquimula—the only encounter they won—as a noble victory: "seven hours of fighting against forces ten times larger than ours."[63] For his part, Lt. Colonel Hernández, grasping for excuses if not for glory, claims that at Chiquimula he fought a hard battle, resisting for long hours against "five hundred or more" rebels, while Zacapa spurned his pleas for assistance. The morale of his soldiers, he says, was good, and "our weapons were satisfactory."[64]

In truth, what happened at Chiquimula could hardly be called a battle. Hernández, who had only 150 men and received no assistance from Zacapa, was

[59] Interview with Fortuny. My major sources on the Getellá mission are interviews with: Getellá; Lt. Col. Mendizabal and another senior officer (who asked not to be identified), both of whom were at Zacapa; Fortuny, Charnaud, Guerra Borges, and María de Arbenz, all of whom related what they learned from Arbenz; Cols. Parinello, Mendoza, and Lorenzana, all of whom related what they learned from other officers. In 1955, Arbenz noted: "On Friday, June 25, the troops led by officers in whom I had complete trust sent me an ultimatum: either I resign, or they would side with Castillo Armas." (Arbenz, "Jacobo Arbenz relata detalles," p. 9.) Getellá's mission has gone virtually unnoticed in the literature; for two exceptions, see the cursory reference in Sierra Roldán, *Diálogos*, p. 109, and Torres Rivas, "Crisis," p. 65, n. 15.

[60] Interviews with Lt. Col. Mendizabal (quoted) and with the aforementioned senior officer from Zacapa.

[61] Interview with Getellá.

[62] Interview with Fortuny.

[63] Flores Avendaño, *Memorias*, 2:439. See also L.A.H.A., *Así se gestó la Liberación*, pp. 231–35, and the fanciful account in Putzeys Rojas, *Así se hizo la Liberación*, pp. 211–51.

[64] Interview with Hernández.

eager to surrender. Those who resisted—"doggedly," recalls a *Liberacionista*—were a few dozen poorly armed peasants. "They fought with old hunting rifles. They were the ones who killed our people. When we captured them, we shot them. Hernández didn't arm the peasants. If he had, then the capture of Chiquimula would have been much more difficult." After Castillo Armas's victory, Hernández was allowed to remain in the army; the dead peasants were eulogized as innocent victims of communist terror.[65]

TREASON AT ZACAPA

It is difficult to reconstruct the details of the events at Zacapa in the days that preceded Getellá's visit and the surrender of Chiquimula. Two of the three commanding colonels are dead. The third, Pablo Díaz, prefers "not to talk about these things";[66] he has maintained an exemplary discretion—as did, as long as they lived, León and Barzanallana. CIA reports reveal only how little the agency knew. Nevertheless, the story can be reconstructed, even though many details will be forever hazy.

When the invasion began, observes Eduardo Taracena, a senior *Liberacionista*, "a group of officers was on our side." They were, however, "very few," and they occupied posts of secondary importance. Their leaders were Enrique Closse de León, a lieutenant colonel who had a desk job, and Antonio Montenegro, a young lieutenant.[67] Other officers, such as Colonels Cruz Salazar, Elfego Monzón, and Mauricio Dubois, "were sapping the spirit of the army, but for their own ends, not to help Castillo Armas," remembers Taracena. Cruz Salazar concurs: "My friends and I were on bad terms with Castillo Armas due to personal differences."[68]

Although Castillo Armas garnered more respect among the officers than did his rivals in the exile movement, the dominant attitude toward him was hostility. Officers like Monzón and Cruz Salazar, who hoped that someday, somehow, they would replace Arbenz, saw Castillo Armas as a rival. But the hostility had other roots as well: many still liked or respected Jacobo Arbenz; others, though unsympathetic to the regime, resented the exiles' strident as-

---

[65] Particularly useful were interviews with Taracena (quoted)—a *Liberacionista* who fought at Chiquimula—and with Col. Parinello and Lt. Silva Girón. In his memoirs, Col. Monzón mentions "the defection of the officer in command at Chiquimula." (Sierra Roldán, *Diálogos*, p. 107; see also pp. 109, 116.)

[66] Telephone conversation with Col. Pablo Díaz.

[67] Interviews with Taracena (quoted) and Montenegro. The only difference between them is that Montenegro claimed that he had not been plotting with Castillo Armas—a denial that greatly amused former *Liberacionistas* and army officers when they were told of it. Bissell noted that very few Guatemalan officers were involved in the plot. (Interview with Bissell.)

[68] Quotations from interviews with Taracena and Cruz Salazar.

sertions that the army was serving a communist government; the exiles' blatant courtship of Trujillo and Somoza offended many Guatemalan officers who were proud that their country was no longer Ubico's tropical dictatorship. Moreover, by seeking to overthrow the Arbenz regime, Castillo Armas and his fellow exiles threatened the well-being of the officer corps.

Those officers who disliked Arbenz even more than they resented Castillo Armas were but a small minority. Had they felt free to choose, most Guatemalan officers would have rallied to Arbenz in June 1954 and crushed the rebels. But fear gnawed at them—fear of the United States.

When the invasion began, the planners of PBSUCCESS knew that they had shaken the morale of the Guatemalan army, but they could not assess to what degree. In addition to the handful of active plotters, "various officers" had promised that they would "take action against the regime given just a little more time or just a little more justification," the CIA reported with some exasperation.[69] Washington did not know when these officers would act—or if they would ever act. Hence they had to be prodded, cattlelike, with the spark of Castillo Armas's invasion.

It is striking, in retrospect, how unsure U.S. Intelligence was of how the army would respond to the rebel attack. A CIA official who participated in the operation has stated that he had thought the chances of success to be about even.[70] A June 17 analysis, cast in a slightly more optimistic mold, reveals the tentativeness of Washington's predictions:

> The political scene [in Guatemala] is dominated by President Arbenz, his Communist advisors, and his sizable but relatively passive popular following. . . . In a position to decide the political issue is the 6,000-man Guatemalan Army. This is a newly professionalized Army, proud of its military efficiency developed during the past ten years. Its officers and men enjoy numerous privileges granted by the Arbenz government. The officer corps has personal ties to Arbenz who emerged from it into political life. . . .
>
> So far as the Army is concerned, its preferred choice unquestionably would be to keep Arbenz and dispose of his Communist Advisors. If the leaders of the officer corps could not persuade Arbenz to go along, they might carry off a coup and set up an Army regime as at least a stop-gap. Or, if they came to believe that opposition political groups could command some popular support and also could be counted on to protect the Army's position and perquisites, then the officers might install a new civilian government manned by members of the present opposition.
>
> The probability is that the Army will take one of these three courses. Its officers will calculate, as will Latin Americans generally, that the US could not embark on

[69] DCI to President, "The Situation in Guatemala as of 20 June," *FRUS*, 1952–1954, 4:1175.

[70] Bissell, "Oral History Interview," p. 13.

the project of ridding Guatemala of Communist domination without intending to carry through any action necessary. This being the case, the Guatemalan Army can be expected . . . to exert its dominant power to the end of preventing a showdown with the US.[71]

That very day, the *Liberacionistas* entered Guatemala. They advanced a few miles, unopposed, were defeated at Gualán and Puerto Barrios, and settled down on their puny strip of "liberated" territory. Meanwhile, the fifth column failed to materialize, and the country remained under government control. The cautious optimism of Castillo Armas's American patrons gave way to uneasiness. A CIA memorandum to Eisenhower warned:

As of 20 June the outcome of the efforts to overthrow . . . Arbenz . . . remains very much in doubt. The controlling factor in the situation is still considered to be the position of the Guatemalan armed forces, and thus far this group has not given any clear indication of whether it will move, and if so, in which way. . . . If it remains loyal . . . Castillo Armas . . . will be defeated. . . .

The position of the top-ranking military officers is constantly shifting. . . . It is probable that the rising pressure of events will compel this group to declare its position, one way or the other, at any time from now on—although the possible result could be a split in the ranks. . . . The action of Colonel Castillo Armas is not in any sense a conventional military operation. . . . The entire effort is thus more dependent upon psychological impact rather than actual military strength, although it is upon the ability of the Castillo Armas effort to create and maintain for a short time the *impression* of very substantial military strength that the success of this particular effort primarily depends. . . . If the effort does not succeed in arousing the other latent forces of resistance within the next period of approximately twenty-four hours, it will probably begin to lose strength.[72]

From his command post in the U.S. embassy, Peurifoy "was like a ship running through a dense fog."[73] His dispatches show that he attempted, with some success, to intimidate Guatemalan officials—not a new game for him.[74] But Peurifoy's dispatches also betray his frustration. On June 20, he cabled Washington: "Embassy is able to report accurately only on events in Guatemala City and even here it is difficult to verify enormous numbers of rumors mostly false which are circulating. . . . No reliable information is available

[71] OIR, Intelligence Report, June 17, 1954, pp. 2–3, NA 714.00.

[72] "The Situation in Guatemala as of 20 June" (see n. 69 above), quoted from pp. 1174–75, 1176 (italics in the original).

[73] Interview with Krieg.

[74] See, for instance, Peurifoy to SecState, no. 1053, June 20, 1954, NA 714.00; Peurifoy to SecState, June 23, 1954, *FRUS*, 1952–1954, 4:1180–82; Peurifoy to SecState, no. 1120, June 26, 1954, NA 714.00. Throughout the invasion, no U.S. official spoke with Arbenz. (Interviews with María de Arbenz, Fortuny, and Krieg.)

about progress of rebels but they are not known to hold any important town."[75]
The capital was but a secondary front. Those army officers who had remained
in the city were unwilling to act on their own, and while they waited for news
of Zacapa, their sullen passivity and nervousness were little comfort to an
ambassador who craved action.[76] Meanwhile, Castillo Armas's supporters in
Guatemala City were beginning to fear that the invasion might collapse.
Among them was the proud Rossell y Arellano, archbishop of Guatemala,
who on June 21 appealed to Peurifoy "for direct U.S. intervention."[77] Until
the twenty-fifth, the mood in the embassy was one of pessimism: "It looked
as if Arbenz had won. . . . We were all very discouraged."[78]

In Washington, too, the mood was somber. On the twenty-second, Assistant
Secretary Holland stated that Castillo Armas had "counted on the defection of
the Guatemalan Army, [and] that since this defection did not occur he would
probably lose."[79] CIA headquarters was equally grim: "The feeling was that
things were going very badly."[80] Addressing the situation up to and including
the twenty-fourth, the CIA observed that Castillo Armas had occupied "only
limited and relatively unimportant territory," and that "local recruiting" by
his forces appeared to be "slow." Little was known of developments at Zacapa, but "there appear to have been no wholesale desertions from the Guatemalan army and key commanders apparently remain loyal."[81] And yet, it
was on the twenty-fourth that Chiquimula fell!

Only on the twenty-fifth did the CIA discern some grounds for optimism:
"Guatemalan army officers are reported . . . to be 'slowly realizing' the extreme gravity of the situation and are becoming convinced that getting rid of
President Arbenz and the Communists would be 'an easy way out.' " However, there was still "no evidence of defections from the Guatemalan army."[82]
And yet, it was on the twenty-fifth that Getellá delivered the army's ultimatum
to Arbenz!

[75] Peurifoy to SecState, no. 1052, June 20, 1954, NA 714.00.

[76] On the mood of the officers in the capital, interviews with the following officers,
all of whom were in the capital, were helpful: Parinello, Cruz Salazar, Paiz Novales,
González Siguí, Getellá, Montenegro, and Peralta Méndez. Parinello adds an interesting story that illustrates the demoralization of the officers. A few days after the beginning of the invasion, "the G-2 of the army, Colonel Víctor Manuel Gordillo, told me:
'Colonel, things are very bad. It's very hard to make ends meet. Why don't you ask
the President to give us two months' salary in advance?' In other words," Parinello
explains, "he knew that the government would not last long."

[77] Peurifoy to SecState, no. 1063, June 21, 1954, NA 714.00.

[78] Interview with Krieg.

[79] DOS, Meeting of Guatemalan Group, June 22, 1954, p. 1.

[80] Interviews with Amory (quoted) and Bissell.

[81] CIA, *Current Intelligence Digest*, June 25, 1954, p. 16.

[82] CIA, *Current Intelligence Digest*, June 28, 1954, p. 15.

Thus, throughout the first week of the invasion, the CIA underestimated the confusion and demoralization that gripped Zacapa. All the available evidence indicates that when the senior officers left the capital for Zacapa, on June 19, they had not yet decided to turn against Arbenz. They were, however, angry: why had they been chosen? "I can't understand Carlos Enrique [Díaz]. Why is he sending his friends to fight against Castillo Armas?" Colonel Pablo Díaz complained before leaving the capital. "Why can't he send someone else?"[83]

At Zacapa the colonels neither surrendered nor fought. "They were paralyzed." They kept Arbenz at bay with reassuring telegrams, and they avoided any move—such as crushing the rebels—that might further provoke the Americans. "The High Command was made of jelly."[84] A few junior officers complained about their superiors, but only among themselves.[85] And so, the troops remained at Zacapa, many kilometers from the "front." This was not due to any secret deal with the CIA. The reason for the army's behavior is more prosaic: "Fear defeated them," a Guatemalan officer explains. "They were terrorized by the idea that the United States was looming behind Castillo Armas." The U.S. army attaché concurs: "The Guatemalan officers were definitely afraid of the possibility of U.S. intervention against Arbenz and with good reason. That fear was the stabilizing influence that kept them from coming to Arbenz's support when the chips were down."[86] This is why the only battle the army fought was at Gualán, where a young lieutenant had acted on his own initiative.[87]

The situation was indeed untenable. The army at Zacapa was lying to Arbenz, and these lies could not long remain hidden. Every day, every hour increased the gravity of this disobedience and led, inexorably, to betrayal.

[83] Interview with Lt. Col. Cruz Salazar, to whom Díaz was speaking. In addition, my most important sources for this paragraph are interviews with: Cols. Mendoza, Parinello, González Siguí, Lorenzana, and Getellá; Lt. Cols. Paiz Novales and Hernández; Maj. Paz Tejada; Lt. Montenegro; and Taracena.

[84] Quotations from interviews with Lt. Col. Mendizabal and Lt. Silva Girón.

[85] Of these officers, those most often mentioned are Lt. Juan García and Captain Prudencio López.

[86] Quotations from interviews with Lt. Col. Mendizabal and Col. McCormick.

[87] After the army at Zacapa had surrendered to Castillo Armas, Silva Girón was assisted by Lt. Col. Mendizabal to return to the capital disguised as a nurse. Later, he was arrested and jailed for a year without trial and then sent into exile. He returned in 1957 after Castillo Armas's death and was eventually reinstated into the army. But while several officers, including some of Arbenz's foes, respected him for his resistance at Gualán, his military career was in fact over. He retired in 1972. He had finally made it to colonel, but had never again been given command over troops. "They made me into a desk officer." (Quoted from interview with Silva Girón. Interviews with Col. González Siguí, and Lt. Cols. Mendizabal and Paiz Novales were particularly useful. See also Silva Girón, *Cuando gobiernan las armas*, esp. pp. 79–115.)

Then Castillo Armas attacked Chiquimula. Hernández surrendered and Zacapa remained aloof. The surrender of the one and the passivity of the other were treason. Getellá arrived at Zacapa: Arbenz was demanding an account. The charade could be sustained no longer. Zacapa told Arbenz to step down.

Only against this backdrop of officers who were demoralized before they reached the front, officers who feared the consequences of victory more than defeat, can the significance of the rebels' air force and superior communication equipment be appreciated.

If Castillo Armas's air force was puny, that of the government was practically nonexistent. Guatemala's planes were as antiquated and unsuited for battle as their pilots were unreliable. With the exception of Lieutenant Juan Adolfo Castillo, who died on June 18 when his AT-6 crashed, the pilots had no desire to fight. One defected with his aircraft to Castillo Armas, several sought asylum in foreign embassies, and the remaining few were grounded to prevent more desertions.[88]

The rebel air force inflicted only minimal damage. In the capital, a P-47 knocked out a radio station, but the station belonged to an American evangelist.[89] The intended target, the nearby government radio transmitter, emerged from the war unscathed. Rebel aircraft also damaged a few bridges and railroad tracks between the capital and Zacapa, but none too seriously. Little harm was done at the front—at Zacapa, Gualán, Puerto Barrios, and Chiquimula. The American pilots were apparently reluctant to risk their lives; the Guatemalans had more ardor, but less skill; the planes were old, and on occasion they met "very heavy anti-aircraft fire."[90]

By June 22 the rebels had lost two planes. One had been brought down by hostile fire, and the other had run out of gas. On that day Eisenhower met with the Dulles brothers and Assistant Secretary Holland to decide whether the planes should be replaced. Nearly a decade later, in an account of the meeting, Eisenhower acknowledged that the United States had provided material assistance to Castillo Armas: "I considered the matter carefully," he wrote. "It seemed to me that to refuse to cooperate in providing indirect support to a strictly anti-Communist faction in this struggle would be contrary to the letter

[88] "The Situation in Guatemala as of 20 June" (see n. 69 above), p. 1175; Peurifoy to SecState, no. 1045, June 19, 1954, NA 714.00; AmEm San Salvador to SecState, no. 192350Z, June, NA 714.00; AmEm San Salvador, McDermott to SecState, no. 160, June 22, 1954, NA 714.00; "Advance 9 Miles," *NYT*, June 20, 1954, p. 1.

[89] "Estragos por avión pirata en la radio La Voz Evangelica," *El I*, June 22, 1954, p. 1; "Wrong Radio Bombed," *NYT*, June 25, 1954, p. 3.

[90] "The Situation in Guatemala as of 20 June" (see n. 69 above), p. 1175. My main sources for this paragraph are (1) interviews with protagonists; (2) reports of the U.S. embassy; (3) press reports (the *New York Times* had a reporter, Paul Kennedy, in Guatemala City during the invasion, as did other major newspapers).

and spirit of the Caracas resolution. I had faith in the strength of the inter-American resolve therein set forth. . . . our proper course of action—indeed my duty—was clear to me. We would replace the airplanes.'' The original planes, Eisenhower averred disingenuously, had been provided to Castillo Armas by another (unnamed) country.[91]

In material terms, the major achievement of the rebel air force was the sinking of a British freighter on June 27. ''Someone gave us the information that there was an unidentified ship in San José [Guatemala],'' recalls Phil Roettinger, a CIA agent who was involved in the incident. ''Robertson [another CIA agent], who was a wild man, said: 'They must be unloading weapons. Let's sink it.' So we got Schupp, and he did it.''[92] In fact, there were no weapons on board, only bales of cotton and bags of coffee. It was this incident that the general counsel of the CIA first remembered when asked about PBSUCCESS. ''Dealing with it was my office's main task associated with PBSUCCESS. I remember the captain of the ship well. He was a nice man.''[93] This ''sub-incident,'' as Bissell called it, ''mercifully turned out to be of little significance and to do no political, and minor financial damage to [the] United States.''[94] The British government was eager not to antagonize Washington, U.S. responsibility was not publicly discussed, and the claim was eventually settled *sub rosa* for $1 million.[95]

Another bombing error did no financial damage to the United States and was, in fact, a political boon. On June 22, a P-47 dropped a couple of bombs on the Honduran town of San Pedro de Copán, eight miles from the Guatemalan border. Secretary Dulles, who knew better, transformed this mistake of a rebel pilot into a Guatemalan attack on its peace-loving neighbor. The Honduran government enthusiastically denounced this Guatemalan ''aggression'' and threatened retaliation.[96]

---

[91] Eisenhower, *Mandate*, pp. 425–26. For the loss of the two planes, see ''Guatemala Links U.S. Fliers to Raid,'' *NYT*, June 21, p. 2; ''Capturada en Puerto Barrios goleta enemiga,'' *DCA*, June 21, p. 1; Peurifoy to SecState, no. 1067, June 21, NA 714.00; ''Aviador americano se estrelló,'' *La Prensa*, Managua, June 22, p. 3; AmEm Tegucigalpa, ALUSNA to SecState, DTG 030230Z, July 3, NA 714.00. All 1954.

[92] Interview with Roettinger.

[93] Interview with Houston.

[94] Bissell, quoted in ''The Science of Spying,'' May 4, 1965, p. 9, AWD Papers, Box 141, ML.

[95] For the incident, see: Tiburcio Avila, Alcalde Municipal San José, to Charnaud, June 27, 1954, CO:G, June 1954, p. 640, AGCA; TelConv (JFD, AWD), June 28, 1954, 9:39 a.m., DP, JFD:CS, Box 8, EL; Peurifoy to SecState, no. 1127, June 28, 1954, NA 714.00; ''British Ship Sunk Off Guatemala,'' *NYT*, June 28, 1954, p. 1; ''Pérdida completa del barco Springfjord,'' *El I*, June 29, 1954, p. 1; AmEmG to DOS, ''Economic Summary—June 1954,'' no. 10, July 9, 1954, p. 2, NA 814.00; Meers, ''Pebble on the Beach,'' pp. 81–82.

[96] TelConv (Holland, JFD), June 22, 1954, 5:12 p.m., DP:TCS, Box 2, EL; Tel-

The rebels' planes and broadcasts have often been presented as the decisive psychological weapons that brought Arbenz and his army to their knees. This is hardly plausible. Arbenz, the PGT, and the other leaders of the government coalition remained confident of Castillo Armas's defeat until the betrayal of the army had become plain, rebel planes and radio broadcasts notwithstanding. Nor did the planes and broadcasts disrupt military operations. They were of no value against those who were willing to fight: Lieutenant Silva Girón with his handful of soldiers at Gualán, the police and the armed civilians at Puerto Barrios, and the peasants at Chiquimula. (Indeed, in his colorful account of the battle, Lt. Colonel Hernández did not even mention the planes.)[97] "Chiquimula stands in its entirety," wrote Marroquín Rojas. "Not one house, not one building, not one shack was destroyed. The capital, as we all know, suffered not at all, except for the bomb that fell on the old Fort Matamoros and the strafing of some gasoline storage tanks. All the rest, except for the sinking of the ship in San José harbor, is pure fantasy."[98] If León failed to attack, this was not because he believed that Castillo Armas had thousands of men, as the *Voz de la Liberación* claimed, or because rebel planes were sowing panic and death among his troops. The Guatemalan officers knew "very well" that the rebel force was paltry, and, at Zacapa, Castillo Armas's aircraft provoked neither desertions nor panic among the rank and file. On the contrary, the soldiers patiently awaited their officers' orders.[99]

The planes and radio broadcasts have been useful, however, to a Guatemalan officer corps that has sought to justify its surrender to Castillo Armas. In conversation after conversation with Guatemalan officers, the rebel air force and radio broadcasts were initially cited as the critical causes of defeat, but they receded as the conversations proceeded, and the true explanation emerged: "The officers were aware," Colonel Paiz Novales admitted with marked understatement, "that it might be better if Arbenz stepped down. . . . The propaganda of the U.S. was devastating. . . . This is why Zacapa did not fight."[100] The broadcasts and the planes were a sideshow. Washington pro-

---

Conv (JFD, Holland), June 23, 1954, 6:24 p.m., DP, JFD:CS, Box 8, EL; "Tres bombas dejó caer el avión en San Pedro de Copán," *El Día*, Tegucigalpa, June 23, 1954, p. 1; "Honduras Reports Bombing," *NYT*, June 23, 1954, p. 1; "Honduran Regime Protests to U.N. on Town Bombing," *NYT*, June 24, 1954, p. 1; "Guatemala rechazó la protesta de Honduras," *El I*, June 24, 1954, p. 1; "Honduran Ouster of Envoy Hinted," *NYT*, June 25, 1954, p. 3; AmEm Tegucigalpa, ALUSNA to SecState, DTG 030230Z, July 3, 1954, NA 714.00.

[97] Interview with Hernández.

[98] Marroquín Rojas, *La derrota*, p. 129.

[99] Interviews with Krieg (quoted), Montenegro, Mendizabal, González Siguí, Parinello, Silva Girón, Hernández.

[100] Interview with Paiz Novales. In a three-hour conversation, Col. González Siguí also began by stressing the impact of the rebels' planes and radio broadcasts. Then, after noting that "actually it was not an impressive invasion," he went on to explain

vided Castillo Armas with a far more powerful weapon: the Guatemalan officers' conviction that the defeat of the motley rebel band would lead to prompt and cruel revenge.

THE RESIGNATION OF ARBENZ

On the night of June 25, Jacobo Arbenz summoned the leaders of the government parties and the labor confederations to the presidential palace; also present was Colonel Carlos Enrique Díaz. The army at Zacapa had deserted, Arbenz explained; the population must be armed; the political parties and the trade unions must gather their supporters at dawn to receive weapons and training. Díaz raised no objections. He asked only that the distribution of weapons be orderly. The party leaders pledged four to five thousand volunteers; the CGTG at least as many.[101]

Of the thousands of volunteers anticipated by the party leaders and the CGTG, no more than two hundred materialized. At the Campo de Marte, where the CGTG had called its troops, only two hundred showed up. There they waited for weapons that never came. All that appeared "was a decrepit colonel who began to lead them in exercises"—and so they passed the day, doing push-ups.[102] A similar scene took place at the Maya Club, where the revolutionary parties had summoned their members. Those few who arrived waited in vain for weapons. They were spared, however, the calisthenics; the few officers who were present "kept them anxious and huddled together doing nothing—yet these were people who could have been organized."[103]

An equally depressing scene occurred at the Hipódromo del Norte, where the teachers of the STEG (one of the country's most combative unions) had been called by their secretary general, Rafael Tischler, a member of the PGT's Central Committee. Many teachers arrived, but when Tischler told them that the army at Zacapa had rebelled and asked for volunteers, only three or four came forward. The others explained that they had families and that it was hopeless anyway. For Arbenz and the PGT, it was "another disheartening blow."[104]

On two earlier occasions—on October 20, 1944 and July 18, 1949—the population of the capital had been summoned to fight, and it had done so

---

that it was fear of the United States that brought about the surrender of the Guatemalan officers.

[101] Interviews with Fortuny and Charnaud, who were present, and with María de Arbenz, who related what Arbenz told her. See also Fortuny, "Observaciones," p. 66.

[102] Interviews with Fortuny (quoted) and Pellecer. Pellecer, who was also at the Campo de Marte, asserts that "no more than one hundred volunteers came."

[103] Interviews with Maj. Rosenberg (quoted) and Paz Tejada.

[104] Interview with Fortuny (quoted), and Cardoza, "A treinta años," p. 92.

eagerly. On this twenty-sixth of June, 1954, however, the response was apathetic.

On those two previous occasions, troops had fought alongside civilians; they had passed out the weapons, and officers had led the volunteers. This time, the military had no intention of fighting, and it opposed arming the people. Moreover, the government's sudden appeal for volunteers—when communiqué after communiqué had spoken of victory—gave credence to the rebel radio's claims that Castillo Armas was advancing with thousands of well armed men. Above all, in October 1944 and July 1949, Guatemalans had been fighting Guatemalans. Now, they faced a formidable foe. Rumors were rife: the Marines had landed on the Caribbean coast and would march on the capital to eliminate Arbenz; "at the front it was raining U.S. paratroopers."[105] Why else, it was asked, would Arbenz call so abruptly for volunteers?

Some have argued that had Arbenz addressed the people on that twenty-sixth of June, had he convoked a mass demonstration, thousands of civilians would have marched on the military barracks in the capital to seize the weapons. But this is highly unlikely. A week of mounting rumors, of growing tensions, had sapped the will of a population bruised by months of psychological warfare. Guatemala City was no Madrid. There were no International Brigades, and the fledgling labor unions had not been hardened in a daily, bloody struggle like their Spanish counterparts eighteen years earlier. Nor was the capital the bastion of the young revolution. It was to the countryside, rather than the cities, that Arbenz had brought the greatest benefits. Thousands of peasants might have fought on that twenty-sixth of June. For them, Arbenz meant freedom and land. But they had no weapons. Unaware that their government was collapsing, they continued to man roadblocks, to search for weapons dropped by rebel planes, and to flood the capital with telegrams pledging their loyalty.[106]

Jacobo Arbenz was exhausted. He remained closeted in his office on the twenty-sixth of June, listening to hourly reports that were increasingly disheartening: the population was immobilized, and the officers in the capital were becoming mutinous. Perhaps, he began to think, he should step down. Perhaps, then, the army would rout Castillo Armas. Perhaps, if he accepted Zacapa's ultimatum, some part of the revolution could be saved. In the late afternoon, Arbenz told Fortuny that he was considering resigning. That evening, the Secretariat of the PGT met in his office. "Several of us spoke. We told Arbenz that resistance was still possible, that we could still win—if we

[105] Lt. Eugenio Dedette of the Presidential Guard quoted by Paz Tejada. (Interview with Paz Tejada.) On the role of the U.S. embassy in this disinformation campaign, see Schlesinger and Kinzer, *Bitter Fruit*, pp. 192–93.

[106] See *GT*, esp. Boxes 5, 11, and 71.

armed the people." As if he were shaking off a trance, Arbenz said, "You've convinced me. Now help me. We have to start at once."[107]

It was 11 p.m. when the leaders of the PGT left the presidential palace. They had talked with Arbenz about organizing a group of about a hundred PGT members who would be armed with machine guns, but they had no suggestions as to how to seize the weapons from the army and transform untrained civilians into an effective fighting force. They were ready to die for their beliefs, and many have died since, under torture.[108] They had no idea, however, how to organize the defense of the capital. In the words of Guerra Borges, "The situation was so grave and so complex that the party could no longer deal with it. We were overtaken by events."[109]

Fortuny stayed with Arbenz. They talked for two or three hours, "discussing the telegrams and messages of support that had arrived from abroad. We talked about how we should handle the U.N. and the diplomatic offensive. We talked about how we could make the military arm the people." But Arbenz took no action during those hours he spent with Fortuny, "other than talking."[110]

Nearly thirty years later, Fortuny comments: "We were escaping from reality. Arbenz was exhausted; he didn't even try to implement the plans he had discussed with the leaders of the PGT." The same was true of Fortuny, who failed (as he acknowledges) to point out to Arbenz that they had to do more than talk.[111] After months of terrible tension, two brave men were unwilling to concede defeat and were paralyzed by despair.

It was to be Arbenz's last night in the presidential palace. While he daydreamed with Fortuny, others in the capital prepared to act—all with one objective, to remove the president and appease the United States. On the morning of Sunday the twenty-seventh, Foreign Minister Toriello, on his own initiative and without informing Arbenz, sought out Peurifoy. He asked whether the United States would be satisfied if Arbenz were replaced by a military *junta*, but not by Castillo Armas. He too would resign, if Washington so desired, although, he hastened to add, "he personally . . . had always been very anti-Communist and . . . as far as he was concerned the Junta could take all the Communists in Guatemala and send them to Moscow."[112]

As Toriello pleaded with Peurifoy, several unconnected plots were brewing

[107] Interviews with Fortuny (quoted) and Guerra Borges, who were both present, and with María de Arbenz, who relates what Arbenz told her. See also Fortuny, "Observaciones," pp. 67–68. The major discrepancy is that in Fortuny's account, Gutiérrez and one or two other members of the PGT's Political Commission were also present.

[108] See below, p. 388.

[109] Interview with Guerra Borges.

[110] Interview with Fortuny.

[111] Interview with Fortuny.

[112] Peurifoy to SecState, June 27, 1954, 2 p.m., *FRUS*, 1952–1954, 4:1188–89.

among the officer corps in the capital. There was the handful of supporters of Castillo Armas, biding time and busily spreading rumors. There were also those perennial plotters who were hostile to both Arbenz and Castillo Armas—senior officers like Cruz Salazar, Monzón, and Dubois, who were ambitious yet had lacked the courage to act. And there were those senior officers who were considered particularly loyal to Arbenz and who had never plotted against him—men like Armed Forces Chief Díaz, Defense Minister Sánchez, Army Chief of Staff Parinello, Air Force Chief Luis Girón, and the president of the Consejo Superior de la Defensa, Carlos Sarti. These five colonels met on the morning of the twenty-seventh at Díaz's house, and their conclusion was swift and unanimous: Jacobo must go.[113] Thereupon Díaz phoned Peurifoy, who had just finished listening to Toriello's entreaties. "Situation appears breaking rapidly," commented the ambassador, after listening to Díaz's plea that they meet "at earliest possible moment." It was 2 p.m., June 27, 1954.[114]

Accompanied by Colonels Martin and McCormick, and by DCM Krieg, Peurifoy went to Díaz's house. There he met Díaz and his four confederates. Díaz said that he and his colleagues were ready to force Arbenz to resign; he would become president and would immediately outlaw the PGT and exile its leaders. In return, the United States must no longer champion Castillo Armas. In ringing tones (rather hollow under the circumstances), Díaz, "strongly seconded by others, [stated] that direct negotiations with Castillo [Armas] were out of question; they would rather die than talk with him." Washington would no longer need Castillo Armas, they pledged: their Guatemala would be stable, anticommunist and pro-American.[115]

The first order of business was the removal of Arbenz, Peurifoy pointed out. The rest could be settled later. Nor did his interlocutors think to insist on a guarantee as to the future role of Castillo Armas. Finding solace in Peurifoy's promise that as soon as Arbenz had been deposed he would arrange a truce with the rebels, "Díaz said that they had decided to act at once." There was, however, one last problem, Díaz added, "the tough problem. Who is going to bell the cat? Who will talk to Jacobo?" Peurifoy's report continues:

> With but moment's hesitation he [Díaz] made decision: "Col. Sánchez will visit all garrisons and announce I have assumed presidency. Colonel Girón will inform air force. I will go to Palace with Parinello and Sarti and we will tell Jacobo." After some other talk, Díaz said, "Arbenz may answer two ways. He will either say 'Yes,'

[113] Interview with Parinello.

[114] Peurifoy to SecState, June 27, 1954, 2 p.m., *FRUS*, 1952–1954, 4:1188–89.

[115] Peurifoy to SecState, June 27, 1954, 11 p.m., ibid., pp. 1189–91, quoted from p. 1190. "At one point Díaz asked whether any members of present Cabinet were unacceptable to US. I said I could not attempt to dictate his Cabinet and that if he appointed reasonable men I was sure all our secondary problems could be worked out, such as difficulties of American Companies." (Ibid., p. 1191.)

or he will say, 'This is insubordination,' and call the guard. In latter case we will not emerge from Palace. If we are not out in reasonable period, Sánchez will bring up artillery.''[116]

Díaz and his friends departed, with Peurifoy insisting on the "necessity of acting quickly to round up leading Communists."[117]

Peurifoy's account is confirmed by two of the U.S. officials who were present and by Colonel Parinello.[118] Once the meeting had ended, Parinello went with Díaz and Girón to the presidential palace: "I was trembling, Arbenz could have had us shot."[119] (The possibility was remote: the small Presidential Guard, the only military force within the presidential palace, was commanded by Lt. Colonel Dubois, who was himself busily plotting against Arbenz.)

In the palace, they found the president virtually alone. While Parinello and Girón waited, Díaz went into Arbenz's office and emerged half an hour later. "It's settled. He will resign today." Leaving the palace, they rushed to tell the good news to Peurifoy: Arbenz had agreed to step down in favor of Díaz and would announce his resignation at 9 p.m. It was approximately 5 p.m.[120]

Fortuny, who had arrived at the palace while Arbenz was with Díaz, saw his friend as soon as the colonels had left. This time, Arbenz refused to reconsider his decision. Instead, he asked Fortuny to write his resignation speech. At first Fortuny refused, but Arbenz insisted: "Please, do this last favor for me, the last favor I will ask you in my life." Fortuny relented, and together they outlined the speech.[121]

Shortly thereafter, in the late afternoon, Arbenz met with the cabinet. At least two ministers were absent. Aldana Sandoval had already sought asylum in the Salvadoran embassy,[122] and Defense Minister Sánchez was busy drumming up support for his friend Carlos Enrique Díaz in the barracks of the capital.

Throughout the Arbenz presidency, the cabinet had been an institution of only modest importance. It had not met since the beginning of the invasion.

[116] Ibid., pp. 1190–91.

[117] Ibid., p. 1191.

[118] McCormick to SecState, no. C-14, 280145Z, NA 714.00; interviews with Krieg, Parinello, and McCormick.

[119] Interview with Parinello, who says that Girón, not Sarti, went with them to the palace.

[120] Interview with Parinello. See also Peurifoy to SecState, no. 1123, June 27, 1954, 7 p.m.; McCormick to SecState, no. C-14, 280145Z. Both NA 714.00.

[121] Interviews with Fortuny (quoted) and María de Arbenz.

[122] Krieg to DOS, no. 41, July 21, 1954, p. 3, NA 714.00; "Expresidente Arbenz ya se encuentra en México," *Tribuna Libre*, San Salvador, Sept. 11, 1954, p. 5. On Aldana Sandoval's demoralization and his fears, see also Peurifoy to SecState, no. 1107, June 25, 1954, NA 714.00, and CIA, *Current Intelligence Digest*, June 28, 1954, p. 15.

As the ministers convened, at Arbenz's request, not one knew he intended to resign. Interior Minister Charnaud, perhaps the most influential cabinet member, had not seen Arbenz since the twenty-fifth; others had not seen him since June 17. Now they were informed of his decision. Arbenz did not ask for their advice, nor did they offer it.[123] The session was short, which suited many of the ministers who were in a hurry to leave—to seek asylum in foreign embassies.

Arbenz also left, but for his personal residence, Casa Pomona. It was 8 p.m., June 27, 1954. He had already taped the short speech that Fortuny had prepared. It was broadcast at 9 p.m. Speaking "with a voice full of emotion,"[124] President Arbenz bade farewell to the Guatemalan people: "I say goodbye to you, my friends, with bitterness and pain, but firm in my convictions." He was resigning to eliminate "the pretext for the invasion of our country." He had reached his decision with his "eyes on the welfare of the people" and he would hand over power to his friend Carlos Enrique Díaz "with the hope of saving the democratic gains of the October revolution. . . . A government that, although different from mine, is still inspired by our October revolution is preferable to twenty years of bloody tyranny under the men whom Castillo Armas has brought into the country."[125]

Arbenz's words, words of immense sadness and dignity, were as enigmatic as the man himself. He did not explain his decision, he remained silent about developments at the front, and he made no reference to any ultimatum from his officers. Indeed his speech included no attack on the army that had betrayed him. His criticism, and it was scathing, was reserved for Castillo Armas and the United States.

Many have branded Arbenz's resignation as the surrender of a frightened man. These critics include Guatemalans and foreigners, people of the right and of the left. They have passed judgment but have seldom sought to understand what hopes and what fears might have led him to this desperate step. Even Peurifoy's dispatches show greater insight into Arbenz's motivations.

[123] Interviews with Charnaud and Toriello, who were at the meeting. Their account is confirmed by Monzón, who was also present (see Sierra Roldán, *Diálogos*, pp. 89, 99), and by interviews with Fortuny and María de Arbenz (providing Arbenz's version of the session). Also at the meeting were a number of party leaders and trade union officials, one of whom has left a self-serving account of it. (See Díaz Rozzotto, *El carácter de la Revolución Guatemalteca*, pp. 291–92.)

[124] "Sucesivos cambios en el Ejecutivo," *El I*, June 29, 1954, p. 1.

[125] The Guatemalan press printed only short excerpts of the speech. The full text, from the original tape, was later published in Putzeys Rojas, *Así se hizo la Liberación*, pp. 297–300. Arbenz's previous broadcast, on June 19, had been full of confidence. ("Tenemos confianza en la unidad del pueblo, en el ejército, en la victoria," *DCA*, June 21, 1954, p. 5.)

As Peurifoy reported, Díaz and his four cohorts had offered to get rid of Arbenz but had insisted that the United States abandon Castillo Armas. Peurifoy had "avoided any comment."[126] The five colonels transformed this ambiguity into a promise.[127]

Díaz went to the presidential palace. He told Arbenz that the army units in the capital would attack the palace by 5 p.m. unless he resigned. Whether out of fear or shame, Díaz stressed that he was merely "the messenger"[128] and that he remained loyal to his friend and president: "This was decided without me, Jacobo, and I was merely asked to inform you; I will not participate in this coup."[129]

Beyond these lies, Díaz told Arbenz the truth, or rather, his version of the truth: Peurifoy had promised, he asserted, that the United States would accept him as Guatemala's next president if Arbenz resigned and the PGT was banned.

Díaz said that he had been sent by the officers in the capital; in fact, he represented no one but himself and his four colonel cronies.[130] Earlier he had told the same tale to Peurifoy. ("Solution desired by all army officers was that he should assume presidency," the ambassador had cabled, quoting Díaz.)[131] Vain and unintelligent, Díaz overestimated his influence in the army. Mistaking superficial camaraderie for loyalty and respect, he believed that the army would rally behind him; his four confederates shared his illusions. ("We, too, believed that Díaz could hold onto power," recalls Parinello.)[132] Díaz was not consciously lying. He was stating what he thought would occur, and his confidence was reinforced by what he believed to be Peurifoy's blessing. He would prove wrong, on both counts.

Arbenz knew even less about the true feelings of the officers than did Díaz. He believed that Díaz was his friend, and he believed that he was telling him the truth. Díaz was the most senior officer in the armed forces and was, Arbenz thought, well regarded by his fellow officers. Had he not been selected as the new president? Furthermore, according to Getellá, the officers at Zacapa were rebelling against Arbenz because they refused to be dragged into "his" war

[126] Interview with Krieg.

[127] Interview with Parinello.

[128] Interview with María de Arbenz.

[129] Interview with Fortuny, confirmed by interviews with María de Arbenz and Charnaud (all giving Arbenz's account) and interview with Parinello (giving Díaz's account); see also Arbenz, "Jacobo Arbenz relata detalles." Several months later, Arbenz still believed Díaz's tale and praised his "exemplary conduct." (Arbenz, "Tiene la palabra Jacobo Arbenz," p. 50.)

[130] Confirmed by interview with Parinello.

[131] Peurifoy to SecState, June 27, 1954, 11 p.m., FRUS, 1952–1954, 4:1190 (quoted); McCormick to SecState, no. C-14, 280145Z, NA 714.00 ("Díaz claimed entire support army"); interviews with Krieg and Parinello.

[132] Interview with Parinello.

against the United States. They had not attacked Díaz; indeed León and his two colleagues were Díaz's friends. Therefore, Arbenz concluded, if the United States was willing to accept Díaz, Zacapa would follow suit, and the ascent of Castillo Armas would be blocked.[133]

Díaz had told Arbenz that as president he would have to ban the PGT, exile its leaders, and halt the agrarian reform; but he had stressed that he would retain as many of the benefits of the revolution as he could—including leaving the land that had been distributed under Decree 900 in the peasants' hands. Arbenz saw himself confronted with a cruel choice. A Díaz presidency would spell the end of the revolution, and it would abort his attempt to transform Guatemala into an independent nation. The alternative, however, was worse. A victory of Castillo Armas meant the surrender of all national dignity, the obliteration of all the reforms undertaken since 1944, the return to power of the landed elite, and an orgy of repression. Reports were already coming in that the *Liberacionistas* were killing "subversives." Arbenz could no longer protect the Guatemalan peasants. He had lost, and they with him. His timely resignation could lighten the burden of their defeat.[134]

And so Arbenz was lulled by Díaz's promises. Later, he said: "I agreed to withdraw in favor of a loyal officer, Colonel Díaz, under two conditions: that there were no deals with Castillo Armas and that the achievements of the October revolution were preserved."[135] Corroboration is afforded by the embassy of the United States. After listening to Díaz's account of his conversation with Arbenz, Colonel McCormick cabled that "Arbenz had accepted Díaz ultimatum provided Díaz promise not [to] negotiate with Castillo Armas. Díaz agreed." In the same vein, Peurifoy reported: "As condition for peaceful turnover Arbenz demanded and Díaz gave his word of honor that he would not enter into negotiations with Castillo Armas."[136]

[133] Interviews with María de Arbenz, Fortuny, and Charnaud were particularly helpful for this paragraph.

[134] For Arbenz's perceptions, interviews with María de Arbenz, Fortuny, Guerra Borges, and Charnaud were particularly useful. (Charnaud was not close to Arbenz at the time, but they became close in the 1960s.) See also PGT, *La intervención*, p. 20. The reports of peasant executions were confirmed in interviews with officers who were in the Zacapa area, such as Hernández, Silva Girón, and Mendizabal; see also Peurifoy to SecState, no. 1157, June 30, 1954, NA 814.062, and Santa Cruz Morales, "La invasión a Guatemala." Putzeys Rojas blandly refers to "those peasants who fled in fear to the mountains." (*Así se hizo la Liberación*, p. 265.) The fate of the peasants, the main beneficiaries of his government, weighed particularly heavily on Arbenz in those dark hours. "Arbenz was afraid that if he resisted the army's ultimatum there would be a bloodbath in the countryside, and he knew that the peasants had no way to defend themselves." (Interview with Charnaud.)

[135] Arbenz, "Tiene la palabra Jacobo Arbenz," p. 50; see also Arbenz, "Jacobo Arbenz relata detalles."

[136] Quoted from McCormick to SecState, no. C-14, 280145Z, and Peurifoy to

This explains why, in his resignation speech, Arbenz did not condemn the officers who had betrayed him. "It is as if Jacobo had said to the army, 'I am resigning, but please continue to fight against this traitor [Castillo Armas]. Do not surrender to these bandits.' Clinging to his last hope, he was appealing to the army's sense of honor."[137]

What alternative was open to Jacobo Arbenz at that late hour? Should he, as some have claimed, have left the capital and become a guerrilla leader? His failure to do so "was a crude error of grave historical consequences," stated Luis Cardoza y Aragón, a Guatemalan writer who lived in Mexico.[138]

But even if Arbenz had been able to leave the capital for the countryside (not a foregone conclusion, since the army could have tried to prevent his departure, and the Presidential Guard was commanded by the disloyal Dubois), how could he have built his guerrilla force? True, many peasants would have joined him, but they had neither weapons nor training. The adventure would have ranked among the most senseless of the many guerrilla efforts attempted in the hemisphere in the twentieth century. Arbenz would have led a host of peasants to their slaughter in the name of what? Revolutionary glory? Personal heroism?

Is the argument that Arbenz should have ennobled the collapse of the revolution through his own death? If such were the aim, rather than staining his own martyrdom with the blood of defenseless peasants, he should have met his fate by attempting to hold out in the presidential palace. As with Salvador Allende, death in the palace would have glorified his memory. And death might have been preferable, for Arbenz, to the seventeen years that awaited him.

But Arbenz's decision must be seen in the light of the alternatives as they appeared to him on that fateful twenty-seventh of June: he believed that his timely resignation would lead to the presidency of Carlos Enrique Díaz and thwart the triumph of Castillo Armas. His resignation was not an act of cowardice, but the desperate attempt to save what might still be saved. "Perhaps many people will think that I am making a mistake," he conceded in his farewell speech. "From the bottom of my heart I do not believe this. Only history will decide."[139]

As his words were broadcast on the evening of the twenty-seventh, Arbenz was at his home, Casa Pomona, where he spent the night—he had no need to seek refuge, he reasoned, since Díaz was in command.[140]

SecState, no. 1123, June 27, 1954, 7 p.m. Both NA 714.00. See also Burrows to Woodward, June 28, 1954, NA 714.00 and CIA, *Current Intelligence Digest*, June 28, 1954, p. 16.

[137] Interview with María de Arbenz.

[138] *La Revolución Guatemalteca*, p. 187.

[139] Putzeys Rojas, *Así se hizo la Liberación*, p. 300.

[140] Interviews with María de Arbenz, Fortuny, and Lilly Zachrisson (who was living

Before leaving the presidential palace, he had urged the revolutionary politicians present to assist the new president. Some did not dally; they fled to foreign embassies. Others stayed, among them Charnaud and Castillo Flores, who remained "calm"—confident that Díaz would remain in control.[141]

"The peasant organizations," Castillo Flores proclaimed, "must cooperate fully with Colonel Díaz, since he has promised to uphold the laws of the October Revolution."[142] In a speech that was broadcast immediately after that of Arbenz, Díaz had indeed pledged that he would honor the social reforms enacted since 1944, and he had also promised that he would continue to fight against Castillo Armas "until he is defeated."[143]

FROM DÍAZ TO CASTILLO ARMAS

Díaz was an opportunist, but he was not utterly disloyal to the men with whom he had hobnobbed when he had been Arbenz's protegé. On the evening of the twenty-seventh, he freed Gutiérrez, who had been arrested a few hours earlier. "You, Pellecer and Gutiérrez should seek asylum tonight," he warned Fortuny, who was still lingering in the presidential palace. "Your lives are in danger, and there are things I cannot control." Díaz, concludes Fortuny, "was not prepared to kill communists."[144]

Díaz was doomed. The United States had not launched Castillo Armas's invasion in order to hand the presidency to a friend of Arbenz. Washington intended to impose its own man, a man with unblemished anticommunist credentials, a man who would not urge communist leaders to seek asylum, but who would destroy them.

A game of musical chairs began. By the time the music stopped, on July 7, Castillo Armas was in control.

To accomplish this feat, the United States, in Secretary Dulles's apt words, had to "crack some heads together,"[145] a task for which Peurifoy was partic-

---

at Casa Pomona). Their version is confirmed by a fiery supporter of Castillo Armas: "Arbenz went to 'Pomona.' " (Del Valle Matheu, *La verdad*, p. 30.) Arbenz sought asylum in the Mexican embassy the following day, once it had become obvious that Díaz was unable to maintain control. He did so under strong pressure from his wife, who urged him: "Don't let them kill you for no reason. Don't make a vain sacrifice. You're still young; you can fight again for Guatemala." (Interview with María de Arbenz.) The fact that Arbenz sought asylum only on the twenty-eighth is also confirmed by the testimony of a Mexican official who was at the embassy: see Guillén, *Guatemala*, p. 77.

[141] Interviews with Fortuny (quoted), who was still at the palace, and with Charnaud.

[142] Castillo Flores to Sec. Gen. de la Unión Campesina "La Brigada," June 28, 1954, *GT*, Box 5.

[143] "Exito en la gestión del nuevo gobierno," *DCA*, June 28, 1954, p. 1.

[144] Interview with Fortuny.

[145] Peurifoy, "Memorandum of Negotiations Leading to Signing of Pact of San Salvador, July 2, 1954," July 7, 1954, *FRUS*, 1952–1954, 4:1202.

ularly well suited. It was not an exacting undertaking. Arbenz and his communist friends had been removed from the stage, and a crowd of officers had rushed into their places. Deeply demoralized, fragmented, aware that their conduct appeared ignominious—but too worried about their own survival to behave with dignity—the Guatemalan officers were easy prey.

In the eleven days following Arbenz's resignation, five provisional governments (staffed entirely by officers) succeeded one another, each more amenable to Castillo Armas than its predecessor. Some officers served in more than one *junta*. (Colonel Monzón set the record by serving in four.) In this squalid minuet, the dancers jostled one another, each with his hopes and delusions, moving to a foreign beat. Some, damned by their *Arbencista* past, were quickly shoved off the floor by an impatient Peurifoy. Others met with his approval: the fervent anticommunists who had disliked Arbenz and had served him only out of opportunism. But theirs was only a supporting role: to pave the way for Castillo Armas. Those who performed gracefully were later rewarded. None proved more supple than Lt. Colonel Cruz Salazar (two *juntas*). When the invasion began, he was hostile to Castillo Armas; two weeks later he was working on his behalf. According to Cruz Salazar, he was "under unbelievable psychological pressure": John Doherty, the CIA station chief, "would appear at any hour, day and night; he didn't let me sleep."[146] But the Americans were reasonable men. Doherty's threats were accompanied by promises, and the promises would be kept. Cruz Salazar became Castillo Armas's first ambassador to the United States and received a generous "bonus"—the beginning of an enriching career.[147]

Colonel Monzón was not as astute as Cruz Salazar. Peurifoy and other U.S. officials had praise for him: he was a fervent anticommunist and a hard worker. Had Monzón understood his role, he too could have savored the sweet blessings of obedience. But he persisted in believing that he could deal with Castillo Armas as an equal. He was soon brought to heel, of course, and his importunities cost him dearly. On September 1, 1954, he was forced out of the *junta*; a few months later he was eased out of the country. When he tried to return, in August 1955, he was informed "that his papers were not in order, and that he regretfully could not be permitted to enter the country."[148] He even

---

[146] Interview with Cruz Salazar.

[147] "Most reports place the figure at $100,000." (Cehelsky, "Guatemala's Frustrated Revolution," p. 63.) "The new Ambassador has expended his efforts in directions which appear to offer little general benefit to Guatemala," a U.S. official reported. (Leddy to Mann, Nov. 12, 1954, p. 1, NA 611.14.)

[148] Cehelsky, "Guatemala's Frustrated Revolution," p. 107. See also Sierra Roldán, *Diálogos*, p. 125. For U.S. impressions of Monzón, see Peurifoy to SecState, no. 1142, June 29, 1954, NA 714.00; CIA, *Current Intelligence Digest*, June 30, 1954, p. 7; Dulles to AmEm Paris, June 30, 1954, NA 714.00/6-2354; Bowdler to Pearson,

suffered the indignity—for a man of his stamp—of being refused a U.S. visa.[149] Monzón's memoirs, *Diálogos con el coronel Monzón*, are the bitter lamentations of a failed opportunist.

The dance that brought Castillo Armas from Chiquimula to the presidency can be quickly described; it is a sordid footnote to Arbenz's resignation. On the night of June 27, Colonel Díaz was awakened by two CIA agents who ordered him to resign at once. Stunned—hadn't Peurifoy given him his word?—Díaz asked to see the ambassador. But when he was brought to Peurifoy, it was only to hear the same sentence again: he must resign. "They were quite rough with Díaz that night," recalls DCM Krieg.[150] Peurifoy upbraided the hapless colonel for having allowed Arbenz to denounce the United States in his resignation speech and told him to step aside in favor of Monzón, who was "well-known for his anti-Communist feelings."[151] In his illusion that Peurifoy would accept him as president of Guatemala, Díaz had chased the mirage of a promise. The tone of Arbenz's farewell speech only abbreviated the span of a presidency that would, in any case, have been ephemeral.

Chastened, Díaz withdrew. He dared not disobey Peurifoy, but neither was he ready to jettison his ambitions. He reappeared before the ambassador a few hours later, flanked by his friend, Colonel Sánchez, and by Monzón. Hoping to placate Peurifoy, Díaz had traded the presidential mantle for that of the head of a three-man *junta* composed of himself, Sánchez and Monzón. Stressing that Monzón would be completely in charge of security matters—that is, of "carrying out vigorous program [to] clean out Communists"—Díaz and Sánchez "promised [to] take no action without his approval."[152]

The *junta* lasted less than twenty-four hours. Peurifoy continued to insist that Díaz resign. His threats were delicately summed up by Monzón in his memoirs: "There will be no peace in Guatemala until the men in power can guarantee the eradication of communism." This was why, Monzón argued,

---

"ARA Monthly Report for July," Aug. 4, 1954, NA 714.00; Memo for Record ("Situation in Guatemala"), Aug. 24, 1954, NA 714.00.

[149] See Sierra Roldán, *Diálogos*, p. 130. Monzón was allowed to return to Guatemala in 1957, after Castillo Armas's death.

[150] Interview with Krieg.

[151] Peurifoy to SecState, June 28, 1954, noon, *FRUS*, 1952–1954, 4:1192.

[152] Quotations from Peurifoy to SecState, June 28, 1954, 5 p.m., ibid., p. 1193. Peurifoy's view of the Díaz *junta* was shared by the CIA: "It would appear that the Guatemalan government is attempting by the maneuver of ousting Arbenz and outlawing the Workers' Party [PGT] to remove the stigma of Communism from the government and thereby take from Castillo Armas the reason for his campaign. Most of those calling for support of the new government have long pro-Communist records." (*Current Intelligence Digest*, June 29, 1954, p. 15.)

"I suggested to Carlos Enrique Díaz that he resign in my favor."[153] Díaz hesitated, and was overtaken by events. On the night of the twenty-eighth, a group of officers arrived unbidden at the house of his ally, Army Chief of Staff Parinello. Unceremoniously, they woke him up: "You are dismissed. Give us the keys to your office."[154] Parinello docilely handed over the keys, thereby exiting from center stage. Meanwhile, another group of officers rose against Díaz and Sánchez. At 4:45 a.m. a new *junta* was proclaimed, composed of Monzón (as president), Cruz Salazar, and Dubois. Not one drop of blood had been shed and no resistance had been offered. Díaz and Sánchez meekly hastened off the stage. Their departure was described by the indefatigable Peurifoy: "Returning to Díaz's office at 4 a.m., I found Monzón had not yet appeared. Just as I was about to leave, Díaz received telephone call from Palace and he and Sánchez left to confer with several officers. . . . Shortly thereafter Díaz returned and wearily informed me that things had changed: he and Sánchez had decided resign from Junta."[155]

This was, applauded Peurifoy, a healthy change, which guaranteed that there would no longer be any wavering in the persecution of communists.[156] Castillo Armas, however, was still at Chiquimula and still waiting for his turn.

When Monzón installed himself in the presidential palace, Castillo Armas controlled only a speck of Guatemalan territory. His was the parody of an invasion, but he faced the parody of an army. In any case, his strength was elsewhere: he was the candidate of the United States in a country that was rapidly regressing to a banana republic. Negotiations had opened on June 27 between Castillo Armas and the colonels at Zacapa. They ended, three days later, with the *Pacto de las Tunas*, whereby the troops at Zacapa placed themselves under Castillo Armas, receiving in exchange "full guarantees . . . of life and property" and the assurance that "they would suffer no discrimination . . . in their military careers." The pact asserted that "the honor and the dignity of the army were untarnished"[157]—a fantasy that convinced no one, and

[153] Sierra Roldán, *Diálogos*, p. 101; see also Peurifoy to SecState, June 28, 1954, 8 p.m., *FRUS*, 1952–1954, 4:1194–95, and Peurifoy to SecState, no. 1138, June 28, 1954, 9 p.m., NA 714.00.

[154] Interview with Parinello.

[155] Quoted from Peurifoy to SecState, June 29, 1954, 7 p.m., *FRUS*, 1952–1954, 4:1197; see also Peurifoy to SecState, no. 1139, June 29, 1954, NA 714.00, and Urist, "Monday Night Meeting," June 29, 1954, RG84 G&C, Box 3, NA-S. For Monzón's account, see Sierra Roldán, *Diálogos*, pp. 105–6. Interview with Cruz Salazar was useful.

[156] MemoTel (Peurifoy, Leddy), June 30, 1954, NA 714.00; Peurifoy to SecState, no. 1153, June 30, 1954, NA 714.00.

[157] The full text of the pact is published in Putzeys Rojas, *Así se hizo la Liberación*, pp. 309–11; for the negotiations, see pp. 98, 100, 118, 293–96, and 300. See also Sierra Roldán, *Diálogos*, p. 117, and Flores Avendaño, *Memorias*, 2:441–45.

certainly not the officers at Zacapa. Within a few days, they returned to their barracks "despondent, with a terrible sense of defeat."[158]

Though eager to crush communists and relentless in his professions of loyalty to the United States, Monzón was reluctant to hand power to Castillo Armas. He enjoyed the timid support of a great many officers who felt that they would be better protected by a *junta* of fellow colonels than by their erstwhile foes; none, however, was willing to challenge the United States. Meanwhile other officers, including *junta* members Dubois and Cruz Salazar, were discreetly working for the triumph of Castillo Armas.

The United States opened the next act. The State Department asked President Osorio to invite Monzón and Castillo Armas to talks in San Salvador. Osorio complied, and the two rivals arrived on June 30 aboard U.S. planes; both were disgruntled, wary, and anxious.[159] Two days of quarrels ensued. Then, at 4:45 a.m. on July 2, Monzón and Castillo Armas embraced, to the edification of a crowd of photographers, and signed the *Pacto de San Salvador*; they had, wrote the *New York Times*, "tears in their eyes."[160] The pact established a new *junta*, which included Monzón, Dubois, and Cruz Salazar, as well as Castillo Armas and another *Liberacionista*, Major Enrique Trinidad Oliva. For the moment, Monzón would continue as president, "but the *junta* would select a new president in not more than two weeks."[161] In Washington, Holland concluded, "Since Cruz [Salazar] and Oliva are Castillo men, Castillo has control."[162]

The most colorful character at San Salvador was Peurifoy, who arrived in the early afternoon of July first, with a planeload of journalists. Acting like a stern father, he brought the recalcitrant pair to a swift agreement. He first received Castillo Armas, whom he had never met. Setting diplomatic niceties aside, he scolded the Guatemalan for his intransigence. Peurifoy explained:

[158] Interview with Col. Mendoza, who was appointed army chief of staff in early July. "Therefore," as he said, "I saw all this very closely."

[159] AmEm San Salvador, McDermott to DOS, "Negotiation in San Salvador of Guatemalan Peace Pact," July 5, 1954, NA 714.00. See also: MemoTel (McDermott, Holland), June 29, 1954, NA 714.00; MemoTel (Willauer, Holland), June 29, 1954, NA 714.00; MemoTel (Peurifoy, Holland), June 29, 1954, *FRUS*, 1952–1954, 4:1195; MemoTel (Peurifoy, Holland, Whelan, McDermott, Castro), June 29, 1954, NA 714.00; Peurifoy to SecState, no. 1148, June 29, 1954, NA 714.00.

[160] "Guatemala Chiefs Vow to Fight Reds," *NYT*, July 3, 1954, p. 1.

[161] Point 6 of the *Pacto de San Salvador*. The best sources on the negotiations are McDermott, "Negotiation" (see n. 159 above), and Peurifoy, "Memorandum of Negotiations" (see n. 145 above), pp. 1202–8. For Monzón's account see Sierra Roldán, *Diálogos*, pp. 114–23, 132–34; for the Salvadoran government's account see El Salvador, *De la neutralidad vigilante a la mediación con Guatemala*.

[162] DOS, "Meeting of Guatemalan Group," July 2, 1954, p. 1.

I then told him I was going to speak with absolute frankness. "You know, and I know," I told him, "how the American people feel about you. Many American people think you should be the president of Guatemala, and . . . I personally will do all in my power to help you. For the present, I think you should be taken into the Junta. And, confidentially, I'll tell you something else. Col. Cruz Salazar . . . told me that he was on your side, so you should have no problem at all." He seemed to be pleased and reassured by these last statements.[163]

Next it was Monzón's turn to be lectured by the ambassador. "In all due modesty," Peurifoy later boasted to Holland, "within an hour—after talking for about 30 minutes with each man . . . [I] had a basic agreement. The rest of the time—all night long—they were fighting over details."[164]

While Peurifoy held center stage, Somoza bombarded the State Department with suggestions and complaints, claiming that Castillo Armas was being placed "at a disadvantage" in the negotiations with Monzón.[165] Ambassador Whelan cabled that Somoza was "hurt and angry" because Castillo Armas had been told upon landing in Managua while enroute to San Salvador "that he was under orders see no one but me. . . . I told President [Somoza] I knew of no such order and thought it misunderstanding. I then phoned airport and learned such order had been received from somewhere. . . . I told airport disregard their orders."[166]

In San Salvador Peurifoy was interrupted in his peacemaking by the untimely visit of the Nicaraguan ambassador, Carlos Duque, who carried an urgent message from his master. Peurifoy reported:

President Somoza wished to advise me that in view of the "breakdown" in negotiations between Castillo Armas and Monzón, he urged the entire negotiating party to come to Managua as his guests to continue their discussions there. If this were not feasible, he said, then he strongly advised that Col. Castillo Armas be made president of Guatemala, and that Col. Monzón be made Minister of Defense. He mentioned several other Cabinet appointments, which I do not recall. I thanked Ambassador Duque. . . . I told him, however . . . that I did not believe it would be necessary to trouble President Somoza with any of the negotiations.[167]

Eager to mask its interference, the State Department downplayed its role at San Salvador. Thus, it was initially thought that Peurifoy should not attend the meeting, much to his disappointment; but the stubbornness of Castillo Armas

[163] Peurifoy, "Memorandum of Negotiations" (see n. 145 above), pp. 1203–4.

[164] MemoTel (Peurifoy, Holland), July 2, 1954, 10:50 a.m., p. 2, NA 714.00.

[165] AmEm Managua, Whelan to SecState, no. 237, June 29, 1954, 9 p.m., NA 714.00.

[166] AmEm Managua, Whelan to SecState, no. 240, June 30, 1954, 4 p.m., NA 714.00.

[167] Peurifoy, "Memorandum of Negotiations" (see n. 145 above), p. 1206.

and Monzón forced Washington to reconsider.[168] Once Peurifoy had done the job, U.S. officials informed Osorio, who had merely housed and fed the guests, that the credit for the agreement was all his. Commendable modesty also led the United States to abstain from signing the pact, "thus giving the Salvadoran government recognition as the principal mediator." The agreement was signed by only Castillo Armas, Monzón, and El Salvador's acting foreign minister. (The foreign minister was " 'indisposed' because of alcoholic excesses.")[169]

On July 3, a triumphant Peurifoy brought Monzón and Castillo Armas—with a crowd of boisterous journalists—back to Guatemala City in the embassy plane. If Castillo Armas still doubted that he had won, his misgivings were soon dispelled. On July 7, in accordance with their secret pledges, Cruz Salazar and Dubois resigned from the *junta*. To Monzón, it came as a surprise; to Peurifoy, as a foreordained conclusion. Left with Castillo Armas and Oliva, the hapless Monzón dutifully added his vote, a few hours later, to theirs, making Castillo Armas's election as *junta* president unanimous. "Things are going to work out beautifully," a confident Peurifoy told Holland the following day.[170] And so they did. On September 1, again by unanimous vote, the *junta* dissolved itself, and Castillo Armas became president of Guatemala.

Only one incident disturbed the careful choreography that brought Castillo Armas from Chiquimula to Guatemala City. At dawn, on August 2, "a vigorous exchange of gunfire awoke those who lived in the southeastern sector of the capital." About a hundred of the 136 cadets of the Escuela Politécnica were attacking the Roosevelt Hospital, which housed seven hundred armed *Liberacionistas* who had come from Zacapa and Chiquimula to participate in a victory parade.[171]

[168] See McDermott, "Negotiation" (see n. 159 above), p. 4; Dulles to Peurifoy, no. 259, June 29, 1954, 8:07 p.m.; MemoTel (Peurifoy, Holland), June 30, 1954, 10 a.m.; MemoTel (Holland, McDermott), June 30, 1954, 9 p.m.; Holland to Wisner, no. 371, June 30, 1954, 9:25 p.m. All NA 714.00.

[169] Quoted from Peurifoy, "Memorandum of Negotiations Leading to Signing of Pact of San Salvador, July 2, 1954," July 7, 1954, p. 4, NA 714.00. The parenthetical sentence has been deleted in *FRUS* 1952–1954 (see 4:1206); see also MemoTel (Peurifoy, Holland), July 2, 1954, 10:50 a.m., NA 714.00.

[170] MemoTel (Peurifoy, Holland), July 8, 1954, NA 714.00; see also Peurifoy to SecState, no. 32, July 6, 1954, NA 714.00. Apparently Dubois received the same financial reward as Cruz Salazar. (See Cehelsky, "Guatemala's Frustrated Revolution," p. 63.)

[171] "Información sobre los sucesos habidos hoy temprano en el sur de la ciudad," *La Hora*, Aug. 2, 1954, p. 1 (quoted). Castillo Armas's troops swelled "with imaginary combatants" after his victory. "These new recruits, many of them children of the upper class, had never fired a shot because they had never been near the fighting." (Col. Pinto Recinos, "Sublevación," July 23, 1988, p. 3.)

Peurifoy, Castillo Armas, and the officers in the city were caught by surprise. Also surprised were the cadets' officers, who did not join their charges in the attack on the hospital.[172]

Taking off from the nearby military airport, Castillo Armas's planes strafed the cadets, who had been reinforced by about two hundred soldiers sent by the Base Militar. But the cadets and soldiers held their ground, demonstrating once again that the rebel air force was of little use against troops willing to fight.

The *Liberacionistas* were isolated. No army unit came to their assistance. On the contrary, the Base Militar sent a detail to occupy the military airport later in the morning, thus grounding Castillo Armas's planes. The Base Militar, however, "never openly raised the banner of insurrection against Castillo Armas." During the day, the army units in the capital broadcast both proclamations of loyalty to the ruling *junta* and words of praise for "the glorious efforts of the cadets to vindicate the honor of the army."[173]

It was Peurifoy who dominated the scene in Guatemala City. He held court, appropriately enough, in the presidential palace. He threatened, cajoled, admonished. He told the officers who came to pledge their loyalty that the United States was irrevocably behind Castillo Armas.[174] He was not unduly excited by the rebellion. It had no leftist tinges, he told Holland, and "there were no signs of Communist activity"; rather, he stressed, "anti-Communists were fighting anti-Communists"[175]—and Guatemala's anticommunists had a comforting tendency to obey U.S. orders.

The immediate cause of the revolt, Peurifoy cabled, was a tawdry incident that had occurred on the night of August 1: "Liberation elements forced two cadets into local bawdy house, made them strip and attempted perpetuate gross indignities on their persons and reportedly killing one of them in ensuing brawl."[176] His information was accurate except for a few details. The unlucky cadets—who were four or five rather than two—had gone to the brothel on

---

[172] The best sources on the revolt are (1) Peurifoy's cables to DOS and memos of telephone conversations between him and Holland, Aug. 2–4, 1954, in NA 714.00; *JW* 32, Aug. 6, 1954; (2) *El I* and *La Hora* (despite a pronounced bias in favor of Castillo Armas); (3) Second Lt. Girón, "La rebelión de los cadetes"; Santa Cruz Morales, "Secuela"; Pinto Recinos, "Sublevación." Also useful are Monzón's account in Sierra Roldán, *Diálogos*, pp. 140–44, and Samayoa Coronado, *La Escuela Politécnica*, 2:243–49. Interviews with Lorenzana, Mendizabal, Peralta Méndez, and Krieg were particularly valuable.

[173] Quotations from *JW* 32, Aug. 6, 1954, p. 3, and Santa Cruz Morales, "Secuela," p. 9.

[174] Interview with Krieg, who acted as Peurifoy's interpreter.

[175] Quotations from: MemoTel (Peurifoy, Holland), Aug. 2, 1954, 11:05 p.m.; Peurifoy to SecState, no. 146, Aug. 2, 1954, 11 p.m. Both NA 714.00.

[176] Peurifoy to SecState, no. 142, Aug. 2, 1954, 6 p.m., NA 714.00.

their own initiative, and, although they were forced to dance naked in front of the prostitutes and other clients, none had been killed.[177]

This was merely one in a series of humiliations. Castillo Armas's supporters had found it difficult to hide their contempt for an army that had surrendered without fighting. On August 6, the U.S. embassy pointed out that behind the cadets' uprising

> was dissatisfaction in the Army resulting from the rankling sense of humiliation of the Officer's Corps, . . . the uneasiness which naturally extended through the armed forces as officers wondered what their fate would be in the shake-up expected from the new government, . . . and the jeers to which uniformed Army personnel are reported to have been subjected by the populace, and especially by the swaggering youngsters carrying the brassard of the "Liberation Army."[178]

The rebellious cadets were not challenging the United States. Even as they besieged the Roosevelt Hospital, they informed Peurifoy of their loyalty to the junta—they wanted only an "end to insults" from the *Liberacionistas*.[179]

At 5:30 p.m. on August 2, while his men still held out at the Roosevelt Hospital against a smaller force,[180] Castillo Armas informed Peurifoy that he intended to go to Zacapa where he had another five hundred men under arms, but Peurifoy told him to stay in the capital.[181]

One hour later, the besieged *Liberacionistas* surrendered. They were disarmed and forced "to rip off their military badges . . . and throw them on the floor."[182] Then they were "marched as prisoners of war through the city, and loaded into trains."[183] After spending the night in the wagons, the defeated rabble departed for Zacapa, from whence it had come as conquerors a few days earlier.

At dusk, on August 3, the confidence of the ambassador was vindicated. The commander of the Base Militar and his deputy went meekly to the presidential palace to give themselves up while the other army units in the capital declared that they were ready to attack the cadets. Obligingly, the cadets sur-

[177] See esp. Santa Cruz Morales, "Secuela," p. 10. Among the dancers was Benedicto Lucas, a future general and chief of staff (1980–1982) of the Guatemalan army. (Villagrán Kramer, "Los pactos," July 19, 1987, pp. 18–19.)

[178] *JW* 32, Aug. 6, 1954, p. 2.

[179] Peurifoy to SecState, no. 138, Aug. 2, 1954, 1 p.m., NA 714.00.

[180] With the passing of the years, the attackers have multiplied in the *Liberacionista* lore; by 1986, they had grown from some three hundred to 1,800 ("2 de agosto: versión del MLN," *La Hora*).

[181] Peurifoy to SecState, no. 145, Aug. 2, 1954, 9 p.m., NA 714.00; see also Peurifoy to SecState, no. 146, Aug. 2, 1954, 11 p.m., NA 714.00.

[182] Santa Cruz Morales, "Secuela," p. 9.

[183] *JW* 32, Aug. 6, 1954, p. 2.

rendered forthwith in exchange for a guarantee that they would not be punished.

The Guatemalan press, which was no longer free, celebrated the end of the revolt as another glorious *Liberacionista* victory: "Second Battle against Communism Won," crowed *El Imparcial*.[184] The U.S. embassy was more sober: the events had demonstrated "that there was very little active support for Castillo Armas in the Armed Forces"; Castillo Armas himself had shown "little imagination or resolution," and the "civilian anti-Communist and 'Liberation' organizations [had] lost all semblance of discipline [during the crisis]."[185]

The cadets had attempted the impossible. They had tried to recover the dignity of the army without standing up to the United States. As in June, opportunism proved stronger than honor; fear of Washington more powerful than national pride. One hundred Guatemalans, including many innocent bystanders, were killed or wounded on August 2 and 3 as the cadets indulged in their senseless pursuit of the lost dignity of the Guatemalan army. Castillo Armas's retribution followed. In violation of the terms of surrender, the Escuela Politécnica was closed, and the rebellious cadets and several officers were cashiered or jailed. The Pax Americana was reestablished.

[184] "Segunda batalla contra el comunismo ganada," *El I*, Aug. 5, 1954, p. 1.
[185] *JW* 32, Aug. 6, 1954, pp. 4, 1.

CHAPTER 15

Conclusion

EVER SINCE Jefferson cast his gaze toward Cuba, three forces have shaped U.S. policy toward the Caribbean: the search for economic gain, the search for security, and imperial hubris. These were the forces that shaped the American response to the Guatemalan revolution. Consider the stage: there is Jack Peurifoy, that "abusive, arrogant ambassador,"[1] there is the Red Jacobo, and there are the bananas.

Behind the bananas looms the United Fruit Company, with its platoon of "influential lobbyists and talented publicists."[2] In Washington, a Republican president heads a probusiness administration whose upper echelon is studded with friends of United Fruit. Foster Dulles had been a senior partner in the law firm that had represented UFCO. His deputy, Walter Bedell Smith, was toying with the idea of taking a job with UFCO (which he indeed did when he retired in 1955). The assistant secretary for Latin America was a Cabot, as was the ambassador to the United Nations—and the Cabots were major UFCO stockholders. Eisenhower's personal secretary, Ann Whitman, was the wife of UFCO's director of public relations.

From Washington's perspective, Arbenz perpetrated outrages against UFCO. If one recalls the fury of the Truman administration when Arévalo sought to enforce the labor code, one can appreciate the gravity of Arbenz's crime when he seized UFCO's lands. It is not surprising, then, that some critics have seen in the decision to overthrow Arbenz the heavy hand of UFCO. "Without United Fruit's troubles," write the authors of *Bitter Fruit*, "it seems probable that the Dulles brothers might not have paid such intense attention to the few Communists in Guatemala, since larger numbers had taken part in political activity on a greater scale during the postwar years in Brazil, Chile and Costa Rica without causing excessive concern in the U.S. government."[3]

[1] Quoted from interview with Col. González Siguí.

[2] Schlesinger and Kinzer, *Bitter Fruit*, p. 77.

[3] Ibid., p. 106. The view that United Fruit was instrumental in the U.S. decision to overthrow Arbenz has its legion of ardent adherents—from Schlesinger and Kinzer, who provide its most compelling presentation, to lovers of the sensational, such as Rodman, "Operation Diablo," who scarcely bothers to cover his lies. Some portray a U.S. government that is putty in the hands of the company, conveniently overlooking evidence that might temper or complicate their thesis, including the fact that the government initiated an antitrust suit against UFCO shortly after the fall of Arbenz. On this, see Miller to Attorney General, Dec. 4, 1951, NA 814.062; Redmond to Miller,

UFCO had a motive, and it had the contacts. It is tempting to survey the scene of the crime, find this smoking gun, and arrest the fruit company. There is, however, more evidence. After studying the Guatemalan primary sources and juxtaposing them with U.S. reports, it becomes clearer and clearer that while the U.S. embassy's concern with communism under Arévalo owed much to UFCO's smoke and mirrors, its concern with communism under Arbenz owed little to the company.

Arbenz's sympathy for the communist cause was obvious, as was the growth in strength and prestige of the Community party. It is true, as *Bitter Fruit* points out, that the communist parties of Brazil, Chile, and Costa Rica had acquired significant influence in their respective countries. The Communist Party of Chile had ministers in the cabinet, that of Costa Rica was an important part of the government coalition, and that of Brazil won 10 percent of the vote in the December 1945 presidential elections. By 1948, however, all three parties had been banned. The PGT, by contrast, gained influence in the early 1950s, when in the United States, McCarthyism was at a peak and when, in Latin America, all other communist parties were waning. Not in Brazil or in Chile or in Costa Rica had the communists ever been the president's intimates; never had they been part of his inner circle, privy to his most closely guarded secrets.[4] In no country of Latin America had the communists ever been as influential as they were in Guatemala. And no president had ever been as close to the communists as was Arbenz. It required no manipulations by UFCO minions for U.S. officials to appreciate these truths. As Ambassador Schoenfeld noted, "One had only to read the articles carried by the official *Diario de Centro America.*"[5]

Just as scholars frequently fail to see the depth of the change from Arévalo to Arbenz, so they have failed to see the change in the U.S. government's reporting on Guatemala from the late forties to the early fifties. The reports of the late forties reveal, beyond their arrogance and ethnocentrism, immense ignorance. Many are simply bizarre, particularly those discussing the communist issue—those convoluted papers, for example, on whether Arévalo was

Dec. 4, 1951, NA 814.062; MemoConv (Barnes, Phleger, Metzger), May 22, 1953, NA Lot 58D18 & 58D78; TelConv (JFD, Brownell), June 30, 1954, DP, JFD:CS, Box 8, EL; "United Fruit Sued," *NYT*, July 3, 1954, p.1; "Oil on the Fire," *Business Week*, July 10, 1954, p. 128. See also Leddy to Holland, Oct. 12, 1954; Barnes to Baggett, Nov. 9, 1954; Sparks to Murphy, Nov. 18, 1954; Sparks to JFD, Dec. 3, 1954; Sherwood to Radius and Pearson, Dec. 6, 1954, and enclosed memo by Cutler. All NA Lot 58D18 & 58D78.

[4] See Alexander, *Communism*, and Goldenberg, *Kommunismus*. See also Halperin, *Nationalism and Communism in Chile*, pp. 52–59; Skidmore, *Politics in Brazil*, pp. 60–67; Aguilar Bulgarelli, *Costa Rica*.

[5] MemoConv (Schoenfeld, Toriello), Feb. 5, 1953, p. 2, RG84 G&C, Box 8, NA-S.

a communist. These reports bear no relationship to the reality of Guatemala; they inhabit a deranged world of nightmares. In the fifties, the embassy dispatches, despite their inaccuracies and ethnocentrism, reveal a grasp of the country and of the situation. A core of Guatemala hands had emerged in the Office of Intelligence and Research of the State Department, in the Directorate of Intelligence of the CIA, and in the embassy in Guatemala. Very often, when these people pointed to cases of communist influence, they were right. This shift from an embassy that knew nothing to an embassy that was reasonably well informed reduced UFCO's power to influence the picture of Guatemala. In the forties, UFCO was, to a great extent, the interpreter of matters Guatemalan. In the fifties, its role had become marginal.

The figure of the loud and arrogant Jack Peurifoy distorts a temperate assessment of U.S. reporting on Guatemala in the months before the overthrow of Arbenz. It is difficult not to be overwhelmed by this embodiment of imperial hubris, particularly when he is contrasted with his poised and urbane predecessor, Rudolph Schoenfeld. Schoenfeld is remembered to this day as a gentleman;[6] the contrast with Peurifoy could not be more stark. There was no contrast, however, between Schoenfeld's and Peurifoy's assessment of Guatemalan politics. Schoenfeld had hardened his stance on the Arbenz administration with each passing year, and his reports to the Department were increasingly hard-hitting. "During the first year of its application the Agrarian Reform caused a perceptible alteration in the political balance in Guatemala," Schoenfeld reported in 1953. "In its simplest terms, this change was the progressive atrophy of the opposition and a further growth and consolidation of Communist influence. This was the natural result of the Communists' position in the Agrarian Reform, of President Arbenz' attitude and of the continued unawareness and indifference of the Guatemalan Army to the currents of the time."[7] Temperamentally, Schoenfeld was not the man to oversee the bullying warfare of PBSUCCESS, but his analysis of what was happening in Guatemala helped to provide the operation's impetus.

Peurifoy was well cast for his role. His bad manners shine through his own report of the conversation he had with Arbenz when the two officials and their wives dined together on December 16, 1953. This oft-cited report has clinched the man's reputation, and indeed, it is difficult not to feel sympathy for Arbenz and respect for his quiet dignity as he faced the American's cross-examination.

---

[6] Interview with María de Arbenz. Schoenfeld's reports of his conversations with Arbenz reveal two men who were able to converse politely but were utterly unable to converse meaningfully. Arbenz would express his interest in technical assistance programs; Schoenfeld would respond with comments about communism. They were two ships in the night. (See: MemoConv [Arbenz, Schoenfeld], May 7, 1952, RG84 CF, Box 15; MemoConv [Arbenz, Schoenfeld], Sept. 25, 1952, ibid.; MemoConv [Arbenz, Schoenfeld], Mar. 4, 1953, RG84 G&C, Box 2. All NA-S.)

[7] Schoenfeld to DOS, no. 31, July 31, 1953, p. 11, NA 814.20.

This is not, however, the only conclusion to be derived from the report. It is also undeniable that the ambassador had been well briefed.

"Our talks lasted approximately six hours," wrote Peurifoy, six hours during which the focus of his interest was communist influence in Guatemala—not UFCO's plight. Indeed, when Arbenz sought to raise the subject of UFCO, Peurifoy retorted that "we should consider first things first."[8]

First things first. As Peurifoy pressed Arbenz with precise questions about communists in the administration, the pro-Soviet slant of the government media, the PGT's influence in the agrarian reform, Arbenz's answers were lame, unconvincing. Nor was he helped by his wife who acted as interpreter and volunteered answers that were manifestly untrue. This was the case when María stated, in response to Peurifoy's questioning, that neither the deputy director of the agrarian reform department nor the director general of radio broadcasting was a communist—only to be quickly corrected by Arbenz. (It was public knowledge that both officials belonged to the PGT.) Further, when Peurifoy asked why the Guatemalan Congress had held memorial services for Stalin, "Mrs. Arbenz interjected to state that the reason for this was that the people of Guatemala had regarded Roosevelt, Churchill and Stalin as saviors of the world and that perhaps when Mr. Churchill passes on, Congress will hold memorial services for him"[9]—a singularly ecumenical position.

Twenty-eight years later, after reading Peurifoy's report, María de Arbenz commented ruefully that on that most unpleasant evening she and her husband had not been persuasive. "The truth," she explained, "is that we were in a very difficult situation because Peurifoy's information was essentially correct."[10]

Survey the scene again. There is UFCO, boasting from the sidelines; there is Peurifoy loudly, rudely, reporting home. These two cloud the crux of the is-

[8] MemoConv (Pres. Arbenz, Mrs. Arbenz, Amb. Peurifoy, Mrs. Peurifoy), Dec. 17, 1953, p. 1, enclosed in Peurifoy to DOS, no. 522, Dec. 18, 1953, NA 611.14.

[9] Ibid., p.4.

[10] Interview with María de Arbenz. In Washington, as ambassador, the able Willy Toriello had been in a somewhat similar predicament. Relentlessly questioned by State Department officials about communist influence in Guatemala, he tried to placate them with a patently incredible message: "Arbenz's policy was directed toward allowing the Communists to discredit themselves," he told Acheson in December 1952; "the Guatemalan government was following a policy of discrediting the Communists and thereby containing their influence," he told State Department officials the following January, and again and again until his departure from Washington. (Quotations from Schoenfeld to Clark, Dec. 19, 1952, p. 1, NA 611.14, and from MemoConv [Toriello, Clark, Leddy], Jan. 27, 1953, p. 1, NA 714.001. See also MemoConv [Toriello, Schoenfeld], Feb. 5, 1953, RG84 G&C, Box 8, NA-S; MemoConv [Toriello, Rubottom, Leddy, Fisher], Mar. 11, 1953, NA 714.001; MemoConv [Toriello, Mann, Fisher], June 26, 1953, NA 611.14.)

sue: U.S. officials were alarmed by the rising influence of communism in Guatemala. And yet they knew that the communists were not in control of Guatemala. Neither the CIA nor embassy officials nor the military attachés ever claimed that the Guatemalan army was infiltrated by communists—and the army, they noted, was Guatemala's key institution.

But they were worried about the future. "The Communists," the CIA had warned as early as 1952, "will attempt to subvert or neutralize the Army."[11] The agency also feared that, under pressure from Arbenz and the PGT, the army "might eventually be unable to retain the monopoly of weapons, and, although very reluctantly, agree to release weapons to a people's militia."[12]

More immediately, Arbenz's Guatemala threatened the stability of the region. It was the only country in the hemisphere that offered a friendly abode to persecuted communists, and it was actively engaged, U.S. officials believed, in subverting its neighbors. On this point, Washington was wrong. Unlike Arévalo, Arbenz did not meddle in the internal affairs of other countries.[13] But his agrarian reform was far more dangerous than Arévalo's Caribbean Legion had ever been: "Guatemala has become an increasing threat to the stability of Honduras and El Salvador. Its agrarian reform is a powerful propaganda weapon; its broad social program of aiding the workers and peasants in a victorious struggle against the upper classes and large foreign enterprises has a strong appeal to the populations of Central American neighbors where similar conditions prevail." Central America was small, the borders were porous, news traveled fast. "It was impossible to escape the contagion," asserted Marroquín Rojas, as the May 1954 strike paralyzed the north coast of Honduras, while from El Salvador, Osorio sent a message of fear. His country, he warned, "would be next on the list."[14]

Even without the hazy prospect of a communist takeover of Guatemala— and the more real threat to Guatemala's neighbors—Arbenz posed an intolerable challenge. In the heart of the American sphere of influence, in an upstart

[11] CIA, "Present Political Situation in Guatemala and Possible Developments during 1952," NIE-62, March 11, 1952, p. 5, Truman Papers, President's Secretary's File, Intelligence File, Box 254, TL.

[12] Interview with Bissell.

[13] Not surprisingly, neither U.S. officials nor Guatemala's neighbors were able to garner any proof of Guatemala's subversive efforts. The following is representative: "Despite repeated efforts on our part in Washington and San Salvador, the Salvadoran Government has not produced any . . . concrete evidence of Guatemalan aggression." (Leddy to Cabot, "Salvadoran Evidence of Guatemalan Aggression," July 31, 1953, p. 1, NA 714.00. See also AmEm San Salvador, McDermott to Cabot, Oct. 2, 1953, NA Lot 58D18 & 58D78, Box 1.)

[14] Quotations from: Burrows to Cabot, Dec. 23, 1953, NA Lot 57D95, Box 5; Clemente Marroquín Rojas, "Tal como lo dijimos está sucediendo," La Hora, May 17, 1954, p. 4; MemoConv (Krieg, Trigueros), May 13, 1954, RG84 G&C, Box 6, NA-S.

banana republic, there stood—proud, defiant—a president whose procommunist sympathies were obvious, a president whose closest collaborators were communists. Worse, this president and his communist friends were successful. The agrarian reform was proceeding well, the PGT was gaining popular support, and basic freedoms were being upheld. It was an intolerable challenge to America's sense of self-respect. Fortuny was right when he said, "They would have overthrown us even if we had grown no bananas."[15]

Eisenhower's Guatemala policy was no aberration; it was derailed neither by UFCO nor by Peurifoy nor by Senator Joseph McCarthy. It fit within a deeply held tradition, shared by Democrats and Republicans alike and centered on the intransigent assertion of U.S. hegemony over Central America and the Caribbean. This intransigence, which climaxed in the series of military interventions linking the presidencies of Theodore Roosevelt, William Taft, and Woodrow Wilson, seemed tempered in the 1930s by the Good Neighbor Policy of Franklin D. Roosevelt. But FDR's neighborliness was tested only once, for the dictators who infested the area during his presidency never questioned Washington's hegemony. The exception was Cuba, where in late 1933 the United States worked for the downfall of a young nationalist government, helping to usher in the long era of Batista's tyranny.[16]

Would Truman, had he remained in the White House for another term, have tried to overthrow Arbenz? In this realm of speculation, there are several guideposts. His administration became fiercely hostile to Arévalo, yet Arévalo's sins were trifling compared to those of Arbenz. Truman did approve a plan to unseat Arbenz, OPERATION FORTUNE, that was canceled only at Acheson's urging. Would he have reactivated it as the agrarian reform unfolded? Would he have held back, as communist influence in Guatemala grew?[17]

[15] Interview with Fortuny. Many have explained the difference in attitude of the Eisenhower administration vis-à-vis the Guatemalan and the Bolivian revolutions by pointing out that there were no U.S. economic interests affected in Bolivia—a proof *a contrario*, therefore, of the economic motivation behind the U.S. intervention in Guatemala. In fact, as the U.S. government correctly understood, the administration of Paz Estenssoro was not procommunist. It is also interesting, in this context, to note that Bolivia voted "correctly" at Caracas, that Bolivia agreed to cosponsor the Montevideo resolution and that it pledged its vote in advance to the United States.

[16] See Aguilar, *Cuba 1933*, pp. 152–229; Thomas, *Cuba*, pp. 634–88; Pérez, *Cuba*, pp. 266–75.

[17] The contrast between Truman's and Eisenhower's use of covert operations should not be drawn too starkly. While the heyday of covert operations was during the Eisenhower administration, under Truman the agency launched a number of covert operations in the Soviet Bloc, including the attempt to overthrow the government of Albania. Helms's comment is apt: "Truman okayed a good many decisions for covert operations

What is certain is that Truman never considered a *modus vivendi* with Guatemala except on his own terms: an end to the "persecution" of American companies and a comprehensive purge of those whom Washington deemed communists. This is what he had demanded of Arévalo, and this is what he demanded of Arbenz. Truman and Eisenhower, Democrats and Republicans were unable to think of Guatemala in terms other than the relationship between metropole and banana republic. America's imperial hubris was no aberration. It preceded Truman and continues well beyond Eisenhower.

As the Eisenhower administration's broadsides against Guatemala reached their crescendo, Republicans and Democrats sang the appropriate chorus in impressive bipartisan harmony. On June 22, as the invasion was underway, the minority leader, Lyndon Johnson, addressed the Senate. The Soviet Union had supported Guatemala's demand that the United Nations, rather than the OAS, handle the crisis. This, he declared, "was open, flagrant notice that the Communists are reserving the power to penetrate the Western Hemisphere by every means—espionage, sabotage, subversion, and ultimately open aggression." Johnson introduced Senate Concurrent Resolution 91, which reaffirmed that the United States must "prevent interference in Western Hemisphere affairs by the Soviet Communists."[18] The resolution was approved with a lone negative vote, that of William Langer, the maverick senator from North Dakota. "The Senate," Langer warned, "does not know all the facts."[19] This was the one expression of humility and the one call for restraint in U.S. policy toward Guatemala heard in the U.S. Congress between 1949—when the attacks on Arévalo began—and 1954. (In the House, Johnson's resolution was lauded as the expression of "the true courage and resolve which is embedded so strongly in the hearts of our countrymen." It passed without dissent.)[20]

If the Congress of the United States mistook the aggressor for the victim, so too did the American press. It had paid very little attention to the country in the Arévalo years. As a result, it had been easy prey for the helpful UFCO representatives. Then came Arbenz. As the "Red Jacobo" became notorious in the United States, journalists began to visit Guatemala more frequently. Many remained ignorant, ethnocentric, and shrouded in Cold War paranoia. Others relied less on obliging sources and gained a better understanding of the

---

that in later years he said he knew nothing about. It's all presidential deniability." (Interview with Helms.)

[18] June 22, 1954, *CR*-Senate, p. 8564. In its final form, the words "Soviet Communists" were replaced by "International Communist movement." (See ibid., June 25, 1954, pp. 8921–27.)

[19] Langer (R-N.Dak.), June 28, 1954, ibid., p. 9066.

[20] Jackson, June 29, 1954, *CR*-House, p. 9177; for the vote see p. 9179.

country.[21] But even they remained convinced that, whatever the peccadillos of a receding past, U.S. respect for the principle of nonintervention had been exemplary since Franklin Delano Roosevelt.

This self-righteousness became all the more shrill as PBSUCCESS gathered momentum: brutal Guatemala was bullying the long-suffering United States. When, in January 1954, the Arbenz government provided proof that the United States was plotting against it, the American press leaped into collective self-delusion and ardently embraced the lies of the State Department. While the Latin Americans stood transfixed in the weeks that followed Caracas, American journalists scoffed at their fears.

Given this attitude, the CIA did not have to do much to mask the involvement of the United States. "The figleaf was very transparent, threadbare," in the words of a CIA official.[22] During the invasion of Guatemala and after Arbenz's overthrow, a magic curtain was drawn around the United States. "There is no evidence that the United States provided material aid or guidance," Milton Bracker assured his readers. Castillo Armas, the *New York Times* explained, had enjoyed merely "the moral support of the United States," just as Arbenz had "the moral support of the Soviet Union."[23] The *New Republic*'s comment was equally penetrating: "It was just our luck that Castillo Armas did come by some second-hand lethal weapons from Heaven knows where."[24]

Even those journalists who hinted that they were not so gullible heeded what John Kennedy later called "the duty of self-restraint."[25] *Newsweek*'s remark

[21] Among these journalists was Sydney Gruson, of the *New York Times*. Gruson was intellectually honest, and by 1952 he knew Guatemala well. His articles "infuriated" Peurifoy, for they told of the popularity of the Arbenz regime, the success of the agrarian reform, the dedication of the Guatemalan communists, and the sterility of the opposition; in a May 1954 NSC meeting, Secretary Dulles "expressed very great concern about the Communist line" of Gruson's articles. Clearly, Gruson was not a mouthpiece of United Fruit, yet he himself had announced, in a November 1953 article, that Arbenz had become "a prisoner of the embrace he so long ago gave the Communists"— the kiss of death in the America of the 1950s. (Quotations from: Salisbury, *Without Fear*, p. 479; "Memorandum of Discussion at the 199th Meeting of the National Security Council," May 27, 1954, *FRUS*, 1952–1954, 4:1132; "Guatemala Reds Increase Powers," *NYT*, Nov. 6, 1953, p. 3.) In early June, the Dulles brothers successfully asked the *Times* to remove Gruson from the Guatemalan story. (See Salisbury, *Without Fear*, pp. 478–83.)

[22] Interview with Kirkpatrick.

[23] Bracker, "The Lessons of the Guatemalan Struggle," *New York Times Magazine*, July 11, 1954, p. 39; "Guatemala: Out Leftists" (edit.), *NYT*, July 4, 1954, D2.

[24] "We Won't Turn the Clock Back—Maybe," *New Republic*, July 19, 1954, p. 10.

[25] Kennedy to newspaper publishers, Apr. 27, 1961, quoted by Houghton, "The Cuban Invasion," p. 426. "The press," Richard Bissell observed dryly, "had not yet gotten into the habit of blaming everything on the CIA." (Interview with Bissell.)

is typical of this style of the fleeting and unprobed innuendo: "The United States, aside from whatever gumshoe work the Central Intelligence Agency may or may not have been busy with, had kept hands strictly off." Washington could have cleaned up the situation "overnight if necessary: by halting coffee purchases, shutting off oil and gasoline from Guatemala, or as a last resort, by promoting a border incident and sending Marines to help the Hondurans. Instead it followed the letter of the law." Arbenz had been overthrown "in the best possible way: by the Guatemalans."[26] James Reston adopted a similar, cryptic style: "If somebody wants to start a revolution against the Communists in, say, Guatemala, it is no good talking to Foster Dulles. But Allen Dulles, head of the Central Intelligence Agency, is a more active man. He has been watching the Guatemalan situation for a long time."[27] Reston quickly moved onto other, less contentious subjects. The discreet works of the CIA were of no concern to patriotic journalists.[28]

The credulity and the complicity of the American press allowed the Eisenhower administration to broadcast the big lie, to present the fall of Arbenz "as dramatic evidence that the idea of freedom was one for which men were willing to fight and die."[29] For Eisenhower, notes one of his closest aides, "it was very important not only to achieve the objective, but how it would be achieved."[30] It was important, that is, for Eisenhower to be able to boast: "The people of Guatemala in a magnificent effort have liberated themselves from the shackles of international communist direction and reclaimed their right of self-determination."[31] The press took up his cry, joining in the celebration of what the *New York Times* called "the first successful anti-Communist revolt since the last war."[32] It was a time for rejoicing, not for questioning. What Oswald Garrison Villard wrote in 1918 about the American press's handling of the U.S. occupations of Haiti and the Dominican Republic, held true thirty-six years later:

[26] "Guatemala: The Price of Prestige," *Newsweek*, July 26, 1954, p. 40. For articles in a comparable vein, see "A Place where Reds Didn't Win," *U.S. News and World Report*, July 30, 1954, pp. 44–45 and "Guatemala," *Time*, July 12, 1954, pp. 38–39. Even *The Nation*, which had been critical of U.S. policy in Guatemala, drew back at the moment of intervention with the lame, "but now we simply do not know the facts." ("Guatemala Guinea Pig," edit., July 10, 1954, pp. 21–23, quote p. 22.)

[27] "With the Dulles Brothers in Darkest Guatemala," *NYT*, June 20, 1954, D8.

[28] There is no study of the failure of the American press to investigate beneath the figleaf of PBSUCCESS, but there are several studies of its similar blindness during the months that preceded the Bay of Pigs. See Bernstein and Gordon, "Press"; Aronson, *Press*, pp. 153–69; Salisbury, *Without Fear*, pp. 137–64.

[29] Vice President Nixon quoted in "Nixon Leads Fiesta on Party Centenary," *NYT*, July 7, 1954, p. 1, quoted from p. 16.

[30] Interview with Goodpaster.

[31] "Transcript of Eisenhower Press Conference," *NYT*, July 1, 1954, p. 10.

[32] "Red Defeat in Guatemala" (edit.), *NYT*, July 1, 1954, p. 24.

There were not more than five journals in this country which took the trouble to examine into the facts, or the reasons for the Government's action, or that sought for independent knowledge as to what led up to this development. There was the usual chorus of absolute approval. America could do no wrong; why inquire? If the desideratum is a watchful, well-informed, intelligent, and independent press, bent upon preserving the liberties of ourselves and our neighbors, then truly are our newspapers sorely lacking.[33]

The press in Western Europe and Latin America was not so flaccid. The figleaf allowed those who did not want to see the truth to avert their eyes, but the others—the majority—were not so coy. "At a time when diplomatic successes are rare in the United States," remarked *Le Monde* on July 2,

it was predictable that the Secretary of State would not forego the opportunity to celebrate the victory of Good versus Evil in Guatemala. This he did in last night's televised speech. . . . The speech will not endure as a masterpiece of eloquence. But it will endure as evidence of the Americans' "clean conscience," of the hypocrisy with which some Americans condemn the colonialism and the subversive plots of others, but never reflect on the modern forms of economic colonialism or on the methods they themselves use to get rid of governments that they do not like.[34]

Few in Western Europe believed that Guatemala had been on the verge of becoming a communist bastion. Many thought that Eisenhower had brought down Arbenz on behalf of United Fruit; others thought his behavior that of the lord of the manor using "a cannon . . . to render a poacher harmless."[35] It is not surprising, then, that Assistant Secretary Holland complained of "the bad European press."[36]

But the irritation of the Europeans was tempered by fatalism: the Caribbean was the Americans' backyard. The Europeans might wish that the United States behaved in a more mature, more generous manner in the region, but in the final analysis, it was Washington's affair. Europe was a distant bystander, and no direct European interests were at stake. "Criticism of and doubts about U.S. policy" are widespread, reported the Foreign Broadcast Information Ser-

[33] "The Press and the International Situation," *The Nation*, Mar. 21, 1918, p. 315. Nancy Mitchell, currently working on a book on Wilson's Caribbean policy, kindly called this article to my attention.

[34] "M. Foster Dulles célèbre le succès de la vertu," *Le Monde*, Paris, July 2, 1954, p. 4. For the text of Dulles' speech, see the *NYT*, July 1, 1954, p. 2.

[35] *Nieuwe Rotterdammer* (edit.), quoted in Foreign Broadcast Information Service (FBIS), "World Comment on the Guatemalan Revolution," June 25, 1954, p. 8.

[36] TelConv (Holland, JFD), June 28, 1954, 5:45 p.m., DP, JFD:CS, Box 8, EL. Franco's Spain, Salazar's Portugal and autocratic Greece were significant exceptions. (FBIS [see n. 35 above], p. 8.)

vice, but the criticism "is neither heated nor large in volume."[37] A U.S. official predicted calmly, "It will die within the next few days."[38] And so it did.

The one European country in which the Guatemala story left more than a fleeting impression was England. For the British, who prided themselves on their "special relationship" with the United States, the crisis had been doubly humiliating. The quarantine had been a slap to England's maritime pride and American browbeating for their Security Council vote had added to the insult. For several weeks, the opposition kept the issue alive, but by late summer it had faded from the British press and from the minds of the British people.[39]

The Latin Americans were less philosophical. "Washington was shocked by the wave of pro-Guatemalan and anti-U.S. demonstrations that swept over Latin America," noted *Newsweek*.[40] Only those countries where the dictator's rule was absolute, like Trujillo's Dominican Republic and Somoza's Nicaragua,[41] remained quiet. "Our people . . . are frightened by reactions all over," Foster Dulles told his brother,[42] while the *New York Times* reported from Brazil that it was "difficult" to find anyone who did not believe that the United States was involved in the fall of Arbenz.[43] PBSUCCESS, most analysts now agree, left a lasting legacy of anti-Americanism in the region.

This conclusion must be tempered. Those who spat on Vice President Nixon in Lima in May 1958 and those who threw stones at him a few days later in Caracas did surely reflect Latin America's deep anger at the Eisenhower administration and, more generally, at the United States. But grievances beyond

[37] FBIS (see n. 35 above), p. 6.

[38] McBride to Merchant and Tyler, "French Reactions to Guatemalan Affair," June 29, 1954, NA Lot 58D18 & 58D78, Box 3.

[39] See the excellent account in Meers, "Pebble on the Beach," pp. 68–82.

[40] "Guatemala: The Strange Revolt," *Newsweek*, July 5, 1954, p. 46.

[41] Even the independent Nicaraguan daily *La Prensa* espoused the U.S. position with enthusiasm worthy of Somoza. During the Caracas conference, it lambasted Toriello, accusing him of "being Moscow's plaything, disrupting inter-American solidarity, and hurling ridiculous charges against the United States." ("Ha sido un fracaso diplomático el del canciller Toriello," Mar. 13, 1954, p. 2.) According to *La Prensa*, no one could accuse the United States of one single violation of the principle of nonintervention. Since the days of FDR, Washington had, if anything, "erred on the side of caution, scared of awakening even the slightest suspicion of interventionism." ("El tabú de la no intervención," Mar. 16, 1954, p. 2.) Not once did *La Prensa* consider the possibility that the United States might be behind the Guatemalan rebels. It praised the overthrow of Arbenz as "the liquidation of the Red threat." ("Guatemala: índice y termometro," July 6, 1954, p. 2.)

[42] TelConv (JFD, AWD), June 24, 1954, 2:01 p.m., DP:TCS, Box 2, EL. See also "Unofficial Reactions in Latin America to the Guatemalan Situation, June 18–22," enclosed in Burgin to Raine, June 23, 1954, NA 714.00 and CIA, *Current Intelligence Review*, SC no. 13342, July 8, 1954, pp. 8–9.

[43] "U.S. Prestige Ebbs in Latin America," *NYT*, June 27, 1954, p. 10.

PBSUCCESS had stoked this fury: the embrace of Latin America's dictators, the support for any and all American companies, the denial of economic aid. Had Eisenhower refrained from PBSUCCESS and maintained the rest of his hemispheric policy, it is doubtful that the reception of Nixon in Lima and Caracas would have been less angry. Furthermore, given his hemispheric policy, had Eisenhower refrained from ousting Arbenz, his restraint would have been seen by many as weakness.

No doubt, geography and history made Guatemala's plight more poignant in Havana than, say, in Buenos Aires. The Guatemalan drama contributed to the radicalization of Che Guevara—who was in Guatemala when Arbenz fell. And it embittered Cuban nationalists like Fidel Castro. The fall of Arbenz, we are told, taught the Cubans and Che Guevara a precious lesson: "We cannot guarantee the Revolution before cleansing the armed forces," Che told Castro.[44]

The Cubans' quarrel with the United States, however, had deep roots. What would have been different had PBSUCCESS not occurred? Not the bitterness over the past—the Platt amendment, the overthrow of Grau, the coddling of Batista. Not the shame of seeing Havana a brothel for American tourists and vast sectors of the country's economy in U.S. hands. The nationalism of Fidel Castro and those who surrounded him had no need of Arbenz's drama. Nor did Castro need to learn from Arbenz's experience that he should not trust Batista's army.

PBSUCCESS had, however, a more real cost for the United States. It inflated the self-confidence of the CIA. ("It induced euphoria: we can do anything if we want to!")[45] Coming in the wake of the overthrow of Mossadegh, it strengthened confidence in the agency's abilities and so contributed to the disaster of the Bay of Pigs, the Cuban nemesis of Washington's victory in Guatemala.

"I don't think that when we were planning the Bay of Pigs we had a clear understanding of why Arbenz had resigned," Richard Bissell muses. "All too seldom," he adds, "did the CIA conduct postmortems of successful covert operations. I never saw a postmortem of AJAX and, to the best of my knowledge, there was no postmortem of PBSUCCESS."[46] His point is enlarged by Lyman Kirkpatrick, the inspector general of the CIA, whose office was expressly excluded from PBSUCCESS. "After I got wind of the operation," he recalls, "I wrote a memo to Allen Dulles: I wanted him to let two men from my office observe PBSUCCESS. That memo got the fastest turnaround I've ever seen. Within an hour the thing was back on my desk: 'Permission refused,'

[44] Schlesinger and Kinzer, *Bitter Fruit*, p. 184 (quoted); Immerman, *CIA in Guatemala*, pp. 187–88.

[45] Interview with Kirkpatrick.

[46] Interviews with Bissell (quoted), Helms, and Kirkpatrick.

signed AWD.''[47] After Arbenz fell, the CIA made no effort to probe the Guatemalan officers and other protagonists to find out what really had happened in Guatemala, what really had brought down Arbenz. Even in the absence of this, notes Bissell, a careful internal study would have been very useful. It was not done.[48]

Flushed with victory, the CIA transformed PBSUCCESS into an impressive exploit. Relief swept away any consideration of the flaws of the operation—the failure to penetrate the military, the failure of the fifth column,[49] the failure to plan beyond the first stage of the invasion. Only seven years later was there a postmortem of sorts of the Guatemalan operation. In his review of the Bay of Pigs, Inspector General Kirkpatrick looked back at PBSUCCESS. ''I can still remember Allen Dulles' face after I had gone over everything and told him: 'The Agency did a miserable job.' ''[50]

Boastful operatives have spun the image of an omnipresent CIA that had penetrated every nook and cranny of Guatemala—the army, in particular. We are told, for example, ''a CIA staff officer, documented and disguised as a European businessman, entered Guatemala and achieved the defection of a senior officer on Arbenz's staff. Through him we were able to gain up-to-the-minute situation intelligence concerning Arbenz's intentions and the disposition of his troops.'' Elsewhere we read that during the invasion ''the CIA had authorized its paramilitary teams at the front lines to promise cash payments to any officer thinking of defecting, and one army commander reportedly accepted $60,000 to surrender his troops.''[51]

The truth is more banal. Throughout PBSUCCESS, the CIA was poorly informed about developments in the Guatemalan army; once the invasion began, it was unsure how the officers would respond. As for the authorization to the CIA ''paramilitary teams on the front lines,'' notes Bissell, ''we couldn't have done it, because we didn't have anyone on the government side at the front.''[52] Nor, for that matter, did the CIA have anyone on the rebel side at the front.

[47] Interview with Kirkpatrick.

[48] Interview with Bissell.

[49] ''From the beginning, I thought that those who were counting on a fifth column were a bit unrealistic,'' comments Bissell. The arrests of January, May, and June 1954 destroyed whatever shaky infrastructure the CIA had managed to build in Guatemala. Yet the hope remained that Arbenz's foes would be galvanized into action by the invasion, by the radio propaganda, and by the saboteurs who had infiltrated the country. ''I don't know how much the CIA appreciated that it could not succeed,'' DCM Krieg remarked later. (Interviews with Bissell and Krieg.)

[50] Interview with Kirkpatrick. On Kirkpatrick's postmortem of the Bay of Pigs, see Ranelagh, *Agency*, pp. 380–81 and Kirkpatrick, ''Paramilitary Case Study.''

[51] Quotations from Hunt, *Undercover*, pp. 99–100, and Schlesinger and Kinzer, *Bitter Fruit*, p. 189.

[52] Interview with Bissell.

"We weren't allowed to go with them," recalls a CIA agent who had trained the rebels in Honduras. "We weren't supposed to have anything to do with them. It would have been a disaster if one of us had been captured."[53]

But this nod to the figleaf was not what caused the agency to remain ignorant, over the next week, of what went on in Zacapa and even in the capital. Very few officers had joined PBSUCCESS, and not one of them occupied a sensitive position. This failure is illuminated by Richard Bissell. In the Directorate of Plans, he explains, there was

> a lack of expertise about Central America. I would be surprised if there was anyone at Opa Locka—or at the CIA Washington headquarters of PBSUCCESS—who had a thoughtful understanding of what was going on in Guatemala. Once PBSUCCESS started rolling, the CIA sent more agents to Guatemala. But they were new to the country, so they weren't the best men to penetrate the armed forces. This is a slow, professional job that requires a lot of time; all our concentration was on things that could bring quick results. The CIA gained very few officers for PBSUCCESS. In fact, to the very limited extent that the U.S. was able to penetrate the Guatemalan armed forces, this was mainly through the military attachés and the military missions, rather than through the CIA.[54]

But the military attachés, too, had their problems. Like the embassy and the State Department, they understood the obvious: the Guatemalan army was not communist; it was opportunistic, nationalistic (especially the younger officers), and loyal to Arbenz despite its uneasiness about his ties to the communists. PBSUCCESS demanded that the military attachés scare the Guatemalan officers, and they were the right men for the job—brash and burly.[55] Subtlety was not their strong card. They succeeded in scaring, but not in understanding. "Socially, we knew the Guatemalan officers very well," the army attaché remembers. "They were very gracious, easy to talk to, but when you tried to pin them down, it was very difficult." DCM Krieg concurs, "For decades, the fear of speaking against the government had been instilled in the officer corps. It was extremely difficult to break down their exterior friendliness. They didn't mind coming to your house, having a drink—but when it came to important questions, they hid behind a wall of clichés and generalities."[56] This broad failure to penetrate the Guatemalan armed forces and to grasp the extent of their demoralization led the CIA to underestimate the chances of success before Castillo Armas crossed the border and to grow increasingly despondent during the first week of the invasion. It explains why Eisenhower's decision

[53] Interview with Roettinger.
[54] Interview with Bissell. Confirmed by interview with Kirkpatrick.
[55] Based on the reports of the military attachés, on Col. Hanford's "Communist Beachhead," and interviews with Col. McCormick and Maj. Chavez.
[56] Quotations from interviews with Col. McCormick and Krieg.

on June 22 to replace the two planes lost by the rebels has been presented as an historic moment when the fate of the operation hung in the balance.[57] This notion that, as Kirkpatrick himself has written, the Guatemalan operation "only succeeded by the narrowest of margins," remains the established truth.[58] In fact, Castillo Armas had won before he crossed the border. He had won because the Guatemalan army was convinced that his defeat would trigger a U.S. intervention.

Taking into account how insecure the CIA had been about the operation, it is striking how little contingency planning had been done. To some degree this was inevitable: "In a covert operation," argues Bissell, "one can plan the first phases, but not what happens next." In PBSUCCESS, the detailed planning of the CIA had extended only until the moment Castillo Armas's force crossed into Guatemala. And after that? "Very little." Through the first week of the invasion, "as the fog of war was pretty dense," and Castillo Armas floundered, the CIA waited passively and with growing pessimism. Finally, as the second week began, Allen Dulles and Wisner spun into action. In a meeting in Allen Dulles' office, they decided "to take all Castillo Armas' troops, to withdraw them from Guatemala, and to shift the attack around into a seaborne operation against Puerto Barrios." This was a plan born of despair. "We thought Armas was going to lose," comments Bissell, who was at the meeting and was told "to go to New York to commission a ship." The operation, he recalls, was called off "when we learned that Arbenz was resigning."[59] Whatever it might say about the CIA's lack of foresight, it is eloquent testimony to the agency's ignorance of developments at the front.

Likewise, Bissell remarks, "No thought had been given to what to do should Castillo Armas fail."[60] Given the U.S. assessment of the threat posed by the Arbenz government, the humiliation that Castillo Armas's defeat would have represented, and the fact that it would have strengthened Arbenz, it is hard to imagine that Eisenhower would have accepted failure. Passivity would have been humiliating abroad. The Guatemalan military and the Latin American governments, who knew that Castillo Armas was Washington's man, would have seen it as weakness, not wisdom. And passivity would have been humiliating at home, where Republicans and Democrats would have railed against the administration that had come to power promising to roll back communism.

[57] Eisenhower, *Mandate*, pp. 425–26. See also Schlesinger and Kinzer, *Bitter Fruit*, pp. 177–78; Ambrose and Immerman, *Ike's Spies*, pp. 232–33; Ranelagh, *Agency*, pp. 266–67; Higgins, *Perfect Failure*, p. 32.

[58] Kirkpatrick, "Paramilitary Case Study," p. 37.

[59] Quoted from interview with Bissell. An operation against Puerto Barrios had been attempted, with disastrous results, on June 21 (see above, p. 327).

[60] Interview with Bissell.

Domestic pressure and the immense imbalance between the two countries would have sparked Eisenhower's imagination. Perhaps he would have imposed unilateral sanctions. Guatemala was totally dependent on imported oil, shipped in by three American companies and Shell. As the general counsel of the CIA remarked, "The oil companies were very cooperative at that time. Very cooperative." On June 16, 1954, Allen Dulles met with representatives of one of the four to discuss "the small country down south."[61] Was this a harbinger, should Castillo Armas fail? Or perhaps a direct military intervention would have been justified by inventing, first, a border incident between Honduras and Guatemala. Eisenhower "firmly believed that the presence of a communist-controlled regime in our backyard was unacceptable," a close aide recalls. "He had a great inventory of principles in order, some would say, to rationalize whatever he wanted to do."[62]

Eisenhower faced no awkward decision. Arbenz fell. The ease with which his regime collapsed helped pave the way for the Bay of Pigs. Overconfidence, lack of reflection on the lessons of PBSUCCESS, and what Kirkpatrick has called the "amateurishness" of the young agency[63] caused the CIA to launch the Cuban operation as if it were a grand sequel to the Guatemalan one. This, despite the fact that the two situations were fundamentally different: Castro had his own army; Arbenz did not. Therefore, PBSUCCESS was a psychological operation that needed only a minimum paramilitary component—the "spark"; the Bay of Pigs was, or should have been, a military operation. If the CIA had paused to reflect on the former, they would have recoiled from the latter. Instead, the agency wallowed in euphoria.

The ease with which Arbenz collapsed held another cost for U.S. policymakers. As Eisenhower's assistant secretary of state for Latin America said, it "tended to blind a little bit the eyes of all us."[64] It reinforced Washington's complacency: no radical challenge would succeed in the American Mediterranean; no changes were necessary in U.S. policy toward the region. It is conceivable that, had Eisenhower refrained from PBSUCCESS, the United States might have learned that an unsympathetic regime need not represent a threat to its security, that coexistence was possible. It might further be argued that,

[61] Quotations from interview with Houston and from TelConv (JFD, AWD), June 16, 1954, 11:20 a.m., DP:TCS, Box 2, EL. Commenting on this document, Bissell stressed that to the best of his knowledge, the oil weapon had never been considered as part of PBSUCCESS. (Interview with Bissell.) As already noted, the United States wanted to appear to be refraining from unilateral sanctions and to be scrupulously respecting the OAS charter.

The three American companies were California Standard, Esso, and Texaco. (Peurifoy, Jan. 26, 1954, U.S. Congress, HCFA, pp. 466, 476.)

[62] Interview with Goodpaster.

[63] Interview with Kirkpatrick.

[64] Rubottom, "Oral History Interview," p. 48.

had Arbenz been allowed to end his term, the example of Guatemala's successful agrarian reform would have forced the neighboring regimes—in El Salvador, above all—to introduce reforms. One might retort, however, that without PBSUCCESS, Washington would have remained just as intransigent and narrow-minded, and that the Hondurans and the Salvadorans would have responded to the Guatemalan contagion with repression, not reform. Beyond these speculations, one conclusion remains: the cost of victory was, for the United States, very low. Those who paid were the Guatemalans.

In 1944, the fall of the dictators had opened the possibility of hope in the country of eternal tyranny. To the eloquent and charismatic Juan José Arévalo fell the task of defining the meaning of the revolution. Arévalo was honest, eager, and confident. His immense ego shines through his countless speeches, his flowery statements about Spiritual Socialism, and the adulatory biographies that rolled off the government presses during his presidency. Yet he failed to address the problem of American control of vital sectors of the country's infrastructure; he failed to address the problem of the country's retrogressive tax structure; and he failed to address the problem of land distribution. He benefited from a period of high coffee prices, and he enacted some worthwhile economic measures, but he lacked a coherent economic program. As the World Bank noted in 1950, "The developmental efforts are so haphazard that resources are dissipated in a number of inadequate and uncoordinated projects."[65]

There could have been no Arbenz, however, without first an Arévalo who introduced political freedoms and social reforms. The men who would form Arbenz's kitchen cabinet—and Arbenz himself—awoke politically in the Arévalo years. Yet there is a clear break between the two presidencies. "Arevalismo and Arbencismo were two very different things—two very different ways of governing," Arévalo himself has stated. "Arbencismo warped the revolution . . . and welcomed the communist leaders into the president's office."[66]

Arbenz did more than welcome the communist leaders into his office. With their help, he brought agrarian reform to the Guatemalan countryside. This is the crucial difference between the two leaders. As the Office of Intelligence and Research had concluded, "no positive action" had been taken by the Arévalo administration to correct the extremely skewed land tenure system that rotted the Guatemalan countryside, home to 80 percent of the country's population.[67] The "revision of the Labor Code was virtually the only incursion which the revolution made in the countryside under Arévalo."[68]

[65] MemoConv (Britnell, Miller, Siracusa), Aug. 28, 1950, p. 1, NA 714.00.
[66] Arévalo, *Carta Política*, pp. 2–3.
[67] OIR, "Agrarian Reform in Guatemala," no. 6001, Mar. 5, 1953, p. 1, NA.
[68] Alexander, "Guatemalan Revolution," pp. 5–6.

True, it would have been very difficult for Arévalo to implement a comprehensive agrarian reform program, at least until the death of Arana, since he did not control the army. The impression that emerges from the written evidence, however, and from Arévalo's own statements on the land tenure problem in Guatemala, and from interviews with men who were close to Arévalo is that it was neither the army nor the upper class that restrained him. He was a middle class Ladino; his family owned land. The world of the Indian was distant and fearsome. Agrarian reform was not in his plans—whether on privately owned lands or on the Fincas Nacionales. This should provoke neither surprise nor indignation; it was typical of his class.

Less typical was Arbenz's behavior. Like Arévalo before him, he wanted Guatemala to be a nation, not a banana republic. But unlike Arévalo, Arbenz—this white son of a Swiss-German father, this military officer—loosened the knots that stifled his country. As he prepared Decree 900, he was moved by his own beliefs, not by external pressure. The revolutionary parties had no desire for such a step, and the rural masses were too weak to demand it. When Arbenz sought to justify the agrarian reform to his officers by saying, "If we don't do it ourselves, the peasants will do it themselves—with machetes,"[69] they rightly understood that he was dissembling: the peasants, so long oppressed, were not demanding what they so desperately needed. Indeed, many peasants were initially deeply wary of Decree 900. The impetus came from Arbenz.

Arbenz's partner was the PGT. No other partner was possible, for no political party shared Arbenz's commitment to social reform and his willingness to put the interests of the nation before his own. The dedication, honesty, and selflessness of the leaders of the PGT were noted even by the U.S. embassy.

A hybrid regime evolved that was unprecedented in the region. A small group of idealists—Arbenz and the leaders of the Communist party—promoted a revolution from above, but not a doctrinaire program that would have been disastrous for their country. The communists spearheaded the agrarian reform, but they did not seek collectivization.

Some American intellectuals who were sympathetic to the reforms complained at the time that the PGT was perverting the revolution. How nice it would have been to have the revolution without the communists![70] This is

[69] Interview with Col. Guillén, quoting Arbenz.

[70] Alexander, for example, wrote, "The Communists . . . were able to divert the Guatemalan Revolution from its course and convert it into one more weapon of Soviet foreign policy." (*Communism*, p. 362.) Alexander, then a young professor at Rutgers University, had been one of the most sensitive U.S. observers of the Guatemalan revolution, clearly sympathetic to social reform and critical of United Fruit and the State Department's support of it. His several excellent articles include: "Revolution in Guatemala," "The Guatemalan Revolution and Communism," "Communists Gain Strength in Guatemala," and "The Guatemalan Communists."

unrealistic. The PGT's role—as advisers and as implementors—was essential. As Arbenz's widow observed, "Alone, he could not have done it."[71]

Granted, Arbenz could have had communists as allies and not been one of them. The evidence, however, indicates that the communists were his closest personal and political friends and that, at least by 1952, he felt like one of them, even though he did not join the party until 1957.

Nearly forty years after his overthrow, Jacobo Arbenz remains an elusive, enigmatic figure. He left no books and no articles presenting his views, arguing his case—only a few reticent interviews. His photographs as an officer, as president, show a teutonic man—good looking but with a distant expression. A different Arbenz emerges in conversations with his few close friends and in yellowed letters that his wife may read aloud but will not lend—personal passages that provide a glimpse of the man who had a soft smile and who had wanted to be a reformer without knowing exactly what it meant, a man who did not become a cold ideologue, but who dreamed a passionate dream. Introverted and brilliant, as the CIA noted.[72] And shy, and modest. "Jacobo never talked of Arbencismo," his wife has written. "Very rarely, in fact almost never, did he give interviews to the television, press or radio. He abhorred personality cults."[73] During his presidency, the government presses printed no book extolling his merits. Here, too, he was unlike Arévalo.

Jacobo Arbenz is not one of history's giants. He made serious mistakes; he was naive. Irrespective of his political beliefs, he should have kept a tight rein on the administration media. The tone of *DCA*, other government publications, and the radio was needlessly provocative, as were actions such as the minute of silence for Stalin. He underestimated the threat from the United States until late 1953 when the documents provided by Delgado made it irrefutable that the United States was plotting against him.

Arbenz, who had renounced Arévalo's activist foreign policy, failed to grasp how completely the Inter-American system was dominated by the United States, how completely Bolívar had been replaced by Monroe. He believed—tenaciously, naively—that other Latin American governments would stand up to Foster Dulles at Caracas. Later, he turned his hopes to the United Nations, blind to the fact that international law was as impotent to help him as it would be for the Hungarians in 1956, the Dominicans in 1965, or the Czechs in 1968.

The complexities of Arbenz's personality and of his position are distilled in his relationship with the army, a relationship that embodied the strain, the distance he had traveled in his own life. He was a respected officer, and, in-

[71] Interview with María de Arbenz.

[72] CIA, "Guatemala," SR-46, July 27, 1950, p. 39, Truman Papers, President's Secretary's File, Intelligence File, Box 261, TL.

[73] María de Arbenz, letter to the author, Jan. 27, 1988, p. 19.

creasingly, he was a communist. These two worlds—the communist and the military—were bridged by Arbenz alone. He alone was the fulcrum. His handling of the officers was deft. By doling out perks, by maintaining the army's monopoly of weapons, by not spreading communist propaganda in the ranks, and by wielding his prestige and power, he established an effective *modus vivendi* with them. This was the best that could have been expected: there was no way he could have subverted the army, that is, indoctrinated the officers. Nevertheless, the officers—conservative, contemptuous of the Indians, anticommunist—accepted Decree 900.

Arbenz's behavior was also naive and contradictory, traits that are crystallized in the story of the *Alfhem*. His decision to break the army's monopoly of the weapons reveals his doubts and fears that the army, under the strain of growing U.S. pressure, would betray him; at the same time, however, he had earmarked some of the weapons to strengthen the very army he was beginning to distrust. Furthermore, he continued to overestimate the loyalty and the nationalism of his officers. He failed to grasp the meaning of their list of demands of June 5, 1954, and persisted in his belief that the army would fight an exile invasion as long as there was no direct U.S. participation.

If Arbenz underestimated the U.S. threat and overestimated the loyalty of the military, so too did the PGT. If Arbenz believed that the Organization of American States and the United Nations could give pause to the American aggressor, so too did the PGT. "If we had been more mature, we would have faced the threat of intervention squarely, and we would have gotten organized to work underground. That would have been the true mark of maturity: to have prepared for winter."[74]

And so we return to the words of Alfredo Guerra Borges with which this book began: "It wasn't a great conspiracy, and it wasn't a child's game. We were just a group of young men searching for our destiny."[75] It was a revolution from above; it was the feat of a small group of men. They proceeded alone, in an international environment that became increasingly inhospitable. "We were a little skiff in a raging tempest," recalls María de Arbenz. "We were pitted against enormous waves."[76] These waves, this tempest were not of Guatemalan origin. For one fact is clear, and makes the Guatemalan tragedy all the more poignant, just as it made intervention seem all the more necessary to the United States: the civilian opposition had no chance of overthrowing the government, and there was no hope that the military would move against Arbenz. The plotters within the army were weak and ineffectual. The officers' betrayal had one cause only: fear of U.S. intervention.

Jacobo Arbenz provided Guatemala with the best government it has ever

---

[74] Interview with Fortuny.

[75] Interview with Guerra Borges.

[76] Interview with María de Arbenz.

had. He embarked on the first comprehensive development plan in the history of Guatemala whereas his predecessor had not even outlined such a plan, and he presided over the most successful agrarian reform in the history of Central America. Within eighteen months, "the agrarian reform had reached its half-way mark":[77] five hundred thousand peasants had received land without disrupting the country's economy. Decree 900 brought more than land to the poor: it broadened political freedom in the countryside. Serfs were becoming citizens.

By the end of Arbenz's term, hundreds of thousands of peasants would have been solidly established on land granted them by Decree 900. In a fundamental sense, Arbenz's successor would have inherited a Guatemala far different from that Arévalo had bequeathed to him in 1951. But the Pax Americana prevailed. Nowhere in Central America or the Caribbean has U.S. intervention been so decisive and so baneful in shaping the future of a country.

By the time Castillo Armas died, in July 1957, he had accomplished, in the words of a close aide, a "herculean feat": all but two hundred of the "squatters"—the beneficiaries of Decree 900—had been chased off the land they had received under Arbenz.[78]

In the early summer of 1954, several American newspapers had demanded that Arbenz not be replaced by a regime of the far right. The *New York Times* had intoned, "We have a right to expect . . . that revolts against the tyranny of the Left shall not bring in a tyranny of the Right."[79] Many U.S. officials had also expressed the hope that the new regime would not be embarrassingly reactionary. Castillo Armas, cabled Peurifoy, should proceed at once to "some land distribution" and a "prompt reorganization of non-Communist labor movement should be genuinely and intelligently encouraged to prevent workers from looking back on Communist unions as only protectors of their rights."[80]

There was no way, however, that the United States could have replaced Arbenz with a centrist, moderate government—even if it had truly wanted to—for the center and the moderates had supported Arbenz. The only Guatemalans who had been eager to overthrow him, and the only Guatemalans who were not tainted by collaboration with his regime, were those who bitterly opposed all social reform. To oust Arbenz was to return them to power.

Neither the press nor U.S. officials faced this unpleasant fact. Waving the

[77] Krieg to DOS, no. 818, Mar. 29, 1954, p. 1, NA 814.20.

[78] Montenegro, "El capitán Montenegro defiende." The figure is approximate; see also Handy, "Reform," esp. pp. 11–12. On the Castillo Armas government see Handy, *Gift*, pp. 149–52; Bishop, "Guatemalan Labor," pp. 162–99; McClintock, *American Connection*, 2:28–45; Toriello, *A dónde va Guatemala?*

[79] "As Guatemala Settles Down" (edit.), *NYT*, July 6, 1954, p. 22.

[80] Peurifoy to SecState, no. 157, Aug. 4, 1954, p. 2, NA 714.00.

wand of rhetoric, American journalists eagerly transformed Castillo Armas into a progressive leader—or one who was, at least, not altogether unsavory. Castillo Armas, pronounced the *New York Times* in a September 1954 editorial, "has made a number of sound decisions and is following progressive policies."[81]

The U.S. embassy was, initially, more honest. In the summer of 1954, it noted "the mass arrests of small agrarian leaders," the flouting of the labor laws and "panic, bitterness and disillusionment" among urban and rural workers. After Castillo Armas enacted "a statute reversing the Agrarian Reform Law," DCM Krieg commented, "there is no blinking at the fact that the new Statute is a long step backwards from the agrarian policies of the previous regime."[82] Some embassy officials were not surprised. In a 1952 memo calling for the overthrow of Arbenz, Second Secretary Hill had concluded, "the Department must . . . face up to the probability that an 'undemocratic' regime is the only one which in the near future could hope to succeed the present one. There will be no immediate 'salvaging of the original aims of the revolution.' "[83]

What mattered, however, was that Castillo Armas be fervently anticommunist and pro-American. As U.S. officials decided that there was no longer any immediate communist threat in Guatemala, their lingering hesitations about Castillo Armas's social policies were papered over with complacency. Within a year, they had convinced themselves that their man was a moderate.[84]

---

[81] "Guatemala without Arbenz" (edit.), *NYT*, Sept. 11, 1954, p. 16. *The Nation* and *Christian Century* stated that Arbenz had been replaced by a tyranny of the right, but they were the exceptions. (See "The Right of Asylum," *The Nation*, July 17, 1954, pp. 41–42; "Guatemala Bulletin," *The Nation*, July 24, 1954, pp. 63–64; "Guatemala Takes Land From Peasants," *Christian Century*, Sept. 8, 1954, p. 1060; "Second Thoughts on Guatemala," *Christian Century*, Dec. 8, 1954, p. 1490.)

[82] Quotations from: Hill to SecState, no. 231, Sept. 1, 1954, p. 1, NA 714.00/9-2154; *JW* 33, Aug. 20, 1954, p. 5; Krieg to DOS, no. 73, July 29, 1954, p. 2, NA 814.20. See also Peurifoy to SecState, no. 160, Aug. 4, 1954; Krieg to SecState, no. 181, Aug. 11, 1954; Peurifoy to SecState, no. 194, Aug. 17, 1954; Peurifoy to SecState, no. 238, Sept. 2, 1954 (all NA 814.062); MemoConv (Hill, Celli), Dec. 29, 1954, RG84 G&C, Box 3, NA-S. Cursory references to peasant protests against the regime appear in the press in the first month after the fall of Arbenz: "Grupos rojos hacen masacres," *La Prensa*, Managua, July 2, 1954, p. 1; "Los campesinos levantan a los propietarios en contra del ejército," ibid., p. 3; "Troops Ordered Out," *NYT*, July 5, 1954, p. 3; "Castillo trasladará por aire a sus tropas," *La Prensa*, Managua, July 6, 1954, p. 3; "Nuevo zafarrancho comunista en Covadonga, Chiquimulilla," *La Hora*, July 26, 1954, p. 1.

[83] Hill to Ambassador, Oct. 2, 1952, p. 3, RG84 CF, Box 15, NA-S.

[84] One of the few exceptions was a June 19, 1956, CIA memo that bluntly noted that Castillo Armas "removed the Communists . . . but he has failed thus far to offer peasants and workers a constructive alternative." (*FRUS*, 1955–1957, 7:120–21.) A sense

In October 1954, Castillo Armas had himself enthroned as president for a six-year term after a plebiscite in which he received 99.99 percent of the vote.[85] He ruled with the support of the upper class, a purged army, and the Eisenhower administration[86] until his death in a murder that has never been solved. By then, the peace and social harmony that Arbenz had disturbed had returned to Guatemala, and the country had long ceased to be in the news in the United States. It was again the joy of American tourists with its pro-American elite, its Mayan ruins and its smiling, humble Indians who lived their quaint traditional life.

This comforting image masks the reality of Guatemala since the "liberation." Guatemala is a foreboding world of repression and violence; it holds the macabre record for human rights violations in Latin America.

Torture and death have been the final arbiters of Guatemalan society, the gods that determine behavior. Fear torments the oppressed and the oppressor. Fear gnaws even at the upper class: fear of the communists and fear of the Indians, fear of the military and fear of the future. Guatemala is ruled by the culture of fear.

It is the keynote that cuts through the cacophony of the many Guatemalan cultures—the Indian and the Ladino, the elite few and the miserable many, the town dweller and the peasant, the civilian and the military. It hails from the long night that began with the Spanish conquest, a conquest that is, for the Indians, a trauma from which they have not yet recovered.[87]

The Guatemalan revolution—Arbenz, above all, with his communist friends—challenged the culture of fear. In eighteen months, five hundred thousand people were given land. The culture of fear was loosening its grip over the great masses of the Guatemalan people. In a not distant future, it might have faded away, a distant nightmare.

---

of urgency returned to State Department dispatches only in the wake of Castillo Armas's death, as the acting president allowed a number of exiles, such as Guillermo Toriello, to return to Guatemala: "You should seek audience immediately with President Flores and emphasize to him my own concern over communist threat and potential which return of these undesirable elements presents for Guatemala," Foster Dulles ordered the American ambassador. "There is no room for complacency." (Dulles to AmEmG, Nov. 8, Dec. 6 [quoted] and Dec. 12, 1957, ibid., pp. 147–48, 150–52.)

[85] Conceding that the election had not been free, the New York Times advised its readers: "It is doubtless unfair to expect anything else so soon after a revolution against a Communist-dominated regime." ("Voting in Guatemala" [edit.], Oct. 12, 1954, p. 26.)

[86] The Eisenhower administration gave the Castillo Armas government close to $100 million in direct aid. "This was during a period when total U.S. aid to all of Latin America was under $60 million annually." (Handy, Gift, p. 189.)

[87] On the culture of fear, see Gleijeses, Politics and Culture.

The Guatemalan upper class responded with cries of pain and anger and fear, and the United States intervened. Arbenz was overthrown, the communists were persecuted, the army was purged, the peasants were thrown off the land they had received. As the culture of fear descended again over the great many, the elite few strengthened their resolve. Never had they felt as threatened as they had under Arbenz; never before had they lost land to the Indians; never would it happen again. For them, the 1944–1954 interlude had confirmed that democracy was dangerous, that reformers were communists, that concession was surrender. To this belief they have held, with fierce resolve, to this day.

And so Guatemala has grown—like a deformed body, wracked with pain and fear—with a land tenure system that is the most skewed in Latin America, a fiscal system that is among the most regressive in the hemisphere, a labor force that suffers from illiteracy, malnutrition, and ill health. Meanwhile, barbarians press at the gates, threatening the enchanted world of the Guatemalan upper class: guerrillas, seeking to destroy the system; middle-class politicians, seeking to reform it; priests, who no longer seek charity from the rich, but justice for the poor.[88]

Under such conditions, violence alone could maintain the status quo. Journalists, professors, priests, men and women of the political center lost their lives to feed the culture of fear. They died alongside members of rural cooperatives, grassroots organizers, labor leaders, left-wing students and armed guerrillas. "Tortures and murders are part of a deliberate and long-standing program of the Guatemalan Government," Amnesty International stated in 1981.[89] Periods of selective violence have alternated with waves of greater violence. The particular characteristics of the man who sat in the presidential palace have not been decisive. The intensity of the repression has depended on the intensity of the fear felt by the upper class and the military.[90]

---

[88] On the post-1954 period, see Handy, *Gift*, pp. 149–281; Aguilera Peralta, *Dialéctica del terror*; Brintnall, *Revolt of the Dead*; Falla, *Quiché rebelde*; Gleijeses, *Politics and Culture*; Hough, *Land and Labor*; Lovell, "Surviving Conquest"; McClintock, *American Connection*, vol. 2; Jonas, *Battle for Guatemala*.

[89] Amnesty International, *Guatemala . . . Political Murder*, p. 3.

[90] Thus, as a presidential candidate, Julio César Méndez Montenegro was a well-respected moderate of the centrist *Partido Revolucionario* (PR). But upon winning the election, Méndez Montenegro was allowed to assume the presidency only after signing a written guarantee that the armed forces—not he—would in fact rule the country. For four long years (1966–1970), he provided a veneer of legitimacy while the social reforms promised by the PR never materialized and the armed forces massacred thousands of peasants in order to eliminate a handful of guerrillas. (The text of the secret pact was eventually published in *La Hora* of Nov. 26 and 27, 1973, by Clemente Marroquín Rojas, who, as Méndez Montenegro's vice president, had been a signatory to it.)

I remember an evening in September 1982 in the house of Ricardo Barrios Peña, Arana's upper-class friend and adviser. "Look how beautiful all this is," he said as he took me to a window that overlooked his luxuriant garden. "I know that it won't last forever, but I will fight as long as I can to preserve it for myself and for my children." Barrios Peña spoke calmly, with no sense of guilt—just as he had when telling me of his plotting with Arana in 1949.[91]

As he spoke, a whirlwind of death was swirling through the Indian highlands of Guatemala. Left-wing guerrillas had mounted an unprecedented challenge and "the repression was pitiless." The mountains and the valleys were littered with corpses of men, women, infants. Rape was a banal event; charred villages a fact of life.[92]

Terror proved effective, but victory carried a price: the drama of the Guatemalan upper class is that, alone, it cannot safeguard its world. The privileged have sought a series of protectors: dictators to control the masses; the United States to topple Arbenz; and now, the army to defeat the guerrillas. They would like the army to be humble, subordinate—as it was to Ubico. But the mercenaries have grabbed power for themselves; they have encroached upon the political and economic preserves of the upper class.

In June 1954, the Guatemalan officers had returned from the "front" after their surrender to Castillo Armas "despondent, and with a terrible sense of defeat."[93] They, who had sympathized with the nationalism of the revolutionary years, had capitulated like officers of a banana republic. They were subjected to the contempt of those whom they had betrayed and of those who had benefited from their betrayal. On August 1, in a military parade, the army was jeered by the masses and by the upper class, by the defeated and by the victors alike, traitors to the former and cowards to the latter. It was a moment that the Guatemalan officers neither forgot nor forgave. Henceforth, they vowed, they might be cursed, but never again would they be jeered.[94]

It was the far left, the guerrillas, that helped them to recover their pride. As

[91] Interview with Barrios Peña. For Barrios Peña and Arana, see above pp. 62–63.

[92] Interview with the Guatemalan Bishop Juan Gerardi, Guatemala City, Jan. 5, 1985. On the slaughter of the early 1980s, see the reports of Americas Watch and Amnesty International listed in the bibliography; Carmack, *Harvest of Violence*; Davis and Hodson, *Witnesses*; Gleijeses, *Guatemala: The Struggle for Democracy*; Montejo, *Testimony*; Capt. Ruiz Morales, "Por qué solos?" According to the Guatemalan government, "the violence left no fewer than forty thousand widows and two hundred thousand orphans in its wake." ("40 mil viudas y 200 mil huérfanos," *La Hora*, Sept. 24, 1988, p. 3.) Since married men were not the only victims, an estimate of fifty thousand dead is conservative.

[93] Interview with Col. Mendoza.

[94] This paragraph is based on interviews with the following officers: González Siguí, Mendoza, Paiz Novales, Peralta Méndez, Silva Girón, Getellá, Lorenzana.

their pride swelled, so did their power. Until 1944, they had been the instrument of the dictators; after 1954, they were the bride of the upper class. As the army battled successfully against the guerrillas, the marriage underwent a subtle transformation: "the army gradually grew whiskers and developed strong muscles."[95] By the late 1970s, the army controlled both the country and the national budget. It had become the country's strongest "political party," ruled by a Central Committee of a few senior officers. It even instituted its own agrarian reform: the State gave land to generals and colonels.

The army is still the *macho* in Guatemalan society. It wields awesome power, and it exudes an institutional pride and a mystique that set it sharply apart from its counterparts in Honduras and El Salvador. The Guatemalan officers are proud of their impunity; they are not prosecuted for crimes against civilians. They are proud of the fear they inspire. "The army is untouchable. They are mightier than God. They are everywhere, they see everything, they know everything."[96] And yet, the army cannot escape the culture of fear. Too much blood has been shed in Guatemala for its officers to sleep peacefully; too many enemies lurk.

In 1985, the army organized elections to lend an aura of legitimacy to a regime in which it would retain power but be relieved of the burden of coping with the economic morass into which it had sunk the country. A "democratic" Guatemala, moreover, would be better able to obtain foreign economic assistance. And so, in January 1986, a civilian president was inaugurated. He boasts about Guatemala's new human rights legislation and its new institutions to protect human rights. But the laws are not enforced and the institutions are spineless. Torture and murder are still the alternative to social reform in Guatemala, and the human sacrifice continues. Hence the cry of pain of the chief justice of Guatemala: "In this country we are drowning in demagoguery and in laws that will never be enforced. I say this in full knowledge of the situation, and it pains me to say it. . . . As a judge, I am filled with shame."[97]

Perhaps someday the process that the United States crushed in 1954 will resume.[98] Perhaps someday the social reforms that the upper class and the

[95] Interview with a Guatemalan intellectual, who prefers to remain anonymous. Guatemala City, Jan. 15, 1985.

[96] Interview with a Guatemalan priest, who prefers to remain anonymous. Guatemala City, Jan. 2, 1985.

[97] Chief Justice Edmundo Vásquez Martínez, quoted in " 'Pena y vergüenza . . .' en Presidente del Poder Judicial," *La Hora*, Nov. 15, 1988, p. 6. See also, Americas Watch, *Closing the Space*; Americas Watch, *Persecuting*; OAS, *Informe anual*; Castellanos Cambranes, *Democratización*; Gleijeses, "Guatemala."

[98] In the 1960s, the Johnson and Nixon administrations provided the Guatemalan army with military assistance against the guerrillas and winked at its crimes, but U.S. assistance was in no way decisive. Unlike Carter, Reagan sought to assist the Guate-

military now oppose will become possible, and the culture of fear will, again, loosen its grip over the land of Guatemala. At present, there is the reality, a reality that was expressed in the 1988 Pastoral of the Guatemalan bishops: "The cry for land is, without any doubt, the loudest, the most dramatic and the most desperate sound in Guatemala. . . . The hunger for land is the root of the injustice of our society." The bishops paid homage to the man their predecessors had reviled: Arbenz's agrarian reform program, they asserted, was "the only serious attempt to reform this situation of profound injustice."[99] Since 1954, at least one hundred thousand Guatemalans have been killed, and over forty thousand have disappeared to preserve the fruits of Castillo Armas's victory.

---

malan army against the guerrillas, but could not overcome congressional resistance and was obliged to cheer from the sidelines.

[99] Penados del Barrio, *El clamor por la tierra*, p. 1.

The Fate of the Defeated

THROUGH the summer and the autumn of 1954, while Castillo Armas arrested thousands in the name of anticommunism, the U.S. embassy bitterly complained that five of the eleven members of the PGT's Political Commission were still at large.[1]

Of these eleven men, three are alive today. Not one of the others died a natural death; all were murdered by their government in cold blood. Víctor Manuel Gutiérrez, the "Franciscan," was seized by the police on March 5, 1966. He was tortured and killed. His corpse and those of several other prisoners were "sewn into burlap sacks and dropped into the ocean from an army transport plane."[2]

Bernardo Alvarado Monzón, Mario Silva Jonama, and other PGT leaders "disappeared" in September 1972. Six weeks later, *Le Monde* told their story:

> Eight leaders of the PGT . . . disappeared on September 26 from the capital of Guatemala. Since then, no one . . . has been able to say where they are or even whether they are still alive. . . . Except for the feeble protests, quickly hushed, of family members and a few friends, silence has reigned. . . . Yet there were witnesses to the "disappearance" of September 26. The eight PGT leaders were attending a secret meeting . . . when the police came to abduct them. Witnesses wrote down the license plate numbers of the police cars. . . . Nevertheless, Colonel Alvarado Robles, chief of police, has denied that the eight were arrested, and officials claim that the allegations are a "plot" to discredit the government. "Many people," they explain, "disappear because they have left illegally for the United States in search of work; others have accidents in inaccessible places; others die in shoot-outs with the forces of law and order and must be buried at once because they don't have identity papers." . . .
>
> The "disappeared of September," are they still alive? Or, as the U.S. Embassy suggests, have they been tortured, killed, hacked in pieces and tossed from a plane into the grey waters of the Pacific ocean—the discreet and welcoming grave of so many "disappeared" more anonymous than these men of the PGT?[3]

[1] See *JW* 33, Aug. 13, 1954, p. 4; *JW* 35, Sept. 3, 1954, p. 3; *JW* 38, Sept. 4, 1954, p. 3; *JW* 43, Oct. 29, 1954, p. 6; *JW* 47, Nov. 26, 1954, p. 3.

[2] "28 in Guatemala Reported Slain by Police in Peralta's Regime," *NYT*, July 18, 1966, p. 12.

[3] "Peut-être en prison, peut-être dans le Pacifique," *Le Monde*, Paris, Dec. 13, 1972, p. 2. See also Cáceres, *Aproximación*, pp. 184–90.

While his former friends were tortured, killed, and hacked in pieces, Carlos Manuel Pellecer lived well. In the Arbenz years, he had been an influential member of the PGT's Political Commission, but he broke with the party in 1962.[4] Not only did he turn into a rabid anticommunist, he soon began to sing the praises of those who ruled Guatemala and to applaud the liberation of 1954. He was appointed ambassador to Israel, consul general in Houston, and chargé d'affaires in Paraguay.[5]

Alfredo Guerra Borges, too, broke with the party in the mid-1960s.[6] But he never recanted, and he never praised the liberators. Although he was allowed to live in Guatemala, he lived in fear, and he subjected himself to rigorous self-censorship. In 1981 he left his country, as the repression rose to a new frenzy, threatening even a man who had long ago renounced all political activity, but who had refused to surrender his dignity.

Unlike Pellecer, Fortuny never betrayed his beliefs; unlike Guerra Borges, he never ceased fighting for them. He has remained pugnacious, stubborn, cantankerous—a poor diplomat and a warm human being. He demonstrated his political courage in Cuba in the 1960s. As the PGT's representative, he clashed repeatedly and doggedly with his hosts on behalf of his party's independence. And he demonstrated his physical courage during four years of clandestine life in Guatemala (1971–1974), where capture meant death.

Fortuny now lives in Mexico—modestly, as he always has. He earns his living as a journalist and freelance editor. In mediocre health, but always active politically, far more attracted by the evolution of the Italian Communist Party than by the dogmatism of the Cubans, Fortuny looks with pride at his forty years of political struggle—from the heady days of the Guatemalan revolution to the long exile that began as he left his country with the defeated Jacobo Arbenz.

ARBENZ

Guatemala City, September 11, 1954, 10 p.m.: several cars speed from the Mexican embassy. Jacobo Arbenz and his wife are driven to the plane that will

---

[4] See "Carlos M. Pellecer rompe con el comunismo," *El I*, Nov. 27, 1962, p. 1, and Pellecer, "Repudio al comunismo."

[5] I draw this portrait reluctantly, as Pellecer received me graciously and is a witty and intelligent conversationalist. Contrary to what many have asserted, there is no indication that he worked for the CIA in the Arbenz years. At least until the fall of Arbenz, the CIA was unable to infiltrate the hierarchy of the PGT. After his "conversion," Pellecer published several turgid diatribes, including: *Renuncia al comunismo*; . . . *camino equivocado, Che!* and *Caballeros sin esperanza*. For a revealing interview of Pellecer, see "Utiles después de muertos."

[6] The portraits of Guerra Borges and Fortuny are based on interviews with them and with a broad spectrum of individuals who have seen them at various times in their years of exile. This spectrum spans Guatemalans and non-Guatemalans, friends and enemies.

take them to Mexico; after a delay of more than two months, Castillo Armas has granted them safe-conduct. At the airport, Arbenz is searched. The defeated president "had to take off all his clothes and hand them to the Immigration officials." As he undressed, journalists and photographers pressed around him, "the former taking notes; the latter, photos of every step of the proceedings: the surrender of the overcoat, the surrender of the jacket, the surrender of the pants, etc." Throughout the ordeal, Arbenz remained composed, and when he spoke, briefly responding to the questions of the immigration officials, he did so "in a sober and serene manner."[7] He left his country with dignity.

In Mexico, "the welcome was cold." The Mexican authorities were sensitive to pressure from Washington, and they had, in any case, little sympathy for the Red Jacobo. They told him that he could remain in the country only if he abstained from all political activity. They wanted to be rid of Arbenz, but without the opprobrium of deporting him. Thus, when he told them in December 1954 that he wanted to go to Europe for a few weeks, they promised that he would be allowed back, but when he tried to return, the Mexican embassy in Paris refused to give him a visa. "The time is not right," they told him. He must wait.[8]

And wait he did: a year in Prague, a few months in Moscow and Paris. At last, in 1957, he and his wife were able to return to the Western Hemisphere. They settled in Uruguay, the only Latin American country willing to receive them. It was there that Arbenz formally joined the PGT.[9]

Those were painful years. Arbenz had to endure more than the hatred and the scorn of those whom Washington had enthroned in Guatemala. When he had been president, Guatemala's revolutionary politicians had been respectful. Now they vented their anger and their frustration: had Arbenz been like Arévalo, had he not unleashed the agrarian reform and befriended the communists, he would still be in power, and they with him. "You are to blame for the defeat of the revolution," a former friend told him in early 1955; "Jacobo was deeply hurt," his wife remembers.[10] And, in a widely read book, the prominent Gua-

[7] Quoted from "Expresidente Arbenz ya se encuentra en México," *Tribuna Libre*, San Salvador, Sept. 11, 1954, pp. 1, 4. See also Arbenz's terse account in "Arbenz revela su secreto a 'Siempre!' "

[8] Quotations from interview with María de Arbenz. For Arbenz's reception in Mexico, see "Guatemalan Ex-President in Exile," *NYT*, Sept. 11, 1954, p. 1; "México acogió ayer al desterrado ex presidente J. Arbenz," *Excelsior*, Mexico City, Sept. 11, 1954, p. 1; "Salió a descansar el ex presidente Jacobo Arbenz," *Excelsior*, Mexico City, Sept. 12, 1954, p. 1.

[9] See above, p. 147.

[10] Quoted from interview with María de Arbenz. Interviews with Fortuny, Capuano, and Paz Tejada were also helpful.

temalan writer Cardoza y Aragón—a self-proclaimed revolutionary who sat out the revolution—pronounced Arbenz a coward and a petty bourgeois.[11]

In 1960, Jacobo and María moved to Havana. Cuba offered Arbenz a place to live, the fleeting hope that he could be useful, and enduring humiliations. For the triumphant Castroites, he was the symbol of failure. In their exuberant arrogance, they overlooked that Arbenz, unlike Castro, had come to power without his own army and had received no support from the Soviet Union. They paid him brief homage for his efforts as president of Guatemala and then stressed how they would avoid his mistakes. "The Cubans were very condescending," recalls María. "It was humiliating for Jacobo." He asked them "to give him something constructive to do, even if it wasn't related to politics—he offered to teach math in a school." But the Cubans demurred. "They made him feel useless. All they did was to call on him every once in a while to give interviews or to deliver speeches."[12]

While Arbenz was in Cuba, young guerrilla leaders raised the flag of revolt in Guatemala. They had been children in 1954; they grew to manhood as Castro triumphed. To them, Fidel was the present and the future; Arbenz, the past. Arbenz respected their courage but was critical of the *foco* theory they had borrowed from the Cubans. His relations with them were friendly but distant; his offer to join them was accepted in principle but postponed to a future that never arrived.[13]

Personal tragedy struck. Arabella, the eldest of Arbenz's three children, shot herself in October 1965, at age twenty-seven. She was, like her mother, beautiful and very intelligent, and she was renowned for her high-strung spirits. In Mexico, at the funeral, friends who had not seen Arbenz in ten years remarked how he had aged. "He was very thin and smoking like a chimney." He looked haggard and sick, "like a tired old man."[14]

[11] Cardoza y Aragón, *La Revolución Guatemalteca*. Cardoza y Aragón had missed the boat from the beginning: he had crossed the border into Guatemala, "ready for anything," on October 22, 1944. (Cardoza y Aragón, *Guatemala*, p. 7.) As Marroquín Rojas has pointed out in a sardonic essay, Cardoza y Aragón's bravery was unnecessary. The struggle against the dictators was over; Ponce had been overthrown on October 20. (*En el mundo de la polémica*, pp. 129-36.)

[12] Interviews with María de Arbenz (quoted) and Fortuny, who was also in Cuba. Che Guevara, who had been in Guatemala as a "revolutionary tourist" in the last months of the Arbenz regime and had witnessed Arbenz's fall from the sidelines, shared this condescending attitude: "We must thank Arbenz and the democracy that perished for the valuable lessons we have learned from our correct analysis of all the weaknesses that that government was unable to overcome." ("Al Primer Congreso Latino Americano de Juventudes," Aug. 1960, in Guevara, *Che*, p. 309.) For embellished accounts of Guevara's stay in Guatemala, see Gadea, *Ernesto*, pp. 1–72, and Mencía, "El Che Guevara en Guatemala."

[13] Interviews with María de Arbenz, Fortuny, and a Guatemalan guerrilla leader.

[14] Quotations from interviews with Paz Tejada and Guillén. See also "Fue sepultada

A few months later, Arbenz left Cuba for Paris and then Lausanne. He was still a member of the PGT, but his health was declining, and he was increasingly lost in his own thoughts, tormented by a sense of failure—and by the ghost of Arabella. At last, in 1970, he was allowed back into Mexico, but on a visa that had to be renewed abroad every six months. "My longing is to live the last moments of my life near Guatemala," he told a journalist in October.[15]

He died on January 27, 1971, in Mexico, a lonely man. He was alone the night he died, for his wife had gone to El Salvador on family business.[16] His last known conversation had been with Fortuny, his loyal friend in success and in defeat.[17]

ARÉVALO

Soon after his inauguration, Arbenz appointed Arévalo roving ambassador—a pleasant sinecure. For the next three years, the ex-president passed his time in Europe and Latin America at his government's expense. He was neither consulted about policy in Guatemala nor did he influence developments there.[18]

Arévalo was in Chile when Arbenz fell. He remained there, later moving to Uruguay and, in 1959, to Venezuela. He resumed his academic career and wrote three books that constituted a passionate—if clumsy—indictment of U.S. policy in the hemisphere.[19] By 1961, however, his criticism of Eisenhower and Foster Dulles was accompanied by attacks on Castro and praise for Kennedy.[20]

In 1963, Arévalo joined in a bizarre tango with his old foe, General Ydígoras, who had been president of Guatemala since 1958. The stench of corruption and incompetence permeated his administration. As the end of his term

---

ayer la actriz Arabella Arbenz," *Excelsior*, Mexico City, Oct. 12, 1965, p. 24. Arbenz received an eight-day visa to attend the funeral of his daughter. (Interviews with María de Arbenz and Ernesto Capuano, a Guatemalan lawyer who had become a Mexican citizen and was instrumental in obtaining the visa for Arbenz.)

[15] "Murió el ex Presidente Arbenz, de Guatemala," *Excelsior*, Mexico City, Jan. 28, 1971, p. 1. On Arbenz's visa, interviews with María de Arbenz and Capuano were helpful.

[16] María's share of the family estate had been their sole source of income since 1954.

[17] Interviews with Fortuny and María de Arbenz.

[18] Interviews with Arévalo, Osegueda, Galich, Charnaud, Toriello, Fortuny, Guerra Borges, and María de Arbenz. See also Arévalo, *Escritos complementarios*, pp. 9–33. These memoirs cover 1951 to 1963. They provide useful, if not always accurate information, and are eloquent testimony to the resilience of Arévalo's ego.

[19] *Guatemala: La democracia y el imperio; Fábula del tiburón y las sardinas; Antikomunismo en América Latina.*

[20] See Arévalo, *Escritos complementarios*, pp. 71–73, 76–77, 100–101.

grew close, Ydígoras groomed his successor, Roberto Alejos, who was unpopular in his own right and further burdened by his champion's disrepute. The upper class opposed Alejos and splintered its support among half a dozen other hopefuls. Elections were scheduled for November 1963. Ydígoras intimated that he would allow Arévalo to run and announced that the elections would be free.

From Mexico, where he had lived since early 1962, Arévalo was campaigning. Seeking to assuage the fears of the upper class and the military, he stressed that he was—and had always been—an anticommunist. For good measure, he indulged in personal attacks on Arbenz. He also swore that he, Arévalo, had had nothing to do with the death of his good friend, Arana. "Everybody in Guatemala knows who killed Arana, why he was killed and who benefited from it."[21] Arévalo made no apology for his past criticism of the United States, but he explained that it was different now: "There has been a changing of the guard. The dinosaurs have been defeated, and the Great Republic is ruled by new men—men who studied at Harvard."[22]

In Guatemala, tensions rose. If Arévalo were to run in unfettered elections, he would win, reported the U.S. embassy, for he would receive the votes of all those who were critical of the liberation of 1954. Yet neither the upper class nor the army would countenance a second presidency of Juan José Arévalo, the man who had delivered them to the Red Jacobo.[23]

On March 30, 1963, the country awoke to the news that Arévalo had returned. He had come to lead his supporters, he announced, and he would remain in Guatemala "even if it cost him his skin."[24] Two days later, however, Arévalo was back in Mexico. On March 31, the army had ousted Ydígoras and installed a military *junta*. The elections were canceled.

Poor Ydígoras. Free elections had never been in his thoughts. He had merely hoped to blackmail the upper class and the military: "He raised the specter of Arévalo in order to frighten us into accepting his candidate," observes an upper-class Guatemalan. "But his little ploy backfired."[25]

---

[21] Arévalo, *Carta política*, p. 4. This is Arévalo's most detailed campaign statement. For an interesting diatribe in response by a prominent conservative, see Marroquín Rojas, La *"Carta política."*

[22] Arévalo, *Carta política*, p. 10.

[23] See McNeil to SecState, A-283, Nov. 10, 1962; Bell to SecState, no. 521, Feb. 28, 1963; *JW* 9, Mar. 2, 1963; Corrigan to SecState, no. 551, Mar. 12, 1963; *JW* 11, Mar. 16, 1963; *JW* 14, Apr. 5, 1963. See also the press of the first four months of 1963, and Marroquín Rojas, La *"Carta política."*

[24] "Arévalo en Guatemala," *Prensa Libre*, Mar. 30, 1963, p. 2. On the evening of the twenty-ninth, Arévalo had given a press conference to selected journalists in the house of a "crony" of Ydígoras. (*JW* 14, Apr. 5, 1963, p. 2.)

[25] Interview with Barrios Peña, another presidential candidate.

The coup neither surprised nor displeased Washington.[26] More than a decade had passed since Truman's days, and much had changed in the world. But Central America was still at the heart of the American empire, and imperial reflexes die hard. For Guatemala, the "dinosaurs" were still in power in Washington, Harvard educated or not.[27] "The Department considers Arévalo's return to power adverse to U.S. interests," Undersecretary George Ball wrote on January 5, 1963. As president, Arévalo "had allowed the infiltration of Communists," Secretary Dean Rusk noted, while from Guatemala the U.S. ambassador joined the chorus: "Arévalo is totally bad from U.S. standpoint."[28]

Arévalo may have been deprived of the presidency, but he had no intention of enduring the lonely fate of Jacobo Arbenz. Lesser honors were available to him, if he was willing to pay the price.

He was willing. In 1969, Guatemala's president offered Arévalo the ambassadorship to Chile. Arévalo accepted the kind offer, turning a blind eye to the fact that the army had just slaughtered thousands of unarmed civilians.[29] Through the next decade, he served under military governments that were notorious for their brutality, their venality, and their illegitimacy.[30] Juan José Arévalo, the honored elder statesman, lives today in Guatemala; he has adjusted well to fear, repression, and forgetting.

[26] Many plotters had visited the U.S. embassy in the preceding weeks. They had been received by very discreet officials who had expressed no disapproval of their schemes. See MemoConv (Dreyfuss, Maldonado), Nov. 25, 1962; Corrigan to SecState, no. 551, Mar. 12, 1963; *JW* 11, Mar. 16, 1963; Bell to SecState, no. 605, Mar. 30, 1963.

[27] In 1963, the Kennedy administration condemned Juan Bosch, the moderate president of the Dominican Republic, as soft on communism in terms strikingly similar to those Truman had earlier used against Arévalo. See Gleijeses, *Dominican Crisis*, pp. 86–99, and Martin, *Overtaken by Events*, pp. 282–614.

[28] Quotations from: Ball, "Telegram to all American Diplomatic Posts in Central America, Caracas, Mexico, Panama and Santo Domingo," Jan. 5, 1963, p. 1; Rusk to All ARA Diplomatic Posts, Jan. 24, 1963, NA 714.00; Bell to SecState, no. 511, Feb. 22, 1963.

[29] See "Doctor Juan J. Arévalo por ser designado embajador en Chile," *El I*, Jan. 13, 1969, p. 1, and "Guatemala Names Arévalo, Long Exiled, Envoy to Chile," *NYT*, Jan. 16, 1969, p. 4.

[30] In the 1970s, Arévalo served as ambassador to Chile, Venezuela, and Israel. He retired in 1978 due to poor health.

Bibliography

THE AIM of this bibliography is to provide the reader with a readily accessible list of the sources I have used and to give the full citation of sources which, for simplicity's sake, have been cited in abbreviated form in the footnotes.

Every book cited in the footnotes, including those that are incidental, is listed in the bibliography. When the author is the same as the publisher, I list only the place and date of publication.

Given the quantity of newspaper and magazine articles cited in the notes, it seemed sensible to follow a different procedure: no article that appeared between January 1, 1930, and January 1, 1955, is listed unless it is of particular historical importance; articles that appeared after January 1, 1955, are included only when they would be of use to a scholar of the revolution.

Articles that appeared in scholarly journals between January 1, 1930, and January 1, 1955, are listed in the bibliography.

UNPUBLISHED PAPERS AND DOCUMENTS

I have used six major depositories of documents.

The *Eisenhower Library* in Abilene, Kansas, is a researcher's dream. Superbly organized, with a staff of highest quality, its only drawback is that it deprives the researcher of the pleasure of the search. Upon arrival, I was handed a list of the files that would be relevant to my study—and whenever I ventured beyond these files, I came up empty-handed. Thus, I had been warned that the library's massive Walter Bedell Smith collection would be of no use to me. I tried anyway, acquired an intimate knowledge of the general's love of fishing—but not a whisper about Guatemala.

In the *Truman Library*, Independence, Missouri, the researcher will have to show some spirit of initiative and search for files on his own, but this, too, is a well-organized, professionally run library.

In the *National Archives* in Washington, the researcher should go systematically through all the decimal files relating, even peripherally, to Guatemala. Particularly valuable is the generally overlooked *Joint Weeka*, especially for the 1952–1954 period, when it not only sheds light on U.S. perceptions, but also presents a reasonably accurate picture of Guatemala. Whenever appropriate, I have also looked at the decimal files of the other Central American countries and the general file for Central America. The researcher should also look beyond the decimal files to the usually neglected lot files.

If the Eisenhower Library is the Concorde, the *National Archives at Suitland, Maryland*, are an Edsel. The confusion of the staff is surpassed only by that of their files. It is, however, worth the considerable pain. Suitland houses the reports of the military attachés, internal embassy memos, and reports that were never sent to Washington, as well as other material that by some mysterious plan of Providence has found its way there.

The Guatemalan Transcripts are located in the Manuscript Division, *Library of Congress*, Washington D.C. They consist of ninety-four boxes of documents (sixty-three reels of microfilm) captured by the CIA in Guatemala after the fall of Arbenz. A mishmash, they include some truly trivial detritus and a mass of important documents. They are indispensable to the study of Guatemala in 1944–1954.

The *Archivo General de Centro América* in Guatemala City houses documents that help to convey the flavor of the time, but the researcher will have to weed through unorganized files to find them.

In addition to these six major depositories, I acquired documents through the Freedom of Information Act and benefited from the generosity of Steven Schlesinger and Blanche Wiesen Cook, who shared their FOIA documents with me. I have also had access to the private papers of some individuals—such as several letters by Jacobo Arbenz and his wife, and the personal papers of other Guatemalans.

Eisenhower Library

John Foster Dulles Papers.
Eisenhower: Papers as President, 1953–1961 (Ann Whitman File).
Eisenhower: Records as President, 1953–1961 (White House Central Files).
Milton Eisenhower Papers.
James Hagerty Papers.
C. D. Jackson Papers.
Bernard Shanley Diary.
White House Office, Office of the Special Assistant for National Security Records.

Truman Library

Nathaniel P. Davis Papers.
Edward G. Miller, Jr. Papers.
Richard Patterson Papers.
Harry S. Truman Papers: Official File.
Harry S. Truman Papers: President's Secretary's Files, Intelligence File.

National Archives

RG59 Decimal Files
RG59 Lot Files
RG59 Research and Analysis Files

National Archives at Suitland (Washington National Record Center)

RG84 Foreign Service Posts: Guatemala, Confidential File. (The box for 1949–1952 is labeled ''Classified, General Records,'' but it is clearly part of the Confidential File.)
RG84 Foreign Service Posts: Guatemala, General and Classified Records.
RG84 Foreign Service Posts: Guatemala, General Records.
RG165 Military Intelligence Division, Regional Files 1922–1944: Guatemala.
RG319 Army Intelligence, Project Decimal File: Guatemala.
RG319 Records of the Army Staff, Intelligence Document Files.

Library of Congress

Guatemalan Transcripts

Archivo General de Centro América

Correspondencia del Presidente de la República (through 1947)
Departamento Administrativo del Trabajo:
  Contratos de Trabajo
  Correspondencia Sindical Campesina
Gobernación:
  Copiador de Oficios
  Correspondencia Dirigida al Señor Ministro (through 1947)
  Informes Mensuales de Jefes Políticos (through Oct. 1947)
  Ministerio Público (through 1946)
Inspección General de Trabajo
Jefaturas Políticas (through 1947)
Organismo Judicial de la República

Other Depositories

Archives of the Nicaraguan Embassy, Washington, D.C.: following the overthrow of Somoza, I was given access to the documents stored in the embassy. They were of modest use.

Archivo Histórico Arquidiocesano "Francisco de Paula García Pelaez," Guatemala City: some useful documents are buried among the baptismal records in the Correspondencia file.

Adolf Berle Papers, Franklin D. Roosevelt Library, Hyde Park, New York.

Allen W. Dulles Papers, Seeley G. Mudd Library, Princeton University.

Edwin J. Kyle Papers, Cornell University: unilluminating memorabilia.

Bernardo Vega File: documents from the Private Archive of Rafael Trujillo (Archivo Particular del Generalisimo), National Palace, Santo Domingo. These documents were culled by the Dominican historian, Bernardo Vega, who, with characteristic generosity, shared them with me.

Whiting Willauer Papers, Seeley G. Mudd Library, Princeton University.

THE PRESS

The Guatemalan press has never been freer than in the 1944–1954 decade—particularly the Arbenz years, when all shades of opinion were expressed openly. The contrast with the Guatemalan press of the 1980s—officially uncensored, but crippled by self-censorship—is striking.

The essential newspapers are the official *Diario de Centro América*, the leading opposition daily *El Imparcial*, the opposition *La Hora* (especially the editorials of its owner, Clemente Marroquín Rojas), the communist weekly *Octubre*, and the communist daily *Tribuna Popular*. I have read these Guatemalan newspapers systematically. I have also consulted about twenty others; they are cited in the footnotes.

I have consulted several newspapers from elsewhere in Central America—both for incidents that involved their countries, and for their slant on Guatemalan developments. Again, they are cited in the footnotes.

I have used South American and European newspapers only very occasionally. Mexican coverage of Guatemala was disappointingly shallow.

The U.S. press covered Guatemala very poorly during most of the revolutionary period. Over time, however, some newspapers improved, particularly the *New York Times* and the *Christian Science Monitor*. But the U.S. press is not the place to learn about the Guatemalan revolution. Nor is it even the place to learn about U.S. policy toward Guatemala. Its usefulness lies in its reflection of American perceptions of matters Guatemalan. This applies equally to American magazines—with the exception of a handful of articles that soar above the rest and are cited in the bibliography.

INTERVIEWS

Unless otherwise noted, the position given for each person interviewed is that held on June 1, 1954. Individuals interviewed about post-1954 Guatemala are not listed.

Alejandro [pseud. of Severo Aguirre Cristo]: Member of the Central Committee of the Cuban Communist Party. Adviser to the Secretariat of the Guatemalan Communist Party, 1951–1954. Havana, Feb. 24, 1982; Mar. 20, 1986.

Aldana Sandoval, Carlos: Colonel (ret.), Guatemalan army. A leader of the 1944 revolution. Chief of Staff of the Guatemalan army (1945–1948). Minister of Public Works (1948–1951; 1952–1954). Ambassador to Washington (1951–1952). Guatemala City, Aug. 22, 1990.

Amory, Robert: CIA, Deputy Director for Intelligence. Washington, D.C., Oct. 17, 1983.

Arévalo Bermejo, Juan José: President of Guatemala, 1945–1951. Guatemala City, Aug. 25, 1979.

Arriola Ligorría, Jorge Luis: Colleague of Jacobo Arbenz when a professor at the Escuela Politécnica under Ubico. Minister of Education in the Revolutionary *Junta*. Minister of Health (1951–1953). Guatemala City, Oct. 13, 1988.

Arvelo Delgado, Tulio: Dominican exile involved in the Caribbean Legion in the late 1940s. Santo Domingo, Dominican Republic, May 24, 1971.

Barrios Peña, Ricardo: Adviser to Col. Francisco Arana in the late 1940s. A leader of the *Liberacionistas*. Guatemala City, Sept. 8, 1982.

Bauer Paiz, Alfonso: President of the National Agrarian Bank. Senior administration politician. Managua, Nov. 26, 1982.

Bendaña Perdomo, Ricardo: A Jesuit priest who is an authority on the Church in the revolutionary period. Guatemala City, Aug. 21 and 22, 1978.

Bissell, Richard: CIA, assistant to Allen Dulles. Participated in PBSUCCESS. Farmington, Conn., Nov. 10, 1983; May 24, 1989.

Capuano del Vecchio, Ernesto: Senior administration politician. Senior official of the National Agrarian Bank. Mexico City, Aug. 11, 16, 20, 1981; Aug. 7, 13, 18, 1982.

Cardoza y Aragón, Luis: Leading Guatemalan intellectual. Mexico City, Aug. 15, 1982.

Castañeda de Guerra Borges, Elsa: Mid-level official of the Guatemalan Communist Party. Mexico City, Aug. 10, 1982.

Charnaud MacDonald, Augusto: Minister of the Interior. One of the most powerful administration politicians. Mexico City, Aug. 12, 15, 18, 23, 1982.

Chavez, Manuel: Major, assistant U.S. Air Force Attaché, 1950–1953. Telephone interview, June 2, 1989.

Coerr, Wimberley: Deputy Chief of Mission, U.S. embassy in Honduras. Telephone interview, May 23, 1985.

Cruz Salazar, José Luis: Lt. Colonel, Guatemalan army. Guatemala City, Aug. 20, 1978; Sept. 6, 1982.

Dillon, Dorothy: CIA analyst. Washington, D.C., Sept. 15, 1984.

Figueres Ferrer, José: President of Costa Rica. San José, Costa Rica, June 6, 1982.

Fortuny Arana, José Manuel: Secretary General of the Guatemalan Communist Party. Mexico City, frequently in Aug. 1980, in Aug. 1981, Aug. 1982; July 16, 1984; Jan. 17–19, 1985; Jan. 19–20, 1987; Apr. 21–23, 1988.

Galich López, Manuel: Senior administration politician in the Arévalo years. Foreign Minister of Guatemala, 1951–1952. Havana, Aug. 25, 1980; Jan. 11, 1981.

García Zepeda, Amadeo: Lieutenant, Guatemalan army and aide to Arbenz, 1945–1950. Guatemala City, Aug. 8, 10, 13, 18, 24, 1978; Aug. 24, 1979; Aug. 21, 22, 1990.

Getellá Amezquita, Anselmo: Colonel, Guatemalan army. Guatemala City, Sept. 4, 1982.

González Orellana, Carlos: Senior official of the Guatemalan Foreign Ministry. Member of the Guatemalan delegation to Caracas. San José, Costa Rica, May 20, 1986.

González Siguí, Rubén: Colonel, Guatemalan army. Guatemala City, Sept. 11, 1982.

Goodpaster, Andrew: General, Staff Secretary to President Eisenhower (Oct. 1954–Jan. 1961). Washington, D.C., Sept. 24, 1983.

Guerra Borges, Alfredo: Member of the Secretariat of the Guatemalan Communist Party. Guatemala City, Jan. 9–13, 1973; Aug. 22, 1979. Mexico City, Aug. 10, 14, 19, 22, 28, 30, 1982.

Guillén Corletto, Terencio: Colonel, Guatemalan army. Governor of Escuintla. Mexico City, Aug. 11, 13, 16, 1981; Aug. 13, 1982.

Helms, Richard: CIA, Chief of Operations, Directorate of Plans. Washington, D.C., Sept. 7, 1989.

Hernández Méndes, Jorge: Lt. Colonel, Guatemalan army. Guatemala City, Sept. 5, 1982.

Houston, Lawrence: CIA, General Counsel. Washington, D.C., Sept. 14, 1989.

Hyman, Elizabeth: State Department, Office of Intelligence and Research. Alexandria, Va., Oct. 25, 1984.

Jamison, Edward: State Department, Deputy Director of the Office of Regional Latin American Affairs. Washington, D.C., Oct. 6, 1983.

Kirkpatrick, Lyman: CIA, Inspector General. Middleburg, Va., June 2, 1989.

Krieg, William: Deputy Chief of Mission, U.S. embassy in Guatemala. Washington, D.C., June 18, 20, 23, 1983; Sept. 22, 26, 29, 1983.

Lorenzana Salazar, Roberto: Colonel, Guatemalan army. Antigua, Guatemala: Aug. 20, 23, 1978.

McCormick, Aloysius: Colonel, U.S. Army Attaché. Telephone interview, June 12, 1989.

Martínez Bonilla, José Rolando: a Dominican exile involved in the Caribbean Legion in the late 1940s. Santo Domingo, Dominican Republic, Jan. 3, 1975.

Mendizabal Pérez, Antonio: Lt. Colonel, Guatemalan army. Mexico City, Aug. 28, 1982.

Mendoza Azurdia, Oscar: Colonel, Guatemalan army. Guatemala City, Sept. 6, 1982.

Monteforte Toledo, Mario: Senior administration politician in the Arévalo years. President of the Congress, 1948–1950. Guatemala City, Oct. 13, 1988.

Montenegro Morales, Manuel Antonio: Lieutenant, Guatemalan army. A leader of the *Liberacionistas*. Guatemala City, Sept. 7, 1982.

Morgan García, Héctor: Senior administration politician. Guatemala City, Aug. 21, 1990.

Noriega Morales, Guillermo: Senior official of the National Agrarian Bank. Member of the Guatemalan delegation to Caracas. Guatemala City, Sept. 6, 1982.

Osegueda Palala, Raúl: Foreign Minister of Guatemala (Nov. 1952–Jan. 1954). Guatemala City, Sept. 3, 5, 1982.

Paiz Novales, Ernesto: Lt. Colonel, Guatemalan army. Guatemala City, Sept. 8, 1982.

Parinello de León, Enrique: Colonel, Chief of Staff of the Guatemalan army. Guatemala City, Sept. 9, 1982.

Paz Tejada, Carlos: Major (ret.), Guatemalan army. Chief of the Armed Forces, 1949–1951. Mexico City, frequently in Aug. 1980, Aug. 1981, Aug. 1982; July 17, 1984; Jan. 17–19, 1985; Jan. 19, 1987; Apr. 22–24, 1988.

Pellecer Durán, Carlos Manuel: Member of the Political Commission of the Guatemalan Communist Party. Antígua, Guatemala, Aug. 15, 19, 1990.

Peralta Méndez, Ricardo: Lieutenant, Guatemalan army. Washington, D.C., Mar. 4, 1986.

Phillips, David: CIA official who participated in PBSUCCESS. Washington, D.C., Nov. 14, 1984.

Ramírez Alcantara, Miguel Angel: a Dominican exile involved in the Caribbean Legion in the late 1940s. Santo Domingo, Dominican Republic, May 16, 1971.

Roettinger, Phillip: CIA agent who participated in PBSUCCESS. Washington, D.C., March 21, 22, 1990.

Rolz Bennett, Federico: A civilian leader of the 1944 revolution and a childhood friend of Arbenz. Guatemala City, Aug. 17, 1990.

Rosenberg Rivera, Jaime: Deputy Chief of the Guatemalan police. Mexico City, Aug. 20, 1980.

Silva Girón, César Augusto: Lieutenant, Guatemalan army. Guatemala City, Sept. 9, 1982.

Sol Castellanos, Jorge: Finance Minister of El Salvador, 1951–1953. Washington, D.C., Nov. 7, 1983.

Steins, Kenedon: Political officer, U.S. embassy in Guatemala, 1947–1951. Washington, D.C., Oct. 15, 1983.

Taracena de la Cerda, Eduardo: a leader of the *Liberacionistas*. Guatemala City, Aug. 15, 18, 23, 1978; Sept. 4, 10, 1982; Aug. 17, 1990.

Toriello Garrido, Guillermo: Guatemalan Ambassador to Washington (Sept. 1952–Jan. 1954). Foreign Minister of Guatemala. Cuernavaca, Mexico, Aug. 21, 1982.

Torres Espinoza, Edelberto: Nicaraguan exile involved in the Caribbean Legion in the late 1940s. San José, Costa Rica, Mar. 4, 1982; Nov. 28, 1982.

Vásquez, Miguel Angel: A leader of Guatemala's first Communist party, 1923–1932. Mexico City, Aug. 24, 1982.

Vilanova de Arbenz, María: Wife of President Arbenz. San José, Costa Rica, March 1–9, 1982; June 1–13, 1982; June 6–15, 1984; May 18–21, 1985; May 14–17, 1986; Aug. 12–13, 1989.

Wardlaw, Andrew: First Secretary, U.S. embassy in Guatemala. Telephone interview, May 29, 1989.

Woodward, Robert: Deputy Chief of Mission, U.S. embassy in Guatemala, 1944–1946; Deputy Assistant Secretary of State for inter-American affairs. Washington, D.C., Oct. 6, 10, 13, 18, 1983; Dec. 12, 1988.

Wright, Lydia: Cultural Attaché, U.S. embassy in Guatemala. Washington, D.C., July 31, 1984.

Ydígoras Fuentes, Miguel: Guatemalan exile leader. Major rival of Castillo Armas. Guatemala City, Aug. 15, 1978.

Zachrisson de Vilanova, Lilly: Sister-in-law of President Arbenz. San José, Costa Rica, Feb. 28, 1982; Mar. 4, 1982.

Works Cited

Acuña, Miguel. *El 48*. San José, C.R.: Lehmann, 1974.

Adams, Richard [Stokes Newbold, pseud.]. "Receptivity to Communist Fomented Agitation in Rural Guatemala." *Economic Development and Cultural Change* 5, no. 4 (July 1957): 338–61.

Adams, Richard. *Crucifixion by Power: Essays on Guatemalan National Social Structure, 1944–1966*. Austin: University of Texas Press, 1970.

Adler, John, Eugene Schlesinger, and Ernest Olson. *Public Finance and Economic Development in Guatemala*. Stanford, Calif.: Stanford University Press, 1952.

Aguilar, Luis. *Cuba 1933: Prologue to Revolution*. Ithaca, N.Y.: Cornell University Press, 1972.

Aguilar Bulgarelli, Oscar. *Costa Rica y sus hechos políticos de 1948*. San José: Editorial Costa Rica, 1978.

Aguilar P., J. Humberto. *Vida y muerte de una dictadura*. Mexico City: Linotipografía Nieto, 1944.

Aguilera Peralta, Gabriel, Jorge Romero Imery, et al. *Dialéctica del terror en Guatemala*. San José, C.R.: EDUCA, 1981.

Alexander, Robert. *Communism in Latin America*. New Brunswick, N.J.: Rutgers University Press, 1957.

———. "Communists Gain Strength in Guatemala." *New Leader*, May 24, 1954.

———. "The Guatemalan Communists." *Canadian Forum*, Toronto, July 1954, pp. 81–83.

———. "The Guatemalan Revolution and Communism." *Foreign Policy Bulletin* 33 (Apr. 1954): 5–7.

———. "Revolution in Guatemala." *New Leader*, Jan. 5, 1953, pp. 6–8.

Alonso, Isidoro, and Gines Garrido. *La Iglesia en América Central y el Caribe*. Madrid: Centro de Información y Sociología de la Obra de Cooperación Sacerdotal Hispanoamericana, 1962.

Altolaguirre Ubico, Arturo. "Entrevistamos al coronel Altolaguirre." *La Hora*, Oct. 3, 1962, p. 4.

Alvarado Arellano, Huberto. *Apuntes para la historia del Partido Guatemalteco del Trabajo*. Guatemala City: Ediciones del PGT, 1975.

―――. *Esbozo histórico del PGT*. Guatemala City: n.p., 1971.

Alvarado Rubio, Mario. *El asesinato del coronel Arana*. Guatemala City: n.p., 1983.

Alvarez Elizondo, Pedro. *El Presidente Arévalo y el retorno a Bolívar*. Mexico City: Ediciones Rex, 1947.

Ambrose, Stephen. *Eisenhower*. Vol. 1: *Soldier, General of the Army, President-Elect, 1890–1952*. Vol. 2: *The President*. New York: Simon and Schuster, 1983, 1984.

Ambrose, Stephen, and Richard Immerman. *Ike's Spies: Eisenhower and the Espionage Establishment*. Garden City, N.Y.: Doubleday, 1981.

Americas Watch. *Closing the Space: Human Rights in Guatemala, May 1987–October 1988*. New York, 1988.

―――. *Creating a Desolation and Calling It Peace*. New York, 1983.

―――. *Guatemala: A Nation of Prisoners*. New York, 1984.

―――. *Human Rights In Guatemala: No Neutrals Allowed*. New York, 1982.

―――. *Persecuting Human Rights Monitors*. New York, 1989.

Ameringer, Charles. *The Democratic Left in Exile*. Coral Gables, Fla.: University of Miami Press, 1974.

―――. *Don Pepe: A Political Biography of José Figueres of Costa Rica*. Albuquerque: University of New Mexico Press, 1978.

Amnesty International. *Guatemala: A Government Program of Political Murder*. London, 1981.

―――. *Guatemala: Massive Extrajudicial Executions in Rural Areas under the Government of General Efraín Ríos Montt*. London, 1982.

Anderson, Thomas. *Matanza: El Salvador's Communist Revolt of 1932*. Lincoln: University of Nebraska Press, 1971.

Arbenz, Jacobo. "Arbenz revela su secreto a 'Siempre!'" *Siempre!* Mexico City, Oct. 27, 1954, pp. 8–11.

―――. *Exposición del Presidente de la República, ciudadano Jacobo Arbenz, ante la opinión pública nacional y el Consejo Nacional de Economía sobre su programa de gobierno*. Guatemala City: Secretaría de Publicidad de la Presidencia de la República, 1951.

―――. "Habla Arbenz." *Alero* 8 (Sept./Oct. 1974): 116–24. (Interview by Marta Cehelsky.)

―――. *Informe del ciudadano Presidente de la República coronel Jacobo Arbenz Guzmán*. Guatemala City: Secretaría de Propaganda y Divulgación de la Presidencia, 1954.

―――. *Informe del ciudadano Presidente de la República, coronel Jacobo Arbenz Guzmán, al Congreso Nacional en su primer periodo de sesiones ordinarias del año de 1953*. Guatemala City: Tipografía Nacional, 1953.

―――. "Jacobo Arbenz relata detalles de la causa de su caída del gobierno de Guatemala." *La Prensa Libre*, San José, C.R., Oct. 25, 1955, pp. 9, 14. (Interview by Ronaldo Ramírez.)

———. "Tiene la palabra Jacobo Arbenz." *Bohemia*, Havana, Nov. 14, 1954, pp. 48–50. (Interview by Raúl Roa.)

Ardón, Enrique. *El señor general Ubico*. Guatemala City: n.p., 1968.

Arévalo, Juan José. *Antikomunismo en América Latina*. Buenos Aires: Editorial Palestra, 1959.

———. *La Argentina que yo viví (1927–1944)*. Mexico City: Costa-Amic, 1974.

———. *El candidato blanco y el huracán. 1944–1945*. Guatemala City: EDITA, 1984.

———. *Carta política al pueblo de Guatemala*. Guatemala City: El Imparcial, 1963.

———. *Discursos del doctor Juan José Arévalo y del teniente coronel Jacobo Arbenz Guzmán en el acto de transmisión de la Presidencia de la República, 15 de marzo de 1951*. Guatemala City: Tipografía Nacional, 1951.

———. *Discursos en la presidencia (1945–1948)*. Guatemala City: Tipografía Nacional, 1948.

———. *Escritos complementarios*. Guatemala City: José de Pineda Ibarra, 1988.

———. *Escritos pedagógicos y filosóficos*. Guatemala City: Tipografía Nacional, 1945.

———. *Escritos políticos*. Guatemala City: Tipografía Nacional, 1945.

———. *Fábula del tiburón y las sardinas*. Santiago de Chile: Ediciones América Nueva, 1956.

———. *Guatemala: la democracia y el imperio*. Rev. ed., Buenos Aires: Editorial Renacimiento, 1955.

———. *La inquietud normalista*. San Salvador: Editorial Universitaria de El Salvador, 1970.

———. "De Juan José Arévalo a Carlos Manuel Pellecer." *El Imparcial*, Sept. 9, 1982, p. 2.

———. *Memorias de aldea*. Mexico City: Editorial Orión, 1963.

———. "La revolución le enseñó al pueblo que se puede luchar." *7 Días*, Oct. 22, 1988, p. 9.

———. "No sé si la ayuda que dimos a Figueres en 1948 fué para bien." *Diario de Costa Rica*, San José, Jan. 31, 1972, p. 16.

Arévalo Martínez, Rafael. *Ecce Pericles!* 1945. 2 vols. San José, C.R.: EDUCA, 1971.

———. *Ubico*. Guatemala City: Tipografía Nacional, 1984.

Argüello, Rosendo hijo. *Quiénes y cómo nos traicionaron*. N.p., n.d.

Arias Gómez, Jorge. *Farabundo Martí*. San José, C.R.: EDUCA, 1972.

Aronson, James. *The Press and the Cold War*. New York: Bobbs-Merrill, 1970.

Arvelo, Tulio. *Cayo Confite y Luperón: Memorias de un expedicionario*. Santo Domingo, D.R.: Universidad Autónoma de Santo Domingo, 1981.

Asociación General de Agricultores. *Proyecto de ley agraria de la Asociación General de Agricultores*. Guatemala City: Sánchez & de Guise, 1952.

Avila Ayala, Manuel María. "La muerte del coronel Arana." *La Hora*, 14 articles, July 27–Aug. 13, 1954.

Aybar de Soto, José. *Dependency and Intervention: The Case of Guatemala in 1954*. Boulder, Colo.: Westview, 1978.

Baker, George. "The Woodrow Wilson Administration and Guatemalan Relations." *The Historian* 27, no. 2 (Feb. 1965): 155–69.

Barrios Archila, Jaime. *Biografía mínima del doctor Juan José Arévalo Bermejo*. Guatemala City: Ministerio de Educación, 1985.

Bauer Paiz, Alfonso. *Como opera el capital yanqui en Centroamérica: El caso de Guatemala*. Mexico City: Ed. Ibero Mexicana, 1956.

———. "La Electric Bond and Share Company." *Alero* 2.2 (Nov. 1970): 20–34.

———. *La Frutera y la discriminación*. Guatemala City: Ministerio de Economía y Trabajo, 1949.

Bayo, Alberto. *Tempestad en el Caribe*. Mexico City: n.p., 1950.

Bell, John Patrick. *Crisis in Costa Rica: The 1948 Revolution*. Austin: University of Texas Press, 1971.

Bemis, Samuel. *The Latin American Policy of the United States*. 1940. New York: Norton, 1967.

Bendaña Perdomo, Ricardo. "Historia general de la Iglesia de América Latina: Parte correspondiente a Guatemala, 1821–1976." Unpublished ms. in author's files.

Benites, Tulio. *Meditaciones de un católico ante la reforma agraria*. Guatemala City: Ministerio de Educación Pública, 1952.

Berle, Beatrice Bishop, and Travis Beal Jacobs, eds. *Navigating the Rapids, 1918–1971*. New York: Harcourt, Brace, Jovanovich, 1973.

Bernays, Edward. *Biography of an Idea: Memoirs of a Public Relations Counsel*. New York: Simon and Schuster, 1965.

Bernstein, Barton. "Election of 1952," in Arthur Schlesinger Jr., ed., *History of American Presidential Elections, 1789–1968*. New York: Chelsea House, 1971, 4:3215–66.

Bernstein, Victor, and Jesse Gordon. "The Press and the Bay of Pigs." *Columbia University Forum* 10, no. 3 (Fall 1967): 5–13.

Betancourt, Rómulo. "La opinión continental frente a la X Conferencia Interamericana." *Cuadernos Americanos*, Mexico City, vol. 71 (Sept.–Oct. 1953): 7–37.

Biechler, Michael. "The Coffee Industry of Guatemala: A Geographic Analysis." Ph.D. diss., Michigan State University, 1970.

Birkett, Blair. "Confidence in Guatemala Restored by Settlement of Labor Dispute." *Foreign Trade*, Ottawa, no. 124 (May 14, 1949): 1008–11.

Bishop, Edwin. "The Guatemalan Labor Movement, 1944–1959." Ph.D. diss., University of Wisconsin, 1959.

Bishop, Jefferson Mack. "Arévalo and Central American Unification." Ph.D. diss., Louisiana State University and Agricultural and Mechanical College, 1971.

Bissell, Richard. "Oral History Interview." Columbia University, 1973.

Blanco, Ramón. *25 galeras*. Guatemala City: Unión Tipográfica, 1954.

Blasier, Cole. *The Hovering Giant: U.S. Responses to Revolutionary Change in Latin America*. Pittsburgh: University of Pittsburgh Press, 1976.

Bosch, Juan. "Errores de la política norteamericana en el Caribe." *Bohemia*, Havana, Oct. 16, 1949, pp. 57, 62.

Bosch, Juan, et al. "Cayo Confites y la lucha contra Trujillo." *Política: teoría y acción*, Santo Domingo, D.R., 44 (Nov. 1983): 1–28.

Brands, H. W. *Cold Warriors: Eisenhower's Generation and American Foreign Policy*. New York: Columbia University Press, 1988.

Brintnall, Douglas. *Revolt of the Dead: The Modernization of a Mayan Community in the Highlands of Guatemala*. New York: Gordon and Breach, 1979.

Bulmer-Thomas, Victor. *The Political Economy of Central America since 1920*. Cambridge: Cambridge University Press, 1987.

Bush, Archer. "Organized Labor in Guatemala, 1944–1949." M.A. thesis, Colgate University, 1950.

Cabot, John Moors. *First Line of Defense: Forty Years' Experiences of a Career Diplomat*. Washington D.C.: School of Foreign Service, Georgetown University, [1979].

——. *Toward Our Common American Destiny*. Boston: Fletcher School of Law and Diplomacy, [1955].

Cáceres, Carlos. *Aproximación a Guatemala*. Culiacán, Mexico: Universidad Autónoma de Sinaloa, 1980.

Calder, Bruce. *Crecimiento y cambio de la Iglesia Católica Guatemalteca, 1944–1966*. Guatemala City: José de Pineda Ibarra, 1970.

Cardona, Rokael. "Cooperativismo y modernización agrícola en Guatemala (1945–1975)." Thesis, University of Costa Rica, 1977.

Cardoza, José Alberto. "A treinta años de la Revolución de Octubre de 1944." *Alero* 8 (Sept./Oct. 1974): 89–93.

Cardoza y Aragón, Luis. *Guatemala, las líneas de su mano*. Mexico City: Fondo de Cultura Económica, 1955.

——. *Retorno al futuro*. Mexico City: Letras de México, 1948.

——. *La Revolución Guatemalteca*. Mexico City: Cuadernos Americanos, 1955.

Carmack, Robert. *Historia social de los Quichés*. Guatemala City: Seminario de Integración Social Guatemalteca, 1979.

Carmack, Robert, ed. *Harvest of Violence: The Maya Indians and the Guatemalan Crisis*. Norman: University of Oklahoma Press, 1988.

Carpio, Cayetano. *Secuestro y capucha*. San José, C.R.: EDUCA, 1979.

Carrillo Ramírez, Alfredo. *Evolución histórica de la educación secundaria en Guatemala*. 2 vols. Guatemala City: José de Pineda Ibarra, 1971, 1972.

Casey, Dennis. "Indigenismo: The Guatemalan Experience." Ph.D. diss., University of Kansas, 1979.

Castellanos Cambranes, Julio. *Café y campesinos en Guatemala, 1853–1897*. Guatemala City: Editorial Universitaria, 1985.

——. *Democratización y movimientos campesinos pro-tierra en Guatemala*. Madrid: Centro de Estudios Rurales Centroamericanos, 1988.

——. *Desarrollo económico y social de Guatemala: 1868–85*. Guatemala City: IIES, Universidad de San Carlos, 1975.

——. "Los empresarios agrarios modernos y el Estado en Guatemala." *Mesoamérica* 10 (Dec. 1985): 243–91.

——. *El imperialismo alemán en Guatemala*. Guatemala City: IIES, Universidad de San Carlos, 1977.

Castillo Armas, Carlos. "Organización del ataque a la Base Militar." *El Espectador*, July 3, 1955, p. 3.

Catalán M., Juan Carlos. "Huelga universitaria contra Ubico." *La calle donde tú vives*, Sept. 16, 1977, pp. 10–15.

Cehelsky, Marta. "Guatemala's Frustrated Revolution: The 'Liberation' of 1954." M.A. thesis, Columbia University, [1967].

Childs, Marquis. *Eisenhower, Captive Hero: A Critical Study of the General and the President*. New York: Harcourt, Brace, Jovanovich, 1958.

Cline, Ray. *Secrets, Spies and Scholars: Blueprint of the Essential CIA*. Washington, D.C.: Acropolis Books, 1976.

Clissold, Stephen, ed. *Soviet Relations with Latin America 1918–1960: A Documentary Record*. New York: Oxford University Press, 1970.

Colby, Benjamin, and Pierre van den Berghe. *Ixil Country: A Plural Society in Highland Guatemala*. Berkeley: University of California Press, 1969.

Comisión permanente del primer congreso contra la intervención soviética en América Latina. *El libro negro del comunismo en Guatemala*. Mexico City, 1954.

Comité Interamericano de Desarrollo Agrícola. *Tenencia de la tierra y desarrollo socio-económico del sector agrícola*. Washington, D.C.: Unión Panamericana, 1965.

Connell-Smith, Gordon. *The Inter-American System*. London: Oxford University Press, 1966.

Cook, Blanche Wiesen. *The Declassified Eisenhower: A Divided Legacy*. Garden City, N.Y.: Doubleday, 1981.

Corado, Carlos Daniel. "Yo no firmé la rendición el 20 de octubre." *La Tarde*, Oct. 17, 1970, p. 9.

Corominas, Enrique. *In the Caribbean Political Areas*. New York: University Press of Cambridge, 1954.

Couloumbis, Theodore. *Greek Political Reaction to American and NATO Influences*. New Haven: Yale University Press, 1966.

Crassweller, Robert. *Trujillo: The Life and Times of a Caribbean Dictator*. New York: Macmillan, 1966.

Cruz Salazar, José Luis. "El ejército como una fuerza política." *Estudios Sociales* 6 (Apr. 1972): 74–98.

Dalton, Roque. *Miguel Mármol*. San José, C.R.: EDUCA, 1982.

Davis, Shelton, and Julie Hodson. *Witnesses to Political Violence in Guatemala: The Suppression of a Rural Development Movement*. Boston: Oxfam America, 1982.

Dawson, Frank Griffith. "Labor Legislation and Social Integration in Guatemala: 1871–1944." *American Journal of Comparative Law* 14 (1965–1966): 124–42.

De la Guarda, Manuel César. *Castillo Armas, libertador y mártir*. Lima: Editorial Indoamérica, 1957.

De León Aragón, Oscar. *Los contratos de la United Fruit Company y las compañías muelleras en Guatemala*. Guatemala City: Ministerio de Educación Pública, 1950.

Delli Sante-Arrocha, Angela. *Juan José Arévalo: Pensador contemporáneo*. Mexico City: Costa-Amic, 1962.

De los Rios, Efraín. *Ombres contra hombres*. 2 vols. Guatemala City: Tipografía Nacional, 1969.

Del Valle Matheu, Jorge. *La verdad sobre el "caso de Guatemala."* Guatemala City: n.p., 1956.

De Santis, Vincent. "Eisenhower Revisionism." *Review of Politics* 38 (Apr. 1976): 190–207.

De Wiche, Josefina. "El comunismo en Guatemala." *Estudios sobre el comunismo*. Santiago de Chile, vol. 1, no. 1 (July/Sept. 1953): 92–96.

De Zirión, Grace H. *Datos biográficos del general e ingeniero Miguel Ydígoras Fuentes*. Guatemala City: José de Pineda Ibarra, 1961.

Díaz Rozzotto, Jaime. *El carácter de la Revolución Guatemalteca*. Mexico City: Ediciones Revista "Horizonte," 1958.

Dinerstein, Herbert. *The Making of a Missile Crisis: October 1962*. Baltimore: Johns Hopkins University Press, 1976.

Dinwoodie, David. "Expedient Diplomacy: The United States and Guatemala, 1898–1920." Ph.D. diss., University of Colorado, 1966.

Dion, Marie Berthe. *Las ideas sociales y políticas de Arévalo*. Mexico City: Editorial América Nueva, 1958.

Divine, Robert. *Eisenhower and the Cold War*. New York: Oxford University Press, 1981.

———. *Foreign Policy and U.S. Presidential Elections, 1952–1960*. New York: New Viewpoints, 1974.

Dominican Republic, Ministry for Home Affairs. *White Book of Communism in Dominican Republic*. Madrid: Gráficas Rey, n.d.

Donaldson, Robert. *Soviet Policy toward India*. Cambridge: Harvard University Press, 1974.

Dosal, Paul. "The Political Economy of Guatemalan Industrialization, 1871–1948: The Career of Carlos F. Novella." *Hispanic American Historical Review* 68, no. 2 (May 1988): 321–58.

Early, John. *The Demographic Structure and Evolution of a Peasant System: The Guatemalan Population*. Boca Raton: University Presses of Florida, 1982.

Ebaugh, Cameron. *Education in Guatemala*. Washington, D.C.: GPO, 1947.

Eden, Anthony. *Full Circle*. London: Cassell, 1960.

Eisenhower, Dwight. *Mandate for Change, 1953–1956*. Garden City, N.Y.: Doubleday, 1963.

El Espectador. July 3, 1955. (Special issue on Castillo Armas.)

El Salvador, Secretaría de Información de la Presidencia. *De la neutralidad vigilante a la mediación con Guatemala*. Rev. ed. San Salvador, 1955.

Escuela Politécnica. *Centenario de la Escuela Politécnica, 1873–1973*. Guatemala City, 1973.

———. *La Escuela Politécnica, 1 de Septiembre 1873–1 de Septiembre 1941*. Guatemala City, 1941.

Estrada Monroy, Agustín. *Datos para la historia de la Iglesia en Guatemala*. 3 vols. Guatemala City: Sociedad de Geografía e Historia de Guatemala, 1973, 1978, 1979.

Fabela, Isidro. "La conferencia de Caracas y la actitud anticomunista de México." *Cuadernos Americanos*, Mexico City, vol. 75, no. 3 (May–June 1954): 7–44.

Falla, Ricardo. *Quiché rebelde*. Guatemala City: Editorial Universitaria, 1978.

Ferrell, Robert, ed. *The Diary of James C. Hagerty*. Bloomington: Indiana University Press, 1983.

———, ed. *The Eisenhower Diaries*. New York: Norton, 1981.

Figueres, José. *El espiritu del 48*. San José, C.R.: Editorial Costa Rica, 1987.
———. "Oral History Interview." Truman Library, 1970.
Figueroa Ibarra, Carlos. "Contenido de clase y participación obrera en el movimiento antidictatorial de 1920." *Política y Sociedad* 4 (July–Dec. 1977): 5–51.
———. "La insurrección armada de 1920 en Guatemala." *Política y Sociedad* 8 (July–Dec. 1979): 91–146.
Flores Avendaño, Guillermo. *Memorias (1900–1970)*. 2 vols. Guatemala City: Editorial del Ejército, 1974.
Fortuny, José Manuel. "Autocrítica." Mexico City, Feb. 15, 1955, unpublished ms. in author's files.
———. *Informe sobre la actividad del Comité Central del Partido Comunista de Guatemala, 11 de diciembre de 1952*. Guatemala City: Ediciones del Partido Guatemalteco del Trabajo, 1953.
———. "Observaciones al trabajo de Edelberto Torres Rivas." *Historia y Sociedad*, Mexico City, 15 (1977): 55–69.
———. *Por un frente único de masas: Informe al Pleno Ampliado del Comité Central del Partido Guatemalteco del Trabajo: 16 de octubre de 1953*. Guatemala City: n.p., 1953.
Frankel, Anita. "Political Development in Guatemala, 1944–1954: The Impact of Foreign, Military and Religious Elites." Ph.D. diss., University of Connecticut, 1969.
Fuentes Mohr, Alberto. "Land Settlement and Agrarian Reform in Guatemala." *International Journal of Agrarian Affairs*, London, vol. 2, no. 1 (Jan. 1955): 24–32.
Gadea, Hilda. *Ernesto: A Memoir of Che Guevara*. Garden City, N.Y.: Doubleday, 1972.
Gaitán, Héctor. "Los mártires del sindicalismo." *La calle donde tú vives*, Apr. 28, 1978, pp. 2–9.
Galich, Manuel. *Del pánico al ataque*. 1949. Guatemala City: Editorial Universitaria, 1977.
———. *Por qué lucha Guatemala?* Buenos Aires: Elmer, 1958.
García, Graciela. *Las luchas revolucionarias de la nueva Guatemala*. Mexico City: n.p., 1952.
———. *Páginas de lucha revolucionaria en Centroamérica*. Mexico City: Ediciones Linterna, 1971.
García Añoveros, Jesús. "El 'caso Guatemala' (junio de 1954): La Universidad y el campesinado." *Alero* 28 (Jan./Feb. 1978): 133–234.
———. *Jacobo Arbenz*. Madrid: Historia 16 Quorum, 1987.
———. *La reforma agraria de Arbenz en Guatemala*. Madrid: Ediciones Cultura Hispánica, 1987.
García Granados, Jorge. *Evolución sociológica de Guatemala*. Guatemala: Sánchez & de Guise, 1927.
Geiger, Theodore. *Communism versus Progress in Guatemala*. Washington, D.C.: National Planning Association, 1953.
Gillin, John, and K. H. Silvert. "Ambiguities in Guatemala." *Foreign Affairs* 34 (Apr. 1956): 469–82.
Girón, José Ernesto. "La rebelión de los cadetes." *La Hora Dominical*, July 27, 1975, pp. 19–22.

Gleijeses, Piero. *The Dominican Crisis*. Baltimore: Johns Hopkins University Press, 1978.

―――. "Guatemala." In James Malloy and Eduardo Gamarra, eds., *Latin America and Caribbean Contemporary Record*. Vol. 7. New York: Holmes & Meier, 1990, pp. B259–74.

―――. *Guatemala: The Struggle for Democracy*. Cork, Ireland: University College, 1986.

―――. *Politics and Culture in Guatemala*. Ann Arbor: Center for Political Studies, University of Michigan, 1988.

Goldenberg, Boris. *Kommunismus in Lateinamerika*. Stuttgart: Kohlhammer, 1971.

Góngora, Mayra. *Introducción a la sociedad guatemalteca contemporánea*. Havana: Centro de Estudios sobre América, 1982.

González, Mario Aníbal. "Recuerdos de la dictadura del general Jorge Ubico." *La Hora*, Feb. 15, 1986, pp. 3, 11.

González Campo, José. "La caída del presidente Jorge Ubico." *Estudios Centroamericanos*, San Salvador, vol. 19, no. 192 (Apr. 1964): 84–98.

―――. "El general Jorge Ubico, un dictador progresista." *Estudios Centroamericanos*, San Salvador, vol. 18, no. 187 (Nov. 1963): 345–55.

González Orellana, Carlos. *Historia de la educación en Guatemala*. Guatemala City: José de Pineda Ibarra, 1970.

Greenstein, Fred. *The Hidden-Hand Presidency: Eisenhower as Leader*. New York: Basic Books, 1982.

Grieb, Kenneth. "American Involvement in the Rise of Jorge Ubico," *Caribbean Studies* 10, no. 1 (Apr. 1970): 5–21.

―――. *Guatemalan Caudillo: The Regime of Jorge Ubico*. Athens: Ohio University Press, 1979.

Griffith, William. "A Recent Attempt at Educational Cooperation between the United States and Guatemala." *Middle American Research Records* 1, no. 12 (May 15, 1949): 171–92.

―――. "Santo Tomás, anhelado emporio del comercio en el Atlántico." *Anales de la Sociedad de Geografía e Historia*, Jan./Dec. 1958, pp. 40–61.

Guatemala, Congress of. "Actas del Congreso," 1952–1953.

―――. *Diario de las Sesiones del Congreso de la República de Guatemala*. 1953–1954.

Guatemala, Government of. *Censo agropecuario 1950*. Guatemala City: Dirección General de Estadística, 1954.

―――. *Crítica al proyecto de ley agraria de la Asociación General de Agricultores*. Guatemala City: Secretaría de Propaganda y Divulgación de la Presidencia de la República, May 1952.

―――. *La democracia amenazada. El caso de Guatemala*. Guatemala City: Tipografía Nacional, Secretaría de Propaganda y Divulgación de la Presidencia de la República, 1954.

―――. *Efemerides del Movimiento de Liberación Nacional: junio y julio de 1954*. Guatemala City: Secretaría de Divulgación, Cultura y Turismo, 1955.

―――. *Primera colonia agrícola de Poptún*. Guatemala City: Departamento de Publicidad de la Presidencia de la República, 1950.

Guatemala, Government of. *El triángulo de Escuintla*. Guatemala City: Tipografía Nacional, 1946.

Guerra Borges, Alfredo. "Apuntes para una interpretación de la Revolución Guatemalteca y de su derrota en 1954." *Anuario de Estudios Centroamericanos*, San José, C.R., vol. 14, no. 1–2 (1988): 109–20.

———. *Pensamiento económico social de la Revolución de Octubre*. Guatemala City: Universidad de San Carlos, 1977.

Guevara, Ernesto. *Che: Obra revolucionaria*. Mexico City: ERA, 1967.

Guillén, Fedro. *Guatemala: prólogo y epílogo de una revolución*. Mexico City: Cuadernos Americanos, 1964.

Gunther, John. *Inside Latin America*. New York: Harper & Brothers, 1941.

Gutiérrez, Víctor Manuel. *Apuntes para la historia del Partido Comunista de Guatemala*. Guatemala City: n.p., 1965.

———. *Breve historia del movimiento sindical de Guatemala*. Mexico City: n.p., 1964.

Halperin, Ernst. *Nationalism and Communism in Chile*. Cambridge: MIT Press, 1965.

Handy, Jim. *Class and Community in Rural Guatemala: Village Reaction to the Agrarian Reform Law, 1952–1954*. Occasional Papers Series, no. 59. Miami: Latin American and Caribbean Center, Florida International University, 1985.

———. *Gift of the Devil: A History of Guatemala*. Boston: South End Press, 1984.

———. "The Guatemalan Revolution and Civil Rights." *Canadian Journal of Latin American and Caribbean Studies*, Toronto, vol. 10, no. 19 (1985): 3–21.

———. " 'The Most Precious Fruit of the Revolution': The Guatemalan Agrarian Reform, 1952–54." *Hispanic American Historical Review* 68, no. 4 (Nov. 1988): 675–705.

———. "Reform and Counter-Reform: Agrarian Policy in Guatemala, 1952–1957." Presented at Latin American Studies Association, 15th Congress, Miami, Dec. 1989.

Hanford, Thomas. "The Communist Beachhead in the Western Hemisphere." Presented at Army War College, Carlisle Barracks, Pa., Mar. 15, 1955.

Hendon, Robert. "Some Recent Economic Reforms in Guatemala." M.A thesis, Colgate University, 1949.

Hennessey, John. "National Economy of Guatemala." *Commercial Pan America* 16, no. 2 (Feb. 1947): 43–96.

Henríquez Vásquez, Alberto. "Cayo Confites (ahora más completo y menos dulce)." *Ultima Hora*, Santo Domingo, D.R., 26 articles, Jan. 2–Apr. 13, 1984.

Hernández de León, Federico. *Viajes presidenciales*. 2 vols. Guatemala City: Publicaciones del Partido Liberal Progresista, 1940, 1943.

Hernández Sifontes, Julio. *Realidad jurídica del indígena guatemalteco*. Guatemala City: José de Pineda Ibarra, 1965.

Higbee, Edward. "The Agricultural Regions of Guatemala." *Geographic Review* 38 (Apr. 1947): 177–201.

———. "Guatemala's Agrarian Problem." Ph.D. diss., Johns Hopkins University, 1949.

Higgins, Trumbull. *The Perfect Failure: Kennedy, Eisenhower, and the CIA at the Bay of Pigs*. New York: Norton, 1987.

Hill, Robert. "Oral History Interview." Princeton University, 1964.

———. "Oral History Interview." Columbia University, 1973.

"History: Damn Good and Sure." *Newsweek*, Mar. 4, 1963, p. 17.

Holleran, Mary. *Church and State in Guatemala*. New York: Columbia University Press, 1949.

Hough, Jerry. *The Struggle for the Third World: Soviet Debates and American Options*. Washington, D.C.: Brookings, 1986.

Hough, Richard, et al. *Land and Labor in Guatemala: An Assesssment*. Guatemala City: United States Agency for International Development and Development Associates, 1982.

Houghton, Neal. "The Cuban Invasion of 1961 and the U.S. Press, in Retrospect." *Journalism Quarterly* 42 (Summer 1965): 422–32.

Hughes, John Emmet. *The Ordeal of Power: A Political Memoir of the Eisenhower Years*. New York: Atheneum, 1963.

Hunt, Howard. *Undercover: Memoirs of an American Secret Agent*. New York: Putnam, 1974.

Hurtado Aguilar, Luis Alberto. *Así se gestó la Liberación*. Guatemala City: Secretaría de Divulgación, Cultura y Turismo de la Presidencia de la República, 1956.

Immerman, Richard. *The CIA in Guatemala: The Foreign Policy of Intervention*. Austin: University of Texas Press, 1982.

———. "Eisenhower and Dulles: Who Made the Decisions?" *Political Psychology* 1 (Autumn 1979): 21–38.

Inman, Samuel Guy. *Inter-American Conferences, 1826–1954: History and Problems*. Washington, D.C.: University Press of Washington D.C. and the Community College Press, 1965.

———. *A New Day in Guatemala*. Wilton, Conn.: Worldover Press, 1951.

International Bank for Reconstruction and Development (World Bank). *The Economic Development of Guatemala*. Washington, D.C., 1951.

James, Daniel. *Red Design for the Americas: Guatemalan Prelude*. New York: John Day, 1954.

Jimenez, Ernesto. *La educación rural en Guatemala*. Guatemala City: José de Pineda Ibarra, 1967.

Joes, Anthony James. "Eisenhower Revisionism: The Tide Comes In." *Presidential Studies Quarterly* 15 (Summer 1985): 561–71.

Jonas, Susanne. *Battle for Guatemala*. Boulder, Colo.: Westview, 1991.

———. "Guatemala: Land of Eternal Struggle." In Ronald Chilcote and Joel Edelstein, eds. *Latin America: The Struggle with Dependency and Beyond*. New York: John Wiley, 1974, pp. 89–219.

Jonas, Susanne, and David Tobis, eds. *Guatemala*. New York: North American Congress on Latin America, 1974.

Jones, Chester Lloyd. *Guatemala: Past and Present*. Minneapolis: University of Minnesota Press, 1940.

Kanet, Roger, ed. *The Soviet Union and the Developing World*. Baltimore: Johns Hopkins University Press, 1974.

Kaufman, Burton. *Trade and Aid: Eisenhower's Foreign Economic Policy, 1953–1961*. Baltimore: Johns Hopkins University Press, 1982.

Kepner, Charles. *Social Aspects of the Banana Industry*. New York: Columbia University Press, 1936.

Kepner, Charles, and Jay Soothill. *The Banana Empire: A Case Study of Economic Imperialism*. New York: Vanguard Press, 1935.

Kirkpatrick, Lyman. "Paramilitary Case Study: The Bay of Pigs," *Naval War College Review*, Nov.–Dec. 1972, pp. 32–42.

———. *The Real CIA*. London: Macmillan, 1968.

Kolb, Glen. *Democracy and Dictatorship in Venezuela, 1945–1958*. Hamden, Conn.: Archon Books, 1974.

Krehm, William. *Democracies and Tyrannies of the Caribbean*. Westport, Conn.: Lawrence Hill, 1984.

LaBarge, Richard. "Impact of the United Fruit Company on the Economic Development of Guatemala, 1946–1954." In LaBarge, et al., *Studies in Middle American Economics*. New Orleans: Middle American Research Institute, Tulane University, 1968, pp. 1–72.

———. "A Study of United Fruit Company Operations in Isthmian America, 1946–1956." Ph.D. diss., Duke University, 1959.

LaCharite, Norman, et al. *Case Study in Insurgency and Revolutionary Warfare: Guatemala, 1944–1954*. Washington D.C.: American University, 1964.

L.A.H.A.: See Hurtado Aguilar.

Larsen, Douglas. " 'Sulfato': Nemesis of the Guatemalan Reds." *Flying*, July 1957, pp. 50–51, 86–88.

Leary, William. *Perilous Missions: Civil Air Transport and CIA Covert Operations in Asia*. University: University of Alabama Press, 1984.

LeBaron, Alan. "Impaired Democracy in Guatemala, 1944–1951." Ph.D. diss., University of Florida, 1988.

López Larrave, Mario. *Breve historia del movimiento sindical guatemalteco*. Guatemala City: Editorial Universitaria, 1976.

López Villatoro, Mario. *Por los fueros de la verdad histórica, una voz de la patria escarnecida*. Guatemala City: n.p., 1956.

———. *Por qué fué derrotado el comunismo en Guatemala?* Guatemala City: n.p., 1957.

Lovell, George. "Surviving Conquest: The Maya of Guatemala in Historical Perspective." *Latin American Research Review* 23, no. 2 (1988): 25–57.

McAuliffe, Mary. "Eisenhower, The President." *Journal of American History* 68 (1981): 625–32.

McCann, Thomas. *An American Company: The Tragedy of United Fruit*. New York: Crown Publishers, 1976.

McClintock, Michael. *The American Connection*. Vol. 1: *State Terror and Popular Resistance in El Salvador*. Vol. 2: *State Terror and Popular Resistance in Guatemala*. London: Zed Books, 1985.

McCreery, David. "Debt Servitude in Rural Guatemala, 1876–1936." *Hispanic American Historical Review* 63, no. 4 (1983): 735–59.

———. *Development and the State in Reforma Guatemala 1871–1885*. Athens: Ohio University Center for International Studies, 1983.

———. "An 'Odious Feudalism': *Mandamiento* Labor and Commercial Agriculture in Guatemala, 1858–1920." *Latin American Perspectives* 13, no. 1 (Winter 1986): 99–117.

McLellan, David, and David Acheson, eds. *Among Friends: Personal Letters of Dean Acheson*. New York: Dodd, Mead, 1980.

McMahon, Robert. "Eisenhower and Third World Nationalism: A Critique of the Revisionists." *Political Science Quarterly* 101, no. 3 (1986): 453–73.

Macaulay, Neill. *The Sandino Affair*. New York: Quadrangle Books, 1967.

Marroquín Rojas, Clemente [Canuto Ocaña, pseud.]. *La "Carta política" del ciudadano Juan José Arévalo*. Guatemala City: Editorial San Antonio, 1965.

Marroquín Rojas, Clemente. *Crónicas de la Constituyente del 45*. 1945. Guatemala City: Tipografía Nacional, 1970.

————. *La derrota de una batalla*. Guatemala City: n.p., n.d.

————. *En el mundo de la polémica*. Guatemala City: n.p., 1971.

Martin, John Bartlow. *Overtaken by Events: The Dominican Crisis from the Fall of Trujillo to the Civil War*. Garden City, N.Y.: Doubleday, 1966.

Martínez Estévez, Alfonso. "En México se pelea duro el arevalismo y Martínez Estévez," *La Hora*, Mar. 4, 1963, pp. 4, 7.

Martz, John. *Central America: The Crisis and the Challenge*. Chapel Hill: University of North Carolina Press, 1959.

————. *Communist Infiltration in Guatemala*. New York: Vantage Press, 1956.

Matthews, Herbert. *A World in Revolution*. New York: Scribner's, 1971.

May, Stacy, and Galo Plaza. *The United Fruit Company in Latin America*. Washington, D.C.: National Planning Association, 1958.

Meers, Sharon. "A Pebble on the Beach: Guatemala, British Decline and the Fall of Jacobo Arbenz." B.A. thesis, Harvard University, 1988.

Mejía, Medardo. *Juan José Arévalo o el humanismo en la presidencia*. Guatemala City: Tipografía Nacional, 1951.

————. *El movimiento obrero en la Revolución de Octubre*. Guatemala City: Tipografía Nacional, 1949.

Melville, Thomas, and Marjorie Melville. *Guatemala—Another Vietnam?* Harmondsworth: Penguin Books, 1971.

————. *Guatemala: The Politics of Land Ownership*. New York: Free Press, 1971.

Mencía, Mario. "El Che Guevara en Guatemala." *Alero* 27 (Nov.–Dec. 1977): 99–111.

Méndez Montenegro, Julio César. *444 años de legislación agraria, 1513–1957*. Guatemala City: Imprenta Universitaria, 1960.

Meza, Víctor. *Historia del movimiento obrero hondureño*. Tegucigalpa: Editorial Guaymuras, 1980.

Miller, Hubert. "Catholic Leaders and Spiritual Socialism during the Arévalo Administration in Guatemala, 1945–1951." In Ralph Lee Woodward, Jr., ed., *Central America: Historical Perspectives on the Contemporary Crises*. New York: Greenwood Press, 1988, pp. 85–105.

Monroe, Keith. "Guatemala: What the Reds Left Behind." *Harper's*, July 1955, pp. 60–65.

Monteforte Toledo, Mario. *Una democracia a prueba de fuego*. Guatemala City: Tipografía Nacional, 1949.

————. *Guatemala: Monografía sociológica*. Mexico City: Universidad Nacional Autónoma de México, 1959.

Montejo, Victor. *Testimony: Death of a Guatemalan Village*. Willimantic, Conn.: Curbstone Press, 1987.

Montenegro, Arturo. "El capitán Montenegro defiende la obra del ex-Presidente Castillo Armas." *La Hora*, Apr. 1, 1958, p. 4.

Morales, Baltasar. *Derrocamiento de una tiranía*. Guatemala City: Tipografía Nacional, 1958.

Morán, Francisco. *Las jornadas cívicas de abril y mayo de 1944*. San Salvador: Editorial Universitaria, 1979.

Morazán, Francisco. "Apuntes de Francisco Morazán." Unpublished ms. in author's files.

————. "Los siete primeros y el hombre de la CIA." 2 vols. Unpublished ms. in author's files.

Mosley, Leonard. *Dulles: A Biography of Eleanor, Allen, and John Foster Dulles and Their Family Network*. New York: Dial Press, 1978.

Moya Posas, Emma. *La jornada épica de Castillo Armas vista desde Honduras*. Tegucigalpa: Imprenta La República, 1955.

Muñoz Meany, Enrique. *El hombre y la encrucijada*. Guatemala City: Tipografía Nacional, 1950.

Munro, Dana. *Intervention and Dollar Diplomacy in the Caribbean, 1900–1921*. Princeton: Princeton University Press, 1964.

Munro, Leslie Knox. "Oral History Interview." Princeton University, 1964.

Nájera Farfán, Mario Efraín. *Cuando el árbol cae . . . (un presidente que murió para vivir)*. Guatemala City: n.p., 1958.

————. *Los estafadores de la democracia: Hombres y hechos en Guatemala*. Buenos Aires: Editorial Glem, 1956.

Náñez Falcón, Guillermo. "Erwin Paul Dieseldorff, German Entrepreneur in the Alta Verapaz of Guatemala, 1889–1937." Ph.D. diss., Tulane University, 1970.

Noval, Joaquín. *Tres problemas de la educación rural en Guatemala*. Guatemala City: José de Pineda Ibarra, 1959.

Obando Sánchez, Antonio. *Memorias*. Rev. ed. Guatemala City: Editorial Universitaria, 1978.

Oquelí, Ramón. "Un señor Juan Pablo Wainwright." *Revista Ariel*, Tegucigalpa, May–June 1974, pp. 11–13.

Ordóñez Argüello, Alberto, ed. *Arévalo visto por América*. Guatemala City: Ministerio de Educación Pública, 1951.

Organization of American States. *Annals of the Organization of American States*. Vol. 5. Washington D.C., 1953.

————. *Informe anual de la Comisión Interamericana de Derechos Humanos 1987–1988*. Washington, D.C., 1988.

————. *Tenth Inter-American Conference, Caracas, Venezuela, 1954. Chronological Collection of Documents*. Washington, D.C., 1954.

Ornes, Horacio. *Desembarco en Luperón*. Mexico City: Ediciones Humanismo, 1956.

Osegueda, Raúl. *Operación Guatemala $$ OK $$*. Mexico City: Editorial América Nueva, 1955.

Ovalle, N. K. *Industrial Report on the Republic of Guatemala*. Washington, D.C.: Inter-American Development Commission, 1946.

Palacios, José Antonio. "Formas de redistribución del ingreso en Guatemala." *Trimestre Económico*, Mexico City, vol. 19 (July–Sept. 1952): 422–51.

Paredes Moreira, José Luis. "Aspectos y resultados económicos de la reforma agraria en Guatemala." *Economía* 12 (Dec. 1966): 26–61.

———. *Aplicación del Decreto 900*. Guatemala City: IIES, Universidad de San Carlos, 1964.

———. *Reforma agraria: Una experiencia en Guatemala*. Guatemala City: Imprenta Universitaria, 1963.

Parkman, Patricia. *Nonviolent Insurrection in El Salvador: The Fall of Maximiliano Hernández Martínez*. Tucson: University of Arizona Press, 1988.

Parmet, Herbert. *Eisenhower and the American Crusade*. New York: Macmillan, 1972.

Partido Guatemalteco del Trabajo. *Estatutos del Partido Guatemalteco del Trabajo*. Guatemala City, 1952.

Partido Guatemalteco del Trabajo, Comisión Política del Comité Central. *La intervención norteamericana en Guatemala y el derrocamiento del régimen democrático*. Guatemala City, 1955.

Pearson, Neale. "The *Confederación Nacional Campesina de Guatemala* (CNCG) and Peasant Unionism in Guatemala, 1944–1954." M.A. thesis, Georgetown University, 1964.

———. "Guatemala: The Peasant Union Movement, 1944–1954." In Henry Landsberger ed., *Latin American Peasant Movements*. Ithaca, N.Y.: Cornell University Press, 1969, pp. 323–73.

Pellecer, Carlos Manuel. *Caballeros sin esperanza*. Guatemala City: Editorial del Ejército, 1973.

———. *. . . camino equivocado, Che!* Guatemala City: Editorial del Ejército, 1971.

———. "Crónica de mi lucha por la tierra." Unpublished ms. in author's files.

———. "Dos yanquis más contra Guatemala." *El Imparcial*, 10 articles, Aug. 27–Sept. 7, 1982.

———. *Memoria en dos geografías*. Mexico City: Costa-Amic, 1964.

———. *Renuncia al comunismo*. Mexico City: Costa-Amic, 1963.

———. "Repudio al comunismo." *El Imparcial*, 8 articles, Nov. 28–Dec. 6, 1962.

———. "Utiles después de muertos." *La Hora*, Feb. 20, 1986, p.3.

Pellicer de Brody, Olga. *México y la Revolución Cubana*. Mexico City: El Colegio de México, 1972.

Pellicer de Brody, Olga, and Esteban Mancilla. *Historia de la Revolución Mexicana, 1952–1960*. Mexico City: El Colegio de México, 1978.

Penados del Barrio et al. *El clamor por la tierra*. (Pastoral Letter of the Guatemalan Bishops.) Guatemala: n.p., 1988.

Pérez, Luis. *Cuba: Between Reform and Revolution*. New York: Oxford University Press, 1988.

Pérez, Silverio. "Los oscuros acontecimientos de hace 37 años." *La Hora*, July 21, 1986, pp. 4, 11.

Phillips, David A. *The Night Watch: 25 Years of Peculiar Service*. New York: Atheneum, 1977.

Piedra-Santa, Rafael. "La construcción de ferrocarriles en Guatemala y los problemas financieros de la IRCA." *Economía* 15 (Jan.–Mar. 1968): 5–48.

Pike, Frederick. "The Catholic Church in Central America." *Review of Politics* 21 (Jan. 1959): 83–113.

Pinto Recinos, Ricardo Alberto. "Lo que yo sé del '20 de Octubre de 1944.' " *La Hora*, Oct. 25, 1984, pp. 2, 11.

———. "Sublevación de los caballeros cadetes." *La Hora*, 14 articles, July 22–Aug. 8, 1988.

———. "La rebelión de la Guardia de Honor, el 18 de Julio de 1949." *La Hora*, 15 articles, June 18–July 4, 1985.

Pitti, Joseph. "Jorge Ubico and Guatemalan Politics in the 1920's." Ph.D. diss., University of New Mexico, 1975.

Pollan, A. A. *The United Fruit Company and Middle America*. New York: New School for Social Research, 1944.

Posas, Mario. *Luchas del movimiento obrero hondureño*. San José, C.R.: EDUCA, 1981.

Powers, Thomas. *The Man Who Kept the Secrets*. New York: Pocket Books, 1981.

"Proyecciones de la Revolución del 44." *El Gráfico*, May 20, 1982, p. 5.

Pruessen, Ronald. *John Foster Dulles: The Road to Power*. New York: The Free Press, 1982.

Putzeys Rojas, Guillermo. *Así se hizo la Liberación*. Guatemala City: Tipografía Nacional, 1976.

Quan Rossell, Stella de la Luz. *Guatemala: una cultura de la ignominía*. 2 vols. Mexico City: Escuela Nacional de Antropología e Historia, 1972.

"Que pasó el 20 de Octubre?" *El Gráfico*, Oct. 20, 1973, p. 7.

Quintana, Epaminondas. *La generación de 1920*. Guatemala City: Tipografía Nacional, 1971.

Rabe, Stephen. *Eisenhower and Latin America: The Foreign Policy of Anticommunism*. Chapel Hill: University of North Carolina Press, 1988.

———. "The Elusive Conference: United States Economic Relations with Latin America, 1945–1952." *Diplomatic History* 2 (Summer 1978): 279–94.

Ramos Guzmán de Schmoock, María Eugenia. "El movimiento sindical en el decenio revolucionario (1944–1954)." Thesis, Universidad de San Carlos (Guatemala City), Escuela de Historia, 1978.

Ranelagh, John. *The Agency: The Rise and Decline of the CIA*. Rev. ed. New York: Touchstone, 1987.

Reichard, Gary. "Eisenhower as President: The Changing View." *South Atlantic Quarterly* 77 (Summer 1978): 265–81.

Reina, Ruben. "Chinautla, A Guatemalan Indian Community." In Richard Adams, ed., *Community Culture and National Change*. New Orleans: Middle American Research Institute, Tulane University, 1972, pp. 55–110.

"Resumen seleccionado del 'Estudio económico-contable sobre los Ferrocarriles Internacionales de Centro América, correspondiente a los años 1954 a 1957.' " *Economía* 16 (Apr.–June 1968): 30–55.

Richard, Pablo, and Guillermo Meléndez, eds. *La Iglesia de los Pobres en América Central*. San José, C.R.: Departamento Ecuménico de Investigaciones, 1982.

Rivas, Ernesto. "Versión inédita sobre la renuncia del general Ubico." *La Tarde*, Oct. 16, 1970, p. 9.

Rodman, Robert. "Operation Diablo." *Soldier of Fortune*, Summer 1976, pp. 16–19, 28, 58, 60, 77–78.

Rodríguez Loeche, Enrique. "Por qué fracasó la expedición a Santo Domingo." *Bohemia*, Havana, Aug. 21, 1949, pp. 58–59, 80–81, 89–90.

Roosevelt, Kermit. *Countercoup: The Struggle for the Control of Iran*. New York: McGraw-Hill, 1979.

Rosenthal, Mario. *Guatemala*. New York: Twayne Publishers, 1962.

Rostow, W. W. *Eisenhower, Kennedy, and Foreign Aid*. Austin: University of Texas Press, 1985.

Roy, M. N. *M. N. Roy's Memoirs*. Bombay: Allied Publishers, 1964.

Rubio Sánchez, Manuel. "Breve historia del desarrollo del cultivo del café en Guatemala." *Anales de la Sociedad de Geografía e Historia* 27 (Mar. 1953–Dec. 1954): 169–238.

Rubottom, Richard. "Oral History Interview." Princeton University, 1966.

Ruiz Franco, Arcadio. *Hambre y miseria*. Guatemala City: Tipografía Nacional, 1950.

Ruiz Morales, César Augusto. "Por qué solos?" *Revista Militar* 4 (1981): 89–93.

Saker-Ti. *Enrique Muñoz Meany*. Guatemala City, 1952.

Salazar, Carlos. *Memoria de los servicios prestados a la nación por el licenciado Carlos Salazar*. Guatemala City: Tipografía Sánchez & de Guise, 1945.

Salisbury, Harrison. *Without Fear or Favor: An Uncompromising Look at the New York Times*. New York: Ballantine Books, 1980.

Samayoa Chinchilla, Carlos. *El dictador y yo*. Guatemala City: Imprenta Iberia, 1950.

———. *El Quetzal no es rojo*. Guatemala City: n.p., 1956.

Samayoa Coronado, Francisco. *La Escuela Politécnica a través de su historia*. 2 vols. Guatemala City: Tipografía Nacional, 1964.

Sandoval Vásquez, Carlos Alberto. *Leifugados*. Mexico City: Impresora Periodística y Comercial, 1946.

Santa Cruz Morales, Raúl. "El Ejército de Liberación." *La Hora Dominical*, Aug. 20, 1978, pp. 5–16.

———. "Hace 42 años: Levantamiento indígena en Patzicía." *La Hora*, Oct. 31, 1986, pp. 7, 26.

———. "La invasión a Guatemala." *La Hora*, June 21, 1986, pp. 4, 11.

———. "Secuela del 2 de agosto." *La Hora Dominical*, Aug. 6, 1978, pp. 7–14.

Schifter, Jacobo. *Las alianzas conflictivas: Las relaciones de Costa Rica y Estados Unidos de la segunda guerra mundial a los inicios de la guerra civil*. San José, C.R.: Libro Libre, 1986.

Schlesinger, Arthur, Jr. "The Ike Age Revisited." *Reviews in American History* 9 (Mar. 1983): 1–11.

Schlesinger, Jorge. *Revolución comunista*. Guatemala City: Unión Tipográfica Castañeda, Avila y Cia, 1946.

Schlesinger, Stephen, and Stephen Kinzer. *Bitter Fruit: The Untold Story of the American Coup in Guatemala*. Garden City, N.Y.: Doubleday, 1982.

Schneider, Ronald. *Communism in Guatemala: 1944–1954*. New York: Praeger, 1959.

Selser, Gregorio. *El guatemalazo: La primera guerra sucia.* Buenos Aires: Iguazú, 1961.

Shoup, Laurence, and William Minter. *Imperial Brain Trust: The Council on Foreign Relations and United States Foreign Policy.* New York: Monthly Review Press, 1977.

Sierra Roldán, Tomás. *Diálogos con el coronel Monzón.* Guatemala City: Editorial San Antonio, 1958.

Silfa, Nicolás. *Guerra, traición y exilio.* 3 vols. Barcelona: n.p., 1980–1981.

Silva Girón, César Augusto. *La batalla de Gualán.* Guatemala City: n.p., 1977.

―――. *Cuando gobiernan las armas.* Guatemala City: Oscar de León Palacios, 1987.

―――. *12 horas de combate.* Guatemala City: Oscar de León Palacios, 1981.

Silva Jonama, Mario. Unpublished diary in author's files.

Silvert, Kalman. *A Study in Government: Guatemala.* New Orleans: Middle American Research Institute, Tulane University, 1954.

Skidmore, Thomas. *Politics in Brazil, 1930–1964.* New York: Oxford University Press, 1967.

Skinner-Klée, Jorge. *Legislación indigenista de Guatemala.* Mexico City: Instituto Indigenista Interamericano, 1954.

Slater, Jerome. *The OAS and United States Foreign Policy.* Columbus: Ohio State University Press, 1967.

Smith, Robert F. *The United States and Cuba.* New Haven, Conn.: College and University Press, 1960.

Solis, César. *Los ferrocarriles en Guatemala.* Guatemala City: Tipografía Nacional, 1952.

Stewart, Watt. *Keith and Costa Rica.* Albuquerque: University of New Mexico Press, 1964.

"Los sucesos de 1932." *Abra,* San Salvador, no. 13 (June 1976): 1–48.

Suslow, Leo. "Aspects of Social Reforms in Guatemala, 1944–1949." M.A. thesis, Colgate University, 1949.

―――. "Social Security in Guatemala." Ph.D. diss., University of Connecticut, 1954.

Szulc, Tad. *Compulsive Spy: The Strange Career of E. Howard Hunt.* New York: The Viking Press, 1974.

Taracena Arriola, Arturo. "Les Origines du Mouvement Ouvrier au Guatemala, 1878–1932." Ph.D. diss., Ecole des Hautes Etudes en Sciences Sociales (Paris), 1982.

―――. "El primer Partido Comunista de Guatemala (1922–1932)." *Araucaria de Chile,* Madrid, no. 27 (1984): 71–91.

Tax, Sol. *Penny Capitalism: A Guatemalan Indian Economy.* Chicago: University of Chicago Press, 1963.

Thomas, Hugh. *Cuba: The Pursuit of Freedom.* New York: Harper & Row, 1971.

Toriello, Guillermo. *La batalla de Guatemala.* Santiago de Chile: Editorial Universitaria, 1955.

―――. *A dónde va Guatemala?* Mexico City: Editorial América Nueva, 1956.

Toriello, Jorge. "Revelaciones de Jorge Toriello." *La Semana,* Oct. 9, 1970, pp. 15–21.

Torres Moss, Clodoveo. "La justicia salomónica del general Jorge Ubico." *La Hora* (Suplemento cultural), Feb. 8, 15, 22, and Mar. 1, 1986.

Torres Rivas, Edelberto. "Crisis y coyuntura crítica: La caída de Arbenz y los contratiempos de la revolución burguesa." *Política y Sociedad* 4 (July–Dec. 1977): 53–83.

Travis, Helen Simon, and A. B. Magil. *The Truth about Guatemala*. New York: New Century Publishers, 1954.

Treverton, Gregory. *Covert Action: The Limits of Intervention in the Postwar World*. New York: Basic Books, 1987.

Tully, Andrew. *CIA: The Inside Story*. New York: William Morrow, 1962.

Turner, Frederick. *Catholicism and Political Development in Latin America*. Chapel Hill: University of North Carolina Press, 1971.

"2 de agosto: Versión del MLN." *La Hora*, Aug. 9, 1986, p. 4.

Unión Panamericana, Departamento de Estudios Jurídicos. *Tratado Interamericano de Asistencia Recíproca*. Vol. 1. Washington, D.C., 1973.

Unión Patriótica Guatemalteca. *Guatemala contra el imperialismo*. Havana, 1964.

United Nations. *El transporte en el istmo centroamericano*. Mexico City, 1953.

United Nations, Economic Commission for Latin America. *Economic Development of Guatemala*. Mexico City, 1951.

———. *La política tributaria y el desarrollo económico en Centroamérica*. Mexico City, 1956.

United Nations, Food and Agriculture Organization. *The World Coffee Economy*. Rome, 1961.

United Nations, Security Council. *Official Records*.

United States Congress. *Congressional Record*.

United States Congress, House Committee on Foreign Affairs. *Selected Executive Session Hearings of the Committee, 1951–1956*. Vol. 16: *Middle East, Africa, and Inter-American Affairs*. Washington, D.C.: GPO, 1980.

United States Congress, House Select Committee on Communist Aggression. *Communist Aggression in Latin America*. Hearings before the Subcommittee on Latin America, 83rd Congress, 2d session, Washington, D.C.: GPO, 1954.

United States Congress, Senate Committee of the Judiciary. *Communist Threat to the United States Through the Caribbean*. Hearings before the Subcommittee to Investigate the Administration of the Internal Security Act and Other Internal Security Laws, 87th Congress, 1st session, Washington, D.C.: GPO, 1961.

United States Congress, Senate Committee on Foreign Relations. *Executive Sessions of the Senate Foreign Relations Committee (Historical Series), 1951–1954*. Washington, D.C.: GPO, 1976–1977.

United States, Department of State. *Department of State Bulletin*. Washington, D.C.: GPO.

———. *Foreign Relations of the United States*. Washington, D.C.: GPO.

———. *Intervention of International Communism in Guatemala*. Washington, D.C.: GPO, 1954.

———. *Penetration of the Political Institutions of Guatemala by the International Communist Movement*. Washington, D.C.: GPO, 1954.

———. *Tenth Inter-American Conference*. Washington, D.C.: GPO, 1955.

United States Tariff Commission. *Economic Controls and Commercial Policy in Guatemala*. Washington, D.C.: GPO, 1947.

———. *Mining and Manufacturing Industries in Guatemala*. Washington, D.C.: GPO, 1949.

United States Treasury Department. *Census of American-Owned Assets in Foreign Countries*. Washington, D.C.: GPO, 1947.

Urquhart, Brian. *Hammarskjöld*. New York: Knopf, 1973.

Valdes López, Julia. "Aspectos socioculturales de la educación en Guatemala." Thesis, Universidad de San Carlos (Guatemala City), Facultad de Humanidades, 1976.

Vega, Bernardo, ed. *Los Estados Unidos y Trujillo–1947*. 2 vols. Santo Domingo: Fundación Cultural Dominicana, 1984.

Vilanova de Arbenz, María. "Aclaración." *La Prensa Libre*, San José, C.R., July 26, 1984, p. 3.

Villagrán Kramer, Francisco. "Los pactos políticos en la historia contemporánea." *Prensa Libre Domingo*, July 12, 19, and 26, 1987.

Villegas Rodas, Miguel. "Como se produjo la renuncia del general Jorge Ubico." *El Imparcial*, July 26, 1961, pp. 3, 11.

Wagner, Regina. "Actividades empresariales de los alemanes en Guatemala, 1850–1920." *Mesoamérica* 13 (June 1987): 87–123.

Wangüemert y Máiquez, J. L. "El diario de Cayo Confites." *Carteles*, Havana, Oct. 12, 19, 26, and Nov. 2, 1947.

Wasserstrom, Robert. "Revolution in Guatemala: Peasants and Politics under the Arbenz Government." *Comparative Studies in Society and History* 17 (Oct. 1975): 443–78.

Whetten, Nathan. *Guatemala: The Land and the People*. New Haven: Yale University Press, 1961.

———. "Land Reform in a Modern World." *Rural Sociology* 19 (1954): 329–36.

Williams, John. "The Rise of the Banana Industry and Its Influence on Caribbean Countries." M.A. thesis, Clark University, 1925.

Wise, David, and Thomas Ross. *The Invisible Government*. New York: Bantam, 1965.

Wood, Bryce. *The Dismantling of the Good Neighbor Policy*. Austin: University of Texas Press, 1985.

———. "Self-Plagiarism and Foreign Policy." *Latin American Research Review* 3, no. 3 (1968): 184–91.

Ydígoras Fuentes, Miguel. *My War with Communism*. Englewood Cliffs, N.J.: Prentice-Hall, 1963.

Young, John. "Great Britain's Latin American Dilemma: The Foreign Office and the Overthrow of 'Communist' Guatemala, June 1954." *International History Review* 8, no. 4 (Nov. 1986): 573-92.

Zamora Alvarez, José. *Las memorias de Andrés*. Guatemala City: Editorial del Ejército, 1975.

Zamora Castellanos, Pedro. *Nuestros cuarteles*. Guatemala City: n.p., 1972.

Zea Carrascosa, Manuel Octavio. *Semblanzas: Ministros de la guerra y de la defensa nacional de Guatemala*. Guatemala City: Ministerio de la Defensa Nacional, 1971.

Zea González, Emilio. *El espejismo de la democracia en Guatemala*. Guatemala City: n.p., 1989.

Zorrilla, Luis. *Relaciones de México con la República de CentroAmérica y con Guatemala*. Mexico City: Editorial Porrúa, 1984.

Zoumaras, Thomas. "Eisenhower's Foreign Economic Policy: The Case of Latin America." In Richard Melanson and David Mayers, eds., *Reevaluating Eisenhower*. Urbana: University of Illinois Press, 1987, pp. 155–91.

Index